Lecture Notes in Computer Science 850

Lecture Notes in Computer Science 850
Edited by G. Goos, J. Hartmanis and J. van Leeuwen

Giorgio Levi
Mario Rodríguez-Artalejo (Eds.)

Algebraic and Logic Programming

4th International Conference, ALP '94
Madrid, Spain, September 14-16, 1994
Proceedings

Springer-Verlag
Berlin Heidelberg New York
London Paris Tokyo
Hong Kong Barcelona
Budapest

Series Editors

Gerhard Goos
Universität Karlsruhe
Postfach 69 80, Vincenz-Priessnitz-Straße 1, D-76131 Karlsruhe, Germany

Juris Hartmanis
Department of Computer Science, Cornell University
4130 Upson Hall, Ithaka, NY 14853, USA

Jan van Leeuwen
Department of Computer Science, Utrecht University
Padualaan 14, 3584 CH Utrecht, The Netherlands

Volume Editors

Giorgio Levi
Department of Computer Science, University of Pisa
Corso Italia 40, I-56125 Pisa, Italy

Mario Rodríguez-Artalejo
Departamento de Informática y Automática
Facultad de Matemáticas, Universidad Complutense
Av. Compultense s/n, E-28040 Madrid, Spain

CR Subject Classification (1991): D.3, F.3-4, I.2.3

ISBN 3-540-58431-5 Springer-Verlag Berlin Heidelberg New York

CIP data applied for

Printed in Germany

Typesetting: Camera-ready by author
SPIN: 10475508 45/3140-543210 - Printed on acid-free paper

Foreword

This volume contains the Proceedings of the Fourth International Conference on Algebraic and Logic Programming (ALP), held in Madrid (Spain) on September 14-16, 1994.

Following the intention of the three previous ALP meetings in Gaussig (1988), Nancy (1990) and Volterra (1992), the conference aims at strengthening the connections between algebraic techniques and logic programming. Logic programming has been very successful during the last decades. Many efforts have been made to enhance its expressive power and efficiency, including in particular the emergence of constraint logic programming. On the other hand, the algebraic approach is very well suited to deal with such key notions as functions, types, equational theories, and modularity. As on previous occasions, ALP offers a unique opportunity to promote the application of algebraic tools within logic programming and the cross-fertilizing exchange of ideas among researchers from the algebraic and logic communities.

On this occasion, ALP is held concurrently with the Sixth International Symposium on Programming Language Implementation and Logic Programming (PLILP), which aims at stimulating research on new declarative concepts, methods, and techniques relevant for the implementation of programming languages, with particular emphasis on declarative ones.

The ALP Program Committee met in Madrid on May 6, 1994, and selected 17 papers from 41 submissions, coming from 17 countries. The selected contributions mainly cover the following topics:

algebraic specification, theorem proving
term rewriting, narrowing, resolution
program semantics, analysis, transformations
equational logic programming
concurrent logic programming
higher-order features

In addition to the selected papers, the scientific program includes three invited lectures (shared with PLILP) by Dale Miller (Univ. of Pennsylvania, USA), Catuscia Palamidessi (Univ. of Genova, Italy), and Robert Paige (Univ. of New York, USA). Abstracts of the invited talks are included both in this volume and in the proceedings volume of PLILP '94. A full version of Paige's invited paper can be found in the proceedings of PLILP '94

We would like to thank all members of the Program Committee and all the referees for their careful work in the reviewing and selection process.

Last but not least, we express our gratitude to all members of the local organizing committees, both of ALP and PLILP, for the effort they have invested.

July 1994

Giorgio Levi, Mario Rodríguez-Artalejo
Co-chairmen

Program Committee

Krzysztof Apt (Amsterdam)
Egidio Astesiano (Genova)
Harald Ganzinger (Saarbrücken)
Claude Kirchner (Nancy)
Giorgio Levi (Pisa), Co-chair
Michael Maher (Yorktown Heights)
Fernando Orejas (Barcelona)
Laurence Puel (Orsay)
Mario Rodríguez-Artalejo (Madrid), Co-chair
Jerzy Tiuryn (Warsaw)
Andrei Voronkov (Uppsala)

Local Organization

Lourdes Araujo Serna, Francisco Bueno Carrillo, Daniel Cabeza Gras, Manuel Carro Liñares, Julio García Martín, Angel Herranz Nieva, María Teresa Hortalá González, Javier Leach Albert (organizing co-chair), Francisco López Fraguas, Julio Mariño Carballo, Juan José Moreno Navarro (organizing co-chair), Germán Puebla Sánchez.

List of Referees

I.Alouini, M.Alpuente, A.Amadio, S.Anantharaman, R.Bagnara, R.Barbuti, J.Barklund, H.Baumeister, A.Bockmayr, A.Bossi, M.Bugliesi, M.Cerioli, J.Chabin, A.Cichon, E.Contejean, R.Cousot, F.S.de Boer, Ph.de Groote, P.Dell'Acqua, R.di Cosmo, K.Doets, E.Domenjoud, A.Dovier, W.Drabent, E.Engel, M.Falaschi, M.Fernandez, G.File, M.Fitting, M.Gabbrielli, D.Galmiche, A.Gavilanes, I.Gnaedig-Antoine, A.Gil, P.Graf, M.Hanus, N.Heintze, C.Hintermeier, M.T.Hortalá, J.Hsiang, P.Inverardi, D.Kesner, Z.Khasidashvili, H.Kirchner, T.Lindgren, G.Longo, D.Lugiez, P.Mancarella, V.Manca, C.Marché, M.Martelli, A.Masini, S.Michaylov, A.Middeldorp, H.Millroth, E.Moggi, U.Montanari, F.Morando, U.Neumerkel, R.Nieuwenhuis, S.Nieva, D.Niwiński, S.O.Nyström, M.Ortega, C.Palamidessi, E.Palmgren, M.Parigot, D.Pedreschi, K.Rao, G.Reggio, C.Ringeissen, J.J.Ruz, P.Réty H.Seki, V.Stoltenberg-Hansen, J.Stuber, A.Szałas, F.Sáenz, A.Tarlecki, E.Tick, J.Torán, Y.Toyama, P.Urzyczyn, P.van Emde Boas, F.van Raamsdonk, G.Vidal, M.Vittek, U.Waldmann, E.Waller, H.Zantema.

Supporters (of ALP & PLILP)

The Association of Logic Programming
Universidad Complutense de Madrid (UCM)
Universidad Politécnica de Madrid (UPM)
CICYT
European Comission - Esprit Basic Research
Esprit COMPULOG-NET
Esprit BR WG CCL (EP 6028)
Comunidad Autónoma de Madrid
ATI
SUN Microsystems - Spain

Contents

Logic Programming I

Term Rewriting

Higher-Order Programming

Logic Programming II

Concurrent Constraint Programming

(Abstract of Lecture)

Catuscia Palamidessi

Dipartimento di Informatica e Scienze dell'Informazione (DISI)
Università di Genova
via Benedetto XV 3, 16132, Genova, Italy
catuscia@di.unipi.it

In the last years there have been several proposals to extend logic programming with the constructs for concurrency, aiming at the development of a concurrent language which would maintain the typical advantages of logic programming: declarative reading, computations as proofs, amenability to meta-programming etc. Examples of concurrent logic languages include PARLOG [6], Concurrent Prolog [12], Guarded Horn Clauses [15] and their so-called *flat* versions.

Concurrent constraint programming (ccp) [11, 13, 14] represents one of the most successful proposals in this area. Basically, ccp presents two new perspectives on the underlying philosophy of logic programming. One is the replacement of the concept of unification over the Herbrand universe by the more general notion of *constraint* over an arbitrary domain. This is in a sense a 'natural' development, and the idea was already introduced in 'sequential' logic programming by Jaffar and Lassez [8]. The other is the introduction of explicit *operators* typical of the traditional concurrent paradigms, like CCS, TCSP and ACP [10, 5, 1]; in particular, the *choice* (+), the *action prefixing* (→), and the *hiding* operator (∃). Communication and synchronization are achieved by means of two kinds of actions: *ask* (originally introduced by Maher in [9]), which checks wether a store entails a certain constraint, and *tell*, which adds a constraint to the store. Also in concurrent logic languages these control features were present, but in an"implicit" way: the choice was represented by alternative clauses, hiding by local (existentially quantified) variables, prefixing by commitment, communication by sharing of variables, and synchronization by restrictions on the unification algorithm.

With respect to the other concurrent logic languages, ccp has a clean algebraic structure, and it is based on a 'minimal' set of concepts. With respect to other concurrent paradigms, ccp is characterized by the logical interpretation of computations [3], and by the monotonic evolution of the store. This last feature allows an agent to be representable as a Scott's closure operator and denoted by the set of its fixpoints. For the so-called confluent ccp [7], where process scheduling doesn't affect the results, closure operators corresponding to agents can be defined in a structural way, thus leading to a very simple denotational semantics. In the full ccp, on the contrary, the parallel composition of processes requires structures encoding the various behaviors relative to different interleaving possibilities, like *reactive sequences* [4] or *bounded trace operators* [14].

Concerning expressiveness, monotonicity imposes a heavy limitation, at least in the basic paradigm where the tell is *eventual*. The alternative proposal, based on *atomic* tell, on the other hand, is not very suitable for distributed implementation. We argue that a good compromise could be obtained by enriching the language with an action removing information from the store [2].

References

1. J.A. Bergstra and J.W. Klop. Process algebra: specification and verification in bisimulation semantics. In *Mathematics and Computer Science II*, CWI Monographs, pages 61 – 94. North-Holland, 1986.
2. F.S. de Boer, E. Best, and C. Palamidessi. Concurrent Constraint Programming with Information Removal. Technical Report, Dipartimento di Informatica, Università di Genova, Genova. 1994.
3. F.S. de Boer, M. Gabbrielli, E. Marchiori, and C. Palamidessi. Proving Concurrent Constraint Programs Correct. In *Proc. Eighteenth Annual ACM Symp. on Principles of Programming Languages*, 1993.
4. F.S. de Boer and C. Palamidessi. A fully abstract model for concurrent constraint programming. In S. Abramsky and T.S.E. Maibaum, editors, *Proc. of TAPSOFT/CAAP*, volume 493 of *Lecture Notes in Computer Science*, pages 296–319. Springer-Verlag, 1991.
5. S.D. Brookes, C.A.R. Hoare, and W. Roscoe. A theory of communicating sequential processes. *Journal of ACM*, 31:499–560, 1984.
6. K.L. Clark and S. Gregory. PARLOG: parallel programming in logic. *ACM Trans. on Programming Languages and Systems*, (8):1–49, 1986.
7. M. Falaschi, M. Gabbrielli, K. Marriott, and C. Palamidessi. Confluence and Concurrent Constraint Programming. Technical Report, Dipartimento di Informatica, Università di Pisa, Pisa. 1994.
8. J. Jaffar and J.-L. Lassez. Constraint logic programming. In *Proc,. of ACM Symposium on Principles of Programming Languages*, pages 111–119. ACM, New York, 1987.
9. M. J. Maher. Logic semantics for a class of committed-choice programs. In Jean-Louis Lassez, editor, *Proc. of the Fourth International Conference on Logic Programming*, Series in Logic Programming, pages 858–876, Melbourne, 1987. The MIT Press.
10. R. Milner. *A Calculus of Communicating Systems*, volume 92 of *Lecture Notes in Computer Science*. Springer-Verlag, New York, 1980.
11. V.A. Saraswat. *Concurrent Constraint Programming Languages*. PhD thesis, Carnegie-Mellon University, January 1989. Published by The MIT Press, U.S.A., 1990.
12. E.Y. Shapiro. A subset of Concurrent Prolog and its interpreter. Technical Report TR-003, Institute for New Generation Computer Technology (ICOT), Tokyo, 1983.
13. V.A. Saraswat and M. Rinard. Concurrent constraint programming. In *Proc. of the seventeenth ACM Symposium on Principles of Programming Languages*, pages 232–245. ACM, New York, 1990.
14. V.A. Saraswat, M. Rinard, and P. Panangaden. Semantics foundations of Concurrent Constraint Programming. In *Proc. of the eighteenth ACM Symposium on Principles of Programming Languages*. ACM, New York, 1991.
15. K. Ueda. Guarded Horn Clauses. In E. Y. Shapiro, editor, *Concurrent Prolog: Collected Papers*. The MIT Press, 1987.

Specifications using multiple-conclusion logic programs *

(Abstract of Lecture)

Dale Miller

Computer Science Department
University of Pennsylvania
Philadelphia, PA 19104-6389 USA
dale@saul.cis.upenn.edu

Multiset rewriting has proved to be a useful presentation of process synchronization [1, 2, 3, 6]. Since sequent calculus presentations of logics that do not use the structural rules of contractions and weakening are based on using multisets of formulas as left and right contexts, it is natural to identify processes with formulas, multisets with sequent contexts, and multiset rewriting as an inference rule. Given earlier work on using sequent calculus to describe logic programming as goal-directed search for proofs [8], it is most natural to use right-hand contexts of sequents to represent multisets of processes. This choice requires the identification of the multiset constructor and the empty multiset with the multiplicative disjunction and false (the $\parr$ and $\bot$ of linear logic [4]), and backchaining with a single step of multiset rewriting. While the logic programming language λProlog [10] and its linear logic refinement Lolli [5] contain rich sources of abstraction (such as modular programming, abstract data types, and higher-order programming), they contain no primitives for specifying concurrency, communications, or synchronization. If multiset rewriting is added to Lolli via the logical connectives $\parr$ and $\bot$, the result is a language that contains primitives for both abstraction and concurrency. Surprisingly, the resulting logic, called Forum [7], is a presentation of all of linear logic in the sense that all of the connectives of linear logic can be defined via logical equivalences using only the connectives of Forum. Thus the rich meta-theory of linear logic, for example, the de Morgan dualities and cut-elimination, can be applied to the analysis of Forum programs. Several examples to illustrate the expressiveness of this presentation of linear logic will be given. These examples will involve a specification of sequent calculi for object-level logics, a specification of the π-calculus [9], and a specification of a functional programming language that contains side-effects and concurrency operators. In each of these examples, we shall argue that the specification is perspicuous and modular and that the meta-theory of linear logic can be used to derive properties of the specification.

---

* The work presented here is supported in part by grants ONR N00014-93-1-1324, NSF CCR-91-02753, NSF CCR-92-09224, and DARPA N00014-85-K-0018.

References

1. J.M. Andreoli and R. Pareschi. Linear objects: Logical processes with built-in inheritance. *New Generation Computing*, 9:3-4, 1991.
2. J-P. Banâtre, A. Coutant, and D. Le Metayer. A parallel machine for multiset transformation and its programming style. *Future Generation Computer Systems*, 4(2):133–145, 1988.
3. G. Berry and G. Boudol. The chemical abstract machine. In *Proceedings of the 17th Annual Symposium of Programming Languages*, pages 81–94, 1990.
4. Jean-Yves Girard. Linear logic. *Theoretical Computer Science*, 50:1–102, 1987.
5. Joshua Hodas and Dale Miller. Logic programming in a fragment of intuitionistic linear logic. *Journal of Information and Computation*, 1994. (To appear). Available from ftp.cis.upenn.edu, pub/papers/miller/ic94.ps.Z.
6. Naoki Kobayashi and Akinori Yonezawa. ACL - a concurrent linear logic programming paradigm. In Dale Miller, editor, *Logic Programming - Proceedings of the 1993 International Symposium*, pages 279–294. MIT Press, October 1993.
7. Dale Miller. A multiple-conclusion meta-logic. In S. Abramsky, editor, *Ninth Annual Symposium on Logic in Computer Science*, Paris, July 1994. (To appear). Available from ftp.cis.upenn.edu, pub/papers/miller/lics94.dvi.Z.
8. Dale Miller, Gopalan Nadathur, Frank Pfenning, and Andre Scedrov. Uniform proofs as a foundation for logic programming. *Annals of Pure and Applied Logic*, 51:125–157, 1991.
9. Robin Milner, Joachim Parrow, and David Walker. A calculus of mobile processes, Part I. *Information and Computation*, pages 1–40, September 1992.
10. Gopalan Nadathur and Dale Miller. An Overview of λProlog. In *Fifth International Logic Programming Conference*, pages 810–827, Seattle, Washington, August 1988. MIT Press.

Viewing A Program Transformation System At Work

(Abstract of Lecture)

Robert Paige*

Computer Science Department, New York University/Courant Institute,
251 Mercer St., New York, NY 10012, USA
E-mail: paige@cs.nyu.edu

How to decrease labor and improve reliability in the development of efficient implementations of nonnumerical algorithms and labor intensive software is an increasingly important problem as the demand for computer technology shifts from easier applications to more complex algorithmic ones; e.g., optimizing compilers for supercomputers, intricate data structures to implement efficient solutions to operations research problems, search and analysis algorithms in genetic engineering, complex software tools for workstations, design automation, etc. It is also a difficult problem that is not solved by current CASE tools and software management disciplines, which are oriented towards data processing and other applications, where the implementation and a prediction of its resource utilization follow more directly from the specification.

Recently, Cai and Paige reported experiments suggesting a way to implement nonnumerical algorithms in C at a programming rate (i.e., source lines per second) that is at least five times greater than a conventional approach in which C programs are written entirely by hand. The runtime performance of the C programs produced by this new approach was shown to be comparable to good hand code. The proposed software development methodology makes use of fully automatic, generic program transformations that capture algorithm design principles. This paper discusses some of the ideas underlying the transformational methodology, and illustrates these ideas through explanatory examples of the APTS system at work.

* Part of this work was done while the author was visiting DIKU at the University of Copenhagen. This research is partially supported by Office of Naval Research Grant N00014-93-1-0924, Air Force Office of Scientific Research Grant AFOSR-91-0308, and National Science Foundation Grant MIP-9300210.

Proving Implications by Algebraic Approximation

Michael Codish Grigory Mashevitzky

Department of Mathematics and Computer Science
Ben-Gurion University of the Negev
PoB 653, Beer-Sheba
84105, Israel
{codish,gmash}@bengus.bgu.ac.il

Abstract. This paper applies techniques of algebraic approximation to provide effective algorithms to determine the validity of universally quantified implications over lattice structures. We generalize the known result which states that any semilattice is approximated in the two element lattice. We show that the validity of a universally quantified implication ψ over a possibly infinite domain can be determined by examining its validity over a simpler domain the size of which is related to the number of constants in ψ. Both the known as well as the new results have high potential in providing practical automated techniques in various areas of application in computer science.

1 Introduction

This paper applies techniques of algebraic approximation to provide effective algorithms to determine the validity of universally quantified implications between identities over lattice structures. Approximation is one of the main methods in the scientific process and is common practice also in various branches of mathematics and computer science. The basic idea in approximating one (mathematical) structure by another is that properties of the objects from a perhaps complex structure may be investigated by examination of a simpler structure which preserves some important features of the first structure. The methods of approximation in algebra are developed in the works of Malcev [17, 19] and Birkhoff [2, 3]. In computer science, approximation is applied in the context of semantic based program analysis as formalized in terms of Galois connections [23, 20] by Cousot and Cousot [10].

Given a universally quantified formula ψ of the form $(\forall)\ p \rightarrow q$ over a domain D which corresponds to some theory (e.g. set theory, propositional logic, group theory, etc.), we are familiar with two general approaches which can be applied when trying to determine if ψ is valid. The *proof theoretic* approach, in which a suitable system of axioms is used to reduce ψ to some solved form; and the *model theoretic* approach in which interpretations are enumerated and every interpretation which satisfies p is checked to determine if it satisfies also q. Both approaches are, in general, computationally hard, even in the case of a finite domain. The proof theoretic approach generally seeks a proof in an exponential search space. The number of interpretations examined in the model theoretic approach typically grows exponentially with the number of variables occurring in the formulae. From a programmer's perspective, the model theoretic approach is attractive because it is straightforward in almost any programming language to enumerate interpretations. Examples 1 and 3 below illustrate an almost trivial implementation in Prolog. On the other hand, the proof theoretic approach is attractive because it enables the consideration of search strategies and heuristics.

To show that an implication ψ is valid in a given class of algebraic structures $\mathcal{K}$, we do not need to check all substitutions of variables in ψ to elements of these structures or for all structures in $\mathcal{K}$. It follows from results of algebraic approximation [3, 19], that it is sufficient to check the validity of ψ for the so called subdirectly irreducible structures which generate the given ones and which are much less complicated. For example, the only subdirectly irreducible boolean algebra is the 2-element boolean algebra. Often the required subdirectly irreducible structures are substructures of members of $\mathcal{K}$ and in this case the validity of a ψ in $\mathcal{K}$ is exactly defined by its validity in the corresponding subdirectly irreducible structures. In other words *ψ is valid in $\mathcal{K}$ if and only if it is valid in the corresponding subdirectly irreducible structures.*

We know the description of subdirectly irreducible structures for many subclasses of classical algebraic structures: semigroups, groups, lattices and so on (see for example [3, 12, 24]). But if we want to apply these results to determine the validity of implications for specific structures which contain constants (the names of elements of the structure), we run into problems. In the classical algebraic theories, formulae do not explicitly reference arbitrary elements of the underlying structures. For example, in lattice theory, we may mention only the top or bottom elements of a given lattice, but we do not usually refer explicitly to other elements. The signature consists of a few special operations. E.g., in the case of lattices: $\bot, \top, \sqcup, \sqcap$.

In contrast, when proving theorems in the context of specific applications, it is common to refer explicitly to arbitrary elements of the underlying structure. For example, consider a lattice of types in the context of a programming language with type declarations. In this context it is natural to reason about the correctness of the type of a specific construct in a given program. Consequently, we may question the validity of an implication which contains explicit reference to elements of the underlying lattice of types. To express or validate theorems which refer to explicit constants from the underlying structure we must enrich the signature of our language. If we wish to discuss lattice structures with explicit constants, we are no longer within the classic lattice theory. Instead, we are dealing with a structure consisting of *marked elements*. *Note that to determine the validity of a given formula we do not need to consider all of the elements of the underlying domain as marked elements. It is sufficient to consider as marked only those elements which correspond to the constant symbols in the given formula.*

In this paper we investigate a practical approach to determine the validity of implications in which quantified variables range over a (possibly infinite) (semi) lattice D. For any such formula ψ, we identify the smallest sub- (semi) lattice D' of D such that validity of ψ over D' implies the validity of ψ over D. The size of D' is related to the number of constants from D occurring in ψ. We investigate the case with a small number of constants (less than three). In particular, if ψ contains no constants then D' is the two valued Boolean lattice. In this case, the result is well-known and it provides a decision procedure for implications even if the underlying structure of D is infinite or if the underlying theory is undecidable. Even in this case, the problem remains, of course, exponential. However, the cost of enumeration is reduced from $|D|^n$ to 2^n (where n is the number of variables in the formula). Moreover, in many cases there exist efficient techniques to determine the validity of the specific types of propositional formula. Examples include the use of Binary Decision Diagrams in circuit design [5, 6] and the use of propositional formulae in program analysis [15, 9, 7]. These techniques have been shown to remain effective when the domain is extended to contain a small number of additional constants [9].

Lattices (semilattices) play a central role in domain theory and provide the foundation for denotational semantics and various semantic based techniques in computer science. The need to determine the validity of an implication is also common in various application areas of computer science and hence also the general applicability of our results. In particular these results are of importance in: (a) the context of static program analysis (e.g. [21]), where for example a central question is to determine if a program state implies the precondition of a conditional statement [13]; (b) type analysis, where set constraints and implications between set constraints often arise (e.g [1]); and (c) semantic based techniques (e.g [10]), where successive approximations to a solution are evaluated as long as the next approximation is not implied by the previous. Another potential area of application is in the context of constraint based languages where constraint satisfaction is one of the basic operations in computations.

The following examples illustrate the spirit of the results presented in this paper.

Example 1. To prove an equality of the form,

$$E_1 \equiv \quad (A \cap B) \cup (C \cap D) = (A \cup C) \cap (B \cup C) \cap (A \cup D) \cup (B \cup D); \quad or$$

$$E_2 \equiv \quad \overline{A \cap B} = \overline{A} \cup \overline{B}$$

where A, B, C, D range over a (possibly infinite) boolean algebra of sets, it is sufficient to test the equality for values of A, B, C, D ranging over $\{0, 1\}$ viewing set union, intersection and completion respectively as propositional disjunction, conjunction and negation. This in itself is not surprising as it is well known that the Boolean algebra of sets is approximated by the two element Boolean algebra. However, it is interesting to observe that the following concise Prolog program P can be used to prove or disprove equations of this form:

```
equiv(A,B) :- imply(A,B), imply(B,A).
imply(A,B) :- \+( (A,\+(B)) ).

and(0,0,0).     or(0,0,0).     neg(0,1).
and(0,1,0).     or(0,1,1).     neg(1,0).
and(1,0,0).     or(1,0,1).
and(1,1,1).     or(1,1,1).
```

where **and(A,B,C)**, **or(A,B,C)** and **neg(A,B)** are relations which correspond respectively to $A \wedge B = C$, $A \vee B = C$ and $\neg A = B$ and "\+" is Prolog's negation as failure[1]. To check if E_1 is valid, we query the program P with the goal:

```
?- equiv( ( and(A,B,T1),and(C,D,T2),or(T1,T2,T3) ),
          ( or(A,C,T4),or(B,C,T5),or(A,D,T6),or(B,D,T7),
            and(T4,T5,T8),and(T6,T7,T9),and(T8,T9,T3) ) ).
```

To check the validity of E_2 we query P with the goal:

```
?- equiv( ( and(A,B,T1), neg(T1,T2) ),
          ( neg(A,T3), neg(B,T4), or(T3,T4,T2) ) ).
```

Example 2. A *comparison network* is a network constructed from *wires* and *comparators* with n inputs and n outputs. A comparator is a device with two inputs x and y and two outputs $min(x,y)$ and $max(x,y)$. We typically refer to the *sequences* of inputs and outputs of a comparison network. A *sorting network* is a comparison network for which the output sequence is monotonically increasing for every input sequence. The *zero-one principle* (cf [14]) states that a comparison network is a sorting network if and only if it correctly sorts all 2^n sequences of 0's and 1's. Namely if the network correctly sorts 0's and 1's then it correctly sorts any numeric inputs.

We can generalize the notion of comparison network to accept inputs from any distributive lattice. A comparator is then a device with two inputs x and y and two outputs $x \sqcup y$ and $x \sqcap y$. It follows that if such a comparison network transforms all sequences of 0's and 1's to an ordered chain, then it transforms any sequence of inputs to an ordered chain. To see this consider a comparison network which transforms the inputs $x_1, \ldots, x_n$ to the outputs $x'_1, \ldots, x'_n$. Each output x'_i can be expressed as a formula w_i involving the inputs $\{x_1, \ldots, x_n\}$ and the two operators $\sqcup$ and $\sqcap$ (exercise 5.3.4-28 in [14]). To prove that the comparison network transforms its inputs to a chain we must prove that $w_i \sqcup w_{i+1} = w_{i+1}$ for $1 \leq i < n$. This paper illustrates that if this is true for inputs ranging over $\{0,1\}$ then it is true for inputs ranging over any distributive lattice. In particular this proves the zero-one principle for sorting networks.

[1] The knowledgeable Prolog programmer will observe that this program is incorrect for queries of the form **imply(A,B)** where B contains variables not occurring in A. We will assume without loss of generality that A and B contain the same sets of variables. If A does not contain a variable X we can replace it by $A \wedge (X \vee \neg X)$.

A less known application which will be justified by our results involves implications which contain constants from the underlying domain and is illustrated by the following,

Example 3. Consider an arbitrary (possibly infinite) semi-lattice which contains an element 'a'. We will show that to prove the implication

$$\psi \equiv \quad (D \sqcup E = A) \wedge (F \sqcup D = C) \wedge (E \sqcup B = F) \wedge (a \sqcup B = B) \quad \rightarrow \quad (a \sqcup C = C)$$

it is sufficient to test the implication over the three-element chain $0 < a < 1$. A Prolog program which implements a theorem prover for implications involving a constant 'a' and the least upper bound operation is obtained by adding the following facts to the program from Example 1.

```
lub(0,0,0).      lub(a,1,1).      lub(0,a,a).
lub(1,0,1).      lub(0,1,1).      lub(1,a,1).
lub(a,0,a).      lub(1,1,1).      lub(a,a,a).
```

where `lub(A,B,C)` corresponds to $A \sqcup B = C$. The Prolog query to determine if ψ is valid is

```
?- imply( ( lub(D,E,A),lub(F,D,C),lub(E,B,F),lub(a,B,B) ),
          ( lub(a,C,C) ) ).
```

We also prove that in order to prove implications of this kind, it is sufficient to test the implication over two two-element chains $0 < a$ and $a < 1$ instead of over a three-element chain. For an implication with n variables, this reduces the cost from $O(3^n)$ to $O(2^n)$. Moreover, since the two two-element chains are dual we may consult a single two-element chain twice replacing the above definition of `lub(A,B,C)` by:

```
lub1(0,0,0).    lub1(a,0,a).    lub2(0,0,0).    lub2(a,0,0).
lub1(0,a,a).    lub1(a,a,a).    lub2(0,a,0).    lub2(a,a,a).
```

To prove ψ we check the following two (dual) queries:

```
?- imply( ( lub1(D,E,A),lub1(F,D,C),lub1(E,B,F),lub1(a,B,B) ),
          ( lub1(a,C,C) ) ).
?- imply( ( lub2(D,E,A),lub2(F,D,C),lub2(E,B,F),lub2(a,B,B) ),
          ( lub2(a,C,C) ) ).
```

It is easy to verify that ψ is not valid in a single two element lattice and that is why it is not enough to test this implication for a two element chain.

The main contribution of this paper is the formal justification which enables us to provide effective algorithms to determine the validity of universally quantified implications, possibly containing less than three constants, in the spirit of the above examples. It is important to consider the case with constants as this is a common case in practical applications. Our approach becomes quickly impractical as the number of constants increases. Consequently, the approach is mainly applicable in cases where the number of constants which appear in formulae is small. This is the case, for example, in the context of polymorphic type analysis recently investigated in [8] which involves implications of the form illustrated by Example 3. An implementation for this application based on the principles described here has illustrated considerable improvements. The only other application we are aware of is the zero-one principle as described in Example 2 (which does not involve marked elements). We believe that the results described here are of general interest and have high potential for applications in computer science.

The rest of this paper is organized as follows. Section 2 provides the necessary preliminary background. Section 3 provides our main contribution. Section 4 describes an application and Section 5 presents a short conclusion.

2 Preliminaries

We review here the basic algebraic concepts which are used to obtain our results. For a more detailed discussion see for example [11, 12].

Semilattices and lattices

A *lattice* is an algebra $(\mathcal{L}, \sqcup, \sqcap)$ with two binary operations which are associative, commutative, idempotent and satisfy the axioms: $\forall_{a,b\in\mathcal{L}}.\ a \sqcap (a \sqcup b) = a$ and $\forall_{a,b\in\mathcal{L}}.\ a \sqcup (a \sqcap b) = a$. If we add also the axiom of distributivity, $a \sqcup (b \sqcap c) = (a \sqcup b) \sqcap (a \sqcup c)$ (or its dual which is equivalent), then we obtain a *distributive lattice*.

A *semilattice* is an algebra $(\mathcal{L}, \sqcup)$ with a single binary operation which is associative, commutative and idempotent. In this paper when we write "semilattice" we refer to an *upper semilattice* in which the binary operation corresponds to a least upper bound operator. All results can be equally stated also for a *lower semilattice* in which the binary operation corresponds to a greatest lower bound operator. The identity between lattices (semilattices) and partially ordered sets in which every pair of elements has a least upper bound and a greatest lower bound (a least upper bound) is well known. The correspondence between the operations $\sqcup$ and $\sqcap$ and the partial order $\sqsubseteq$ is characterized by: $\forall_{a,b\in\mathcal{L}}.\ a \sqsubseteq b \Leftrightarrow a \sqcup b = b$ and $\forall_{a,b\in\mathcal{L}}.\ a \sqsubseteq b \Leftrightarrow a \sqcap b = a$.

Let x and y be different elements of a (semi) lattice. Then, either $x \not\sqsubseteq y$ or $y \not\sqsubseteq x$. That is why we may assume without loss of generality that $x \not\sqsubseteq y$.

Marked elements

When we consider a concrete structure such as $L = (\mathcal{L}, \sqcup)$ (for example in computer science applications) we usually assume that every element of $\mathcal{L}$ has a name in the language (of formulae). Typically, the formulae of interest contain explicitly referenced constants from $\mathcal{L}$. Of course, ground formula pose no problem, as each symbol has a unique interpretation in the given domain. In the case, when a formula contains some variables and some constants we are confronted with a problem when attempting to determine the validity of the formula in a non-classical object. That is, the given structure L with the additional 0-ary operations — marked elements, which correspond to the constants of the formula.

Let us notice, that adding even one 0-ary operation to a signature may change greatly the properties. For example, it is obvious, that the implication from Example 3 is not valid in any two-element lattice. Another example is nontrivial: the well known fact, that every finite group has a finite basis of identities [22] turns out to be wrong for finite groups with one marked element [4].

A lattice with marked elements is a lattice $(\mathcal{L}, \sqcup, \sqcap, E)$, together with the set $E \subseteq \mathcal{L}$ of additional 0-ary operations, namely the set of names of the marked elements. For the purposes of this paper we may assume that there are finitely many marked elements. This because we are reasoning about the validity of a given formula which may contain only finitely many constants. For any (semi) lattice L with marked elements E we denote by L_0 the sub(semi) lattice of L generated by E. We denote the unit of L_0 by $e = \sqcup E$.

Homomorphisms and congruences

Let $L_1 = (\mathcal{L}_1, \sqcup, \sqcap, E_1)$ and $L_2 = (\mathcal{L}_2, \sqcup, \sqcap, E_1)$ be two lattices with marked elements. A mapping $\varphi : \mathcal{L}_1 \to \mathcal{L}_2$ is called a ***homomorphism***, if

1. $\varphi : E_1 \to E_2$ is one-to-one and on;
2. $\forall_{x,y \in \mathcal{L}_1}.\ \varphi(x \sqcup y) = \varphi(x) \sqcup \varphi(y)$; and
3. $\forall_{x,y \in \mathcal{L}_1}.\ \varphi(x \sqcap y) = \varphi(x) \sqcap \varphi(y)$.

Note that we do not add any new axioms with marked elements to the definitions of classical structures. This is why homomorphisms of structures with marked elements are required to preserve marked elements (condition 1). For semilattices we have the same definition but without the third condition. It follows from the definition that L_1 and L_2 have the same number of marked elements and that a homomorphism preserves not only the marked elements but also any element from the sub(semi) lattice, generated by the marked elements.

We associate with a homomorphism $\varphi : L_1 \to L_2$ the binary relation $\sim_\varphi$ on $\mathcal{L}_1$ defined by $a \sim_\varphi b \Leftrightarrow \varphi(a) = \varphi(b)$. It is well known that $\sim_\varphi$ is a congruence on L_1 (cf [11]). Namely, $\forall_{x,y,z \in L_1}.\ x \sim_\varphi y \ \rightarrow\ z \sqcup x \sim_\varphi z \sqcup y$. This congruence is named the ***kernel*** of the homomorphism φ. We say that a congruence $\sim$ on L_1 is ***trivial*** if $\forall_{x,y \in L_1}.\ x \sim y \Leftrightarrow x = y$.

Ideals, filters and closed filters

Let $L = (\mathcal{L}, \sqcup)$ be a semilattice. If L is an upper or lower semilattice we refer to its filters or ideals respectively. A filter $\mathcal{F}$ will be named a *closed filter* if $\forall_{x,y \in L}.\ x \sqcup y \in \mathcal{F} \ \rightarrow\ x \in \mathcal{F} \vee y \in \mathcal{F}$. One can observe, that a filter $\mathcal{F}$ is closed if and only if its complement is in L, that is $L \setminus \mathcal{F}$ is subsemilattice.

If $\varphi : L_1 \to L_2$ is a homomorphism of semilattices and 1 is the unit of L_2 which is join-irreducible then $\varphi^{-1}(1)$ is a closed filter. If L_2 is nontrivial, 1 is the unit of L_2 which is join-irreducible and $\mathcal{F}$ is a closed filter of L_1, then there exists a homomorphism $\varphi : L_1 \to L_2$ such that $\varphi^{-1}(1) = \mathcal{F}$.

For every $\ell \in L$, we denote the *ideal* and the *filter* of ℓ by

$$\mathcal{I}_\ell = \{\, x \mid x \sqsubseteq \ell \,\}; \quad \textit{and} \quad \mathcal{F}_\ell = \{\, x \mid \ell \sqsubseteq x \,\}.$$

Let $x \in L$. Let us denote by $\mathcal{F}^x$ the maximal filter of L which does not contain x. One can observe, that $\mathcal{F}^x = L \setminus \mathcal{I}_x$ and that $\mathcal{F}^x$ is a closed filter. Let $y \in L$, such that $x \not\sqsupseteq y$, then $y \in \mathcal{F}^x$.

Let $x, y \in L$. Let us denote by $\mathcal{F}^{x,y}$ the maximal filter of L which does not contain x and y. Observe that $\mathcal{F}^{x,y} = \mathcal{F}^x \cap \mathcal{F}^y$.

Algebraic approximation

We say that a universal algebra $\mathcal{U}$ is *approximated* in a class of universal algebras $\mathcal{K}$ if for every $a, b \in \mathcal{U}$ such that $a \neq b$ there exists a homomorphism φ of $\mathcal{U}$ onto an algebra from $\mathcal{K}$ such that $\varphi(a) \neq \varphi(b)$. Such a homomorphism is said to *separate* the elements a and b.

Let L be a lattice with marked elements approximated in a class $\mathcal{K}$ of lattices. It follows from the definition of approximation that the intersection of all congruences corresponding to the homomorphisms separating elements of L is trivial.

Quasi-identities

Let Σ_L and $\mathcal{V}$ denote the signature of an algebra L and a set of variable symbols. Then, $\mathcal{T}_L(\mathcal{V})$ denotes the term algebra over Σ_L and $\mathcal{V}$ which is the corresponding free algebra. Any mapping $\varphi : \mathcal{V} \to L$ can be uniquely extended to a homomorphism $\mathcal{T}_L(\mathcal{V}) \to L$ which is also denoted φ.

A *quasi-identity* of L is a universally quantified formula of the form

$$\psi \equiv \quad (\forall)\ u_1 = v_1 \wedge \cdots \wedge u_n = v_n \to u_0 = v_0$$

where $u_i, v_i \in \mathcal{T}_L(\mathcal{V})$ $(0 \leq i \leq n)$. We say that ψ is *valid* in a L, denoted $L \models \varphi$, if for every homomorphism $\varphi : \mathcal{T}_L(\mathcal{V}) \to L$, $\varphi(\psi)$ is true.

It is well known that the validity of a quasi-identity τ is preserved by direct products and subsystems. In particular, if $L_i \models \tau$ for a class of semilattices L_i with marked elements $(i \in I)$ and L is a subsemilattice of the product $\prod_{i \in I} L_i$, then $L \models \tau$.

3 Approximating (semi) lattices

Let ψ be a quasi-identity over a semilattice L. In this section we show that the validity of ψ can be determined by inspection in a smaller (sub) semilattice

L' of L the size of which is determined by the number of constants from L occurring in ψ. It is well known that any semilattice is approximated in the class of isomorphic copies of the two-element semilattice. We show that any semilattice L with marked elements (constants) is approximated in the class of semilattices which are constructed from the semilattice generated by the marked elements. We distinguish several cases depending on the number of marked elements: *none*, *one* and *two*. We also show that the result is minimal with respect to the size of L'. Ongoing research addresses the general result. All of the results given below hold for distributive lattices as well as for semilattices. The proofs are similar.

Our approach to the problem of determining the validity of a quasi-identity is based on the following proposition which follows from Birkhoff's well known theorem on subdirect decomposition [3].

Proposition 1.
Let L be a semilattice with marked elements approximated by a class K of semilattices with marked elements. If a quasi-identity τ is valid in every semilattice from K then it is valid in L.

Proof.
As stated in Section 2, the validity of a quasi-identity is preserved by direct products and subsystems. As L is approximated by K, it follows from the definition of algebraic approximation that the intersection of the kernels of homomorphisms of L onto semilattices from K which separate elements of L is trivial. Thus, it follows from Birhoff's Theorem [2, 3] that L can be represented as a subdirect product of semilattices from K. Hence, if τ is valid in every semilattice from K then it is valid in L.

Remark.
Let L be a semilattice with marked elements approximated by a class K of subsemilattices of L. Then Proposition 1 can be reformulated as follows: A quasi-identity τ is valid in L if and only if it is valid in K.

Remark.
The word "semilattice" in Proposition 1 can be replaced by the word "universal algebra". In particular, the result is true for distributive lattices with marked elements as well.

Remark.
Malcev [19] proves that for an axiomatizable class K of universal algebras the quasivariety generated by K coincides with the prevariety generated by K. A class K_0, consisting of a finite number of finite (semi)lattices with marked elements is axiomatizable. Consequently, *every quasi-identity which is valid in K_0 is valid in a (semi)lattice A if and only if A is approximated in K_0.*

Remark.
If a semilattice contains the elements 0 or 1 then these elements are preserved by any homomorphism and hence may also be viewed as marked elements. In this paper by "marked elements" we mean additional elements besides 0 and 1.

3.1 Semilattice with no marked elements

The results for this case are known and are included here for completeness. Let C_2 be a two element chain $0 \sqsubset 1$.

Proposition 2. *Birkhoff [3]*
Every distributive lattice is approximated by $\{C_2\}$.

Proposition 3. *folklore*
Every semilattice is approximated by $\{C_2\}$.

3.2 Semilattice with one marked element

Let $L = (\mathcal{L}, \sqcup, E)$ be a semilattice with one marked element and C_3 a three element chain: $0 \sqsubset a \sqsubset 1$. If possible we consider the semilattices by which we approximate L as subsemilattices of L. In particular we denote the marked element of C_3 by the same letter as in L.

Proposition 4.
A semilattice L with one marked element is approximated in the class of subsemilattices of C_3.

Proof.
Let $x, y \in L$, $x \not\sqsubseteq y$, that is $y \notin \mathcal{F}_x$. That is why $x \in \mathcal{F}^y$. Let us consider two cases:

1. $a \notin \mathcal{F}^y$. In this case let us consider the mapping $\varphi : L \to C_3$ defined by:
$$\varphi(z) = \begin{cases} 1 & \text{if } z \in \mathcal{F}^y \\ a & \text{if } z \in L \setminus \mathcal{F}^y. \end{cases}$$
2. $a \in \mathcal{F}^y$. In this case let us consider the mapping $\varphi : L \to C_3$ defined by:
$$\varphi(z) = \begin{cases} a & \text{if } z \in \mathcal{F}^y \\ 0 & \text{if } z \in L \setminus \mathcal{F}^y. \end{cases}$$

In both cases φ is a homomorphism which separates x from y.

Remark.
A three-element chain $0 \sqsubset a \sqsubset 1$ is approximated by two two-element chains $0 \sqsubset a$ and $a \sqsubset 1$. Let ψ be a formula containing n variables and 1 marked letter (constant). To examine the validity of ψ in a three-element chain we are to fulfill 3^n examinations. To examine the validity of ψ in two two-element chains we are to fulfill 2^{n+1} examinations. Thus, the approximation of a semilattice L with one marked element by two two-element chains is usually more efficient.

In some cases L does not contain a subsemilattice which is isomorphic to C_3. Moreover, some semilattices with one marked element can be approximated by a two-element chain. We prove that we can always use for approximation a subsemilattice of L which is minimal in the number of elements. Let us assume that L contains more than one element. In this case L contains a subsemilattice which is isomorphic to C_2.

Proposition 5.
Let L be a semilattice with one marked element 'a'. Then, L is approximated in $\{C_2\}$ if and only if $\mathcal{I}_a$ or $\mathcal{F}_a$ contains exactly one element.

Proof.

$\Leftarrow$ The proof of this direction is analogous to the proof of the Proposition 4;
$\Rightarrow$ To prove this direction we observe the following:
- to separate an element x such that $x \sqsubset a$ from a we need a two-element chain $0 \sqsubset a$;
- to separate an element x such that $x \sqsupset a$ from a we need a two-element chain $a \sqsubset 1$;
- these two chains are not approximated one by another.

Remark.
We can change in the previous statements the word "semilattice" for the word "distributive lattice". The proofs are the same. This is because we can define $\mathcal{F}^x$ for a distributive lattice as well and also in this case $\mathcal{F}^x$ will be a closed filter.

3.3 Semilattice with two marked elements

Let L be a semilattice with two marked elements a and b. Without lost of generality we assume that $a \not\sqsupseteq b$. Let us denote the three-element chains $a \sqsubset b \sqsubset 1$ and $0 \sqsubset a \sqsubset b$ by $\overline{C}_3$ and $\underline{C}_3$ respectively and the the three-element semilattice $\{a, b, c\}$ where $b = a \sqcup c$ by V_3. The four-element lattice $\{a, b, c, 0\}$ denoted S_4 is obtained by adding a bottom element to V_3 and the lattice S_5 is obtained by adding a top element to S_4. These semilattices are illustrated in Figure 1.

Proposition 6.
A semilattice L with two marked elements is approximated in the class of five semilattices: C_2, $\overline{C}_3$, $\underline{C}_3$, V_3 and S_4.

Proof.
Let $x, y \in L$, $x \not\sqsubseteq y$, that is $y \notin \mathcal{F}_x$ and hence $x \in \mathcal{F}^y$. Let us consider three cases:

1. $a \notin \mathcal{F}^y$ and $b \notin \mathcal{F}^y$. In this case consider the mapping $\varphi : L \rightarrow \overline{C}_3$ defined by:

$$\varphi(z) = \begin{cases} 1 & \text{if } z \in \mathcal{F}^y \\ b & \text{if } z \in \mathcal{F}^b \setminus \mathcal{F}^y \\ a & \text{otherwise.} \end{cases}$$

   To prove that φ is a homomorphism we have to show that (*) for any $z_1, z_2 \in L$

$$\varphi(z_1 \sqcup z_2) = \varphi(z_1) \sqcup \varphi(z_2) : \qquad (1)$$

   We consider three cases:

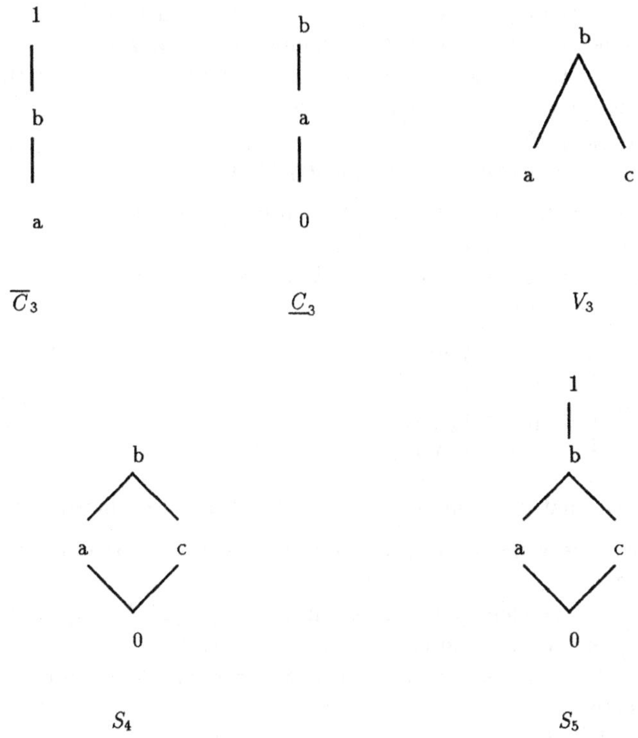

Fig. 1. The semilattices $\overline{C}_3$, $\underline{C}_3$, V_3, S_4 and S_5.

(a) If one of the elements z_1, z_2 is in $\mathcal{F}^y$ then so is $(z_1 \sqcup z_2)$ and consequently (1) is true. Let us assume that $z_1, z_2 \notin \mathcal{F}^y$.

(b) If both of elements z_1, z_2 are in $\mathcal{F}^b \setminus \mathcal{F}^y$ or in $L \setminus (\mathcal{F}^y \cup \mathcal{F}^b)$ then so is $(z_1 \sqcup z_2)$ and consequently (1) is true.

(c) The remaining case is $z_1 \in (\mathcal{F}^b \setminus \mathcal{F}^y)$, $z_2 \in L \setminus (\mathcal{F}^y \cup \mathcal{F}^b)$. In this case $(z_1 \sqcup z_2) \in (\mathcal{F}^b \setminus \mathcal{F}^y)$, consequently (1) is true.

Hence, φ is a homomorphism and it separates x from y.

2. $a \in \mathcal{F}^y$ and $b \in \mathcal{F}^y$.

We consider three subcases: $b \not\sqsubseteq a \sqcup y$, $a \not\sqsubseteq b \sqcup y$, and $b \sqsubseteq a \sqcup y$ & $a \sqsubseteq b \sqcup y$, that is $a \sqcup y = b \sqcup y$.

In the first case we consider the mapping $\varphi : L \to \underline{C}_3$ defined by:

$$\varphi(z) = \begin{cases} a & \text{if } z \in \mathcal{I}_{a \sqcup y} \cap \mathcal{F}^y \\ b & \text{if } z \in \mathcal{F}^y \setminus \mathcal{I}_{a \sqcup y} \\ 0 & \text{if } L \setminus \mathcal{F}^y. \end{cases}$$

Let us prove, that φ is a homomorphism: let $z_1, z_2 \in L$ and consider the following three cases.

(a) If one of the elements z_1, z_2 is in $\mathcal{F}^y \setminus \mathcal{I}_{a \sqcup y}$ then so is $(z_1 \sqcup z_2)$ and consequently (1) is true. Let us assume that $z_1, z_2 \notin \mathcal{F}^y \setminus \mathcal{I}_{a \sqcup y}$.
(b) If both of the elements z_1, z_2 is in $\mathcal{I}_{a \sqcup y} \cap \mathcal{F}^y$ or in $L \setminus \mathcal{F}^y$ then so is $(z_1 \sqcup z_2)$ and consequently (1) is true.
(c) If $z_1 \in \mathcal{I}_{a \sqcup y} \cap \mathcal{F}^y$, $z_2 \in L \setminus \mathcal{F}^y$ then $(z_1 \sqcup z_2) \in \mathcal{I}_{a \sqcup y} \cap \mathcal{F}^y$ since $z_1 \sqcup z_2 \not\sqsubseteq y$ and $z_1 \sqcup z_2 \sqsubseteq a \sqcup y$ and consequently (1) is true.

Hence, φ is a homomorphism and it separates x from y.
The second case is similar to the first.
To examine the third case, $b \sqsubseteq a \sqcup y$ & $a \sqsubseteq b \sqcup y$, we consider the mapping $\varphi : L \to S_4$ defined by:

$$\varphi(z) = \begin{cases} b & \text{if } z \in \mathcal{F}^{a,y} \\ 0 & \text{if } z \in \mathcal{I}_a \cap \mathcal{I}_y \\ a & \text{if } z \in \mathcal{I}_a \setminus \mathcal{I}_y \\ c & \text{if } z \in \mathcal{I}_y \setminus \mathcal{I}_a. \end{cases}$$

Let us prove that φ is a homomorphism. Consider the following five cases:

(a) If one of the elements z_1, z_2 is in $\mathcal{F}^{a,y}$ then so is $(z_1 \sqcup z_2)$ and consequently (1) is true.
(b) If both of the elements z_1, z_2 are in $\mathcal{I}_a \cap \mathcal{I}_y$ or in $\mathcal{I}_a \setminus \mathcal{I}_y$ or in $\mathcal{I}_y \setminus \mathcal{I}_a$ then so is $(z_1 \sqcup z_2)$ and consequently (1) is true.
(c) If $z_1 \in \mathcal{I}_a \cap \mathcal{I}_y$, $z_2 \in \mathcal{I}_a \setminus \mathcal{I}_y$ then $(z_1 \sqcup z_2) \in \mathcal{I}_a \setminus \mathcal{I}_y$ and consequently (1) is true.
(d) If $z_1 \in \mathcal{I}_a \cap \mathcal{I}_y$, $z_2 \in \mathcal{I}_y \setminus \mathcal{I}_a$ then $(z_1 \sqcup z_2) \in\in \mathcal{I}_y \setminus \mathcal{I}_a$ and consequently (1) is true.
(e) If $z_1 \in \mathcal{I}_a \setminus \mathcal{I}_y$, $z_2 \in \mathcal{I}_y \setminus \mathcal{I}_a$ then $(z_1 \sqcup z_2) \not\sqsubseteq y$ and $(z_1 \sqcup z_2) \not\sqsubseteq a$. That is, $(z_1 \sqcup z_2) \in \mathcal{F}^{a,y}$ and consequently (1) is true.

Hence, φ is a homomorphism and it separates x from y.
One can observe that if $\mathcal{I}_a \cap \mathcal{I}_y$ is empty then we have obtained a homomorphism $\varphi : L \to V_3$.

3. $a \notin \mathcal{F}^y$ and $b \in \mathcal{F}^y$. In this case consider the mapping $\varphi : L \to C_2$ defined by:

$$\varphi(z) = \begin{cases} 1 & \text{if } z \in \mathcal{F}_y \\ 0 & \text{if } z \in L \setminus \mathcal{F}^y. \end{cases}$$

It is obvious that φ is a homomorphism which separates x from y.

Remark.
One can observe that none of the semilattices mentioned in Proposition 6 is approximated by the others. All of these semilattices except $\underline{C}_3$ are subsemilattices of $\underline{S}_4$. Consequently, to determine the validity of a quasi-identity ψ with less than three constants in a semilattice it is sufficient to determine its validity in $\underline{C}_3$ and S_4. Sometimes it is convenient to present these semilattices as subsemilattices of S_5 and to determine the validity of ψ in S_5 only.

Remark.
It is worthy to notice that the statement of Proposition 6 does not depend on the relationship between the elements a and b. That is, in general we can not simplify the class of semilattices in which we approximate even in the case when $a \leq b$ or in the case $a \not\leq b$ and $b \not\leq a$.

Proposition 7.
A distributive lattice with two marked elements is approximated in the class of the following distributive lattices: C_2, $\underline{C}_3$, $\overline{C}_3$ *and* S_4.

Proof. The proof is similar to that of Proposition 6.

4 An Application

In [8] we describe a polymorphic type analysis for logic programs in which types are represented by *lub-clauses*. Namely by Horn clauses of the form

$$h \leftarrow \ell_1, \ldots, \ell_n$$

in which each ℓ_i is an atom of the form $lub(t_1, t_2, t_3)$ which specifies a least upper bound $t_1 \sqcup t_2 = t_3$ on the given domain of types. For example, the lub-clause

$$append(list(A), list(B), list(C)) \leftarrow lub(A, B, C)$$

specifies a type for the append/3 relation in which the three arguments are respectively lists of type A, B and C such that $A \sqcup B = C$. A type of this form can be applied to determine that the result of concatenating a list of `real` numbers with a list of `integer` numbers is a list of `number`'s (assuming that `integer` $\sqcup$ `real` $=$ `number` in the given lattice of types).

At each stage in our type analysis we have a a set C of lub-clauses and a new candidate lub-clause $c \equiv h \leftarrow lubs$ and we are required to determine if c is *subsumed* by C. An approximation is obtained by checking if there exists a renaming of a clause c' in C of the form $h \leftarrow lubs'$ such that $lubs' \Rightarrow lubs$. In practice, there are more details. However, this is the topic of another paper. At the bottom line we need to determine the validity of an implication of the form $lubs' \Rightarrow lubs$ in which $lubs'$ and $lubs$ are conjunctions of least upper bound operations which typically contain a small number of marked elements. The application of the principles described in this paper have led to substantial (2-3 orders of magnitude on the examples we have tested) gains in the efficiency of our type analysis.

5 Conclusion

We have addressed the question of determining the validity of universally quantified implications over algebraic structures such as semilattices and distributive lattices. Our approach is based on the fact that the validity of a quasi-identity

ψ in a universal algebra $\mathcal{L}$ is preserved under direct products and subalgebras. That is why it is sufficient to decompose $\mathcal{L}$ into a subdirect product and to determine the validity of ψ on the components of this decomposition. This paper applies techniques of algebraic approximation to obtain such decompositions.

Birkhoff [3] proves that every universal algebra $\mathcal{L}$ can be decomposed into the subdirect product of subdirectly irreducible universal algebras and that all subdirectly irreducible components belong to the variety generated by $\mathcal{L}$. For example, it is well known [12] that the only subdirectly irreducible Boolean algebra is a two-element Boolean algebra and that the only subdirectly irreducible Stone algebras are two-element and three-element Stone algebras. Hence to determine the validity of a quasi-identity (without constants) in any Boolean or Stone algebra it is sufficient to determine the validity for the two-element Boolean algebra or the two- and three- element Stone algebras. The corresponding results for these algebras with a signature enriched by marked elements and for quasi-identities with less than three constants follow from the results of this paper.

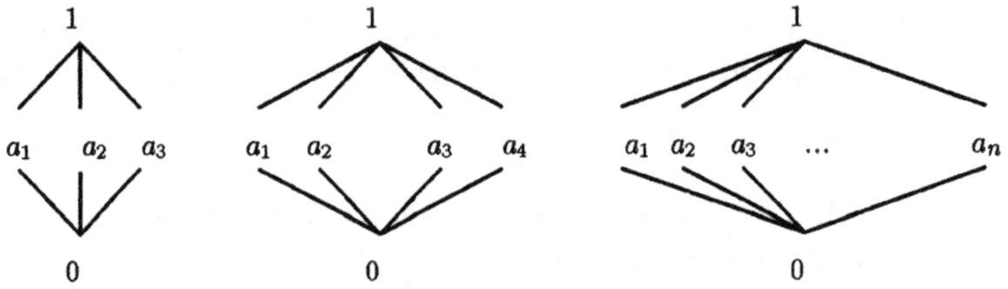

Fig. 2. A family of subdirectly irreducible lattices

Let us mention, that for some other classes of lattices the approach described in this paper fails and the proof theoretic approach should be preferred. For example, it is easily verified that each of the lattices depicted in Figure 2 are subdirectly irreducible. Such domains cannot be simplified when trying to determine implications (even in the case with no constants). On the other hand, in the proof theoretic approach it is straightforward to observe that for any two distinct elements a, b (not including 0 or 1), $a \sqcup b = 1$ and $a \sqcap b = 0$. Observe that if the structures in Figure 2 are viewed as semi-lattices then they are obviously subdirectly irreducible.

The results of Birkhoff are generalized by Malcev [16] who proves, under very general assumptions on the class of models, that models can be decomposed into subdirect products of subdirectly irreducible models. Hence we might apply the same approach to determine the validity of quasi-identities of the general form

$$p_1(t_1^1, \ldots, t_{k_1}^1) \wedge \cdots \wedge p_n(t_1^n, \ldots, t_{k_n}^n) \rightarrow p_0(t_1^0, \ldots, t_{k_0}^0)$$

which are also known as definite Horn clauses. Of particular interest is to consider the predicates of set inclusion and set membership instead of the predicate of equality. However, in this case it is still not clear (even for the case with no marked elements) how to decompose the given algebraic structure and still obtain useful results. This is the topic of ongoing research.

Acknowledgments

The useful discussions with Bart Demoen are gratefully acknowledged. Avraham Melkman pointed out the reference to the zero-one principle for sorting networks.

References

1. A. Aiken and E. L. Wimmers. Solving systems of set constraints (extended abstract). In *Proceedings, Seventh Annual IEEE Symposium on Logic in Computer Science*, pages 329–340, Santa Cruz, California, June 22–25 1992. IEEE Computer Society Press.
2. G. Birkhoff. Subdirect unions in univeral algebras. *Bull. Amer. Math. Soc.*, 50:764–768, 1944.
3. G. Birkhoff. Lattice Theory. In *AMS Colloquium Publication, third ed.*, 1967.
4. R. Bryant. The laws of finite pointed groups. *Bull. London Math. Soc.*, 14(2), 1982.
5. R. Bryant. Graph based algorithms for boolean function manipulation. *IEEE Transactions on Computers*, 35(8):677–691, 1986.
6. R. Bryant. Ordered binary-decision diagrams. *ACM Computing Surveys*, 24(3), 1992.
7. M. Codish and B. Demoen. Analysing logic programs using "Prop"-ositional logic programs and a magic wand. In D. Miller, editor, *Logic Programming - Proceedings of the 1993 International Symposium*, pages 114–129, Massachusetts Institute of Technology, Cambridge, Massachusetts 021-42, 1993. The MIT Press.
8. M. Codish and B. Demoen. Deriving polymorphic type dependencies for logic programs using multiple incarnations of prop. Technical report, Department of Mathematics and Computer Science, Ben-Gurion University of the Negev, Beer-Sheva 84105, Israel, 1994. Anonymous ftp: black.bgu.ac.il:pub/codish/type.dvi.
9. M. Corsini, K. Musumbu, A. Rauzy, and B. Le Charlier. Efficient bottom-up abstract interpretation of Prolog by means of constraint solving over symbolic finite domains. In *Proceedings of the Fifth International Symposium on Programming Language Implementation and Logic Programming*, Lecture Notes in Computer Science, Talin, Aug. 1993. Springer Verlag.
10. P. Cousot and R. Cousot. Abstract interpretation: A unified lattice model for static analysis of programs by construction or approximation of fixpoints. In *Proceedings of the Fourth ACM Symposium on Principles of Programming Languages*, pages 238–252, Jan. 1977.
11. G. Grätzer. *Universal Algebra.* D. van Nostrand Company, Inc., 1968.
12. G. Grätzer. *General Lattice Theory.* Akademie-Verlag, Berlin, 1978.
13. K. Kennedy. A survey of data flow analysis techniques. pages 5–54. Chapter 1 in [21].
14. D. E. Knuth. *The Art of Computer Programming*, volume 3. Addison-Wesley, 1973.

15. B. Le Charlier and P. V. Hentenryck. Groundness analysis for Prolog: implementation and evaluation of the domain Prop. In *Proceedings Symposium on Partial Evaluation and Semantics-based Program Manipulation*, 1993.
16. A. Malćev. Subdirect products of models. *Dokl. Akad. Nauk SSSR*, 109:264–266, 1956. In Russian and Chapter 5 in [18] (English translation).
17. A. Malćev. About homomorphisms on finite groups. In *Učenye Zapiski Ivanov*, volume 28, pages 49–60. Ped. Inst., 1958. In Russian.
18. A. Malćev. *The Metamathematics of Algebraic Systems*. North-Holland Publishing Company, 1971.
19. A. Malćev (Maltsev). *Algebraic Systems*. Springer-Verlag, 1973.
20. A. Melton, D. Schmidt, and G. Strecker. Galois connections and computer science applications. In D. P. *et al.*, editor, *Category Theory and Computer Programming*, pages 299–312. Springer-Verlag, 1986. Lecture Notes in Computer Science 240.
21. S. S. Muchnick and N. D. Jones. *Program Flow Analysis: Theory and Applications*. Prentice Hall, 1981.
22. H. Neuman. Varieties of groups. Springer-Verlag, Berlin-Heidelberg-New York, 1967.
23. O. Ore. Galois connections. In *Trans. AMS*, volume 55, pages 493–513, 1944.
24. B.M. Schein. On subdirectly irreducible semigroups. *Dokl. Akad. Nauk SSSR*, 144:999–1002, 1962. In Russian.

Sufficient Completeness and Parameterized Proofs by Induction

Adel Bouhoula
CRIN & INRIA-Lorraine
BP 239, 54506 Vandœuvre-lès-Nancy, France
email: bouhoula@loria.fr

Abstract. Theorem proving in parameterized specifications allows for shorter and more structured proofs. Moreover, a generic proof can be given just once and reused for each instantiation of the parameters. We present procedures to test sufficient completeness and to prove and disprove inductive properties automatically in parameterized conditional specifications. This new method when limited to non-parameterized conditional specifications, can refute general clauses; refutational completeness is also preserved for boolean ground convergent rewrite systems even if the functions are not sufficiently complete and the constructors are not free. The method has been implemented in the prover SPIKE. Based on computer experiments, the method appears to be more practical and efficient than inductive theorem proving in non-parameterized specifications. Moreover, SPIKE offers facilities to check and complete definitions.

Keywords: Theorem Proving, Sufficient completeness, Implicit induction, Parameterized Conditional Specifications, Term rewriting systems.

1 Introduction

Algebraic specifications (see [Wir90]) provide a powerful method for the specification of abstract data types in programming languages and software systems. Often, algebraic specifications are built with conditional equations. Semantically, the motivation for this is the existence of initial models; operationally, the motivation is the ability to use term rewriting techniques for computing and automatic prototyping. One of the most important issues within the theory of algebraic specifications is the specification of parameterized data types. Most common data types like *list* are in fact parameterized types, *list(data)*. The key idea is to consider the parameter part *data* as a formal algebraic specification which can be actualized (i.e. instantiated) by other predefined algebraic specifications like *nat*, *int* or *bool*. Hence, we can obtain from the parameterized specification *list(data)* the three value specifications corresponding to lists of natural numbers, lists of integers and lists of boolean values. The benefit of this process is not only an economy of presentation but also the automatic correctness of all the value specifications provided that the parameterized specification *list(data)* is correct and the actual instantiation is valid. These are very important properties for building up larger data types and software systems from small pieces in a correct way. Sufficient completeness and consistency are fundamental notions for guaranteeing correctness of a parameterized specification. Also, they are very useful in proofs by induction. Informally, given a conditional specification S and a set of distinguished operators C, called *constructors*, S is said to be sufficiently complete, if any normal form of a ground term is a primitive term, i.e. a term built only from constructors. J. Guttag showed that this property is undecidable. However, some syntactic criteria can be given. Most of them are based on rewriting methods [GH78; Kou85; Com86; LLT90]. In the context of conditional parameterized specifications, the art is less developed. This is mostly due to the fact that the problem is much harder. In this paper, we give an effective method for testing this

property for parameterized conditional specifications [1]. This method is inspired by [Kou85; BKR92] and it is based on the notion of *Pattern* trees.
Another direction is to make use of parameterization at the proof level and to develop a generic proof method. This approach allows us to have shorter and more structured proofs. A generic proof for a parameterized specification must be given only once and can be reused for each instantiation of the parameter. We are interested in automating proof by induction. Many tools for proof by induction have been developed for non-parameterized specifications: The first type applies explicit induction arguments on the term structure [BM79]. The second type involves a proof by consistency [Mus80; HH82; JK86; Bac88]. More recently, new methods were developed that do not rely on the completion framework [KR90; Red90; BR93; BR94].

Inductive theory of a parameterized specification have been studied by Navarro and Orejas [NO87]; their results generalize [Pad84]. But they do not give effective methods to prove inductive theorems. Ganzinger [Gan87] considered parametric conditional equational specifications which allow arbitrary first order formulas as "parameter constraints", but he was interested in ground confluence results and not in inductive theorem proving. H. Kirchner has studied proofs by induction in the unconditional case (where the parameter theory is equational) [Kir91] using techniques of proof by consistency. K. Becker has dealt with proof by consistency in parameterized positive/negative conditional equational specifications [Bec92]. To conclude, most of the work in proof by induction only considers the technique of proof by consistency. It is generally accepted that such techniques may be very inefficient since the completion procedure often diverges. For that reason, we adopt here a method which does not require completion.

The system SPIKE [Bou94b] has been developed in this framework. It incorporates many optimizations such as powerful simplification techniques. To our knowledge, our system is the only one that can disprove non-trivial inductive theorems in conditional theories without any interaction. None of the well-known induction prover has been designed to refute false conjectures. SPIKE has proved the challenging Gilbreath card trick with only 2 easy lemmas [BR94]. This example was treated by B. Boyer in NQTHM and H. Zhang in RRL. Unlike SPIKE, they require a lot of lemmas, some of them being non-obvious.

We give in this paper a new procedure for proof by induction in parameterized conditional specifications. Our procedure relies on the notion of *test set* which can be seen as a special induction scheme that allows us to refute false conjectures by the construction of a counterexample. Our definition of test set is more general than the previous one given in [BR94]. It permits us to obtain a smaller test set, which improves efficiency. As in our previous procedure [BR94], to prove conjectures, we just instantiate them with terms from the test set at induction positions and simplify them by axioms, other conjectures or induction hypotheses. The method does not require any hierarchy between the lemmas. They are all stored in a single list and using conjectures for mutual simplification simulates *simultaneous induction*. Unlike our previous method [BR94], this new procedure when limited to non-parameterized conditional specifications, can refute general clauses; refutational completeness is also preserved for boolean ground convergent rewrite systems even if the functions are not sufficiently complete and the constructors are not free. The method has been implemented in the prover SPIKE. Experiments illustrate the improvements in length and structuration of proofs, due to parametrisation.

The organization of this paper is as follows: In section 2, we briefly introduce basic con-

[1] To our knowledge, no previous implementation was able to check the sufficient completeness of parameterized conditional specifications.

cepts about term rewriting. In section 3, we characterize the inductive theory defined by a parameterized specification. We present in section 4 the procedure for testing sufficient completeness and we prove its correctness and completeness. We also describe a session with SPIKE to give an idea about the interaction with the user if the specification is not sufficiently complete. In section 5, we define the notions of induction variables and test sets. In section 6, we give a general inference system to perform induction and to refute false conjectures and we show its correctness. The strategy is proved refutationally complete for conditional equations with boolean preconditions (subsection 6.3). Section 7 is dedicated to a computer experiment with our SPIKE system. We give a comparison with our previous method for non-parameterized specifications and we show how proofs in parameterized specifications are shorter and more structured.

2 Basic concepts

We assume that the reader is familiar with the basic concepts of term rewriting, equational reasoning and mathematical logic. We introduce the essential terminology below and refer to [DJ90] for a more detailed presentation.

A many sorted signature Σ is a pair (S, F) where S is a set of *sorts* and F is a finite set of function symbols. For short, a many sorted signature Σ will simply denoted by F. We assume that we have a partition of F in two subsets, the first one, C, contains the *constructor symbols* and the second, D, is the set of *defined symbols*.

Let X be a family of sorted variables and let $T(F,X)$ be the set of well-sorted F-terms. $Var(t)$ stands for the set of all variables appearing in t and $\sharp(x,t)$ denotes the number of occurrences of the variable x in t. A variable x in t is *linear* iff $\sharp(x,t) = 1$. If $Var(t)$ is empty then t is a *ground* term. By $T(F)$ we denote the set of all ground terms. From now on, we assume that there exists at least one ground term of each non-parameter sort.

Let N^* be the set of sequences of positive integers. For any term t, $occ(t) \subseteq N^*$ denotes its set of positions and the expression t/u denotes the *subterm of t at a position u*. We write $t[s]_u$ (resp. $t[s]$) to indicate that s is a subterm of t at position u (resp. at some position). The top position is written ε. Let $t(u)$ denote the symbol of t at position u. A position u in a term t is said to be *a strict position* if $t(u) = f \in F$, a *linear variable position* if $t(u) = x \in X$ and $\sharp(x,t) = 1$, a *non-linear variable position* if $t(u) = x \in X$ and $\sharp(x,t) > 1$. We use $sdom(t)$ to denote the set of strict positions in t. If t is a term, then the *depth* of t is the maximum of the depths of the positions in t and denoted *depth(t)*. The *strict depth* of t, written as *sdepth(t)*, is the maximum of the depths of the strict positions in t. The symbol $\equiv$ is used for syntactic equality between two objects.

A F-substitution assigns F-terms of appropriate sorts to variables. Composition of substitutions σ and η is written by $\sigma\eta$. The F-term $t\eta$ obtained by applying a substitution η to t is called an *instance* of t. If η applies every variable of its domain to a ground term then we say that η is a ground substitution. If $t\eta$ is ground then it is a *ground instance* of t. A term t unifies with a term s if there exists a substitution σ such that $t\sigma \equiv s\sigma$.

A *conditional* F-equation is a F-equation of the following form: $s_1 = t_1 \wedge \cdots \wedge s_n = t_n \Rightarrow s_0 = t_0$ where $n \geq 0$ and $s_i, t_i \in T(F,X)$ are terms of the same sort. A F-clause is an expression of the form:

$$\neg(s_1 = t_1) \vee \neg(s_2 = t_2) \vee \cdots \vee \neg(s_n = t_n) \vee (s'_1 = t'_1) \vee \cdots \vee (s'_m = t'_m).$$

When F is clear from the context we omit the prefix F. A clause is *positive* if $\neg$ does not occur in it. Let c_1 and c_2 be two clauses such that $c_1\sigma$ is a subclause of c_2 for some substitution

σ, then we say that c_1 subsumes c_2. Let H be a set of clauses and C be a clause, we say that C is a logical consequence of H if C is valid in any model of H. This will be denoted by $H \models C$.

In the following, we suppose that $\succ$ is a transitive irreflexive relation on the set of terms, that is noetherian, monotonic ($s \succ t$ implies $w[s] \succ w[t]$), stable ($s \succ t$ implies $s\sigma \succ t\sigma$) and satisfy the proper subterm property ($f(\cdots,t,\cdots) \succ t$, for all $t \in T(F,X)$). We also assume that the ordering $\succ$ can be extended consistently when adding new constants to the signature. The multiset extension of $\succ$ will be denoted by $\gg$. Let $\succ_c$ be a well-founded ordering on clauses (see [BR93]).

A conditional equation $a_1 = b_1 \wedge \cdots a_n = b_n \Rightarrow l = r$ will be written as $a_1 = b_1 \wedge \cdots \wedge a_n = b_n \Rightarrow l \rightarrow r$ if $\{l\sigma\} \gg \{r\sigma, a_1\sigma, b_1\sigma, \cdots, a_n\sigma, b_n\sigma\}$ for each substitution σ and $Var(l)$ contains $Var(r) \cup Var(p)$ where $p \equiv \wedge_{i=1}^{n} a_i = b_i$; in that case we say that $a_1 = b_1 \wedge \cdots a_n = b_n \Rightarrow l \rightarrow r$ is a *conditional rule*. The term l is the *left-hand side* of the rule. A rewrite rule $c \Rightarrow l \rightarrow r$ is *left-linear* if l is linear. A rewrite system R is *left-linear* if every rule in R is left-linear, otherwise R is said to be *non-left-linear*. The *depth of a rewrite system* R, denoted *depth(R)*, is defined as the maximum of the depths of the left-hand sides of R. Similarly, the *strict depth* of R denoted by *sdepth(R)*, is the maximum of the depths of the strict positions in the left-hand sides of R.

From now on, we assume that for each conditional rule $p \Rightarrow l \rightarrow r$, if $l \in T(C,X)$, then $r \in T(C,X)$. A conditional rule is used to rewrite terms by replacing an instance of the left-hand side with the corresponding instance of the right-hand side (but not in the opposite direction) provided the conditions hold. The conditions are checked recursively. Termination is ensured because the conditions are smaller (w.r.t. to $\succ$) than the conclusion. A set of conditional rules is called a conditional rewrite system. We can define the one-step rewrite relation $\rightarrow_R$ and its reflexive-transitive closure $\rightarrow_R^*$ as follows:

Definition 2.1 (Conditional Rewriting) *Let R be a set of conditional equations. Let t be a term and u a position in t. We write: $t[l\sigma]_u \rightarrow_R t[r\sigma]_u$ if there is a substitution σ and a conditional equation $\wedge_{i=1}^{n} a_i = b_i \Rightarrow l = r$ in R such that:*

1. *$l\sigma \succ r\sigma$.*
2. *for all $i \in [1 \cdots n]$ there exists c_i such that $a_i\sigma \rightarrow_R^* c_i$ and $b_i\sigma \rightarrow_R^* c_i$.*
3. *$\{t[l\sigma]_u\} \gg \{a_1\sigma,\ b_1\sigma,\ \cdots,\ a_n\sigma,\ b_n\sigma\}$.*

A term t is *R-irreducible* (or in *normal form*) if there is no term s such that $t \rightarrow_R s$. Let R be a set of conditional rules. A term t is *strongly* irreducible by R (or *strongly R-irreducible*) if none of its non-variable subterms matches a left-hand side of R. Otherwise, we say that t is *strongly reducible* by R. We say that two terms s and t are joinable, denoted by $s \downarrow_R t$, if $s \rightarrow_R^* v$ and $t \rightarrow_R^* v$ for some term v. The rewrite relation $\rightarrow_R$ is said to be noetherian if there is no infinite chain of terms $t_1,\ t_2, \cdots, t_k, \cdots$ such that $t_i \rightarrow_R t_{i+1}$ for all i. The rewrite relation $\rightarrow_R$ is said to be *ground convergent* if the terms u and v are joinable whenever $u,\ v \in T(F)$ and $R \models u = v$.

3 Parameterized conditional specifications

A parameterized conditional specification is a pair $PS = (PAR, BODY)$ of specifications: $PAR = (F_{PAR}, E_{PAR})$ and $BODY = (F_{BODY}, E_{BODY})$ where E_{PAR} is the set of parameter *constraints* consisting of equational clauses in F_{PAR} and E_{BODY} is the set of axioms of the parameterized specification. We assume that these axioms are conditional rules over $F = F_{PAR} \cup F_{BODY}$, where F_{PAR} and F_{BODY} are signatures.

Example 3.1 *Consider the following parameterized specification:* $S_{PAR} = \{bool, elem\}$, $F_{PAR} = \{true :\rightarrow bool,\ false :\rightarrow bool,\ \leq : elem \times elem \rightarrow bool,\ dif : elem \times elem \rightarrow bool\}$, E_{PAR} *contains the following* constraints:

$$
\begin{gathered}
true \neq false \\
x \leq x = true \\
x \leq y = true \vee x \leq y = false \\
x \leq y = true \vee y \leq x = true \\
x \leq y = false \vee y \leq z = false \vee x \leq z = true \\
dif(x,x) = false \\
dif(x,y) = true \vee dif(x,y) = false
\end{gathered}
$$

$S = S_{PAR} \cup S_{BODY}$ *where* $S_{BODY} = \{nat, list\}$, $F = F_{PAR} \cup C_{BODY} \cup D_{BODY}$ *where* $C_{BODY} = \{0 :\rightarrow nat,\ s : nat \rightarrow nat,\ nil :\rightarrow list,\ cons : elem \times list \rightarrow list\}$ *and* $D_{BODY} = \{length : list \rightarrow nat,\ count : elem \times list \rightarrow nat,\ sorted : list \rightarrow bool,\ insert : elem \times list \rightarrow list,\ isort : list \rightarrow list\}$, E_{BODY} *contains the following conditional rules:*

$$
\begin{aligned}
length(nil) &\rightarrow 0 \\
length(cons(x,y)) &\rightarrow s(length(y)) \\
count(x,nil) &\rightarrow 0 \\
dif(x,y) = false \Rightarrow count(x,cons(y,t)) &\rightarrow s(count(x,t)) \\
dif(x,y) = true \Rightarrow count(x,cons(y,t)) &\rightarrow count(x,t) \\
sorted(nil) &\rightarrow true \\
sorted(cons(x,nil)) &\rightarrow true \\
x \leq y = false \Rightarrow sorted(cons(x,cons(y,z))) &\rightarrow false \\
x \leq y = true \Rightarrow sorted(cons(x,cons(y,z))) &\rightarrow sorted(cons(y,z)) \\
insert(x,nil) &\rightarrow cons(x,nil) \\
x \leq y = true \Rightarrow insert(x,cons(y,z)) &\rightarrow cons(x,cons(y,z)) \\
x \leq y = false \Rightarrow insert(x,cons(y,z)) &\rightarrow cons(y,insert(x,z)) \qquad (1) \\
isort(nil) &\rightarrow nil \\
isort(cons(x,l)) &\rightarrow insert(x,isort(l))
\end{aligned}
$$

To prove the termination of E_{BODY}, *we can use the* lrpo *ordering* $\prec$ *(see [Der87]) with the following precedence on functions:*

$false \prec true \prec 0 \prec s \prec Nil \prec Cons \prec dif \prec count \prec length \prec \leq \prec sorted \prec insert \prec isort$ ♦

3.1 The canonical term algebra

An actualization (see [EM85]) of the parameter theory E_{PAR} is a model $\mathcal{A}$ of E_{PAR}. We shall describe $\mathcal{A}$ by its diagram (see [EM85; Pad87]). For this reason we enrich the signatures by adding new constants $\underline{a}$ for each element a of the carrier A of $\mathcal{A}$. Let $\mathcal{N}(\mathcal{A})$ be the set of new constants and let $F(\mathcal{A}) = F \cup \mathcal{N}(\mathcal{A})$. The diagram $\mathcal{D}(\mathcal{A})$ of $\mathcal{A}$ is the set of (directed) equations $f(\underline{a}_1, \cdots, \underline{a}_n) = \underline{a}$ such that $f \in F_{PAR}$; a_i, $a \in A$ and $f^{\mathcal{A}}(a_1, \cdots, a_n) = a$. We denote by $E_{BODY}(\mathcal{A})$ the set $E_{BODY} \cup \mathcal{D}(\mathcal{A})$. For any model $\mathcal{A}$ of E_{PAR}, we define a canonical term algebra $\mathcal{T}(\mathcal{A})$ representing the semantics of the result of an actualization: $\mathcal{T}(\mathcal{A}) = T(F(\mathcal{A}))_{/=_{E_{BODY(\mathcal{A})}}}$ where $=_{E_{BODY(\mathcal{A})}}$ is the smallest congruence on $T(F(\mathcal{A}))$ generated by

$E_{BODY(\mathcal{A})}$. An interesting case is when $\mathcal{T}(\mathcal{A})$ is an initial model in the class of $F(\mathcal{A})$-algebras that are models of $E_{BODY}(\mathcal{A})$ for any model $\mathcal{A}$ of E_{PAR}. To guarantee this fact we need that $E_{BODY}(\mathcal{A})$ is consistent (i.e. has a model) for any model $\mathcal{A}$ of E_{PAR}. This result is shown by the following theorem which is analogous to theorem 2.8 from [Pad87].

Theorem 3.2 *If $E_{BODY}(\mathcal{A})$ is consistent for any model $\mathcal{A}$ of E_{PAR}, then $\mathcal{T}(\mathcal{A})$ is initial in the class of $F(\mathcal{A})$-algebras that are models of $E_{BODY}(\mathcal{A})$ for any model $\mathcal{A}$ of E_{PAR}.*

Many works have been done on checking consistency of parameterized specifications (see for instance [EM85; Pad87; Kir91; Bec92]).

3.2 Proving inductive theorems w.r.t. parameterized specifications

We shall now define what is an inductive theorem in parameterized specifications. Note that the theorems to be proved are *F-clauses.*

Definition 3.3 *A* F-clause *Γ is an inductive theorem for a parameterized specification PS (or inductively valid w.r.t. PS) iff $\mathcal{T}(\mathcal{A})$ is a model of Γ for any model $\mathcal{A}$ of E_{PAR}. This will be denoted by $PS \models_{ind} \Gamma$ or $E_{BODY}(\mathcal{A}) \models_{ind} \Gamma$ for any model $\mathcal{A}$ of E_{PAR}.*

The next lemma which is similar to lemma 9 from [Bec92], gives us a useful characterization of inductive theorems.

Lemma 3.4 *Let Γ be a* F-clause,

$$\Gamma \equiv \neg(u_1 = v_1) \vee \cdots \vee \neg(u_n = v_n) \vee (s_1 = t_1) \vee \cdots \vee (s_m = t_m)$$

Then Γ is an inductive theorem w.r.t. PS iff for any model $\mathcal{A}$ of E_{PAR} and for any ground substitution σ over $T(F(\mathcal{A}))$:

(for all i : $E_{BODY}(\mathcal{A}) \models u_i\sigma = v_i\sigma$) implies (there exists j such that $E_{BODY}(\mathcal{A}) \models s_j\sigma = t_j\sigma$)

4 Sufficient completeness for parameterized specifications

The property of sufficient completeness is in general undecidable. We now give a method for testing this property for conditional parameterized specifications. This method is inspired by [Kou85; BKR92] and based on the notion of *Pattern* trees. Let $\mathcal{A}$ be a model of E_{PAR}. If any ground term in $T(F(\mathcal{A}))$ can be expressed only with constructors and elements of $\mathcal{N}(\mathcal{A})$, we say that PS is complete w.r.t. the constructors and parameter (or sufficiently complete). Here is a more formal definition:

Definition 4.1 (sufficient completeness) *We say that PS is sufficiently complete if and only if for any model $\mathcal{A}$ of E_{PAR}, for all t in $T(F(\mathcal{A}))$ there exists t' in $T(C_{BODY} \cup \mathcal{N}(\mathcal{A}))$ such that $t \rightarrow^*_{E_{BODY}(\mathcal{A})} t'$.*

4.1 How to check sufficient completeness

The main idea behind our test for sufficient completeness is to compute a pattern tree for every f in D_{BODY}. The leaves of the tree give a partition of the possible arguments for f. If all the leaves are "pseudo-reducible by PS", then the answer is affirmative. To compute pattern trees, we use the following notions: Let f be a function symbol in F_{BODY}, a term t is in $Def(f)$, if t is of the form $f(w_1, \cdots, w_n)$ with for all i, $w_i \in T(F, X)$. A sort S is *nullary* [2], if for any model $\mathcal{A}$ of E_{PAR}, there is no infinite set of terms in $T(F(\mathcal{A}))$ of sort S that are irreducible by $E_{BODY}(\mathcal{A})$. Let t be a term and u a variable position in t, u is *nullary* if the sort of $t(u)$ is *nullary*.

In the following, we present a definition which characterizes induction positions of function symbols in F.

Definition 4.2 (induction positions) *Let f in F_{BODY}, we define the set of induction positions of functions as follows: $pos\_ind(f) = \{u \mid$ there is $p \Rightarrow g \rightarrow d \in E_{BODY}$ such that $g \in Def(f)$ and u is either a strict and non-top position in g or a non-parameter and non-linear variable position in $g\}$.*

Example 4.3 (example 3.1 continued) *The output of the SPIKE procedure that computes induction positions of functions is given in figure 6.* ♦

From any node of the tree labeled by the term $t = f(w_1, \cdots, w_n)$, with $w_i \in T(C_{BODY}, X)$ for all $i \in [1 \cdots n]$, we build the sons of this node by choosing a variable position u of t that is nullary or that is an induction position of f and by making a graft at this occurrence. Each son is thereby labeled by an element of a set of terms called $sons(t, u)$. In this case, we say that t is extensible.

Definition 4.4 *Let t be a term of the form $f(w_1, \cdots, w_n)$ where for all i, $w_i \in T(C_{BODY}, X)$. Let u be a variable position of t, that is nullary or that belongs to $pos\_ind(f)$. Suppose that $t(u)$ is of sort s. We define $sons(t, u)$ as follows: $sons(t, u) = \{t[u \leftarrow c] \mid c \equiv c_i(x_1, \cdots, x_n)$ where c_i is a constructor with codomain s, n the arity of c_i and $x_1, \cdots, x_n$ are distinct variables $\}$.*

We say that u is an extension position and that t is extensible. The transformation operation of t to $sons(t, u)$ is called the graft of t at the occurrence u. We denote by $pos\_ext(t)$ the set of extension positions of t.

The construction of the pattern tree is based on the notion of *case rewriting* which can be defined as follows:

Definition 4.5 (case rewriting) *Let t be a term. Assume there exists a non-empty sequence of conditional rules $C_1 \Rightarrow t_1 \rightarrow r_1$, $C_2 \Rightarrow t_2 \rightarrow r_2$, $\cdots$, $C_n \Rightarrow t_n \rightarrow r_n$ in E_{BODY} and a sequence of positions $u_1, u_2, \cdots, u_n$ in t such that $t/u_1 = t_1\sigma_1$, $t/u_2 = t_2\sigma_2$, $\cdots$, $t/u_n = t_n\sigma_n$ and $C_1\sigma_1 \vee C_2\sigma_2 \vee \cdots \vee C_n\sigma_n$ is an inductive theorem w.r.t. PS. Then, we write:*

$$case\_rewriting(t) = \{C_1\sigma_1 \Rightarrow t[r_1\sigma_1]_{u_1}, \cdots, C_n\sigma_n \Rightarrow t[r_n\sigma_n]_{u_n}\}$$

In this case, t is said to be pseudo-reducible *by PS. Otherwise, t is said to be* pseudo-irreducible *by PS. This definition can be generalized to the case where t is a clause in a straightforward way.*

[2] This property is decidable if the functions in D_{BODY} are sufficiently complete over free constructors.

Thus, if a term t is *pseudo-reducible* by PS, then all its ground instances are reducible.

Example 4.6 *Consider the following specifications which define* odd *and* even *for non-negative integers:* $S_{PAR} = \emptyset$, $F_{PAR} = \emptyset$, $E_{PAR} = \emptyset$. $S_{BODY} = \{nat, bool\}$, $C_{BODY} = \{0 :\rightarrow nat,\ s : nat \rightarrow nat,\ true :\rightarrow bool,\ false :\rightarrow bool\}$ *and* $D_{BODY} = \{even : nat \rightarrow bool,\ odd : nat \rightarrow bool\}$. E_{BODY} *contains the following conditional rules:*

$$even(0) \rightarrow true$$
$$even(s(0)) \rightarrow false$$
$$even(s(s(x))) \rightarrow even(x)$$
$$even(x) = true \Rightarrow odd(x) \rightarrow false$$
$$even(s(x)) = true \Rightarrow odd(x) \rightarrow true$$

The term $odd(x)$ *is* pseudo-reducible *by* PS *since* $even(x) = true \vee even(s(x)) = true$ *is an inductive theorem w.r.t.* PS. *However, the term* $even(x)$ *is* pseudo-irreducible *by* PS. ♦

It is useless to continue the graft process when we meet a node labeled by a term which is pseudo-reducible by PS. Then, we can describe the construction of the pattern tree in the following way: from the tree initially constituted from the root $t = f(x_1, \cdots, x_n)$, where n is the arity of f and $x_1, \cdots, x_n$ are distinct variables. We check the pseudo-reducibility by PS of t. If t is pseudo-irreducible by PS, we build at every step the sons of a node s of the tree by choosing an occurrence in $pos\_ext(s)$ and by making a graft operation on s at this occurrence. The construction of the tree stops if each of its sons is either pseudo-reducible by PS or we can no more split it.

stop: $(\emptyset,\ Red,\ Irred) \vdash_C stop$

delete reducible leaf: $(Candidates \cup \{t\},\ Red,\ Irred) \vdash_C (Candidates,\ Red \cup \{t\},\ Irred)$
if t is pseudo-reducible

decompose: $(Candidates \cup \{t\},\ Red,\ Irred) \vdash_C (Candidates \cup sons(t,u),\ Red,\ Irred)$
if t is pseudo-irreducible and $u \in pos\_ext(t)$.

delete irreducible leaf: $(Candidates \cup \{t\},\ Red,\ Irred) \vdash_C (Candidates,\ Red,\ Irred \cup \{t\})$
if t is pseudo-irreducible and $pos\_ext(t) = \emptyset$.

Fig. 1. Inference System C

4.2 Inference rules

To check if an operator f in E_{BODY} is sufficiently complete, we apply the rules given in figure 1. *Candidates* is the set of terms used for the reducibility check. *Red* is the set of leaves of the tree which are pseudo-reducible. *Irred* is the set of leaves of the tree which are pseudo-irreducible and not extensible. The initial state is $(\{f(x_1, \cdots, x_n)\}, \emptyset, \emptyset)$, where

n is the arity of f and $x_1, \cdots, x_n$ are distinct variables. The rule ***stop*** is applied if the set ***candidates*** is empty. Then, if *Irred* is empty, we conclude that all the leaves of the pattern tree are pseudo-reducible by PS. Consequently, the operator f is sufficiently complete (see theorem 4.7). If we meet a term t that is pseudo-reducible by PS, then the *delete reducible leaf* rule add it to the set *Red* and we continue the check of the pseudo-reducibility of the other leaves of the tree. The *decompose* rule expresses the operation of decomposition of a term t at the occurrence u. This rule applies, if we meet a term t that is extensible and pseudo-irreducible by PS. The graft operation produces the sons of t, for which we must check pseudo-reducibility. Finally, the *delete irreducible leaf* rule is applied if we meet a leaf of the tree that is not extensible and pseudo-irreducible by PS. In this case we add the term t to the set *Irred* and we continue the check of the pseudo-reducibility of the other leaves of the tree.

The rules of E_{BODY} which have the function symbol f at the top is finite. This involves that the set *pos_ind(f)* is finite too. As a consequence the set *occ_var(t)* $\cap$ *pos_ind(f)* decreases during the construction of the tree since consecutive grafts in the same branch of the tree are made at deeper and deeper occurrences. On the other hand, a nullary position correspond to a finite set of constructor terms. Consequently, the height of the pattern tree is bounded.

4.3 Correctness and completeness

In the following we denote by $C_{BODY}(\mathcal{A})$ the set $C_{BODY} \cup \mathcal{N}(\mathcal{A})$.

Theorem 4.7 *Let PS be a parameterized specification such that for every model $\mathcal{A}$ of E_{PAR} $\rightarrow_{E_{BODY(\mathcal{A})}}$ is ground convergent over $T(F(\mathcal{A}))$. If for all f in D_{BODY}, there exists a sequence of states $(\{f(x_1, \cdots, x_n)\}, \emptyset, \emptyset) \vdash_C \cdots \vdash_C (\emptyset, Red, \emptyset)$, then PS is sufficiently complete.*

proof: Let f be a function symbol and suppose that there exists a sequence of states $(\{f(x_1, \cdots, x_n)\}, \emptyset, \emptyset) \vdash_C \cdots \vdash_C (\emptyset, Red, \emptyset)$. Let $\mathcal{A}$ be a model of E_{PAR}, we have to prove the following property $\mathcal{P}(t)$: $\forall t \in T(F(\mathcal{A}))$, $\exists t' \in T(C_{BODY}(\mathcal{A}))$ *such that* $t \rightarrow^*_{E_{BODY}(\mathcal{A})} t'$. We proceed by induction on t w.r.t. $\succ$ which is compatible [3] with $\rightarrow_{E_{BODY}(\mathcal{A})}$. Without loss of generality, we can assume that $t = f(t_1, \cdots, t_n)$ with f in D_{BODY} and for all i we have t_i in $C_{BODY}(\mathcal{A})$. Then, there exists a leaf s of the pattern tree and a ground substitution σ over $T(C_{BODY}(\mathcal{A}))$ such that $s\sigma = t$. Since s is pseudo-reducible by PS, then there exists a non-empty sequence of conditional rules $C_1 \Rightarrow t_1 \rightarrow r_1$, $C_2 \Rightarrow t_2 \rightarrow r_2$, $\cdots$, $C_n \Rightarrow t_n \rightarrow r_n$ in E_{BODY} and a sequence of positions $u_1, u_2, \cdots, u_n$ in s such that $s/u_1 = t_1\sigma_1$, $s/u_2 = t_2\sigma_2$, $\cdots$, $s/u_n = t_n\sigma_n$ and $C_1\sigma_1 \vee C_2\sigma_2 \vee \cdots \vee C_n\sigma_n$ is an inductive theorem w.r.t. PS. Then, there exists k such that $t_k\sigma_k \rightarrow_{E_{BODY}(\mathcal{A})} r_k\sigma_k$ since for every model $\mathcal{A}$ of E_{PAR} $\rightarrow_{E_{BODY}(\mathcal{A})}$ is ground convergent over $T(F(\mathcal{A}))$. On the other hand, $\rightarrow_{E_{BODY}(\mathcal{A})}$ is stable by substitution, therefore $t_k\sigma_k\sigma \rightarrow_{E_{BODY}(\mathcal{A})} r_k\sigma_k\sigma$. Finally, we have $r_k\sigma_k\sigma \prec t$ and $r_k\sigma_k\sigma \in T(F(\mathcal{A}))$ since $C_k \Rightarrow t_k \rightarrow r_k$ is a conditional rule. Then by induction hypothesis, we conclude that there exists t' in $T(C_{BODY}(\mathcal{A}))$ such that $r_k\sigma_k\sigma \rightarrow^*_{E_{BODY}(\mathcal{A})} t'$ and therefore there exists t'' in $T(C_{BODY}(\mathcal{A}))$ such that $t \rightarrow^*_{E_{BODY}(\mathcal{A})} t''$. □

The completeness of the procedure is shown by the following theorem:

Theorem 4.8 *Let PS be a parameterized specification. Suppose that the constructors are free, all parameter variables in the left-hand sides of E_{BODY} are linear and if the defined*

[3] Two noetherian orders $\succ_1$ and $\succ_2$ are compatible if they are both included in a noetherian order.

function g *appears in a left-hand side of a conditional rule in* E_{BODY}*, then every rule in* E_{BODY} *that contains* g *in its left-hand side is linear. If* PS *is sufficiently complete, then for all* f *in* D_{BODY}*, there exists a sequence of states* $(\{f(x_1, \cdots, x_n)\}, \emptyset, \emptyset) \vdash_C \cdots \vdash_C (\emptyset, Red, \emptyset)$.

proof: Assume that PS is sufficiently complete. Suppose that there exists a leaf t which is not extensible and pseudo-irreducible by PS. Then there exists a model $\mathcal{A}$ of E_{PAR} and a substitution ϕ over $T(F(\mathcal{A}))$ such that $t\phi$ is ground and irreducible by $E_{BODY}(\mathcal{A})$. This contradicts the assumption. The detailed proof can be found in [Bou93]. □

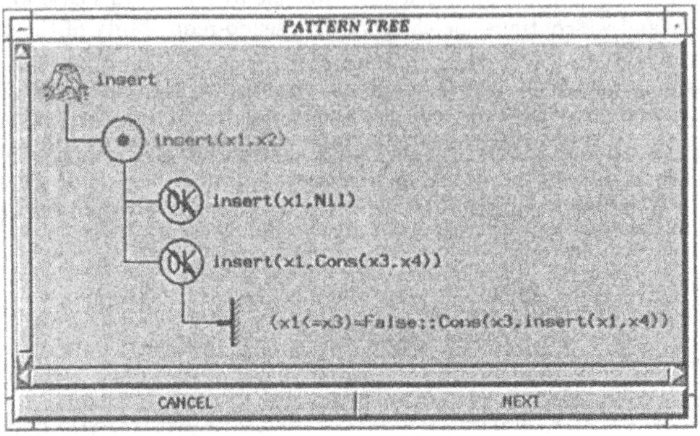

Fig. 2. The function *insert* is not sufficiently complete

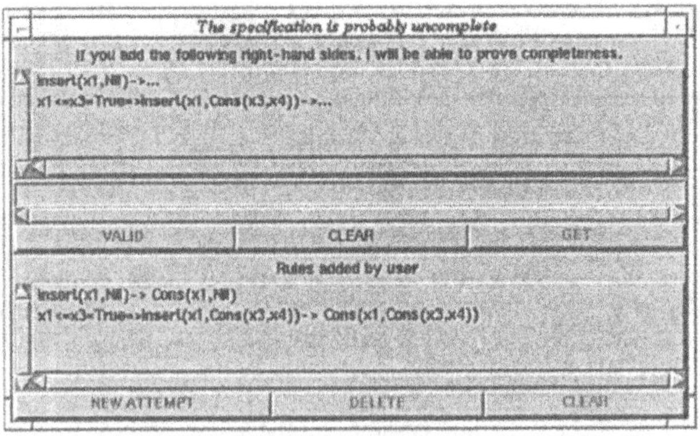

Fig. 3. Suggestions

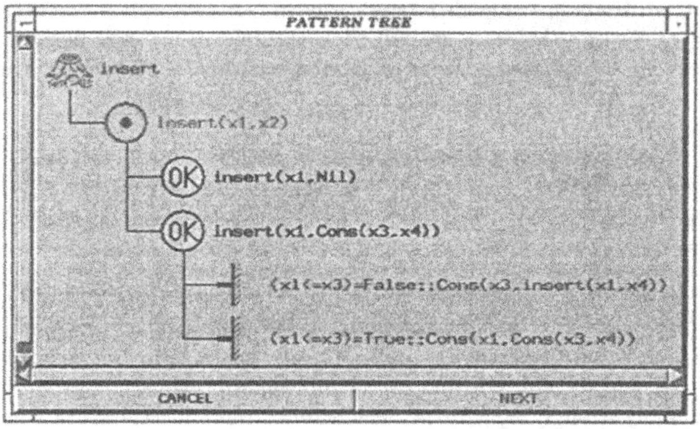

Fig. 4. The function *insert* is now sufficiently complete

4.4 Sufficient completeness with SPIKE

SPIKE checks automatically if an operator f in a specification PS is sufficiently complete. The program builds a pattern tree for f. The leaves of the tree give a partition of the possible arguments for f. If all the leaves are *pseudo-reducible* by PS, the answer is affirmative. If one of the leaves is not extensible and *pseudo-irreducible* by PS, then SPIKE suggests new rules for completing the specification. These rules are not entirely determined but rather possible schemes for them are proposed, every rule is of the form: *(condition, left-hand-side)*. Once the user has chosen the new rules, usually by simply giving their right-hand sides, SPIKE replays the test. Consider example 3.1 and suppose that *insert* is defined by the rule 1 and therefore it is not sufficiently complete. Here we describe a session with SPIKE to give an idea about the interaction with the user if the specification is not sufficiently complete (see figure 2 and figure 3). Then we add two rules and try again (see figure 4).

Note that this procedure is combined with an inductive theorem proving to check the pseudo-reducibility of the leaves of the tree. Therefore, the efficiency of our procedure depends of the one of the inductive theorem prover. Sometimes, the suggestions given by SPIKE are not useful since the pseudo-reducibility test can fail because of the divergence of the procedure of proof by induction. In the next sessions, we propose a new procedure to prove and disprove inductive properties automatically in parameterized conditional specifications.

5 Selection of induction schemes

To perform a proof by induction, it is necessary to provide some induction schema. In our framework these schema are defined *first* by a function which, given a conjecture, selects the positions of variables where induction will be applied and *second* by a special set of terms called a test set with which the induction variables are instantiated.

Given a specification, we start by computing a set of induction positions of function symbols (see definition 4.2). This computation is done only once and it permits us to determine whether a variable position of a term t is an induction variable or not.

Definition 5.1 (induction variable) *Given a term t and let x be a variable of t of non-parameter sort s. We say that x is an* induction variable *of t if s is* nullary *or x occurs at a position $u.v$ of t such that v is an induction position of $t(u)$ (if t is a variable of non-parameter sort, then it is considered as an induction variable).*

Example 5.2 (example 3.1 continued) *Let $t \equiv insert(x, insert\ (x, y))$, y is the only induction variable of t because y occurs at position 2 of the subterm $insert(x, y)$ and 2 in an induction position of insert. The term $insert(x, cons(y, cons(z, t)))$ does not contain any induction variable.* ♦

To define test set, we use the following notions: The *bound* for PS, denoted $D(PS)$, is equal to $depth(E_{BODY}) - 1$ if $sdepth(E_{BODY}) < depth(E_{BODY})$ and E_{BODY} is left linear, otherwise $D(PS)$ is equal to $depth(E_{BODY})$. We say that a term t is *infinitary* if for any model $\mathcal{A}$ of E_{PAR} and for any position u in t for which t/u is a non-ground term, there exists infinitely many strongly $E_{BODY}(\mathcal{A})$-irreducible ground instances of t whose subterms at position u are distinct.

Definition 5.3 (test set) *A test set $S(PS)$ for a parameterized specification PS is a finite set of terms over $T(F, X)$ that has the following properties:*

1. *For any model $\mathcal{A}$ of E_{PAR} and for any $E_{BODY}(\mathcal{A})$-irreducible term s in $T(F(\mathcal{A}))$, there exist a term t in $S(PS)$ and a substitution σ such that $t\sigma = s$;*
2. *any non-ground term in $S(PS)$ is* infinitary *and has non-parameter variables at depth greater than or equal to $D(PS)$;*

The first property allows us to prove theorems by induction on the domain of irreducible terms rather than on the whole set of terms. Sets of terms with the property *1.* are usually called *cover sets* in the literature. Several proof procedures have been built on cover sets [Red90; ZKK88]. Note that our method is also valid if we use cover sets rather than test set. However, *cover sets* cannot be used to refute false conjectures. The second property of test sets is fundamental for this purpose (see theorem 5.5). The next definition provides us with a criteria to reject false conjectures.

Definition 5.4 (provably inconsistent) *Given a parameterized specification PS and a test $S(PS)$, then a clause $C \equiv \neg(s_1 = t_1) \vee \cdots \vee \neg(s_m = t_m) \vee (g_1 = d_1) \vee \cdots \vee (g_n = d_n)$ is provably inconsistent with respect to PS if there is a test substitution σ of C (i.e. that maps any induction variable of C to a renaming of an element of $S(PS)$) such that:*

1. *$E_{PAR} \not\models (g_1 = d_1 \vee \cdots \vee g_n = d_n)\sigma$;*
2. *for all $i \in [1 \cdots m]$: $s_i\sigma = t_i\sigma$ is an inductive theorem w.r.t. PS;*
3. *for all $j \in [1 \cdots n]$: the maximal elements of $\{g_j\sigma, d_j\sigma\}$ w.r.t. $\succ$ are strongly E_{BODY}-irreducible.*

The next result shows that a provably inconsistent clause cannot be inductively valid w.r.t. PS. This is proved by building a well-chosen ground instance of the clause which gives us a counterexample (see [Bou93]).

Theorem 5.5 *Given a parameterized specification PS such that all parameter variables in the left-hand sides of E_{BODY} are linear and $\rightarrow_{E_{BODY}(\mathcal{A})}$ is ground convergent for every model $\mathcal{A}$ of E_{PAR}. If a clause C is provably inconsistent, then C is not inductively valid w.r.t. PS.*

We can compute a test set in a parameterized conditional specification if the constructors are free.

Proposition 5.6 *Assume that $\rightarrow_{E_{BODY}(\mathcal{A})}$ is noetherian* [4], *PS is sufficiently complete and the constructors are free. Then, the set $\mathcal{T}$ of constructor terms (up to variable renaming) of depth $\leq D(PS)$ where the variables of non-parameter and non-nullary sort may occur only at depth $D(PS)$ is a test set for PS.*

proof: Let $\mathcal{A}$ be a model of E_{PAR} and t in $T(F(\mathcal{A}))$. As PS is sufficiently complete, then there exists t' in $T(C_{BODY}(\mathcal{A}))$ such that $t \rightarrow^{*}_{E_{BODY}(\mathcal{A})} t'$. On the other hand, $\rightarrow_{E_{BODY}(\mathcal{A})}$ is noetherian and for each conditional rule $p \Rightarrow l \rightarrow r \in E_{BODY}$, if $l \in T(C_{BODY}, X)$, then $r \in T(C_{BODY}, X)$. Therefore, there exists $t'' \in T(C_{BODY}(\mathcal{A}))$ such that, $t' \rightarrow^{*}_{E_{BODY}(\mathcal{A})} t''$ and t'' is irreducible by $E_{BODY}(\mathcal{A})$. This implies that $t \rightarrow^{*}_{E_{BODY}(\mathcal{A})} t''$. So any irreducible term in $T(F(\mathcal{A}))$ is built only with constructors and elements of $\mathcal{N}(\mathcal{A})$ and therefore is an instance of an element of $\mathcal{T}$. By construction, any non-ground term in $\mathcal{T}$ has non-parameter variables at depth greater than or equal to $D(PS)$. Since the constructors are free, any variable of non-parameter and non-nullary sort may be replaced by infinitely many different constructor terms. Therefore, any non-ground term in $\mathcal{T}$ is infinitary. □

Example 5.7 (example 3.1 continued) *The output of the SPIKE procedure that computes the test set is given in figure 6.* ♦

6 An inductive procedure for parameterized specifications

6.1 Inference rules

Our procedure is defined by a set of transition rules (see figure 5) which are applied to pairs (E, H), where E is the set of conjectures and H is the set of inductive hypotheses. The *generate* [5] rule allows us to derive lemmas and initiates induction steps. The *case simplify* rule simplifies a conjecture with conditional rules where the disjunction of all conditions is inductively valid (note that this case analysis is more general than our previous definition given in [BR94]). The *simplify* rule reduces a clause C with axioms from $E_{BODY} \cup E_{PAR}$, induction hypotheses from H, other conjectures which are not yet proved. Note that *simplify* permits mutual simplification of conjectures. This rule implements *simultaneous induction* and is crucial for efficiency. The *subsumption* rule deletes clauses C subsumed by an element of $E_{BODY} \cup E_{PAR} \cup H \cup E$. The role of *deletion* is obvious. The *disproof* rule is applied if a provably inconsistent clause is detected. The *fail* rule is applied to (E, H) if no other rule can be applied to $C \in E$.

An I-derivation is a sequence of states:

$$(E_0, H_0) \vdash_I (E_1, H_1) \vdash_I \cdots \vdash_I (E_n, H_n) \vdash_I \cdots$$

An I-derivation fails if it terminates with the rule *fail* or *disproof*.

[4] to guarantee that $\rightarrow_{E_{BODY}(\mathcal{A})}$ is noetherian, it is sufficient to assume that $\rightarrow_{E_{BODY}}$ is noetherian and no left-hand side of an equation of E_{BODY} contains a symbol from F_{PAR}.

[5] Let R' be a set of clauses and suppose that R is the set of all conditional rules of R'. By abuse of notation, the relation $\rightarrow_R$ will be denoted by $\rightarrow_{R'}$.

generate: $(E \cup \{C\}, H) \vdash_I (E \cup (\cup_\sigma E_\sigma), H \cup \{C\})$
if $C \equiv p \Rightarrow q$ and for every test substitution σ of C
if $E_{PAR} \models q\sigma$, then $E_\sigma = \emptyset$;
if $C\sigma \rightarrow_{E_{BODY} \cup E_{PAR}} C'$, then $E_\sigma = \{C'\}$;
otherwise, $E_\sigma = case\_rewriting(C\sigma)$.

case simplify: $(E \cup \{C\}, H) \vdash_I (E \cup E', H)$
if $E' =$ case_rewriting(C)

simplify: $(E \cup \{C\}, H) \vdash_I (E \cup \{C'\}, H)$
if $C \rightarrow_{E_{BODY} \cup E_{PAR} \cup H \cup E} C'$
and for each instance $S\tau$ of clauses of H used in the simplification, we have $S\tau \preceq_c C$, while for each instance $S'\theta$ of clauses of E, we have $S'\theta \prec_c C$.

subsumption: $(E \cup \{C\}, H) \vdash_I (E, H)$
if C is subsumed by another clause of $E_{BODY} \cup E_{PAR} \cup H \cup E$.

delete: $(E \cup \{C\}, H) \vdash_I (E, H)$
if C is a tautology.

disproof: $(E \cup \{C\}, H) \vdash_I$ *Disproof*
if C is provably inconsistent.

fail: $(E \cup \{C\}, H) \vdash_I \square$
if no condition of the previous rules hold for C.

Fig. 5. Inference System I

6.2 Correctness

The correctness of a procedure based on our inference system relies on a fairness assumption: every conjecture to be checked must be considered at some step. More formally, a derivation $(E_0, H_0) \vdash_I (E_1, H_1) \vdash_I \cdots$ is *fair* if either it fails or it is infinite and the set of persisting clauses $(\cup_{i \geq 0} \cap_{j \geq i} E_j)$ is empty. Then we reason by contradiction: if a non-valid clause is generated in an unfailing derivation then a minimal one is generated too. We show that no inference step can apply to this clause. In other words, this clause persists in the derivation. This contradicts the fairness hypothesis (see [Bou93]). Therefore, we obtain the following result:

Theorem 6.1 (correctness) *Let $(E_0, \emptyset) \vdash_I (E_1, H_1) \vdash_I \cdots$ be a fair I-derivation. If it does not fail then $PS \models_{ind} E_0$.*

If *disproof* is applied at step k, then a provably inconsistent clause is detected and therefore, from theorem 5.5, we conclude that some conjecture in E_k is false, if for every model $\mathcal{A}$ of $E_{PAR} \rightarrow_{E_{BODY(\mathcal{A})}}$ is ground convergent over $T(F(\mathcal{A}))$ and all parameter variables in the left-hand sides of E_{BODY} are linear. The initial conjectures E_0 is not inductively valid in PS too. This is a consequence of the next result:

Lemma 6.2 *Let* $(E_0, \emptyset) \vdash_I (E_1, H_1) \vdash_I \cdots$ *be an I-derivation. If for all* i *such that* $i \leq j$ *we have* $PS \models_{ind} E_i$ *then* $PS \models_{ind} E_{j+1}$.

proof: If $(E_j, H_j) \vdash_I (E_{j+1}, H_{j+1})$ by *generate* on C. Let σ be a test substitution of C. If $E_{PAR} \not\models C\sigma$, then there are two cases to consider: i) if there exists C' such that $C\sigma \rightarrow_{E_{BODY} \cup E_{PAR}} C'$. Then, we have $PS \models_{ind} C'$. ii) otherwise, there exists a sequence of conditional rules $P_1 \Rightarrow t_1 \rightarrow r_1$, $P_2 \Rightarrow t_2 \rightarrow r_2$, ... $P_n \Rightarrow t_n \rightarrow r_n$ in E_{BODY} and a sequence of positions $u_1, u_2, \ldots, u_n$ in $C\sigma$ such that $C\sigma/u_1 = t_1\tau_1$, $C\sigma/u_2 = t_2\tau_2$, ... $, C\sigma/u_n = t_n\tau_n$ and $P_1\tau_1 \vee P_2\tau_2 \vee \ldots \vee P_n\tau_n$ is an inductive theorem w.r.t. PS. Assume that there exists k such that: $PS \not\models_{ind} C_k \equiv P_k\tau_k \Rightarrow C\sigma[r_k\tau_k]_{u_k}$. In other words there is a ground instance $C_k\theta$ over $T(F(\mathcal{A}))$ (without loss of generality, we can assume that $C\sigma\theta$ is ground) such that: $PS \not\models_{ind} C_k\theta$, then $PS \models_{ind} P_k\tau_k\theta$ and $PS \not\models_{ind} C\sigma\theta[r_k\tau_k\theta]$. Therefore, $PS \models_{ind} t_k\tau_k\theta = r_k\tau_k\theta$. This implies that $PS \not\models C\sigma\theta[t_k\tau_k\theta]$, which is absurd. For case simplify the argument is the same as above. If $(E_j, H_j) \vdash_I (E_{j+1}, H_{j+1})$ by *simplify*, then the equations which are used for simplification occur in some E_j $(j < k)$ and therefore are inductively valid in PS by hypothesis. Hence, E_{j+1} is inductively valid too in PS. A more detailed proof is given in [Bou93]. □

The next theorem is a straightforward consequence of the above results:

Theorem 6.3 (refutation) *Given a parameterized specification* PS *such that for every model* $\mathcal{A}$ *of* E_{PAR}, $\rightarrow_{E_{BODY(\mathcal{A})}}$ *is ground convergent over* $T(F(\mathcal{A}))$ *and all parameter variables in the left-hand sides of* E_{BODY} *are linear. Let* $(E_0, \emptyset) \vdash_I (E_1, H_1) \vdash_I \cdots$ *be an I-derivation. If there exists* j *such that* disproof *applies to* (E_j, H_j) *then* $PS \not\models_{ind} E_0$.

6.3 Refutational completeness for parameterized boolean specifications

In this section, we shall consider axioms that are conditional rules with boolean preconditions. To be more specific, we assume there exists a sort *bool* with two free constructors $\{true,\ false\}$. Every rule in E_{BODY} is of type: $\wedge_{i=1}^{n} p_i = p'_i \Rightarrow s \rightarrow t$ where for all i in $[1 \cdots n]$, $p'_i \in \{true,\ false\}$. For $\alpha \in \{true,\ false\}$ we denote by $\overline{\alpha}$ the complementary *bool* symbol of α. Conjectures will be *boolean clauses*, i.e. clauses whose negative literals are of type $\neg(p = p')$ where $p' \in \{true, false\}$. Let f be a function symbol in D_{BODY}. If for all the rules in E_{BODY} of the form $p_i \Rightarrow f(\vec{t_i}) \rightarrow r_i$ whose left-hand sides are identical up to a renaming μ_i, we have $PS \models_{ind} \vee_i p_i \mu_i$, then f is weakly complete w.r.t. PS. We say that PS is weakly complete if any function in D_{BODY} is weakly complete w.r.t. PS. Note that a *weakly complete* specification is not necessary *sufficiently complete* [Bou93].

Now, we can define a new inference system J from I by adding the following complement rule which transforms negative clauses to positive clauses that are easier to refute.

complement: $(E \cup \{\neg(a = \alpha) \vee r\}, H) \vdash_J (E \cup \{(a = \overline{\alpha}) \vee r\}, H)$ if $\alpha \in \{true,\ false\}$.

We also remove the *fail* rule and reformulate *disproof* as follows:

disproof: $(E \cup \{C\}, H) \vdash_J$ *Disproof* if no condition of the previous rules hold for C.

Let us assume that E_0 only contains boolean clauses. The only rule that permits us to introduce negative clauses is *case_rewriting*. Since the axioms have boolean preconditions, all the clauses generated in a J-derivation are boolean. If *disproof* is applied in a J-derivation, then there exists a positive clause C such that *generate* cannot be applied to C. Therefore there exists a test substitution σ such that $E_{PAR} \not\models C\sigma$. Moreover $C\sigma$ does not match any left-hand side of E_{BODY}. Otherwise, the *inductive rewriting* or the *case rewriting* rule can be applied to $C\sigma$ since PS is weakly complete. As a consequence, C is a provably inconsistent clause. So, the new inference system J can be proved refutationally complete for boolean clauses.

Theorem 6.4 *Given a weakly complete parameterized specification PS such that all parameter variables in the left-hand sides of E_{BODY} are linear and $\rightarrow_{E_{BODY}(\mathcal{A})}$ is ground convergent for every model $\mathcal{A}$ of E_{PAR}. Let $(E_0, \emptyset) \vdash_J (E_1, H_1) \vdash_J \cdots$ be a fair J-derivation such that E_0 only contains boolean clauses. Then $PS \not\models_{ind} E_0$ iff the derivation ends with disproof.*

7 Implementation and experimental results

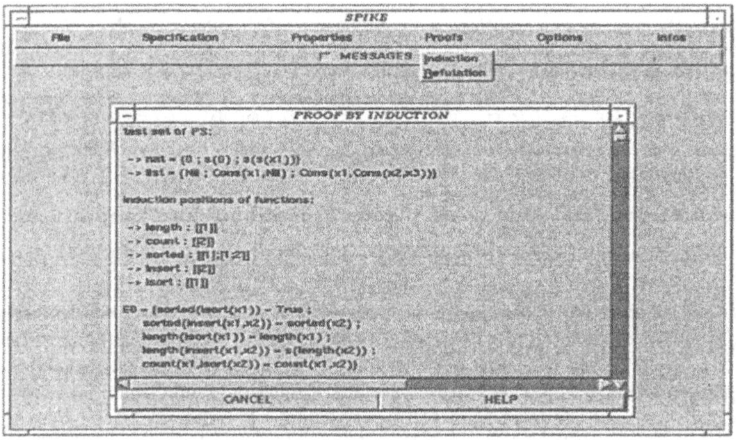

Fig. 6. Example

Our implementation is based on the previous inference system. The program is able to prove the validity of a set of clauses in parameterized conditional specifications. Here is an overview of the algorithm. The main data structures are: the list E_{BODY} of axioms, that are conditional rules built with the constructor discipline, the list E of conjectures (clauses) to be checked, the list E_{PAR} of parameter constraints, that are equational clauses in Σ_{PAR} and finally, the set H of induction hypotheses (initialized by $\emptyset$). The first step in a proof session is to check if all defined functions are completely defined. The second step is to compute a test set for PS and also induction positions. After these preliminary tasks, the proof starts.

Consider example 3.1 with E_0 the set of conjectures to be proved (see figure 6). SPIKE can prove these conjectures in a completely automatic way, using *112* steps. Note that one lemma (generated automatically) is sufficient to prove the initial conjectures. Now consider the same example with lists of natural numbers, using the method in [BR94]. To prove the same conjectures without parameters, SPIKE used *326* steps. In addition, *50* lemmas were generated automatically during the proof. This example illustrates that with parameterized specifications we obtain shorter and structured proofs.

8 Conclusion

We have proposed a new procedure for proof by induction in parameterized conditional specifications. It allows ***simultaneous induction*** and can handle non-orientable equations. Our method is also compatible with simplification rules given in [BR94]. An extension to theories that are presented by non-Horn clauses along the lines of [Bec92] should be easy. Unlike our previous procedure [BR94], this new one, when limited to non-parameterized conditional specifications, can refute general clauses; refutational completeness is also preserved for boolean ground convergent rewrite systems even if the functions are not sufficiently complete and the constructors are not free. Note that our method remains valid in theories without constructors. The property of sufficient completeness is very important in specification systems but is in general undecidable. We have given a procedure for testing this property for parameterized conditional specifications.

The method is implemented in the prover SPIKE. This system has proved interesting examples in a completely automatic way [Bou94a], that is, without interaction with the user and without ad-hoc heuristics. Experiments illustrate the improvements in length and structuration of proofs, due to parametrisation. Unlike the well-known induction prover, SPIKE guarantees when it fails that one of the initial conjectures is not an inductive theorem provided that the axioms are boolean and ground convergent with weakly complete defined functions. Moreover, SPIKE offers facilities to check and complete definitions.

We plan to generalize the method to get refutational completeness for a larger class of rewrite systems. Another powerful extension is to allow for generalization techniques, such as in the traditional induction method. How this can be done and the possible implications with respect to soundness and refutational completeness, still have to be studied very carefully.

Acknowledgment: I am very grateful to Michaël Rusinowitch, Hélène Kirchner, Toby Walsh and Pierre Lescanne for valuable discussions and comments on an earlier version of this paper. I would also like to thank Peter Padawitz and Jürgen Avenhaus for stimulating discussions and the anonymous referees for their constructive remarks. This work is partially supported by the Esprit Basic Research working group 6112, COMPASS.

References

[Bac88] L. Bachmair. *Proof by consistency in equational theories.* In *Proceedings 3rd IEEE Symposium on Logic in Computer Science, Cambridge (Mass., USA)*, pages 228–233, 1988.

[Bec92] K. Becker. Inductive Proofs in Specifications Parameterized by a Built-in Theory. SEKI-Report, SR-92-02, 1992.

[BKR92] A. Bouhoula, E. Kounalis, and M. Rusinowitch. Automated mathematical induction. Technical Report 1636, INRIA, 1992.

[BR93] A. Bouhoula and M. Rusinowitch. Automatic Case Analysis in Proof by Induction. In *Proccedings of the 13th International Joint Conference on Artificial Intelligence*, volume 1, page 88–94. Chambéry France, 1993.

[BR94] A. Bouhoula and M. Rusinowitch. Implicit Induction in Conditional Theories. *Journal of Automated Reasoning*, accepted in June 1994. To appear.

[Bou93] A. Bouhoula. Parameterized Specifications: Sufficient Completeness and Implicit Induction. Technical Report 2129, INRIA, 1993.

[Bou94a] A. Bouhoula. *Preuves Automatiques par Récurrence dans les Théories Conditionnelles.* PhD thesis, Université de Nancy I, Mars 1994.

[Bou94b] A. Bouhoula. Spike: a system for sufficient completeness and parameterized inductive proof. In *Proceedings 12th International Conference on Automated Deduction, Nancy (France)*, Lecture Notes in Artificial Intelligence. Springer-Verlag, June 1994. To appear.

[BM79] R. S. Boyer and J. S. Moore. *A Computational Logic.* Academic Press, New York, 1979.

[Com86] H. Comon. Sufficient Completeness, Term rewriting Systems and "Anti-Unification". In *Proceedings 8th International Conference on Automated Deduction*, Oxford, England, July 1986.

[Der87] N. Dershowitz. Termination of rewriting. *Journal of Symbolic Computation*, 3(1 & 2):69–116, 1987.

[DJ90] N. Dershowitz and J.-P. Jouannaud. Rewrite systems. In J. van Leuven, editor, *Handbook of Theoretical Computer Science.* Elsevier Science Publishers North-Holland, 1990.

[EM85] H. Ehrig, B. Mahr. Fundamentals of Algebraic Specification 1. Equations and Initial Semantics. Springer Verlag, 1985.

[Gan87] H. Ganzinger. Ground Term Confluence in Parametric Conditional Rewrite Systems. In *STACS'87*, volume 247 of *LNCS*, pages 286–298. Springer-Verlag, 1987.

[GH78] J. V. Guttag and J. J. Horning The Algebraic Specification of Abstract Data Types. In *Acta Informatica*, 10:27-52, 1978.

[HH82] G. Huet and J.-M. Hullot. Proofs by induction in equational theories with constructors. *Journal of Computer and System Sciences*, 25(2):239–266, October 1982.

[JK86] J.-P. Jouannaud and E. Kounalis. Proof by induction in equational theories without constructors. In *Proceedings 1st IEEE Symposium on Logic in Computer Science, Cambridge (Mass., USA)*, pages 358–366, 1986.

[Kir91] H. Kirchner. Proofs in Parameterized Specifications. In *4th RTA*, volume 488 of *LNCS*, pages 174–187. Springer-Verlag, 1991.

[Kou85] E. Kounalis. Completeness in Data Type Specifications. In *Proceeding EUROCAL Conference.* Springer-Verlag, Linz (Austria), 1991.

[KR90] E. Kounalis and M. Rusinowitch. Mechanizing inductive reasoning. In *Proceedings of the American Association for Artificial Intelligence Conference, Boston*, pages 240–245. AAAI Press and MIT Press, July 1990.

[LLT90] A. Lazrek, P. Lescanne, and J.-J. Thiel. Tools for proving inductive equalities, relative completeness and ω-completeness. *Information and Computation*, 84(1):47–70, January 1990.

[Mus80] D. R. Musser. On proving inductive properties of abstract data types. In *Proceedings 7th ACM Symp. on Principles of Programming Languages*, pages 154–162. Association for Computing Machinery, 1980.

[NO87] M. Navarro and F. Orejas. Parameterized Horn clause specifications: proof theory and correctness. In *Proceeding TAPSOFT Conference*, volume 249 of *LNCS*. pages 202–216, Springer-Verlag, 1987.

[Pad84] P. Padawitz. Towards a proof theory of parameterized specifications. In *Semantics of data type's*, volume 173 of *LNCS*, pages 375–391. Springer-Verlag, 1984.

[Pad87] P. Padawitz. Parameter-Preserving Data Type Specifications. In *Journal of Computer and System Science*, volume 34, pages 179–209, 1987.

[Red90] U. S. Reddy. Term rewriting induction. In M. E. Stickel, editor, *Proceedings 10th ICADE, Kaiserslautern (Germany)*, volume 449 of *LNCS*, pages 162–177. Springer-Verlag, 1990.

[Wir90] M. Wirsing. Algebraic specification. In J. van Leeuwen, editor, *Handbook of Theoretical Computer Science B: Formal Methods and Semantics*, chapter 13, pages 675–788. Elsevier, Amsterdam, 1990.

[ZKK88] H. Zhang, D. Kapur, and M. S. Krishnamoorthy. A mechanizable induction principle for equational specifications. In *Proceedings 9th ICADE, Argonne (Ill., USA)*, volume 310 of *LNCS*, pages 162–181. Springer-Verlag, 1988.

Proving Behavioural Theorems with Standard First-Order Logic

Michel Bidoit[1] and Rolf Hennicker[2]

[1] LIENS, C.N.R.S. U.R.A. 1327 & Ecole Normale Supérieure
45, Rue d'Ulm, F-75230 Paris Cedex 05, France
[2] Institut für Informatik, Ludwig-Maximilians-Universität München
Leopoldstr. 11B, D-80802 München, Germany

Abstract. Behavioural logic is a generalization of first-order logic where the equality predicate is interpreted by a behavioural equality of objects (and not by their identity). We establish simple and general sufficient conditions under which the behavioural validity of some first-order formula with respect to a given first-order specification is equivalent to the standard validity of the same formula in a suitably enriched specification. As a consequence any proof system for first-order logic can be used to prove the behavioural validity of first-order formulas.

1 Introduction

Observability plays a prominent role in formal software development, since it provides a suitable basis for defining adequate correctness concepts. For instance, for proving the correctness of a program with respect to a given specification, many examples show that it is essential to abstract from internal implementation details and to rely only on the observable behaviour of the program. A similar situation is the notion of equivalence between concurrent processes and the abstraction from single step transitions to input-output operational semantics.

Behavioural correctness concepts can be formalized by using a behavioural logic, where the usual satisfaction relation of first-order logic with equality is generalized to a *behavioural satisfaction relation* (cf. e.g. [14, 12]). The key idea is to interpret the equality predicate symbol by a *behavioural equality*, where two objects are behaviourally equal if they cannot be distinguished by experiments with observable results. Hence to prove the behavioural validity of a formula we have to consider in general infinitely many observable experiments which are formally represented by an infinite set of "observable contexts".

The problem considered in this paper is how to prove the behavioural validity of some first-order formula ϕ with respect to a given first-order specification *SP*. We prove that, when the (first-order) specification *SP* satisfies some general and simple property (called the "Observability Kernel assumption"), the behavioural validity of the first-order formula ϕ (w.r.t. *SP*) is equivalent to the standard validity of the same formula ϕ with respect to the specification *SP* enriched by an adequate **finitary** first-order formula that represents the infinite set of all observable experiments. To this end, we use a general characterization of behavioural theories that we established in [5], and we show that the behavioural first-order theory of *SP* is equal to the standard first-order theory of the class of the fully abstract (standard) models of *SP*. Then we provide an infinitary axiomatization of full abstractness, and finally we show that, under the "Observability Kernel assumption", this infinitary axiomatization is equivalent to a finitary one.

The main significance of our result is that any available theorem prover for standard first-order logic with equality can be used, first to discharge the "Observability Kernel assumption", and then to prove the behavioural validity of first-order formulas. The soundness and completeness of behavioural proofs only rely on the soundness and completeness of the actually used standard proof system. Our result is fairly general since we do not need any restriction neither on the first-order specification *SP* nor on the first-order formula ϕ to be proved.

In the literature several approaches formalize behavioural correctness concepts by introducing some kind of behavioural semantics (cf. e.g. [8], [14], [12], [15], [2], [13]). The main drawback of these approaches is that they either do not provide a proof-theoretical framework or suggest technically complicated proof techniques which are only of limited interest for practical applications (cf. the context induction principle in [10] or the correspondance relation in [16]). [4] can be considered as a preliminary result, but restricted to the behavioural proof of equations w.r.t. equational specifications, with only one non observable sort.

This paper is organized as follows. In Section 2 we briefly summarize the basic notions of algebraic specifications that will be used later on. In Section 3 we define the behavioural equality and the associated behavioural satisfaction relation, we explain how all usual notions can be generalized in a behavioural framework and we point out the crucial role of fully abstract algebras. In Section 4 we study sufficient conditions (the "Observability Kernel" assumption) under which it is enough to consider a finite number of observable experiments. In Section 5 we show how the "Observability Kernel" assumption leads to a general method to prove behavioural theorems using any theorem prover for standard first-order logic.

2 Basic Notions

We assume that the reader is familiar with algebraic specifications [9, 6]. The basic concepts and notations that will be used hereafter are briefly summarized in this section.

A (many sorted) *signature* Σ is a pair (S, F) where S is a set of *sorts* and F is a set of *function symbols*.[3] To each function symbol $f \in F$ is associated an *arity*

[3] In this paper we assume that both S and F are finite.

$s_1 \dots s_n \to s$ with $s, s_1, \dots, s_n \in S$. If $n = 0$ then f is called *constant* of sort s. A *total Σ-algebra* $A = ((A_s)_{s\in S}, (f^A)_{f\in F})$ over a signature $\Sigma = (S, F)$ consists of a family of carrier sets $(A_s)_{s\in S}$ and a family of functions $(f^A)_{f\in F}$ such that, if f has arity $s_1 \dots s_n \to s$, then f^A is a (total) function from $A_{s_1} \times \dots \times A_{s_n}$ to A_s (if $n = 0$ then f^A denotes a constant object of A_s). Σ-morphisms are defined as usual. The category of all Σ-algebras is denoted by $Alg(\Sigma)$.

Throughout this paper, given a signature $\Sigma = (S, F)$, we assume given an arbitrary but fixed family $X = (X_s)_{s\in S}$ of countably infinite sets X_s of variables of sort $s \in S$. $T_\Sigma(X)$ denotes the *Σ-term algebra freely generated by X*, the carrier sets of which are the sets $T_\Sigma(X)_s$ of *terms* of sort s (and with variables in X). Given a Σ-algebra A, a *valuation* $\alpha : X \to A$ is a family of mappings $(\alpha_s : X_s \to A_s)_{s\in S}$. Any valuation $\alpha : X \to A$ uniquely extends to a Σ-morphism $I_\alpha : T_\Sigma(X) \to A$, called the *interpretation* associated to α.

Given a Σ-algebra A, a *Σ-congruence* on A is a family $\approx_A = (\approx_{A,s})_{s\in S}$ of equivalence relations $\approx_{A,s}$ on A_s compatible with the signature Σ, i.e. for all $f \in F$ of arity $s_1 \dots s_n \to s$, for all $a_i, b_i \in A_{s_i}$, if $a_i \approx_{A,s_i} b_i$ then $f^A(a_1, \dots, a_n) \approx_{A,s} f^A(b_1, \dots, b_n)$.[4]

In practice it is often useful to consider instead of arbitrary Σ-algebras those algebras that are finitely generated by a distinguished subset Ω of the function symbols, called *constructors*. In these algebras all elements can be denoted by a constructor term (which is built only by constructor symbols and by variables of those sorts for which no constructor is defined). More precisely, let $\Sigma = (S, F)$ be a signature and $\Omega \subseteq F$ be a distinguished subset of constructors. A term t is called a *constructor term* if $t \in T_{\Sigma'}(X')$, where $\Sigma' = (S, \Omega)$, $X' = (X'_s)_{s\in S}$ with $X'_s = X_s$ if s is not the result sort of some constructor $f \in \Omega$ and $X'_s = \emptyset$ otherwise. The set of constructor terms is denoted by T_Ω. A Σ-algebra A is called *finitely generated by Ω* if for any $a \in A$ there exists a constructor term $t \in T_\Omega$ and a valuation $\alpha : X' \to A$ such that $I_\alpha(t) = a$. In particular, if $\Omega = \emptyset$, then any algebra $A \in Alg(\Sigma)$ is finitely generated by the empty set of constructors. (Note also that the definition of the generation principle is independent of X because X_s is countably infinite for all $s \in S$.)

Given a signature Σ and a set of variables X, the set WFF(Σ, X) of (well-formed) *finitary first-order Σ-formulas* is defined as usual, from equations $l = r$, the logical connectives $\neg, \wedge, \dots$ and the quantifiers $\forall, \exists$. Here the only predicate symbol is equality. In some occasions we will also use *infinitary Σ-formulas* of the form $\bigwedge_{i\in I} \phi_i$, where $(\phi_i)_{i\in I}$ is a countable family of Σ-formulas. A *Σ-sentence* is a Σ-formula which contains no free variable. In the sequel we will use the following abbreviations: For any term $t \in T_\Sigma(X)$, $var(t)$ denotes the set of variables occurring in t, and similarly $var(l, r)$ for a couple of terms l, r.

[4] In the sequel, for sake of clarity, we will omit the subscript s and write $a \approx_A b$ instead of $a \approx_{A,s} b$.

Hence a universally quantified equation will be denoted by $\forall var(l,r) \,.\, l = r$.

The *(standard) satisfaction* of a Σ-formula ϕ (finitary or not) by a Σ-algebra A, denoted by $A \models \phi$, is defined as usual in the first-order predicate calculus: the only predicate symbol $=$ is interpreted by the set-theoretic equality over the carrier sets of the algebra.

A *standard algebraic specification* SP is a tuple (Σ, Ω, Ax) where $\Sigma = (S, F)$ is a signature, $\Omega \subseteq F$ is a distinguished subset of constructors and Ax is a set of Σ-sentences, called *axioms* of SP. The *model class* of SP, denoted by $Mod(SP)$, is the class of all Σ-algebras which satisfy the axioms of SP and which are finitely generated by Ω, i.e. $Mod(SP) \stackrel{\text{def}}{=} \{A \in Alg(\Sigma) \mid A \models \phi$ for all $\phi \in Ax$ and A is finitely generated by $\Omega\}$.

Remember that if $\Omega = \emptyset$ then any algebra $A \in Alg(\Sigma)$ is finitely generated by the empty set of constructors. Hence in that case $Mod(SP)$ is simply the class of all Σ-algebras satisfying the axioms of SP. Therefore our assumption that any specification includes a declaration of a set of constructors is not a restriction but, on the contrary, it allows to apply our results to specifications with or without reachability constraints.

The *(standard) theory* of a class $\mathbf{C} \subseteq Alg(\Sigma)$ of Σ-algebras, denoted by $Th(\mathbf{C})$, is defined by $Th(\mathbf{C}) \stackrel{\text{def}}{=} \{\phi \in \mathrm{WFF}(\Sigma, X) \mid A \models \phi$ for all $A \in \mathbf{C}\}$.
In the following $SP \models \phi$ is an equivalent notation for $\phi \in Th(Mod(SP))$.

Example. Let us consider the following **CONTAINER** specification.

```
spec : CONTAINER
 use : ELEM, NAT, BOOL
 sort : Container
 generated by :
  ∅ : → Container
  insert : Elem Container → Container
 operations :
  _∪_ : Container Container → Container
  remove : Elem Container → Container
  _∈_ : Elem Container → Bool
  card : Container → Nat
  subset : Container Container → Bool
 axioms :
   ∀ S,S' : Container, e,e' : Elem .
  ∅ ∪ S = S
  insert(e,S) ∪ S' = insert(e,S ∪ S')
  remove(e,∅) = ∅
  remove(e,insert(e,S)) = remove(e,S)
  not(e = e') ⇒ remove(e,insert(e',S)) = insert(e',remove(e,S))
```

```
e ∈ ∅ = false
e ∈ insert(e',S) = ((e eq e') | (e ∈ S))
card(∅) = 0
(e ∈ S = true) ⇒ card(insert(e,S)) = card(S)
(e ∈ S = false) ⇒ card(insert(e,S)) = succ(card(S))
(subset(S,S') = true) ⇔
                    (∀ e : Elem . (e ∈ S = true) ⇒ (e ∈ S' = true))
```
end CONTAINER.

We do not detail the subspecifications **ELEM, NAT** and **BOOL** which are the usual ones. Note that the models of **CONTAINER** are finitely generated by the operations ∅ and **insert**. Since the **CONTAINER** specification is rather loose, its model class contains, among other algebras, the algebra of finite sets of elements, the algebra of finite multisets of elements, as well as the algebra of finite sequences of elements. It is quite easy to show (by structural induction w.r.t. the constructors ∅ and **insert**) that[5] **CONTAINER** $\models$ `S ∪ ∅ = S`, for instance, or that **CONTAINER** $\models$ `e ∈ S ∪ S' = (e ∈ S) | (e ∈ S')`, but it is important to note that **CONTAINER** $\not\models$ `insert(x,insert(x,S)) = insert(x,S)` and that **CONTAINER** $\not\models$ `insert(x,insert(y,S)) = insert(y,insert(x,S))`. As a consequence, the (standard) **CONTAINER** specification cannot be considered as a correct abstract implementation of a (standard) specification of sets. ◊

3 Behavioural Specifications and Behavioural Theories

As explained in the Introduction, we want to reflect the following idea: Some data structures are observable with respect to some *observable sorts*. (For instance, in the example given in the previous section, **Containers** are observable with respect to **Booleans** and **Natural** numbers by means of the ∈, **subset** and **card** operations.) The underlying intuition of our approach is that two objects are *behaviourally equal* if they cannot be distinguished by experiments with observable results. In the definitions below, experiments are formalized through *contexts* and experiments with observable results through *observable contexts*. Then we will generalize first-order logic to *behavioural first-order logic*: Instead of the set-theoretic equality, we use the *behavioural equality* for the interpretation of the = predicate symbol. This behavioural equality is defined with respect to the observable contexts (hence the observable sorts) and is used to define a *behavioural satisfaction relation*. Similar approaches can be found in [14, 12, 10, 2, 3]. We provide now the necessary technical definitions:

Definition 1 (Context). Let $\Sigma = (S, F)$ be a signature and $Y = (Y_s)_{s \in S}$ be an S-sorted family of countably infinite sets Y_s of variables of sort s.[6] Let

[5] For sake of clarity the variables occurring in the equations used in our examples are implicitly universally quantified.

[6] For sake of clarity we assume that the sets of variables Y_s used for contexts are disjoint from the sets of variables X_s used for formulas.

$Z = \{z_s \mid s \in S\}$ be an S-sorted set of variables such that $z_s \notin Y_s$ for all $s \in S$.[7]

1. A *context* is a term $C \in T_\Sigma(Y \cup Z)$ that contains, besides variables in Y, one or many occurrences of exactly one variable $z_s \in Z$, called the *context variable* of C.
2. By exception, $var(C)$ will denote the set of variables occurring in C *but* the context variable of C.
3. The arity of a context C is $s \to s'$, where s is the sort of the context variable of C and s' is the sort of C.
4. $C[t]$ denotes the term obtained by substituting the term t (of sort s) for the context variable z_s (of sort s) of C.
5. Given a distinguished subset S_D of S and a sort s in S, we denote by $\mathcal{C}_s^{S_D}$ the set of all contexts C of arity $s \to s_d$, with $s_d \in S_D$.

Definition 2 (Contextual equality). Let $\Sigma = (S, F)$ be a signature, $\mathcal{C}$ be an arbitrary set of contexts and A be a Σ-algebra. The *contextual equality* on A induced by $\mathcal{C}$, denoted by $\approx_{\mathcal{C},A}$, is defined as follows:
Two elements $a, b \in A_s$ of sort s are contextually equal (w.r.t. $\mathcal{C}$), i.e. $a \approx_{\mathcal{C},A} b$, if and only if, for all contexts $C \in \mathcal{C}$ with context variable z_s of sort s, for all valuations $\alpha : Y \to A$, we have $I_{\alpha_1}(C) = I_{\alpha_2}(C)$, where $\alpha_1, \alpha_2 : Y \cup \{z_s\} \to A$ are the unique extensions of α defined by $\alpha_1(z_s) = a$ and $\alpha_2(z_s) = b$.
Note that, if there is no context $C \in \mathcal{C}$ with context variable of sort s, then we have $a \approx_{\mathcal{C},A} b$, for all $a, b \in A_s$ of sort s.

The intuition behind this definition is that two elements a and b are contextually equal w.r.t. a given set $\mathcal{C}$ of contexts if they cannot be distinguished by at least one of the computations represented by the contexts of $\mathcal{C}$. Note that $\approx_{\mathcal{C},A}$ is a family of equivalence relations (one for each sort $s \in S$), in particular $\approx_{\mathcal{C},A}$ always contains the set-theoretic equality. However, $\approx_{\mathcal{C},A}$ is not necessarily a congruence relation, i.e. $\approx_{\mathcal{C},A}$ is not necessarily compatible with the signature Σ. From our definition of the contextual equality induced by a given set of contexts $\mathcal{C}$ we immediately deduce the following characterization:

Lemma 3. *Let $\Sigma = (S, F)$ be a signature and $\mathcal{C}$ be an arbitrary set of contexts. For any Σ-algebra A, any sort $s \in S$ and any $a, b \in A_s$, let $x_L, x_R \in X_s$ and $\beta : \{x_L, x_R\} \to A$ be the valuation defined by $\beta(x_L) = a$ and $\beta(x_R) = b$. Then $a \approx_{\mathcal{C},A} b$ if and only if $A, \beta \models \bigwedge_{C \in \mathcal{C}(s)} \forall var(C) \,.\, C[x_L] = C[x_R]$
where $\mathcal{C}(s)$ denotes the subset of all the contexts in $\mathcal{C}$ with context variable of sort s. As usual, when $\mathcal{C}(s)$ is empty, then the empty conjunction $\bigwedge_{C \in \mathcal{C}(s)} \cdots$ is equivalent to true.
Note that the formula axiomatizing the contextual equality is an infinitary one if $\mathcal{C}(s)$ is an infinite set of contexts.*

In the following we assume given a signature $\Sigma = (S, F)$ and a subset of *observable sorts* $S_{Obs} \subseteq S$. $S_{\neg Obs}$ denotes the complementary subset of non observable sorts, i.e. $S_{\neg Obs} = S \backslash S_{Obs}$.

[7] We assume as well that $z_s \notin X_s$.

Definition 4 (Observable context and behavioural equality). The set $C_{Obs} \stackrel{\text{def}}{=} \bigcup_{s \in S} C_s^{S_{Obs}}$ denotes the set of all *observable contexts*.
Let A be a Σ-algebra. The contextual equality on A induced by C_{Obs} (cf. Definition 2) is called the *behavioural equality* on A and is denoted by $\approx_{Obs,A}$.

Lemma 5. *The behavioural equality $\approx_{Obs,A}$ on A is a Σ-congruence.*

Note that, on observable sorts, the behavioural equality coincides with the set-theoretic equality, since $C_s^{S_{Obs}}$ always contains the "trivial" context z_s when s is an observable sort. For the non observable sorts, the behavioural equality contains the set-theoretic equality, but there may be also distinct values which are behaviourally equal.

Now we can define the behavioural satisfaction relation with respect to S_{Obs}:

Definition 6 (Behavioural satisfaction relation). The *behavioural satisfaction relation* w.r.t. S_{Obs}, denoted by $\models_{Obs}$, is defined as follows:
Let A be a Σ-algebra.

1. For any couple $l, r \in T_\Sigma(X)_s$ of terms of sort s, for any valuation $\alpha : X \to A$, $A, \alpha \models_{Obs} l = r$ if and only if $I_\alpha(l) \approx_{Obs,A} I_\alpha(r)$.
2. For any arbitrary Σ-formula ϕ, for any valuation $\alpha : X \to A$, $A, \alpha \models_{Obs} \phi$ is defined by induction over the structure of the formula ϕ in the usual way.
3. For any arbitrary Σ-formula ϕ, $A \models_{Obs} \phi$ if and only if, for all valuations $\alpha : X \to A$, $A, \alpha \models_{Obs} \phi$.

Hence Definition 6 is quite similar to the definition of the standard satisfaction relation $\models$, the only difference concerns (1) where $I_\alpha(l) \approx_{Obs,A} I_\alpha(r)$ replaces $I_\alpha(l) = I_\alpha(r)$.

Lemma 7. *Let A be a Σ-algebra and $\forall var(l,r) \,.\, l = r$ be a universally quantified equation. Let s be the common sort of l and r.*
If s is an observable sort, then $A \models_{Obs} \forall var(l,r) \,.\, l = r$ if and only if $A \models \forall var(l,r) \,.\, l = r$.
If s is a non observable sort, then $A \models_{Obs} \forall var(l,r) \,.\, l = r$ if and only if, for all observable contexts $C \in C_s^{S_{Obs}}$, $A \models \forall var(C) \cup var(l,r) \,.\, C[l] = C[r]$.

Remark. Lemma 7 is often used in the literature to define directly (i.e. without introducing explicitly the behavioural equality) the behavioural satisfaction of equations. However the explicit definition we have chosen is necessary to define the behavioural satisfaction of arbitrary first-order formulas. On the other hand, this lemma suggests that to prove the behavioural satisfaction of an equation $l = r$ (between non observable terms), it is equivalent to prove the standard satisfaction of the infinite set of equations $C[l] = C[r]$, for all $C \in C_s^{S_{Obs}}$. *Context Induction* (a specialized version of structural induction) was introduced by R. Hennicker in [10] as a means to prove such infinite sets of equations and has been implemented in the ISAR system (cf. [1]). In [4] it is explained how an explicit use of context induction can be avoided under some assumptions. Unfortunately, none of these ideas directly extends to the proof of the behavioural satisfaction of arbitrary first-order formulas.

In a similar way to what was done for the satisfaction relation we also generalize the generation principle of algebras to take into account the behavioural equality:

Definition 8 (Behaviourally finitely generated algebra). Let $\Omega \subseteq F$ be a distinguished subset of constructors and A be a Σ-algebra. A is called *behaviourally finitely generated by* Ω (w.r.t. S_{Obs}) if for any $a \in A$ there exists a constructor term $t \in T_\Omega$ and a valuation $\alpha : var(t) \rightarrow A$ such that $I_\alpha(t) \approx_{Obs,A} a$. In particular, if $\Omega = \emptyset$, then any algebra $A \in Alg(\Sigma)$ is behaviourally finitely generated by the empty set of constructors.

Behavioural specifications can be built on top of standard specifications as follows:

Definition 9 (Behavioural specification).

1. A *behavioural specification* is a tuple $SP\text{--}Obs = (SP, S_{Obs})$ such that $SP = (\Sigma, \Omega, Ax)$ is a standard specification (with signature $\Sigma = (S, F)$), and $S_{Obs} \subseteq S$ is a distinguished subset of observable sorts.
2. The *model class of SP–Obs*, denoted by *Mod*(*SP–Obs*), is the class of all Σ-algebras which behaviourally satisfy the axioms of *SP* and which are behaviourally finitely generated by Ω, i.e.:
   $$Mod(SP\text{--}Obs) \stackrel{\text{def}}{=} \{A \in Alg(\Sigma) \mid A \models_{Obs} \phi \text{ for all } \phi \in Ax \text{ and } A \text{ is behaviourally finitely generated by } \Omega\}.$$

Now we can consider the behavioural theory with respect to S_{Obs} of a given class **C** of Σ-algebras:

Definition 10 (Behavioural theory). Let $\mathbf{C} \subseteq Alg(\Sigma)$ be a class of Σ-algebras. The *behavioural theory* of **C** w.r.t. S_{Obs}, denoted by $Th_{Obs}(\mathbf{C})$, is defined by $Th_{Obs}(\mathbf{C}) \stackrel{\text{def}}{=} \{\phi \in \mathrm{WFF}(\Sigma, X) \mid A \models_{Obs} \phi \text{ for all } A \in \mathbf{C}\}$.
In the following, $SP\text{--}Obs \models_{Obs} \phi$ means $\phi \in Th_{Obs}(Mod(SP\text{--}Obs))$. In this case ϕ is called a *behavioural theorem* (w.r.t. *SP–Obs*).

Example. Let us consider again our **CONTAINER** specification and assume that the observable sorts are `Elem`, `Nat` and `Bool`. Then we obtain a behavioural specification (**CONTAINER**, {`Elem, Nat, Bool`}). Two objects of sort `Container` will be considered as behaviourally equal if they cannot be distinguished by observable contexts. Here, all observable contexts (with context variable of sort `Container`) must contain either $\in$, `subset` or `card`. If we consider the algebra of finite sequences of elements, it is intuitively clear that two distinct sequences will be behaviourally equal if they contain the same elements (not necessarily with the same number of occurrences or in the same order), because these sequences cannot be distinguished by the operations $\in$, `subset` or `card`. For the same reasons, it is intuitively clear that the two characteristic equations of sets, **insert(x,insert(x,S)) = insert(x,S)** and **insert(x,insert(y,S)) = insert(y,insert(x,S))**, are behaviourally satisfied by all models of the behavioural specification (**CONTAINER**, {**Elem, Nat, Bool**}). Indeed no observable experiment (done with the $\in$, **card** and **subset** operations) can distinguish the left and right-hand sides of these equations. The aim of this paper is to provide a proof technique to formally establish that this intuition is right. ◊

Fully abstract algebras play an important role for the characterization of behavioural theories. Following Milner's notion (cf. [11]), we define full abstractness with respect to the observable sorts S_{Obs} as follows:

Definition 11 (Fully abstract algebra).

1. A Σ-algebra A is called ***fully abstract*** with respect to S_{Obs} if $\approx_{Obs,A}$ coincides with the set-theoretic equality over the carrier sets of A.
2. For any class $\mathbf{C} \subseteq Alg(\Sigma)$ of Σ-algebras, $FA_{Obs}(\mathbf{C})$ denotes the subclass of the fully abstract algebras of $\mathbf{C}$, i.e.
$FA_{Obs}(\mathbf{C}) \stackrel{\text{def}}{=} \{A \in \mathbf{C} \mid A \text{ is fully abstract w.r.t. } S_{Obs}\}$.

Example. Consider again our behavioural specification (**CONTAINER**, {**Elem, Nat, Bool**}). The algebra of finite sequences of elements is not fully abstract (we have pointed out above that two distinct sequences may be behaviourally equal), while the algebra of finite sets of elements is fully abstract. ◊

Since an algebra A is fully abstract if and only if all behaviourally equal objects are identical, we have:

Proposition 12 (Infinitary characterization of fully abstract algebras). *A Σ-algebra A is fully abstract w.r.t. S_{Obs} if and only if A satisfies (in the standard sense) the following infinitary formula FA^{∞}_{Obs} : $\bigwedge_{s \in S_{\neg Obs}} FA^{\infty}_{Obs}(s)$, where, for each non observable sort $s \in S_{\neg Obs}$, $FA^{\infty}_{Obs}(s)$ is:*
$\forall x_L, x_R : s \,.\, \Big[\Big(\bigwedge_{C \in C^{s_{Obs}}_{s}} \forall var(C) \,.\, C[x_L] = C[x_R]\Big) \Longrightarrow x_L = x_R\Big]$

Proof. Straightforward from Definition 11 and Lemma 3. □

The crucial role of fully abstract algebras is outlined by the following result:

Theorem 13 (Characterization of behavioural theories). *Let SP–Obs = (SP, S_{Obs}) be a behavioural specification.*

1. *$Th_{Obs}(Mod(SP\text{–}Obs)) = Th(FA_{Obs}(Mod(SP)))$.*
2. *Let SP–FA^{∞}_{Obs} be the (standard) specification SP augmented by the infinitary axiom FA^{∞}_{Obs} defined in Proposition 12. Then:*
$Th_{Obs}(Mod(SP\text{–}Obs)) = Th(Mod(SP\text{–}FA^{\infty}_{Obs}))$ i.e.
SP–Obs $\models_{Obs} \phi$ if and only if SP–$FA^{\infty}_{Obs} \models \phi$, for all $\phi \in WFF(\Sigma, X)$.

Proof. (1) is a special case of a more general theorem given in [5]. (2) is a direct consequence of (1) and of Proposition 12. □

According to Theorem 13, the behavioural satisfaction of a given first-order formula ϕ by the model class of the behavioural specification *SP–Obs* is equivalent to the standard satisfaction of the same formula ϕ by the standard specification $SP\text{–}FA^{\infty}_{Obs}$. Unfortunately this result is up to now of limited practical interest, since Proposition 12 only provides an infinitary axiomatization of fully abstract algebras, hence the specification $SP\text{–}FA^{\infty}_{Obs}$ contains an infinitary axiom. In the sequel we study sufficient conditions for getting rid of this infinitary axiomatization.

4 The Observability Kernel

Since the behavioural equality is defined with respect to an infinite set of observable contexts which represent the infinitely many experiments with observable results, it is not surprising that our characterization of fully abstract algebras involves an infinitary formula (cf. Proposition 12). A natural idea to get rid of this infinitary formula is to check whether, under some conditions, it would be enough to consider some adequate finite set of observable contexts instead of the infinite set of all observable contexts.

In a first step we will study some sufficient conditions under which the contextual equality induced by an arbitrary set of contexts $\mathcal{C}$ coincides with the behavioural equality.

Lemma 14. *Let A be a Σ-algebra and $\approx_A$ be an arbitrary congruence on A. If $\approx_A$ coincides with the set-theoretic equality on the carrier sets of all observable sorts $s \in S_{Obs}$, then $\approx_A \subseteq \approx_{Obs,A}$.*

Proof. Let a, b be two elements of A_s, for some sort $s \in S$ and assume that $a \approx_A b$. Since $\approx_A$ is a congruence (hence is compatible with the signature Σ), we have, for any observable context $C \in \mathcal{C}_s^{S_{Obs}}$ and for any valuation $\alpha : Y \to A$, $I_{\alpha_1}(C) \approx_A I_{\alpha_2}(C)$, where $\alpha_1, \alpha_2 : Y \cup \{z_s\} \to A$ are the unique extensions of α defined by $\alpha_1(z_s) = a$ and $\alpha_2(z_s) = b$, where z_s is the context variable of C. Since C is an observable context, both $I_{\alpha_1}(C)$ and $I_{\alpha_2}(C)$ belong to the carrier set of some observable sort. But since we have assumed that $\approx_A$ coincides with the set-theoretic equality on the carrier sets of the observable sorts, $I_{\alpha_1}(C) \approx_A I_{\alpha_2}(C)$ implies $I_{\alpha_1}(C) = I_{\alpha_2}(C)$, hence we have $a \approx_{Obs,A} b$. Therefore $\approx_A \subseteq \approx_{Obs,A}$. □

Remark. Indeed it is easy to prove that the set of all congruences on A that coincides with the set-theoretic equality on each observable sort is a complete lattice, the smallest element of which is the set-theoretic equality, the greatest element being the behavioural equality.

Lemma 15. *Let $\mathcal{C} \subseteq \mathcal{C}_{Obs}$ be an arbitrary subset of observable contexts such that, for any observable sort $s \in S_{Obs}$, $z_s \in \mathcal{C}$ and let A be a Σ-algebra. Then $\approx_{\mathcal{C},A} = \approx_{Obs,A}$ if and only if $\approx_{\mathcal{C},A}$ is a Σ-congruence.*

Proof. Assume that $\approx_{C,A}$ is a Σ-congruence. Since $C \subseteq C_{Obs}$, obviously we have $\approx_{Obs,A} \subseteq \approx_{C,A}$. To prove that $\approx_{C,A} \subseteq \approx_{Obs,A}$, by Lemma 14, it is enough to prove that $\approx_{C,A}$ coincides with the set-theoretic equality for each carrier set of an observable sort. But this holds since C contains by assumption all the "trivial" contexts z_s when s is an observable sort. The converse direction is trivial. □

Notation. In the following, C_k^f denotes a context of the form $f(y_1, \ldots, y_{k-1}, z_{s_k}, y_{k+1}, \ldots, y_n)$ built from a function symbol $f \in F$ of arity $s_1 \ldots s_{k-1}\, s_k\, s_{k+1} \ldots s_n \rightarrow s$, an integer k with $1 \leq k \leq n$, a context variable z_{s_k} of sort s_k, and pairwise distinct variables $y_i \in Y$. Provided they are pairwise distinct, the actual names of the variables y_i are irrelevant and these variables can be left implicit in the notation C_k^f. Moreover, when the context C_k^f is substituted for the context variable of another context C to form the context $C[C_k^f]$, we assume w.l.o.g. that the variables y_i of C_k^f are distinct from the variables y_j occurring in C (i.e. we assume that $var(C) \cap var(C_k^f) = \emptyset$).

Proposition 16. *Let C be an arbitrary set of contexts and A be a Σ-algebra. The contextual equality $\approx_{C,A}$ on A induced by C is a Σ-congruence if and only if A satisfies the following (possibly infinitary) formulas, for each $s \in S$, for each function symbol $f \in F$ of arity $s_1 \ldots s_n \rightarrow s'$, for each integer k with $1 \leq k \leq n$ and $s_k = s$:*

$$\forall x_L, x_R : s\ .\ \Big[\Big(\bigwedge_{C \in C(s)} \forall var(C)\ .\ C[x_L] = C[x_R]\Big) \Longrightarrow \bigwedge_{C' \in C(s')} \forall var(C') \cup var(C_k^f)\ .\ C'[C_k^f[x_L]] = C'[C_k^f[x_R]]\Big]$$

where $C(s)$ ($C(s')$ resp.) denotes the subset of all the contexts in C with context variable of sort s (s' resp.).[8]

Proof. For the proof we use the following lemma:

Lemma 17. *Given a Σ-algebra A, a family $\approx_A$ of equivalence relations is a Σ-congruence on A if and only if, for all $s \in S$, for all $f \in F$ of arity $s_1 \ldots s_n \rightarrow s'$, for all k with $1 \leq k \leq n$ and $s_k = s$, for all $a, b \in A_s$, if $a \approx_A b$ then for all $c_i \in A_{s_i}$, $f^A(c_1, \ldots, c_{k-1}, a, c_{k+1}, \ldots, c_n) \approx_A f^A(c_1, \ldots, c_{k-1}, b, c_{k+1}, \ldots, c_n)$.*

Now let A be a Σ-algebra, and C be an arbitrary set of contexts. Let $s \in S$ and let $f \in F$ be an arbitrary function symbol of arity $s_1 \ldots s_n \rightarrow s'$, let k be an arbitrary integer with $1 \leq k \leq n$ and $s_k = s$. According to the lemma above, $\approx_{C,A}$ is a Σ-congruence if and only if for all $a, b \in A_s$, $a \approx_{C,A} b$ implies that $f^A(c_1, \ldots, c_{k-1}, a, c_{k+1}, \ldots, c_n) \approx_{C,A} f^A(c_1, \ldots, c_{k-1}, b, c_{k+1}, \ldots, c_n)$ holds for all $c_i \in A_{s_i}$. We will now show that this implication is equivalent to the fact that A satisfies the formula given in the proposition. According to Lemma 3, $a \approx_{C,A} b$ iff $A, \beta \models \bigwedge_{C \in C(s)} \forall var(C)\ .\ C[x_L] = C[x_R]$, where $\beta : \{x_L, x_R\} \rightarrow A$ is the valuation defined by $\beta(x_L) = a$ and $\beta(x_R) = b$. Similarly, $f^A(c_1, \ldots, c_{k-1}, a, c_{k+1}, \ldots, c_n) \approx_{C,A} f^A(c_1, \ldots, c_{k-1}, b, c_{k+1}, \ldots, c_n)$ iff $A, \beta' \models \bigwedge_{C' \in C(s')} \forall var(C')\ .\ C'[x'_L] = C'[x'_R]$, where $\beta' : \{x'_L, x'_R\} \rightarrow A$ is

[8] Remember that an empty conjunction is as usual equivalent to true.

the valuation defined by $\beta'(x'_L) = f^A(c_1, \ldots, c_{k-1}, a, c_{k+1}, \ldots, c_n)$ and $\beta'(x'_R) = f^A(c_1, \ldots, c_{k-1}, b, c_{k+1}, \ldots, c_n)$. Now let $\alpha : var(C^f_k) \to A$ be the valuation defined by $\alpha(y_i) = c_i$. Then $\beta'(x'_L) = I_{\beta \cup \alpha}(C^f_k[x_L])$ and $\beta'(x'_R) = I_{\beta \cup \alpha}(C^f_k[x_R])$. Hence $f^A(c_1, \ldots, c_{k-1}, a, c_{k+1}, \ldots, c_n) \approx_{C,A} f^A(c_1, \ldots, c_{k-1}, b, c_{k+1}, \ldots, c_n)$ holds for all $c_i \in A_{s_i}$ iff $A, \beta \cup \alpha \models \bigwedge_{C' \in C(s')} \forall var(C') \,.\, C'[C^f_k[x_L]] = C'[C^f_k[x_R]]$ holds for all $\alpha : var(C^f_k) \to A$, i.e. iff $A, \beta \models \bigwedge_{C' \in C(s')} \forall var(C') \cup var(C^f_k) \,.\, C'[C^f_k[x_L]] = C'[C^f_k[x_R]]$, which shows that the required implication is exactly the one provided by the proposition. □

Lemma 15 points out that we can replace the infinite set C_{Obs} of all observable contexts by any subset $C \subseteq C_{Obs}$ (in particular by any finite subset C), provided that C contains the trivial observable contexts and that the contextual equality induced by C is a congruence. Moreover, Proposition 16 provides a necessary and sufficient condition for this contextual equality to be a Σ-congruence. The problem now is to find an adequate finite subset of C_{Obs}. Remember that observable contexts represent experiments with observable results. A typical experiment will start by some computations involving mainly non observable values and providing non observable results, then there will be a computation providing an observable result, possibly followed by more computations over observable values. The crucial idea is that intuitively only the step going from non observable values to observable ones is critical. Hence our intuition suggests that, in addition to the trivial observable contexts, it would be enough to consider the contexts of the form C^f_k, with $f \in \Sigma$ of arity $s_1 \ldots s_{k-1}\, s_k\, s_{k+1} \ldots s_n \to s$, $s \in S_{Obs}$ and $s_k \in S_{\neg Obs}$, provided that the contextual equality induced by these contexts is a Σ-congruence. To make this intuition more precise we start by introducing some useful notations.

Notation. According to the partition of the sorts S into S_{Obs} and $S_{\neg Obs}$, the set of function symbols F can be split into:

1. The subset F_O of function symbols of arity $f_O : s_1 \ldots s_n \to s$, with $s \in S_{Obs}$, and at least one $s_i \in S_{\neg Obs}$;
2. The subset F_I of function symbols of arity $f_I : s_1 \ldots s_m \to s$, with $s \in S_{\neg Obs}$, and at least one $s_j \in S_{\neg Obs}$;
3. The subset of all other function symbols.

Definition 18 (Crucial observable contexts). The set of the *crucial observable contexts*, denoted by CC_{Obs}, is defined by:

$$CC_{Obs} = \{C^{f_O}_i \mid f_O : s_1 \ldots s_{i-1}\, s_i\, s_{i+1} \ldots s_n \to s \in F_O \text{ and } i \text{ is such that } s_i \in S_{\neg Obs}\} \cup \{z_s \mid s \in S_{Obs}\}.$$

Note that, for each adequate choice of $f_O \in F_O$ and i, we make an arbitrary choice for the (pairwise distinct) variables y_k left implicit in the notation $C^{f_O}_i$. Hence the set of the crucial observable contexts is finite.

Example. Consider again our behavioural specification (`CONTAINER`, {`Elem`, `Nat`, `Bool`}). We have F_O = {∈, `card`, `subset`} and F_I = {`insert`, ∪, `remove`}.

$CC_{Obs} = \{x \in z_{Cont}$, $\mathbf{card}(z_{Cont})$, $\mathbf{subset}(S, z_{Cont})$, $\mathbf{subset}(z_{Cont}, S)$, z_{Bool}, z_{Nat}, $z_{Elem}\}$. ◊

Before stating the main result of this section we observe the following property:

Lemma 19. *The contextual equality induced by the set of the crucial observable contexts CC_{Obs} is always compatible with the function symbols $f_O \in F_O$.*

Proof. Let A be a Σ-algebra and $\approx_{CC_{Obs},A}$ be the contextual equality induced over A by the crucial contexts CC_{Obs}. We know that $\approx_{CC_{Obs},A}$ coincides with the set-theoretic equality on the carrier sets of the observable sorts. Hence it is enough to check the compatibility w.r.t. non observable sorts. Let $s \in S_{\neg Obs}$ and $a, b \in A_s$ such that $a \approx_{CC_{Obs},A} b$. Let $f_O \in F_O$ of arity $f_O : s_1 \ldots s_n \to s$, and let k such that $s_k = s$. Let $c_i \in A_{s_i}$ be arbitrary values. Then $f_O^A(c_1, \ldots, c_{k-1}, a, c_{k+1}, \ldots, c_n)$ ($f_O^A(c_1, \ldots, c_{k-1}, b, c_{k+1}, \ldots, c_n)$ resp.) is equal to $I_{\alpha_1}(C_k^{f_O})$ ($I_{\alpha_2}(C_k^{f_O})$ resp.), where $\alpha : var(C_k^{f_O}) \to A$ is the valuation defined by $\alpha(y_i) = c_i$ and $\alpha_1, \alpha_2 : Y \cup \{z_s\} \to A$ are the unique extensions of α defined by $\alpha_1(z_s) = a$ and $\alpha_2(z_s) = b$. By definition, $a \approx_{CC_{Obs},A} b$ implies $I_{\alpha_1}(C_k^{f_O}) = I_{\alpha_2}(C_k^{f_O})$, i.e. $f_O^A(c_1, \ldots, c_{k-1}, a, c_{k+1}, \ldots, c_n) = f_O^A(c_1, \ldots, c_{k-1}, b, c_{k+1}, \ldots, c_n)$. Hence $f_O^A(c_1, \ldots, c_{k-1}, a, c_{k+1}, \ldots, c_n) \approx_{CC_{Obs},A} f_O^A(c_1, \ldots, c_{k-1}, b, c_{k+1}, \ldots, c_n)$ and Lemma 17 shows that $\approx_{CC_{Obs},A}$ is a (S, F_O)-congruence. □

We have now the necessary ingredients to state our main result:

Theorem 20 (Observability Kernel). *Let A be a Σ-algebra. The contextual equality $\approx_{CC_{Obs},A}$ on A induced by the set of the crucial observable contexts CC_{Obs} coincides with the behavioural equality $\approx_{Obs,A}$ if and only if the algebra A satisfies (in the standard sense) the following finitary first-order formula $OK_{\Sigma,S_{Obs}}$, called the Observability Kernel associated to Σ and S_{Obs}, and defined by $OK_{\Sigma,S_{Obs}} \stackrel{\text{def}}{=} \bigwedge_{s \in S_{\neg Obs}} OK_\Sigma(s)$, where for each non observable sort $s \in S_{\neg Obs}$, $OK_\Sigma(s)$ is the following implication:*

$$\forall x_L, x_R : s \,.\, \Big[\Big(\bigwedge\nolimits_{f_O \in F_O}^{\wedge i} \forall var(C_i^{f_O}) \,.\, C_i^{f_O}[x_L] = C_i^{f_O}[x_R]\Big) \Longrightarrow$$
$$\bigwedge\nolimits_{f_I \in F_I}^{\wedge j} \bigwedge\nolimits_{f_O \in F_O}^{\wedge i} \forall var(C_i^{f_O}) \cup var(C_j^{f_I}) \,.\, C_i^{f_O}[C_j^{f_I}[x_L]] = C_i^{f_O}[C_j^{f_I}[x_R]]\Big]$$

and where:

1. *$\bigwedge_{f_O \in F_O}^{\wedge i}$ is an abbreviation for the conjunction over all contexts $C_i^{f_O}$, for all $f_O \in F_O$ and all choices of i such that the sort of the context variable of the context $C_i^{f_O}$ is s.*
2. *Similarly $\bigwedge_{f_I \in F_I}^{\wedge j} \bigwedge_{f_O \in F_O}^{\wedge i}$ is an abbreviation for the conjunction over all contexts $C_j^{f_I}$ and $C_i^{f_O}$, for all $f_I \in F_I$, $f_O \in F_O$ and all choices of j and i such that the sort of the context variable of the context $C_j^{f_I}$ is s and the sort of the context variable of the context $C_i^{f_O}$ is the sort of the context $C_j^{f_I}$.*

Proof. According to Lemma 15, the contextual equality induced by CC_{Obs} coincides with the behavioural equality if and only if it is a Σ-congruence, i.e. if it is compatible with all $f \in F$. Since the contextual equality induced by $\mathcal{CC}_{Obs}$ coincides with the set-theoretic equality on the carrier sets of the observable sorts, and since it is compatible with F_O (cf. Lemma 19), it is enough to check the compatibility w.r.t. non observable sorts and function symbols in F_I. But then the Observability Kernel is exactly the conjunction, for all non observable sorts and for all $f_I \in F_I$, of the formulas given in Proposition 16 (with $\mathcal{CC}_{Obs}$ as a special case for $\mathcal{C}$). □

It is important to note that, since the signature Σ is finite, $OK_{\Sigma,S_{Obs}}$ is a finitary first-order formula.

Example. Consider again our behavioural specification (**CONTAINER**, {**Elem, Nat, Bool**}). The Observability Kernel is the following formula (here there is just one non observable sort, `Container`):[9]

```
∀ CL, CR : Container .
  [ (∀ x : Elem, S : Container .
     x ∈ CL = x ∈ CR ∧
     card(CL) = card(CR) ∧
     subset(S,CL) = subset(S,CR) ∧
     subset(CL,S) = subset(CR,S) )
   ⟹ (∀ y, z : Elem, S1, S2 : Container .
       z ∈ insert(y,CL) = z ∈ insert(y,CR) ∧
       z ∈ (S1 ∪ CL) = z ∈ (S1 ∪ CR) ∧
       z ∈ (CL ∪ S1) = z ∈ (CR ∪ S1) ∧
       z ∈ remove(y,CL) = z ∈ remove(y,CR) ∧
       card(insert(y,CL)) = card(insert(y,CR)) ∧
       card(S1 ∪ CL) = card(S1 ∪ CR) ∧
       card(CL ∪ S1) = card(CR ∪ S1) ∧
       card(remove(y,CL)) = card(remove(y,CR)) ∧
       subset(S1, insert(y,CL)) = subset(S1, insert(y,CR)) ∧
       subset(S1, S2 ∪ CL) = subset(S1, S2 ∪ CR) ∧
       subset(S1, CL ∪ S2) = subset(S1, CR ∪ S2) ∧
       subset(S1, remove(y,CL)) = subset(S1, remove(y,CR)) ∧
       subset(insert(y,CL), S1) = subset(insert(y,CR), S1) ∧
       subset(S2 ∪ CL, S1) = subset(S2 ∪ CR, S1) ∧
       subset(CL ∪ S2, S1) = subset(CR ∪ S2, S1) ∧
       subset(remove(y,CL), S1) = subset(remove(y,CR), S1) ) ]
```

Note that in the next section we will study further simplifications that will considerably improve the Observability Kernel, and as a consequence will lead to much more simpler formulas to be proved. ◇

[9] For sake of clarity we have chosen more adequate names for the variables and we have moved the universal quantifiers in front of the conjunctions.

Corollary 21. *Let A be a Σ-algebra.* **If** $A \models OK_{\Sigma,S_{Obs}}$ **then** *for any non observable sort $s \in S_{\neg Obs}$, for any $a, b \in A_s$ and valuation $\beta : \{x_L, x_R\} \to A$ with $\beta(x_L) = a$ and $\beta(x_R) = b$, the following conditions are equivalent:*

1. $a \approx_{Obs,A} b$
2. $a \approx_{CC_{Obs},A} b$
3. $A, \beta \models \bigwedge_{C \in C_s^{S_{Obs}}} \forall var(C) \,.\, C[x_L] = C[x_R]$
4. $A, \beta \models \bigwedge_{f_O \in F_O}^{\wedge i} \forall var(C_i^{f_O}) \,.\, C_i^{f_O}[x_L] = C_i^{f_O}[x_R]$

Proof. Follows immediately from Theorem 20 and Lemma 3. In particular, according to Lemma 3 we know that $a \approx_{CC_{Obs},A} b$ is equivalent to $A, \beta \models \bigwedge_{C \in CC_{Obs}(s)} \forall var(C) \,.\, C[x_L] = C[x_R]$. Since s is a non observable sort, the latter formula is the same as the one given in 4. □

5 How to Prove Behavioural Theorems

We assume given a behavioural specification *SP–Obs* $= (SP, S_{Obs})$ with signature $\Sigma = (S, F)$ and with observable sorts $S_{Obs} \subseteq S$. We keep the notations F_O and F_I introduced in the previous section. CC_{Obs} denotes the set of the crucial observable contexts.

We can now combine the results obtained in Section 3 (especially Proposition 12 and Theorem 13) with the simplifications induced by the Observability Kernel assumption (cf. Theorem 20 and Corollary 21).

Proposition 22 (Finitary characterization of fully abstract algebras). *Let A be a Σ-algebra.* **If** $A \models OK_{\Sigma,S_{Obs}}$ **then** *A is fully abstract w.r.t. S_{Obs} if and only if A satisfies (in the standard sense) the following finitary formula $FA_{Obs} : \bigwedge_{s \in S_{\neg Obs}} FA_{Obs}(s)$, where, for each non observable sort $s \in S_{\neg Obs}$, $FA_{Obs}(s)$ is:*
$\forall x_L, x_R : s \,.\, \left[\left(\bigwedge_{f_O \in F_O}^{\wedge i} \forall var(C_i^{f_O}) \,.\, C_i^{f_O}[x_L] = C_i^{f_O}[x_R]\right) \Longrightarrow x_L = x_R\right]$

Proof. Follows from Proposition 12 and Corollary 21 (3 ⇔ 4). □

Now we obtain our final result:

Theorem 23. *Let SP* **partitioned by** *F_O be the (standard) specification SP augmented by the finitary axiom FA_{Obs} defined in Proposition 22.*
If $SP \models OK_{\Sigma,S_{Obs}}$ **then**
$Th_{Obs}(Mod(SP\text{–}Obs)) = Th(Mod(SP$ **partitioned by** $F_O))$, *i.e. for all $\phi \in WFF(\Sigma, X)$, SP–Obs $\models_{Obs} \phi$ if and only if SP* **partitioned by** $F_O \models \phi$.

Proof. By Theorem 13.1 we have $Th_{Obs}(Mod(SP\text{–}Obs)) = Th(FA_{Obs}(Mod(SP)))$. The assumption $SP \models OK_{\Sigma,S_{Obs}}$ and Proposition 22 imply that $FA_{Obs}(Mod(SP)) = Mod(SP$ **partitioned by** $F_O)$. □

Theorem 23 provides a very general and powerful method to prove the behavioural satisfaction of arbitrary first-order formulas by *SP*-Obs: First we compute the Observability Kernel $OK_{\Sigma,S_{Obs}}$ and we prove, once for all, that:

$$(A)\ SP \models OK_{\Sigma,S_{Obs}}$$

Then, for any first-order formula ϕ, to prove $SP\text{–}Obs \models_{Obs} \phi$ we prove:

$$(B)\ SP\ \textbf{partitioned by}\ F_O \models \phi$$

The result is general since we have made no assumption neither on the axioms of *SP* nor on the number of non observable sorts. The result is powerful since for both (A) and (B) we can use any available theorem prover for first-order logic. Our method has been successfully applied to various examples using the Larch Prover V3.0 [7].[10]

A last improvement can be obtained using the following remark. In most cases it is possible to split F_O into two sets F_{O1} and F_{O2}, with the following property (for all $s \in S_{\neg Obs}$):

$$(R)\ SP \models \forall x_L, x_R : s\ .\ \Big[\Big(\bigwedge\nolimits^{\wedge i}_{fo \in F_{O1}} \forall var(C_i^{fo})\ .\ C_i^{fo}[x_L] = C_i^{fo}[x_R]\Big) \Longrightarrow \bigwedge\nolimits^{\wedge i}_{fo \in F_{O2}} \forall var(C_i^{fo})\ .\ C_i^{fo}[x_L] = C_i^{fo}[x_R]\Big]$$

Then the proof of (A) is split into the proof of (R) (for all $s \in S_{\neg Obs}$) and the proof of the Reduced Observability Kernel, which is similar to the Observability Kernel, but where the conjunctions $\bigwedge^{\wedge i}_{fo \in F_O}$ are restricted to $\bigwedge^{\wedge i}_{fo \in F_{O1}}$.

Example. Consider again our behavioural specification (**CONTAINER**, {**Elem**, **Nat**, **Bool**}). Using our last improvement, we can split F_O into $F_{O1} = \{\in\}$ and $F_{O2} = \{$**card**, **subset**$\}$. Then the proof of the Observability Kernel is split into the proof of the *Simplifiability of the Observability Kernel*:

```
∀ CL, CR : Container .
  [ (∀ x : Elem . x ∈ CL = x ∈ CR )
   ⟹ (∀ S : Container .
        card(CL) = card(CR) ∧
        subset(S,CL) = subset(S,CR) ∧
        subset(CL,S) = subset(CR,S) ) ]
```

and the proof of the *Reduced Observability Kernel*:

```
∀ CL, CR : Container .
  [ (∀ x : Elem . x ∈ CL = x ∈ CR )
   ⟹ (∀ y, z : Elem, S : Container .
        z ∈ insert(y,CL) = z ∈ insert(y,CR) ∧
        z ∈ (S ∪ CL) = z ∈ (S ∪ CR) ∧
        z ∈ (CL ∪ S) = z ∈ (CR ∪ S) ∧
        z ∈ remove(y,CL) = z ∈ remove(y,CR) ) ]
```

[10] Indeed the **partitioned by** construct was inspired by the Larch Prover where it is available.

It is not difficult to show that **CONTAINER** $\models$ "Simplifiability of the Observability Kernel" and that **CONTAINER** $\models$ "Reduced Observability Kernel". Hence we now consider the enriched specification **CONTAINER partitioned by** $\in$, i.e. the specification **CONTAINER** enriched by the axiom:
$\forall$ `CL, CR : Container . [ (`$\forall$` x : Elem . x` $\in$ `CL = x` $\in$ `CR )` $\Longrightarrow$ `CL = CR ]`
and it is then very easy to prove that:
`CONTAINER partitioned by` $\in \models$ `insert(x,insert(x,S)) = insert(x,S)`
and that:
`CONTAINER partitioned by` $\in \models$
`insert(x,insert(y,S)) = insert(y,insert(x,S))`
which means that these two equations are behaviourally valid in the model class of the behavioural specification (**CONTAINER**, {`Elem, Nat, Bool`}). This means as well that this behavioural specification can be considered as a correct abstract implementation of sets. $\diamondsuit$

6 Conclusion

We have provided a technique that allows us to reduce the infinitary characterization of behavioural equality to a finitary one. Hence to prove behavioural theorems we can use arbitrary theorem provers for standard first-order logic. Our technique relies on the so-called "Observability Kernel Assumption". Unfortunately there are interesting examples where this condition is not satisfied (like the usual specification of stacks.) However, in all such cases that we have considered so far we can define a conservative extension of the given specification by introducing appropriate auxiliary function symbols such that the extended specification satisfies the Observability Kernel Assumption. It is an interesting objective of further research to study under which conditions appropriate conservative extensions exist and to develop a general method for the construction of such extensions.

Acknowledgements: This work is partially supported by the French-German cooperation program Procope, a joint CNRS-NSF grant, the E.C. ESPRIT Working Group COMPASS, the E.C. HCM project MeDiCis, and the German BMFT project SPECTRUM. Special thanks are due to Fernando Orejas, Andrzej Tarlecki and Martin Wirsing for fruitful discussions, to Steve Garland for suggesting improvements in our LP scripts and to Franck Vedrine for running the examples with LP. It is a pleasure to acknowledge also Hubert Baumeister who pointed out that the proofs of our results could be simplified by avoiding any reference to the context induction principle.

References

1. B. Bauer and R. Hennicker. Proving the correctness of algebraic implementations by the ISAR system. In *Proc. of DISCO'93*, pages 2–16. Springer-Verlag L.N.C.S. 722, 1993.

2. G. Bernot and M. Bidoit. Proving the correctness of algebraically specified software: modularity and observability issues. In *Proc. of AMAST'91*, pages 216–242. Springer-Verlag Workshops in Computing Series, 1992.
3. G. Bernot, M. Bidoit, and T. Knapik. Towards an adequate notion of observation. In *Proc. of ESOP'92*, pages 39–55. Springer-Verlag L.N.C.S. 582, 1992.
4. M. Bidoit and R. Hennicker. How to prove observational theorems with LP. In *Proc. of the First International Workshop on Larch*. Springer-Verlag Workshops in Computing Series, 1993.
5. M. Bidoit, R. Hennicker, and M. Wirsing. Characterizing behavioural semantics and abstractor semantics. In *Proc. of ESOP'94*, pages 105–119. Springer-Verlag L.N.C.S. 788, 1994.
6. H. Ehrig and B. Mahr. *Fundamentals of algebraic specification 1. Equations and initial semantics*, volume 6 of *EATCS Monographs on Theoretical Computer Science*. Springer-Verlag, 1985.
7. S. Garland and J. Guttag. An overview of LP, the Larch Prover. In *Proc. of the Third International Conference on Rewriting Techniques and Applications*, pages 137–151. Springer-Verlag L.N.C.S. 355, 1989.
8. J. Goguen and J. Meseguer. Universal realization, persistent interconnection and implementation of abstract modules. In *Proc. of 9th ICALP*, pages 265–281. Springer-Verlag L.N.C.S. 140, 1982.
9. J.A. Goguen, J.W. Thatcher, and E.G. Wagner. *An initial approach to the specification, correctness, and implementation of abstract data types*, volume 4 of *Current Trends in Programming Methodology*. Prentice Hall, 1978.
10. R. Hennicker. Context induction: a proof principle for behavioural abstractions and algebraic implementations. *Formal Aspects of Computing*, 3(4):326–345, 1991.
11. R. Milner. Fully abstract models of typed λ-calculi. *Theoretical Computer Science*, 4:1–22, 1977.
12. P. Nivela and F. Orejas. Initial behaviour semantics for algebraic specification. In *Recent Trends in Data Type Specification*, pages 184–207. Springer-Verlag L.N.C.S. 332, 1988.
13. F. Orejas, M. Navarro, and A. Sànches. Implementation and behavioural equivalence: A survey. In *Recent Trends in Data Type Specification*, pages 93–125. Springer-Verlag L.N.C.S. 655, 1993.
14. H. Reichel. Initial restrictions of behaviour. In *Proc. of IFIP Working Conference, The Role of Abstract Models in Information Processing*, 1985.
15. D. Sannella and A. Tarlecki. On observational equivalence and algebraic specification. In *Proc. of TAPSOFT'85*, pages 308–322. Springer-Verlag L.N.C.S. 185, 1985.
16. O. Schoett. Behavioural correctness of data representation. *Science of Computer Programming*, 14:43–57, 1990.

How to Realize LSE Narrowing*

Andreas Werner[1], Alexander Bockmayr[2], Stefan Krischer[3]

[1] SFB 314, Univ. Karlsruhe, D-76128 Karlsruhe, werner@ira.uka.de
[2] MPI Informatik, Im Stadtwald, D-66123 Saarbrücken, bockmayr@mpi-sb.mpg.de
[3] CRIN & INRIA-Lorraine, B.P.239, F-54506 Vandœuvre-lès-Nancy, krischer@loria.fr

Abstract. Narrowing is a complete unification procedure for equational theories defined by canonical term rewriting systems. It is also the operational semantics of various logic and functional programming languages. In [BKW93], we introduced the LSE narrowing strategy which is complete for arbitrary canonical rewriting systems and optimal in the sense that two different LSE narrowing derivations cannot generate the same narrowing substitution. LSE narrowing improves all previously known strategies for arbitrary systems. According to their definition, LSE narrowing steps seem to be very expensive, because a large number of subterms has to be checked for reducibility. In this paper, we first show that many of these subterms are identical. Then we describe how using left-to-right basic occurrences the number of subterms that have to be tested can be reduced drastically. Finally, based on these theoretical results, we develop an efficient implementation of LSE narrowing.

1 Introduction

Narrowing allows us to solve equations in equational theories defined by canonical term rewriting systems. It is also the operational semantics of various logic and functional programming languages [DG86, Han94]. In its original form, it is very inefficient. Therefore, many optimizations have been proposed in the past. In [BKW92, BKW93], we introduced a new narrowing strategy called LSE narrowing and its normalizing variant. LSE narrowing is complete for arbitrary canonical rewriting systems and it is optimal in the sense that two different LSE narrowing derivations cannot generate the same narrowing substitution.

LSE narrowing detects redundant derivations by reducibility tests. According to their definition, LSE narrowing steps seem to be very expensive, because a large number of subterms has to be checked for reducibility. However, many of these terms are identical. In this paper, we analyze which subterms are equal.

* The first author's work was supported by the *Deutsche Forschungsgemeinschaft* as part of the SFB 314 (project S2). The second author's work was supported by the German Ministry for Research and Technology (BMFT) (contract ITS 9103) and the ESPRIT Working Group CCL (contract EP 6028). The third author's work was supported by the *Centre National de la Recherche Scientifique* (CNRS), and the *Conseil Régional de Lorraine.*

Since each LSE narrowing derivation is left-to-right basic, we can use left-right-basic narrowing to rule out in advance a lot of derivations that are not LSE. We show that using left-to-right basic occurrences also the number of subterms that have to be tested can be reduced drastically. Finally, we present two concepts for the realization of LSE narrowing and compare them. These results illustrate why the benefits of the reducibility tests surpass their costs and explain the success of the strategy in empirical experiments.

The organization of the paper is as follows. Section 2 contains an introduction to LSE narrowing and its normalizing variant. In Section 3, we explain how LSE narrowing and left-to-right basic narrowing are related. The main results about the occurrences that have to be considered by the LSE-Tests are given in Section 4. We develop a method that checks only left-to-right basic occurrences. Based on these results we explain how an efficient implementation of LSE narrowing can be obtained by modifying an implementation of left-to-right basic narrowing. In Section 5, we introduce the notion of test occurrences which are a refinement of non-left-to-right-basic occurrences and develop a second method for the realization of the LSE-Tests. In Section 6, we compare both methods and give recommendations concerning their application. Finally we illustrate our results by some empirical experiments in Section 7.

2 LSE Narrowing

Throughout this paper we use the standard terminology of term rewriting as it can be found for example in [HO80, DJ90]. In this section, we recall the basic ideas of narrowing and LSE narrowing. More details can be found in [BKW93].

Narrowing allows us to find complete sets of E-unifiers for equational theories E that can be defined by a canonical term rewriting system $\mathcal{R}$. Let $\mathcal{R}$ be a canonical rewriting system that contains the (additional) rule $x \doteq x \rightarrow true$ where $\doteq$ does not occur in any other rule. A substitution μ is an $\mathcal{R}$-unifier of G iff there exists a rewriting derivation $\mu(G) \xrightarrow{*}_R true \wedge \ldots \wedge true$. Narrowing simulates such a derivation by instantiating the variables of the goals as far as necessary to rewrite them.

Definition 1 (Narrowing). A system of equations $G : s_1 \doteq t_1 \wedge \ldots \wedge s_n \doteq t_n$ is *narrowable* to a system of equations G' with *narrowing substitution* δ, $G \rightsquigarrow_{[v,l \rightarrow r,\delta]} G'$, iff there exist a non-variable occurrence $v \in Occ(G)$ and a rule[4] $\pi : l \rightarrow r$ in $\mathcal{R}$ such that G/v and l are syntactically unifiable with most general unifier δ and $G' = \delta(G)[v \leftarrow \delta(r)]$.

A *narrowing derivation* $G_0 \rightsquigarrow^*_\sigma G_n$ with *narrowing substitution* σ is a sequence of narrowing steps $G_0 \rightsquigarrow_{\delta_1} G_1 \rightsquigarrow_{\delta_2} \cdots \rightsquigarrow_{\delta_n} G_n$, $n \geq 0$, where $\sigma = (\delta_n \circ \ldots \circ \delta_1)\mid_{Var(G_0)}$. The narrowing substitution leading from G_i to G_j, for $0 \leq i \leq j \leq n$, will be denoted by $\lambda_{i,j} \stackrel{\text{def}}{=} \delta_j \circ \ldots \circ \delta_{i+1}$. In particular, $\lambda_{i,i} = id$, for $i = 0, \ldots, n$.

[4] We always assume that $Var(l) \cap Var(G) = \emptyset$.

It is well-known that the set of all substitutions σ such that there exists a narrowing derivation $G = G_0 \rightsquigarrow^*_\sigma G_n = true \wedge \ldots \wedge true, n \geq 0$ is a complete set of R-unifiers of G [Hul80].

A substitution μ is called *normalized* if $\mu(x)$ is in normal form for all variables x. To ensure completeness it suffices to guarantee that for each normalized substitution μ there is *one* reduction $\mu(G) \xrightarrow{*}_R true \wedge \ldots \wedge true$ for which a corresponding narrowing derivation exists. The idea of LSE narrowing is to select a unique reduction called *left reduction* (a special form of leftmost-innermost rewriting derivation) and to use reducibility tests such that only narrowing derivations corresponding to left reductions are generated [BKW93]. In *normalizing narrowing* the systems of equations are normalized after each narrowing step. To treat ordinary narrowing and normalizing narrowing in common we introduce the notion of *reducing narrowing* (cf. [Rét87]):

Definition 2 (Reducing and Normalizing Narrowing). A *reducing narrowing step* $G \rightsquigarrow^r_{[v, l \to r, \delta]} G''$ is given by a narrowing step followed by a (possible empty) sequence of reduction steps: $G \rightsquigarrow_{[v, l \to r, \delta]} G' \xrightarrow{*}_R G''$ where G'' is not necessarily in normal form. We call $G \rightsquigarrow^r G''$ *a normalizing narrowing step* if G'' is the normal form of G'.

In ordinary narrowing we have $G' = G''$, in normalizing narrowing G'' is the normal form of G', but there are also ("mixed") reducing narrowing steps that are neither ordinary nor normalizing steps. Next we define LSE narrowing.

Definition 3 (Left, Below).

- An occurrence ω is *left* of an occurrence ω', denoted $\omega \lhd \omega'$, iff there exist occurrences o, v, v' and natural numbers i, i' such that $i < i', \omega = o.i.v$ and $\omega' = o.i'.v'$.
- An occurrence ω is *below* an occurrence ω', denoted $\omega > \omega'$ iff there exists an occurrence $v \neq \epsilon$ such that $\omega = \omega'.v$.

We assume that the rules are ordered by a total well-founded ordering $<_{\mathcal{R}}$.

Definition 4 (LSE Narrowing). In a reducing narrowing derivation

$$G'_0 \rightsquigarrow^r_{[v_1, \pi_1, \delta_1]} G'_1 \rightsquigarrow^r_{[v_2, \pi_2, \delta_2]} \cdots G'_{n-1} \rightsquigarrow^r_{[v_n, \pi_n, \delta_n]} G'_n$$

the step $G'_{n-1} \rightsquigarrow^r_{[v_n, \pi_n, \delta_n]} G'_n$ is called *LSE* iff the following three conditions are satisfied:

(Left-Test) For all $i \in \{1, \ldots, n\}$ the subterms of $\lambda_{i-1,n}(G'_{i-1})$ which lie left of v_i are in normal form.

(Sub-Test) For all $i \in \{1, \ldots, n\}$ the subterms of $\lambda_{i-1,n}(G'_{i-1})$ which lie below v_i are in normal form.

(Epsilon-Test) For all $i \in \{1, \ldots, n\}$ the term $\lambda_{i-1,n}(G'_{i-1}/v_i)$ is not reducible at occurrence ϵ with a rule smaller (w.r.t. $<_R$) than π_i.

A (normalizing) narrowing derivation is *LSE* iff every single (normalizing) narrowing step is LSE.

LSE narrowing and its normalizing variant have the following fundamental properties [BKW93]:

- Both strategies are complete for arbitrary canonical rewriting systems.
- Two different derivations cannot generate the same narrowing substitution. Especially both strategies enumerate each solution at most once.
- Finally, the narrowing substitution of any derivation is normalized.

LSE narrowing for conditional term rewrite systems is studied in [BW94].

3 Left-to-Right Basic Occurrences

To perform a single new LSE step we have to apply the LSE-Tests to all narrowing steps done before. This means that we have to check for each system of equations in the derivation whether the narrowing substitution has produced a reducible subterm left of or below the narrowing occurrence and whether the Epsilon-Test succeeds. Hence, LSE narrowing steps seem to be very expensive. In particular the Left- and the Sub-Test cause problems, since there are a lot of occurrences that have to be checked. In the following sections, we show how the number of occurrences which have to be considered can be reduced drastically using *left-to-right basic occurrences.*

First, we give the definition of reducing left-to-right basic narrowing (cf. [Hul80, Her86, Rét87]).

Definition 5 (Antecedent, Residual). Let $G \rightsquigarrow_{[v,l \to r,\delta]} G'$ be a narrowing step. We say that the occurrence ω in G is an *antecedent* of the occurrence ω' in G' (and ω' is a *residual* of ω respectively) iff

- $\omega = \omega'$ and neither $\omega \leq v$ nor $v \geq \omega$ or
- there exists an occurrence ρ' of a variable x in r such that $\omega' = v.\rho'.o$ and $\omega = v.\rho.o$ where ρ is an occurrence of the same variable x in l.

Consider a narrowing step $G \rightsquigarrow G'$. If ω' is a residual of ω then G'/ω' is an instance of G/ω. For rewriting steps, which are special narrowing steps, both terms are equal.

The idea of *left-to-right basic narrowing* is to discard those occurrences which have been introduced by a *narrowing* substitution or which are left of a *narrowing* occurrence. In the initial goal G'_0 all non-variable occurrences are *left-to-right basic.* After a narrowing step, all occurrences left of or below the narrowing occurrence are removed and the non-variable occurrences of the (non-instantiated) right-hand side of the rule are added. After a rewriting step, the occurrences below the rewriting occurrence are replaced by the occurrences that are non-variable in the (non-instantiated) right-hand side or whose antecedents are left-to-right basic.

Definition 6 (Reducing Left-to-Right Basic Narrowing). Given the reducing narrowing derivation

$$
\begin{array}{l}
G'_0 \quad \rightsquigarrow_{[v_1,l_1 \to r_1,\delta_1]} G_1 = G_{10} \to \ldots \to_{[v_{1k_1},l_{1k_1} \to r_{1k_1},\delta_{1k_1}]} \quad G_{1k_1} = G'_1 \\
\vdots \\
G'_{n-1} \rightsquigarrow_{[v_n l_n \to r_n,\delta_n]} G_n = G_{n0} \to \ldots \to_{[v_{nk_n},l_{nk_n} \to r_{nk_n},\delta_{nk_n}]} G_{nk_n} = G'_n
\end{array}
$$

for $i = 1, \ldots n$ and $j = 1, \ldots, k_i$, the sets of *left-to-right basic occurrences* are inductively defined as follows:

$$
\begin{array}{lll}
LB'_0 & \stackrel{\text{def}}{=} & FuOcc(G'_0) \\
LB_i & \stackrel{\text{def}}{=} & (LB'_{i-1} \ \setminus \ \{v \in LB'_{i-1} \mid v \lhd v_i \text{ or } v \geq v_i\}) \\
 & & \quad \cup \ \{v_i.v \mid v \in FuOcc(r_i)\} \\
LB_{ij} & \stackrel{\text{def}}{=} & (LB_{i,j-1} \setminus \ \{v \in LB_{i,j-1} \mid v \geq v_{ij}\}) \\
 & & \quad \cup \ \{v_{ij}.o \mid o \in FuOcc(r_{ij})\} \\
 & & \quad \cup \ \{v_{ij}.o \mid o \in FuOcc(\delta_{ij}(r_{ij})) \setminus FuOcc(r_{ij}) \text{ and} \\
 & & \qquad \qquad \text{all antecedents of } v_{ij}.o \text{ are in } LB_{i,j-1}\}
\end{array}
$$

where $LB_{i0} = LB_i$ and $LB'_i = LB_{i,k_i}$. $FuOcc(t)$ denotes the set of non-variable occurrences of t. For a *reducing left-to-right basic narrowing derivation* we require that $v_i \in LB'_{i-1}$, for all $i = 1, \ldots, n$ and $v_{ij} \in LB_{i,j-1}$, for all $i = 1, \ldots, n$ and $j = 1, \ldots, k_i$.

In a simple way, left-to-right basic narrowing eliminates a priori many narrowing derivations that are not LSE. Every LSE narrowing derivation is left-to-right basic. However, the converse does not hold [BKW93].

We now give the basic intuition for the two methods of realizing LSE narrowing that we will present in the rest of the paper. Let us consider a left-to-right basic narrowing derivation

$$(G_0, LB_0) \rightsquigarrow_{[v_1,l_1 \to r_1,\delta_1]} (G_1, LB_1) \quad \ldots \quad \rightsquigarrow_{[v_n,l_n \to r_n,\delta_n]} (G_n, LB_n).$$

If v is an occurrence left of v_i in G_{i-1} then v is an occurrence left of or below v_{i+1} in G_i by Definition 6 and $\lambda_{i,n}(G_i)/v = \lambda_{i,n}(\delta_{i-1}(G_{i-1}[v_i \leftarrow r_i]))/v = \lambda_{i-1,n}(G_{i-1})/v$ by Definition 1. Note that the occurrence v is always non-left-to-right-basic in G_i. A naive implementation of LSE narrowing would check both $\lambda_{i-1,n}(G_{i-1})/v$ and $\lambda_{i,n}(G_i)/v$ for reducibility. Since they are identical, it suffices to perform the tests on one of them only. There are two possibilities now, which can be distinguished using the notion of left-to-right basic occurrences: we may apply the reducibility tests either to left-to-right basic occurrences or non-left-to-right-basic occurrences only.

Example 1. Consider the rules

$$
\begin{array}{ll}
\pi_1: \ 0 + y \ \to y & \pi_3 : p(x) + y \to p(x + y) \\
\pi_2 : s(x) + y \to s(x + y) & \pi_4 : s(p(x)) \ \to x
\end{array}
$$

and the derivation

$$s(x) + (y + 0) \quad \rightsquigarrow_{[2,\pi_1,\{y \mapsto 0\}]} \quad s(x) + 0 \quad \rightsquigarrow_{[\epsilon,\pi_2,id_V]} \quad s(x + 0).$$

$s(x)$ lies left of the narrowing occurrence 2 in the first term and below the narrowing occurrence ϵ in the second term. The occurrence of $s(x)$ in the first term is left-to-right basic whereas the one in the second term is non-left-to-right-basic.

The concept developed in Section 4 applies the tests to the left-to-right basic occurrences whereas the concept in Section 5 is based on non-left-to-right-basic occurrences. First we describe how the occurrences in a reducing left-to-right basic narrowing derivation are related to each other. This will provide the basis for both methods.

4 Testing Basic Occurrences For Reducibility

In Example 1, we motivated that the notion of left-to-right basic occurrences may be used to reduce the number of occurrences that have to be considered by the LSE-Tests. The method proposed in this section tests only left-to-right basic occurrences. If an occurrence lies left of or below a narrowing occurrence or if it is non-left-to-right-basic then all its residuals are non-left-to-right-basic (cf. Definition 6 and Definition 5). Thus the method developed in this section tests the subterms where they get for the first time into the scope of the LSE-Tests.

We begin by a lemma which shows that the subterms introduced by a most general unifier of two terms s and s' contain only function symbols occurring in s and s'. The lemma will allow us to neglect almost all occurrences that have been introduced by the narrowing substitutions δ_i.

Lemma 7 [WBK93]. *Let δ be a most general unifier of s and s'. Then for each $x \in Dom(\delta)$ and for every non-variable subterm t of $\delta(x)$ there exists a non-variable occurrence u in s or in s' such that $t = \delta(s/u)$ or $t = \delta(s'/u)$ respectively.*

Next, we show that all non-left-to-right-basic occurrences in the current goal have been checked for reducibility while we applied the tests to one of the preceding narrowing steps. Intuitively, these occurrences either have an antecedent that lies left of a narrowing occurrence or they originate from a variable instantiation. Remember that the occurrences that originate from variable instantiation have been characterized in Lemma 7.

Proposition 8. *Consider a reducing left-to-right basic narrowing derivation*

$$(G'_0, LB'_0) \quad \rightsquigarrow^{r}_{[v_1,l_1 \to r_1,\delta_1]} \quad \cdots \quad \rightsquigarrow^{r}_{[v_n,l_n \to r_n,\delta_n]} \quad (G'_n, LB'_n).$$

- *If $t = G'_n/u$ for some occurrence $u \notin LB'_n$, $n \geq 0$ or*
- *if t is a subterm of $\delta_n(x)$ for some variable x, $n \geq 1$,*

then

- *there exist* $j \in \{1,\ldots,n\}$ *and an occurrence* $\omega \in LB'_{j-1}$ *left of or below* v_j *such that* $t = \lambda_{j-1,n}(G'_{j-1}/\omega)$ *or*
- *there exist* $j \in \{1,\ldots,n\}$ *and an occurrence* $\omega \in FuOcc(l_j)\backslash FuOcc(G'_{j-1}/v_j)$ *such that* $t = \lambda_{j-1,n}(l_j/\omega)$ *or*
- t *is a variable.*

Proof. We use induction on n. The case $n = 0$ is trivial. Assume that the proposition holds for the narrowing derivation $(G'_0, LB'_0) \rightsquigarrow^{\mathcal{T}*} (G'_n, LB'_n)$ and suppose $(G'_n, LB'_n) \rightsquigarrow_{[v_{n+1}, l_{n+1} \to r_{n+1}, \delta_{n+1}]} (G_{n+1}, LB_{n+1})$. Hence, we have $G_{n+1} = \delta_{n+1}(G'_n[v_{n+1} \leftarrow r_{n+1}])$ and $LB_{n+1} = (LB'_n \backslash \{v \in LB'_n \mid v \lhd v_{n+1} \text{ or } v \geq v_{n+1}\}) \cup \{v_{n+1}.v \mid v \in FuOcc(r_{n+1})\}$. We show that the proposition holds for G_{n+1}, LB_{n+1}, and δ_{n+1}. Let $u \in Occ(G_{n+1})$ be not in LB_{n+1}.

(1) First, we consider the case $u \in FuOcc(G'_n[v_{n+1} \leftarrow r_{n+1}])$.
  - Assume that $u \lhd v_{n+1}$ or $u \rhd v_{n+1}$. Then $G_{n+1}/u = \delta_{n+1}(G'_n/u)$.
    If $u \notin LB'_n$ then by induction hypothesis
    - there exist $j \in \{1,\ldots,n\}$ and an occurrence $\omega \in LB'_{j-1}$ left of or below v_j such that $G'_n/u = \lambda_{j-1,n}(G'_{j-1}/\omega)$ or
    - there exist $j \in \{1,\ldots,n\}$ and $\omega \in FuOcc(l_j) \setminus FuOcc(G'_{j-1}/v_j)$ such that $G'_n/u = \lambda_{j-1,n}(l_j/\omega)$.

    Hence, we have
    - $G_{n+1}/u = \delta_{n+1}(G'_n/u) = \lambda_{j-1,n+1}(G'_{j-1}/\omega)$ or
    - $G_{n+1}/u = \delta_{n+1}(G'_n/u) = \lambda_{j-1,n+1}(l_j/\omega)$ respectively.

    If $u \in LB'_n$ then u is left of v_{n+1} and $G_{n+1}/u = \lambda_{n,n+1}(G'_n/u)$. Hence, we choose $\omega \stackrel{\text{def}}{=} u$ and $j \stackrel{\text{def}}{=} n+1$.
  - All occurrences $u \geq v_{n+1}$ in $FuOcc(G'_n[v_{n+1} \leftarrow r_{n+1}])$ are in LB_{n+1} by definition.
  - Also all $u < v_{n+1}$ are in LB_{n+1} (which can be shown by induction on n).

(2) Now, suppose that t (for example G_{n+1}/u) is a subterm of $\delta_{n+1}(x)$ for some variable x. If t is a variable then the proposition trivially is true. Therefore, assume that t is not a variable. By Lemma 7, there exists a non-variable occurrence v in G'_n/v_{n+1} or l_{n+1} such that $t = \delta_{n+1}(G'_n/v_{n+1}.v)$ or $t = \delta_{n+1}(l_{n+1}/v)$.
  - If $v_{n+1}.v \in LB'_n$ then we choose $\omega \stackrel{\text{def}}{=} v_{n+1}.v$ and $j \stackrel{\text{def}}{=} n+1$, since $t = \delta_{n+1}(G'_n/v_{n+1}.v) = \lambda_{n,n+1}(G'_n/v_{n+1}.v)$.
  - If $v_{n+1}.v \notin LB'_n$ but $v_{n+1}.v \in FuOcc(G'_n)$ then by induction hypothesis
    - there exist $j \in \{1,\ldots,n\}$ and an occurrence $\omega \in LB'_{j-1}$ left of or below v_j such that $G'_n/v_{n+1}.v = \lambda_{j-1,n}(G'_{j-1}/\omega)$ or
    - there exist $j \in \{1,\ldots,n\}$ and a $\omega \in FuOcc(l_j) \setminus FuOcc(G'_{j-1}/v_j)$ such that $G'_n/v_{n+1}.v = \lambda_{j-1,n}(l_j/\omega)$.

    Hence, we have
    - $t = \delta_{n+1}(G'_n/v_{n+1}.v) = \lambda_{j-1,n+1}(G'_{j-1}/\omega)$ or
    - $t = \delta_{n+1}(G'_n/v_{n+1}.v) = \lambda_{j-1,n+1}(l_j/\omega)$ respectively.

- Finally, if $v_{n+1}.v \notin FuOcc(G'_n)$ but $v \in FuOcc(l_{n+1})$ then we choose $\omega \stackrel{\text{def}}{=} v$ and $j \stackrel{\text{def}}{=} n+1$, since $t = \delta_{n+1}(l_{n+1}/v) = \lambda_{n,n+1}(l_{n+1}/v)$.

Therefore, the proposition holds for G_{n+1}, LB_{n+1}, and δ_{n+1}.

Suppose $(G_{n+1}, LB_{n+1}) \stackrel{*}{\rightarrow}_R (G'_{n+1}, LB'_{n+1})$. By induction on the number of rewrite steps it follows that for every occurrence u' of G'_{n+1} such that $u' \notin LB'_{n+1}$ there exists an occurrence u in G_{n+1} such that $G'_{n+1}/u' = G_{n+1}/u$ and $u \notin LB_{n+1}$. Thus, the proposition holds for $n+1$. □

Now, we are able to show that it suffices to test for reducibility only the left-to-right-basic occurrences and some occurrences of the left-hand sides of the used rules. We obtain this result by induction based on the previous results.

Theorem 9. *Consider a reducing left-to-right basic narrowing derivation*

$$(G'_0, LB'_0) \;\rightsquigarrow^{r}_{[v_1,l_1 \to r_1,\delta_1]} \;\cdots\; \rightsquigarrow^{r}_{[v_n,l_n \to r_n,\delta_n]} \;(G'_n, LB'_n).$$

For all $i \in \{1,\ldots,n\}$ and for all occurrences u in $\lambda_{i-1,n}(G'_{i-1})$ left of or below v_i

(1) *there exist $j \in \{1,\ldots,n\}$ and an occurrence $\omega \in LB'_{j-1}$ left of or below v_j such that $\lambda_{i-1,n}(G'_{i-1})/u = \lambda_{j-1,n}(G'_{j-1}/\omega)$ or*
(2) *there exist $j \in \{1,\ldots,n\}$ and an occurrence $\omega \in FuOcc(l_j) \setminus FuOcc(G'_{j-1}/v_j)$ such that $\lambda_{i-1,n}(G'_{i-1})/u = \lambda_{j-1,n}(l_j/\omega)$ or*
(3) *$\lambda_{i-1,n}(G'_{i-1})/u$ is a variable.*

Proof. Again, we use induction on n. If $n = 0$ then the theorem trivially holds, since there are no narrowing steps. Assume that the theorem holds for n. First we show that the statement is true for $i = 1,\ldots,n$ and for all occurrences u in $\lambda_{i-1,n+1}(G'_{i-1})$ left of or below v_i.

- If u is an occurrence in $\lambda_{i-1,n+1}(G'_{i-1})$ left of or below v_i that is a non-variable occurrence in $\lambda_{i-1,n}(G'_{i-1})$, then by induction hypothesis
  - there exist $j \in \{1,\ldots,n\}$ and an occurrence $\omega \in LB'_{j-1}$ left of or below v_j such that $\lambda_{i-1,n}(G'_{i-1})/u = \lambda_{j-1,n}(G'_{j-1}/\omega)$ or
  - there exist $j \in \{1,\ldots,n\}$ and an occurrence $\omega \in FuOcc(l_j) \setminus FuOcc(G'_{j-1}/v_j)$ such that $\lambda_{i-1,n}(G'_{i-1})/u = \lambda_{j-1,n}(l_j/\omega)$.

  Hence, we have
  - $\lambda_{i-1,n+1}(G'_{i-1})/u = \lambda_{j-1,n+1}(G'_{j-1}/\omega)$ or
  - $\lambda_{i-1,n+1}(G'_{i-1})/u = \lambda_{j-1,n+1}(l_j/\omega)$ respectively.
- If $\lambda_{i-1,n+1}(G'_{i-1})/u$ is a subterm of $\delta_{n+1}(x)$ for some variable x then the theorem is true due to Proposition 8.

Now we show that the theorem holds for $i = n+1$. Therefore, let u be an occurrence of $\lambda_{n,n+1}(G'_n)$ left of or below v_{n+1}.

- If $u \in LB'_n$ then we choose $\omega \stackrel{\text{def}}{=} u$ and $j \stackrel{\text{def}}{=} n+1$.
- If $u \notin LB'_n$ but $u \in FuOcc(G'_n)$ then by Proposition 8

  - there exist $j \in \{1, \ldots, n\}$ and an occurrence $\omega \in LB'_{j-1}$ left of or below v_j such that $G'_n/u = \lambda_{j-1,n}(G'_{j-1}/\omega)$ or
  - there exist $j \in \{1, \ldots, n\}$ and an occurrence $\omega \in FuOcc(l_j) \setminus FuOcc(G_{j-1}/v_j)$ such that $G'_n/u = \lambda_{j-1,n}(l_j/\omega)$.

  Hence, we have
  - $\lambda_{n,n+1}(G'_n/u) = \lambda_{j-1,n+1}(G'_{j-1}/\omega)$ or
  - $\lambda_{n,n+1}(G'_n/u) = \lambda_{j-1,n+1}(l_j/\omega)$ respectively.
- Finally, if G'_n/u is a subterm of $\delta_{n+1}(x)$ for some variable x then the theorem is true due to Proposition 8.

Therefore, the theorem is true for $n + 1$. □

Note that the terms $\lambda_{j-1,n}(G'_{j-1}/\omega)$ and $\lambda_{j-1,n}(l_j/\omega) = \lambda_{j-1,n}(G'_{j-1})/v_j.\omega$ mentioned in the last theorem are subterms of $\lambda_{j-1,n}(G'_{j-1})$ lying left of or below v_j. Hence, we do not lose completeness if we check these occurrences for reducibility.

We summarize the results of this section by giving a first method to perform the LSE-Tests:

Method 1 Consider an ordinary or a normalizing left-to-right basic narrowing derivation of the form

$$(G'_0, LB'_0) \quad \rightsquigarrow^{r}_{[v_1, l_1 \to r_1, \delta_1]} \quad \cdots \quad \rightsquigarrow^{r}_{[v_n, l_n \to r_n, \delta_n]} \quad (G'_n, LB'_n).$$

In the n-th step one tests for each step $j = 1, \ldots, n$

- $\lambda_{j-1,n}(G'_{j-1})$ for reducibility at occurrence ω iff ω is a *left-to-right basic occurrence* in G'_{j-1} lying left of or below v_j,
- $\lambda_{j-1,n}(l_j)$ for reducibility at occurrence ω iff ω is a non-variable occurrence in l_j but $v_j.\omega$ is not a non-variable occurrence in G'_{j-1},

and carries out the Epsilon-Test.

Example 2. Consider the rules given in Example 1 and the derivation

$$x_0{+}y \;\rightsquigarrow_{[\epsilon, \pi_2, \delta_1]}\; s(x_1{+}y) \;\rightsquigarrow_{[1, \pi_2, \delta_2]}\; \cdots \;\rightsquigarrow_{[1.\cdots.1, \pi_2, \delta_n]}\; s^n(x_n{+}y)$$

where $\delta_i = \{x_{i-1} \mapsto s(x_i)\}$. Since $\lambda_{i-1,n}(x_{i-1}) = s^{n-i+1}(x_n)$ we have to test $n(n+1)/2$ non-variable occurrences for the Left- and Sub-Test in the n-th step by the definition of LSE narrowing. Method 1 allows us to restrict these tests to n occurrences: the top of $\lambda_{i-1,n}(l_i)/1 = s^{n-i+1}(x_n)$ for $i = 1, \ldots, n$. Note that we obtain a redundant derivation if we apply rule π_3 in step $n + 1$.

It is advisable to compute the occurrences needed in l_j during the unification of G'_{j-1}/v_j and l_j. If this is not possible then it may be very costly to determine $FuOcc(l_j) \setminus FuOcc(G'_{j-1}/v_j)$. Instead of testing these occurrences for reducibility one may then check whether $\lambda_{0,n}|_{Var(G'_0)}$ is normalized [WBK93].

In the following, we sketch how Theorem 9 can be used to obtain easily an efficient implementation of LSE narrowing by modifying a WAM-based implementation of left-to-right basic narrowing. For example, the functional-logic languages ALF [Han91] and KANN [GS92] provide implementations of left-to-right basic narrowing on the level of an extended Warren Abstract Machine (WAM) [War83]. Most of the ideas that we will present may also help to modify other implementations of left-to-right basic narrowing - for example implementations in Prolog.

Storing the Terms Needed for the LSE-Tests. To perform the tests for the n-th narrowing step, we need subterms of $G'_0, \ldots, G'_{n-1}$ (cf. Theorem 9). Especially the Epsilon-Test has to be applied to the subterms that have been replaced by the narrowing steps. If we use a WAM-based implementation (of left-to-right basic narrowing) then all the terms that are needed are available on the *heap*:

(a) Although G'_{i-1}/v_i has been replaced in the i-th step, it has not been removed since it will be needed for backtracking. Only the reference to G'_{i-1}/v_i has been removed in the i-th step.
(b) If v is left of v_i in G'_{i-1} then its residual (and any occurrence below it) is non-left-to-right-basic in G'_i and the following systems of equations until it will be replaced by a narrowing step j applied above of it. Recall that left-to-right basic narrowing steps never take place at non-left-to-right-basic occurrences. Hence, G'_{i-1}/v is available in the current system of equations G'_n (if there is no step $j \leq n$ above of v_i) or in G'_{j-1}/v_j (see (a)).

By the definition of the LSE-Tests, we have to apply $\lambda_{i-1,n} = \delta_n \circ \ldots \circ \delta_i$ to the subterms G'_{i-1}/v of G'_{i-1} that have to be checked for reducibility. It is not necessary to do this explicitly. By the concept of term representation in WAM-based machines, if a variable is instantiated then all of its occurrences are instantiated wherever the variable occurs. Hence, in the j-th narrowing step, δ_j is applied to all terms on the heap (cf. Definition 1). Thus, G'_{i-1}/v has been successively instantiated to $\lambda_{i-1,n}(G_{i-1}/v)$ by the steps $i, \ldots, n$. A crucial point is that it may happen that a narrowing step is applied to an occurrence that originates from a variable instantiation. This narrowing step would reduce one of the subterms that have to be checked for reducibility. But then the corresponding derivation will be detected as non-LSE (see Theorem 9).

Determining the Occurrences that Have to Be Tested. The Epsilon-Test is not crucial since for the n-th step we need just the occurrences v_i and the rules π_i that have been used in the first n steps. The occurrences that have to be considered by the Left-Test and the Sub-Test in the n-th step are those in item (1) - (3) of Theorem 9. We suggest to use an additional data structure called *test stack* which always contains the occurrences that are needed for the Left-Test and the Sub-Test. Initially, this stack is empty.

(1) Usually left-to-right basic narrowing is implemented as follows [Han91, GS92]: each narrowing step j consists of a sequence of applications of *skip innermost* followed by a proper narrowing step at an occurrence v_j. *Skip innermost* removes successively all occurrences left of and below v_j from the set of left-to-right basic occurrences. These removed occurrences are just the ones for step j in item (1) of Theorem 9. Hence, instead of removing the occurrences, we just have to push them on the test stack by *skip innermost.*

(2) Item (2) in Theorem 9 consists of occurrences of the left-hand sides l_j of the rules that have no counterpart or that have a variable as counterpart in G'_{j-1}. Hence, we just have to modify the unification algorithm in such a way that these occurrences are pushed on the test stack.

(3) Since the given rewriting system is canonical, variables are not reducible. Hence, they need not be considered by the LSE-Tests.

Thus, by slight modifications we can achieve that the first n narrowing steps push in a very efficient way all those occurrences on the test stack which are needed to perform the Left-Test and Sub-Test for step n. It should be pointed out that this technique allows us to compute the test stack incrementally. Hence, after the unification of l_n and G'_{n-1} all the informations needed for the LSE-Tests in step n are available and we just have to perform them. Further optimizations are discussed in [WBK93].

5 Testing Non-basic Occurrences for Reducibility

In Proposition 8, we have seen that if an occurrence is non-left-to-right-basic in G'_n then the corresponding subterm will be tested for reducibility by the LSE-Tests. In [Rét87], it already has been shown that completeness is preserved if we consider only left-to-right basic narrowing derivations $G'_0 \rightsquigarrow^* G'_n$ where the non-left-to-right-basic occurrences of the current goal G'_n are normalized (*SL left-to-right basic narrowing*). The idea of our second method is to restrict the reducibility tests to non-left-to-right-basic occurrences in G'_n as far as possible. This means that the LSE-Tests may be seen as a generalization of Réty's SL-Condition. In fact, originally LSE narrowing was introduced in [KB91] as *LSE-SL left-to-right basic narrowing*. The SL-Condition only has to be tested for the current goal whereas the LSE-Tests also have to be applied to the preceding goals. This has important consequences on the search space, since LSE narrowing detects more redundant derivations. In [BKW93] we compared both strategies.

If an occurrence lies left of or below a narrowing occurrence then all its residuals are non-left-to-right-basic. Also the residuals of a non-left-to-right-basic occurrence are again non-left-to-right-basic. Therefore, we do not have to check an occurrence in a goal if there exists a residual of it. This means that we will test a subterm as late as possible. The method which will be derived in this section checks for reducibility only

- non-basic-occurrences in the current goal G'_n and
- occurrences in the preceding goals that have no residuals.

The first implementation of LSE narrowing sketched in [KB91] tests *all* those occurrences for reducibility. This is not necessary as we will see now.

We first introduce a refinement of the notion of non-left-to-right-basic occurrences which describes exactly which occurrences of the current system have to be tested.

Definition 10 (Test Occurrences). Given the reducing left-to-right basic narrowing derivation

$$\begin{pmatrix} G'_0 \\ LB'_0 \end{pmatrix} \rightsquigarrow_{[v_1,\pi_1,\delta_1]} \begin{pmatrix} G_1 = G_{10} \\ LB_1 = LB_{10} \end{pmatrix} \to \ldots \to_{[v_{1k_1},\pi_{1k_1},\delta_{1k_1}]} \begin{pmatrix} G_{1k_1} = G'_1 \\ LB_{1k_1} = LB'_1 \end{pmatrix}$$
$$\vdots$$
$$\begin{pmatrix} G'_{n-1} \\ LB'_{n-1} \end{pmatrix} \rightsquigarrow_{[v_n,\pi_n,\delta_n]} \begin{pmatrix} G_n = G_{n0} \\ LB_n = LB_{n0} \end{pmatrix} \to \ldots \to_{[v_{nk_n},\pi_{nk_n},\delta_{nk_n}]} \begin{pmatrix} G_{nk_n} = G'_n \\ LB_{nk_n} = LB'_n \end{pmatrix}$$

the sets of *test occurrences* are inductively defined as follows:

$$\begin{aligned} T'_0 &\stackrel{\text{def}}{=} \emptyset \\ T_i &\stackrel{\text{def}}{=} (T'_{i-1} \setminus \{v \mid v \geq v_i\}) \\ &\qquad \cup \{v_i.o \mid o \in FuOcc(\delta_i(r_i)) \setminus FuOcc(r_i) \text{ and} \\ &\qquad\qquad \text{at least one antecedent of } v_i.o \text{ is in } T'_{i-1} \cup LB'_{i-1}\} \\ &\qquad \cup \{v \mid v \lhd v_i \text{ and } v \in LB'_{i-1}\} \\ T_{ij} &\stackrel{\text{def}}{=} (T_{i,j-1} \setminus \{v \mid v \geq v_{ij}\}) \\ &\qquad \cup \{v_{ij}.o \mid o \in FuOcc(\delta_{ij}(r_{ij})) \setminus FuOcc(r_{ij}) \text{ and} \\ &\qquad\qquad \text{at least one antecedent of } v_{ij}.o \text{ is in } T_{i,j-1}\} \end{aligned}$$

where $\pi_i : l_i \to r_i$ and $\pi_{ij} : l_{ij} \to r_{ij}$ for $i = 1, \ldots n$ and $j = 1, \ldots, k_i$.

If $n = 0$ then there does not exist any narrowing step, consequently the set of test occurrences is empty. We update the set of test occurrences after a narrowing step in the following way. All the occurrences of the replaced subterm have to be removed or replaced by their residuals. Residuals of occurrences left of or below the narrowing occurrence have to be added. In this context, we use again Theorem 9 to reduce the number of occurrences that have to be considered. Finally, after a rewriting step we have to replace occurrences by their residuals.

Theorem 11. *Consider the reducing left-to-right basic narrowing derivation*

$$\begin{pmatrix} G'_0 \\ LB'_0 \\ T'_0 \end{pmatrix} \rightsquigarrow_{[v_1,l_1 \to r_1,\delta_1]} \begin{pmatrix} G_{10} \\ LB_{10} \\ T_{10} \end{pmatrix} \to \ldots \to_{[v_{1k_1},l_{1k_1} \to r_{1k_1},\delta_{1k_1}]} \begin{pmatrix} G'_1 \\ LB'_1 \\ T'_1 \end{pmatrix}$$
$$\vdots$$
$$\begin{pmatrix} G'_{n-1} \\ LB'_{n-1} \\ T'_{n-1} \end{pmatrix} \rightsquigarrow_{[v_n l_n \to r_n,\delta_n]} \begin{pmatrix} G_{n0} \\ LB_{n0} \\ T_{n0} \end{pmatrix} \to \ldots \to_{[v_{nk_n},l_{nk_n} \to r_{nk_n},\delta_{nk_n}]} \begin{pmatrix} G'_n \\ LB'_n \\ T'_n \end{pmatrix}$$

For all $i \in \{1, \ldots, n\}$ and for each occurrence u in $\lambda_{i-1,n}(G'_{i-1})$ left of or below v_i

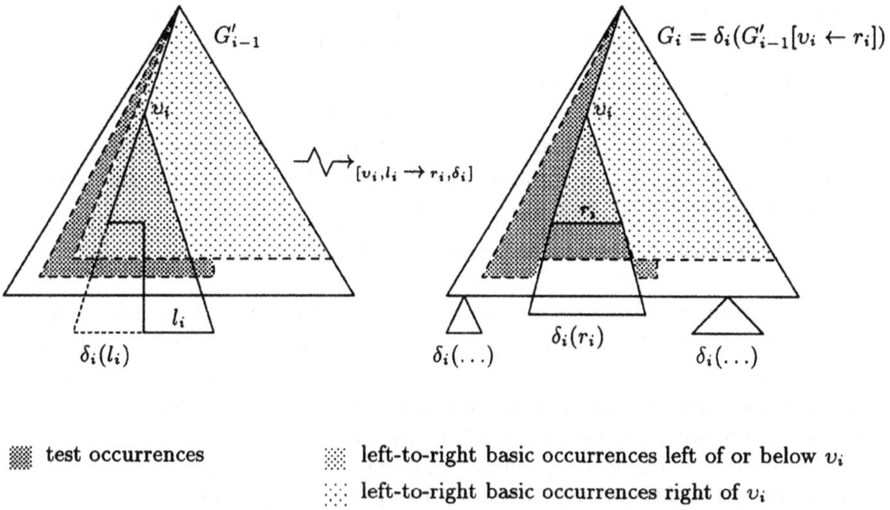

Fig. 1. One left-to-right basic narrowing step with test occurrences

(1) *there exists an occurrence* v *in* T'_n *such that* $\lambda_{i-1,n}(G'_{i-1})/u = G'_n/v$ *or*
(2) *there exist* $j \in \{1,\ldots,n\}$ *and* $\omega \in \mathit{FuOcc}(l_j)\backslash\{\epsilon\}$ *such that* $\lambda_{i-1,n}(G'_{i-1})/u = \lambda_{j-1,n}(l_j/\omega)$ *and* $(v_j.\omega \in T'_{j-1} \cup \mathit{LB}'_{j-1}$ *or* $v_j.\omega \notin \mathit{FuOcc}(G'_{j-1}))$ *or*
(3) *there exist* $j \in \{1,\ldots,n\}$, *a variable* $x \in \mathit{Var}(l_j) \setminus \mathit{Var}(r_j)$ *at an occurrence* o *in* l_j *and a non-variable occurrence* ω *in* $\delta_j(x)$ *such that* $\lambda_{i-1,n}(G'_{i-1})/u = \lambda_{j-1,n}(x)/\omega$ *and* $v_j.o.\omega \in T'_{j-1} \cup \mathit{LB}'_{j-1}$ *or*
(4) *there exist* $j \in \{1,\ldots,n\}$, $k \in \{1,\ldots,k_j\}$ *and an occurrence* $\omega \in \mathit{FuOcc}(l_{jk})$ *such that* $\lambda_{i-1,n}(G_{i-1})/u = \lambda_{j,n}(\delta_{jk}(l_{jk}/\omega))$ *and* $v_{jk}.\omega \in T_{jk}$ *or*
(5) *there exist* $j \in \{1,\ldots,n\}$, $k \in \{1,\ldots,k_j\}$, *a variable* $x \in \mathit{Var}(l_{jk}) \setminus \mathit{Var}(r_{jk})$ *at an occurrence* o *in* l_{jk} *and a non-variable occurrence* ω *in* $\delta_{jk}(x)$ *such that* $\lambda_{i-1,n}(G'_{i-1})/u = \lambda_{j,n}(\delta_{jk}(x)/\omega)$ *and* $v_{jk}.o.\omega \in T_{jk}$ *or*
(6) $\lambda_{i-1,n}(G'_{i-1})/u$ *is a variable.*

The proof is rather long and can be found in [WBK93]. Using this theorem we give a second method for performing the LSE-Tests:

Method 2 Consider the narrowing derivation of Theorem 11. After the n-th narrowing step the following has to be done:

- It has to be checked whether G'_n is reducible at an occurrence in T'_n.
- For each narrowing step $j = 1,\ldots,n$,
  - $\lambda_{j-1,n}(l_j)$ has to be tested for reducibility at occurrence ω if ω is a non-variable occurrence in l_j .
  - $\lambda_{j-1,n}(x)$ has to be tested for reducibility at occurrence ω if $x \in \mathit{Var}(l_j)\setminus \mathit{Var}(r_j)$ and ω is a non-variable occurrence in $\delta_j(x)$.

In both cases it is possible to restrict the tests to the occurrences defined in Theorem 11. Additionally for each each rewriting step jk

- $\lambda_{j,n}(\delta_{jk}(l_{jk}))$ has to be tested for reducibility at occurrence ω if ω is a non-variable occurrence in l_{jk} and $v_{jk}.\omega \in T_{jk}$, and
- $\lambda_{j,n}(\delta_{jk}(x))$ has to be tested for reducibility at occurrence ω if x is in $Var(l_{jk}) \setminus Var(r_{jk})$, ω is a non-variable occurrence in $\delta_{jk}(x)$ and there exists an occurrence o such that $l_{jk}/o = x$ and $v_{jk}.o.\omega \in T_{jk}$.

Moreover the Epsilon-Test has to be carried out.

In the sequel we discuss the realization of the second method. We already have shown that in WAM-based implementations all the terms which we need to perform the tests are available on the heap. In this case the terms are automatically instantiated. Other forms of implementations may make it necessary to store and instantiate the needed left-hand sides explicitly.

The occurrences needed in the instantiated left-hand sides may be marked or stored in an additional data structure like the test stack above.

- If we check all non-variable occurrences in l_j then these occurrences can be computed in advance. Sometimes it is cheaper to check some terms more than necessary instead of performing too expensive occurrence computations. This also holds for the occurrences in G'_n which we will discuss below.
- Disappearing variables may occur several times in a left-hand side as for example x in the rule $x * inv(x) \rightarrow 1$. It suffices to check the occurrence in the instance of the variable only once. Disappearing variables that occur more than once in a left-hand side may be detected in advance.

Besides the occurrences of the left-hand-sides the test occurrences in the current goal G'_n are needed. Again they can be marked or stored. Storing the occurrences in an additional data structure is always possible. However, updating after a narrowing or rewriting step may be expensive. On the other hand, it depends on how left-to-right-basic occurrences are realized whether marking is possible.

- If narrowing and rewriting occurrences are handled using an occurrence stack [Han91] then marking is not advisable since we have to search the marked terms which in this case is too expensive.
- But, if we normalize a term by searching left-to-right basic occurrences in it, then normalization and testing the occurrences in T'_n may be combined. The test occurrences lie directly below the basic occurrences. However, combining testing and normalization also causes some problems. Applying first the reducibility tests to the preceding goals and then normalizing and testing the current goal has the disadvantage that many redundancies are detected very late (see left column of Method 2 in Figure 2, Section 7). On the other hand, first normalizing and testing the current goal and then applying the tests to the preceding goals has the disadvantage that if we detect in one of the preceding goals a redundancy then the normalization of the current goal was superfluous (see right column of Method 2 in Figure 2).

6 Comparison

In this section, we compare the two methods for the realization of LSE narrowing proposed in Section 4 and 5.

The Terms That Have To Be Tested. First we show that in principle both methods test the same number of occurrences.

Theorem 12 [WBK93]. *Let $\mathcal{R}$ be a left- and right-linear rewriting system. Given any reducing left-to-right basic narrowing derivation there is a bijective mapping from the set of non-variable occurrences determined by Theorem 9 to the set of non-variable occurrences determined by Theorem 11 such that the corresponding subterms are identical.*

The theorem is not true if $\mathcal{R}$ contains non-linear rules. However, the differences can be eliminated if an appropriate form of *structure sharing* is used [WBK93].

Order of the Tests. As mentioned above the first method checks terms as soon as possible where they get into the scope of the tests for the first time. The second method checks them as late as possible, if possible in the last goal or where they get lost.

Storage. If we implement LSE narrowing on the level of an extended WAM then for both methods all occurrences needed for the tests are available on the heap. But if we have to store the terms that are needed explicitly then the order in which the tests are performed has important consequences. In this case the second method is better since fewer terms have to be stored. If we implement narrowing in Prolog then unification, instantiation and backtracking are supplied by the implementation language, but the terms needed for the tests have to be kept explicitly.

There are different possibilities to determine the occurrences that have to be tested. These occurrences can be kept in an additional data structure (e.g. the test stack), or we can just mark them. Marking can be expensive since we have to search for the marks. On the other hand, if we use an additional data structure then we have to update it. This causes more problems for the second method than for the first one. In [Gol92] the problem of handling occurrences is discussed for basic occurrences.

Complexity of Narrowing and Rewriting Steps. The main problem of the first method is the computation of the occurrences needed in the left-hand sides. In languages that support unification like Prolog this computation may be expensive. However, if it is possible to obtain these occurrences by a modified unification algorithm then this should be no problem. An advantage of the first method is that rewriting steps are not influenced by the tests.

Narrowing steps and even rewriting steps are complex compared to the first method if we use the second one. Even simplifying the formulas for the occurrences that have to be tested by adding some non-left-to-right-basic occurrences does not solve the problem completely.

Recommendation and Summary. Both methods have been implemented in the Karlsruhe Narrowing Laboratory KANAL [Kri90] which is written in the Prolog dialect KA-Prolog. In the implementation of Method 2 we checked all non-left-to-right-basic occurrences in the current goal and nearly all lost occurrences. The empirical results published in [BKW93, KB91] are based on this implementation. Method 1 was developed later. In principle, its Prolog implementation is slower than the implementation of Method 2. Computing the occurrences needed in the left-hand sides is too expensive in Prolog. Furthermore, in Prolog the subterms in the preceding goals have to be stored explicitly. Since Method 1 has to store more such terms, storing is more expensive. However, we also had some problems with Method 2 due to the order which we used to test the terms (see next section).

Above we described how to integrate the LSE-Tests in a WAM-based implementation of left-to-right basic narrowing. In principle the number of occurrences that have to be considered are the same for both methods. We have seen above that in the WAM case the computation and the handling of the test occurrences for Method 1 is simple and cheap. On the other hand, some problems arise for Method 2 as discussed above. Therefore, we expect better results for Method 1.

In summary, we recommend for WAM-based implementations Method 1 and for Prolog implementations Method 2.

7 Empirical Results

In [BKW93, KB91] we compared LSE narrowing with other narrowing strategies and demonstrated the benefits of our strategy on empirical results. In this section, we compare four different methods to realize normalizing LSE narrowing. We show that it makes a big difference which of these methods is chosen. This means that it is not enough to choose a good narrowing strategy. It is also very important how this strategy is implemented.

In the first implementation we used normalizing narrowing and added the LSE-Tests. In the second implementation, we added them to an implementation of normalizing left-to-right basic narrowing, whereas the third and the fourth version are the original implementations of Method 1 and Method 2 in KANAL.

We use the family R_n of canonical systems for arithmetic modulo an integer number $n \geq 1$ introduced in [BKW93] to solve the equation $x * y + x \doteq s(0)$. For the systems R_n, each normalizing LSE derivation is at most $2n + 1$ steps long whereas neither normalizing narrowing nor normalizing left-to-right basic narrowing terminates. The following table shows the number of nodes in the tree up to the given depth for the normalizing variant of the strategies and the number of occurrences that had to be tested to perform the tests:

System	Depth	Nodes of the Tree			Occurrences Tested				
		ord.	ltrb	LSE	ord.+LSE	ltrb+LSE	Meth. 1	Method 2	
R_2	5	474	69	12	181	143	99	134	126
R_3	7	14720	243	26	660	532	318	481	421
R_4	9	907882	918	46	1689	1369	720	1297	986
R_5	11	*	3865	72	3670	3002	1403	3053	2001
R_6	13	*	16946	104	6793	5555	2352	6224	3472
R_7	15	*	74954	142	11940	9832	3776	11923	5825
R_8	17	*	330604	186	19052	15684	5546	20913	8878
R_9	19	*	1449219	236	29311	24191	7899	34964	13158
R_{10}	21	*	6310334	292	42775	35297	10738	55538	18546

Fig. 2. Comparison of different implementations of LSE narrowing.

This figure also shows that the number of occurrences that have to be tested depends on the ordering in which they are tested. Method 1 mainly reduces the number of occurrences that have to be tested. Thus, it was possible to use the same strategy for the first three implementations - we started the tests below the last narrowing occurrences. For Method 2 we tested the occurrences in two different orders. In the left column the occurrences in the current goal are checked last (see discussion in Section 5). This is the reason why some redundancies are detected very late. Therefore, even more occurrences have to be tested than in the naive implementation. In the right column we started the reducibility tests at the current goal. Since Method 2 rearranges the occurrences that have to be checked, both implemented strategies are not comparable with the strategy used for Method 1. Although the second version of Method 2 has to test more occurrences it nearly achieves the same running time as Method 1.

8 Summary

LSE narrowing is based on reducibility tests. The strategy is complete for arbitrary canonical systems. Moreover, it enumerates any solution at most once. The number of occurrences that have to be considered by the LSE-Tests can be reduced drastically. It is possible to realize LSE narrowing by a slight modification of an implementation of left-to-right basic narrowing. In [BKW93] we demonstrated the benefits of the strategy on empirical results.

Acknowledgments: We are grateful to Michael Gollner for reading an earlier version of this paper and for discussions about the Warren Abstract Machine.

References

[BKW92] A. Bockmayr, S. Krischer and A. Werner. An Optimal Narrowing Strategy for General Canonical Systems. In *Conditional Term Rewriting Systems*, CTRS 1992, Pont-à-Mousson, France, LNCS 656, Springer-Verlag, 1993.

[BKW93] A. Bockmayr, S. Krischer and A. Werner. *Narrowing Strategies for Arbitrary Canonical Systems.* Interner Bericht 22/93, Fakultät für Informatik, University of Karlsruhe, 1993. To appear in *Fundamenta Informaticae.*

[BW94] A. Bockmayr and A. Werner. LSE Narrowing for Decreasing Conditional Term Rewrite Systems. To appear in *Conditional Term Rewriting Systems*, CTRS 1994, Jerusalem, Israel, 1994.

[GS92] M. Gollner and C. Scharnhorst. Integration logischer und funktionaler Sprachkonzepte mit dem normalisierenden Narrowing-System KANN. In *Proc. Workshop "Sprachen für KI-Anwendungen"*, Bericht 12/92-I, Univ. Münster, 1992.

[DG86] D. DeGroot and G. Lindstrom. Logic Programming. Functions, Relations, and Equations. Prentice Hall, 1986.

[DJ90] N. Dershowitz, J.P. Jouannaud. Rewrite Systems, in: *Handbook of Theoretical Computer Science*, Volume B, Chapter 6, pages 244 - 320, Elsevier Science Publishers North-Holland, 1990.

[Gol92] M. Gollner. Implicit, Explicit and Consistent-Explicit Basic-Indexing. In *Implementation of Logical-Functional Languages.* Interner Bericht 10/92, Fakultät für Informatik, Univ. Karlsruhe, 1993.

[Han91] M. Hanus. Efficient Implementation of Narrowing and Rewriting. In Proc. International Workshop on *Processing Declarative Knowledge*, Kaiserslautern, LNAI 567, Springer-Verlag, 1991.

[Han94] M. Hanus. Integration of Funtions into Logic Programming: A Survey. MPI-Report MPI-I-94-201, Max-Planck-Institut für Informatik, Saarbrücken, 1994. To appear in *Journal of Logic Programming.*

[Her86] A. Herold. *Narrowing Techniques Applied to Idempotent Unification.* SEKI Report SR-86-16, Univ. Kaiserslautern, 1986.

[HO80] G. Huet and D.C. Oppen. Equations and Rewrite Rules: A Survey. In R. Book, editor, *Formal Languages: Perspectives and Open Problems*, Academic Press, 1980.

[Hul80] J. M. Hullot. Canonical Forms and Unification, In Proc. *5th Conference on Automated Deduction*, Les Arcs, France, 1980, LNCS 87, Springer-Verlag.

[Kri90] S. Krischer: *Vergleich und Bewertung von Narrowing-Strategien.* Diplomarbeit, Fakultät für Informatik, Univ. Karlsruhe, 1990.

[KB91] S. Krischer and A. Bockmayr. Detecting Redundant Narrowing Derivations by the LSE-SL Reducibility Test. In Proc. 4th International Conference on *Rewriting Techniques and Applications*, RTA-91, Como, LNCS 488, Springer-Verlag, 1991.

[Rét87] P. Réty: Improving Basic Narrowing Techniques. In Proc. 2nd International Conference on *Rewriting Techniques and Applications*, RTA-87, Bordeaux, LNCS 256, Springer-Verlag, 1987.

[War83] D. H. Warren: *An Abstract Prolog Instruction Set.* Technical Report 309, Artificial Intelligence Center, SRI International, 1983.

[WBK93] A. Werner, A. Bockmayr and S. Krischer. How to Realize LSE Narrowing, Interner Bericht 6/93, Fakultät für Informatik, Univ. Karlsruhe, 1993.

Compositional Analysis for Equational Horn Programs*

María Alpuente[1], Moreno Falaschi[2] and Germán Vidal[1]

[1] Departamento de Sistemas Informáticos y Computación,
Universidad Politécnica de Valencia,
Camino de Vera s/n, Apdo. 22012, 46020 Valencia, Spain.
e.mail:{alpuente,gvidal}@dsic.upv.es
[2] Dipartimento di Elettronica e Informatica,
Università di Padova,
Via Gradenigo 6/A, 35131 Padova, Italy.
e.mail: falaschi@di.unipi.it

Abstract. We introduce a compositional characterization of the operational semantics of equational Horn programs. Then we show that this semantics and the standard operational semantics based on (basic) narrowing coincide. We define an abstract narrower mimicking this semantics, and show how it can be used as a basis for efficient AND-compositional program analysis. As an application of our framework, we show a compositional analysis to detect the unsatisfiability of an equation set with respect to a given equational theory. We also show that our method allows us to perform computations and analysis incrementally in a Constraint Equational setting and that the test of satisfiability in this setting can be done in parallel.

Keywords: Semantic analysis, compositionality, equational logic programming, term rewriting systems.

1 Introduction

Compositionality is a desirable property which has been recognised as fundamental in the semantics of programming languages [11]. Compositionality has to do with a (syntactic) composition operator $\diamond$, and holds when the meaning (semantics) $\mathcal{S}(C_1 \diamond C_2)$ of a compound construct is defined by composing the meanings of the constituents $\mathcal{S}(C_1)$ and $\mathcal{S}(C_2)$, i.e. for a suitable function $f_\diamond$, $\mathcal{S}(C_1 \diamond C_2) = f_\diamond(\mathcal{S}(C_1), \mathcal{S}(C_2))$. In the case of logic programs [11], one could be concerned with AND-composition (of atoms in a goal or in a clause body) or with OR-composition, i.e. composition of (sets of) clauses. In the context of equational logic programming [15,19], consideration has been given to the problem of defining a compositional semantics for the direct union of complete theories which correctly models the computational properties related to the use of logical variables [4]. In this paper, we address the problem of solving equations

* This work has been partially supported by CICYT under grant TIC 92-0793-C02-02

in equationally defined theories but, unlike [4], we want to define compositionally the meaning of the union of $\mathcal{E}$-unification problems. Let a theory $\mathcal{E}$ be fixed and consider two finite equation sets Γ_1, Γ_2. We want to define the meaning of $\Gamma_1 \cup \Gamma_2$ (with respect to $\mathcal{E}$) in terms of the meanings of Γ_1 and Γ_2. Throughout the paper, $\mathcal{E}$ is assumed to be axiomatized as an equational Horn theory, which is called the 'program' [12,15,19]. We do not consider compositionality with respect to the union of programs in this paper. For this topic we refer to [4].

The semantics of equational Horn programs is usually defined as some variant of *narrowing*, a method for generating complete sets of $\mathcal{E}$-unifiers with respect to a canonical set of clauses. Simple restrictions on narrowing, like narrowing only at basic positions, are still complete for theories which satisfy some additional properties [25]. The use of narrowing as the operational mechanism for computing leads to a powerful extension of ordinary logic programs [15,28] and the computation model has many opportunities for parallelism. For example, [10] describes a kind of OR-parallelism in which, for each position in the term and each rule in the program, alternative narrowings are explored concurrently according to some heuristic function. Our work concerns an AND-parallel computation model of equational Horn programs, where all subexpressions can be narrowed independently and the computed substitutions obtained so far can then be composed. This mechanism of computation was also mentioned in [28]. We extend the notion of *parallel composition* of substitutions introduced in [17,27] to the case of equational logic programs. Hence we show how complete sets of $\mathcal{E}$-unifiers for a given goal $\Leftarrow \Gamma_1, \Gamma_2$ can be generated by composing the complete sets of $\mathcal{E}$-unifiers computed by narrowing the separate subgoals $\Leftarrow \Gamma_1$ and $\Leftarrow \Gamma_2$. This allows us to model the combination of substitutions computed by AND-parallel 'narrowing processes', i.e. by agents which narrow subexpressions in parallel. We show that for unrestricted narrowing a "semantic" composition operator would be necessary. However, for basic narrowing we achieve a stronger result and show that the substitutions can be composed syntactically.

We have recently defined an equational logic language [1] as an instance of Constraint Logic Programming [18], where the equations to be solved with respect to an equational theory are considered as constraints. For a computational step in this framework, it is essential to be able to (semi-)decide if a set of equations is satisfiable. The computation of complete sets of $\mathcal{E}$-unifiers is less striking in this context, while it is essential a mechanism to evaluate the satisfiability of the constraints incrementally. In [2] we have defined a lazy procedure which does not prove the satisfiability of the equational constraint c but just checks that c is not unsatisfiable by means of an approximated narrower. We show that a compositional narrowing can be taken as a basis for a compositional analysis for the problem of unsatisfiability. Then we show that compositionality leads, as a by-product, to an incremental implementation for the analysis. Therefore, while OR-compositionality, i.e. compositionality w.r.t. union of programs, has proven significant for programming with modules [4,11], we show that AND-compositionality can lead to incremental computations.

This paper is organized as follows. After introducing some preliminary notions in Section 2, Section 3 defines an operator which describes the operational semantics of equational Horn programs in a compositional way. In Section 4, we introduce *compositional conditional narrowing*, an AND-parallel computation model for equational Horn programs. We characterize the *success* set of a goal, i.e. the set of the computed answer substitutions corresponding to all successful narrowing derivations. That is, we prove that the meaning of a composite goal can be obtained by composing the meanings of its conjuncts, when considering the success set as observable. Then we state the completeness of our semantics. In Section 5 we recall an abstract algorithm for the static analysis of unsatisfiability of equation sets [2] and modify it to perform the analysis compositionally. Section 6 formulates an incremental analyzer for equational constraints and presents some encouraging results from the implementation of the analyzer. Section 7 concludes. More details and missing proofs can be found in [5].

2 Preliminaries

We briefly recall some known results about equations, conditional rewrite systems and equational unification. For full definitions refer to [9,20]. Throughout this paper, V will denote a countably infinite set of variables and Σ denotes a set of function symbols, each with a fixed associated arity. $\tau(\Sigma \cup V)$ and $\tau(\Sigma)$ denote the sets of terms and ground terms built on $\Sigma \cup V$ and Σ, respectively. A Σ-equation $s = t$ is a pair of terms $s, t \in \tau(\Sigma \cup V)$. Terms are viewed as labelled trees in the usual way. Occurrences are represented by sequences, possibly empty, of natural numbers used to address subterms of t, and they are ordered by the prefix ordering $u \leq v$ if there exists a w such that $uw = v$. $\bar{O}(t)$ denotes the set of nonvariable occurrences of a term t. $t_{|u}$ is the subterm at the occurrence u of t. $t[r]_u$ is the term t with the subterm at the occurrence u replaced with r. These notions extend to equations in a natural way. Identity of syntactic objects is denoted by $\equiv$. $Var(s)$ is the set of distinct variables occurring in the syntactic object s. A *fresh* variable is a variable that appears nowhere else. The symbol $\tilde{}$ denotes a finite sequence of symbols.

We describe the lattice of equation sets following [7]. We let *Eqn* denote the set of possibly existentially quantified finite sets of equations over terms. We let *fail* denote the unsatisfiable equation set, which (logically) implies all other equation sets. Likewise, the empty equation set, denoted by *true*, is implied by all elements of *Eqn*. We write $E \leq E'$ if E' logically implies E. Thus *Eqn* is a lattice ordered by $\leq$ with bottom element *true* and top element *fail*. An equation set is *solved* if it is either *fail* or it has the form $\exists y_1 \ldots \exists y_m . \{x_1 = t_1, \ldots, x_n = t_n\}$, where each x_i is a distinct variable not occurring in any of the terms t_i and each y_i occurs in some t_j. Any set of equations E can be transformed into an equivalent one $solve(E)$ which is solved. We restrict our interest to the set of idempotent substitutions over $\tau(\Sigma \cup V)$, which is denoted by *Sub*. There is a natural isomorphism between substitutions and unquantified equation sets. The equational representation of a substitution $\theta = \{x_1/t_1, \ldots, x_n/t_n\}$ is the set of equations $\widehat{\theta} = \{x_1 = t_1, \ldots, x_n = t_n\}$. The identity function on V is called the empty substitution and denoted ϵ. Given a substitution θ and a set of variables $W \subseteq V$, we denote by $\theta_{\upharpoonright W}$ the substitution obtained from θ by restricting its domain, $Dom(\theta)$, to W.

We consider the usual preorder on substitutions $\leq$: $\theta \leq \sigma$ iff $\exists \gamma. \sigma \equiv \theta\gamma$. Note that $\theta \leq \sigma$ iff $\widehat{\sigma} \Rightarrow \widehat{\theta}$ [27]. A substitution $\{x_1/t_1, \ldots, x_n/t_n\}$ is a *unifier* of an equation set E iff $\{x_1 = t_1, \ldots, x_n = t_n\} \Rightarrow E$. We denote the set of unifiers of E by *unif*(E) and *mgu*(E) denotes the *most general unifier* of the unquantified equation set E. In abuse of notation, we let *fail* denote failure when computing the *mgu*(E). While every unquantified equation set has a *most general unifier* [23], this is not generally true for equation sets with existentially quantified variables [7].

An equational Horn theory $\mathcal{E}$ consists of a finite set of equational Horn clauses of the form $e \Leftarrow e_1, \ldots, e_n,\ n \geq 0$, where $e, e_i, i = 1, \ldots, n$, are equations. An equational goal is an equational Horn clause with no head. We let *Goal* denote the set of equational goals. The set of *states* is defined by $State = Goal \times Sub$.

A Term Rewriting System (TRS for short) is a pair $(\Sigma, \mathcal{R})$ where $\mathcal{R}$ is a finite set of reduction (or rewrite) rule schemes of the form $(\lambda \rightarrow \rho \Leftarrow \widetilde{e})$, λ, $\rho \in \tau(\Sigma \cup V)$, $\lambda \notin V$ and $Var(\rho) \subseteq Var(\lambda)$. The condition $\widetilde{e}$ is a possibly empty conjunction $e_1, \ldots, e_n,\ n \geq 0$, of equations. Variables in $\widetilde{e}$ that do not occur in λ are called extra-variables. If a rewrite rule has no condition we write $\lambda \rightarrow \rho$. We will often write just $\mathcal{R}$ instead of $(\Sigma, \mathcal{R})$.

An equational Horn theory $\mathcal{E}$ which satisfies the above assumptions can be viewed as a term rewriting system $\mathcal{R}$ where the rules are the heads (implicitely oriented from left to right) and the conditions are the respective bodies. We assume that these assumptions hold for all theories we consider in this paper. The equational theory $\mathcal{E}$ is said to be canonical (complete) if the binary one-step conditional rewriting relation $\rightarrow_{\mathcal{R}}$ defined by $\mathcal{R}$ is noetherian and confluent. For TRS $\mathcal{R}$, $r \ll \mathcal{R}$ denotes that r is a new variant of a rule in $\mathcal{R}$ such that r contains no variable previously met during computation (standardised apart). Given a conditional TRS $\mathcal{R}$, an equational goal clause $\Leftarrow g$ conditionally narrows into a goal clause $\Leftarrow g'$ (in symbols $\Leftarrow g \overset{\theta}{\hookrightarrow} \Leftarrow g'$) if there exists an equation $e \in g$, $u \in \bar{O}(e)$, a standardised apart variant $(\lambda \rightarrow \rho \Leftarrow \widetilde{e}) \ll \mathcal{R}$ and a substitution θ such that $\theta = mgu(\{e_{|u} = \lambda\})$ and $g' = ((g \sim \{e\}) \cup \{e[\rho]_u\} \cup \widetilde{e})\theta$. A *narrowing derivation* is defined by $\Leftarrow g \overset{\theta}{\hookrightarrow}{}^* \Leftarrow g'$ iff $\exists \theta_1, \ldots, \theta_n.\ \Leftarrow g \overset{\theta_1}{\hookrightarrow} \ldots \overset{\theta_n}{\hookrightarrow} \Leftarrow g'$ and $\theta = \theta_1 \ldots \theta_n$. We say that the derivation has length n. In order to treat syntactical unification as a narrowing step, we add to the TRS $\mathcal{R}$ the rule $x = x \rightarrow true \Leftarrow$, $x \in V$. Then $t = s \overset{\sigma}{\hookrightarrow} true$ holds iff $\sigma = mgu(\{t = s\})$. A successful derivation for $\Leftarrow g$ in $\mathcal{R} \cup \{x = x \rightarrow true \Leftarrow\}$ is a narrowing derivation $\Leftarrow g \overset{\theta}{\hookrightarrow}{}^* \Leftarrow true$ and $\theta_{\upharpoonright Var(g)}$ is called a computed answer substitution for $\Leftarrow g$ in $\mathcal{R}$. If $n = 0$ then $\theta = \epsilon$.

Each equational Horn theory $\mathcal{E}$ generates a smallest congruence relation $=_{\mathcal{E}}$ called *$\mathcal{E}$-equality* on the set of terms $\tau(\Sigma \cup V)$ (the least equational theory which contains all logic consequences of $\mathcal{E}$ under the entailment relation $\models$ obeying the axioms of equality for $\mathcal{E}$). $\mathcal{E}$ is a presentation or axiomatization of $=_\mathcal{E}$. In abuse of notation, we sometimes speak of the equational theory $\mathcal{E}$ to denote the theory axiomatized by $\mathcal{E}$. $\mathcal{E}$-equality is extended to substitutions by $\sigma =_\mathcal{E} \theta$ iff $\forall x \in V.\ x\sigma =_\mathcal{E} x\theta$.

A finite set of equations $\Gamma = \{s_1 = t_1, \ldots, s_n = t_n\}$ together with an equational theory $\mathcal{E}$ is called an ***$\mathcal{E}$-unification*** problem. A substitution σ is an ***$\mathcal{E}$-unifier*** or a ***solution*** of the equation set Γ iff $\mathcal{E} \models (\widehat{\sigma} \Rightarrow \Gamma)$ [24]. The set $\mathcal{U}_\mathcal{E}(\Gamma)$ of all ***$\mathcal{E}$-unifiers*** of Γ is recursively enumerable [12,15,29].

For ***$\mathcal{E}$-unification*** problems, the notion of most general unifier generalizes to complete sets of minimal (incomparable) ***$\mathcal{E}$-unifiers***. A set S of $\mathcal{E}$-unifiers of the equation set Γ is complete iff every $\mathcal{E}$-unifier σ of Γ factors into $\sigma =_\mathcal{E} \theta\gamma$ for some substitutions $\theta \in S$ and γ. A complete set of $\mathcal{E}$-unifiers of a system of equations may be infinite. Minimal complete sets $\mu\mathcal{U}_\mathcal{E}(\Gamma)$ of ***$\mathcal{E}$-unifiers*** of Γ do not always exist. An ***$\mathcal{E}$-unification*** procedure is complete if it generates a complete set of ***$\mathcal{E}$-unifiers*** for all input equation system. Conditional narrowing has been shown to be a complete $\mathcal{E}$-unification algorithm for canonical theories satisfying different restrictions [15,25].

3 Equational Parallel Composition

In the following, we recall the notion of ***parallel composition*** of substitutions, denoted by $\Uparrow$. Roughly speaking, parallel composition is the operation of unification generalized to substitutions.

Parallel composition corresponds to one of the basic operations performed by the AND-parallel execution model of logic programs [17,27]. Namely, when two subgoals (of the same goal) are run in parallel, the answer substitutions (computed independently) have to be combined to get the final result. This 'combination' can be done as follows [17,27]. Given two idempotent substitutions θ_1 and θ_2, we let $\theta_1 \Uparrow \theta_2 = mgu(\widehat{\theta_1} \cup \widehat{\theta_2})$. Parallel composition is idempotent, commutative, associative and has a null element *fail* and an identical element ϵ. $\Uparrow$ is lifted to sets of substitutions by

$$\Theta_1 \Uparrow \Theta_2 = \begin{cases} \bigcup_{\theta_1 \in \Theta_1, \theta_2 \in \Theta_2} \theta_1 \Uparrow \theta_2 & \text{if it is different from } \{fail\} \\ \emptyset & \text{otherwise.} \end{cases}$$

Parallel composition was proposed in [27] as a basis for a compositional characterization of the semantics of Horn Clause Logic. We are able to generalize the notion of parallel composition to the case when unification in equational theories is considered. In the following definition we formalize the notion of ***equational parallel composition***, denoted by $\Uparrow_\mathcal{E}$.

Definition 1. Let $\theta_1, \theta_2 \in Sub$. We define the operator $\Uparrow_\mathcal{E} : Sub \times Sub \rightarrow \wp(Sub)$ as follows:

$$\theta_1 \Uparrow_\mathcal{E} \theta_2 = \mathcal{U}_\mathcal{E}(\widehat{\theta_1} \cup \widehat{\theta_2}).$$

Example 1. Let $\mathcal{E} = \{f(0) = 0,\ f(g(X)) = g(X),\ g(0) = c(0),\ g(c(X)) = g(X)\}$.

1. Let $\theta_1 = \{X/g(Z)\}$ and $\theta_2 = \{X/c(Z)\}$. Then $\{X/c(0), Z/0\} \in \theta_1 \Uparrow_{\mathcal{E}} \theta_2$.
2. Let $\theta_1 = \{X/f(0)\}$ and $\theta_2 = \{X/g(Z)\}$. Then $\theta_1 \Uparrow_{\mathcal{E}} \theta_2 = \emptyset$.

It is straightforward to show that $\Uparrow_{\mathcal{E}}$ is commutative and associative and has a null element $\{fail\}$ and an identical element $\{\epsilon\}$. The operator $\Uparrow_{\mathcal{E}}$ can be lifted to sets of substitutions as follows.

Definition 2. Given $\Theta_1, \Theta_2 \in \wp(Sub)$, let:

$$\Theta_1 \Uparrow_{\mathcal{E}} \Theta_2 = \bigcup_{\theta_1 \in \Theta_1, \theta_2 \in \Theta_2} \theta_1 \Uparrow_{\mathcal{E}} \theta_2.$$

Given an $\mathcal{E}$-unification problem $\Gamma = \Gamma_1 \cup \Gamma_2$, a compositional characterization of the set of all $\mathcal{E}$-unifiers of Γ is given in the following proposition.

Proposition 3. *Let* $\Gamma = \Gamma_1 \cup \Gamma_2$, $\Theta_1 = \mathcal{U}_{\mathcal{E}}(\Gamma_1)$ *and* $\Theta_2 = \mathcal{U}_{\mathcal{E}}(\Gamma_2)$. *Then* $\mathcal{U}_{\mathcal{E}}(\Gamma) = \Theta_1 \Uparrow_{\mathcal{E}} \Theta_2$.

We note that it is much more complex to evaluate $\Uparrow_{\mathcal{E}}$ than the much simpler operation $\Uparrow$. However, equational parallel composition can be redefined in terms of 'most general' unifiers in the case of *finitary* theories, for which the solutions to an $\mathcal{E}$-unification problem Γ can always be represented by a complete and minimal finite set $\mu\mathcal{U}_{\mathcal{E}}(\Gamma)$ of (maximally general) $\mathcal{E}$-unifiers, which is unique up to equivalence [29]. Equational theories which are of finitary *unification type* play an important role in logic programming with equality [19]. In general, the unification type of an equational theory is undecidable. On the other hand, for a finitary theory the minimality requirement is often too strong, since an algorithm which generates a superset of $\mu\mathcal{U}_{\mathcal{E}}(\Gamma)$ may be far more efficient than a minimal one and hence sometimes preferable. In the following section, we will show that we can still work with ordinary parallel composition $\Uparrow$ when we consider the class of (level-)canonical equational theories, for which the problem of $\mathcal{E}$-unification reduces to ordinary (syntactic) unification plus narrowing [16].

4 Compositional Conditional Narrowing

In this section we recall the operational semantics of our language, following [4]. We specify the *observables*, that is, the property we are interested to "observe" in a computation (e.g. the set of successes, the finite failure set, the infinite failure set, etc.) and that has to be reflected in the semantics. In this paper we are interested in the success set. We describe the *success* set of a goal, i.e. the set of all computed answer substitutions corresponding to all successful narrowing derivations, by a formal operational semantics $\mathcal{O} : Goal \mapsto \wp\, Sub$, based on a (labelled) transition relation, which associates a set of substitutions with a goal.

Basic conditional narrowing has been proposed as the operational model of equational logic programs [15,25]. Basic conditional narrowing gives a complete set of solutions for level-canonical sets of conditional rewrite rules [25]. Compared to ordinary narrowing, the basic strategy leads to a smaller search space by eliminating some search paths that lead to reducible solutions. In the rest of this paper, we assume the level-canonical program $\mathcal{R}$ to be fixed. We formulate basic conditional narrowing as a transition system $(State, \leadsto)$ whose transition relation $\leadsto \subseteq State \times State$ is defined as the smallest relation satisfying

$$\langle \Leftarrow g, \theta\rangle \leadsto \langle \Leftarrow g', \theta\sigma\rangle \text{ iff } e \in g \;\wedge\; u \in \bar{O}(e) \;\wedge (\lambda \rightarrow \rho \Leftarrow \tilde{e}) \ll \mathcal{R} \;\wedge$$
$$\sigma = mgu(\{(e_{|u})\theta = \lambda\}) \;\wedge\; g' = (g \sim \{e\}) \cup \{e[\rho]_u\} \cup \tilde{e}.$$

Note that, in the above inference rule, the computed substitution σ is not applied to the equations in the derived state, as opposed to ordinary (unrestricted) narrowing (cf. Section 2). This ensures that no narrowing step will reduce any expression brought by a substitution computed in a previous step.

A *basic conditional narrowing derivation* is a sequence of states $s_1 \leadsto s_2 \leadsto \ldots$, where $s_i \equiv \langle \Leftarrow g_i, \theta_i\rangle$ is the ith state in the sequence.

Based on this transition system, we define the operational semantics of an equational goal $\Leftarrow g$ in the TRS $\mathcal{R} \cup \{x = x \rightarrow true \Leftarrow\}$ by the (non ground) set (*success set*)

$$\mathcal{O}_{\mathcal{R}}(\Leftarrow g) = \{\theta \mid \langle \Leftarrow g, \epsilon\rangle \leadsto^* \langle \Leftarrow true, \theta\rangle\}^3.$$

Now we are ready to give a compositional characterization of the operational semantics of equational Horn programs in a style similar to that of [27] for logic programs. We define a new narrowing procedure by means of a transition relation from equational goals to equational goals, labeled on substitutions.

Definition 4. (Compositional Conditional Narrowing)
We define *compositional conditional narrowing* as a labelled transition system $(Goal, Sub, \longmapsto)$ whose transition relation $\longmapsto \subseteq Goal \times Sub \times Goal$ is the smallest relation which satisfies

$$(1)\ \frac{u \in \bar{O}(e) \;\wedge\; (\lambda \rightarrow \rho \Leftarrow \tilde{e}) \ll \mathcal{R} \;\wedge\; \sigma = mgu(\{e_{|u} = \lambda\})}{\Leftarrow \{e\} \overset{\sigma}{\longmapsto} \Leftarrow \{e[\rho]_u\} \cup \tilde{e}}$$

$$(2)\ \frac{\Leftarrow g_1 \overset{\theta_1}{\longmapsto} \Leftarrow g_1' \;\wedge\; \Leftarrow g_2 \overset{\theta_2}{\longmapsto} \Leftarrow g_2'}{\Leftarrow g_1, g_2 \overset{\theta_1 \Uparrow \theta_2}{\longmapsto} \Leftarrow g_1', g_2'}$$

Roughly speaking, in the computation model formalized by the transition system above, all equations in the equational goal to be solved are reduced at the same time. Then, the substitutions resulting from these local computations are combined by means of the operator of *parallel composition* to obtain the global result of the computation. By abuse, we consider $\Leftarrow true \overset{\epsilon}{\longmapsto} \Leftarrow true$.

[3] We often write $\mathcal{O}(\Leftarrow g)$ instead of $\mathcal{O}_{\mathcal{R}}(\Leftarrow g)$ when $\mathcal{R}$ is understood.

Note that, by not applying the substitutions to the goal at each derivation step, compositional conditional narrowing may have to overcompute when compared to (basic) conditional narrowing thus possibly causing execution to slow down (see Example 2 below).

The computation model formalized in Definition 4 could be taken as a basis for an AND-parallel computation model of equational Horn programs. We note that the model has not been devised to achieve maximal parallelism in the sense that not all redexes in a given goal are allowed to perform one narrowing step independently. Namely, redexes which occur in a same equation are not reduced in parallel, while they could. To overcome this lack, it suffices to introduce the following *flattening* rule, which preserves the reachable solutions

$$(3)\ \frac{e \in g \ \wedge\ u \in \bar{O}(e)\ \wedge\ x \text{ is a new variable}}{\Leftarrow g \overset{\epsilon}{\longmapsto} \Leftarrow (g \sim \{e\}) \cup \{e[x]_u\} \cup \{e_{|u} = x\}}$$

provided that both $e_{|u}$ and $e[x]_u$ contain at least one function symbol [26]. Note that we need not determine the level of granularity [22] (as it neither affects correctness nor completeness); this we consider to be an implementation issue that could enable (more) effective parallelizations.

Our approach differs from other AND-parallel execution models, such as e.g. [22], where subexpressions are only narrowed in parallel if they are *independent*, i.e. if they do not share (unbound) variables. A 'need-driven' syncronization model is imposed which compels processes to wait for the value of a parallel subexpression if such a value is needed. In [21], a *dependent* AND-parallel execution model is exploited, but the imposed syncronization mechanisms produce too much overhead.

A new operational semantics of an equational goal $\Leftarrow g$ in the TRS $\mathcal{R} \cup \{x = x \rightarrow \mathit{true} \Leftarrow\}$ can now be defined by

Definition 5. $\mathcal{O}'(\Leftarrow g) = \{\theta \mid \Leftarrow g \overset{\theta_1}{\longmapsto} \ldots \overset{\theta_n}{\longmapsto} \Leftarrow \mathit{true}$ and $\theta = \theta_1 \Uparrow \ldots \Uparrow \theta_n$, $\theta \not\equiv \mathit{fail}\}$.

In Definition 5 we use parallel composition because, in the transition system in Definition 4, the computed substitution is not applied to either the derived goal or to the redex $e_{|u}$ selected to be narrowed, as opposed to the standard semantics. Therefore, the next computation step will not take this substitution into account and the next substitution that is computed has to be combined with the previous one.

The new success set semantics $\mathcal{O}'$ is compositional w.r.t. the AND operator. Formally,

Theorem 6. $\mathcal{O}'(\Leftarrow g_1, g_2) = \mathcal{O}'(\Leftarrow g_1) \Uparrow \mathcal{O}'(\Leftarrow g_2)$.

The following result states that the compositional conditional semantics and the standard basic conditional semantics coincide. The correspondence is restricted to successes, namely to the substitutions computed by all successfully terminating derivations. The compositional semantics and the standard basic semantics have a different failure behaviour: the latter delivers finite failure for more goals than the former, as illustrated in the following example.

Example 2. Let $\mathcal{R} = \{f(0) \to 0 \Leftarrow, f(c(X)) \to c(f(X)) \Leftarrow\}$ and consider the goal $\Leftarrow g \equiv \Leftarrow f(c(0)) = 0$. Then there is only one (failed) basic narrowing derivation for $\Leftarrow g$ in $\mathcal{R}$:

$$\langle \Leftarrow f(c(0)) = 0, \epsilon\rangle \leadsto \langle \Leftarrow c(f(X)) = 0, \{X/0\}\rangle \leadsto \langle \Leftarrow c(0) = 0, \{X/0\}\rangle,$$

whereas there exists the nonterminating compositional narrowing derivation:

$$\Leftarrow f(c(0)) = 0 \overset{\{X/0\}}{\longmapsto} \Leftarrow c(f(X)) = 0 \overset{\{X/c(Y)\}}{\longmapsto} \Leftarrow c(c(f(Y))) = 0 \longmapsto \ldots$$

Corollary 7. *$\langle \Leftarrow g, \epsilon\rangle \leadsto^* \langle \Leftarrow true, \theta\rangle$ iff $\Leftarrow g \overset{\theta_1}{\longmapsto} \ldots \overset{\theta_n}{\longmapsto} \Leftarrow true$ and $\theta = \theta_1 \Uparrow \ldots \Uparrow \theta_n$, $\theta \not\equiv fail$.*

We note that the equivalence established by Theorem 6 and Corollary 7 does not hold for ordinary (unrestricted) narrowing. Roughly speaking, what is wrong with ordinary narrowing is the fact that it transfers terms from the substitution part into the goal, thus introducing narrowing steps (at *non-basic* positions) that might not be proven when the subgoals are solved independently. As a consequence, ordinary narrowing is not compositional using the parallel composition operator $\Uparrow$. The following example illustrates this point.

Example 3. Let $\mathcal{R}$ be the following program

$$\begin{aligned} \mathcal{R} = \{ \quad z(s(0)) &\to 0 \Leftarrow \\ z(one(X)) &\to 0 \Leftarrow \\ one(0) &\to s(0) \Leftarrow \\ one(s(X)) &\to one(X) \Leftarrow \ \}, \end{aligned}$$

and consider the following (ordinary) narrowing derivation:

$$\begin{aligned} &\Leftarrow X = s(0),\ z(X) = 0 \overset{\{X/one(Y)\}}{\hookrightarrow} \Leftarrow one(Y) = s(0),\ 0 = 0 \overset{\{Y/0\}}{\hookrightarrow} \\ &\Leftarrow s(0) = s(0),\ 0 = 0 \overset{\epsilon}{\hookrightarrow} \Leftarrow true,\ 0 = 0 \overset{\epsilon}{\hookrightarrow} \Leftarrow true \end{aligned}$$

with computed answer substitution $\theta = \{X/one(0)\}$. According to Definition 4, there is no compositional narrowing derivation for $\mathcal{R}$ with initial goal $\Leftarrow X = s(0),\ z(X) = 0$ with computed answer substitution $\{X/one(0)\}$ as the goal $\Leftarrow X = s(0)$ only computes the substitution $\{X/s(0)\}$. Note that basic conditional narrowing does not compute the answer substitution $\{X/one(0)\}$ either.

As a consequence of Corollary 7, every solution found by basic conditional narrowing is found by compositional basic conditional narrowing as well. Hence, we have the following corollary for level-canonical systems.

Corollary 8. (completeness)
The set $\{\vartheta\restriction_{Var(g)} \mid \vartheta \in \mathcal{O}'(\Leftarrow g)\}$ is a complete set of $\mathcal{E}$-unifiers of g.

We note that, by forcing the join of the parallel solutions every time that all equations in the goal have performed a single step independently, the compositional execution model formalized by Definition 4 might not couch all the exploitable AND-parallelism. Corollary 7 suggests that many different computation schemes are possible. For instance, we can solve in parallel all (sub-)goals, joining the AND-parallel (sub-)goals when the (sub-)goals are completely solved, instead of forcing the syncronization of the AND-parallel branches at every single reduction step. In the following section, we show how this execution scheme can be efficiently exploited for program analysis.

5 Abstract Basic Conditional Narrowing

Abstract interpretation is a theory of semantic approximation which is used to provide statically sound answers to some questions about the run-time behaviour of programs [8]. The 'concrete' data and semantic operators are approximated and replaced by corresponding abstract data and operators. The 'answers' obtained by using the abstract data and operators have to be proven sound by exploiting the correspondence with the concrete data and operators. In this section, we recall the framework of abstract interpretation for analysis of equational unsatisfiability we defined in [2]. Then we extend this framework by defining a compositional abstract semantics which safely approximates the observables.

Our analysis of unsatisfiability is an abstraction of the transition system semantics for basic conditional narrowing that we have introduced in Definition 4. We first recall the abstract domains and the associated abstract operators together with some previous results concerning them. We note that a different analysis of unsatisfiability is introduced in [6] for constructor-based programs where the computation is done by *abstract rewriting*. This method is not comparable to ours, since there are examples which can be analyzed by only one of the two methods and our method is able to capture some computational properties related to the use of logical variables that abstract rewriting does not.

5.1 Abstract Domains and Operators

A *description* is the association of an *abstract domain* $(D, \leq)$ (a poset) with a *concrete domain* $(E, \leq)$ (a poset). When $E = Eqn$, $E = Sub$ or $E = State$, the description is called an *equation description*, a *substitution description* or a *state description*, respectively. The correspondence between the abstract and concrete domain is established through a 'concretization' function $\gamma : D \rightarrow \wp E$. We say that *d approximates e*, written $d \propto e$, iff $e \in \gamma(d)$. The approximation relation can be lifted to relations and cross products as usual [2].

We approximate the behaviour of a TRS and initial state by an abstract transition system which can be viewed as a finite transition graph with nodes labeled by state descriptions, where transitions are proved by (abstract) narrowing reduction [2]. State descriptions consist of a set of equations with substitution descriptions. The descriptions for equations, substitutions and term rewriting systems are defined as follows.

Definition 9. By $\mathcal{T} = (\tau(\Sigma \cup V), \leq)$, we denote the standard domain of (equivalence classes of) terms ordered by the standard partial order $\leq$ induced by the preorder on terms given by the relation of being "more general". Let $\perp$ be an irreducible symbol, where $\perp \notin \Sigma$. Let $\mathcal{T}_\mathcal{A} = (\tau(\Sigma \cup V \cup \{\perp\}), \preceq)$ be the domain of terms over the signature augmented by $\perp$, where the partial order $\preceq$ is defined as follows:

(a) $\forall t \in \mathcal{T}_\mathcal{A}. \perp \preceq t$ and $t \preceq t$ and

(b) $\forall s_1, \ldots, s_n, s'_1, \ldots, s'_n \in \mathcal{T}_\mathcal{A}, \forall f/n \in \Sigma.\ s'_1 \preceq s_1 \wedge \ldots \wedge s'_n \preceq s_n \Rightarrow f(s'_1, \ldots, s'_n) \preceq f(s_1, \ldots, s_n)$

This order can be extended to equations: $s' = t' \preceq s = t$ iff $s' \preceq s$ and $t' \preceq t$ and to sets of equations S, S':

1) $S' \preceq S$ iff $\forall e' \in S'. \exists e \in S$ such that $e' \preceq e$.

2) $S' \sqsubseteq S$ iff $(S' \preceq S)$ and $(S \preceq S'$ implies $S' \subseteq S)$.

Roughly speaking, we introduce the special symbol $\perp$ in the abstract domains to represent any concrete term. Logically, $\perp$ stands for an existentially quantified variable [2,24]. Define $[\![S]\!] = S'$, where the n-tuple of occurrences of $\perp$ in S is replaced by an n-tuple of existentially quantified fresh variables in S'.

Definition 10. An abstract substitution is a set of the form $\{x_1/t_1, \ldots, x_n/t_n\}$ where, for each $i = 1, \ldots, n$, x_i is a distinct variable in V not occurring in any of the terms $t_1, \ldots, t_n$ and $t_i \in \tau(\Sigma \cup V \cup \{\perp\})$. The ordering on abstract substitutions can be given as logical implication: let $\theta, \kappa \in Sub_\mathcal{A}$, $\kappa \preceq \theta$ iff $[\![\widehat{\theta}]\!] \Rightarrow [\![\widehat{\kappa}]\!]$.

Let us introduce the abstract domains which we will use in our analysis.

Definition 11. Let $\mathcal{T} = (\tau(\Sigma \cup V), \leq)$ and $\mathcal{T}_\mathcal{A} = (\tau(\Sigma \cup V \cup \{\perp\}), \preceq)$. The *term description* is $\langle \mathcal{T}_\mathcal{A}, \gamma, \mathcal{T} \rangle$ where $\gamma : \mathcal{T}_\mathcal{A} \to \wp \mathcal{T}$ is defined by: $\gamma(t') = \{t \in \mathcal{T} \mid t' \preceq t\}$.

Let *Eqn* be the set of finite sets of equations over $\tau(\Sigma \cup V)$ and $Eqn_\mathcal{A}$ be the set of finite sets of equations over $\tau(\Sigma \cup V \cup \{\perp\})$. The *equation description* is $\langle (Eqn_\mathcal{A}, \sqsubseteq), \gamma, (Eqn, \leq) \rangle$, where $\gamma : Eqn_\mathcal{A} \to \wp\, Eqn$ is defined by: $\gamma(g') = \{g \in Eqn \mid g' \sqsubseteq g$ and g is unquantified $\}$.

Let *Sub* be the set of substitutions over $\tau(\Sigma \cup V)$ and $Sub_\mathcal{A}$ be the set of substitutions over $\tau(\Sigma \cup V \cup \{\perp\})$. The *substitution description* is $\langle (Sub_\mathcal{A}, \preceq), \gamma, (Sub, \leq) \rangle$, where $\gamma : Sub_\mathcal{A} \to \wp\, Sub$ is defined by: $\gamma(\kappa) = \{\theta \in Sub \mid \kappa \preceq \theta\}$.

Define the abstract state domain $State_\mathcal{A}$ induced by $Eqn_\mathcal{A}$ and $Sub_\mathcal{A}$ to be $State_\mathcal{A} = \{\langle \Leftarrow g, \kappa \rangle \mid g \in Eqn_\mathcal{A}, \kappa \in Sub_\mathcal{A}\}$.

In the following, we formalize the idea that abstract narrowing reduction approximates narrowing reduction by replacing concrete states, unification and term rewriting systems with abstract states, abstract unification and abstract term rewriting systems. We define the abstract most general unifier for an equation set $E' \in Eqn_\mathcal{A}$ as follows. First replace all occurrences of $\perp$ in E' by existentially quantified fresh variables. Then take a solved form of the resulting quantified equation set and finally replace the existentially quantified variables again by $\bot$. Formally: let $\exists y_1 \ldots y_n.E = solve([\![E']\!])$ and $\kappa = \{y_1/\bot, \ldots, y_n/\bot\}$. Then $mgu_{\mathcal{A}}(E') = E\kappa$.

We now extend the notion of parallel composition from substitutions to abstract substitutions by replacing unification by abstract unification.

Definition 12. Let $\kappa_1, \kappa_2 \in Sub_{\mathcal{A}}$. We define the abstract parallel composition $\kappa_1 \Uparrow_{\mathcal{A}} \kappa_2$ by:

$$\kappa_1 \Uparrow_{\mathcal{A}} \kappa_2 = mgu_{\mathcal{A}}(\widehat{\kappa}_1 \cup \widehat{\kappa}_2).$$

Our notion of abstract term rewriting system is parametric with respect to a loop-check, i.e. a finite graph of functional dependencies built from the equational theory, which helps to recognize the narrowing derivations which definitely terminate. The purpose of a loop-check is to reduce the search space to end up with a finite search space. Two different instances can be found in [2,3].

Definition 13. A loop-check is a graph $\mathcal{G}_{\mathcal{R}}$ associated with a term rewriting system $\mathcal{R}$, i.e. a relation consisting of a set of pairs of terms, such that: (1) the transitive closure $\mathcal{G}_{\mathcal{R}}^{+}$ is decidable and (2) Let $\overset{\circ}{t} = t'$ be a function which assigns to a term t some node t' in $\mathcal{G}_{\mathcal{R}}$. If there is an infinite sequence:
$\langle \Leftarrow g_0, \theta_0 \rangle \rightsquigarrow \langle \Leftarrow g_1, \theta_1 \rangle \rightsquigarrow \ldots$
then

$$\exists i \geq 0.\ \langle \overset{\circ}{t_i}, \overset{\circ}{t_i} \rangle \in \mathcal{G}_{\mathcal{R}}^{+}, \text{ where } t_i = e_{|u}\theta_i,\ e \in g_i \text{ and } u \in \bar{O}(e).$$

(we refer to $\langle \overset{\circ}{t_i}, \overset{\circ}{t_i} \rangle$ as a 'cycle' of $\mathcal{G}_{\mathcal{R}}$.)

A loop-check can be thought of as a sort of 'oracle' whose usefulness in proving the termination of basic narrowing derivations is stated in the following proposition.

Proposition 14. [2] *Let $\mathcal{R}$ be a term rewriting system and $\mathcal{G}_{\mathcal{R}}$ be a loop-check for $\mathcal{R}$. If there is no cycle in $\mathcal{G}_{\mathcal{R}}$, then every basic conditional narrowing derivation for $\mathcal{R}$ terminates.*

To illustrate our definition, we consider a simple example here.

Example 4. Let $\mathcal{R} = \{X + 0 \rightarrow X \Leftarrow,\ X + s(Y) \rightarrow s(X + Y) \Leftarrow\}$ and define $\overset{\circ}{t} = t'$ the function which, given a graph, assigns to a term t some node t' in the graph such that t' unifies with t (variables are implicitly renamed to be disjoint). Then the graph $\mathcal{G} = \{\langle X + s(Y), X + s(Y) \rangle\}$ is a loop-check for $\mathcal{R}$.

Most papers on loop-checking consider the application of loop-checks at run-time. Static loop-checks have not received that much attention yet. In the following we show how a loop-check can be used to obtain a form of (compiled) abstract program which always terminates and in which the semantics of a given goal can be approximated safely. A TRS is abstracted by simplifying the right-hand side and the body of each rule. This definition is given inductively on the structure of terms and equations. The main idea is that terms which are mapped to a cycle of the loop-check are drastically simplified by replacing them by $\bot$. This enforces termination.

Definition 15. (abstract term rewriting system)
Let $\mathcal{R}$ be a TRS. Let $\mathcal{G}_{\mathcal{R}}$ be a loop-check for $\mathcal{R}$. We define the abstraction of $\mathcal{R}$ using $\mathcal{G}_{\mathcal{R}}$ as follows:
$\mathcal{R}_{\mathcal{A}} = \{\lambda \to sh(\rho) \Leftarrow sh(\tilde{e}) \mid \lambda \to \rho \Leftarrow \tilde{e} \in \mathcal{R}\}$ (we also write $\mathcal{R}_{\mathcal{A}} \propto \mathcal{R}$), where the shell $sh(x)$ of an expression x is defined inductively

$$sh(x) = \begin{cases} x & \text{if } x \in V \\ f(sh(t_1), \ldots, sh(t_k)) & \text{if } x = f(t_1, \ldots, t_k) \text{ and } \langle \mathring{x}, \mathring{x} \rangle \notin \mathcal{G}_{\mathcal{R}}^{+} \\ sh(l) = sh(r) & \text{if } x = (l = r) \\ sh(e_1), \ldots, sh(e_n) & \text{if } x = e_1, \ldots, e_n \\ \bot & \text{otherwise} \end{cases}$$

Example 5. (Continued from Example 4) The abstraction of $\mathcal{R}$ using the loop-check $\mathcal{G}$ is: $\mathcal{R}_{\mathcal{A}} = \{X + 0 \to X \Leftarrow,\ X + s(Y) \to s(\bot) \Leftarrow\}$.

5.2 Compositional Abstract Narrowing

We now introduce compositional abstract (basic) narrowing.

Definition 16. Let $\mathcal{R}_{\mathcal{A}}$ be an abstract *TRS*. We define *compositional abstract (basic) narrowing* as a transition system $(State_{\mathcal{A}}, \leadsto_{\mathcal{A}})$ whose transition relation $\leadsto_{\mathcal{A}} \subseteq State_{\mathcal{A}} \times State_{\mathcal{A}}$ is defined as the smallest relation satisfying:

$$(1)\ \frac{\begin{array}{l} e \in g \ \wedge\ u \in \bar{O}(e)\ \wedge\ (\lambda \to \rho \Leftarrow \tilde{e}) \ll \mathcal{R}_{\mathcal{A}}\ \wedge \\ \sigma = mgu_{\mathcal{A}}(\{(e_{|u})\kappa = \lambda\}) \end{array}}{\langle \Leftarrow g, \kappa \rangle \ \leadsto_{\mathcal{A}}\ \langle \Leftarrow (g \sim \{e\}) \cup \{e[\rho]_u\} \cup \tilde{e}, \kappa\sigma \rangle}$$

$$(2)\ \frac{\langle \Leftarrow g_1, \kappa \rangle \leadsto_{\mathcal{A}}^{*} \langle \Leftarrow true, \kappa_1 \rangle \ \wedge\ \langle \Leftarrow g_2, \kappa \rangle \leadsto_{\mathcal{A}}^{*} \langle \Leftarrow true, \kappa_2 \rangle}{\langle \Leftarrow (g_1, g_2), \kappa \rangle \leadsto_{\mathcal{A}} \langle \Leftarrow true, \kappa_1 \Uparrow_{\mathcal{A}} \kappa_2 \rangle}$$

Example 6. (Continued from Example 5) The sequences

$$\begin{array}{l} \langle \Leftarrow X + 0 = 0, \epsilon \rangle \leadsto_{\mathcal{A}} \langle \Leftarrow X = 0, \epsilon \rangle \leadsto_{\mathcal{A}} \langle \Leftarrow true, \{X/0\} \rangle, \\ \langle \Leftarrow X + s(Y) = s(0), \epsilon \rangle \leadsto_{\mathcal{A}} \langle \Leftarrow s(\bot) = s(0), \epsilon \rangle \leadsto_{\mathcal{A}} \langle \Leftarrow true, \epsilon \rangle, \quad \text{and} \\ \langle \Leftarrow (X + 0 = 0,\ X + s(Y) = s(0)),\ \epsilon \rangle \leadsto_{\mathcal{A}} \langle \Leftarrow true,\ \{X/0\} \rangle \end{array}$$

are three (successful) compositional abstract narrowing derivations for $\mathcal{R}_{\mathcal{A}} \cup \{x = x \to true \Leftarrow\}$. Note that there is no successful compositional abstract narrowing derivation for $\mathcal{R}_{\mathcal{A}}$ with initial goal $\langle \Leftarrow s(0) + Y = 0, \epsilon \rangle$.

The following definition formalizes the *compositional abstract basic narrowing semantics* for the success set.

Definition 17. (abstract semantics)

$$\Delta_{\mathcal{R}_\mathcal{A}}(\Leftarrow g) = \{\kappa \in Sub_\mathcal{A} \mid \langle \Leftarrow g, \epsilon \rangle \leadsto^*_\mathcal{A} \langle \Leftarrow true, \kappa \rangle\}.$$

The main purpose of introducing compositional abstract basic narrowing here is to suggest a mechanism for the static analysis of the run-time behaviour of programs. We now establish a preliminary result that clarifies our interest in compositional abstract basic narrowing reduction. It basically states that in the abstract computations no solutions are lost, that is, each concrete computed answer is still 'represented' by a more general answer in the abstract semantics.

Theorem 18. *Let $\mathcal{R}_\mathcal{A} \propto \mathcal{R}$ and $g' \propto g$. Then, for every solution $\theta \in \mathcal{O}_\mathcal{R}(\Leftarrow g)$ there exists $\kappa \in \Delta_{\mathcal{R}_\mathcal{A}}(\Leftarrow g')$ such that $\kappa \propto \theta$.*

Our analysis of unsatisfiability is formalized in the following theorem.

Corollary 19. *If $\Delta_{\mathcal{R}_\mathcal{A}}(\Leftarrow g) = \emptyset$, then g is unsatisfiable in $\mathcal{R}$.*

The following theorem constitutes the main result in this section and basically states that compositional abstract narrowing is compositional w.r.t. the AND operator.

Theorem 20. $\Delta_{\mathcal{R}_\mathcal{A}}(\Leftarrow g_1, g_2) = \Delta_{\mathcal{R}_\mathcal{A}}(\Leftarrow g_1) \Uparrow_\mathcal{A} \Delta_{\mathcal{R}_\mathcal{A}}(\Leftarrow g_2)$.

As a consequence of Theorem 20, the analysis for a specific goal (the abstract meaning of a goal) can be determined by exploiting the AND-compositionality of the basic narrowing semantics and its abstract version. In Section 6 we will formalize the idea that the compositionality of the abstract semantics w.r.t the union of $\mathcal{E}$-unification problems, as established in Theorem 20, provides for incrementality when dealing with constraint satisfaction problems in the framework of constraint logic programming, where sets of constraints are incrementally added to a solver.

6 Incremental Equational Analyzer

In the context of constraint logic programming [14,18], incremental search consists of proving the solvability of a sequence of constraint problems by transforming the existing solution to each previously solved problem into a solution to the next problem [13].

When dealing with equational constraints [1], the tests of solvability can be extremely redundant. Termination is not even guaranteed. In [2] we propose a lazy resolution procedure [14] which incorporates an analysis of unsatisfiability which allows us to avoid some useless computations. To achieve efficiency, the analyses also need to be incremental, that is, when adding a new equation set $\tilde{c}$ to an already tested set c of constraints, the analysis should not start checking the accumulated constraint $c \cup \tilde{c}$ from scratch. In this section, we formulate an incremental algorithm for analyzing the unsatisfiability of equation sets within a constraint setting [1]. The kernel of the algorithm is the calculus of compositional abstract (basic) narrowing reduction as formulated in Section 5.

We assume that constraints monotonically grow as long as the computation proceeds, and the question we consider is how to deal efficiently with the test of unsatisfiability for the accumulated constraints as long as new equations are added.

Definition 21. (incremental constraint satisfaction problem)
Let $c_0, c_1, \tilde{c}_1, \ldots, c_n, \tilde{c}_n$ be constraints, where $c_i = c_{i-1} \cup \tilde{c}_i$. The incremental constraint satisfaction problem consists of (efficiently) checking the (un)satisfiability of c_i by using some information from the computations of $c_0, \ldots, c_{i-1}$, $i = 1, \ldots, n$.

The idea here is to compute the abstract success set of $\Leftarrow c \cup \tilde{c}$ by combining the sets $\Delta_{\mathcal{R}_\mathcal{A}}(\Leftarrow c)$ and $\Delta_{\mathcal{R}_\mathcal{A}}(\Leftarrow \tilde{c})$ which describe the successes of $\Leftarrow c$ and $\Leftarrow \tilde{c}$, respectively.

We define an *incremental Equational Analyzer (iEA)* as follows.

Definition 22. An *iEA*-state is a pair $\langle c, \Theta \rangle$, where c is a constraint and Θ is a set of substitutions. The empty *iEA*-state is $\langle \emptyset, \emptyset \rangle$.

Definition 23. (*iEA transition relation* $\stackrel{\tilde{c}}{\longrightarrow}_{iEA}$)

$$\frac{\Theta' = \Theta \Uparrow_\mathcal{A} \Delta_{\mathcal{R}_\mathcal{A}}(\Leftarrow \tilde{c})}{\langle c, \Theta \rangle \stackrel{\tilde{c}}{\longrightarrow}_{iEA} \langle c \cup \tilde{c}, \Theta' \rangle}$$

We note that, if the accumulated abstract success set $\Theta' = \emptyset$ then $c \cup \tilde{c}$ is unsatisfiable by Corollary 19. Our strategy proves the unsatisfiability of $c \cup \tilde{c}$, or it builds the (non-empty) abstract success set $\Delta_{\mathcal{R}_\mathcal{A}}(\Leftarrow c \cup \tilde{c})$, as stated by:

Theorem 24. *Let c be a constraint and $\Theta = \Delta_{\mathcal{R}_\mathcal{A}}(\Leftarrow c) \neq \emptyset$. Then,*

1. *if a transition $\langle c, \Theta \rangle \stackrel{\tilde{c}}{\longrightarrow}_{iEA} \langle c \cup \tilde{c}, \Theta' \rangle$ is proven, then $\Theta' = \Delta_{\mathcal{R}_\mathcal{A}}(\Leftarrow c \cup \tilde{c})$;*
2. *if a transition $\langle c, \Theta \rangle \stackrel{\tilde{c}}{\longrightarrow}_{iEA} \langle c \cup \tilde{c}, \emptyset \rangle$ is proven, then the constraint $c \cup \tilde{c}$ is unsatisfiable.*

We note that the computed abstract answer set $\Delta_{\mathcal{R}_\mathcal{A}}(\Leftarrow c \cup \tilde{c})$ can be used to guide the final execution of a 'full' narrower which can find the concrete solutions and possibly recognize the unsatisfiability not detected by this lazy procedure, as described in [3].

The analysis above has been implemented in Prolog and tested on several programs with good results. To demonstrate this point empirically, consider the performance of the simple program `parity`:

```
X + 0        → X          ⇐
X + s(Y)     → s(X + Y)   ⇐
parity(X)    → even       ⇐ X = Y + Y
```

constraint	CAn	ICAn	AbNar	APCom
parity(X) = even	0.42	0.42	0.30	0.00
parity(Y) = even	3.88	2.80	0.32	1.20
X + Y = s^2(0)	**18.24**	**3.44**	0.44	2.92
parity(X) = even	0.40	0.40	0.28	0.00
Y = s(0), Z = X + Y	3.78	1.52	0.46	0.66
X + Z = s^3(0)	**26.36**	**4.44**	fail	
X + Y = s^4(0)	0.72	0.72	0.54	0.00
parity(X) = even	3.66	2.10	0.32	1.46
parity(Y) = even	**19.48**	**3.64**	0.30	2.62
parity(X) = parity(Y)	3.62	3.66	2.30	0.00
X + Y = s(Z)	23.18	12.00	0.46	9.52
Z = 0	**20.26**	**1.14**	fail	
Z = 0, parity(X) = even	0.52	0.54	0.42	0.00
Y + Z = s^2(0)	3.38	1.62	0.62	0.86
Y = X + Z	**10.62**	**5.24**	0.44	4.76

CAn Constraint Analyzer
ICAn Incremental Constraint Analyzer
AbNar Abstract Narrowing
APCom Abstract Parallel Composition

Table 1. *Incremental* vs. *Non-Incremental* constraint analyzer times (secs, using BIM-Prolog, SUN 3/80)

In Table 1 we report on some experiments we have performed for the case of a sequential implementation. We have not tried with the parallel interpreter yet. The time in the second column (ICAn) is the result of the sum of the time in the third and fourth column (AbNar and APCom) plus some extratime for some simplification rules which are only relevant for the implementation. We compare the time performances of the incremental vs. the non-incremental analyzers. If the incrementality was exploited our interpreter was able to achieve up to 95% gain in efficiency.

7 Conclusion and further research

The contribution of this paper is twofold. We have presented a formal compositional semantics for the success set of equational logic programs which is suitable for AND-parallel implementations. We have then shown that this semantics leads to compositional analyses and have given an example of an enhanced analysis of unsatisfiability which is suitable for theories where equations are considered as constraints.

The approach which we have taken is of general interest. In particular it applies to any kind of analysis where we look for properties which are satisfied by all (or some) success paths. For specific analyses, it will be necessary to provide the appropriate abstract domains and approximation of the term rewriting system. A groundness analysis which follows the approach proposed here is defined in [3].

References

1. M. Alpuente, M. Falaschi, and G. Levi. Incremental Constraint Satisfaction for Equational Logic Programming. Technical Report TR-20/91, Dipartimento di Informatica, Università di Pisa, 1991. To appear in *Theoretical Computer Science*.
2. M. Alpuente, M. Falaschi, and F. Manzo. Analyses of Unsatisfiability for Equational Logic Programming. Technical Report DSIC-II/29/92, UPV, 1992. Short version in M. Bruynooghe and M. Wirsing, editors, *Proc. of PLILP'92*, volume 631 of *Lecture Notes in Computer Science*, pages 443-457, Springer-Verlag, Berlin, 1992. To appear in the *Journal of Logic Programming.*
3. M. Alpuente, M. Falaschi, M.J. Ramis, and G. Vidal. Narrowing Approximations as an Optimization for Equational Logic Programs. Technical Report DSIC-II/1/93, UPV, 1993. Short version in J. Penjam and M. Bruynooghe, editors, *Proc. of PLILP'93*, volume 714 of *Lecture Notes in Computer Science*, pages 391-409, Springer-Verlag, Berlin, 1993.
4. M. Alpuente, M. Falaschi, M.J. Ramis, and G. Vidal. A Compositional Semantics for Conditional Term Rewriting Systems. In H.E. Bal, editor, *Proc. Sixth IEEE Int'l Conf. on Computer Languages ICCL'94*, pages 171–182. IEEE Computer Society Press, 1994.
5. M. Alpuente, M. Falaschi, and G. Vidal. Semantics-Based Compositional Analysis for Equational Horn Programs. Technical Report DSIC-II/5/93, UPV, 1993.
6. R. Bert, R. Echahed, and B.M. Østvold. Abstract Rewriting. In *Proc. Third Int'l Workshop on Static Analysis WSA'93*, volume 724 of *Lecture Notes in Computer Science*, pages 178–192. Springer-Verlag, Berlin, 1993.
7. M. Codish, M. Falaschi, and K. Marriott. Suspension Analyses for Concurrent Logic Programs. *ACM Transactions on Programming Languages and Systems*, 1994.
8. P. Cousot and R. Cousot. Abstract Interpretation: A Unified Lattice Model for Static Analysis of Programs by Construction or Approximation of Fixpoints. In *Proc. Fourth ACM Symp. Principles of Programming Languages*, pages 238–252, 1977.
9. N. Dershowitz and J.-P. Jouannaud. Rewrite systems. In J. van Leeuwen, editor, *Handbook of Theoretical Computer Science*, volume B: Formal Models and Semantics, pages 243–320. Elsevier, Amsterdam and The MIT Press, Cambridge, 1990.
10. N. Dershowitz and N. Lindenstrauss. An Abstract Concurrent Machine for Rewriting. In H. Kirchner and W. Wechler, editors, *Proc. Second Int'l Conf. on Algebraic and Logic Programming*, volume 463 of *Lecture Notes in Computer Science*, pages 318–331. Springer-Verlag, Berlin, 1990.
11. M. Gabbrielli and G. Levi. On the Semantics of Logic Programs. In J. Leach Albert, B. Monien, and M. Rodriguez Artalejo, editors, *Automata, Languages and Programming, 18th International Colloquium*, volume 510 of *Lecture Notes in Computer Science*, pages 1–19. Springer-Verlag, Berlin, 1991.
12. J.H. Gallier and S. Raatz. Extending SLD-resolution to equational Horn clauses using E-unification. *Journal of Logic Programming*, 6:3–43, 1989.

13. P. Van Hentenryck and T. Le Provost. Incremental Search in Constraint Logic Programming. *New Generation Computing*, 9:257–275, 1991.
14. M. Höhfeld and G. Smolka. Definite relations over constraint languages. Technical report, IBM Deutschland GmbH, Stuttgart, 1988.
15. S. Hölldobler. *Foundations of Equational Logic Programming*, volume 353 of *Lecture Notes in Artificial Intelligence*. Springer-Verlag, Berlin, 1989.
16. J.M. Hullot. Canonical Forms and Unification. In *5th Int'l Conf. on Automated Deduction*, volume 87 of *Lecture Notes in Computer Science*, pages 318–334. Springer-Verlag, Berlin, 1980.
17. J.-M. Jacquet. *Conclog: A Methodological Approach to Concurrent Logic Programming*. PhD thesis, University of Namur, Belgium, 1989.
18. J. Jaffar and J.-L. Lassez. Constraint Logic Programming. In *Proc. Fourteenth Annual ACM Symp. on Principles of Programming Languages*, pages 111–119. ACM, 1987.
19. J. Jaffar, J.-L. Lassez, and M.J. Maher. A theory of complete logic programs with equality. *Journal of Logic Programming*, 3:211–223, 1984.
20. J.W. Klop. Term rewriting systems. In S. Abramsky, D. Gabbay, and T. Maibaum, editors, *Handbook of Logic in Computer Science*, volume I, pages 1–112. Oxford University Press, 1992.
21. H. Kuchen and W. Hans. An AND-Parallel Implementation of the Functional Logic Language Babel. In *Aachener Informatik-Bericht*, volume 12, pages 119–139, RWTH Aachen, 1991.
22. H. Kuchen, J.J. Moreno-Navarro, and M. Hermenegildo. Independent AND-Parallel Implementation of Narrowing. In M. Bruynooghe and M. Wirsing, editors, *Proc. of PLILP'92, Leuven (Belgium)*, volume 631 of *Lecture Notes in Computer Science*, pages 24–38. Springer-Verlag, Berlin, 1992.
23. J.-L. Lassez, M. J. Maher, and K. Marriott. Unification Revisited. In J. Minker, editor, *Foundations of Deductive Databases and Logic Programming*, pages 587–625. Morgan Kaufmann, Los Altos, Ca., 1988.
24. M. J. Maher. On parameterized substitutions. Technical Report RC 16042, IBM - T.J. Watson Research Center, Yorktown Heights, NY, 1990.
25. A. Middeldorp and E. Hamoen. Completeness results for basic narrowing. *AAECC*, 5:213–253, 1994.
26. W. Nutt, P. Réty, and G. Smolka. Basic narrowing revisited. *Journal of Symbolic Computation*, 7:295–317, 1989.
27. C. Palamidessi. Algebraic properties of idempotent substitutions. In M. S. Paterson, editor, *Proc. of the 17th International Colloquium on Automata, Languages and Programming*, volume 443 of *Lecture Notes in Computer Science*, pages 386–399. Springer-Verlag, Berlin, 1990.
28. U.S. Reddy. Narrowing as the Operational Semantics of Functional Languages. In *Proc. Second IEEE Int'l Symp. on Logic Programming*, pages 138–151. IEEE, 1985.
29. J.H. Siekmann. Unification Theory. *Journal of Symbolic Computation*, 7:207–274, 1989.

Equation Solving in Projective Planes and Planar Ternary Rings

Philippe Balbiani[(a)]

Institut de recherche en informatique de Toulouse

Abstract A geometrical approach to algebraic reasoning is presented. To every system of algebraic equations in the language of planar ternary rings is associated a system of equations in the language of a first order theory with equality equivalent to projective geometry. A narrowing-based mechanism computes the solutions of this geometrical system corresponding to the solutions of the original algebraic problem. As a corollary, unification in planar ternary rings is finitary and constitutes a decidable class of problems for which a type conformal algorithm exists.

1 Introduction

Let $(\Gamma,+,.)$ be an algebraic structure, for example: the field $\mathbb{R}$ of real numbers. Let Π be the geometrical structure which points are pairs (x,y) of elements of Γ and which lines are equations like $y = x.m + b$. By definition of Π, (x,y) belongs to $y = x.m + b$ if y and $x.m + b$ are equal in Γ. The properties of Π are directly related to the properties of Γ: that two non parallel lines of Π intersect in exactly one point is a consequence of the fact that if $m \neq m'$ then the equation $x.m + b = x.m' + b'$ possesses exactly one solution in Γ. The algebraic approaches to geometrical reasoning [7] use this first correspondence between algebra and geometry. Any geometrical problem is translated into a algebraic problem of the form: "does some polynomial g belong to the ideal generated by polynomials $h_1, ..., h_n$?". With the help of Gröbner bases [6] or characteristic sets [22], the answer to this question can be given [9].

Let Π be a geometrical structure, for example: the euclidean plane. Let $(\Gamma,+,.)$ be the algebraic structure which elements are coordinates x and y of points of Π. The properties of Γ are directly related to the properties of Π: that if $m \neq m'$ then the equation $x.m + b = x.m' + b'$ has exactly one solution in Γ is a consequence of the fact that two non parallel lines of Π intersect in exactly one point. The geometrical approach to algebraic reasoning presented in this paper uses this second correspondence between algebra and geometry. Any algebraic problem is translated into a unification problem in some first order theory with equality. Then, with the help of a narrowing-based mechanism, this unification problem can be solved.

The geometrical structure Π considered here is projective geometry. The algebraic structures Γ which elements are coordinates x and y of points of Π are planar ternary rings (section 2). To every system of algebraic equations in planar ternary rings is associated a system of geometrical equations in the language of a first order theory with equality equivalent to projective geometry (section 3.1). A family[(b)] of positive/negative conditional rewrite rules defines for this theory a nœtherian and confluent relation of reduction (section 3.2). A narrowing-based mechanism[c] defines an algorithm for the resolution of the geometrical system of equations (section 4). Every solution of this geometrical system corresponds to a solution of the original algebraic system (section 5). As a corollary, unification in planar ternary rings is finitary and constitutes a decidable class of problems for which a type conformal algorithm exists.

2 Projective geometry

Projective geometry (PG) is made of two sets of geometrical beings: points and lines together with two incidence relations. Points (lines) will be denoted by capital (lower case) letters.

2.1 The postulates

The relations of incidence are defined by the following postulates:

P_0 X is incident with x iff[d] x is incident with X.
P_1 Two distinct points are together incident with exactly one line.
P_2 Two distinct lines are together incident with exactly one point.
P_3 There are four pairwise distinct points such that no three of them are incident with the same line.

The expression "on" is used as a synonym for "incident with". Models of postulates P_0 through P_3 are *projective planes* (PP). A PP contains at least four pairwise distinct lines such that no three of them are incident with the same point[e]. Consequently, if "point" and "line" are interchanged in any theorem, then one still have a theorem. This duality principle is very important for the study of PG and will provide a great help to its axiomatization through a first order theory with equality (section 3).

2.2 Introduction of coordinates

Let A, B, O, I be four points of a PP, such that no three of them are incident with the same line. Let γ' be the correspondence between $i(A)$, the set of lines on A, and $i(B)$, the set of lines on B, obtained by associating a line of $i(A)$ and a line of $i(B)$, provided they intersect on OI. Let Γ be an abstract set in a one-to-one correspondence γ with $i'(A)$, the set obtained by deleting AB from $i(A)$. Let 0 and 1 be two distinct elements of Γ. A correspondence γ^* between Γ and $i'(B)$, the set obtained by deleting AB from $i(B)$, associates to each line of $i'(B)$ the element of Γ that is associated to the line of $i'(A)$ corresponding to it by γ'. Through γ, the set of points incident with OI not on

AB becomes identified with Γ. In this section, lower case letters denote elements of the *coordinate set* Γ. Let $\gamma(AO)=\gamma^*(BO)=0$ and $\gamma(AI)=\gamma^*(BI)=1$. Let *P* be a point not on *AB*. The pair *(a,b)* is associated to *P* as *coordinates* if $\gamma(AP)=a$ and $\gamma^*(BP)=b$. Suppose $Q \neq A$ is a point on *AB*. Line *OQ* intersects *AI* in a point with coordinates *(1,m)*. Let *m* be the unique coordinate of *Q*.

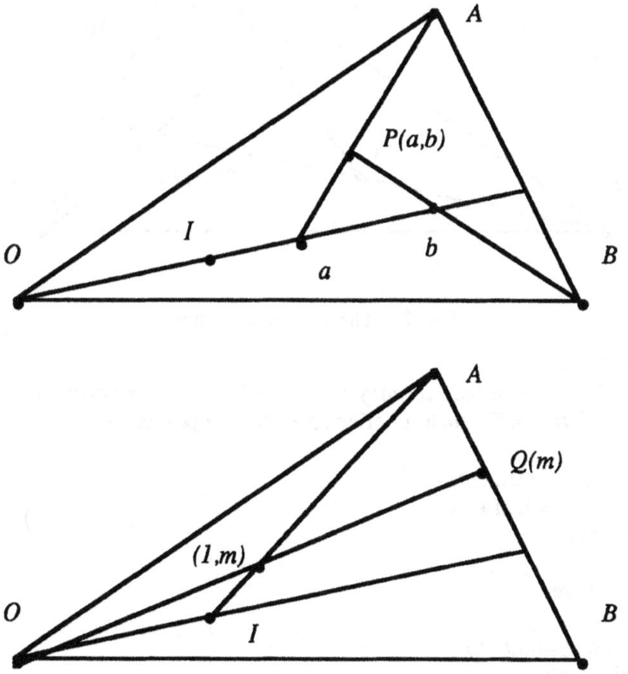

Fig. 1 Introduction of coordinates

2.3 The ternary operation

A ternary operation *T(x,m,b)* is defined in Γ by associating to $x, m, b \in \Gamma$ the second coordinate of the point in which the line of *i'(A)* that corresponds by γ to *x* intersects the line joining *(m)* and *(0,b)*. Every set of four points *A, B, O, I*, no three of them being incident with the same line, determines an abstract set Γ and a ternary operation *T* with the following properties[f]:

(1) Γ contains distinct elements *0* and *1*

(2) for all $a, b, c \in \Gamma$, $T(0,b,c)=T(a,0,c)=c$

(3) for every element *a* of Γ, $T(a,1,0)=T(1,a,0)=a$

(4) if $m, m', b, b' \in \Gamma$, $m \neq m'$, then the equation $T(x,m,b)=T(x,m',b')$ has a unique solution in Γ

(5) if $a, a', b, b' \in \Gamma$, $a \neq a'$, then the system $T(a,x,y)=b$, $T(a',x,y)=b'$ has a unique solution in Γ

(6) for all $a, m, c \in \Gamma$, the equation $T(a,m,x)=c$ has a unique solution in Γ

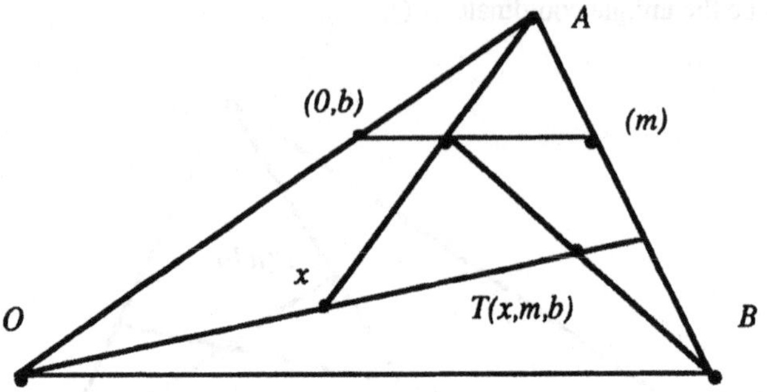

Fig. 2 The ternary operation

The system $[\Gamma,T]$ is a *planar ternary ring* (PTR) or equivalently a *ternary system* (TS). Now, if $[S,t]$ is a TS then it defines a PP which points are:

(i) pairs (a,b) of elements of S
(ii) singletons (m), $m \in S$
(iii) a symbol A

and which lines are:

(iv) equations $y=t(x,m,b)$
(v) equations $x=a$
(vi) a symbol $\mathcal{L}_\infty$

where $a, b, m \in S$. One can proved that, in this PP defined by $[S,t]$, points A, $B=(0)$, $O=(0,0)$ and $I=(1,1)$ are base points of a coordinate system with respect to which $[S,t]$ is the TS. This property gives a complete equivalence[g] between PG and PTR.

3. Positive/negative conditional rewriting[i]

3.1 A typed first order theory with equality

Let E_l be a first order theory with two types: Σ (points) and Λ (lines). Its alphabet contains: *(i)* an infinite set of variables of each type, *(ii)* three function symbols $l : \Sigma\times\Sigma\rightarrow\Lambda$, $i : \Lambda\times\Lambda\rightarrow\Sigma$ and $p : \Sigma\times\Lambda\rightarrow\Sigma$, and *(iii)* two equality predicate symbols of type $\Sigma\times\Sigma$ and $\Lambda\times\Lambda$. Moreover, for each type, there are a universal and an existential quantifiers. Variables of type Σ (Λ) will be denoted by capital (lower case) letters. The first order language of this alphabet is defined as usual and the corresponding set of terms will be denoted by $\mathcal{T}$. The term $l(X,Y)$ denotes the line passing through X and Y while $i(x,y)$ denotes the intersection point of x and y. The term $p(X,x)$ denotes a projection of X onto x. The first order theory with equality of PG is elaborated through the following axioms :

E_{l0} $\forall\,(l(X,Y)=l(Y,X))$

E_{l1} $\forall\,(i(x,y)=i(y,x))$

E_{l2} $\forall\,(X\neq i(x,y) \wedge x\neq y \wedge p(X,x)=X \Rightarrow l(X,i(x,y))=x)$

E_{l3} $\forall\,(X\neq p(Y,x) \wedge p(X,x)=X \Rightarrow l(X,p(Y,x))=x)$

E_{l4} $\forall\,(x\neq l(X,Y) \wedge X\neq Y \wedge p(X,x)=X \Rightarrow i(x,l(X,Y))=X)$

E_{l5} $\forall\,(X\neq Y \Rightarrow p(X,l(X,Y))=X)$

E_{l6} $\forall\,(x\neq y \Rightarrow p(i(x,y),x)=i(x,y))$

E_{l7} $\forall\,(p(p(X,x),x)=p(X,x))$

E_{l8} $\exists\,(X\neq Y \wedge X\neq Z \wedge X\neq T \wedge Y\neq Z \wedge Y\neq T \wedge Z\neq T \wedge \forall x\,(\neg(p(X,x)=X \wedge p(Y,x)=Y \wedge p(Z,x)=Z) \wedge \neg(p(X,x)=X \wedge p(Y,x)=Y \wedge p(T,x)=T) \wedge \neg(p(X,x)=X \wedge p(Z,x)=Z \wedge p(T,x)=T) \wedge \neg(p(Y,x)=Y \wedge p(Z,x)=Z \wedge p(T,x)=T)))$

The geometrical interpretation of these axioms is not difficult. Axiom E_{l2}, for example, means that if X is on x then the line joining X and the intersection of x with any other line y is equal to x. In other respects, axiom E_{l8} means that there are four pairwise distinct points such that no three of them are incident with the same line and corresponds to postulate P_3.

Let * be the function of translation between the languages of PG and E_l defined by : "X is incident with x"* = "x is incident with X"* = $(p(X,x)=X)$. Next proposition says that E_l and PG are equivalent.

proposition 3.1.1(h) If F is a statement in the language of PG and F^* is its translation into the language of E_l then $\vdash_{PG} F$ iff $\vdash_{El} F^*$.

Let A, B, O, I be four variables of type Σ. Let $^\circ$ be the function of translation between the languages of PTR and E_l defined by:

(i) $0^\circ=O$ and $1^\circ=I$

(ii) if x is a variable then x° is a variable of type Σ

(iii) $T(x,y,z)^\circ = i(l(O,I), l(B, i(l(A, x^\circ), l(i(l(A, O), l(B, z^\circ)), i(l(A, B), l(O, i(l(A, I), l(B, y^\circ))))))))$

(iv) $(t_1=t_2)^\circ = (t_1{}^\circ=t_2{}^\circ)$

(v) $(F\wedge G)^\circ = F^\circ \wedge G^\circ$

(vi) $(\neg F)^\circ = \neg F^\circ$

(vii) $(\forall x\, F)^\circ = \forall x^\circ\,(p(x^\circ,l(A,B))\neq x^\circ \wedge p(x^\circ,l(O,I))=x^\circ \Rightarrow F^\circ)$

Next proposition says that E_l and PTR are equivalent.

proposition 3.1.2(h) If F is a statement in the language of PTR and $F°$ is its translation into the language of E_l then $\vdash_{PTR} F$ iff $\vdash_{El} A{\neq}B \wedge p(O,l(A,B)){\neq}O \wedge p(I,l(A,B)){\neq}I \wedge p(I,l(A,O)){\neq}I \wedge p(I,l(B,O)){\neq}I \wedge p(x_1°,l(A,B)){\neq}x_1° \wedge ... \wedge p(x_k°,l(A,B)){\neq}x_k° \wedge p(x_1°,l(O,I))=x_1° \wedge ... \wedge p(x_k°,l(O,I))=x_k° \Rightarrow F°$, where $x_1°$, ..., $x_k°$ are the free variables distinct from A, B occurring in $F°$.

3.2 A conditional term rewriting system

The basic concepts of positive/negative conditional term rewriting systems (P/N CTRS) introduced in this section have been developed by Kaplan [16]. Let R_l be the P/N CTRS made of the following rules:

R_{l1} $X{\neq}i(x,y) \wedge x{\neq}y \wedge p(X,x)=X \Rightarrow l(X,i(x,y)){\rightarrow}x$
R_{l2} $X{\neq}p(Y,x) \wedge p(X,x)=X \Rightarrow l(X,p(Y,x)){\rightarrow}x$
R_{l3} $x{\neq}l(X,Y) \wedge X{\neq}Y \wedge p(X,x)=X \Rightarrow i(x,l(X,Y)){\rightarrow}X$
R_{l4} $X{\neq}Y \Rightarrow p(X,l(X,Y)){\rightarrow}X$
R_{l5} $x{\neq}y \Rightarrow p(i(x,y),x){\rightarrow}i(x,y)$
R_{l6} $p(p(X,x),x){\rightarrow}p(X,x)$

Let C be the first order equational theory generated by $\{l(X,Y)=l(Y,X),\ i(x,y)=i(y,x)\}$. Unification and matching under C are finitary and constitute decidable classes of problems for which type conformal algorithms exist [8]. A partial ordering > on $\mathcal{T}$ is monotonic when: for every term u and for every position p in u, if $t > t'$ then $u[t]_p > u[t']_p$. It possesses the subterm property when: if t' is a proper subterm of t then $t > t'$. Let > be the smallest monotonic ordering on $\mathcal{T}$ possessing the subterm property and such that:

(i) $l(X,i(x,y)) > p(X,x)$
(ii) $l(X,p(Y,x)) > p(X,x)$
(iii) $i(x,l(X,Y)) > p(X,x)$
(iv) if $t > t'$ and $t'=_C t''$ then $t > t''$
(v) if $t > t'$ and $t=_C t''$ then $t'' > t'$

It can be proved that > is well-founded.

Let $\{u_i=v_i\}_i \wedge \{u_j{\neq}v_j\}_j \Rightarrow l{\rightarrow}r$ be a rule in R_l. Since, for every substitution σ, $l\sigma > u_i\sigma, v_i\sigma, u_j\sigma, v_j\sigma, r\sigma$, then the rules of R_l define a decidable and terminating relation $\rightarrow$ of reduction such that, for every term t and t', $t \rightarrow t'$ iff there are:

(i) a position p of t
(ii) a substitution σ
(iii) a variant $Q \Rightarrow l{\rightarrow}r$ of a rule

such that:

(iv) $t_{/p}=_C l\sigma$
(v) $t'=t[r\sigma]_p$

(vi) $Q\sigma\downarrow$, that is to say: for every $u=v$ in Q, $u\sigma\downarrow v\sigma$ and, for every $u\neq v$ in Q, $u\sigma\not\downarrow v\sigma$, the relation $\downarrow$ being defined by $u\downarrow v$ if there are two terms w and w' such that $w=_C w'$, $u \to^* w$ and $v \to^* w'$

A *normal form* is a term that cannot be reduced.

In other respects, it can be proved that $\to$ is confluent(h). Thus, for every term t, the normal forms of t are equal modulo C. For every term t, $NF(t)$ denotes the class modulo C of its normal forms. Let M be the interpretation of E_l defined by $\to$, that is to say : the domain of M is $\{NF(t): t \in \mathcal{T}\}$ and the interpretations of l, i and p are $l^M(NF(X), NF(Y))=NF(l(X, Y))$, $i^M(NF(x), NF(y))=NF(i(x, y))$ and $p^M(NF(X), NF(x))=NF(p(X, x))$. The confluence of $\to$ implies the correctness of this definition. It can be proved that M is a minimal model of E_l. This model is called the *quasi-initial model* of E_l.

3.3 Reduction with respect to a finite set of equations and disequations

From now on, S and T will denote finite sets of equations and disequations in the language of E_l. The expressions S^+ and S^- will respectively denote the set of equations and the set of disequations that appear in S. A set S is *consistent* if it is true in some model of E_l. For every set S and for every substitution σ, if $S\sigma\downarrow$ then $S\sigma$ is true in M and S is consistent.

Any set S defines a sequence $(\to_{S,n})_{n\geq 0}$ of binary relations on $\mathcal{T}$ such that $\to_{S,0}=\emptyset$ and $t \to_{S,n+1} t'$ if either $t \to_{S,n} t'$ or there are:

(i) a position p of t
(ii) a substitution σ
(iii) a variant $Q \Rightarrow l\to r$

such that

(iv) $t_{/p}=_C l\sigma$
(v) $t'=t[r\sigma]_p$
(vi) for every $u=v$ in Q, $u\sigma\downarrow_{S,n} v\sigma$
(vii) for every $u\neq v$ in Q, there is $u'\neq v'$ in S such that $u\sigma\downarrow_{S,n} u'$ and $v\sigma\downarrow_{S,n} v'$

Let $\to_S = \cup_{n\geq 0} \to_{S,n}$. It can be proved that $\to_S$ is decidable and terminating. The rewrite relation $\to$ is not stable under substitution: in general, $t \to t'$ does not imply $t\theta \to t'\theta$.

proposition 3.3.1 For every set S and for every substitution θ, if $t \to_S t'$ then $t\theta \to_{S\theta} t'\theta$.

In other respects, rewrites with $\to_S$ or $\to$ are not related to each other. For example, if $S=\{X\neq X\}$ then $p(X,l(X,X)) \to_S X$ but $p(X,l(X,X)) \not\to X$. This is not the case if $S\downarrow$.

proposition 3.3.2 For every set S, if $S\downarrow$ then $\rightarrow_S \subseteq \rightarrow$.

Moreover, if $t\downarrow_S t'$ then $\vdash_{El} S \Rightarrow t=t'$.

proposition 3.3.3 For every set S, if $t\downarrow_S t'$ then $\vdash_{El} S \Rightarrow t=t'$.

This last proposition is of fundamental importance for the proof that the consistency of S is a sufficient condition making $\rightarrow_S$ confluent.

proposition 3.3.4 For every consistent set S, $\rightarrow_S$ is confluent.

proof A CCP $Q \Rightarrow t_1=t_2 \{t_0\}$ is almost S-convergent if, for every substitution σ, $Q\sigma\downarrow_S$ and confluence of $\rightarrow_S$ for every term smaller than $t_0\sigma$ imply $t_1\sigma\downarrow_S t_2\sigma$. As a lemma, it can be proved that $\rightarrow_S$ is locally confluent (and thus confluent) iff every CCP is almost S-convergent (see, for examples, Kaplan [16]). Now, it should be proved that every CCP $Q \Rightarrow t_1=t_2 \{t_0\}$ weakly S-converges. Many cases should be considered, depending on which rules are used to rewrite t_0 into t_1 and t_2. The case where $t_0=l(p(X,x),p(Y,y))$ such that $p(p(Y,y),x)\downarrow_S p(Y,y)$, $p(p(X,x),y)\downarrow_S p(X,x)$, $t_1=x$ and $t_2=y$, and such that there is $u'\neq v'$ in S with $p(X,x)\downarrow_S u'$ and $p(Y,y)\downarrow_S v'$ is considered here. Let $X°$, $Y°$, $x°$ and $y°$ be the normal forms of X, Y, x and y. Let A and B be the normal forms of $p(X°,x°)$ and $p(Y°,y°)$. Then, either A is $p(X°,x°)$ or A is $X°$, in which case either $x°$ is $l(A,.)$, A is $i(x°,.)$ or A is $p(.,x°)$. Similarly, either B is $p(Y°,y°)$ or B is $Y°$, in which case either $y°$ is $l(.,B)$, B is $i(.,y°)$ or B is $p(.,y°)$. Moreover, since $t_0>p(p(X,x),y)$ and $t_0>p(p(Y,y),x)$, then $p(A,y°) \rightarrow_S A$ and $p(B,x°) \rightarrow_S B$. Then, either $y°$ is $l(A,.)$, A is $i(.,y°)$ or A is $p(.,y°)$. Similarly, either $x°$ is $l(.,B)$, B is $i(x°,.)$ or B is $p(.,x°)$. Now, $4\times4\times3\times3=144$ cases have to be considered. For example, if A is $i(x°,.)$, B is $i(.,y°)$, A is $i(.,y°)$ and B is $i(x°,.)$ then either $x°$ and $y°$ are equal modulo C, in which case $x\downarrow_S y$, or A and B are equal modulo C. If A and B are equal modulo C then $p(X,x)\downarrow_S p(Y,y)$. Thus, according to proposition 3.3.3, $\vdash_{El} S \Rightarrow p(X,x)=p(Y,y)$, $\vdash_{El} S \Rightarrow p(X,x)=u'$ and $\vdash_{El} S \Rightarrow p(Y,y)=v'$. Then, $\vdash_{El} S \Rightarrow u'=v'$, a contradiction with the consistency of S.

3.4 Saturated sets

The functions denoted by the symbols l and i are only partial, that is to say: they are not properly defined when their two arguments are equal. A set S is *saturated* if, for every of its subterms of the form $l(u,v)$ or $i(u,v)$, it contains a disequation $u'\neq v'$ such that $u\downarrow_S u'$ and $v\downarrow_S v'$. It is always decidable to check whether a finite set of equations and disequations is saturated or not.

It is remarkable that saturation is preserved by unification modulo C.

proposition 3.4.1 For every saturated set S and for every mgu(j) μ of S^+ modulo C, $S\mu$ is saturated.

proof The following unification algorithm à la Martelli-Montanari [18] calculates a mgu of a given set modulo C. It repeatedly performs any of the following transformations. If no transformation applies then it stops with success.

(i) Select any equation of the form $t=x$ where t is not a variable and x is a variable and rewrite it as $x=t$.

(ii) Select any equation of the form $x=x$ where x is a variable and erase it.

(iii) Select any equation of the form $l(X_{11},X_{12})=l(X_{21},X_{22})$ and replace it either with the equations $X_{11}=X_{21}$, $X_{12}=X_{22}$ or with the equations $X_{11}=X_{22}$, $X_{12}=X_{21}$.

(iv) Select any equation of the form $i(x_{11},x_{12})=i(x_{21},x_{22})$ and replace it either with the equations $x_{11}=x_{21}$, $x_{12}=x_{22}$ or with the equations $x_{11}=x_{22}$, $x_{12}=x_{21}$.

(v) Select any equation of the form $p(X_{11},x_{12})=p(X_{21},x_{22})$ and replace it with the equations $X_{11}=X_{21}$, $x_{12}=x_{22}$.

(vi) Select any equation of the form $x=t$ where x is a variable which occurs somewhere else in the set of equations and where $t \neq x$. If x occurs in t then stop with failure otherwise apply the substitution $\{x=t\}$ to both terms of all other equations in the set.

(vii) Select any equation of the form $f(t_{11},t_{12})=g(t_{21},t_{22})$ where f and g are distinct function symbols and stop with failure.

Let it be proved that any transformation performed by this algorithm preserves the saturation property. This is obvious for transformations *(i)* to *(v)*. Let $x=t$ be an equation in S where x is a variable which occurs somewhere else in S and where $t \neq x$. If x does not occur in t then the substitution $\sigma=\{x=t\}$ is applied to S. Let $l(u,v)$ be a subterm in $S\sigma$. Then, either there is a subterm of the form $l(u',v')$ in S such that $u'\sigma=u$ and $v'\sigma=v$ or $l(u,v)$ is a subterm of t. In the first case, since S is saturated, it contains some disequation $u'' \neq v''$ such that $u' \downarrow_S u''$ and $v' \downarrow_S v''$. Therefore, $S\sigma$ contains some disequation $u''\sigma \neq v''\sigma$ such that, according to proposition 3.3.1 $u'\sigma \downarrow_{S\sigma} u''\sigma$ and $v'\sigma \downarrow_{S\sigma} v''\sigma$. In the second case, since S is saturated, it contains some disequation $u'' \neq v''$ such that $u \downarrow_S u''$ and $v \downarrow_S v''$. Therefore, $S\sigma$ contains some disequation $u''\sigma \neq v''\sigma$ such that $u\sigma \downarrow_{S\sigma} u''\sigma$ and $v\sigma \downarrow_{S\sigma} v''\sigma$. In both case, $S\sigma$ contains some disequation $u''\sigma \neq v''\sigma$ such that $u \downarrow_{S\sigma} u''\sigma$ and $v \downarrow_{S\sigma} v''\sigma$. As a consequence, $S\sigma$ is saturated.

In other respects, for every saturated set S and for every subterm w of S, it can be proved that if $w \rightarrow w'$ then $w \rightarrow_S w'$.

proposition 3.4.2 For every saturated set S and for every subterm w of S, if $w \rightarrow w'$ then $w \rightarrow_S w'$.

proof Let it be proved by induction on w that if $w \rightarrow w'$ then $w \rightarrow_S w'$. If $w \rightarrow w'$ then there are a position p of w, a substitution σ and a variant $Q \Rightarrow l \rightarrow r$ such that $w_{/p}=Cl\sigma$, for every $u=v$ in Q, $u\sigma \downarrow v\sigma$ and, for every $u \neq v$ in Q, $u\sigma \not\downarrow v\sigma$. Let $u=v$ be in Q. Then $u\sigma=p(X,x)$ and $v\sigma=X$, X and x being proper subterms of w. Let $X°=NF(X)$ and $x°=NF(x)$. Then, by induction hypothesis, $X \rightarrow_{S,*} X°$ and $x \rightarrow_{S,*} x°$. Consequently, $p(X,x) \rightarrow_{S,*} p(X°,x°)$. Moreover, $p(X°,x°) \rightarrow X°$. Then, either

$x^\circ = c_l(X^\circ, Y^\circ)$ or $X^\circ = c_i(x^\circ, y^\circ)$ or $X^\circ = c_p(Y^\circ, x^\circ)$. If $x^\circ = c_l(X^\circ, Y^\circ)$ then, since S is saturated, there is $u' \neq v'$ in S such that $X^\circ \downarrow_S u'$ and $Y^\circ \downarrow_S v'$. If $X^\circ = c_i(x^\circ, y^\circ)$ then there is $u' \neq v'$ in S such that $x^\circ \downarrow_S u'$ and $y^\circ \downarrow_S v'$. Consequently, in any case, $p(X^\circ, x^\circ) \rightarrow_S X^\circ$. Then, $p(X,x) \downarrow_S X$ and $u\sigma \downarrow_S v\sigma$. Let $u \neq v$ be in Q. Then, $l(u\sigma, v\sigma)$ or $i(u\sigma, v\sigma)$ is a subterm of w and there is $u' \neq v'$ in S such that $u\sigma \downarrow_S u'$ and $v\sigma \downarrow_S v'$. Finally, $w \rightarrow_S w'$.

As a consequence, a saturated set S of disequations is consistent iff $S \downarrow_S$.

proposition 3.4.3 A saturated set S of disequations is consistent iff $S \downarrow_S$.

Next proposition is a straightforward consequence of proposition 3.4.3.

proposition 3.4.4 For every consistent set S of disequations, if S is saturated then $S\downarrow$ and $\rightarrow_S \subseteq \rightarrow$.

Consequently, if S is a saturated set of disequations then its consistency can be decided. Finally, it is remarkable that if $S \rightarrow_S T$ and if the reduction occurs in some equation of S then $\vdash_{El} S \Leftrightarrow T$.

proposition 3.4.5 For every set S, if $S \rightarrow_S T$ and if the reduction occurs in some equation of S then $\vdash_{El} S \Leftrightarrow T$.

proof If $S \rightarrow_S T$ then, according to proposition 3.3.3, $\vdash_{El} S \Rightarrow T$. Moreover, there are a position p of S, a substitution σ and a variant $Q \Rightarrow l \rightarrow r$ such that $S_{/p} = c_l\sigma$, $T = S[r\sigma]_p$, for every $u=v$ in Q, $u\sigma \downarrow_S v\sigma$ and, for every $u \neq v$ in Q, there is $u' \neq v'$ in S such that $u\sigma \downarrow_S u'$ and $v\sigma \downarrow_S v'$. If the reduction occurs in some equation of S then $S^- = T^-$ and $\rightarrow_S = \rightarrow_T$. Let $u=v$ be in Q. Then, $u\sigma \downarrow_T v\sigma$ and, according to proposition 3.3.3, $\vdash_{El} T \Rightarrow u\sigma = v\sigma$. Let $u \neq v$ be in Q. Then, there is $u' \neq v'$ in T such that $u\sigma \downarrow_T u'$ and $v\sigma \downarrow_T v'$ and, according to proposition 3.3.3, $\vdash_{El} T \Rightarrow u\sigma = u'$ and $\vdash_{El} T \Rightarrow v\sigma = v'$. Since $\vdash_{El} T \Rightarrow u' \neq v'$, then $\vdash_{El} T \Rightarrow u\sigma \neq v\sigma$. Consequently, $\vdash_{El} T \Rightarrow Q\sigma$. Since $\vdash_{El} Q\sigma \Rightarrow l\sigma = r\sigma$, then $\vdash_{El} T \Rightarrow l\sigma = r\sigma$ and $\vdash_{El} T \Rightarrow S$.

As a consequence, if S is saturated, if $S \rightarrow_S T$, if either S or T is consistent and if the reduction occurs in some equation of S then T is saturated.

proposition 3.4.6 For every saturated set S, if $S \rightarrow_S T$, if either S or T is consistent and if the reduction occurs in some equation of S then T is saturated.

This proposition will be of great importance for the proof that saturation is preserved by narrowing.

4 Equation solving in projective planes

This section examines the problem of solving equations in M, that is to say : given any set S, find a substitution σ such that $S\sigma\downarrow$. Narrowing is a complete unification procedure for any equational theory defined by a canonical rewriting system [13]. It has been extended to conditional theories by Hußmann [14] and Kaplan [15]. Middeldorp and Hamoen [19] has given completeness results for basic narrowing in conditional theories. This section presents the extension of narrowing to R_l. One of its basic specializations terminates and provides a unification algorithm in M.

4.1 Conditional narrowing

A substitution σ is an *R_l-unifier* of a set S if:

$$S\sigma\downarrow$$

A substitution σ is *normalized* if, for every variable x in $D(\sigma)$, $\sigma(x)$ is not reducible. Let W be a set of "protected variables". The *narrowing relation* $\Rightarrow$ is defined in the following way. For every set S, $S \Rightarrow_{[p,\, Q \Rightarrow l \to r,\, \sigma,\, W]} T$ iff there are:

(i) an equation $s=t$ in S
(ii) a non variable position p in s
(iii) a variant $Q \Rightarrow l \to r$
(iv) a mgu σ of $s_{/p}$ and l modulo C away from W such that $T=S\sigma[r\sigma]_p \cup Q\sigma$

The set T is called a *surreduction* of S.

theorem 4.1.1(h) *(soundness of narrowing)* For every saturated set S, for every narrowing sequence $S_0=S \Rightarrow_{\sigma 1} S_1 \Rightarrow_{\sigma 2} \dots \Rightarrow_{\sigma n} S_n$ and for every R_l-unifier μ of S_n, the substitution $\sigma=\sigma_1 o \sigma_2 \dots o \sigma_n o \mu$ is an R_l-unifier of S.

It can be proved, as a consequence of proposition 3.4.6, that saturation is preserved by surreduction: for every saturated set S, if $S \Rightarrow T$ and if T is consistent then S is consistent and T is saturated. As a consequence, for every saturated set S, for every narrowing sequence $S_0=S \Rightarrow_{\sigma 1} S_1 \Rightarrow_{\sigma 2} \dots \Rightarrow_{\sigma n} S_n$, for every mgu μ of $S_n{}^+$ modulo C such that $S_n{}^-\mu\downarrow$ and, for every $i=0,\dots,n$, S_i is consistent and saturated. This property is of fundamental importance for the completeness proof of narrowing.

theorem 4.1.2(h) *(completeness of narrowing)* For every saturated set S, for every normalized R_l-unifier θ of S and for every set W of "protected variables" containing $Var(S)$ and $D(\theta)$, there exist a narrowing sequence $S_0=S \Rightarrow_{\sigma 1} S_1 \Rightarrow_{\sigma 2} \dots \Rightarrow_{\sigma n} S_n$ away from W and a mgu μ of $S_n{}^+$ modulo C away from W such that $\sigma=\sigma_1 o \sigma_2 \dots o \sigma_n o \mu \leq_C \theta\ [W]$ and $S_n{}^-\mu\downarrow$.

Let S be a saturated set and W be a set of "protected variables" containing $Var(S)$. A narrowing sequence $S_0=S \Rightarrow_{\sigma 1} S_1 \Rightarrow_{\sigma 2} \dots \Rightarrow_{\sigma n} S_n$ away from W together with a mgu μ of $S_n{}^+$ modulo C away from W such that $S_n{}^-\mu\downarrow$ will be denoted by: $S \Rightarrow_{[\theta, W]}{}^* S_n$ where $\theta=\sigma_1 o \sigma_2 \dots o \sigma_n o \mu$.

corollary 4.1.3 For every saturated set S and for every set W of "protected variables" containing $Var(S)$, the set $CSU_{Rl}(S)\ [W] = \{\theta/Var(S): S \Rightarrow_{[\theta,W],*} S'\}$ is a complete set of R_l-unifiers of S away from W, that is to say: for every normalized R_l-unifier σ of S, there is a substitution θ in $CSU_{Rl}(S)\ [W]$ such that $\theta \leq_C \sigma\ [Var(S)]$.

4.2 Basic conditional narrowing

Basic narrowing [13] restricts surreductions to subterms that have not been introduced by instantiation. A narrowing sequence $S_0=S \Rightarrow_{\sigma 1} S_1 \Rightarrow_{\sigma 2} \ldots \Rightarrow_{\sigma n} S_n$ using variants $Q_1 \Rightarrow l_1 \rightarrow r_1, Q_2 \Rightarrow l_2 \rightarrow r_2, \ldots, Q_n \Rightarrow l_n \rightarrow r_n$ at positions $p_1, p_2, \ldots, p_n$ in equations $e_1, e_2, \ldots, e_n$ is *basic* if, for every $i=1,\ldots,n$, p_i belongs to $B_i(e_i)$ where the sets of positions $B_1(e_1), \ldots, B_n(e_n)$ are inductively defined by: *(i)* B_1 is the set of non variable positions in $S_0{}^+$ and *(ii)* if e' belongs to $S_i \backslash \{e_i\}$ then $B_{i+1}(e)=B_i(e')$ else if e' is the equation $e_i[r_i]_{p_i}$ then $B_{i+1}(e)= \mathfrak{B}(B_i(e_i),p_i,r_i)$ else e' belongs to Q_i and $B_{i+1}(e)$ is equal to the set of non variable positions in e' where $i=1,\ldots,n$ and e is an equation $e'\sigma_i$ belonging to S_{i+1}, the expression $\mathfrak{B}(B_i(e_i),p_i,r_i)$ abbreviating $(B_i(e_i) \backslash \{q \in B_i(e_i): p_i \leq q\}) \cup \{p_i.q: q$ is a non variable position in $r_i\}$.

theorem 4.2.1 *(completeness of basic narrowing)* For every saturated set S, for every normalized R_l-unifier θ of S and for every set W of "protected variables" containing $Var(S)$ and $D(\theta)$, there exist a basic narrowing sequence $S_0=S \Rightarrow_{\sigma 1} S_1 \Rightarrow_{\sigma 2} \ldots \Rightarrow_{\sigma n} S_n$ away from W and a mgu μ of $S_n{}^+$ modulo C away from W such that $\sigma=\sigma_1 o \sigma_2 \ldots o \sigma_n o \mu \leq_C \theta\ [W]$ and $S_n{}^- \mu \downarrow$.

Basic conditional narrowing does not always terminate. For example, the basic sequence:

$S_0=\{p(X^{(0)},x)=Y,\ p(Y,y)=p(X^{(0)},x)\} \Rightarrow_{\sigma 1}$

$S_1=\{p(X^{(1)},x)=Y,\ p(Y,y)=p(p(X^{(1)},x),x)\}$

$S_1 \Rightarrow_{\sigma 2} S_2=\{p(X^{(1)},x)=Y,\ p(Y,y)=p(X^{(1)},x)\}$

$S_2 \Rightarrow_{\sigma 3} S_3=\{p(X^{(2)},x)=Y,\ p(Y,y)=p(p(X^{(2)},x),x)\}$

$S_3 \Rightarrow_{\sigma 4} S_4=\{p(X^{(2)},x)=Y,\ p(Y,y)=p(X^{(2)},x)\} \Rightarrow_{\sigma 5}$ etc ...

is an infinite basic narrowing sequence using R_{16} and substitutions $\sigma_1=\{X^{(0)}=p(X^{(1)},x)\}$, $\sigma_2=\emptyset$, $\sigma_3=\{X^{(1)}=p(X^{(2)},x)\}$, $\sigma_5=\emptyset$, etc.

4.3 Termination of basic narrowing

A complete strategy preventing infinite surreductions is presented here. A substitution σ is *saturated* if, for every variable x in $D(\sigma)$ and for every subterm in $\sigma(x)$ of the form $l(u,v)$ or $i(u,v)$, $u \not\downarrow v$. It goes without saying that non saturated R_l-unifiers have no geometrical interest. It can be proved that[h], for every saturated set S and for every set W of "protected variables" containing $Var(S)$, every substitution σ in $CSU_{Rl}(S)$

$[W]$ is saturated. Moreover, for every saturated and normalized R_l-unifier θ of S, every substitution σ in $CSU_{Rl}(S)$ $[W]$ such that $\sigma \leq_C \theta$ $[W]$ is normalized. Similarly, if $\sigma=\sigma_1 o \sigma_2 ... o \sigma_n o \mu$ then one can proved that, for every $i=1,...,n$, the substitution $\sigma_1 o \sigma_2 ... o \sigma_i$ is normalized.

Let θ be a saturated and normalized R_l-unifier of some saturated S. The basic narrowing mechanism which computes $\sigma_1, \sigma_2, ..., \sigma_n$ can be constrained in such a way that, for every narrowing sequence $S_0=S \Rightarrow_{\sigma 1} S_1 \Rightarrow_{\sigma 2} ... \Rightarrow_{\sigma i} S_i$ already computed, every narrowing step $S_i \Rightarrow_{\sigma i+1} S_{i+1}$ such that $\sigma_1 o \sigma_2 ... o \sigma_i o \sigma_{i+1}$ is not normalized should not be considered. Therefore, the definition of basic narrowing has to be modified so that: (C_1) if rule R_{l6} is used on some subterm $p(X,x)$ at a position p_i in some equation e_i of S_{i-1} and if X is a variable then R_{l6} should not be applied again at the same position in the same equation since, otherwise, the substitution computed by the narrowing process would not be normalized. Thus, in this case solely, the expression $\mathfrak{B}(B_i(e_i),p_i,r_i)$ abbreviates $B_i(e_i)\backslash\{q \in B_i(e_i): p_i \leq q\}$. In all other cases, $\mathfrak{B}(B_i(e_i),p_i,r_i)$ remains unchanged. Moreover: (C_2) if a narrowing step $S \Rightarrow_\sigma T$ is applied on some equation $p(X,x)=X$ of S to the term $p(X,x)$ then the resulting equation $X\sigma=X\sigma$ is deleted from T. From now on, every basic narrowing sequence will satisfy the constraints C_1 and C_2 above.

theorem 4.3.3 For every saturated set S, there is no infinite basic narrowing sequence starting with S satisfying the constraints C_1 and C_2 above.

Consequently, the set of normalized R_l-unifiers in $CSU_{Rl}(S)$ $[W]$ is finite and R_l-unifiability of saturated sets can always be decided.

corollary 4.3.4 R_l-unification is finitary and constitutes a decidable class of problems for which a type conformal algorithm exists: for every saturated set S and for every set W of "protected variables" containing $Var(S)$, the set of normalized R_l-unifier in $CSU_{Rl}(S)$ $[W]$ is finite ; moreover, there is an algorithm that, given S and W, terminates and computes the set of normalized R_l-unifiers in $CSU_{Rl}(S)$ $[W]$.

4.4 Equation solving in projective geometry

This section analyses what it means for a substitution to be an R_l-unifier. Let S be a saturated set. For every narrowing sequence $S_0=S \Rightarrow_{\sigma 1} S_1 \Rightarrow_{\sigma 2} ... \Rightarrow_{\sigma n} S_n$ and for every mgu μ of S_n^+ modulo C such that $S_n^-\mu\downarrow$, the following sets are defined: $\Sigma_i=((...(S_i\sigma_{i+1} \cup S_{i+1})\sigma_{i+2} \cup ...)\sigma_{n-1} \cup S_{n-1})\sigma_n \cup S_n$, $i=1,...,n$. One can prove by induction on i that, for every $i=0,...,n$, Σ_i is saturated. Consequently, it can be proved that $\vdash_{El} S_n^-\mu \Rightarrow S\sigma_1 o \sigma_2 ... o \sigma_n o \mu$. Therefore, narrowing computes two things: an R_l-unifier $\sigma=\sigma_1 o \sigma_2 ... o \sigma_n o \mu$ of a given saturated set S and a finite set $S_n^-\mu$ of negative conditions such that $\vdash_{El} S_n^-\mu \Rightarrow S^+\sigma$. The negative conditions $S_n^-\mu$ can be considered as *nondegenerate conditions* that the variables in $S^+\sigma$ have to satisfy.

example The narrowing sequence:

$S_0=\{l(i(x,y),X)=x,\ i(x,y)\neq X,\ x\neq y\} \Rightarrow_{\sigma 1} S_1=\{p(X,x)=X,\ i(x,y)\neq X,\ x\neq y\}$
$S_1 \Rightarrow_{\sigma 2} S_2=\{i(x,y)\neq p(X',x),\ x\neq y\}$

using R_{11}, R_{16} and substitutions $\sigma_1=\emptyset$, $\sigma_2=\{X=p(X',x)\}$ proves that $\vdash_{E1} i(x,y)\neq p(X',x) \wedge x\neq y \Rightarrow l(i(x,y),p(X',x))=x$.

5 Equation solving in planar ternary rings

Any algebraic system S of equations in the language of TS can be expressed as a set S_0 of equations and disequations in the language of E_1. Every geometrical solution for S_0 corresponds to some algebraic solution for S.

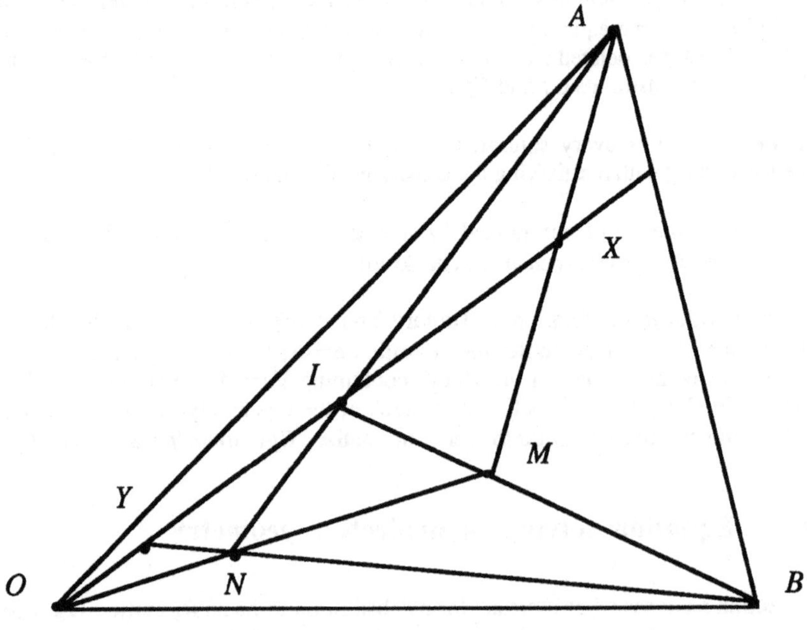

Fig. 3 A geometrical solution to the equation $x.y=1$

Let $[\Gamma,T]$ be a PTR. The binary operations + and . are defined in Γ by $x+y=T(x,1,y)$ and $x.y=T(x,y,0)$. Let S be a set of equations in the language of TS of the form $T(x,y,z)=t$ where x, y, z and t are either variables or the constants 0 and 1. Let $x_1, x_2, \ldots, x_k$ be the variables occurring in S. Let Π be the PP associated to $[\Gamma,T]$ with points A, $B=(0)$, $O=(0,0)$ and $I=(1,1)$ as base points of a coordinate systems. Let $X_1, X_2, \ldots, X_k$ be pairwise distinct variables of type Σ. To every equation $T(x_1,x_2,x_3)=x_4$ in S is associated the equation

$i(l(O,I),l(B,i(l(A,X_1),l(i(l(A,O),l(B,X_3)),i(l(A,B),l(O,i(l(A,I),l(B,X_2)))))))) = X_4$

Let S_0 be the smallest saturated set in the language of E_l containing these equations, the disequations $A \neq B, p(O,l(A,B)) \neq O, p(I,l(A,B)) \neq I, p(I,l(A,O)) \neq I, p(I,l(B,O)) \neq I$, the equations $p(X_i,l(O,I))=X_i$, $i=1,\ldots,k$, and the disequations $p(X_i,l(A,B)) \neq X_i$, $i=1,\ldots,k$.

example Let $S=\{x.y=1\}$. Then, the associated saturated set S_0 contains the equation $i(l(O,I),l(B,i(l(A,X),l(i(l(A,O),l(B,O)),i(l(A,B),l(O,i(l(A,I),l(B,Y))))))))=I$ which, in the context of the disequations contained in S_0, is equivalent to

$$i(l(O,I),l(B,i(l(A,X),l(O,i(l(A,B),l(O,i(l(A,I),l(B,Y))))))))=I$$

The substitution $\sigma=\{X=p(X',l(O,I)), Y=i(l(O,I),l(B,i(l(A,I),l(O,i(l(A,p(X',l(O,I))),l(B,I))))))\}$ can be computed by the basic narrowing procedure in the following way. Let:

(0) $S_0 = \{i(l(O,I),l(B,i(l(A,X),l(O,i(l(A,B),l(O,i(l(A,I),l(B,Y)))))))) = I,$
$p(X,l(O,I)) = X, p(Y,l(O,I)) = Y, \ldots\}$

Then, using substitution $\sigma_1=\{Y=i(l(O,I),y_1)\}$ and rule R_{15}, one has $S_0 \Rightarrow_{\sigma 1} S_1$ with:

(1) $S_1 = \{i(l(O,I),l(B,i(l(A,X),l(O,i(l(A,B),l(O,i(l(A,I),l(B,i(l(O,I),$
$y_1)))))))))) = I, p(X,l(O,I)) = X, \ldots\}$

Now, using substitution $\sigma_2=\emptyset$ and rule R_{11}, one has $S_1 \Rightarrow_{\sigma 2} S_2$ with:

(2) $S_2 = \{i(l(O,I),l(B,i(l(A,X),l(O,i(l(A,B),l(O,i(l(A,I),y_1))))))) = I, p(B,y_1) =$
$B, p(X,l(O,I)) = X, \ldots\}$

etc ...

(12) $S_{12} = \{i(l(O,I),y_{11}) = I, p(B,y_{11}) = B, p(X,l(O,I)) = X, \ldots\}$

Then, using substitution $\sigma_{13}=\{y_{11}=l(B,Y_{13})\}$ and rule R_{14}, one has $S_{12} \Rightarrow_{\sigma 13} S_{13}$ with:

(13) $S_{13} = \{i(l(O,I),l(B,Y_{13})) = I, p(X,l(O,I)) = X, \ldots\}$

Now, using substitution $\sigma_{14}=\emptyset$ and rule R_{13}, one has $S_{13} \Rightarrow_{\sigma 14} S_{14}$ with:

(14) $S_{14} = \{Y_{13} = I, p(Y_{13},l(O,I)) = Y_{13}, p(X,l(O,I)) = X, \ldots\}$

Finally, using substitution $\sigma_{15}=\{Y_{13}=I\}$, and rule R_{14}, one has $S_{14} \Rightarrow_{\sigma 15} S_{15}$ with:

(15) $S_{15} = \{p(X,l(O,I)) = X, \ldots\}$

and, using substitution $\sigma_{16}=\{X=p(X',l(O,I))\}$, and rule R_{16}, one has $S_{15} \Rightarrow_{\sigma 16} S_{16}$ with:

(16) $S_{16} = \{p(i(l(O,I), l(B, i(l(A,I), l(O, i(l(A, p(X', l(O,I))), l(B,I))))), l(A,B)) \neq i(l(O,I), l(B, i(l(A,I), l(O, i(l(A, p(X', l(O,I))), l(B,I))))), ...\}$

This geometrical solution to the equation $x.y=1$ can be depicted in the following way. Let X be a point on OI corresponding by γ to x. Let M be the point in which AX intersects BI and N be the point in which AI intersects OM, and let Y be the point in which OI intersects BN. Then, the element in Γ that corresponds by γ to Y is the sole element y in Γ such that $x.y=1$.

In this example, the basic narrowing procedure also computes the finite set S_{16}^- of nondegenerate conditions. One of them:

$p(i(l(O,I), l(B, i(l(A,I), l(O, i(l(A, p(X', l(O,I))), l(B,I))))), l(A,B)) \neq i(l(O,I), l(B, i(l(A, I), l(O, i(l(A, p(X', l(O,I))), l(B,I)))))$

implicitly says that x is distinct from 0. More precisely, $x=0$ which corresponds to $p(X',l(O,I))=O$ is a contradiction since it implies that $p(i(l(O, I), l(B, i(l(A, I), l(O, i(l(A, p(X', l(O,I))), l(B,I))))), l(A,B))$ and $i(l(O,I), l(B, i(l(A,I), l(O, i(l(A, p(X', l(O, I))), l(B,I)))))$ are both equal to $i(l(O,I), l(B,A))$.

6 Conclusion

The narrowing mechanism computes a finite set S_n-μ of nondegenerate conditions. These conditions are geometrical disequations in the language of the first order theory E_l equivalent to PG. It should be questioned whether they can always be translated into the language of PTR. This problem faces algebraic approaches to geometrical reasoning. Buchberger's algorithm [6] and Wu's method [22] both compute polynomial conditions $f_i \neq 0, ..., f_m \neq 0$ that can hardly be translated into geometrical expressions. In other respects, the evaluation of the complexity of the narrowing mechanism is still to be done in order to estimate the operational usability of this geometrical approach to algebraic reasoning in TS. It should be questioned whether strategies like left-to-right basic narrowing [12] and LSE narrowing [5] can improve the efficiency of the unification algorithm.

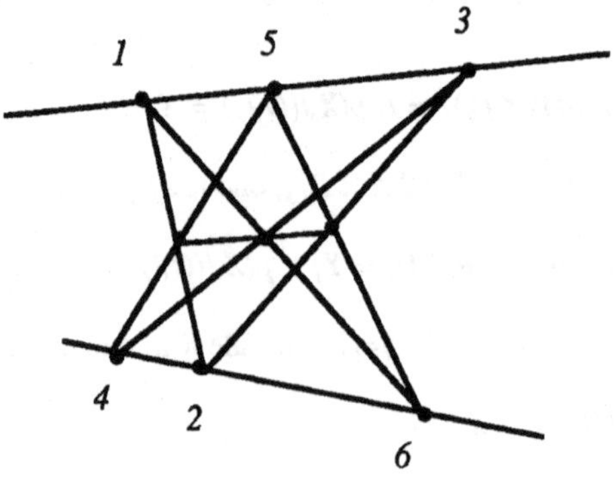

Fig. 4 The Pappus' property

Next remark is of some interest for the unification problem in commutative fields. The mechanism presented in this paper is able to solve every algebraic problems in ternary systems ($x+y=0$, $x.y=1$, $x.y+x=0$, etc). A PP has the Pappus' property if, for any six pairwise distinct points of two distinct lines, labeling three points of one line *1*, *3*, *5* and three points of the other *2*, *4*, *6*, the three pairs *12* and *45*, *23* and *56*, and *34* and *61* of lines intersect in three points of a line. A pappian plane is a PP satisfying the Pappus' property. Any PTR associated to a pappian plane is commutative for multiplication, that is to say: every PTR defined in a pappian plane is a commutative field and every PP defined over a commutative field is pappian [4]. Consequently, solving equations in commutative fields is equivalent to solving equations in pappian planes. It should be asked whether it is possible to extend E_l to a first order theory with equality equivalent to Pappus' geometry. If one answers positively then one might be able to define a unification algorithm for commutative fields.

Notes ***(a)*** Philippe Balbiani, ***1.*** Institut de recherche en informatique de Toulouse, Université Paul Sabatier, 118 route de Narbonne, F-31062 Toulouse Cedex or ***2.*** Institut de recherche en informatique de Toulouse, 58 avenue de la république, F-93110 Rosny-sous-bois. ***(b)*** It should be observed that other first order theories with equality equivalent to affine incidence geometry has been studied in [1], [2] and [3]. ***(c)*** The extension of narrowing to P/N CTRS has been detailed in [1]. ***(d)*** If and only if. ***(e)*** This is a straightforward consequence of the postulates. ***(f)*** Those properties are obvious consequences of postulates P_0 through P_3. ***(g)*** The interested reader is invited to refer to the book from Blumenthal [4] where the abstract equivalence between PG and PTR is fully established. ***(h)*** See [1] for a complete proof. ***(i)*** The reader is assumed to be familiar with the usual conventions and definitions of term rewriting and unification. The interested reader is invited to co nsult Dershowitz and Jouannaud [10], Rusinowitch [20] or Snyder [21] for details. ***(j)*** Most general unifier.

References

1. P. Balbiani, V. Dugat, L. Fariñas del Cerro, A. Lopez: Eléments de géométrie mécanique. Hermès, Paris, France, 1994

2. P. Balbiani, L. Fariñas del Cerro. Affine geometry of collinearity and conditional term rewriting. In: Ecole de printemps d'informatique théorique, Font Romeu, France, mai 1993, Proceedings. Lecture Notes in Computer Science, Springer-Verlag, Berlin, Germany

3. P. Balbiani, A. Lopez: Simplification des figures de la géométrie affine plane d'incidence. In: Neuvième congrès reconnaissance des formes et intelligence artificielle, Paris, France, 11-14 janvier 1994

4. L. Blumenthal: A Modern View of Geometry. Freeman, San Francisco, California, 1961

5. A. Bockmayr, S. Krischer, A. Werner: An optimal narrowing strategy for general canonical systems. In J.-L. Rémy, M. Rusinowitch (editors): Conditional Term Rewriting Systems, 3rd International Workshop, Pont-à-Mousson, France, July 1992, Proceedings. Lecture Notes in Computer Science 656, Springer-Verlag, Berlin, Germany

6. B. Buchberger: Gröbner bases: an algorithmic method in polynomial ideal theory. In N. Bose (editor) : Recent Trends in Multidimensional Systems Theory. Reidel, Dordrecht, Netherlands, 1985

7. B. Buchberger, G. Collins, B. Kutzler: Algebraic methods for geometric reasoning. In: Ann. Rev. Comput. Sci., volume 3, pp. 85-119 (1988)

8. H.-J. Bürckert: Matching - a special case of unification ? In C. Kirchner (editor) : Unification, pages 125-138. Academic Press, London, Great Britain, 1990

9. S.-C. Chou: Mechanical Geometry Theorem Proving. Reidel, Dordrecht, Netherlands, 1988

10. N. Dershowitz, J.-P. Jouannaud: Rewrite systems. In J. van Leeuwen (editor): Handbook of Theoretical Computer Science, volume B, Formal Models and Semantics, pp. 243-320. Elsevier, Amsterdam, Netherlands, 1990

11. H. Ganzinger: A completion procedure for conditional equations. In S. Kaplan, J.-P. Jouannaud (editors): Conditional term Rewriting Systems, 1st International Workshop, Orsay, France, July 1987, Proceedings, pp. 62-83. Lecture Notes in Computer Science 308, Springer-Verlag, Berlin, Germany, 1988

12. A. Herold: Narrowing techniques applied to idempotent unification. Technical report SR-86-16, Universität Kaiserslautern

13. J.-M. Hullot: Canonical forms and unification. In: Fifth International Conference on Automated Deduction, Les Arcs, France, Proceedings, pp. 318-334. Lecture Notes in Computer Science 87, Springer-Verlag, Berlin, Germany, 1980

14. H. Hußmann: Unification in conditional equational theories. Proceedings of the European Conference on Computer Algebra, pp. 543-553. Lecture Notes in Computer Science 204, Springer-Verlag, Berlin, Germany, 1985

15. S. Kaplan: Simplifying conditional term rewriting systems: unification, termination and confluence. In : Journal of Symbolic Computation, volume 4, number 3, pp. 295-334, 1987

16. S. Kaplan: Positive/negative conditional rewriting. In S. Kaplan and J. P. Jouannaud (editors) : Conditional Term Rewriting Systems, 1st International Workshop, Orsay, France, July 1987, Proceedings,

pp. 129-143. Lecture Notes in Computer Science 308, Springer Verlag, Berlin, Germany, 1988

17. S. Kaplan, J.-L. Rémy: Completion algorithms for conditional rewriting systems. In H. Aït-Kaci and M. Nivat (editors): Resolution of Equations in Algebraic Structures, volume 2, Rewriting Techniques, pp. 141-170. Academic Press, San Diego, California, 1989

18. M. Martelli, U. Montanari: An efficient unification algorithm. In: ACM Transactions on Programming Languages and Systems, volume 4, number 2, pp. 258-282 (1982)

19. A. Middeldorp, E. Hamoen: Counterexamples to completeness results for basic narrowing. In H. Kirchner, G. Levi (editors) : Algebraic and Logic Programming, Third International ALP Conference, Volterra, Italy, September 1992, Proceedings, pp. 244-258. Lecture Notes in Computer Science 632, Springer-Verlag, Berlin, Germany, 1992

20. M. Rusinowitch: Démonstration automatique: techniques de réécriture. InterEditions, Paris, France, 1989

21. W. Snyder: A Proof Theory for General Unification. Birkhäuser, Boston, Massachusetts, 1991

22. W.-T. Wu: Basic principles of mechanical theorem proving in elementary geometries. In : Journal of Automated Reasoning, volume 2, number 3, pp. 221-252 (1986)

From Eventual to Atomic and Locally Atomic CC Programs: A Concurrent Semantics

F. Bueno*, M. Hermenegildo*
U. Montanari**, F. Rossi**

*Universidad Politécnica de Madrid (UPM), Facultad de Informática
28660 Boadilla del Monte, Madrid, Spain
E-mail: {bueno,herme}@fi.upm.es
**Università di Pisa, Dipartimento di Informatica
Corso Italia 40, 56125 Pisa, Italy
E-mail: {ugo,rossi}@di.unipi.it

Abstract. We present a concurrent semantics (i.e. a semantics where concurrency is explicitely represented) for CC programs with atomic tells. This allows to derive concurrency, dependency, and nondeterminism information for such languages. The ability to treat failure information puts CLP programs also in the range of applicability of our semantics: although such programs are not concurrent, the concurrency information derived in the semantics may be interpreted as possible parallelism, thus allowing to safely parallelize those computation steps which appear to be concurrent in the net. Dually, the dependency information may also be interpreted as necessary sequentialization, thus possibly exploiting it to schedule CC programs. The fact that the semantical structure contains dependency information suggests a new tell operation, which checks for consistency only the constraints it depends on, achieving a reasonable trade-off between efficiency and atomicity.

1 Introduction

A concurrent constraint (CC) program [Sar93, SR90, SRP91] consists of a set of agents interacting through a shared store, which is a set of constraints on some variables. The framework is parametric w.r.t. the kind of constraints handled. The concurrent agents do not communicate with each other, but only with the shared store, by either checking if it entails a given constraint (ask operation) or adding a new constraint to it (tell operation). Therefore computations proceed by monotonically accumulating information (that is, constraints) into the store.

The semantics of CC programs is usually given following the SOS-style operational semantics [SR90, SRP91, BP91], and thus suffering from the typical pathologies of an interleaving semantics. On the other hand, the concurrent semantics approach introduced in [MR91], which is equipped with a non-monolithic model of the shared store and of its communication with the agents, allows to express uniformly the behavior of the store and that of the agents, and, as a consequence, to derive a semantical structure where it is possible and easy to see the maximal level of both concurrency and nondeterminism in a given program.

Thus it can be much more useful than an interleaving semantics when exploiting semantic information for compile-time optimizations which require knowledge about any one of these two concepts. In fact, an interleaving semantics is not able to express such knowledge correctly, mainly due to the fact that concurrency is not directly expressible but is instead reduced to nondeterminism.

The concurrent semantics in [MR91], from which this paper starts from, is based on an operational semantics described via context-dependent rewrite rules. The evolution of each of the agents in a CC program, as well as the declarations of the program and its underlying constraint system, can all be expressed by sets of such rules. The concurrent semantical structure is then built from the rules by starting from the initial agent and unfolding it applying the rules in all possible ways. The result is a contextual net [MR93a], which is able to represent all the computations of a given CC program (as defined by its operational semantics) in a single structure, and for each of such computations to provide a partial order expressing the dependency pattern among the events of the computation.

There are two ways in which the basic tell operation of CC languages is usually interpreted: either *eventually*, which means that the constraint is added to the current store without any check, or *atomically*, which instead means that the constraint is added only if it is consistent with the current store. The concurrent semantics for CC programs in [MR93b]) follows the eventual interpretation. While the eventual interpretation of the tell operation allows for a completely uniform treatment of agents and constraints and thus a distributed representation of the constraint system, it suffers from the fact that possibly many computation steps of a failing computation are performed while not being needed. Therefore, the semantical structure presented in [MR93b] contained all such useless (and, most crucial, possibly infinite) parts of computations.

Here we modify such semantics to allow for the atomic interpretation of the tell operation. This implies that now we must have the possibility of knowing immediately if a set of constraints is consistent or not. Thus it may seem that we have to go back to the usual notion of a constraint system as a black box which can answer yes/no questions in one step (which is what is used in all the semantics other than [MR91, MR93b]). However, this is not true: the semantical structure we obtain still shows all the atomic entailment steps, thus allowing to derive the correct dependencies among agents.

The new semantics can be obtained from the old one by defining an inconsistency relation on agents and constraints, and then cutting all those parts of the semantical structure which depend on inconsistently "told" constraints. The basic idea is to derive the inconsistency relation from the constraint system, where we assume that an inconsistent set of constraints always entails the token *false*. Then, the inconsistency relation is propagated through the contextual net via the dependency relation. If, as a result of that, some items are inconsistent with themselves, then it means that they could not appear in any computation without creating an inconsistent state of affairs. Therefore we prune such items and everything that depends on them. We also define the new semantics from scratch (instead of first deriving the semantical structure for eventual tells and then pruning it), by adopting a slightly more complicated inference rule.

Since our semantics introduces an explicit representation for failure (i.e. the attempt to add a constraint which is inconsistent with the current store), we can say that we achieve a faithful model for capturing backtracking. In fact, the ability of recognizing independence and/or nondeterminism in CLP programs is crucial when one is interested in parallelizing such programs while retaining their semantic meaning (in terms of input-output relation and time complexity). This is true also for the *dual* task, that of scheduling CC programs [KS92, KT91] (although for such task the treatment of failure is not necessary).

Both such tasks need some knowledge on dependencies (or independence) of goals, since in the first one we want to parallelize only goals which are not dependent on each other, and in the second one we want to schedule later goals which may be dependent on earlier scheduled goals. The attractive point of the proposed semantics is that the dependency relation is an integral part of the semantics and thus parallelization and scheduling decisions can be made by rather direct observations on the semantical structure. Furthermore, the level of granularity offered by the semantics allows scheduling or parallelizing tasks of a new nature and at a new level of detail. For example, it is possible to parallelize across the operations of the constraint solver and thus to create parallel tasks that include part of the solver operations all in the same semantic framework.

While the atomic interpretation of the tell operation allows to recognize, and thus stop, a failing computation possibly much earlier, it has the disadvantage that it can be extremely costly to achieve, especially in a distributed implementation of a CC language. The store could be scattered over many locations, and thus checking its consistency with the new constraint to be told could require locking all the locations and thus all the other operations until the consistency check has been performed. For this reason, it would be reasonable to achieve a convenient trade-off between efficiency and atomicity, thus defining a new interpretation of the tell operation, which just checks some of the constraints in the current store, and not all of them. Our semantics gives a very natural hint on the definition and also the possible implementation of one such interpretation of the tell operation. In fact, being based on dependency information, it is natural to think of checking for consistency only the part of the current store on which the tell operation is dependent on. The interesting, and convenient, thing is that these are the constraints which are in some sense responsible for the presence of the tell agent, and therefore, in a distributed implementation, could be stored in a memory which is local to that agent. This means that they will be the most easily accessible and that thus the tell operation can be performed efficiently. For this locality reason we call this new operation a *locally atomic* tell.

2 Concurrent Constraint Programming

In the CC paradigm, the underlying constraint system can be described [SRP91] as a *partial information system* (derived from the *information system* introduced in [Sco82]) of the form $\langle D, \vdash \rangle$ where D is a set of *tokens* (or primitive constraints) and $\vdash \subseteq \wp(D) \times D$ is the entailment relation which states which tokens are entailed by which sets of other tokens. The relation $\vdash$ has to be reflexive and transitive. Note that there is no notion of consistency in a partial information system. This means that inconsistency has to be modelled through entailment. More precisely, the convention is that D contains a $false$ element, so that an inconsistent set of tokens is that one which entails $false$.

Given D, $\mid D \mid$ is the set of all subsets of D closed under entailment. Then, a constraint in a constraint system $\langle D, \vdash \rangle$ is simply an element of $\mid D \mid$, that is, a set of tokens, closed under entailment. In the rest of the paper we will consider a constraint as simply a set of tokens.

Consider the class of programs P, the class of sequences of procedure declarations F, and the class of agents A. Let c range over constraints, and $\mathbf{x}$ denote a tuple of variables. The following grammar describes the CC language we consider:

$$P ::= F.A \qquad\qquad F ::= p(\mathbf{x}) :: A \mid F.F$$

$$A ::= success \mid failure \mid tell(c) \rightarrow A \mid \sum_{i=1,\ldots,n} ask(c_i) \rightarrow A_i \mid A \parallel A \mid \exists \mathbf{x}.A \mid p(\mathbf{x})$$

Each procedure is defined once, thus nondeterminism is expressed via the + combinator only (which is here denoted by $\sum$). We also assume that, in $p(\mathbf{x}) :: A$, $vars(A) \subseteq \mathbf{x}$, where $vars(A)$ is the set of all variables occurring free in agent A. In a program $P = F.A$, A is called initial agent, to be executed in the context of the set of declarations F.

Agent "$\sum_{i=1,\ldots,n} ask(c_i) \rightarrow A_i$" behaves as a set of guarded agents A_i, where the success of the guard $ask(c_i)$ coincides with the entailment of the constraint c_i by the current store. If instead c_i is inconsistent with the current store, then the guard fails. Lastly, if c_i is not entailed but it is consistent with the current store, then the guarded agent gets suspended. No particular order of selection of the guarded agents is assumed, and only one of the choices is taken. In an "atomic" interpretation of the tell operation, agent "tell(c) $\rightarrow$ A" adds constraint c to the current store and then, if the resulting store is consistent, behaves like A, otherwise it fails; in an "eventual" interpretation of the tell, this same agent adds c to the store (without any consistency check) and then behaves like A (if the resulting store is inconsistent this will result in an uncontrolled behaviour of the system, since from now on all ask operations will succeed).

Given a program P, in the following we will refer to $Ag(P)$ as the set of all agents (and subagents) occurring in P, i.e. all the elements of type A occurring in a derivation of P according to the above grammar.

The CC language we consider in this paper does not use the notion of *cylindric* constraint system, as defined for example in [SRP91]. Therefore, constraints cannot be projected over some of their variables. However, we strongly believe that our whole framework and results can be extended to this more general case. Another extension could be the presence of tell agents in the guards of an indeterministic agent: this would certainly not cause any problem to our approach. We have made a less general choice here for space reasons.

3 The Operational Semantics

Each state of a CC computation consists of a multiset of (active) agents and of (already generated) tokens. Each computation step models either the evolution of a single agent, or the entailment of a new token through the $\vdash$ relation. Such a change in the state of the computation is performed via the application of a rewrite rule. There are as many rewrite rules as the number of agents and declarations in a program (which is finite), plus the number of pairs of the entailment relation (which can be infinite).

Definition 1 (computation state). Given a program $P = F.A$ with a constraint system $\langle D, \vdash \rangle$, a state is a multiset of elements of $Ag(P) \cup D$. □

Definition 2 (rewrite rules). Have the form $r : L(r)(\mathbf{x}) \stackrel{c(r)(\mathbf{x})}{\leadsto} R(r)(\mathbf{xy})$ where $L(r)$ is an agent, $c(r)$ is a constraint, and $R(r)$ is a state. Also, $\mathbf{x}$ is the tuple of variables appearing in both $L(r) \cup c(r)$ and in $R(r)$, while $\mathbf{y}$ is the tuple of variables appearing free only in $R(r)$. □

The intuitive meaning of a rule is that $L(r)$,[1] which is called the left hand side of the rule, is rewritten into (or replaced by) $R(r)$, i.e. the right hand side, if $c(r)$ is present in the current state. $R(r)$ could contain some variables not appearing (free) in $L(r)$ nor in $c(r)$ (i.e. the tuple $\mathbf{y}$). As computations will be defined over *constants*, then the application of r would have to rename such variables $\mathbf{y}$ to constants which are different from all the others already in use. The items in $c(r)$ have to be interpreted as a context, since it is necessary for the application of the rule but it is not affected by such application. In the CC framework, such context is used to represent asked constraints.

Definition 3 (from programs to rules). The rules corresponding to agents, declarations, and entailment pairs are given as follows:

1. $(tell(c) \to A) \leadsto c, A$
2. $A_1 \parallel A_2 \leadsto A_1, A_2$
3. $\exists \mathbf{x}.A \leadsto A$
4. $(\sum_{i=1,\ldots,n} ask(c_i) \to A_i) \stackrel{c_i}{\leadsto} A_i \quad \forall i = 1, \ldots, n$
5. $p(\mathbf{x}) \leadsto A$ for all $p(\mathbf{x}) :: A$
6. $\stackrel{S}{\leadsto} t$ for all $S \vdash t$

Given a CC program $P = F.A$ and its underlying constraint system $\langle D, \vdash \rangle$, we will call $RR(P)$ the set of rewrite rules associated to P, which consists of the rules corresponding to all agents in $Ag(P)$, plus the rules representing the declarations in F, plus those rules representing the pairs of the entailment relation. □

In an eventual CC language, a rule r can be applied to a state S_1 if both the left hand side of r and its context can be found (via a suitable substitution) in S_1. The application of r removes its left and adds its right hand side to S_1.

[1] Note that in a slight abuse of notation we consider $L(r)$ as a set, which will be either a singleton or the empty set.

Definition 4 (eventual computation steps). Let a computation state $S_1(\mathbf{a})$ and a rule $r : L(r)(\mathbf{x}) \overset{c(r)(\mathbf{x})}{\leadsto} R(r)(\mathbf{xy})$, such that $(L(r) \cup c(r))[\mathbf{a}/\mathbf{x}] \subseteq S_1(\mathbf{a})$. The application of r to S_1 is an eventual computation step which yields a new computation state $S_2 = (S_1 \setminus L(r)[\mathbf{a}/\mathbf{x}]) \cup R(r)[\mathbf{a}/\mathbf{x}][\mathbf{b}/\mathbf{y}]$, where the constants in $\mathbf{b}$ are fresh, i.e. they do not appear in S_1. We will write $S_1 \overset{r[\mathbf{a}/\mathbf{x}][\mathbf{b}/\mathbf{y}]}{\Longrightarrow} S_2$. □

Instead, in an atomic CC language, not only the left hand side and the context of a rule have to match some elements in the current state, but also, if the rule implements a tell agent, a check has to be done for the constraints that such tell wants to add to be consistent with the current store.

Definition 5 (atomic computation steps). Let a computation state $S_1(\mathbf{a})$ and a rule $r : L(r)(\mathbf{x}) \overset{c(r)(\mathbf{x})}{\leadsto} R(r)(\mathbf{xy})$, such that

- $(L(r) \cup c(r))[\mathbf{a}/\mathbf{x}] \subseteq S_1(\mathbf{a})$ and
- if $r = ((tell(c) \to A) \leadsto c, A)$, then $c \cup cons(S_1) \not\vdash false$ (where $cons(S)$ is the set of constraints in state S)

The application of r to S_1 is an atomic computation step which yields a new computation state $S_2 = (S_1 \setminus L(r)[\mathbf{a}/\mathbf{x}]) \cup R(r)[\mathbf{a}/\mathbf{x}][\mathbf{b}/\mathbf{y}]$, where the constants in $\mathbf{b}$ are fresh, i.e. they do not appear in S_1. We will write $S_1 \overset{r[\mathbf{a}/\mathbf{x}][\mathbf{b}/\mathbf{y}]}{\Longrightarrow} S_2$. □

Definition 6 (computations). Given a CC program $P = F.A$, an eventual (resp. atomic) computation segment for P is any sequence of eventual (resp. atomic) computation steps $S_1 \overset{r_1[\mathbf{a_1}/\mathbf{x_1}]}{\Longrightarrow} S_2 \overset{r_2[\mathbf{a_2}/\mathbf{x_2}]}{\Longrightarrow} S_3 \ldots$ such that $S_1 = \{A[\mathbf{a_0}/\mathbf{x_0}]\}$ and $r_i \in RR(P)$, i = 1,2, ... Two eventual (resp. atomic) computation segments which are the same except that different fresh constants are employed in the various steps, are called α-equivalent. An eventual (resp. atomic) computation is an eventual (resp. atomic) computation segment CS such that for each eventual (resp. atomic) computation segment CS', of which CS is a prefix, CS' adds to CS only steps applying rules for the entailment relation. □

Definition 7 (successful, suspended, and failing computations). A successful computation is a finite computation where the last state contains only a set of constraints, say S, and $S \not\vdash false$. A suspended computation is a finite computation where the last state does not contain tell agents but contains ask agents, and its set of constraints S is such that $S \not\vdash false$. A failing computation is a computation which is neither successful nor suspended. □

Notice that a computation has been defined as a sequence of computation steps which is maximal w.r.t. the evolution of the agents. This means that there could be some subsequent step due to the entailment relation, but no step due to the agents. The reason for this is that, after all the agents have evolved, there could be an infinite number of entailment steps, and still we do not want to consider such a computation failing just because of that. A consequence of this is that to recognize a successful computation we have to ask the constraint system for a consistency test even in an eventual environment. Thus, the difference between atomic and eventual tell is just *when* such a check is asked for.

In the following we will only consider either finite computations or infinite computations which are fair. Here fairness means, informally, that if a rule can continuously be applied from some point onwards, then it will eventually be applied. This implies that both goal selection (among several goals in the current state) and rule selection (among several rules applicable to a goal) are fair.

Definition 8 (eventual and atomic operational semantics). Given a CC program $P = F.A$, its eventual operational semantics, say $EO(P)$, is the set of all its eventual computations, and its atomic operational semantics, say $AO(P)$, is the set of all its atomic computations. □

4 Contextual Nets and Consistent Contextual Nets

In the following, we assume the reader to be familiar with the classical notions of nets. For the formal definitions missing here we refer to [Rei85] and [MR93a].

4.1 Contextual Nets

The formal technique which we use to introduce contexts consists in adding a new relation, besides the usual flow relation, which we call the *context relation*.

Definition 9 (contextual nets). A contextual net is a quadruple $(B, E; F_1, F_2)$ where elements of B are called conditions and those of E events; $F_1 \subseteq (B \times E) \cup (E \times B)$ is called the flow relation; $F_2 \subseteq (B \times E)$ is called the context relation; and it holds that $B \cap E = \emptyset$ and $(F_1 \cup F_1^{-1}) \cap F_2 = \emptyset$. □

Definition 10 (pre-set, post-set, and context). Given a contextual net $N = (B, E; F_1, F_2)$ and an element $x \in B \cup E$, the pre-set of x is the set $^\bullet x = \{y \mid yF_1x)\}$; the post-set of x is the set $x^\bullet = \{y \mid xF_1y)\}$; the context of x is defined if $x \in E$ and it is the set $\widehat{x} = \{y \mid yF_2x)\}$. □

Contextual nets will be graphically represented in the same way as nets. Thus, conditions are circles, events are boxes, the flow relation is represented by directed arcs from circles to boxes or viceversa, and the context relation by undirected arcs. An example of a contextual net can be seen in Figure 1. In this figure we see four events, of which two of them share a context.

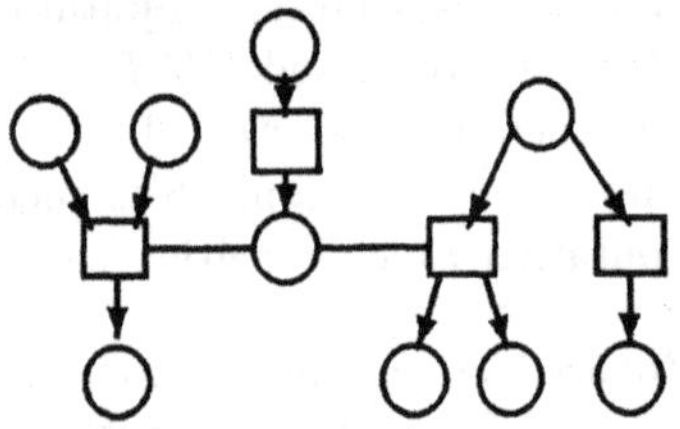

Fig. 1. A contextual net.

In our concurrent semantics the underlying notion is that of a contextual process, which is a contextual occurrence net together with a suitable mapping of the elements of the net to the syntactic objects of the program execution. Through the mapping, each condition of the contextual net represents an agent or a constraint, and each event represents a rule application. Informally, a contextual occurrence net is just an acyclic contextual net, where acyclicity refers to the dependency relation induced by F_1 and F_2.

Definition 11 (dependency). Consider a contextual net $N = (B, E; F_1, F_2)$. Then we define a corresponding structure $(B \cup E, \leq_N)$, where the dependency relation $\leq_N$ is the minimal relation which is reflexive, transitive, and which satisfies the following conditions: xF_1y implies $x \leq_N y$; e_1F_1b and bF_2e_2 implies $e_1 \leq_N e_2$; bF_2e_1 and bF_1e_2 implies $e_1 \leq_N e_2$. □

Therefore in the following we will say that x depends on y whenever $y \leq_N x$. However, a contextual net gives information not only about dependency of events and conditions, but also about concurrency and mutual exclusion (or conflict).

Definition 12 (mutual exclusion and concurrency). Consider a contextual net $N = (B, E; F_1, F_2)$ and the associated dependency relation $\leq_N$. Assume that $\leq_N$ is antisymmetric, and let $\leq\geq \in (B \cup E) \times (B \cup E)$ be defined as $\leq\geq = \{\langle x, y\rangle \mid x \leq_N y \text{ or } y \leq_N x\}$.

- The mutual exclusion relation $\#_N \subseteq ((B \cup E) \times (B \cup E))$ is defined as follows. First we define $x\#'y$ iff $x, y \in E$ and $\exists z \in B$ such that zF_1x and zF_1y. Then, $\#_N$ is the minimal relation which includes $\#'$ and which is symmetric and hereditary (i.e. if $x\#_Ny$ and $x \leq z$, then $z\#_Ny$).
- The concurrency relation co_N is just $((B \cup E) \times (B \cup E)) \setminus (\leq\geq \cup \#_N)$. □

In words, the mutual exclusion is originated by the existence of conditions which cause more than one event, and then it is propagated downwards through the dependency relation. Instead, two items are concurrent if they are not dependent on each other nor mutually exclusive.

Definition 13 (contextual occurrence net). A contextual occurrence net is a contextual net N, where $N = (B, E; F_1, F_2)$ and: $\leq_N$ is antisymmetric; $b \in B$ implies $|\ {}^\bullet b\ | \leq 1$; $\#_N$ is irreflexive. □

A useful special case of a contextual occurrence net occurs when the mutual exclusion relation is empty. This means that, taken any two items in the net, they are either concurrent or dependent. Since no conflict is expressed in such nets, they represent a completely deterministic behaviour.

Definition 14 (deterministic contextual occurrence net). A deterministic contextual occurrence net is a quadruple $N = (B, E; F_1, F_2)$ such that N is a contextual occurrence net with $\#_N = \emptyset$. □

Given a (nondeterministic) contextual occurrence net, it is easy to derive the set of all its subnets which are deterministic. For this we use restrictions defined as $F_{|S} = \{x \in F | x \in S\}$ (set intersection).

Definition 15 (from contextual to deterministic contextual occ. nets). Let a contextual occurrence net $N = (B, E; F_1, F_2)$ and the associated relations $\leq_N$, $\#_N$, and co_N, a deterministic contextual occurrence net of N is a deterministic contextual occurrence net $N' = (B', E'; F_1', F_2')$ where $B' \subseteq B$ and $E' \subseteq E$ and

- $x \in (B' \cup E')$ and $y \in (B \cup E)$ s.t. $y \leq_N x$ implies that $y \in (B' \cup E')$;
- $F_1' = F_{1|(B' \times E') \cup (E' \times B')}$ and $F_2' = F_{2|(B' \times E')}$. □

We are now ready to define contextual processes. We recall that, informally, a contextual process is just a contextual occurrence net plus a suitable mapping from the items of the net (i.e. conditions and events) to the agents of the CC program and the rules representing it.

Definition 16 (contextual process). Given a CC program P with initial agent A, and the associated sets of rewrite rules $RR(P)$, agents $Ag(P)$, and tokens D, consider the sets $RB = \{b\theta\}$ and $RE = \{r\theta\}$, with $b \in (Ag(P) \cup D)$, $r \in RR(P)$ and θ any substitution. Then a contextual process is a pair $\langle N, \pi \rangle$, where

- $N = (B, E; F_1, F_2)$ is a (nondeterministic) contextual occurrence net;
- $\pi : (B \cup E) \rightarrow (RB \cup RE)$ is a mapping where
  - $\forall b \in B,\ \pi(b) \in RB$ and $\forall e \in E,\ \pi(e) \in RE$;
  - $\forall x \in B$ such that $\nexists y \in (B \cup E),\ y \leq_N x,\ \pi(x) = A$;
  - let $\pi(e) = r\theta$, with $r = L \overset{c}{\leadsto} R$, then $\{\pi(x) | x \in {}^\bullet e\} = L\theta$, $\{\pi(x) | x \in \hat{e}\} = c\theta$, $\{\pi(x) | x \in e^\bullet\} = R\theta$. □

4.2 Consistent Contextual Nets

A consistent contextual net is just a contextual net with an additional relation, called the mutual inconsistency relation, which defines, together with the mutual exclusion relation, which items of the net cannot be present in the same computation. In the same way as mutual exclusion, dependency, and concurreny are defined in contextual nets starting from the basic relations F_1 and F_2, the mutual inconsistency relation is defined starting from them and a new basic relation F_3. The addition of such relation has however some heavy consequences, among which the fact that the concurrency relation is not binary any more.

Definition 17 (consistent contextual nets). A consistent contextual net is a quintuple $(B, E; F_1, F_2, F_3)$ where $N = (B, E; F_1, F_2)$ is a contextual net, and $F_3 \subseteq \wp(E)$ s.t. $F_3(S)$ implies $\forall e_1, e_2 \in S,\ e_1\ co_N\ e_2$ and $\forall S' \subset S,\ \neg F_3(S')$. □

Pre-set, post-set, and context are defined as for contextual nets. The same holds also for the dependency ($\leq$ from now on) and the mutual exclusion ($\#$) relation. However, now we have to define the new *mutual inconsistency* relation (@), starting from F_3, and we have to redefine the concurrency relation (co).

Definition 18 (mutual inconsistency and concurrency). Let a consistent contextual net $(B, E; F_1, F_2, F_3)$, and its dependency and mutual exclusion relations $\leq$ and $\#$.

- The mutual inconsistency relation $@ \subseteq \wp(B \cup E)$ is defined as follows:
  - $F_3(S)$ implies $@(S)$, and
  - $@(S \cup \{t\})$ and $t \leq t'$ implies $@(S \cup \{t'\})$.
- The concurrency relation $co \in \wp(B \cup E)$ is defined as follows: $co(S)$ if there is no subset $S' \subset S$ s.t. $@(S')$ and no $s_1, s_2 \in S$ s.t. $s_1 \# s_2$ or $s_1 \leq s_2$. □

In words, the mutual inconsistency relation includes the F_3 relation and it is hereditary. Instead, the concurrency relation is as usually defined by taking what is forbidden by the other relations. However, while usually such relation is binary, now it becomes n-ary, due to the fact that the new mutually inconsistency relation may be n-ary in general.

Since the mutual inconsistency relation is hereditary, there could be items inconsistent with themselves (which will be called *self-inconsistent* in the following). This informally means that they cannot appear in any computation, since they are inconsistent with their parents. We call a net *admissible* if it does not contain any of such items, and from now on we will only consider admissible consistent contextual nets.

Definition 19 (admissible consistent nets). A consistent contextual net $N = (B, E; F_1, F_2, F_3)$ is admissible whenever $\nexists e \in E$ such that $@(\{e\})$. □

An admissible consistent contextual net can be seen in Figure 2. Notice that we choose to represent the mutual exclusion relation by (hyper)arcs which have arrows on all their endings. In this figure, suposse that the inconsistency link was between the event on the left and the one generating its context. Because of inheritance, the leftmost event will then be inconsistent with itself. Therefore, the net will not be admissible.

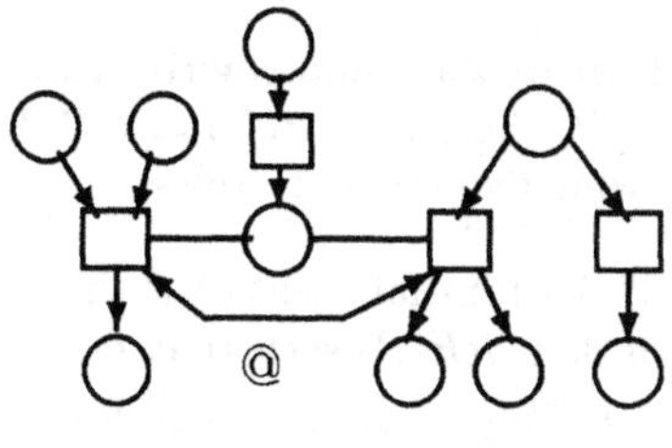

Fig. 2. A consistent contextual net.

As in the previous section, we now define deterministic and occurrence nets for the class of consistent contextual nets. The only difference is that now we define a net to be deterministic whenever both the mutual exclusion and the mutual inconsistency relations are empty.

Definition 20 ((deterministic) consistent contextual occ. nets). A consistent contextual occurrence net is a consistent contextual net $(B, E; F_1, F_2, F_3)$ such that $(B, E; F_1, F_2)$ is a contextual occurrence net. A consistent contextual occurrence net $(B, E; F_1, F_2, F_3)$ is deterministic when $F_3 = \# = \emptyset$. □

Notice that a deterministic consistent contextual occurrence net is just a (deterministic) contextual occurrence net, since $F_3 = \emptyset$. Therefore the way to obtain the deterministic consistent contextual occurrence nets of a given consistent contextual net is the same as in Definition 15.

If instead we just require the absence of mutually exclusive elements, just as in classical and contextual nets, then we still get subnets which have a meaning. In fact, we will see that they will be used to model the *locally atomical* interpretation for the tell operation, in which a computation step just checks the consistency of the constraint told within a local store.

Definition 21 ((deterministic) locally consistent contextual occ. nets). A deterministic locally consistent contextual occurrence net $(B, E; F_1, F_2, F_3)$ is a consistent contextual occurrence net with $\# = \emptyset$. □

Finally, we will relate consistent occurrence nets to CC programs by means of consistent contextual processes, whose definition is straightforward.

Definition 22 (consistent contextual process). A consistent contextual process is a pair $\langle N, \pi \rangle$ such that $N = (B, E; F_1, F_2, F_3)$ is a consistent contextual occurrence net, and $\langle (B, E; F_1, F_2), \pi \rangle$ is a contextual process.□

5 Concurrent Semantics for CC with Eventual Tell

The key idea in the semantics is to take the set of rewrite rules $RR(P)$ associated to a given CC program P and to incrementally construct a corresponding contextual process. A longer description of this semantics is contained in [MR93b].

Definition 23 (from rewrite rules to a contextual process). Given a CC program P, the pair $CP(P) = \langle (B, E; F_1, F_2), \pi \rangle$ is constructed by means of the following two inference rules:

- if $A(\mathbf{a})$ initial agent of P then $\langle A(\mathbf{a}), \emptyset, 1 \rangle \in B$;
- if $\exists r \in RR(P)$ such that $L(r) \cup c(r) = \{B_1(\mathbf{x}_1), \ldots, B_n(\mathbf{x}_n)\}$, and
  - $\exists \{s_1, \ldots, s_n\} \subseteq B$ such that $\forall i, j = 1, \ldots, n$, $s_i \; co_N \; s_j$, and
  - $\forall i = 1, \ldots, n$, $s_i = \langle e_i, B_i(\mathbf{a_i}), k_i \rangle$, and for some $\mathbf{a}$, $B_i(\mathbf{x}_i)[\mathbf{a}/\mathbf{x}] = B_i(\mathbf{a}_i)$

  then
  - $e = \langle r[\mathbf{a}/\mathbf{x}], \{s_1, \ldots, s_n\}, 1 \rangle \in E$,
  - $s_i F_1 e$ for all $s_i = \langle e_i, B_i(\mathbf{a_i}), k_i \rangle$ such that for some $\mathbf{a}$, $B_i(\mathbf{x}_i)[\mathbf{a}/\mathbf{x}] = B_i(\mathbf{a}_i)$ and $B_i(\mathbf{x}_i) \in L(r)$
  - $s_i F_2 e$ for all $s_i = \langle e_i, B_i(\mathbf{a_i}), k_i \rangle$ such that for some $\mathbf{a}$, $B_i(\mathbf{x}_i)[\mathbf{a}/\mathbf{x}] = B_i(\mathbf{a}_i)$ and $B_i(\mathbf{x}_i) \in c(r)$
  - let h be the multiplicity of $B(\mathbf{x}, y_1, \ldots, y_m) \in R(r)$, then $\forall l = 1, \ldots, h$, $b_l = \langle B[\mathbf{a}/\mathbf{x}][\langle e, y_1 \rangle / y_1] \ldots [\langle e, y_m \rangle / y_m], e, l \rangle \in B$, and $e F_1 b_l$.

Moreover, for any item $x = \langle x_1, x_2, x_3 \rangle \in (B \cup E)$, $\pi(x) = x_1$. □

The elements of the net in the contextual process are built in such a way that elements generated by using different sequences of rules are indeed different. In fact, each element is a term consisting of a triple, of which the first element is the *type* of the term, and represents the rule or agent or constraint the term corresponds to, the second element is its *history*, and this is what makes different terms which are generated in different ways, and the third element is its *multiplicity*, and takes care of different copies of the same element in the same computation state.

Each time the inference rule is applied, a rule in RR(P) is chosen whose left hand side and context are *matched* by some elements already present in the partially built process. Such elements have to be concurrent, otherwise it would mean that they cannot be together in a state. Then, a new element representing the rule application is added (as an event), as well as new elements representing the right hand side of the rule (as conditions).

Theorem 24 (**$CP(P)$ is a contextual process**). *Given a CC program P, its corresponding structure $CP(P)$ from Definition 23 is a contextual process.* □

Theorem 25 (**soundness and completeness of $CP(P)$ w.r.t. $EO(P)$**). *Given a CC program P and its corresponding contextual process $CP(P) = \langle N, \pi \rangle$.*

- *For a given computation in $EO(P)$ there are (1) an α-equivalent computation $S_1 \stackrel{r_1[\mathbf{a}_1/\mathbf{x}_1]}{\Longrightarrow} S_2 \stackrel{r_2[\mathbf{a}_2/\mathbf{x}_2]}{\Longrightarrow} S_3 \ldots$, and (2) one linearization (restricted to events), say $e_1 e_2, \ldots$, of the partial order associated to a maximal deterministic contextual occurrence net of N, s.t. $\forall i = 1, 2, \ldots,\ \pi(e_i) = r_i[\mathbf{a}_i/\mathbf{x}_i]$*
- *For any linearization $e_1 e_2 \ldots$ of the partial order associated to a deterministic contextual occurrence net of N, there is a computation in $EO(P)$, say $S_1 \stackrel{r_1[\mathbf{a}_1/\mathbf{x}_1]}{\Longrightarrow} S_2 \stackrel{r_2[\mathbf{a}_2/\mathbf{x}_2]}{\Longrightarrow} S_3 \ldots$, such that, if $e_i = \langle e_{i1}, e_{i2}, e_{i3} \rangle$ and $\pi(e_i) = r$, then $r_i[\mathbf{a}_i/\mathbf{x}_i] = r$ for all $i = 1, \ldots$* □

As just shown by the above theorem, the concurrent semantics defined in this section considers the eventual interpretation of the tell operation: constraints are added to the store without checking their consistency with the current set of constraints already in it. Therefore there may be parts of the net which represent computation sequences which would not happen if taking the atomic interpretation of the tell operation. In the following section we show how to recognize and then delete such parts, obtaining a (possibly much) smaller process. We will also give a new inference rule which allows to not even generate those parts.

6 Concurrent Semantics for CC with Atomic Tell

In order to correctly treat atomic tell, we need to know when a set of constraints is inconsistent. This can be done by just looking at the constraint system, since we assumed that a set of inconsistent constraints entails the token *false*.

Definition 26 (**inconsistent constraints**). Given a constraint system $\langle D, \vdash \rangle$, we say that $u \in \wp(D)$ is inconsistent, and we write $inc(u)$, whenever $u \vdash false$. Moreover, we write $inc_0(u)$ whenever $inc(u)$ holds and also $\nexists v \in \wp(D)$ such that $v \subset u$ and $v \vdash false$. □

From the inconsistency of a set of tokens we can then derive the mutual inconsistency of a set of conditions and/or events in the contextual process. Mutual inconsistency means impossibility of appearing in the same computation without creating an inconsistent store.

Definition 27 (mutual inconsistency). Given a CC program P, a constraint system $\langle D, \vdash \rangle$, and the contextual process $CP(P) = \langle (B, E; F_1, F_2), \pi \rangle$, we define a mutual inconsistency relation $@ \subseteq \wp(B \cup E)$ (and $@'$) as follows:

- if $\{b_1, \ldots, b_n\} \in B$ and $\forall i = 1, \ldots, n, \pi(b_i) \in D$ and $inco_O(\{\pi(b_1), \ldots, \pi(b_n)\})$ and $\nexists i, j = 1, \ldots, n$ such that $b_i \# b_j$, then $@'(\{b_1, \ldots, b_n\})$;
- if $@'(\{b_1, \ldots, b_n\})$ and $\forall i = 1, \ldots, n, \exists e_i \in E$ s.t. $e_i F_1 b_i$, then $@'(\{e_1, \ldots, e_n\})$;
- $@$ is the minimal relation which includes $@'$ and which is hereditary (i.e. if $@(S \cup \{s\})$ and $s \leq s'$, then $@(S \cup \{s'\})$). □

In particular, the elements of the process which are self-inconsistent cannot appear in any computation. Therefore, one step which allows us to change the semantical structure which represents the eventual operational semantics of a CC program and get closer to that which represents the atomic operational semantics of the same program consists in deleting everything that depends on them. In fact, such steps are exactly those tell operations which could be done only because it was not performed any consistency check.

Definition 28 (net pruning). Given a CC program P, a constraint system $\langle D, \vdash \rangle$, the contextual process $CP(P) = \langle (B, E; F_1, F_2), \pi \rangle$, and the relation $@$ of Definition 27, the new process is $CP'(P) = \langle (B', E'; F_1', F_2'), \pi' \rangle$, where

- $B' = B \setminus \{b \mid \exists e \in E \ s.t. \ @(\{e\}) \text{ and } e \leq b\}$,
- $E' = E \setminus \{e \mid \exists e' \in E \ s.t. \ @(\{e'\}) \text{ and } e' \leq e\}$,
- $F_1' = F_{1|B' \times E' \cup E' \times B'}$ and $F_2' = F_{2|B' \times E'}$, and
- π' is the restriction of π to $B' \cup E'$. □

Theorem 29 ($CP'(P)$ is a consistent contextual process). *Consider the process $CP'(P) = \langle (B', E'; F_1', F_2'), \pi' \rangle$ of Definition 28 and the relation $@$ of Definition 27. Then $\langle (B', E'; F_1', F_2', @'_{|\wp(E')}), \pi' \rangle$ is a consistent contextual process.* □

Theorem 30 (soundness and completeness of $CP'(P)$ w.r.t. $AO(P)$). *Given a CC program P and its consistent contextual process $CP'(P) = \langle N, \pi \rangle$.*

- *For any computation in $AO(P)$, there are (1) an α-equivalent computation $S_1 \stackrel{r_1[\mathbf{a}_1/\mathbf{x}_1]}{\Longrightarrow} S_2 \stackrel{r_2[\mathbf{a}_2/\mathbf{x}_2]}{\Longrightarrow} S_3 \ldots$, and (2) one linearization (restricted to events), $e_1, e_2, \ldots$, of the partial order associated to a maximal deterministic consistent contextual occurrence net of N, s.t. $\forall i = 1, 2, \ldots, \pi(e_i) = r_i[\mathbf{a}_i/\mathbf{x}_i]$*
- *For any linearization $e_1 e_2 \ldots$ of the partial order associated to a deterministic consistent contextual occurrence net of N, there is a computation in $AO(P)$, say $S_1 \stackrel{r_1[\mathbf{a}_1/\mathbf{x}_1]}{\Longrightarrow} S_2 \stackrel{r_2[\mathbf{a}_2/\mathbf{x}_2]}{\Longrightarrow} S_3 \ldots$, such that, if $e_i = \langle e_{i1}, e_{i2}, e_{i3} \rangle$ and $\pi(e_i) = r$, then $r_i[\mathbf{a}_i/\mathbf{x}_i] = r$ for all $i = 1, \ldots$* □

It is also possible to characterize failing, successful, and suspended computations directly in the concurrent semantics, instead of having to map them back to the corresponding computations in the operational semantics.

Definition 31 (successful, failing, and suspended nets). Given a CC program P and a constraint system $\langle D, \vdash \rangle$, consider the corresponding consistent contextual process $CP(P) = \langle (B, E; F_1, F_2, F_3), \pi \rangle$. Consider also any maximal deterministic consistent contextual net of $(B, E; F_1, F_2, F_3)$, $DN = (B', E'; F_1', F_2', \emptyset)$, and the elements $DN^\circ = \{b \mid b \in B' \text{ and } \nexists b' \in B',\ b \leq b'\}$. Then DN is:

- successful if the set of events representing agent rules is finite, and $\forall b \in DN^\circ,\ \pi(b) \in (D \setminus \{false\})$;
- suspended if the set of events representing agent rules is finite, and $\forall b \in DN^\circ$ such that $\pi(b) \in Ag(P)$, $\pi(b)$ is an ask agent;
- failing otherwise. □

Theorem 32 (characterization of success, failure, and suspension). *Let P be a CC program and $CP(P) = \langle (B, E; F_1, F_2, F_3), \pi \rangle$ its corresponding consistent contextual process. Consider any maximal deterministic consistent contextual net of $(B, E; F_1, F_2, F_3)$, say $DN = (B', E'; F_1', F_2', \emptyset)$. If DN is successful (resp., suspended, failing) then all the computations in $AO(P)$ corresponding to DN according to Theorem 30 are successful (resp., suspended, failing).* □

Now we will obtain the same consistent contextual process by means of a new inference rule, instead of first producing the contextual process as in Definition 23 and then pruning it. The advantage consists in a possibly much smaller resulting process. However, the drawback is a much more costly condition to check during the generation, each time the inference rule is applied.

Definition 33 (from rewrite rules to a consistent contextual process). Let P be a CC program, $CCP(P) = \langle (B, E; F_1, F_2, F_3), \pi \rangle$ is constructed by means of the following two inference rules:

- if $A(\mathbf{a})$ initial agent of P then $\langle A(\mathbf{a}), \emptyset, 1 \rangle \in B$;
- if $\exists r \in RR(P)$ such that $L(r) \cup c(r) = \{B_1(\mathbf{x}_1), \ldots, B_n(\mathbf{x}_n)\}$, and
  - $\exists \{s_1, \ldots, s_n\} \subseteq B$ such that $co(\{s_1, \ldots, s_n\})$, and
  - $\forall i = 1, \ldots, n,\ s_i = \langle e_i, B_i(\mathbf{a_i}), k_i \rangle$, and for some $\mathbf{a}$, $B_i(\mathbf{x}_i)[\mathbf{a}/\mathbf{x}] = B_i(\mathbf{a}_i)$
  - $\neg inc(ct(\{e\}))$, for $e = \langle r[\mathbf{a}/\mathbf{x}], \{s_1, \ldots, s_n\}, 1 \rangle$, where $ct : \wp(B \cup E) \rightarrow \wp(D)$ is defined as follows: $\forall \langle t_1, t_2, t_3 \rangle \in (B \cup E)$,

$$ct(S \cup \{\langle t_1, t_2, t_3 \rangle\}) = \begin{cases} ct(S \cup t_2) \cup (R(r)[\mathbf{a}/\mathbf{x}] \cap D) & \text{if } t_1 = r[\mathbf{a}/\mathbf{x}] \text{ and } r \text{ is a rule for a tell agent} \\ ct(S \cup t_2) & \text{otherwise} \end{cases}$$

$$ct(\emptyset) = \emptyset$$

  then
  - $e \in E$,

- $s_i F_1 e$ for all $s_i = \langle e_i, B_i(\mathbf{a_i}), k_i\rangle$ such that for some $\mathbf{a}$, $B_i(\mathbf{x}_i)[\mathbf{a}/\mathbf{x}] = B_i(\mathbf{a}_i)$ and $B_i(\mathbf{x}_i) \in L(r)$
- $s_i F_2 e$ for all $s_i = \langle e_i, B_i(\mathbf{a_i}), k_i\rangle$ such that for some $\mathbf{a}$, $B_i(\mathbf{x}_i)[\mathbf{a}/\mathbf{x}] = B_i(\mathbf{a}_i)$ and $B_i(\mathbf{x}_i) \in c(r)$
- let h be the multiplicity of $B(\mathbf{x}, y_1, \ldots, y_m) \in R(r)$, then $\forall l = 1, \ldots, h$, $b_l = \langle B[\mathbf{a}/\mathbf{x}][\langle e, y_1\rangle/y_1]\ldots[\langle e, y_m\rangle/y_m], \{e\}, l\rangle \in B$, and $eF_1 b_l$.
- $F_3(S \cup \{e\})$ for all $S = \{e_1, \ldots, e_n\} \subseteq E$ such that $co(S \cup \{s_1, \ldots, s_n\})$, and $inc(ct(\{e\} \cup S))$, and $\not\exists S' \subseteq E$ such that $S' \cup \{s_1, \ldots, s_n\} \in co$, and $inc(ct(\{e\} \cup S'))$, and $\forall e' \in S'\ \exists e \in S$ such that $e' \leq e$.

Moreover, for any item $x = \langle x_1, x_2, x_3\rangle \in (B \cup E)$, $\pi(x) = x_1$. □

The main difference of the above definition w.r.t. Definition 23 is the condition which has to be checked for applying the second inference rule. It is not enough to check that there are conditions which are concurrent and which match the left hand side and the context of a rule. It is also necessary to check that the constraints which would be added to the process because of the application of the chosen rule are consistent with those which are in the history of the rule itself. In fact, such constraints would be in any store where that rule is applied, no matter which linearization one chooses. Such constraints are retrieved by function *ct*, which traverses a term and gets all the constraints in its history.

Another difference concerns the creation of relation F_3. Inconsistency of the new event e with a set S of events, already in the process, is derived if e and the constraints generated in the history of S are inconsistent. This is done only if e is concurrent with them (checked by looking at the pre-conditions of e, $s_1, \ldots, s_n$, since e is not formally in the process yet). This would create an F_3 relation which is already hereditary. However, we prefer to have F_3 as the base relation, and then to close it by inheritance as by Definition 18 to get the mutual inconsistency relation. This is the reason why we also check that there is no other set S' of events which has the same relation as S with e but on which S depends.

Theorem 34 (equivalence of $CP'(P)$ and $CCP(P)$). *Given a CC program P, its corresponding pruned contextual process $CP'(P)$ and consistent contextual process $CCP(P)$, then $CP'(P) = CCP(P)$.* □

Part of the complexity of this approach to the construction of the consistent contextual process for a given CC program comes from our aim of employing a standard way of selecting the subnets corresponding to (equivalence classes of) computations. In fact, assuming that mutual inconsistency is just another aspect of mutual exclusion (that is, just another reason for certain items not to be in the same computation), then the desired subnets are, as usual, those which are maximal, left-closed, and without mutual exclusion. Simpler approaches could be taken; however, they would require ad hoc subnet selection procedures.

7 Locally Atomic Tell

Let us consider now a *locally atomic* tell operation, where a constraint is added to the store if it is consistent with the set of constraints it depends on. Then, it is easy to see that such operation, and the corresponding resulting computations, are very easily expressed by the same process. It is just a matter of selecting different subnets of the process: the (deterministic) locally consistent contextual occurrence nets instead of the deterministic contextual occurrence nets. Recall that the only difference between these two classes of nets is that in the former only the mutual exclusion relation is empty, while in the latter also the mutual inconsistency relation is so. In fact, if in a computation we allow steps which are mutually inconsistent between them, while still not allowing any self-inconsistent step, it means that the only way a computation can finitely fail is that a self-inconsistent step is tried. But we know that such steps represent tell operations which attempt to add a constraint which is inconsistent with the constraints in their history. Therefore, these subnets only have those computation steps which are allowed by the locally atomic interpretation of the tell operation.

```
p(X) :: tell(X=a), tell(X=b).     p(X) :: tell(X=a) -> tell(X=b).
```

Fig. 3. Simple CC programs: query is `p(X)`.

Consider the very simple CC programs of Figure 3, where the comma represents the parallel composition operator $||$, and the absence of "$\rightarrow A$" after a tell operation means that $A = success$.

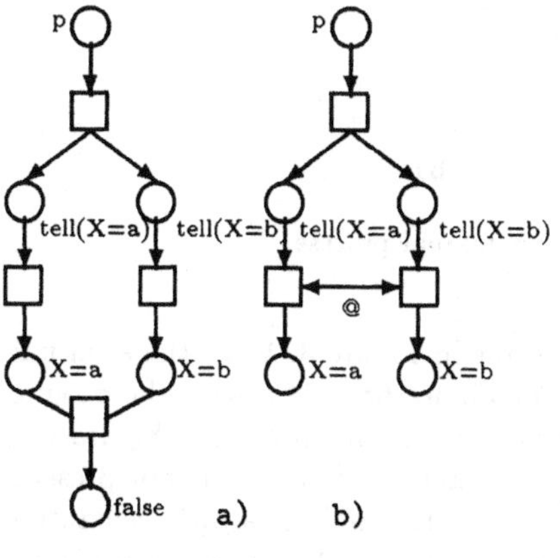

Fig. 4. Contextual and consistent contextual process.

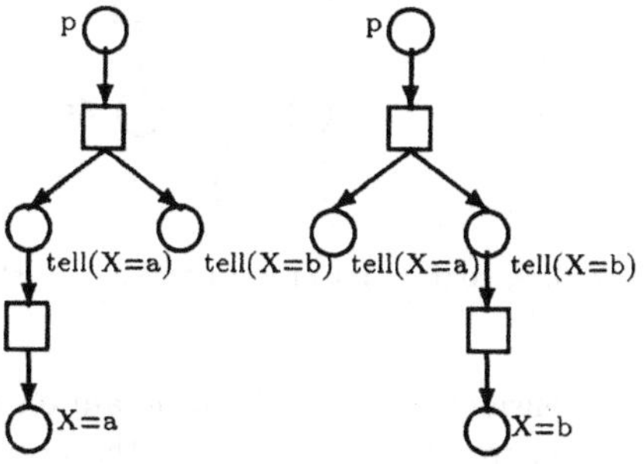

Fig. 5. Consistent contextual nets.

The contextual process corresponding to the program on the left in Figure 3 can be seen in Figure 4a, while its consistent contextual process is that of Figure 4b. Also, the set of subnets corresponding to classes of computations which differ only for the scheduling order is, in the case of eventual tell, a singleton set containing the whole contextual process, and in the case of atomic tell a set of two processes whose nets can be seen in Figure 5. In fact, in the eventual tell interpretation, we just have two computations (depending on the order of execution of the two tell operations), both of them failing. Instead, in the atomic tell interpretation, we have two computations, each one performing just one of the tell operations, and both of them failing (which can be seen from the fact that some tell agent is not "expanded"). Consider now the locally atomic tell operation. In this case there is only one subnet, which incidentally coincides with the contextual process. In fact, with this interpretation, both tells are performed, since there is no constraint they depend on (and thus the *incomplete* consistency check for such tells succeeds).

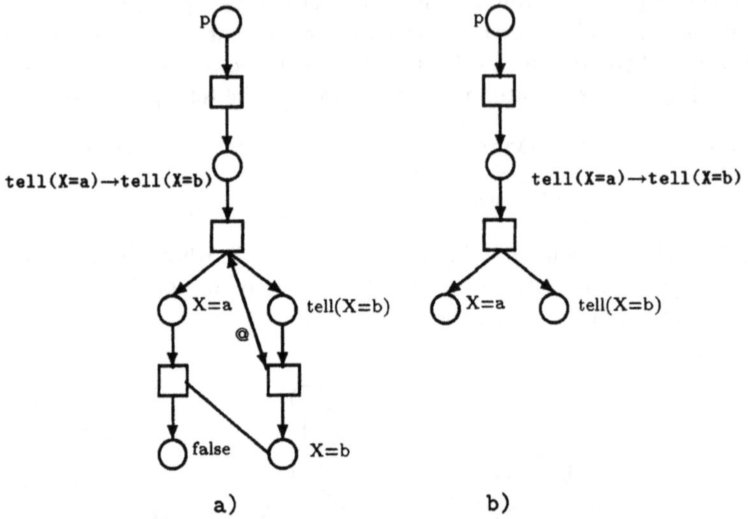

Fig. 6. A contextual process and a consistent contextual process.

Consider now the CC program on the right in Figure 3. With the eventual tell interpretation, we obtain the process in Figure 6a, while with the atomic tell interpretation we obtain the consistent contextual process in Figure 6b. Indeed, the second tell operation is self-inconsistent and thus it is not present in the atomic semantics. The locally atomic semantics and the atomic semantics coincide, since no tell attempts to add a constraint which is inconsistent with the current store but not with the current local store. With the eventual tell, there is only one failing computation, which performs both tells and generates an inconsistent store. Instead, with the (locally) atomic tell there is one computation as well, which however performs just one tell operation and then stops.

8 Applications: CLP parallelization and CC scheduling

Being able to explicitely express concurrency and dependency, our semantics can be exploited in several tasks which need such kind of information. One such task is the (compile-time) scheduling of CC programs, or schedule analysis [KS92].

The goal of schedule analysis is to find maximal linearizations of the program processes (agents in our case) where the efficient compilation techniques of sequential implementations can be applied. The best case would be to obtain a complete total order, but in general we may instead obtain a set of total orders, which specify *threads* of sequential execution which, because of the interdependencies in the program, cannot be sequentialized among them [KS92]. Moreover, in each single thread, one would like to schedule the producer(s) before the corresponding consumer(s), so that the consumers do not need to be suspended and then woken up later. In the specific case of CC programs, the producers are the tell operations and the consumers are the ask operations, so this desirable property of each thread here means that some ask operations could be deleted, if we can be sure that when they will be scheduled the asked constraint has already been told. In [KS92] a framework for this analysis is defined, which is safe w.r.t. the termination properties of the program, and which is based on an input *data-dependency* relation among atoms in the clauses of the program. It is easy to show that in our approach the dependency relation of the contextual process of a program can provide such an input. In fact, it is intuitive to see that the order between two goals in the body of a clause can be easily decided by looking at the contextual net describing the behaviour of the original CC program: if the subnets rooted at these two goals are linked by dependency links which all go in the same direction (from one subnet to the other one), then this direction is the order to be taken for the scheduling; if instead the dependency links go in both directions, then the two goals must belong to two different threads; otherwise (that is, if there are no dependency links between the two subnets), we can order them in any way. Once the order has been chosen, each ask operation which is scheduled later than all the items of the net on which it depends on can safely be deleted. Of course finding the best scheduling is an NP-complete problem. Therefore the optimal solution would require a global analysis of the relationship among the subnets corresponding to all the goals in the body of the considered clause.

Another interesting application is the parallelization of CLP programs. In this task, the problem consists in parallelizing the executions of some of the goals if we are sure that doing that will not change the input-output semantics of the program, nor increase the execution time. What is usually said is that we can parallelize two (or more) goals if we can recognize that they are in some sense "independent," meaning that their executions do not interfere with each other. Instead, for all the goals which do not meet this independence criteria, we resort to the usual left-to-right order. However, the traditional concepts of independence in logic programming [HR93] do not carry over trivially to CLP. In fact, the generalization of the conditions for search space preservation is no longer sufficient for ensuring the efficiency of several optimizations when arbitrary CLP languages are taken into account, and the definition of *constraint independence* in the CLP framework is not trivial [dlBHM93]. Following constraint independence notions, we argue that an efficient parallelization scheme for CLP programs can be developed from the mutual inconsistency relation between events in the consistent contextual processes of the programs. Current work is being devoted towards making this explicit in the (consistent) contextual nets by the new notion of *local independence* [BBHRM93]. In particular, by using our concurrent semantics, we are able to apply the notion of goal independence at a granularity level which, to our knowledge, allows more goals to be safely run in parallel than any other approach. Note that local independence is in general different from concurrency: the idea is that only items which are concurrent (as defined previously in this paper) and which are not dependent because of inconsistency, are locally independent.

References

[dlBHM93] M. García de la Banda, M. Hermenegildo, and K. Marriott. Independence in Constraint Logic Programs. In *Proc. ILPS*. MIT Press, 1993.

[BBHRM93] F. Bueno, M. García de la Banda, M. Hermenegildo, F. Rossi, and U. Montanari. Towards true concurrency semantics based transformation between CLP and CC. TR CLIP2/93.1, UPM, 1993.

[BP91] F.S. De Boer and C. Palamidessi. A fully abstract model for concurrent constraint programming. In *Proc. CAAP*. Springer-Verlag, 1991.

[HR93] M. Hermenegildo and F. Rossi. Strict and Non-Strict Independent And-Parallelism in Logic Programs: Correctness, Efficiency, and Compile-Time Conditions. *Journal of Logic Programming*, 1993. To appear.

[JL87] J. Jaffar and J.L. Lassez. Constraint logic programming. In *Proc. POPL*. ACM, 1987.

[KS92] A. King and P. Soper. Schedule Analysis of Concurrent Logic Programs. In *Proc. JICSLP*, pages 478–492, MIT Press, 1992.

[KT91] M. Koorsloot and E. Tick. Sequentializing parallel programs. In *Phoenix Seminar and Workshop on Declarative Programming*. Hohritt, Sasbachwalden, Germany, Springer-Verlag, 1991.

[MR91] U. Montanari and F. Rossi. True concurrency in concurrent constraint programming. In *Proc. ILPS*. MIT Press, 1991.

[MR93a] U. Montanari and F. Rossi. Contextual nets. Technical Report TR-4/93, CS Department, University of Pisa, Italy, 1993.

[MR93b] U. Montanari and F. Rossi. Contextual occurrence nets and concurrent constraint programming. In *Proc. Dagstuhl Seminar on Graph Transformations in Computer Science*. Springer-Verlag, LNCS, 1993.

[Rei85] W. Reisig. *Petri Nets: An Introduction*. EATCS Monographs on Theoretical Computer Science. Springer Verlag, 1985.

[Sar93] V.A. Saraswat. *Concurrent Constraint Programming*. MIT Press, 1993.

[SR90] V. A. Saraswat and M. Rinard. Concurrent constraint programming. In *Proc. POPL*. ACM, 1990.

[SRP91] V. A. Saraswat, M. Rinard, and P. Panangaden. Semantic foundations of concurrent constraint programming. In *Proc. POPL*. ACM, 1991.

[Sco82] D. S. Scott. Domains for denotational semantics. In *Proc. ICALP*. Springer-Verlag, 1982.

Concurrent Logic Programming as Uniform Linear Proofs

Paolo Volpe
Dipartimento di Informatica
Università di Pisa
Corso Italia, 40 — 56125 Pisa, Italy
e-mail: volpep@di.unipi.it
tel: +39 - 50 - 887246
fax: +39 - 50 - 887226

Abstract. We describe $\mathcal{LC}$, a formalism based on the proof theory of linear logic, whose aim is to specify concurrent computations and whose language restriction (as compared to other linear logic language) provides a simpler operational model that can lead to a more practical language core. The $\mathcal{LC}$ fragment is proveded to be an abstract logic programming language, that is any sequent can be derived by uniform proofs. The resulting class of computations can be viewed in terms of multiset rewriting and is reminiscent of the computations arising in the Chemical Abstract Machine and in the Gamma model.
The fragment makes it possible to give a logic foundation to existing extensions of Horn clause logic, such as Generalized Clauses, whose declarative semantics was based on an ad hoc construction.
Programs and goals in $\mathcal{LC}$ can declaratively be characterized by a suitable instance of the phase semantics of linear logic. A canonical phase model is associated to every $\mathcal{LC}$ program. Such a model gives a full characterization of the program computations and can be obtained through a fixpoint construction.

Keywords: Linear Logic, Uniform Proofs, Concurrency, Phase Semantics, Chemical Abstract Machine.

1 Introduction

The availability of powerful environments for parallel processing has made particularly interesting the field of logic languages. Writing concurrent programs is quite difficult. Therefore it is desirable to have languages with a clear and simple semantics, so as to have a rigorous basis for the specification, the analysis, the transformation and the verification of programs. A programming framework based on logic seems to be well suited.

In this paper we investigate the expressive power of linear logic in a concurrent programming framework. This logic is gaining wide consensus in theoretical computer science and our attempt is not quite new in its kind. Linear logic has already given the basis to many proposals. Our approach is based on the paradigm of computation as proof search, typical of logic programming. We take as foundation the proof theoretical characterization of logic programming given by Miller [24, 23]. The definition of uniformity will lead us to single out a restricted fragment of linear logic capable of specifying an interesting class of parallel computations. We think the simple operational model can lead to a more practical language core.

The resulting framework is strongly related to the paradigm of multiset rewriting lying at the basis of the Gamma formalism [6] and of the Chemical Abstract Machine [7]. Actually it allows to specify a set of transformations that try to reduce an input multiset of goals to the empty multiset, returning as an output an answer substitution for the initial goal. More transformations can be applied concurrently to the multiset, thus making possible efficient implementations in parallel environments.

An important feature of the language is its ability to express in a simple way the synchronization and the communication between different computational flows, opening the way to distributed programming, as has already been showed in [11] and [8] for similar languages. In the case of $\mathcal{LC}$ however we have a declarative semantics for the symmetrical interactions.
In fact in the last part of the paper we propose a semantics for the language obtained by instantiating the phase semantics of linear logic. The resulting abstract structure associated to programs allows to declaratively model the behaviour of our computations. By exploiting the similarities of our fragment with the language of Generalized Clauses [11, 8], a fixpoint characterization of the phase semantics is also presented.

The paper is organized as follows. In subsection 1.1 we introduce linear logic and its proof system. In section 1.2 we introduce the definition of uniformity for multiple conclusions sequent systems. Section 2 shows the fragment $\mathcal{LC}$ and its computational features. In section 3 we relate the $\mathcal{LC}$ framework to actual programming environments. Finally a semantics for $\mathcal{LC}$ programs in the style of the phase semantics will be shown in section 5 together with a fixpoint characterization.

1.1 Linear Logic

Linear logic is becoming an important subject the framework of computational logic. This is due to its interesting expressive features that make it possible to model both sequential and concurrent computations.

The key feature of the formalism is certainly its ability of treating resources through the manipulation of formulas, thus allowing to express in a natural way the notion of consumption and production. This leads to a direct interpretation of computation in linear logic. A process is also viewed as a (reusable) resource. The change of its state is obtained through the consumption (or decomposition) and the production (or construction) of resources. Since the processing of resources is inherently concurrent, multiple parallel flows of computation can be represented.

The sequent calculus allows us to represent in a natural way the resource sensitivity of this logic. A sequent can be thought of as an "action" that consumes the left-hand formulas and produces the right-hand ones. Equivalently a sequent tree makes explicit the consumption of formulas to produce more complex ones or vice versa the destruction of formulas in simpler parts.

The sequent system formalization shows also in a satisfactory way the subtle links between linear and classical logic. in fact we can see the derivation rules of the linear logic sequent system obtained from the classical derivation rules by abolishing the contraction and the thinning rules, which are responsible for the insensitivity of classical logic to formulas multiplicity. This elimination causes the classical connectives and constants to split down into two versions, the additive and the multiplicative one. In order to reach the power of classical logic, two modalities have to be introduced in order to have formulas *reusable* ad libitum. Contraction and thinning rules are recovered for formulas annotated with the modalities.

In Table 1 we show the sequent system $\mathcal{LL}$ of linear logic. A sequent is an expression $\Gamma \vdash \Delta$, where Γ and Δ are multisets of linear formulas, i.e. formulas built on the linear primitives $\otimes, ⅋, \oplus, \&, 1, 0, \bot, \top, \forall, \exists, !, ?$. Notice the use of the multiset structure, which allows us to get rid of an explicit structural rule of exchange. For a more complete account on the $\mathcal{LL}$ system we refer to [13].

The outstanding features of linear logic have soon determined its impact on theoretical computer science. Actually two basic approaches can be recognized. The *functional approach* models computations through normalization, i.e. *cut elimination*, of sequent calculi derivation trees. This approach has allowed the definition of powerful functional languages where we can express concurrent computations and derive program properties (e.g. strictness, sharing), which make it possible the elimination of the garbage collector [1, 19, 20].

We are more concerned with the other approach, the *logic programming approach.* In the following we will illustrate in details how we have instantiated this paradigm. Let us just note that the "proof search as computation" analogy applied to linear logic has already inspired several interesting logic programming frameworks like *LinLog* [2], *Linear Objects* [3, 4], and Miller's linear refinement of hereditary Harrop's formulas [15].

$$\frac{}{\bot \vdash}(\bot L) \qquad \frac{}{\vdash 1}(1R) \qquad \frac{}{0, \Gamma \vdash \Delta}(0L) \qquad \frac{}{\Gamma \vdash \Delta, \top}(\top R)$$

$$\frac{}{A \vdash A}(id) \qquad \frac{\Gamma \vdash A, \Delta \quad A, \Lambda \vdash \Theta}{\Gamma, \Lambda \vdash \Delta, \Theta}(cut) \qquad \frac{\Gamma \vdash \Delta}{1, \Gamma \vdash \Delta}(1L) \qquad \frac{\Gamma \vdash \Delta}{\Gamma \vdash \Delta, \bot}(\bot R)$$

$$\frac{A, B, \Gamma \vdash \Delta}{A \otimes B, \Gamma \vdash \Delta}(\otimes L) \qquad \frac{\Gamma \vdash \Delta, A \quad \Lambda \vdash \Theta, B}{\Gamma, \Lambda \vdash \Delta, \Theta, A \otimes B}(\otimes R) \qquad \frac{A, \Gamma \vdash \Delta \quad B, \Lambda \vdash \Theta}{A \parr B, \Gamma, \Lambda \vdash \Delta, \Theta}(\parr L) \qquad \frac{\Gamma \vdash \Delta, A, B}{\Gamma \vdash \Delta, A \parr B}(\parr R)$$

$$\frac{\Gamma \vdash \Delta, A \quad B, \Lambda \vdash \Theta}{A \multimap B, \Gamma, \Lambda \vdash \Delta, \Theta}(\multimap L) \qquad \frac{A, \Gamma \vdash \Delta, B}{\Gamma \vdash \Delta, A \multimap B}(\multimap R) \qquad \frac{\Gamma \vdash \Delta, A}{A^{\perp}, \Gamma \vdash \Delta}({}^{\perp} L) \qquad \frac{A, \Gamma \vdash \Delta}{\Gamma \vdash \Delta, A^{\perp}}({}^{\perp} R)$$

$$\frac{A, \Gamma \vdash \Delta}{A \& B, \Gamma \vdash \Delta}(\& L) \qquad \frac{B, \Gamma \vdash \Delta}{A \& B, \Gamma \vdash \Delta}(\& L) \qquad \frac{\Gamma \vdash \Delta, A \quad \Gamma \vdash \Delta, B}{\Gamma \vdash \Delta, A \& B}(\& R)$$

$$\frac{A, \Gamma \vdash \Delta \quad B, \Gamma \vdash \Delta}{A \oplus B, \Gamma \vdash \Delta}(\oplus L) \qquad \frac{\Gamma \vdash \Delta, A}{\Gamma \vdash \Delta, A \oplus B}(\oplus R) \qquad \frac{\Gamma \vdash \Delta, B}{\Gamma \vdash \Delta, A \oplus B}(\oplus R)$$

$$\frac{A, \Gamma \vdash \Delta}{!A, \Gamma \vdash \Delta}(!L) \qquad \frac{\Gamma \vdash \Delta, A}{\Gamma \vdash \Delta, ?A}(?R) \qquad \frac{\Gamma \vdash \Delta}{!A, \Gamma \vdash \Delta}(!WL) \qquad \frac{\Gamma \vdash \Delta}{\Gamma \vdash \Delta, ?A}(?WR)$$

$$\frac{!\Gamma, A \vdash ?\Delta}{!\Gamma, ?A \vdash ?\Delta}(?L) \qquad \frac{!\Gamma \vdash A, ?\Delta}{!\Gamma \vdash !A, ?\Delta}(!R) \qquad \frac{!A, !A, \Gamma \vdash \Delta}{!A, \Gamma \vdash \Delta}(!CL) \qquad \frac{\Gamma \vdash \Delta, ?A, ?A}{\Gamma \vdash \Delta, ?A}(?CR)$$

$$\frac{A[t/x], \Gamma \vdash \Delta}{\forall x A, \Gamma \vdash \Delta}(\forall L) \qquad \frac{\Gamma \vdash \Delta, A}{\Gamma \vdash \Delta, \forall x A}(\forall R) \qquad \frac{A, \Gamma \vdash \Delta}{\exists x A, \Gamma \vdash \Delta}(\exists L) \qquad \frac{\Gamma \vdash \Delta, A[t/x]}{\Gamma \vdash \Delta, \exists A}(\exists R)$$

Table 1. The $\mathcal{LL}$ system

1.2 Modeling computations in a sequent system

As already mentioned our approach is based on the notion of computation as proof search. In particular the proofs we search are cut-free derivations in a sequent calculus. As usual a derivation statically represents the evolution of a computation. We want a sequent $\Gamma \vdash G_1, \ldots, G_n$ in that derivation to represent the evolution of a computation. The change of state through the derivation tree is obtained by applying derivation rules. The right side of a sequent is viewed as a multiset of agent formulas that evolves through applications of derivation rules. Each complex agent can be decomposed in a uniform way and independently from the other formulas of the sequent, that is the proof strategy makes evident a fixed operational semantics for the logical connectives. The evolution of atomic agents, possibly together with other atoms, is instead dependent on other formulas of the sequent.
The left side of the sequent is viewed as a set of rules which specifies how simple right formulas (alone or in a group) can be transformed.

In other words we want our proofs to satisfy a suitable "parallel" extension of the notion of *uniformity* [24]. We remember that in [24] the definition of uniformity was given for single conclusion sequent derivations only, so it does not seem suitable to our aim. Miller in [23] has proposed an extension of that definition for multiple conclusions sequent derivations similar to ours. This definition formally singles out exactly the class of derivations we are concerned with.

Definition 1. A sequent proof Ξ is uniform if it is cut-free and for every subproof Ψ of Ξ and for every non atomic formula occurrence B, in the right-hand side of the root sequent of Ψ, there exists a derivation Ψ' which is equal to Ψ up to permutation of inference rules and such that the last inference rule in Ψ' introduces the top level logical connective occurring in B.

It can easily be shown that this definition generalizes the one given in [24]. This definition formalizes a "concurrent" view of derivations where the permutability represents the ideal simultaneous application of several independent right introduction rules. If two or more introduction rules can be applied, all derivations using them can be obtained from each other by simply permuting the order of the application of the rules. In the following we can see a non uniform derivation. As can be easily noticed the two right-hand formulas can not be decomposed in parallel. In fact $A \otimes B$ can not be solved independently from $\top \otimes 1$. If it is decomposed first it would result one of the unprovable sequents $\vdash A$ or $\vdash B$.

$$\frac{\vdash \top, A \otimes B \quad \vdash 1}{\vdash \top \otimes 1, A \otimes B}$$

As mentioned in [24], restricting the proof search we implicitly give a fixed operational meaning to the logical primitives. We can thus define a basic formalism which can specify concurrent computations through the parallel rewriting of agent formulas in the multiset.

Moreover, since we are working in a logical system we have a declarative interpretation for agent-formulas and a notion of logical equivalence and we can give an abstract semantics to computations based on the declarative semantics of the logic we use. However we must be consistent with the declarative meaning of the logical primitives. Thus our task can be stated as follow: Given a logical system we want to single out a subset of the well formed sequents such that if they are derivable they can be derived uniformly. This guarantees that the operational meaning of the logical primitives be consistent with their declarative meaning. In other words, even if we search uniform proofs only we do not lose the completeness.

Fragment enjoying this property are called by Miller *abstract logic programming languages*. Therefore our aim can be stated as the definition of an abstract logic programming language in linear logic, able to model concurrent computations. As we will see, linear logic has such constructive features to allow that.

2 The $\mathcal{LC}$ fragment

In this section we single out a fragment of linear logic that seems to be adequated for specifying an interesting class of computations. We will define a subset of the linear sequents by stepwise approximation, justifying every extension in terms of an improvement of the expressive power. Eventually we will identify a class of uniform proofs for the sequents of the subset. Our aim will be then to show that when considering uniform proofs only we keep the declarative meaning of the logical primitives. This will be done by proving that the fragment is an abstract logic programming language.

Let us remind that we want to represent concurrent computations as the concurrent evolution of the agents $G_1, \ldots, G_n$ in the proof tree of the sequent $\Gamma \vdash G_1, \ldots, G_n$, where Γ contains rules for the evolution of the agents. As a first step we can assume the agents to be simple ground atoms.

First of all we want to have "transformation formulas", like $G \rightarrow A$, that allow a change of state in the evolution of the atomic agent A. The application of this formula transforms the atom A into the agent G. We can easily obtain this behaviour by using linear formulas like $G \multimap A$, where $\multimap$ is linear implication. The above operational meaning can be assigned to those clauses by specifying how a proof search can evolve, once we have an atom A in the multiset and the formula $G \multimap A$ in the right-hand side of the sequent.

$$\dfrac{\begin{array}{c}\vdots\\ \Gamma \vdash G, \Delta\end{array} \quad \dfrac{}{A \vdash A}(id)}{\Gamma, G \multimap A \vdash A, \Delta}(\multimap L)$$

This operational meaning is fixed, by forcing the rule $(\multimap L)$ to be applied only that way. Notice that, due to the loss of the contraction rule (we cannot duplicate formulas), the formula A of the conclusion sequent is no more present in the continuation of the computation (the subproof starting from $\Gamma \vdash G, \Delta$). In fact the loss of this rule creates a problem: as it can easily be noticed, once applied, the formula $G \multimap A$ is no more applicable in the rest of the computation. Since we want these clauses to be usable more than once, we can mark all of them with the modality !, thus making them reusable resources of the computation. Through a clever use of the rules $(!C)$ and $(!D)$ we can specify the multiple reuse of "program" formulas. The following is an example of the resulting behaviour.

$$\dfrac{\dfrac{\dfrac{\begin{array}{c}\vdots\\ !\Gamma, !(G \multimap A) \vdash G, \Delta\end{array} \quad \dfrac{}{A \vdash A}(id)}{!\Gamma, !(G \multimap A), G \multimap A \vdash A, \Delta}(\multimap L)}{!\Gamma, !(G \multimap A), !(G \multimap A) \vdash A, \Delta}(!D)}{!\Gamma, !(G \multimap A) \vdash A, \Delta}(!C)$$

Thus the computation evolves without consuming the clause $!(G \multimap A)$.
Due to the constructive capabilities of linear logic an interesting change can be made to program formulas. The application of a clause can easily be extended to involve more than one atom, that is more than one agent. By considering

formulas like $G \multimap A ⅋ B$ we can obtain the following transition

$$\dfrac{\dfrac{\vdots}{\Gamma, !(G \multimap A ⅋ B) \vdash G, \Delta} \quad \dfrac{\dfrac{}{A \vdash A}(id) \quad \dfrac{}{B \vdash B}(id)}{A ⅋ B \vdash A, B}(⅋ L)}{\dfrac{!\Gamma, !(G \multimap A ⅋ B), G \multimap A ⅋ B \vdash A, B, \Delta}{\dfrac{!\Gamma, !(G \multimap A ⅋ B), !(G \multimap A ⅋ B) \vdash A, B, \Delta}{!\Gamma, !(G \multimap A ⅋ B) \vdash A, B, \Delta}(!C)}(!D)}(\multimap L)$$

Obviously the clauses can have more than two atoms in their heads. The application of these "multiset rewriting rules" can be interpreted in a variety of ways. [11] and [8] suggest to view them as a way to synchronize n computations and to allow them to communicate through a full not constrained unification. [8] also suggests to view them as specifying the consumption of "atomic messages", floating in the multiset, considered as a pool of processes and messages. An asynchronous model of communication is thus achieved. Some example in the following section will show the different forms of communication.

Clauses need not to be ground. It is a straightforward task to lift them to first order clauses by obtaining schemas of transformations. Clauses have then the form $\forall \mathbf{x}(G \multimap A_1 ⅋ \cdots ⅋ A_n)$, with the free variables of G included in the free variables of $A_1 ⅋ \cdots ⅋ A_n$. Obviously the rule $(\forall L)$ will be used in derivations.

The structure of goal formulas can be made more complex, so as to be decomposed in the derivation through the application of right introduction rules.

First of all we can use the connective ⅋ to connect more elementary goal formulas. Consider the $(⅋ R)$ introduction rule.

$$\frac{\Gamma \vdash A, B, \Delta}{\Gamma \vdash A ⅋ B, \Delta}(⅋ R)$$

We can view the previous behaviour as the decomposition of the agent $A ⅋ B$ into the two agents A and B. In other terms we can specify the creation of independent flows of subcomputation inside the overall computation.

Another connective that can be added to our fragment is the connective $\oplus$. The right introduction rules for $\oplus$ are the following:

$$\frac{\Gamma \vdash A, \Delta}{\Gamma \vdash A \oplus B, \Delta}(\oplus R) \quad \frac{\Gamma \vdash B, \Delta}{\Gamma \vdash A \oplus B, \Delta}(\oplus R)$$

We can have then an operator to specify internal nondeterminism. A possible extension can be obtained by introducing guards.

We can also have existentially quantified variables in the agents. This is the basis for a notion of computed substitution as output of the computation (the substitutions will obviously be the bindings of the existentially quantified variables of the starting agents multiset).

Other behaviours can be specified by using the constants of linear logic. In particular we can easily force the termination of a computation or the disappearing of an agent in a multiset. We can use the introduction rule for the constant

$\top$ to specify the termination of the overall computation like in the following derivation:

$$\dfrac{\dfrac{\dfrac{\dfrac{}{!\Gamma,!(\top\multimap A)\vdash \top,B,C}\,(\top R)\qquad \dfrac{}{A\vdash A}\,(id)}{!\Gamma,!(\top\multimap A),\top\multimap A\vdash A,B,C}\,(\multimap L)}{!\Gamma,!(\top\multimap A),!(\top\multimap A)\vdash A,B,C}\,(!D)}{!\Gamma,!(\top\multimap A)\vdash A,B,C}\,(!C)$$

The application of the transformation $\top\multimap A$ ends the computation. We can stop the proof search since we have obtained a correct proof of the final sequent.

The other feature, the disappearing of an agent in the multiset, can be obtained by using the constants 1 and $\bot$. Actually we can use the clauses $1\multimap A$ and $\bot\multimap A$ to state that the agent A can disappear from a multiset. The clause $\bot\multimap A$ makes the agent A disappear in a non empty multiset (see rule $(\bot R)$). The clause $1\multimap A$ makes the agent A end (together the overall computation) in the empty agent multiset (see rule $(1R)$). We will use for the pair of clauses $!(\bot\multimap A),!(1\multimap A)$ the equivalent notation $!(1\oplus\bot\multimap A)$.
Two termination modes (stated in terms of communicating processes) are then made available; i.e. silent termination by using the formula $1\oplus\bot$ and overall termination by using the constant $\top$.

Thus we have singled out an interesting fragment of linear logic with a class of uniform derivations (as it can easily be proved) which can express computations in the style of multiset rewriting. In our derivations the clause formulas act as multiset rewriting rules, while the agent formulas are uniformly decomposed in the derivation, until they are reduced to atomic formulas which can then be rewritten.
We do not want to lose the declarative reading of the logical primitives we use. As we will show in the following this is not the case since our fragment is an abstract logic programming language, that is the search of uniform derivations restricted to the fragment is complete.

In order to state this result we summarize in a more formal way the properties of our fragment. The fragment of linear logic (we will call it $\mathcal{LC}$ for *Linear Chemistry*) we are considerating is composed of the sequent $!\Gamma\vdash\Delta$, where Γ and Δ are finite multisets of formulas of the sets $\mathcal{D}$ and $\mathcal{G}$, respectively, of linear logic formulas. The set $\mathcal{G}$ is composed by the goal formulas G defined as

$$G := A|1\oplus\bot|\top|G\parr G|G\oplus G|\exists xG$$

where A is an atomic formula and G is a goal of $\mathcal{G}$. The set $\mathcal{D}$ is composed by the clause formulas D defined as

$$D = \forall(G\multimap A_1\parr\cdots\parr A_n)$$

where $A_1,\ldots,A_n$ are atomic formulas and G is a formula of $\mathcal{G}$. The free variables of G are included in the free variables of $A_1,\ldots,A_n$.

The following theorem asserts the completeness of a uniform proof search strategy for the sequent of $\mathcal{LC}$.

Theorem 2. *Let Γ be a multiset of formulas of $\mathcal{D}$ and Δ be a multiset of formulas of $\mathcal{G}$. Then $!\Gamma \vdash \Delta$ is derivable in linear logic if and only if $!\Gamma \vdash \Delta$ is uniformly derivable.*

Proof. We have just to prove the "only if" part. Assume without loss of generality we have a cut-free derivation of $!\Gamma \vdash \Delta$. It can be shown by induction that all the applications of the rule $(\multimap L)$ can be constrained to be as follows:

$$\dfrac{\begin{array}{cc}\vdots & \vdots \\ \Gamma \vdash G, \Delta & A_1 \parr \cdots \parr A_n \vdash A_1, \ldots, A_n\end{array}}{\Gamma, G \multimap A_1 \parr \cdots \parr A_n \vdash A_1, \ldots, A_n, \Delta}(\multimap L)$$

All the applications of the linear rules (id) and $(\parr L)$ occur in the right subtree of the instances of $(\multimap L)$ rule only (note that those subproofs are all uniform). By exploiting the permutability of the rules $(\oplus R)$, $(\parr R)$ and $(\exists R)$ with the remaining left rules in the resulting tree, we can easily show that we have a uniform derivation.

The fragment $\mathcal{LC}$ is then an abstract logic programming language. On the basis of theorem **1** we can state that the derivation rule system in Table 2 (we will call it $\mathcal{LC}$ system) is sound and complete w.r.t. linear logic for the sequents of $\mathcal{LC}$. In

$$\dfrac{}{!\Gamma \vdash 1 \oplus \bot}(1 \oplus \bot) \qquad \dfrac{}{\Gamma \vdash \top, \Delta}(\top) \qquad \dfrac{\Gamma \vdash \Delta}{\Gamma \vdash 1 \oplus \bot, \Delta}(1 \oplus \bot)$$

$$\dfrac{\Gamma \vdash A, B, \Delta}{\Gamma \vdash A \parr B, \Delta}(\parr) \qquad \dfrac{\Gamma \vdash A, \Delta}{\Gamma \vdash A \oplus B, \Delta}(\oplus) \qquad \dfrac{\Gamma \vdash B, \Delta}{\Gamma \vdash A \oplus B, \Delta}(\oplus)$$

$$\dfrac{\Gamma \vdash G, \Delta}{\Gamma \vdash A_1, \ldots, A_n, \Delta}(\multimap) \qquad \dfrac{\Gamma \vdash A[t/x], \Delta}{\Gamma \vdash \exists x A, \Delta}(\exists)$$

Table 2. The system $\mathcal{LC}$.

the rule $(\multimap)$ the formula $G \multimap A_1 \parr \cdots \parr A_n$ is an instance of $G' \multimap A'_1 \parr \cdots \parr A'_n$ and $!\forall(G' \multimap A'_1 \parr \cdots \parr A'_n)$ is in Γ. In the rule $(\exists)$ the formula $A[t/x]$ is obtained by substituting all the free occurrences of x in A by a term t.

These rules explicitly convey the computational flavour of the primitives of the language. It can easily be shown that they represent in a compact form exactly the uniform derivations considered introducing the $\mathcal{LC}$ formulas. A sequent $\Gamma \vdash \Delta$ will be $\mathcal{LC}$ derivable ($\Gamma \vdash_{LC} \Delta$) if it can be derived by the $\mathcal{LC}$ derivation rules.

3 $\mathcal{LC}$ and the logic Programming

We think that $\mathcal{LC}$ provides interesting features as a programming language. First of all it can be shown that we can embed in $\mathcal{LC}$ the language of Generalized Horn Clauses ($\mathcal{GC}$), introduced in [21, 22, 25] and further developed in [11] and [8]. $\mathcal{GC}$ allows multiple atoms in the heads of clauses with the aim of synchronizing concurrent computations. The syntax of the clauses is the following

$$A_1 + \cdots + A_n \leftarrow B_1 + \cdots + B_m \quad n \geq 1, m \geq 0$$

The operational semantics is a straightforward generalization of SLD refutation. $\mathcal{GC}$ formulas can easily be translated to formulas of $\mathcal{LC}$ thus preserving the computational behaviour. The translation is the following.

$$\begin{aligned} (A)^o &= A \text{ if A is an atom;} \\ (\Box)^o &= 1 \oplus \bot; \\ (A+B)^o &= (A)^o \parr (B)^o; \\ (A \leftarrow B)^o &= \forall(\exists(B)^o \multimap (A)^o). \end{aligned}$$

The $\exists$ quantifier binds all the variables of $(B)^o$ not included in $(A)^o$. The $\forall$ quantifier binds all the free variables of $\exists(B)^o \multimap (A)^o$. The translation of $\Box$ to $1 \oplus \bot$ is explained by noting that in $\mathcal{GC}$ AND-parallel processes die silently without disturbing the others and that can be obtained through the disappearing of a $\mathcal{LC}$ agent in a multiset. It is not hard to prove the following theorem that relates $\mathcal{GC}$ to $\mathcal{LC}$.

Theorem 3. *Let P be a $\mathcal{GC}$ program and $A_1, \ldots, A_n$ be atomic formulas. The goal $\leftarrow A_1 + \cdots + A_n$ is refutable in P iff $!\Gamma \vdash \exists(A_1 \parr \cdots \parr A_n)$ is $\mathcal{LC}$ -provable, where Γ is the multiset of the translations of the clauses of program P and $\exists$ binds all the variables in $A_1 \parr \cdots \parr A_n$.*

We can now show that $\mathcal{LC}$ can face the same class of problems for which $\mathcal{GC}$ was introduced. In the following we will show some programming examples taken from [11] and [8] to show in practical cases the kind of behaviours $\mathcal{LC}$ can specify.

The application of multiple head clauses can be viewed as a synchronization mechanism between agents. Moreover, if we assume the use of unification in the proof search, this application makes it possible the symmetrical exchange of messages.

Example 1. Let us consider the program $\mathcal{P}$

$$\begin{aligned} & SRB(v,X) \parr bodyA(X) \multimap A \\ & SRA(Y,w) \parr bodyB(Y) \multimap B \\ (*)\ & 1 \oplus \bot \multimap SRB(X,Y) \parr SRA(X,Y) \end{aligned}$$

The computation starts with $\mathcal{P} \vdash A, B$. We have two processes communicating through the application of the program clause $(*)$. This clause will consume in the multiset the two atoms *SRB(v,X)* and *SRA(Y,w)* and at the same time binds Y to v and X to w, thus allowing an exchange of information between the two processes.

This communication model can easily be extended to allow multiple agents to exchange information.

Example 2. The clause

$$p_1(X_1,\ldots,X_k) ⅋ \cdots ⅋\, p_k(X_1,\ldots,X_k) \multimap p_1(X_1,\ldots,X_k) ⅋ \cdots ⅋\, p_k(X_1,\ldots,X_k)$$

when applied in an environment which contains the atoms

$$\ldots, p_1(v_1, Y_1^2,\ldots,Y_1^k),\ldots,p_i(Y_i^1,\ldots,v_i,\ldots,Y_i^k),\ldots,p_k(Y_k^1,\ldots,Y_k^{k-1},v_k),\ldots$$

causes every agent p_i to communicate the value v_i to the other processes and to receive from them $k-1$ messages (we are assuming variables in the agents to be *logical* variables). Obviously the clause has to be opportunely instantiated to preclude it from keeping on reapplying itself.

As already noted, another model of communication can easily be obtained. We can distinguish two types of objects in the right-hand of a sequent. Besides the agent formulas which can be viewed as process activations, we can single out some atomic formulas acting as messages. The application of a multiple head formula can then be seen as the consumption of some message and possibly as the production of new ones. An asynchronous communication paradigm can then be established. This view of $\mathcal{LC}$ computations can improve the modularity of the program design.

Example 3. The following program, taken from [26], defines two processes which cooperate to build a list of squares exploiting the fact that the sum of the first n odd numbers equals n^2:

$o(N,s(0)) \multimap odd(N)$
$end \multimap o(0,I) ⅋\, ok$
$o(N,s(s(I))) ⅋\, num(I) \multimap o(s(N),I) ⅋\, ok$

$ok ⅋\, q(0,K) \multimap sqr(K)$
$1 \oplus \bot \multimap q(Q,Q.nil) ⅋\, end$
$ok ⅋\, \exists R(add(J,Q,R) ⅋\, q(R,K)) \multimap q(Q,Q.K) ⅋\, num(J)$

The computation originated from the initial goal formulas $odd(3), \exists K sqr(K)$, binds the variable K to the list $0.1.4.9.nil$. The *odd* process computes the first 3 odd numbers sending to the environment a *num* message for each one of them. The *sqr* process consumes the *num* message, adds the numbers and stops as soon as it receives the *end* message. The *ok* message has been introduced to synchronize the process.

The resulting communication model is reminiscent of Linda's *generative communication*[12].

Finally, as noted in [8], these two schemes of communication can be used in such a way as to make useless the sharing of variables between different agents. We can easily impose that agents do not share variables without losing any expressive power. This makes it possible the use of $\mathcal{LC}$ in a distributed environment.

4 The semantics

Since our fragment is an abstract logic programming language we can be confident about the use of the semantics of linear logic to characterize the $\mathcal{LC}$ computations. An interesting semantics for $\mathcal{LC}$ programs and goals is obtained by instantiating the phase semantics of linear logic, the semantics proposed by Girard in his seminal paper [13], to which we refer for a complete account.

In the following we consider a *phase semantics* simply as a triple $(M, \bot, s)$, where M is a monoid, $\bot$ is a subset of M, s is a valuation of atomic formulas in M, i.e. a function mapping atoms into specific subsets of M (the *facts*). By structural induction on the linear formulas and by using the distinguished operators $⅋_M, \oplus_M, \ldots$ on the facts of M, the function s can be extended to the whole set of well formed formulas (for example $s(A ⅋ B) = s(A) ⅋_M s(B)$). Finally a formula A is considered valid if it is the case that $1 \in s(A)$.

Given a program P, we obtain a phase semantics $M_P = (\mathcal{M}_{LL}, \bot_P, s)$ which behaves like the canonical Herbrand models of traditional logic programs. Namely the validity of a goal formula in the model amounts to its provability from the program P.
Let us define now in detail the *canonical phase model* of the program P. We associate to a program P the phase model $M_P = (\mathcal{M}_{LL}, \bot_P, s)$ obtained as follows:

- $\mathcal{M}_{LL} = \{\Gamma | \Gamma$ is a finite multiset of closed goal formulas$\}$,
- $\bot_P = \{\Delta | \Delta \in \mathcal{M}_{LL}$ and $P \vdash_{LC} \Delta, 1 \oplus \bot\}$,
- $s(A) = \{\Delta | \Delta \in \mathcal{M}_{LL}$ and $P \vdash_{LC} A, \Delta\}$.

In other words $\bot_P$ is the subset of $\mathcal{M}_{LL}$ composed by all the multisets which start a successful computation. Finally every atom A is mapped by s into the subset of $\mathcal{M}_{LL}$ composed of the complementary environment of A in a successful computation.
It can easily be verified that M_P is a phase semantics.

The phase semantics M_P singles out in a standard way the operators between facts $⅋_M, \oplus_M, \multimap_M$, the function $!_M$ and the distinguished facts $\mathbf{I}, \bot_P, \top$, that allow to extend the valuation s to map every formula of the $\mathcal{LC}$ fragment into a fact of the model.

The following lemma can be proved by a straightforward induction on the structure of the formulas of $\mathcal{G}$.

Lemma 4. *Given a program P and its phase semantics M_P then for each $G \in \mathcal{G}$*

$$s_{\text{ext}}(G) = \{\Delta \in \mathcal{M}_{LL} | P \vdash G, \Delta\}$$

where s_{ext} is the extension of s to linear formulas.

We can now easily prove the following theorem.

Theorem 5. *$P \vdash G$ is $\mathcal{LC}$ -provable if and only if G is valid in M_P.*

We have thus obtained a class of models for the language $\mathcal{LC}$ which generalizes the Herbrand models of traditional logic programming languages [5]. While the latter can be viewed as mapping from classical goal formulas into the set $\{\mathbf{true}, \mathbf{false}\}$, our model maps a goal formula into a fact of M_P. Note that in the case of a single head clauses program P, not using the constant $\top$, the phase model semantics M_P reduces to a boolean evaluation for the closed goals of $\mathcal{LC}$. We show now an example of a canonical phase model for a program.

Example 4. We build the phase model of the program shown in example 3. The base $\mathcal{M}_{LL}$ is the set of multisets of closed goals in the language $\{\{odd/1, o/2, end/0, num/1, sqr/1, q/2, add/3\}, \{0, s/1\}\}$. We get

$$\begin{array}{llll} \bot_P = \{ & [\top], & [1 \oplus \bot], & [\top, 1 \oplus \bot], & \dots \\ & [odd(0), sqr(0.nil)], & [o(0, s(0)), sqr(0.nil)], & [o(0, s(0)), q(0, 0.nil)], & \dots \\ & [odd(s(0)), sqr(0.s(0).nil)], & [o(s(0), s(0)), sqr(0.s(0).nil)], & [o(s(0), s(0)), q(0, 0.s(0).nil)], & \dots\} \end{array}$$

The interpretation of $odd(0)$, for example, can easily be extracted from $\bot_P$.

$$\begin{array}{llll} s(odd(0)) = \{ & [sqr(0.nil)], & [q(0, 0.nil)], & \dots \\ & [sqr(0.nil), 1 \oplus \bot], & [q(0, 0.nil), 1 \oplus \bot] & \dots \\ & [sqr(s^3(0)), \top], & [q(s^3(0)), \top] & \dots\} \end{array}$$

A fixpoint denotation can be given to a program of $\mathcal{LC}$ by viewing it as a set of mutually recursive procedures.
In the following we will use the relations

$$\frac{\Gamma \vdash \Theta}{\Lambda \vdash \Delta}(\mathcal{LC}) \qquad \frac{}{\Lambda \vdash \Delta}(\mathcal{LC})$$

The former states that $\Lambda \vdash \Delta$ can be derived from $\Gamma \vdash \Theta$ by applying a rule of the system $\mathcal{LC}$. The latter states that $\Lambda \vdash \Delta$ can be derived as an axiom of $\mathcal{LC}$.

We are now in the position to define the transformation $T_P : \mathcal{P}(\mathcal{M}_{LL}) \rightarrow \mathcal{P}(\mathcal{M}_{LL})$ associated to the program P.

$$T_P(I) = \{\Delta \in \mathcal{M}_{LL} \mid \frac{}{P \vdash 1 \oplus \bot, \Delta}(\mathcal{LC}) \text{ or } \frac{P \vdash \Theta}{P \vdash \Delta}(\mathcal{LC}) \text{ and } \Theta \in I\}$$

The following theorems give some relevant properties of the transformation T_P.

Theorem 6. *T_P is monotonic and continuous over $(\mathcal{P}(\mathcal{M}_{LL}), \subseteq)$.*

Theorem 7. $min\{I \mid T_P(I) = I\} = T_P \uparrow \omega = \bigcup_{k \geq 0} T_P^k()$.

Finally we can prove the following theorem, which states the equivalence between the fixpoint semantics and the declarative one.

Theorem 8. *Given a program P, its canonical phase semantics $(\mathcal{M}_{LL}, \bot_P, s)$ and its associated operator T_P,*

$$T_P \uparrow \omega = \bot_P$$

The semantics is very similar to that of Distributed Logic and of Generalized Horn Clauses. We remember however that in our case it is obtained through the instantiation of an already studied abstract structure, the phase space, and not as an ad hoc construction. We think this approach can be more useful to understand the primitives of the language in the light of the whole logic. Moreover that semantics can easily support extensions to the paradigm, through the addition of other linear logic constructions.

5 Related works

As already mentioned several languages have been proposed which use linear logic as their underlying logic. Miller [15, 23] uses the concept of uniform proof to characterize computationally interesting fragments of linear logic. In [15] the fragment is included in intuitionistic linear logic. Its main goal is to refine the language of hereditary Harrop Formulae, by exploiting the ability of linear logic to treat limited resource. The differences with our framework lies essentially in the absence of a mechanism of multiple head clauses, whence our fragment lacks a mechanism for the dynamic loading of modules. The areas of application seem indeed quite different. The results in [23] are more closely related to ours. In fact the fragment used to express the π-calculus as a theory of linear logic is essentially a higher order version of $\mathcal{LC}$. However the emphasis is on the use of the fragment as a metatheory of the π-calculus rather than as a logic programming language.

Other related results are [3, 4] and [2]. [3, 4] present Linear Objects (LO), an object-oriented logic programming language based on the proof theory of linear logic. LO can express the concurrent evolution of multiple objects, having complex states (essentially multisets of *slots*). Multiple-head clauses are exploited to express the evolution of our multisets of agents. Our language can be thought of as specifying the evolution of a single object without the powerful knowledge structuring of LO programs. However, in $\mathcal{LC}$ more sophisticated operations on the "single object" can easily be made available.
In [2], LinLog a fragment of linear logic is presented. This language allows a compact representation of the so called *focusing* proofs. It shows that LinLog does not lose expressive power w.r.t. linear logic. Every linear formula can be translated to LinLog preserving its focusing proofs. The $\mathcal{LC}$ language is essentially a fragment of LinLog. It is a compact representation of an *asynchronous* fragment (the ($\parr$, $\perp$, $\top$) fragment) with some synchronous additions (the connectives $\oplus$ and 1). We believe that $\mathcal{LC}$ characterizes a class of applications for a subset of LinLog.
In fact with respect to these languages, $\mathcal{LC}$ can be thought as a low level language, able to express more elementary and simple form of computations. We can think of it as a kernel language for a distributed system.

This is also the relation that $\mathcal{LC}$ has with ACL [17], with which it has some similarities. The difference lies essentially in the multiset rewriting style of the concurrence in $\mathcal{LC}$ and in the stress in $\mathcal{LC}$ on the notion of uniform proofs that assures the full independence in the decomposition of the goal formulas. Moreover the communication in $\mathcal{LC}$ can be obtained also at the term level, differently from ACL, and that can happen without synchronization problems, due to the presence of multiple head clauses. As regards the semantics, our fixpoint construction seems to be more similar than the ACL analogue in [18], to previous constructions in traditional logic programming semantics. That can allows an easier inheritance and adaptation of known results.

Finally we want to mention the relation to [6] and [7]. We think that the $\mathcal{LC}$ framework can easily be related to the general model of multiset rewriting. Indeed $\mathcal{LC}$ computations realize in a very natural way the *chemical metaphor* (as first noted in [14] for a smaller fragment). The multiset are *solutions* in which the *molecules* (agent or messages) can freely move. The *heating* of the solution (the application of the derivation rules) makes the molecules to be *decomposed* until they become simple *atoms.* At this point they are *ions* which by *chemical reactions* (the applications of the rules of the program) form new molecules.

Traditional concurrent logic programming languages ([9, 27, 28]) are quite distant relatives of our language. However we think that $\mathcal{LC}$ allows a more declarative view of concurrent interactions. For example we have not to constraint the unification to obtain synchronizations between parallel agents. Moreover the phase semantics does not seem to have the complexity of other declarative models of concurrent logic languages (see [10], for example).

6 Conclusions

In this paper we have presented a language for the concurrent programming based on the proof theory of linear logic. The $\mathcal{LC}$ framework can be characterized as an abstract logic programming language, which is closely related to the multiset rewriting computational paradigms like Chemical Abstract Machine and the Gamma model. We have proposed a semantics obtained as an instance of phase semantics of linear logic. Such a semantics describes the successful computations of $\mathcal{LC}$ programs. Finally we have given a fixpoint construction of this canonical phase model.

The $\mathcal{LC}$ language deserves further studies. We are currently investigating the possibility of extending the fragment of linear logic, so as to support mechanisms such as guards or hiding operators as proposed in [18].

An important thing to realize is that a program in the $\mathcal{LC}$ fragment is indeed a linear logical theory, while its computations are derivations in a linear proof system. Thus we need not to associate to the language $\mathcal{LC}$ a program logic. $\mathcal{LC}$ is its own program logic. We can use $\mathcal{LC}$ formulas to specify and investigate the properties of $\mathcal{LC}$ programs. We think however that the subject of specification and verification of $\mathcal{LC}$ programs still needs some work. Furthermore it would be interesting to establish to what extent the linear logic and its semantics can describe and model divergent or deadlocked computations (the present semantics simply ignores them). Moreover we think that applying some of the techniques suggested in [6] to build Γ programs we can define a set of tools for the synthesis of $\mathcal{LC}$ programs.

Finally we think an intriguing subject could be the study of abstract interpretations for $\mathcal{LC}$ programs. We think that the work made in [16] regarding an abstract interpretation of Linear Objects could be quite helpful.

Acknowledgements

The author would like to thank Giorgio Levi for his encouragement and support. Thanks are due to Alessio Guglielmi, for valuable comments, and to Andrea Masini, for helpful discussions.

References

1. S. Abramsky. Computational interpretations of linear logic. *Theoretical Computer Science*, 111(1 & 2):3–59, 1993.
2. J. M. Andreoli. Logic programming with focusing proofs in linear logic. *Journal of Logic and Computation*, 2(3):297–347, 1992.
3. J. M. Andreoli and R. Pareschi. Linear Objects: logical processes with built-in inheritance. In D. H. D. Warren and P. Szeredi, editors, *Proc. Seventh Int'l Conf. on Logic Programming*, pages 495–590. The MIT Press, Cambridge, Mass., 1990.
4. J. M. Andreoli and R. Pareschi. Communication as fair distribution of knowledge. In *Proc. of OOPSLA '91*, pages 212–229, 1991.
5. K. R. Apt. Introduction to Logic Programming. In J. van Leeuwen, editor, *Handbook of Theoretical Computer Science*, volume B: Formal Models and Semantics, pages 495–574. Elsevier, Amsterdam and The MIT Press, Cambridge, 1990.
6. J-P. Banâtre and D. Le Metayer. The gamma model and its discipline of programming. *Science of Computer Programming*, 15(1):55–77, 1990.
7. G. Berry and G. Boudol. The chemical abstract machine. In *Proc. Seventeenth Annual ACM Symp. on Principles of Programming Languages*, pages 81–94, 1990.
8. A. Brogi. And-parallelism without shared variables. In D. H. D. Warren and P. Szeredi, editors, *Proc. Seventh Int'l Conf. on Logic Programming*, pages 306–319. The MIT Press, Cambridge, Mass., 1990.
9. K. L. Clark and S. Gregory. PARLOG: parallel programming in logic. *ACM Transactions on Programming Languages and Systems*, 8:1–49, 1986.
10. F. S. de Boer, J. N. Kok, C. Palamidessi, and J. J. M. M. Rutten. Semantic models for concurrent logic languages. *Theoretical Computer Science*, 86:3–33, 1991.
11. M. Falaschi, G. Levi, and C. Palamidessi. A Synchronization Logic: Axiomatics and Formal Semantics of Generalized Horn Clauses. *Information and Control*, 60(1):36–69, 1984.
12. D. Gelernter. Generative Communication in Linda. *ACM Transactions on Programming Languages and Systems*, 7(1):80–113, 1985.
13. J.Y. Girard. Linear logic. *Theoretical Computer Science*, 50:1–102, 1987.
14. A. Guglielmi and G.Levi. Chemical logic programming? In D. Saccà, editor, *Proc. Eight Italian Conference on Logic Programming*, pages 39–51, 1993.
15. J. S. Hodas and D. Miller. Logic programming in a fragment of intuitionistic linear logic. In *Proc. Sixth IEEE Symp. on Logic In Computer Science*, pages 32–42, 1991.

16. R. Pareschi J. M. Andreoli, T. Castagnetti. Abstract Interpretation of Linear Logic Programming. In D. Miller, editor, *Proc. 1993 Int'l Symposium on Logic Programming*, pages 295–314. The MIT Press, Cambridge, Mass., 1993.
17. N. Kobayashi and A. Yonezawa. Acl-a concurrent linear logic programming paradigm. In *Proc. of the 1993 International Symposium on Logic Programming*, pages 279–294, Vancouver, 1993.
18. N. Kobayashi and A. Yonezawa. Asynchronous communication model based on linear logic. Technical report, Department of Information Science, University of Tokyo, July 1992.
19. Y. Lafont. The linear abstract machine. *Theoretical Computer Science*, 59:157–180, 1988.
20. Y. Lafont. Interaction nets. In *Proc. Fifth IEEE Symp. on Logic In Computer Science*, pages 95–108, 1990.
21. G. Levi and F. Sirovich. A problem reduction model for non-independent subproblems. In *Proc. Fourth International Joint Conference on Artificial Intelligence*, pages 340–344, 1975.
22. G. Levi and F. Sirovich. Generalized and-or graphs. *Artificial Intelligence*, 7:243–259, 1976.
23. D. Miller. The π-calculus as a theory in linear logic: Preliminary result. In E. Lamma and P. Mello, editors, *Proc. of Third International Workshop on Extensions of Logic Programming*, volume 660 of *Lecture Notes in Computer Science*, pages 242–264. Springer-Verlag, Berlin, 1992.
24. D. Miller, F. Pfenning, G. Nadathur, and A. Scedrov. Uniform proofs as a foundation for Logic Programming. *Annals of Pure and Applied Logic*, 51:125–157, 1991.
25. L. Monteiro. An extension to horn clause logic allowing the definition of concurrent processes. In G. Goos and J. Hartmanis, editors, *Proc. of International Colloquium on Formalization of Programming Concepts*, volume 107 of *Lecture Notes in Computer Science*. Springer-Verlag, Berlin, 1981.
26. L. Monteiro. A proposal for distributed programming in logic. In J. A. Campbell, editor, *Implementations of Prolog*, pages 329–340. Ellis-Horwood, 1984.
27. E. Y. Shapiro. The family of concurrent logic programming languages. *ACM Computing Surveys*, 21(3):412–510, 1989.
28. K. Ueda. Guarded Horn Clauses. In E.Y. Shapiro, editor, *Concurrent Prolog: Collected Papers*, volume 1, pages 140–156. The MIT Press, Cambridge, Mass., 1987.

Three-Valued Completion for Abductive Logic Programs

Frank Teusink

CWI, P.O. Box 94079, 1090 GB Amsterdam, The Netherlands, email: frankt@cwi.nl

Abstract. There is a growing interest in ways to represent incomplete information in logic programs. It has been shown that limited forms abduction can be used quite elegantly for this purpose. In this paper, we propose a a three-valued completion semantics for abductive logic programs, which solves some problems associated with Console et al's two-valued completion semantics. The semantics is a generalization of Kunen's completion semantics for general logic programs, which is know to correspond very well to a class of effective proof procedures for general logic programs. Secondly, we propose a proof procedure for abductive logic programs, which is a generalization of a proof procedure for general logic programs based on constructive negation. This proof procedure is sound and complete with respect to the proposed semantics. Basically, by generalizing a number of results on general logic programs to the class of abductive logic programs, we present further evidence for the idea that limited forms of abduction can be added quite naturally to general logic programs. One problem that remains, is the occurrence of inconsistencies. We argue that there are cases in which these do not pose a problem.

1 Introduction

In [DDS93], Denecker and De Schreye propose to use abduction as a means to represent incomplete information in logic programs, and present a translation from $\mathcal{A}$ (a language for stating problems in event calculus, proposed by M. Gelfond and V. Lifschitz in [GL92]) to abductive logic programs (or *incomplete logic programs*, as they call them). As a proof procedure, they propose SLDNFA-resolution (see [DDS92]); a proof procedure for abductive logic programs based on SLDNF-resolution. The semantics they use, is the two-valued completion semantics for abductive logic programs, proposed by Console et al in [CDT91].

In the last few years, various forms of constructive negation have been proposed (see for instance [Cha88], [Stu91], [Dra93b] and [Dra93a]), to deal with the problem of *floundering* in SLDNF-resolution. In [Dra93b], W. Drabent introduces SLDFA-resolution, a proof procedure for general logic programs based on SLD-resolution and constructive negation. In [Dra93b], he proves that his proof procedure is sound and complete with respect to Kunen's three-valued completion semantics, and sound with respect to two-valued completion semantics.

In this paper, we generalize SLDFA-resolution and use it as a proof procedure for abductive logic programs. The proposed proof procedure solves some problems associated with SLDNFA-resolution. First of all, by using constructive negation instead of negation as failure, we remove the problem of *floundering*. Secondly, instead of skolemizing non-ground queries, which introduces some technical problems, we use equality to our language, which allows a natural treatment of non-ground queries. Moreover, by generalizing a proof procedure from general logic programming in a straightforward way to abductive logic programming, we show that adding (limited forms of) abduction to logic programs is not too involving. We prove that this proof procedure is (under some restrictions) sound with respect to the two-valued completion semantics of Console et al.

In general logic programming, it has been shown that three-valued semantics are better suited to characterize proof procedures based on SLD-resolution, than two-valued semantics. In [Fit85], M. Fitting proposes a three-valued immediate consequence operator, on which he bases a semantics (*Fitting semantics*). Basically, it states that a formula is true in a program iff it is true in all three-valued Herbrand models of the completion of that program. In [Kun87], K. Kunen proposes an alternative to this semantics (*Kunen semantics*), in which a formula is true in a program iff it is true in all three-valued models of the completion of that program. It is this second semantics with respect to whom Drabent proved his proof procedure sound and complete.

In this paper, we generalize Fitting Semantics and Kunen semantics to abductive logic programs. In the process, we also propose a three-valued immediate consequence operator, and truth- and falseness formulas as presented by J.C. Shepherdson in [She88], for abductive logic programs. Finally, we prove soundness and completeness of the generalized SLDFA-resolution with respect to Kunen semantics. Again, in generalizing these notions to abductive logic programs, we intend to show that general logic programs can be extended quite naturally to incorporate (some limited forms of) abduction.

The class of abductive logic programs on which we concentrate in this paper, is (almost) the same as the class of 'incomplete logic programs' defined by Denecker and De Schreye. They can be seen as a generalization of ordinary general logic programs, in the sense that they are treated as general logic programs in all but the abducible predicates. The abducible predicates can be seen as 'placeholders' for representing incomplete information; the answer of a query (or the explanation of an observation) is an expression in terms (predicates) of concepts that you know exist, but on which you have no knowledge that enable you to reason with them. The proof procedure we present will reflect this view on this class of programs, by reasoning with the non-abducible predicates as if they were part of a general logic program, while the abducible predicates just 'hang around'.

The paper is organized in three more or less separate part. In the first part, we give an introduction to abductive logic programming (section 3), and present two- and three-valued completion semantics (section 4). Then, in the second part, we start with a generalization of SLDFA-resolution to the case of abductive logic programs (section 5), followed by an example of its use in section 6. The last section, section 8, in which we present some soundness and completeness results on SLDFA-resolution, can also be counted as belonging to this part. In the third part (section 7, we present the immediate consequence operator, and use it to characterize Fitting semantics and Kunen semantics for abductive logic programs.

2 Preliminaries and notation

In this paper, we use k, l, m and n to denote natural numbers, f, g and h to denote functions (constants are treated as 0-ary functions), x, y and z to denote variables, s, t and u to denote terms, p, q and r to denote predicate symbols, A, B and C to denote atoms, L, M and N to denote literals, G, H and I to denote goals, θ, δ, σ, τ and ρ to denote abducible formulas (they will be defined later) and ϕ and ψ to denote formulas.

In general, we use underlining to denote finite sequences of objects. Thus, $\underline{L}$ denotes a sequence $L_1, \ldots, L_n$ of literals and $\underline{s}$ denotes a sequence $s_1, \ldots, s_n$ of terms. Moreover, in formulas we identify the comma with conjunction. Thus, $\underline{L}$ (also) denotes a conjunction $L_1 \wedge \ldots \wedge L_n$. Finally, for two sequences $s_1, \ldots, s_k$ and $t_1, \ldots, t_k$ of terms, $(\underline{s} = \underline{t})$ denotes the formula $(s_1 = t_1) \wedge \ldots \wedge (s_k = t_k)$.

Two- and three-valued models are defined as usual, except for the fact that we treat equality as a special predicate with a fixed (two-valued) interpretation (in this, we follow [Doe93]). An *algebra* (or *pre-interpretation*, as it is called in [Llo87]), is the part of a model that interprets the terms of the language. We use $\models$ to denote ordinary two-valued logical consequences, while $\models_3$ is used for three-valued logical consequences ($T \models_3 \phi$ iff ϕ is true in all three-valued models of T).

In this paper, we always use equality in the context of Clark's Equality Theory (CET), which consists of the following *Free Equality Axioms*:

(i) $f(x_1, \ldots, x_n) = f(y_1, \ldots, y_n) \rightarrow (x_1 = y_1) \wedge \ldots \wedge (x_n = y_n)$ (for all f)
(ii) $f(x_1, \ldots, x_n) \neq g(y_1, \ldots, y_m)$ (for all distinct f and g)
(iii) $x \neq t$ (for all x and t where x is a proper subterm of t)

Note, that the fixed interpretation of equality replaces the usual equality axioms, which are normally part of CET.

For a formula ϕ, $FreeVar(\phi)$ denotes the set of free variables in ϕ. A *sentence* is a closed formula (i.e. $FreeVar(\phi)$ is empty). A *ground* formula is a quantifier-free sentence. Given a language $\mathcal{L}$ and an algebra J with domain D, a D-formula is a formula in the language $\mathcal{L}_D$, which is an extension of $\mathcal{L}$ that contains a fresh constant for every domain element of D. We sometimes refer to ground D-formulas as J-ground formulas.

In the remainder of this paper, we will not always specify the language. When no language is given, we assume a fixed 'universal' language $\mathcal{L}_\mathcal{U}$, which has a (countably) infinite number of constant and function symbols of any arity. The advantage of using such a universal language is, among others, that for that language CET is complete.

3 Abductive Logic Programming

Abduction is the process of generating an explanation E, given a theory T and an observation Ψ. More formally, E is an explanation for an abductive problem $\langle T, \Psi \rangle$, if $T \cup E$ is consistent, Ψ is a consequence of $T \cup E$, and E satisfies 'some properties that make it interesting'.

In this paper, we limit ourselves to the context of abductive logic programs, in which T is an *abductive logic program*, Ψ is a formula and E is an *abducible formula.*

An *abductive logic program* P is a triple $\langle \mathcal{A}_P, \mathcal{R}_P, \mathcal{I}_P \rangle$, where

- $\mathcal{A}_P$ is a set of *abducible predicates,*
- $\mathcal{R}_P$ is finite set of clauses $A \leftarrow \theta, \underline{L}$, where A is a non-abducible atom, θ is an abducible formula and $\underline{L}$ is a sequence of non-abducible literals, and
- $\mathcal{I}_P$ is a finite set of first-order integrity constraints.

An *abducible formula* (w.r.t. to a program P) is a first-order formula build out of the equality predicate '=' and the abducible predicates. An abducible formula δ is said to be *(in)consistent,* if $CET \cup \{\delta\}$ is (in)consistent.

In the remainder of this paper, no integrity constraints are used, i.e. $\mathcal{I}_P$ will always be empty. We can make this restriction, because there exist techniques to translate integrity constrains to some set $\mathcal{IR}_P$ of program rules with head *False* (this is a propositional variable). Instead of testing whether a candidate-explanation δ of a problem $\langle P, \phi \rangle$ satisfies the integrity constraints, one can find an explanation of the problem $\langle P', \phi \wedge \neg False \rangle$, where P' is the program $\langle \mathcal{A}_P, \mathcal{R}_P \cup \mathcal{IR}_P, \emptyset \rangle$. We use this technique in the example of section 6.

If we compare our definition of abductive logic programs with the definitions given by Console et al, and by Denecker and DeSchreye, the main difference is, that we add equality to our abducible formulas. Of course, equality is not abducible, in the sense that one can assume two terms to be equal, in order to explain an observation; we use equality in context of CET, which is complete when a universal language is used. However, when one thinks of the class of abducible formulas as the class of formulas that can be used to explain a given observation, it makes perfect sense to include equality.

4 Completion semantics for abductive logic programs

In [Cla78], K. L. Clark introduces the notion of *completion* of a general logic program, and proposes the (two-valued) completion semantics for general logic programs. The central notion in the definition of the completion of a program, is the notion of the *completed definition* of a predicate.

Definition 1. Let P be a program and let p be a predicate symbol in the language of P. Let n be the arity of p and let $x_1, \ldots, x_n$ be a sequence of fresh variables. Let $p(\underline{s}_1) \leftarrow \theta_1, \underline{L}_1 \quad \ldots \quad p(\underline{s}_m) \leftarrow \theta_m, \underline{L}_m$ be the clauses in P with head

p, and let, for $i \in [1..m]$, $y_i = FreeVar(\theta_i, \underline{L}_i) - FreeVar(p(\underline{s}_i))$. The *completed definition of p (w.r.t. P)* is the formula

$$p(\underline{x}) \cong \bigvee_{i \in [1..m]} \exists_{\underline{y}_i}((\underline{x} = \underline{s}_i), \theta_i, \underline{L}_i)$$

Intuitively, the completed definition of a predicate states that "p is **t** *iff* there exists a rule for p whose body is **t**".

The *completion* ($comp(P)$) of a general logic program consists of the completed definitions of its predicates, plus CET to interpret equality correctly. In the (two-valued) completion semantics for general logic programs, a formula is true in a program iff it is true in all (two-valued) models of the completion of that program.

In [CDT91], Console et al propose a two-valued completion semantics for abductive logic programs. The idea is, that the completion of an abductive logic program only contains completed definitions of non-abducible predicates. As a result, the theory $comp(P)$ contains no information on the abducible predicates (i.e. the abducible predicates can be freely interpreted).

Definition 2. Let P be an abductive logic program. The *completion of* P (denoted by $comp(P)$) is the theory that consists of CET and, for every non-abducible predicate p in P, the completed definition of p.

Using this notion of completion for abductive logic programs, Console et al give an object level characterization of the explanation of an abductive problem $\langle P, \phi \rangle$. Intuitively, it is the formula (unique up to logical equivalence) that represents all possible ways of explaining the observation in that abductive problem. Before we can give its definition, we have to introduce the notion of *most specific abducible formula.*

Definition 3. For abducible formulas θ and σ, θ is *more specific* than σ if $CET \models \theta \rightarrow \sigma$. θ is *most specific* if there does not exist a σ (different from θ, modulo logical equivalence) such that σ is more specific than θ.

We now give the definition of explanation, as proposed by Console et al (i.e. the object level characterization of definition 2 in [CDT91]). As we want to reserve the term 'explanation' for an alternative notion of explanation we define later on, we use the term 'full explanation' here.

Definition 4. Let $\langle P, \phi \rangle$ be an abductive problem. Let δ be an abducible formula. Then, δ is *the full explanation of* $\langle P, \phi \rangle$, if δ is the most specific abducible formula such that $comp(P) \cup \{\phi\} \models \delta$, and $comp(P) \cup \{\delta\}$ is consistent.

Note, that in this definition ϕ and δ switched positions with respect to the ordinary characterization of abduction. The advantage of this definition is, that for a given abductive problem, the full explanation is unique (up to logical equivalence).

In their paper, Console et al restrict their abductive logic programs to the class of *hierarchical programs.* As a reason for this, they argue that 'it is useless to explain a fact in terms of itself'. Practical reasons for this restriction seem to be twofold: it ensures consistency of $comp(P)$, and soundness and completeness of their 'abstract' proof procedure ABDUCE. Although we agree that, as is the case with general logic programs, a large class of naturally arising programs will turn out to be hierarchical, we do not want to restrict ourselves to hierarchical programs at this point. Moreover, the problem of checking whether a given program is hierarchical is not always easy (see [AB91] for some techniques). Thus, instead of restricting ourselves to hierarchical programs, in the definition of full explanation, we added the condition that $comp(P) \cup \{\delta\}$ has to be consistent.

We now define an alternative notion of 'explanation'. This second definition is more in line with the normal characterization of abduction. However, it is also weaker, in the sense that there can exist more than one explanation for a given abductive problem.

Definition 5. Let $\langle P, \phi \rangle$ be an abductive problem. An abducible formula δ is *an explanation for* $\langle P, \phi \rangle$, if $comp(P) \cup \{\delta\} \models \phi$ and $comp(P) \cup \{\delta\}$ is consistent.

The following lemma shows that the full explanation of a given abductive problem is less specific than any explanation for that abductive problem.

Lemma 6. *Let $\langle P, \phi \rangle$ be an abductive problem, let δ be the full explanation of $\langle P, \phi \rangle$, and let θ be an explanation for $\langle P, \phi \rangle$. Then, $CET \models \theta \rightarrow \delta$.*

Thus, the difference between the two kinds of explanations is, that the full explanation incorporates all possible ways of explaining a given observation, while an (ordinary) explanation is a formula that is just sufficient to explain that given observation.

In the above, we used two-valued completion as a semantics. In general logic programming, there also exist three-valued completion semantics. In these semantics, the third truth-value models the fact that effective proof procedures cannot determine truth or falsity for all formulas. Thus, the third truth-value ($\perp$) stands for 'truth-value undetermined'. In section 7, we will characterize Fitting semantics and Kunen semantics for abductive logic programs, using a three-valued immediate consequence operator. In the remainder of this section, we present Kunen semantics using a model-theoretic approach.

Fitting semantics and Kunen semantics are based the same notion of completion as used in the two-valued case, but use it in the setting of three-valued models. In this three-valued setting, special care must be taken to interpret the equiv-

$\leftrightarrow$	t	f	$\perp$
t	t	f	$\perp$
f	f	t	$\perp$
$\perp$	$\perp$	$\perp$	$\perp$

$\cong$	t	f	$\perp$
t	t	f	f
f	f	t	f
$\perp$	f	f	t

Fig. 1. Kleene equivalence and strong equivalence

alence operator, used in the completed definition of a predicate, correctly. Intuitively, this equivalence should enforce that the lefthand side and the righthand side of the completed definition have the same truth-value. However, Kleene's three-valued equivalence ($\leftrightarrow$) stands for something like "the truth-values of left and right hand sides are equal and neither one is unknown". Therefore, instead of $\leftrightarrow$, another notion of equivalence ($\cong$) is used, which has the required truth-table (see figure 1). The operator $\cong$ cannot be constructed using Kleene's operators, and therefore has to be introduced separately. Its use will be restricted: it will only be used in the completed definition of a predicate. Note, that $\leftrightarrow$ and $\cong$ are equivalent when restricted to the truth-values **t** and **f**.

Using a model-theoretic approach, Kunen semantics can be stated very succinctly.

Definition 7. Let $\langle P, \phi \rangle$ be an abductive problem. A consistent abducible formula δ is a *three-valued explanation for* $\langle P, \phi \rangle$ if $comp(P) \cup \{\delta\} \models_3 \phi$.

Note, that in this definition only consistency of δ (with respect to *CET*) is required. The reason is, that in three-valued completion the completed definitions of the program-rules are always consistent.

There is a large difference in the handling of inconsistencies between two- and three-valued completion. In the following example, we show how inconsistencies 'disappear' in three-valued completion semantics.

Example 1. Consider the abductive logic program P, with a single abducible predicate a, and the following two clauses:

$$p \leftarrow \neg p, a$$
$$q \leftarrow a$$

Then, $comp(P) \cup \{a\}$ is obviously inconsistent in two-valued completion, because when a is true, the completed definition of p reduces to $p \cong \neg p$. Thus, among others, a is not an explanation for $\langle P, q \rangle$. However, by assigning $\perp$ to p, we can construct three-valued models of $comp(P) \cup \{a\}$, and therefore a *is* a three-valued explanation for $\langle P, q \rangle$.

5 Generalizing SLDFA-resolution

In this section we generalize SLDFA-resolution, as defined by W. Drabent in [Dra93b], to abductive logic programs. The main difference with the definition given in [Dra93b] is, that the answers we compute are abducible formulas instead of constraints. As a result, most definitions in this section are direct copies of definitions in [Dra93b]. Only the definition of *goal* is slightly different.

Drabent defines a *constraint* to be a first-order formula build out of the equality predicate '='. Thus, the definition of abducible formula is a generalization of the definition of constraint. A constraint θ is said to be *satisfiable*, if $CET \models \exists\theta$. Instead of using this notion of satisfiability, we use the notion of *consistency* of abducible formulas (with respect to *CET*). Not only is the notion of abducible formulas a generalization of constraint (as used by Drabent), but, when a universal language is used, also the notion of consistency of abducible formulas generalizes then notion of satisfiability of constraints; because $CET_{\mathcal{L}u}$ is complete, a constraint is consistent iff it is satisfiable.

We will not concern ourselves with reducing abducible formulas to normal forms. We simply assume the existence of normalization procedures that transform a given abducible formula into a format that is intelligible to humans.

SLDFA-resolution is defined by two basic notions: *SLDFA-refutations* and *(finitely failed) SLDFA-trees*. An *SLDFA-refutation* is a sequence of goals, ending in a goal without non-abducible atoms, such that each goal in the sequence is obtained from the previous goal by a *positive* or *negative derivation step*. A *positive derivation step* is the usual one used in SLD-resolution, with the difference that the resolved atom has to be a non-abducible atom. A *negative derivation* step is the replacement of a negative non-abducible literal $\neg A$ in the goal by an abducible formula σ such that $\leftarrow \sigma, A$ is guaranteed to fail finitely. A *finitely failed SLDFA-tree* for a goal G is a proof for the fact that G fails finitely; it is an approximation that is 'save' with respect to finite failure; if a finitely failed SLDFA-tree for G exists, it is guaranteed that G fails finitely, but the fact that that there exists an SLDFA-tree for G that is not finitely failed, does not imply that G is not finitely failed.

We begin the definition of SLDFA-resolution with the definition of a *goal*.

Definition 8. Let P be a program. A *goal* (w.r.t. P) is a formula of the form $\neg(\theta \wedge L_1 \wedge \ldots \wedge L_k)$, usually written as $\leftarrow \theta, L_1, \ldots, L_k$, such that

- θ is a consistent abducible formula, and
- L_i (for $i \in [1..k]$) is a non-abducible literal.

An *s-goal* is a goal in which one of the literals is marked as *selected*.

We start with the definition of *positively derived goals*.

Definition 9. Let P be a program, let G be the s-goal $\leftarrow \theta, \underline{N}, p(\underline{t}), \underline{M}$ (with $p(\underline{t})$ selected) and let $p(\underline{s}) \leftarrow \sigma, \underline{L}$ be a variant of a clause in P. A goal G' is *positively derived* from G using $p(\underline{s}) \leftarrow \sigma, \underline{L}$ if

- $FreeVar(G) \cap FreeVar(p(\underline{s}) \leftarrow \sigma, \underline{L}) = \emptyset$ and
- G' is of the form $\leftarrow \theta, (\underline{t} = \underline{s}), \sigma, \underline{N}, \underline{L}, \underline{M}$.

If G' is positively derived from G using a variant of a clause R, we call R *applicable* to G.

Note that the abducible formula in G' is (by definition) consistent because G' is (by definition) a goal, and by definition the abducible formula in a goal is consistent.

We now give the definitions of *negatively derived goals*, *SLDFA-refutations*, *finitely failed goals* and *(finitely failed) SLDFA-trees*. These definitions are mutually recursive. Therefore, the definitions are defined inductively, using the notion of *rank*.

Definition 10. Let P be a program and let G be the s-goal $\leftarrow \theta, \underline{N}, \neg A, M$ (with $\neg A$ selected). Let the notion of *rank k finitely failed goals* be defined. A goal G' is *rank k negatively derived* from G if

- G' is of the form $\leftarrow \theta, \sigma, \underline{N}, \underline{M}$,
- $\leftarrow \theta, \sigma, A$ is a rank k finitely failed goal, and
- $FreeVar(\sigma) \subseteq FreeVar(A)$.

We call θ, σ a *(rank k) fail answer* for $\leftarrow \theta, A$.

Definition 11. Let P be a program and let G be a goal. Let the notion of *rank $k-1$ negatively derived s-goal* be defined. A *rank k SLDFA-refutation* of G is a sequence of s-goals $G_0, G_1, \ldots, G_n$ such that G is the goal part of G_0, G_n is of the form $\leftarrow \theta$ and, for $i \in [1..n]$,

- G_i is positively derived from G_{i-1} using a variant C of a clause in P such that
  $FreeVar(C) \cap FreeVar(G_0, \ldots, G_{i-1}) = \emptyset$, or
- G_i is rank $k-1$ negatively derived from G_{i-1}.

The abducible formula $\exists \underline{y}\theta$, where $\underline{y} = FreeVar(\theta) - FreeVar(G)$, is a *SLDFA-computed answer* for G.

Definition 12. Let P be a program and let G be a goal. Let the notion of *rank k SLDFA-refutation* be defined. A *rank k finitely failed SLDFA-tree* for G is a tree such that

1. each node of the tree is an s-goal and the goal part of the root node is G,
2. the tree is finite,
3. if $H : \leftarrow \theta, \underline{L}_1, A, \underline{L}_2$ (with A selected) is a node in the tree then, for every clause R in P applicable to H, there exists exactly one son of H that is positively derived from H using a variant of R, and
4. if $H : \leftarrow \theta, \underline{L}_1, \neg A, \underline{L}_2$ (with $\neg A$ selected) is a node in the tree, then it has sons

$$\leftarrow \sigma_1, \underline{L}_1, \underline{L}_2 \ , \ \ldots \ , \ \leftarrow \sigma_m, \underline{L}_1, \underline{L}_2$$

   provided there exist $\delta_1, \ldots, \delta_n$ that are SLDFA-computed answers obtained by rank k SLDFA-refutations of $\leftarrow \theta, A$, such that

$$CET \models \theta \rightarrow \delta_1 \vee \ldots \vee \delta_n \vee \sigma_1 \vee \ldots \vee \sigma_m$$

If no node in an SLDFA-tree is of the form $\leftarrow \theta$, then that tree is called *finitely failed.*

Definition 13. Let P be a program and let G be a goal. Let the notion of *rank k finitely failed SLDFA-tree* be defined. G is a *rank k finitely failed goal* if there exists a rank k finitely failed SLDFA-tree for G.

6 An example: the Murder Mystery Domain

In [DDS93], M. Denecker and D. de Schreye present a translation of the so-called Murder Mystery Domain into an abductive logic program. The Murder Mystery domain is described by the following action system:

Init *Alive*.
$\neg$*Alive* **after** *Shoot*; *Wait*.
Load **causes** *Loaded*.
Shoot **causes** $\neg$*Alive* **if** *Loaded*.
Shoot **causes** $\neg$*Loaded*.

This domain is translated into the following abductive logic program P_{MMD} (we use lists here, instead of *Result/2* terms):

$$Holds(f, []) \leftarrow Init(f).$$
$$Holds(f, [a|s]) \leftarrow Holds(f, s), \neg NonInert(f, a, s).$$
$$Holds(Loaded, [Load|s]).$$
$$NonInert(Loaded, Load, s).$$
$$NonInert(Loaded, Shoot, s).$$
$$NonInert(Alive, Shoot, s) \leftarrow Holds(Loaded, s).$$
$$False \leftarrow \neg Holds(Alive, []).$$
$$False \leftarrow Holds(Alive, [Wait, Shoot]).$$

In this program, *Init*/1, which models the initial situation, is the only abducible predicate. The predicate *NonInert*/3 describes which actions under which situations can influence which fluents. Then, the *Holds*/2 predicate uses *Init*/1 and *NonInert*/3 to describe which fluents hold in which situations. Note, that the first two clauses for *Holds*/2 are standard; the first one uses *Init*/1 to state that there is incomplete information on the initial situation, while the second one defines the law of inertia (whenever a fluent is inert, it doesn't change state). Finally, the clauses with head *False* implement the integrity constraints. They are used to model the *v-propositions* (i.e. the **init** and **after** clauses). Note, that in order to enforce the integrity constraints, the conjunct $\neg False$ should be added to any goal we would like to answer.

Now, consider the goal $\leftarrow \neg Holds(Alive, [x_1, x_0]) \wedge \neg False$. Figure 2 contains an SLDFA-refutation for this goal, together with some subsidiary refutations and trees. In this figure, a label $fail(T_i)$ is used in negative derivation steps to indicate that one can construct a finitely failed SLDFA-tree from the SLDFA-tree T_i, by adding the constraint in the derivant to every goal in T_i. A label $answers(R_1, \ldots, R_n)$ indicates the SLDFA-refutations used in the constructing of the sons of a node in an SLDFA-tree with negative literal selected. We have omitted the SLDFA-tree for $\leftarrow False$, used in refutation R_1, for lack of space. As a fail answer for this goal we use $Init(Alive) \wedge Init(Loaded)$. From refutation R_2 it follows that

$$x_1 = Shoot \wedge x_0 \neq Shoot \wedge Init(Loaded) \wedge Init(Alive)$$

R_1

$\underline{\neg Holds(Alive, [x_1, x_0]),}$
$\underline{\neg False}$
$fail(T_2)$

|

$x_1 = Shoot \wedge x_0 \neq Shoot \wedge Init(Loaded),$
$\underline{\neg False}$
$fail(\leftarrow False)$

|

$x_1 = Shoot \wedge x_0 \neq Shoot \wedge$
$Init(Loaded) \wedge Init(Alive)$

R_3

$\underline{NonInert(Alive, x_1, [x_0])}$

|

$x_1 = Shoot,$
$\underline{Holds(Loaded, [x_0])}$

|

$x_1 = Shoot, x_0 = Load$

R_3

$\underline{NonInert(Alive, x_1, [x_0])}$

|

$x_1 = Shoot,$
$\underline{Holds(Loaded, [x_0])}$

|

$x_1 = Shoot,$
$Holds(Loaded, []),$
$\underline{\neg NonInert(Loaded, x_0, [])}$
$fail(T_4)$

|

$x_1 = Shoot \wedge x_0 \neq Load \wedge x_0 \neq Shoot,$
$\underline{Holds(Loaded, [])}$

|

$x_1 = Shoot \wedge x_0 \neq Load \wedge$
$x_0 \neq Shoot \wedge Init(Loaded)$

T_2

$\underline{Holds(Alive, [x_1, x_0])}$

|

$Holds(Alive, [x_0]),$
$\underline{\neg NonInert(Alive, x_1, [x_0])}$
$answers(R_2, R_3)$

|

$x_1 \neq Shoot \vee x_0 = Shoot \vee \neg Init(Loaded),$
$\underline{Holds(Alive, [x_0])}$

|

$x_1 \neq Shoot \vee x_0 = Shoot \vee \neg Init(Loaded),$
$Holds(Alive, []),$
$\underline{\neg NonInert(Alive, x_0, [])}$
$answers()$

|

$x_1 \neq Shoot \vee x_0 = Shoot \vee \neg Init(Loaded),$
$Holds(Alive, [])$

|

$(x_1 \neq Shoot \vee x_0 = Shoot \vee \neg Init(Loaded))$
$\wedge\ Init(Alive)$

T_4

$\underline{NonInert(Loaded, x_0, [])}$

/ \

$x_0 = Load$ $\qquad$ $x_0 = Shoot$

Fig. 2. Answering $\langle P_{MMD}, \neg Holds(Alive, [x_1, x_0]) \wedge \neg False\rangle$.

is an SLDFA-computed answer for the goal. Note, that in this refutation we both use abducible predicates (in this case only *Init*/1) and constructive negation. In section 8, we prove that it follows that this abducible formula is a three-valued explanation for

$$\langle P_{MMD}, \neg Holds(Alive, [x_1, x_0]) \wedge \neg False \rangle$$

7 Three-valued completion semantics

In definition 7, we generalize Kunen semantics to abductive logic programs. The definition as given there is, however, very succinct. For one thing, it doesn't express the intention behind both Fitting and Kunen semantics. That is, that the third truth-value stands for something like 'truth-valued not determined'.

In [Fit85], M. Fitting proposes the use of three-valued semantics for general logic programs, using the third truth-value ($\perp$) to represent the fact that for some formulas, the truth-value cannot be determined. For this purpose, Fitting introduced a three-valued immediate consequence operator Φ_P, to characterize the meaning of a general logic program. He proves that the fixpoints of this operator are three-valued Herbrand models of the completed program. He takes the least fixpoint of this operator as the meaning of a general logic program (*Fitting semantics*). However, as Fitting points out, in general this semantics is highly non-constructive: the closure ordinal for the least fixpoint can be as high as ω_1, the first non-recursive ordinal.

In [Kun87], K. Kunen proposes a semantics in which the iteration of Fitting's immediate consequence operator is cut-off at ordinal ω. Moreover, he proves that a sentence ϕ is **t** in his semantics iff ϕ is **t** in all three-valued models of *comp*(P).

In this section, we define an immediate consequence operator for abductive logic programs, and use it to characterize Fitting semantics and Kunen semantics for abductive logic programs. In the process, we also generalize Shepherdson's truth- and falseness formulas (see [She88]).

For general logic programs, the immediate consequence operator Φ_P operates on models, and $\Phi_P(M)$ denotes the one-step consequences of M, given a program P. In our definition, $\Phi_{P,\delta}(\mathcal{M})$ denotes the one-step consequences of $\mathcal{M}$, given an abductive logic program P and an abducible formula δ. So, we compute immediate consequences in P, under the assumption that δ holds. However, for arbitrary abducible formulas δ, δ cannot be characterized by a single model. For instance, if δ is of the form $p(a) \vee p(b)$, it has two minimal models. Therefore, $\Phi_{P,\delta}$ will operate on sets of models. In [Fit85] and [Kun87], Φ_P operates on Herbrand models. We however follow K.Doets [Doe93], and define the operators on J-models, given an algebra J.

Thus, the operator $\Phi_{P,\delta}$ operates on sets of models. To facilitate its definition and various proofs, we define the operator $\Phi_{P,\delta}$ in two steps. First, we define an operator $\Phi_{P,\Delta}$, which operates on models. Then, in the second step, we define $\Phi_{P,\delta}$ in terms of $\Phi_{P,\Delta}$. In $\Phi_{P,\Delta}$, Δ models the abducible predicates of P. The idea is that, because Δ is a model instead of an abducible formula, the set of immediate consequences of a model M in P under assumption Δ can be characterized by a single model. Because we want Δ to model the abducible predicates only, we first have to introduce the notion of *abducible models.*

Definition 14. Let P be a program. A model M is an *abducible model* (w.r.t. P), if all non-abducible atoms in P are mapped to $\perp$ in M.

Now, the definition of $\Phi_{P,\Delta}$ is a straightforward generalization of the operator Φ_P for general logic programs. For non-abducible atoms, the definition stays the same. However, for an abducible atom A, A is **t** (resp. **f**) in $\Phi_{P,\Delta}(M)$ iff it is **t** (resp. **f**) in Δ.

Definition 15. Let P be a program. Let J be an algebra and let Δ be a abducible J-model. The three-valued immediate consequence operator $\Phi^J_{P,\Delta}$ is defined as follows:

- $\Phi^J_{P,\Delta}(M)(A) = \mathbf{t}$ iff $\Delta \models_3 A$ or there exists a J-ground instance $A \leftarrow \theta, \underline{L}$ of a clause in P such that $\Delta \models_3 \theta$ and $M \models_3 \underline{L}$.
- $\Phi^J_{P,\Delta}(M)(A) = \mathbf{f}$ iff $\Delta \models_3 \neg A$ or for all J-ground instances $A \leftarrow \theta, \underline{L}$ of clauses in P, either $\Delta \models_3 \neg\theta$ or $M \models_3 \neg\underline{L}$.

The powers of $\Phi^J_{P,\Delta}$ are defined as follows:

$$\Phi^J_{P,\Delta} \uparrow \alpha = \begin{cases} \Delta & \text{, if } \alpha = 0 \\ \Phi^J_{P,\Delta}(\Phi^J_{P,\Delta} \uparrow n-1) & \text{, if } \alpha \text{ is a successor ordinal} \\ \bigcup_{\beta<\alpha} \Phi^J_{P,\Delta} \uparrow \beta & \text{, if } \alpha \text{ is a limit ordinal} \end{cases}$$

Note that this definition is not standard for $\alpha = 0$. We could define $\Phi^J_{P,\delta} \uparrow 0$ to be the empty set, but at the cost of having a special treatment of the base case in some of the lemmas.

Now, we can define $\Phi_{P,\delta}$. We will not define $\Phi_{P,\delta}(\mathcal{M})$ for arbitrary sets of models $\mathcal{M}$. Instead, we only define $\Phi_{P,\delta} \uparrow \alpha$, for arbitrary ordinals α.

Definition 16. Let P be a program and let δ be a consistent abducible formula. Let J be an algebra and let $\mathcal{M}$ be the set of abducible J-models of $\{\delta\}$. Then,

$$\Phi^J_{P,\delta} \uparrow \alpha = \{\Phi^J_{P,\Delta} \uparrow \alpha \mid \Delta \in \mathcal{M}\}$$

In [She88], J.C. Shepherdson defines the notion of truth- and falseness formulas. These formulas give an elegant alternative characterization of what is computed by the immediate consequence operator. We now generalize these formulas to abductive logic programs.

Definition 17. Let P be a program. For a natural number n and a formula ϕ, we define the formulas $T_n(\phi)$ and $F_n(\phi)$ as follows:

- If ϕ is an abducible formula, we define for all n

$$T_n(\phi) \stackrel{def}{=} \phi \qquad F_n(\phi) \stackrel{def}{=} \neg\phi$$

- If ϕ is an atom of the form $p(\underline{s})$, where p is a non-abducible predicate, then $comp(P)$ contains a definition $p(\underline{x}) \cong \psi$, where $FreeVars(\psi) = \underline{x}$. We define

$$T_0(\phi) \stackrel{def}{=} \mathbf{f} \qquad F_0(\phi) \stackrel{def}{=} \mathbf{f}$$

and

$$T_n(\phi) \stackrel{def}{=} T_{n-1}(\underline{x} = \underline{s} \wedge \psi) \qquad F_n(\phi) \stackrel{def}{=} F_{n-1}(\underline{x} = \underline{s} \wedge \psi)$$

- If ϕ is a complex formula, $T_n(\phi)$ and $F_n(\phi)$ are defined by structural induction on ϕ.

The following lemma is a generalization of lemma 4.1 in [She88] to abductive logic programs.

Lemma 18. *Let P be a program and let δ be a consistent abducible formula. Let J be an algebra with domain D and let ϕ be a D-sentence. Then,*

1. $\Phi^J_{P,\delta} \uparrow n \models_3 \phi$ *iff* $J \cup \{\delta\} \models_3 T_n(\phi)$
2. $\Phi^J_{P,\delta} \uparrow n \models_3 \neg\phi$ *iff* $J \cup \{\delta\} \models_3 F_n(\phi)$

Using the three-valued consequence operator, we can generalize the Fitting semantics to abductive logic programs.

Definition 19. Let $\langle P, \phi \rangle$ be an abductive problem. Let δ be a consistent abducible formula. Let $\mathcal{M}$ be the least fixpoint of $\Phi^{HA}_{P,\delta}$. Then, δ is an *explanation* for $\langle P, \phi \rangle$ *in the Fitting semantics*, if $\mathcal{M} \models_3 \phi$.

With Fitting semantics for general logic programs, a formula is true in the Fitting semantics iff it is true in all three-valued Herbrand models. The same holds for Fitting semantics for abductive logic programs.

Theorem 20. *Let $\langle P, \phi \rangle$ be an abductive problem. A consistent abducible formula δ is an explanation for $\langle P, \phi \rangle$ in the Fitting semantics iff ϕ is true in all three-valued Herbrand models of $comp(P) \cup \{\delta\}$.*

In [Kun87], Kunen proposes to stop iteration of the immediate consequence operator at ω, instead of continuing until the least fixpoint is reached. Generalizing this idea to abductive logic programming, we get the following semantics.

Definition 21. Let $\langle P, \phi \rangle$ be an abductive problem. Let δ be a consistent abducible formula. Then, δ is an *explanation* for $\langle P, \phi \rangle$ *in the Kunen semantics* if, for some natural number n, $\Phi^{HA}_{P,\delta} \uparrow n \models_3 \phi$.

Note, that this definition differs from definition 7. The following theorem proves that both definitions give rise to the same semantics. First, we state some results on (recursively saturated) elementary extensions.

Lemma 22. *Let P be a program. Let J be an elementary extension of HA, let Δ be an abducible HA-model and let Δ' be an elementary J-extension of Δ. For every sentence ϕ and natural number n, $\Phi^{HA}_{P,\Delta} \uparrow n \models_3 \phi$ iff $\Phi^J_{P,\Delta'} \uparrow n \models_3 \phi$.*

Property 1 *Every countable model has a countable recursively saturated elementary extension*

Lemma 23. *Let P be a program and let δ be a consistent abducible formula. Let ϕ be a sentence and let J be a recursively saturated CET-algebra. Then, $comp(P) \cup \{\delta\} \models_3 \phi$ implies that, for some finite n, $\Phi^J_{P,\delta} \uparrow n \models_3 \phi$.*

Theorem 24. *Let P be a program and let δ be a consistent abducible sentence. Let ϕ be a sentence. Then, $comp(P) \cup \{\delta\} \models_3 \phi$ iff, for some finite n, $\Phi^{HA}_{P,\delta} \uparrow n \models_3 \phi$.*

Proof.
($\Rightarrow$) Suppose that $comp(P) \cup \{\delta\} \models_3 \phi$. By property 1, there exists a recursively saturated elementary extension J of HA. Because J is an extension of HA, it is a CET-algebra. By lemma 23 there exists an n such that $\Phi^J_{P,\delta} \uparrow n \models_3 \phi$. Let Δ be an arbitrary abducible HA-model of $\{\delta\}$. By property 1, there exists an elementary J-extension Δ' of Δ. Because Δ' is an elementary extension of Δ, δ is a sentence and $\Delta \models_3 \delta$, it follows that $\Delta' \models_3 \delta$. Therefore, it follows from $\Phi^J_{P,\delta} \uparrow n \models_3 \phi$ that $\Phi^J_{P,\Delta'} \uparrow n \models_3 \phi$. But then, by lemma 22, $\Phi^{HA}_{P,\Delta} \uparrow n \models_3 \phi$. Thus, for arbitrary Herbrand models Δ of δ, $\Phi^{HA}_{P,\Delta} \uparrow n \models_3 \phi$. But then, also $\Phi^{HA}_{P,\delta} \uparrow n \models_3 \phi$.

($\Leftarrow$) The proof is by induction on n. For $n = 0$, we have that $\Phi^{HA}_{P,\Delta} \uparrow 0 \models_3 \phi$ implies that ϕ is an abducible formula and that $HA \cup \{\delta\} \models_3 \phi$. Because δ and ϕ are sentences and every model of CET is an extension of a Herbrand model, $CET \cup \{\delta\} \models_3 \phi$ and therefore $comp(P) \cup \{\delta\} \models_3 \phi$.

Assume that the claim holds for all $m < n$. If $p(\underline{s})$ is a non-abducible J-ground atom, there exists a J-ground instance $p(\underline{a}) \cong \psi$ of a formula in $comp(P)$ such that $\Phi^J_{P,\delta} \uparrow n \models_3 p(\underline{s})$ iff $comp(P) \cup \{\delta\} \models_3 p(\underline{s})$.

For complex sentences, the proof is by structural induction.

8 Soundness and completeness of generalized SLDFA-resolution

In this section, we present some soundness and completeness results on SLDFA-resolution for abductive logic programs. We start by proving soundness with respect to three-valued completion semantics for abductive logic programs.

Theorem 25. *Let P be a program and let G be the goal $\leftarrow \theta, \underline{L}$.*

1. *If δ is an SLDFA-computed answer for G then $comp(P) \models_3 \delta \to \theta \wedge \underline{L}$.*
2. *If G finitely fails then $comp(P) \models_3 \theta \to \neg\underline{L}$.*

The proof of this theorem closely resembles the proof of theorem 4.2 in in [Dra93b]. The differences between the two proofs are, that here we prove soundness with respect to three-valued completion semantics, while Drabent's proof proves soundness with respect to two-valued completion, and that we work with abductive formulas instead of constraints.

The following corollary proves soundness of SLDFA-resolution with respect to the three-valued completion semantics for abductive logic programs, as stated in definition 7.

Corollary 26. *(Three-valued Soundness) Let P be a program and let $G : \leftarrow \theta, \underline{L}$ be a goal. If δ is an SLDFA-computed answer for G, then δ is a three-valued explanation for $\langle P, \theta \wedge \underline{L} \rangle$.*

Now that we have proven soundness with respect to three-valued completion semantics, the following result is straightforward.

Corollary 27. *(Two-valued Soundness) Let P be a program and let $G : \leftarrow \theta, \underline{L}$ be a goal. If δ is an SLDFA-computed answer for G and $comp(P) \cup \{\delta\}$ is consistent, then δ is an explanation for $\langle P, \theta \wedge \underline{L} \rangle$.*

We now turn prove completeness of the generalized SLDFA-resolution with respect to three-valued completion semantics.

Theorem 28. *Let P be a program and let $G : \leftarrow \theta, \underline{L}$ be a goal. Let δ be an abducible sentence. Then, for an arbitrary fair selection rule,*

1. *if $comp(P) \cup \{\delta\} \models_3 \theta \wedge \underline{L}$, then there exist computed answers $\delta_1, \ldots, \delta_n$ for G such that $CET \models_3 \delta \rightarrow \delta_1 \vee \ldots \vee \delta_n$, and*
2. *if $comp(P) \models_3 \theta \rightarrow \neg\underline{L}$ then G fails finitely.*

As was the case with theorem 25, the proof of this theorem is (almost) identical to the proof of the corresponding theorem in [Dra93b] (theorem 5.1). The only difference is, that we use results from section 7, where Drabent used results from [Kun87].

Corollary 29. *(Three-valued Completeness) Let P be a program, let $G :\leftarrow \theta, \underline{L}$ be a goal and let δ be an abducible sentence. If δ is a three-valued explanation for $\langle P, \theta \wedge \underline{L} \rangle$, then there exist SLDFA-computed answers $\delta_1, \ldots, \delta_k$ for G such that $CET \models_3 \delta \rightarrow \delta_1 \vee \ldots \vee \delta_k$.*

9 Conclusions

In this paper we present a generalization of Drabent's SLDFA-resolution, and use it as a proof procedure for abductive logic programming. We show that the proof procedure is sound with respect to two-valued completion semantics -provided the union of completed program and answer is consistent- and that it is sound and complete with respect to three-valued completion semantics.

There is quite a difference between SLDFA-resolution for abductive logic programming, and Denecker and De Schreye's SLDNFA-resolution. For one thing, Denecker and De Schreye want the explanations to be ground conjunctions of atoms. For this, they skolemize non-ground goals, and use 'skolemizing substitutions' in the resolution steps. Instead, we allow our explanations to be arbitrary non-ground abducible formulas. These differences would make a close comparison between the two proof procedures a rather technical exercise. However, we are quite confident that, for any answer given by SLDNFA-resolution, there is an 'equivalent' SLDFA-computed answer. We expect this not to hold the other way around, simply because our proof procedure is based on constructive negation, while SLDNFA-resolution is based on negation as failure.

The great similarity between SLDFA-resolution and SLDNFA-resolution is, that they both use deduction, and both do not concern themselves with the consistency of the obtained answers with respect to the completed program. As a result, they cannot be compared with ordinary proof procedures for abductive logic programming, whose main concern *is* consistency of the obtained answers.

In this context, choice between two- and three-valued completion semantics is an important one; if we use two-valued completion semantics, in addition to SLDFA-resolution we do need a procedure to check whether the obtained SLDFA-computed answer is consistent with respect to the completed program. We think that this will mean a considerable increase in computation costs. On the other hand, if we use three-valued completion semantics, the need for this consistency check disappears. However, one can argue that this is a 'fake' solution; in some sense we just disregard inconsistencies, by weakening the notion of a model. In our opinion, the choice of semantics depends on your view on abductive logic programs, and the relation between abducible and non-abducible predicates. If one assumes that a program, i.e. the definition of the non-abducible predicates, can contain implicit information on the abducible predicates, in the form of potential inconsistencies, one should use two-valued completion. On the other hand, if one thinks of abducible predicates as *completely* undefined (apart from integrity constraints), or thinks that only integrity constraints should be used for constraining the abducible predicates, one should use three-valued completion, because then inconsistencies are the result of flaws in the program.

A second reason why it is interesting to look at proof procedures for abductive logic programming that do not check for consistency, is the case where you can guarantee that the union of computed answer and completed program is consistent. An example of this is the translation proposed by Denecker and De Schreye in [DDS93]. The programs resulting from this translation are acyclic (proposition 3.1), which seems to suggest that the union of their completion with a consistent abducible formula is consistent. There might be more of these examples, and it might be interesting to define classes of programs for which this property holds (among others, the above conjecture on acyclic programs should be proven).

Acknowledgements

This paper was supported by a grant from SION, a department of NWO, the Netherlands Organization for Scientific Research. I would like to thank Krzysztof

Apt for his support, and Kees Doets for his help on three-valued completion semantics. Also, I am grateful to the referees, for some valuable comments.

References

[AB91] Krzysztof R. Apt and Marc Bezem. Acyclic programs. *New Generation Computing*, 9:335–363, 1991.

[CDT91] Luca Console, Daniele Theseider Dupre, and Pietro Torasso. On the relationship between abduction and deduction. *Journal of Logic and Computation*, 1(5):661–690, 1991.

[Cha88] David Chan. Constructive negation based on the completed database. In *Proceedings of the International Conference on Logic Programming*, pages 111–125. MIT Press, 1988.

[Cla78] K. L. Clark. Negation as failure rule. In H. Gallaire and G. Minker, editors, *Logic and Data Bases*, pages 293–322. Plenum Press, 1978.

[DDS92] Marc Denecker and Danny De Schreye. SLDNFA: an abductive procedure for normal abductive programs. In *Proceedings of the Joint International Conference and Symposium on Logic Programming*, pages 686–700, 1992.

[DDS93] Marc Denecker and Danny De Schreye. Representing incomplete knowledge in abductive logic programming. In *Proceedings of the International Logic Programming Symposium*, 1993.

[Doe93] Kees Doets. *From Logic to Logic Programming*. The MIT Press series in Foundations of Computing. MIT Press, 1993. forthcomming.

[Dra93a] Wlodzimierz Drabent. SLS-resolution without floundering. In *Proceedings of the workshop on Logic Programming and Non-Monotonic Reasoning*, 1993.

[Dra93b] Wlodzimierz Drabent. What is failure? an approach to constructive negation. Updated version of a Technical Report LITH-IDA-R-91-23 at Linkoping University, 1993.

[Fit85] Melvin Fitting. A Kripke-Kleene semantics for logic programs. *Journal of Logic Programming*, 2(4):295–312, 1985.

[GL90] Michael Gelfond and Vladimir Lifschitz. Logic programs with classical negation. In *Proceedings of the International Conference on Logic Programming*, pages 579–597, 1990.

[GL92] Michael Gelfond and Vladimir Lifschitz. Representing actions in extended logic programming. In *Proceedings of the Joint International Conference and Symposium on Logic Programming*, pages 559–573, 1992.

[KKT92] A.C. Kakas, R.A. Kowalski, and F. Toni. Abductive logic programming. *Journal of Logic and Computation*, 2:719–770, 1992.

[Kun87] Kenneth Kunen. Negation in logic programming. *Journal of Logic Programming*, 4:289–308, 1987.

[Llo87] J.W. Lloyd. *Foundations of Logic Programming*. Symbolic Computation – Artificial Intelligence. Springer-Verlag, 1987. Second, extended edition.

[She88] John C. Shepherdson. Language and equality theory in logic programming. Technical Report PM-88-08, School of Mathematics, University Walk, Bristol, BS8 1 TW, England, 1988.

[Stu91] Peter J. Stuckey. Constructive negation for constraint logic programming. In *Proceedings of the IEEE Symposium on Logic in Computer Science*, pages 328–339. IEEE Computer Society Press, July 1991.

A Sequential Reduction Strategy

Sergio Antoy
Portland State University, U.S.A.
antoy@cs.pdx.edu

Aart Middeldorp
University of Tsukuba, Japan
ami@softlab.is.tsukuba.ac.jp

ABSTRACT

Kennaway proved the remarkable result that every (almost) orthogonal term rewriting system admits a computable sequential normalizing reduction strategy. In this paper we present a computable sequential reduction strategy similar in scope, but simpler and more general. Our strategy can be thought of as an outermost-fair-like strategy that is allowed to be unfair to some redex of a term when contracting the redex is useless for the normalization of the term. Unlike the strategy of Kennaway, our strategy does not rely on syntactic restrictions that imply confluence. On the contrary, it can easily be applied to any term rewriting system, and we show that the class of term rewriting systems for which our strategy is normalizing properly includes all (almost) orthogonal systems. Our strategy is more versatile; in case of (almost) orthogonal term rewriting systems, it can be used to detect certain cases of non-termination. Our normalization proof is more accessible than Kennaway's. We also show that our sequential strategy sometimes succeeds where the parallel-outermost strategy fails.

1 Introduction

This paper is concerned with reductions strategies for term rewriting systems. Given a term rewriting system (TRS for short) and a term, a reduction strategy tells you which redex(es) to contract. The desirable property of reduction strategies is *normalization*: repeated contraction of the redex(es) selected by the reduction strategy leads to a normal form, if the term under consideration has a normal form. For the important subclass of (almost) orthogonal TRSs several positive results are known. An *orthogonal* TRS is left-linear and non-overlapping. If the non-overlapping restriction is relaxed by allowing trivial overlays then we speak of *almost* orthogonal TRSs. A typical example of an almost orthogonal TRS that is not orthogonal is the two-rule system $\{\top \vee x \to \top,\ x \vee \top \to \top\}$. O'Donnell

[7] showed that the *parallel-outermost* strategy—which evaluates all outermost redexes in parallel—is normalizing for all almost orthogonal TRSs. The question whether there exists a computable normalizing *sequential* reduction strategy for all (almost) orthogonal TRSs has received quite a bit of attention. A sequential strategy must choose a single redex for contraction. The main results are summarized below.

(1) Contrary to the situation for λ-calculus, there are orthogonal TRSs for which the *leftmost-outermost* strategy is not normalizing. Consider for instance the orthogonal TRS (from [3])

$$\begin{array}{rcl} a & \to & b \\ c & \to & c \\ f(x,b) & \to & d \end{array}$$

and the term $t = f(c,a)$. The leftmost-outermost strategy will select redex c in t and hence produce the infinite reduction sequence $t \to t \to t \to \cdots$. Nevertheless, parallel-outermost succeeds in normalizing t: $t \to^* f(c,b) \to d$. O'Donnell [7] showed that the leftmost-outermost strategy is normalizing for every *left-normal* orthogonal TRS.[1] Left-normality means that variables do not precede function symbols in the left-hand sides of the rewrite rules. A typical example of a left-normal orthogonal TRS is *combinatory logic.*

(2) Huet and Lévy, in a landmark paper [3], formulated the strong sequentiality criterion and showed that every strongly sequential orthogonal TRS admits a computable normalizing sequential reduction strategy. Every left-normal orthogonal TRS is strongly sequential, but there are many strongly sequential orthogonal TRSs that are not left-normal, one example being the TRS of the preceding paragraph. The strategy of Huet and Lévy is based on the fact that for orthogonal TRSs

- every term not in normal form contains a *needed* redex, and
- repeated contraction of needed redexes leads to the normal form, if it exists.

The latter statement can be strengthened to the *hyper normalization* of needed reduction: there are no infinite reduction sequences starting from a term that has a normal form in which infinitely many needed redexes are contracted. Since needed redexes are in general not computable, this does not give a normalizing sequential strategy for all orthogonal TRSs. Huet and Lévy showed that for strongly sequential orthogonal TRSs at least one of the needed redexes in a term not in normal form can be efficiently computed. The orthogonality requirement cannot be weakened to almost orthogonality, simply because needed redexes may not exist for almost orthogonal TRSs, as observed by Sekar and Ramakrishnan [10].

---

[1] Actually, O'Donnell showed that the leftmost-outermost strategy is normalizing for all left-normal *almost* orthogonal TRSs. However, it is easy to see that if two rewrite rules in a left-normal almost orthogonal TRS overlap, then one of the rules is an instance of the other. Hence for every left-normal almost orthogonal TRS there exists a left-normal orthogonal TRS with the same rewrite relation. Thus nothing is really added by allowing trivial overlays, rather, it would unnecessarily confuse Figure 1 below.

(3) Kennaway [4] showed the remarkable fact that *every* almost orthogonal TRS admits a computable normalizing sequential reduction strategy. Actually, Kennaway doesn't restrict himself to TRSs but obtains his result in the very general setting of ***combinatory reduction systems*** of Klop [5].

(4) Toyama [11] showed that the sequential strategy of Huet and Lévy is normalizing for the larger class of strongly sequential left-linear ***root-balanced joinable*** TRSs. The root-balanced joinability requirement is less restrictive than the trivial overlays allowed by Kennaway, but because of the strong sequentiality requirement Toyama's result does not cover the result of Kennaway. For instance, the almost orthogonal TRS $\{\top \vee x \to \top,\ x \vee \top \to \top\}$ is not strongly sequential.

(5) Oyamaguchi [8] extended the work of Huet and Lévy in a different direction. Strong sequentiality is a property based on the left-hand sides of the rewrite rules. Oyamaguchi showed that by incorporating information in the right-hand sides of the rewrite rules, a less restrictive notion of sequentiality can be obtained, while retaining the good properties of strong sequentiality. The resulting class of ***NV-sequential*** orthogonal TRSs properly contains all strongly sequential orthogonal TRSs. Although Kennaway's result applies to all systems covered by Oyamaguchi's result, the result of Oyamaguchi is of interest because his strategy can be computed in polynomial time, which is not the case for the strategy of Kennaway.[2]

Figure 1 shows the relationships between the above-mentioned results. The area enclosed in the dotted rectangle denotes the class of TRSs for which the parallel-outermost strategy is normalizing. Areas enclosed in numbered solid rectangles correspond to the sequential strategies described above. Observe that parallel-outermost encompasses all known sequential reduction strategies. (The fact that parallel-outermost is normalizing for every strongly sequential left-linear root-balanced joinable TRS follows from the work of Toyama [11].) All systems in area (3) are confluent. Systems in area (4) are not necessarily confluent, but they do have unique normal forms. (Slightly stronger, every term that has a normal form is confluent.)

The starting point of the present paper is Kennaway's result. The strategy of Kennaway is complicated and relies on the confluence property. We define a simpler and intuitive sequential strategy for *every* TRS and we show that the class of TRSs for which our strategy is normalizing properly includes the class of TRSs for which Kennaway's strategy is defined. This class is indicated in Figure 1 as the area between the dashed lines. At present it is unclear whether the shaded area is inhabited. All other areas are inhabited. In particular, we will see that there exist TRSs which cannot be normalized by means of the parallel-outermost strategy but for which our sequential strategy succeeds.

Our strategy is versatile. We will show that in case of almost orthogonal TRSs, it can be used as a sufficient condition for the property of having no

[2] Moreover, Oyamaguchi obtained his results in 1987, two years before Kennaway's paper was published.

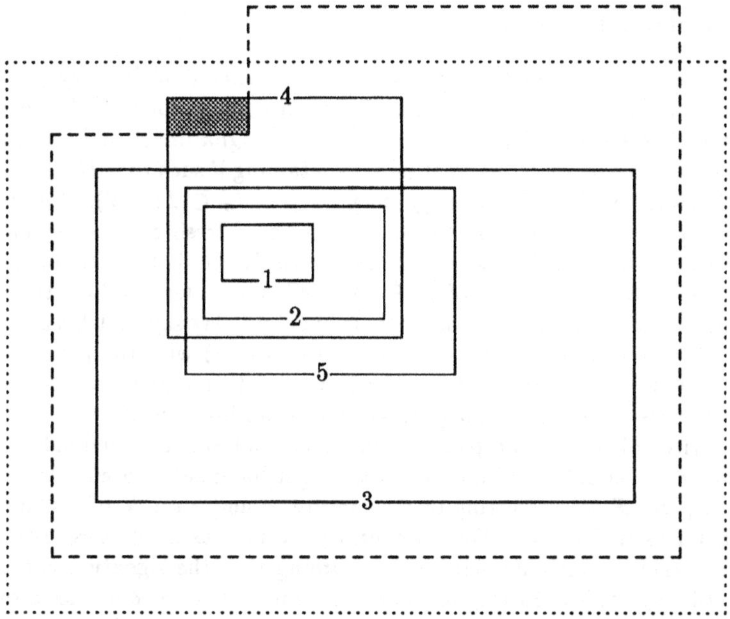

Fig. 1.

normal form. This means that for certain terms our strategy will signal that it is useless to contract any redex as the term under consideration has no normal form.

The remainder of the paper is organized as follows. In the next section we formally define the notion of sequential reduction strategy. In Section 3 we describe an abstract game of Klop which is closely related to our strategy. It is well-known that in general it is undecidable whether a term cycles. In Section 4 we give a sufficient and decidable criterion for cyclicity. Using this result, our computable sequential strategy is defined in Section 5. In Section 6 we present our main theorem: if our strategy fails to normalize a term then there exists an infinite so-called *outermost-fair* reduction sequence starting from that term. This result does not rely on orthogonality, quite to the contrary, it holds for every TRS. Our proof is non-trivial but considerably simpler than the normalization proof of Kennaway. Since for almost orthogonal TRSs it is known (O'Donnell [7]) that terms that admit infinite outermost-fair reduction sequences do not have a normal form, an immediate consequence is the normalization of our strategy for all almost orthogonal TRSs. In Section 7 we explain how, in case of almost orthogonal systems, our strategy can be used to detect certain cases of non-termination. Furthermore, we exhibit a non-left-linear TRS which can be normalized by our sequential strategy, but for which parallel-outermost fails. We also mention some directions for further research. In particular, we address the question how to enhance our strategy in order to enlarge the class of TRSs for which it is normalizing.

2 Preliminaries

A signature is a set $\mathcal{F}$ of function symbols. Associated with every $f \in \mathcal{F}$ is a natural number denoting its arity. Function symbols of arity 0 are called constants. The set $\mathcal{T}(\mathcal{F},\mathcal{V})$ of terms built from a signature $\mathcal{F}$ and a countably infinite set of variables $\mathcal{V}$ is the smallest set containing $\mathcal{V}$ such that $f(t_1,\ldots,t_n) \in \mathcal{T}(\mathcal{F},\mathcal{V})$ whenever $f \in \mathcal{F}$ has arity n and $t_1,\ldots,t_n \in \mathcal{T}(\mathcal{F},\mathcal{V})$. We write c instead of $c()$ whenever c is a constant. Let $\Box$ be a fresh constant symbol. A context C is a term in $\mathcal{C}(\mathcal{F},\mathcal{V})$ containing precisely one hole. The designation term is restricted to members of $\mathcal{T}(\mathcal{F},\mathcal{V})$. If C is a context and t a term then $C[t]$ denotes the result of replacing the hole in C by t. We say that t is a subterm of $C[t]$. A substitution is a map σ from $\mathcal{V}$ to $\mathcal{T}(\mathcal{F},\mathcal{V})$ with the property that the set $\{x \in \mathcal{V} \mid \sigma(x) \neq x\}$ is finite. If σ is a substitution and t a term then $t\sigma$ denotes the result of applying σ to t. We call $t\sigma$ an instance of t.

A rewrite rule $l \to r$ is a pair of terms such that the left-hand side l is not a variable and variables which occur in the right-hand side r occur also in l. A TRS is a pair $(\mathcal{F},\mathcal{R})$ consisting of a signature $\mathcal{F}$ and a set $\mathcal{R}$ of rewrite rules between terms in $\mathcal{T}(\mathcal{F},\mathcal{V})$. We often present a TRS as a set of rewrite rules, without making explicit its signature, assuming that the signature consists of the function symbols occurring in the rewrite rules. A TRS $\mathcal{R}$ defines a rewrite relation $\to_\mathcal{R}$ on terms as follows: $s \to_\mathcal{R} t$ if there exists a rewrite rule $l \to r$ in $\mathcal{R}$, a substitution σ, and a context C such that $s = C[l\sigma]$ and $t = C[r\sigma]$. The subterm $l\sigma$ of s is called a redex and we say that s rewrites to t by contracting the redex $l\sigma$. The subterm $r\sigma$ of t is called a contractum of the redex $l\sigma$. We call $s \to_\mathcal{R} t$ a rewrite step. We usually omit the subscript $\mathcal{R}$. A term without redexes is called a normal form. The set of all normal forms of $\mathcal{R}$ is denoted by $NF(\mathcal{R})$. We say that a term t has a normal form if there exists a reduction sequence starting from t that ends in a normal form.

A position is a sequence of natural numbers identifying a subterm in a term. The set $\mathcal{P}os(t)$ of positions in a term t is inductively defined as follows: $\mathcal{P}os(t) = \{\varepsilon\}$ if t is a variable and $\mathcal{P}os(t) = \{\varepsilon\} \cup \{i{\cdot}p \mid 1 \leqslant i \leqslant n \text{ and } p \in \mathcal{P}os(t_i)\}$ if $t = f(t_1,\ldots,t_n)$. We say that a position p is above a position q if there exists a position r such that $p \cdot r = q$. If p is above q we also say that q is below p and we write $p \leqslant q$. We write $p < q$ if $p \leqslant q$ and $p \neq q$. Positions p, q are disjoint, denoted by $p \parallel q$, if neither $p \leqslant q$ nor $q \leqslant p$. If $p \in \mathcal{P}os(t)$ then $t_{|p}$ denotes the subterm of t at position t and $t[s]_p$ denotes the term that is obtained from t by replacing the subterm at position p by the term s. The size $|t|$ of a term t is the number of symbols occurring in it.

A TRS $\mathcal{R}$ is left-linear if the left-hand side l of every rewrite rule $l \to r \in \mathcal{R}$ doesn't contain multiple occurrences of the same variable. Let $l_1 \to r_1$ and $l_2 \to r_2$ be renamed versions of rewrite rules of a TRS $\mathcal{R}$ such that they have no variables in common. Suppose $l_{1|p}$, for some $p \in \mathcal{P}os(l_1)$ such that $l_{1|p}$ is not a variable, and l_2 are unifiable with most general unifier σ. The pair of terms $\langle l_1[r_2]_p\sigma, r_1\sigma\rangle$ is called a critical pair of $\mathcal{R}$. If $l_1 \to r_1$ and $l_2 \to r_2$ are renamed versions of the same rewrite rule, we do not consider the case $p = \varepsilon$. A critical pair $\langle l_1[r_2]_p\sigma, r_1\sigma\rangle$ with $p = \varepsilon$ is an overlay. A critical pair $\langle s,t\rangle$ is trivial if $s = t$. A left-linear TRS without critical pairs is called orthogonal. An almost orthogonal TRS is a left-linear TRS with the property that all its critical pairs are trivial overlays. Almost orthogonal TRSs are called weakly orthogonal in Kennaway [4], but nowadays weak orthogonality is used to denote the larger class of left-linear TRSs with only trivial critical pairs. A typical example of a weakly orthogonal TRS that is not (almost) orthogonal is the two-rule system $\{s(p(x)) \to x,\ p(s(x)) \to x\}$. Almost all results obtained for orthogonal TRSs (Klop [6] contains a good overview) carry over to almost orthogonal TRSs, with literally the same proofs, the notable exception being the theory of Huet and Lévy [3] on needed reductions. Weakly orthogonal TRSs are more complicated. Much more information on term rewriting can be found in Dershowitz and Jouannaud [2] and Klop [6]. The latter contains an introduction to the study of reduction strategies.

What is a sequential reduction strategy? In the literature one often finds the following definition:

> A sequential reduction strategy is a mapping $\mathcal{S}$ that assigns to every term t not in normal form a redex position in t.

This definition serves if the contractum of a redex is unique, which is the case for any TRS that lacks non-trivial overlays, in particular for all weakly orthogonal TRSs. However, if the TRS under consideration does have non-trivial overlays, we are faced with the problem that there are redexes with more than one contractum. Hence we must also supply the rewrite rule according to which the redex has to be contracted. Given a redex and a rule, the contractum is again uniquely determined. How to choose the rewrite rule? There are two possibilities:

- The rewrite rule depends only on the redex. This means that we are given a mapping that assigns to every redex a rewrite rule of whose left-hand side the redex is an instance.
- The rewrite rule depends on the redex and the surrounding context.

Clearly the latter option is more general. For instance, a (confluent) TRS like

$$\begin{array}{rcl} a & \to & b \\ b & \to & a \\ a & \to & c \\ c & \to & a \\ f(b,c) & \to & d \end{array}$$

cannot be normalized if we opt for the former. (This example also shows that both options lead to *unfairness* in the sense of Porat and Francez [9].) The simplicity of the former option however makes it possible to reason effectively about the strategy we will present later. Therefore we arrive at the following formal definition.

DEFINITION 2.1 Let $\mathcal{R}$ be an arbitrary TRS. A *sequential reduction strategy* for $\mathcal{R}$ consists of the following two components:

- a mapping *rule* that assigns to every redex of $\mathcal{R}$ a rewrite rule of whose left-hand side the redex is an instance, and

- a mapping $\mathcal{S}$ that assigns to every term t not in normal form one of its redex positions.

We require that both *rule* and $\mathcal{S}$ are computable. The mapping *rule* induces a mapping *contract* from redexes to instances of right-hand sides of rewrite rules of $\mathcal{R}$ as follows: if $rule(t) = l \to r$ then $contract(t) = r\sigma$ where σ is any substitution satisfying $t = l\sigma$. If t is not in normal form then $t\mathcal{S}$ denotes the term $t[contract(t_{|\mathcal{S}(t)})]_{\mathcal{S}(t)}$, i.e. the result of applying the strategy to t. We write $t \to_{\mathcal{S}} t'$ if and only if $t' = t\mathcal{S}$.

In the remainder of this paper we identify a sequential reduction strategy with its mapping $\mathcal{S}$, that is, we assume that the mapping *rule* is given but our main results do not depend on its definition. This implies that we cannot prove that our sequential reduction strategy is capable of normalizing the rather simple TRS $\mathcal{R} = \{a \to a,\ a \to b\}$ since this depends on *rule*: a sequential reduction strategy normalizes $\mathcal{R}$ if and only if $rule(a) = a \to b$. For TRSs that do not admit non-trivial overlays, in particular for almost and weakly orthogonal TRSs, the identification of a sequential reduction strategy with its mapping $\mathcal{S}$ entails no loss of generality since the contractum of a redex is independent of the mapping *rule*.

It should be stressed that a sequential reduction strategy has no memory. This means that the decision concerning which redex to contract must be solely based on the term at hand and the given TRS, but the reduction sequence leading from the starting term to the present term may not be used. In particular, parallel-outermost cannot be simulated by a sequential reduction strategy since after contracting one outermost redex there is no way of telling which redexes in the resulting term coincide with the remaining outermost redexes in the starting term.

DEFINITION 2.2 A sequential reduction strategy for a TRS $\mathcal{R}$ is *normalizing* if for every term t that has a normal form there exists a reduction sequence $t = t_1 \to_{\mathcal{S}} t_2 \to_{\mathcal{S}} \cdots \to_{\mathcal{S}} t_n$ (with $n \geqslant 1$) ending in a normal form t_n.

Throughout the following we assume that we are dealing with TRSs that satisfy the following two properties:

- it is decidable whether a term is a redex (and hence it is also decidable whether a term is a normal form),
- in every infinite reduction sequence $t_1 \to t_2 \to \cdots$ in which the size of all terms is uniformly bounded, only finitely many different function symbols and variables occur (and hence the reduction sequence contains a repetition).

These properties are in particular true for all finite TRSs.

We conclude this preliminary section by introducing some notation for manipulating reduction sequences. Let $\mathcal{D}$: $t_1 \to t_2 \to t_3 \to \cdots$ be an arbitrary infinite reduction sequence. We write $\mathcal{D}[i,j]$ $(1 \leqslant i < j)$ to denote the finite portion $t_i \to t_{i+1} \to \cdots \to t_j$ and $\mathcal{D}[i]$ $(i \geqslant 1)$ to denote the term t_i. The concatenation $t_1 \to^+ t_2 \to^+ t_3$ of two finite reduction sequences $\mathcal{D}_1$: $t_1 \to^+ t_2$ and $\mathcal{D}_2$: $t_2 \to^+ t_3$ is denoted by $\mathcal{D}_1;\mathcal{D}_2$. If $\mathcal{D}$: $t \to^+ t$ is a cycle then $\mathcal{D}^\infty$ denotes the infinite reduction sequence $\mathcal{D};\mathcal{D};\mathcal{D};\ldots$. Let $\mathcal{D}$ be an arbitrary (finite or infinite) reduction sequence. If C is a context then $C[\mathcal{D}]$ denotes the reduction sequence obtained from $\mathcal{D}$ by replacing every term t in $\mathcal{D}$ with $C[t]$. Finally, if p is a position in $\mathcal{D}[1]$ such that no redex at a position $q < p$ is contracted in $\mathcal{D}$, then $\mathcal{D}_{|p}$ denotes the reduction sequence extracted from $\mathcal{D}$ by replacing every term t in $\mathcal{D}$ with $t_{|p}$. In this case the resulting sequence may contain fewer rewrite steps.

3 The Game of Klop

The result of Kennaway [4] covers the TRS combinatory logic extended with the parallel-or rules $\{\mathsf{T} \vee x \to \mathsf{T},\ x \vee \mathsf{T} \to \mathsf{T}\}$, which is rather surprising since the term $t_1 \vee t_2$ seems to require parallel evaluation of its arguments t_1 and t_2. In Kennaway [4] (see also Klop [6]) the following abstract game is described which captures the essence of the difficulty of evaluating a term like $t_1 \vee t_2$ with a sequential strategy.

Suppose we are given two total functions f and g from $\mathbb{N}_+$, the set of positive integers, to $\mathbb{N}$. The objects of the game are pairs (x, y) of natural numbers. The search space is defined as a relation between these pairs:

$$\begin{array}{lcl}(x,y) & \to & (f(x),y),\\ (x,y) & \to & (x,g(y)),\\ (x,0) & \to & (0,0),\\ (0,y) & \to & (0,0)\end{array}$$

for all $x, y > 0$. The goal of the game is to reach $(0,0)$ from a given pair of natural numbers by adopting a sequential strategy. Sequential means here that, given a pair of positive integers, we must choose between applying function f to the first argument and applying function g to the second argument. Moreover, the choice can only be based on the pair of positive integers at hand (and the functions f and g of course). In particular, the strategy of alternatively applying f and g until one of the numbers become zero—which is guaranteed to produce $(0,0)$ if this is at all possible—is not allowed. Formally, a *sequential strategy* is a function $\mathcal{S}$ from $\mathbb{N}_+ \times \mathbb{N}_+$ to the set $\{L, R\}$. Every sequential strategy $\mathcal{S}$ defines a subset of the search space as follows:

$$\begin{array}{lcll}(x,y) & \to_{\mathcal{S}} & (f(x),y) & \text{if } \mathcal{S}(x,y)=L,\\ (x,y) & \to_{\mathcal{S}} & (x,g(y)) & \text{if } \mathcal{S}(x,y)=R,\\ (x,0) & \to_{\mathcal{S}} & (0,0), & \\ (0,y) & \to_{\mathcal{S}} & (0,0) & \end{array}$$

for all $x, y > 0$. We say that a sequential strategy $\mathcal{S}$ is *good* if $(x,y) \to_{\mathcal{S}}^{*} (0,0)$ whenever $(x,y) \to^{*} (0,0)$, for all natural numbers x and y.

In Kennaway [4] it is shown that there exists a good strategy for this game.[3] The sequential reduction strategy (for almost orthogonal TRSs) defined in [4]

[3] The solution described in [4] is attributed to M. van Leeuwen and H. Mulder.

however is not related to the solution of this abstract game. We present a slightly different solution. Our solution is very close to the sequential reduction strategy that we define in Section 5.

We define a strategy $\mathcal{S}$ by distinguishing two cases. If $x \leqslant y$ then we compute the sequence x, $f(x)$, $f^2(x)$, ... until we reach an $f^n(x)$ with $n \geqslant 1$ such that

- $f^n(x) = 0$, or
- $f^n(x) > x$, or
- $f^n(x) = f^m(x)$ for some $0 \leqslant m < n$.

Since there are only finitely many different natural numbers less than x, eventually one of these alternatives is satisfied. We define $\mathcal{S}(x, y) = R$ if the last alternative holds with $m = 0$, and $\mathcal{S}(x, y) = L$ in all other cases. If $x > y$ then we compute the sequence y, $g(y)$, $g^2(y)$, ... until we reach a $g^n(y)$ with $n \geqslant 1$ such that

- $g^n(y) = 0$, or
- $g^n(y) > y$, or
- $g^n(y) = g^m(y)$ for some $0 \leqslant m < n$,

and we define $\mathcal{S}(x, y) = L$ if the last alternative holds with $m = 0$, and $\mathcal{S}(x, y) = R$ in all other cases. Before showing that $\mathcal{S}$ is a good strategy, we illustrate the strategy by means of a simple example. Consider the functions

$$f(x) = \begin{cases} x+1 & \text{if } x \neq 7, \\ 6 & \text{if } x = 7 \end{cases}$$

and

$$g(x) = \begin{cases} 2x & \text{if } x < 5, \\ 0 & \text{if } x = 5, \\ x-1 & \text{if } x > 5. \end{cases}$$

Starting from the pair $(1,1)$, the strategy $\mathcal{S}$ produces the following sequence:

$$\begin{aligned} (1,1) &\to_{\mathcal{S}} (2,1) \to_{\mathcal{S}} (2,2) \to_{\mathcal{S}} (3,2) \to_{\mathcal{S}} (3,4) \to_{\mathcal{S}} (4,4) \to_{\mathcal{S}} (5,4) \\ &\to_{\mathcal{S}} (5,8) \to_{\mathcal{S}} (6,8) \to_{\mathcal{S}} (7,8) \to_{\mathcal{S}} (7,7) \to_{\mathcal{S}} (7,6) \to_{\mathcal{S}} (7,5) \\ &\to_{\mathcal{S}} (7,0) \to_{\mathcal{S}} (0,0). \end{aligned}$$

THEOREM 3.1 *The strategy $\mathcal{S}$ just defined is a good strategy.*

PROOF. Suppose to the contrary that there exist functions $f, g\colon \mathbb{N}_+ \to \mathbb{N}$ and a pair $(x, y) \in \mathbb{N} \times \mathbb{N}$ such that $(x, y) \to^* (0,0)$ but not $(x, y) \to^*_{\mathcal{S}} (0,0)$. Without loss of generality we assume that the last step in the finite sequence $(x, y) \to^* (0,0)$ is $(0, \tilde{y}) \to (0,0)$. Hence there exists an $n > 0$ such that $f^n(x) = 0$ while $g^m(y) > 0$ for all $m \geqslant 0$. The infinite $\to_{\mathcal{S}}$-sequence starting from (x, y) must have the following form:

$$(x, y) \to^*_{\mathcal{S}} (x', y') \to_{\mathcal{S}} (x', g(y')) \to_{\mathcal{S}} (x', g^2(y')) \to_{\mathcal{S}} (x', g^3(y')) \to_{\mathcal{S}} \cdots,$$

i.e., we eventually reach a pair (x', y') such that $\mathcal{S}(x', g^i(y')) = R$ for all $i \geqslant 0$. Suppose that all $g^i(y')$ are smaller than x'. This implies that the infinite sequence

y', $g(y')$, $g^2(y')$, ... contains a repetition, say $g^p(y') = g^q(y')$ with $0 \leqslant p < q$. Let $g^l(y')$ be a maximal element in the cycle $g^p(y')$, $g^{p+1}(y')$, ..., $g^q(y')$. It is not difficult to see that $\mathcal{S}(x', g^l(y')) = L$, yielding a contradiction. Hence there exists an $i \geqslant 0$ such that $g^i(y') \geqslant x'$. From $\mathcal{S}(x', g^i(y')) = R$ we infer that $x' = f^k(x')$ for some $k \geqslant 1$, contradicting our assumption that $f^n(x) = 0$. We can only conclude that $\mathcal{S}$ is a good strategy. □

This game and its solution easily generalize to n-tuples ($n > 2$) of natural numbers.

4 Cycle Detection

Let $\mathcal{S}$ be a (sequential) reduction strategy for a TRS $\mathcal{R}$. In general it is undecidable whether a term t cycles with respect to $\mathcal{S}$. However, it is decidable whether there exists a cycle $t \rightarrow_{\mathcal{S}}^{+} t$ in which all terms have size less than or equal to some positive integer n.

DEFINITION 4.1 Let $\mathcal{S}$ be a sequential reduction strategy for a TRS $\mathcal{R}$. We say that a term t *$\mathcal{S}$-cycles within size $n > 0$*, denoted by $cyclic(t, n, \mathcal{S})$, if there exists a cycle

$$t = t_1 \rightarrow_{\mathcal{S}} t_2 \rightarrow_{\mathcal{S}} \cdots \rightarrow_{\mathcal{S}} t_m = t$$

with $m > 1$ such that $|t_i| \leqslant n$ for all $i \in \{1, \ldots, m\}$.

LEMMA 4.2 *Let $\mathcal{S}$ be a sequential reduction strategy for a TRS $\mathcal{R}$. Let t be a term and suppose $n > 0$. It is decidable whether t $\mathcal{S}$-cycles within size n.*

PROOF. Since there are no infinite reduction sequences consisting of pairwise different terms whose size does not exceed n, there exists a finite reduction sequence $t = t_1 \rightarrow_{\mathcal{S}} t_2 \rightarrow_{\mathcal{S}} \cdots \rightarrow_{\mathcal{S}} t_m$ with $m \geqslant 1$ such that $t_1, \ldots, t_{m-1}$ are pairwise different terms whose size does not exceed n, and one of the following alternatives holds:

- $|t_m| > n$,
- $|t_m| \leqslant n$ and $t_m \in NF(\mathcal{R})$, or
- $|t_m| \leqslant n$ and $t_m = t_k$ for some $k \in \{1, \ldots, m-1\}$.

The term t $\mathcal{S}$-cycles within size n if and only if the last alternative holds with $k = 1$. Hence we can decide whether t $\mathcal{S}$-cycles within size n by simply applying the strategy and check which of the above alternatives holds. □

For deciding whether a term $\mathcal{S}$-cycles within size n, we only need to know what the strategy $\mathcal{S}$ does to terms whose size does not exceed n. This observation will be used in the next section where we define our strategy by induction on the size of terms. The proof of Lemma 4.2 suggests the 'algorithm' of Figure 2 to compute the predicate *cyclic*.

$$cyclic(t,n,\mathcal{S}) = \begin{cases} \mathit{false} & \text{if } |t| > n \text{ or } t \in NF(\mathcal{R}), \\ \varphi(t,n,\mathcal{S},\varnothing,t') & \text{if } |t| \leqslant n \text{ and } t \to_{\mathcal{S}} t' \end{cases}$$

$$\varphi(t,n,\mathcal{S},T,t') = \begin{cases} \mathit{true} & \text{if } t' = t, \\ \mathit{false} & \text{if } |t'| > n, \text{ or } t' \in NF(\mathcal{R}), \\ & \text{or } t' \in T, \\ \varphi(t,n,\mathcal{S},T \cup \{t'\},t'') & \text{if } |t'| \leqslant n, \text{ and } t' \notin T \cup \{t\}, \\ & \text{and } t' \to_{\mathcal{S}} t''. \end{cases}$$

Fig. 2.

5 The Strategy

In this section we define our sequential strategy which will be denoted by $\mathcal{S}_\omega$. The strategy $\mathcal{S}_\omega$ only needs to know whether a term t $\mathcal{S}_\omega$-cycles within its own size. From now on we abbreviate $cyclic(t, |t|, \mathcal{S}_\omega)$ with $\odot(t)$.

DEFINITION 5.1 Let t be a reducible term. By induction on $|t|$ we define a redex position $\mathcal{S}_\omega(t) \in \mathcal{P}os(t)$. If $|t| = 1$ then t is a reducible constant and we define $\mathcal{S}_\omega(t) = \varepsilon$. Let $t = f(s_1, \ldots, s_n)$. If t is a redex then we define $\mathcal{S}_\omega(t) = \varepsilon$. Suppose t is not a redex. Let m be the number of reducible terms among $s_1, \ldots, s_n$. We have $1 \leqslant m \leqslant n$. The reducible arguments of t are ordered according to their size. If two reducible arguments have the same size, the one to the left is considered first. Formally, there exists an injective map π from $\{1, \ldots, m\}$ to $\{1, \ldots, n\}$ such that

- $s_{\pi(i)}$ is reducible for all $i \in \{1, \ldots, m\}$,
- $|s_{\pi(1)}| \leqslant |s_{\pi(2)}| \leqslant \cdots \leqslant |s_{\pi(m)}|$, and
- if $|s_{\pi(i)}| = |s_{\pi(j)}|$ with $1 \leqslant i < j \leqslant m$ then $\pi(i) < \pi(j)$.

According to the induction hypothesis, $\mathcal{S}_\omega(s)$ is already defined for all terms s with $|s| < |t|$. Hence we can determine the validity of $\odot(s_{\pi(i)})$ for all $i \in \{1, \ldots, m\}$. If there is an $i \in \{1, \ldots, m\}$ such that $\odot(s_{\pi(i)})$ does not hold then we take the smallest such i and define $\mathcal{S}_\omega(t) = \pi(i) \cdot \mathcal{S}_\omega(s_{\pi(i)})$. If there is no such i then we let $\mathcal{S}_\omega(t) = \pi(m) \cdot \mathcal{S}_\omega(s_{\pi(m)})$.

It is easy to see that $\mathcal{S}_\omega$ only selects outermost redexes. We find it convenient to introduce some terminology relating to the selection of the arguments $s_{\pi(1)}, \ldots, s_{\pi(m)}$ of t in Definition 5.1. If $1 \leqslant i < j \leqslant m$ then we call $s_{\pi(i)}$ a *predecessor* of $s_{\pi(j)}$ and we call $s_{\pi(j)}$ a *successor* of $s_{\pi(i)}$. If $1 \leqslant i < m$ and $\odot(s_{\pi(i)})$ holds then we say that $s_{\pi(i)}$ is *useless* in t. So if $\mathcal{S}_\omega(t) \geqslant \pi(k)$ then all predecessors of $s_{\pi(k)}$ are useless in t. We conclude this section by illustrating the workings of our strategy $\mathcal{S}_\omega$ on a small example.

EXAMPLE 5.2 Consider the (almost orthogonal) TRS

$$\mathcal{R} = \begin{cases} \top \vee x & \to & \top \\ x \vee \top & \to & \top \\ \bot \vee \bot & \to & \bot \\ \infty & \to & \infty \end{cases}$$

and the term $t_1 = (\bot \vee \infty) \vee (\infty \vee (\top \vee \bot))$. We have $\mathcal{S}_\omega(\bot \vee \infty) = 2$ and hence $\bot \vee \infty \to_{\mathcal{S}_\omega} \bot \vee \infty$. So the first argument of t_1 $\mathcal{S}_\omega$-cycles within its own size. Therefore $\mathcal{S}_\omega(t_1) = 2 \cdot \mathcal{S}_\omega(\infty \vee (\top \vee \bot))$. Because $\odot(\infty)$ we have $\mathcal{S}_\omega(\infty \vee (\top \vee \bot)) = 2 \cdot \mathcal{S}_\omega(\top \vee \bot)$. The term $\top \vee \bot$ is a redex, so $\mathcal{S}_\omega(\top \vee \bot) = \varepsilon$. We conclude that $\mathcal{S}_\omega(t_1) = 2{\cdot}2$ and consequently $t_1 \to_{\mathcal{S}_\omega} (\bot \vee \infty) \vee (\infty \vee \top) = t_2$. We already know that $\odot(\bot \vee \infty)$. Hence $\mathcal{S}_\omega(t_2) = 2 \cdot \mathcal{S}_\omega(\infty \vee \top) = 2$ since $\infty \vee \top$ is a redex. Therefore $t_2 \to_{\mathcal{S}_\omega} (\bot \vee \infty) \vee \top = t_3$. The term t_3 is a redex and thus $t_3 \to_{\mathcal{S}_\omega} \top$. So our strategy needs three steps to normalize the term t_1.

6 Its Normalization

In this section we establish a relationship between our strategy $\mathcal{S}_\omega$ and so-called outermost-fair reductions. In O'Donnell [7] this concept—O'Donnell uses the terminology *eventually outermost*—is defined for almost orthogonal TRSs. The definition we give below applies to all TRSs. It is equivalent to the one in Klop [6], except that we only consider *infinite* reduction sequences.

DEFINITION 6.1 An infinite reduction sequence $\mathcal{D}$ is called *outermost-fair* if there do not exist a position p and an index $n \geqslant 1$ such that for all $i \geqslant n$, $\mathcal{D}[i]_{|p}$ is an outermost redex in $\mathcal{D}[i]$ which is not contracted in the reduction step $\mathcal{D}[i, i+1]$. If $\mathcal{D}$ is not outermost-fair then every position p satisfying the above condition is said to be *unfairly treated* by $\mathcal{D}$. If a position is unfairly treated by $\mathcal{D}$ we also say that the corresponding outermost redex is unfairly treated. These notions carry over to a cycle $\mathcal{D}$ via the associated infinite reduction sequence $\mathcal{D}^\infty$.

Let us illustrate the concept of outermost-fairness by means of two examples. The infinite reduction sequence $\mathcal{D}_1$: $f(a) \to g(f(a)) \to g(g(f(a))) \to \cdots$ with respect to the TRS

$$\begin{array}{rcl} a & \to & b \\ f(x) & \to & g(f(x)) \end{array}$$

is outermost-fair since every term in $\mathcal{D}_1$ contains a single outermost redex which is immediately contracted. The infinite reduction sequence $\mathcal{D}_2$: $f(a,c) \to f(a,d) \to f(a,c) \to f(a,d) \to \cdots$ with respect to the TRS

$$\begin{array}{rcl} a & \to & b \\ c & \to & d \\ f(x,d) & \to & f(x,c) \end{array}$$

is also outermost-fair. Observe that redex a in $\mathcal{D}_2$ is only half of the time an outermost redex, even though it is never contracted.

Next we show that if $\mathcal{S}_\omega$ fails to normalize a term t then there exists an (infinite) outermost-fair reduction sequence starting from t. The proof proceeds in three steps. First we show that every outermost redex unfairly treated in an $\mathcal{S}_\omega$-reduction sequence is a subterm of an $\mathcal{S}_\omega$-cyclic subterm (Lemma 6.3). This result is used to show that if a term admits an $\mathcal{S}_\omega$-cycle then it has a cycle in which no position is unfairly treated (Lemma 6.6). Finally we transform a presupposed infinite $\mathcal{S}_\omega$-reduction sequence into an outermost-fair reduction sequence by simply inserting enough cycles (Theorem 6.7).

DEFINITION 6.2 Let $\mathcal{D}$ be an infinite reduction sequence. We say that a property $\mathcal{P}$ of terms *eventually* holds for $\mathcal{D}$ if $\mathcal{P}$ holds for all but a finite number of terms in $\mathcal{D}$.

Observe that a position p is unfairly treated by an infinite $\mathcal{S}_\omega$-reduction sequence $\mathcal{D}$ if and only if the property "$t_{|p}$ is an outermost redex in t and $\mathcal{S}_\omega(t) \parallel p$" eventually holds for $\mathcal{D}$.

LEMMA 6.3 *If a position p is unfairly treated in an $\mathcal{S}_\omega$-reduction sequence $\mathcal{D}$ then there exist a term t, an index $N \geqslant 1$, and a position $\varepsilon < q \leqslant p$ such that t is $\mathcal{S}_\omega$-cyclic and $\mathcal{D}[i]_{|q} = t$ for all $i \geqslant N$.*

PROOF. Suppose $\mathcal{D}$: $t_1 \rightarrow_{\mathcal{S}_\omega} t_2 \rightarrow_{\mathcal{S}_\omega} \cdots$ is an infinite reduction sequence in which position p is unfairly treated. So there exists an $M \geqslant 1$ such that $(t_i)_{|p}$ is an outermost redex in t_i and $\mathcal{S}_\omega(t_i) \parallel p$, for all $i \geqslant M$. Since $\mathcal{S}_\omega$ is an outermost strategy, position ε is fairly treated in $\mathcal{D}$ and hence $p \neq \varepsilon$. There exist a position q and a positive integer k such that

- $q{\cdot}k \leqslant p$,
- $\mathcal{S}_\omega(t_i) > q$ for infinitely many values of $i \geqslant M$, and
- $\mathcal{S}_\omega(t_i) > q{\cdot}k$ for finitely many values of $i \geqslant M$.

Hence there exists an $N \geqslant M$ such that there is no $i \geqslant N$ such that $\mathcal{S}_\omega(t_i) > q{\cdot}k$. Let s_k be the k-th argument of $t_{N|q}$. For all $i \geqslant N$, let $t_{i|q} = f(s^i_1, \ldots, s^i_n)$. Clearly $s^i_k = s_k$ for all $i \geqslant N$. We show that s_k is $\mathcal{S}_\omega$-cyclic. According to the pigeon-hole principle there exists a $j \in \{1, \ldots, n\}$ such that $\mathcal{S}_\omega(t_i) \geqslant q{\cdot}j$ for infinitely many values of $i \geqslant N$. Let I be the set of these values. For all $i \in I$, either s_k is a predecessor of s^i_j, or s_k is a successor of s^i_j. First suppose that s_k is a successor of s^i_j for all $i \in I$. This implies that the sequence

$$s^{i_1}_j \rightarrow_{\mathcal{S}_\omega} s^{i_2}_j \rightarrow_{\mathcal{S}_\omega} s^{i_3}_j \rightarrow_{\mathcal{S}_\omega} \cdots$$

contains a cycle, for otherwise there would be an $l \in I$ such that $|s^l_j| > |s_k|$ and consequently s_k a predecessor of s^l_j. Here $I = \{i_1, i_2, i_3, \ldots\}$ with $i_1 < i_2 < i_3 < \cdots$. Let s^m_j (with $m \in I$) be a biggest term in such a cycle. We clearly have $\odot(s^m_j)$. Hence s^m_j is useless in $t_{m|q}$, which is impossible since $m \in I$. We conclude that there exists an $i \in I$ such that s_k is a predecessor of s^i_j. This implies that s_k is useless in $t_{i|q}$ since a redex in s^i_j is selected by $\mathcal{S}_\omega$. Therefore s_k is $\mathcal{S}_\omega$-cyclic, which proves the lemma. □

The following technical result states that if $\mathcal{S}_\omega$ selects a redex in subterm $t_{|p}$ of t, then instead of applying $\mathcal{S}_\omega$ to t we can also replace its subterm $t_{|p}$ by the result of applying $\mathcal{S}_\omega$ to $t_{|p}$, without changing the final outcome. This does not hold if the contractum of a redex depends on the term in which the redex occurs (cf. the remarks in Section 2).

LEMMA 6.4 *If $\mathcal{S}_\omega(t) \geqslant p$ then $t\mathcal{S}_\omega = t[t_{|p}\mathcal{S}_\omega]_p$.*

PROOF. We use induction on the position p. If $p = \varepsilon$ then the result trivially holds. Suppose $p = i{\cdot}q$. In the following we write t_i instead of $t_{|i}$. From the definition of $\mathcal{S}_\omega$ we infer that $\mathcal{S}_\omega(t) = i \cdot \mathcal{S}_\omega(t_i)$. Hence

$$\begin{aligned} t\mathcal{S}_\omega &= t[contract(t_{|\mathcal{S}_\omega(t)})]_{\mathcal{S}_\omega(t)} \\ &= t[contract(t_{|i\cdot\mathcal{S}_\omega(t_i)})]_{i\cdot\mathcal{S}_\omega(t_i)} \\ &= t[t_i[contract(t_{|i\cdot\mathcal{S}_\omega(t_i)})]_{\mathcal{S}_\omega(t_i)}]_i \\ &= t[t_i[contract(t_{i|\mathcal{S}_\omega(t_i)})]_{\mathcal{S}_\omega(t_i)}]_i \\ &= t[t_i\mathcal{S}_\omega]_i. \end{aligned}$$

Since $\mathcal{S}_\omega(t_i) \geqslant q$, the induction hypothesis yields $t_i\mathcal{S}_\omega = t_i[(t_{i|q})\mathcal{S}_\omega]_q$ and therefore

$$\begin{aligned} t\mathcal{S}_\omega &= t[t_i[t_{i|q}\mathcal{S}_\omega]_q]_i \\ &= t[t_{i|q}\mathcal{S}_\omega]_{i\cdot q} \\ &= t[t_{|p}\mathcal{S}_\omega]_p. \end{aligned}$$

□

LEMMA 6.5 *Let $\mathcal{D}$ be any $\mathcal{S}_\omega$-reduction sequence. If p is a position in $\mathcal{D}[1]$ such that no redex at a position $q < p$ is contracted in $\mathcal{D}$, then $\mathcal{D}_{|p}$ is an $\mathcal{S}_\omega$-reduction sequence.*

PROOF. Let $t \to t\mathcal{S}_\omega$ be an arbitrary reduction step in $\mathcal{D}$. We have to show that $t_{|p} \to^*_{\mathcal{S}_\omega} t\mathcal{S}_{\omega|p}$. If $\mathcal{S}_\omega(t) \parallel p$ then $t\mathcal{S}_{\omega|p} = (t[contract(t_{|\mathcal{S}_\omega(t)})]_{\mathcal{S}_\omega(t)})_{|p} = t_{|p}$. If $\mathcal{S}_\omega(t) \geqslant p$ then $t\mathcal{S}_{\omega|p} = (t[t_{|p}\mathcal{S}_\omega]_p)_{|p} = t_{|p}\mathcal{S}_\omega$ by using Lemma 6.4, and hence $t_{|p} \to_{\mathcal{S}_\omega} t\mathcal{S}_{\omega|p}$. □

LEMMA 6.6 *If a term t $\mathcal{S}_\omega$-cycles then there exists a cycle of t in which every position is fairly treated.*

PROOF. Let $\mathcal{D}$ be an $\mathcal{S}_\omega$-cycle of t. We prove the lemma by structural induction on t. If t is a constant then there are no positions that are unfairly treated by $\mathcal{D}$. Suppose $t = f(s_1, \ldots, s_n)$ and let P be the set of all positions that are unfairly treated by $\mathcal{D}$. Observe that $P \subset \mathcal{P}os(t)$. Let $p \in P$. We show that there exists a cycle $\mathcal{D}_p$ of t in which position p is fairly treated. Since $p = \varepsilon$ is impossible, we have $k \leqslant p$ for some $k \in \{1, \ldots, n\}$. Let $p' = p\backslash k$. We show that s_k $\mathcal{S}_\omega$-cycles. If a redex in s_k is contracted in $\mathcal{D}$ then we obtain an $\mathcal{S}_\omega$-cycle $\mathcal{D}_{|k}$: $s_k \to^+_{\mathcal{S}_\omega} s_k$ with help of Lemma 6.5. If no redex in s_k is contracted in $\mathcal{D}$ then we infer the $\mathcal{S}_\omega$-cyclicity of s_k by applying Lemma 6.3 to the reduction sequence $\mathcal{D}^\infty$. According to the induction hypothesis there exists a cycle of s_k, say $\mathcal{D}_{p'}$, in which position

p' is fairly treated. Let C be the context $t[\square]_k$ and define $\mathcal{D}_p = C[\mathcal{D}_{p'}]$. Clearly $\mathcal{D}_p$ is a cycle of t in which position p is fairly treated. Suppose $P = \{p_1, \ldots, p_m\}$. The reduction sequence $\mathcal{D}; \mathcal{D}_{p_1}; \ldots; \mathcal{D}_{p_m}$ is a cycle of t in which every position is fairly treated. □

Our main theorem is easily derived from the preceding lemma.

THEOREM 6.7 *If $\mathcal{S}_\omega$ fails to normalize some term then there exists an outermost-fair reduction sequence starting from that term.*

PROOF. Suppose $\mathcal{D}$ is an infinite $\mathcal{S}_\omega$-reduction sequence. For every $i \geqslant 1$ we define a reduction sequence $\mathcal{D}_i$: $\mathcal{D}[i] \to^* \mathcal{D}[i]$ as follows. Let $P_i \subseteq \mathcal{P}os(\mathcal{D}[i])$ be the set of all positions p with the property that $\mathcal{D}[i]_{|p}$ $\mathcal{S}_\omega$-cycles. From the preceding lemma we learn that for every $p \in P_i$ there exists a cycle $\mathcal{D}_p$ of $\mathcal{D}[i]$ in which every position is fairly treated. We define $\mathcal{D}_i$ as the concatenation of all those cycles. (If $P_i = \varnothing$ then $\mathcal{D}_i$ is the empty reduction sequence from $\mathcal{D}[i]$ to $\mathcal{D}[i]$, otherwise $\mathcal{D}_i$ is a cycle of $\mathcal{D}[i]$.) Now it is easy to see that the sequence $\mathcal{D}_1; \mathcal{D}[1,2]; \mathcal{D}_2; \mathcal{D}[2,3]; \mathcal{D}_3; \mathcal{D}[3,4]; \ldots$ is outermost-fair. □

O'Donnell [7] obtained the following result.

THEOREM 6.8 *Let $\mathcal{R}$ be an almost orthogonal TRS. If a term admits an outermost-fair reduction sequence then it does not have a normal form.* □

The normalization of the parallel-outermost strategy for almost orthogonal TRSs is an immediate consequence of Theorem 6.8. Combining this result with Theorem 6.7 yields the normalization of $\mathcal{S}_\omega$ for almost orthogonal TRSs.

COROLLARY 6.9 *The strategy $\mathcal{S}_\omega$ is normalizing for almost orthogonal TRSs.* □

7 Concluding Remarks

The ingenious proof of Theorem 6.8 in O'Donnell [7] is not easily digested. In the appendix of Bergstra and Klop [1] O'Donnell's proof is presented in a more accessible setting and is also generalized to combinatory reduction systems. (Although only orthogonal systems are considered in [1], the presence of trivial overlays doesn't cause any problems.) We would like to remark that for orthogonal TRSs Theorem 6.8 is easily derived from the work of Huet and Lévy [3] on needed reduction: it is not difficult to show that in every outermost-fair reduction sequence infinitely many needed redexes are contracted. In Section 2 we already remarked that the restriction to orthogonal TRSs is essential in the work of Huet and Lévy. Sekar and Ramakrishnan [10] showed that by generalizing the concept of needed redex to *necessary set of redexes* the main results of [3] carry over to the almost orthogonal case. In particular, contraction of necessary sets of redexes is hyper normalizing. It seems feasible to reduce Theorem 6.8 to this result.

It is interesting to note that (in the case of almost orthogonal TRSs) the normalization of both the parallel-outermost strategy and our sequential strategy

$\mathcal{S}_\omega$ is based on Theorem 6.8. So it is worthwhile to try to extend Theorem 6.8 to a more general class of TRSs. We believe that Theorem 6.8 holds for all weakly orthogonal TRSs. Also the class of strongly sequential left-linear root-balanced joinable TRSs considered by Toyama [11] should fall within its scope. These questions will be pursued in the near future.

Whereas all infinite reduction sequences produced by the parallel-outermost strategy are outermost-fair, this is not the case for $\mathcal{S}_\omega$. The following example shows that $\mathcal{S}_\omega$ ignores an outermost redex when it 'believes' that there is no reason to contract it.

EXAMPLE 7.1 Consider the TRS

$$\begin{array}{rcl} a & \to & b \\ c & \to & c \\ f(b,x) & \to & f(a,x) \end{array}$$

and the term $t = h(f(a,b), g(g(c)))$. We have $f(a,b) \to_{\mathcal{S}_\omega} f(b,b) \to_{\mathcal{S}_\omega} f(a,b)$, so the first argument of t $\mathcal{S}_\omega$-cycles within its own size. Hence the second argument of t is selected for reduction, which of course gives $t \to_{\mathcal{S}_\omega} t$. Thus $\mathcal{S}_\omega$ produces an an infinite reduction sequence in which position 1·1 (corresponding to outermost redex a) is unfairly treated.

In the above example both arguments of the term under consideration $\mathcal{S}_\omega$-cycle within their own size. Since the TRS is (almost) orthogonal, we might as well stop the evaluation since the term cannot have a normal form. This is justified by our next result.

THEOREM 7.2 *Let $\mathcal{R}$ be an almost orthogonal TRS and $t = f(s_1, \ldots, s_n)$ a term that is neither a redex nor a normal form. If for all $i \in \{1, \ldots, n\}$ s_i is a normal form or $\odot(s_i)$ then $\odot(t)$.*

PROOF. Since all reducible arguments of t are $\mathcal{S}_\omega$-cyclic within their own size, t itself is $\mathcal{S}_\omega$-cyclic within its own size, unless after some contractions in its $\mathcal{S}_\omega$-cyclic arguments a redex is created, say $t \to^{+}_{\mathcal{S}_\omega} f(s'_1, \ldots, s'_n) = t'$ with t' a redex. For all $i \in \{1, \ldots, n\}$ we have $s_i \to^{*}_{\mathcal{S}_\omega} s'_i \to^{*}_{\mathcal{S}_\omega} s_i$, hence redex t' can be rewritten to t by internal (i.e. at positions different from ε) contractions. Because $\mathcal{R}$ is almost orthogonal, redexes cannot be destroyed by internal contractions. Therefore t must be a redex, contrary to the assumption. We conclude that t $\mathcal{S}_\omega$-cycles within its own size. □

According to Corollary 6.9, in the case of almost orthogonal TRSs, $\odot(t)$ implies that t has no normal form. Hence Theorem 7.2 shows how our strategy can be used to detect non-termination. If we are faced with a redex t, we can of course also check whether $\odot(t)$ holds in order to avoid unnecessary infinite computations. These considerations do not generalize to arbitrary TRSs, as shown in the next example.

Example 7.3 Consider the TRS

$$\begin{array}{rcl} a & \to & b \\ b & \to & a \\ c & \to & c \\ f(b,x) & \to & d \end{array}$$

and the term $t = f(a,c)$. Both arguments of t $\mathcal{S}_\omega$-cycle within their own size. Nevertheless t has a normal form which can be reached by means of the outermost reduction sequence

$$f(a,c) \to f(b,c) \to d.$$

Observe that $\mathcal{S}_\omega$ will select redex c in t and hence produce an infinite reduction sequence that is not outermost-fair. It should be noted that the above TRS is not root-balanced joinable (in the terminology of Toyama [11]).

One possibility to extend the class of systems for which our strategy is normalizing is that in the case all reducible arguments of a term that is not a redex $\mathcal{S}_\omega$-cycle within their own size, we may look for a combination of terms in these cycles that creates a redex upwards. For instance, in the above example we see that the combination b and c in the cycles $a \to_{\mathcal{S}_\omega} b \to_{\mathcal{S}_\omega} a$ and $c \to_{\mathcal{S}_\omega} c$ creates the redex $f(b,c)$ which contracts to normal form d. Even if such a combination does not exist we can still test whether it is possible to redefine the mapping *rule*—which assigns rewrite rules to redexes—in such a way that the present deadlock situation disappears, at least temporarily. These idea should be investigated further.

In the final example of the paper we justify our earlier claim that our sequential strategy $\mathcal{S}_\omega$ sometimes succeeds where parallel-outermost fails.

Example 7.4 Consider the non-left-linear TRS

$$\mathcal{R} = \left\{ \begin{array}{rcl} f(x,x) & \to & a \\ g(x) & \to & f(x,g(x)) \\ c & \to & g(c) \end{array} \right.$$

of Klop [5]. This well-known TRS shows that non-left-linearity destroys confluence, even in the absence of critical pairs. The following reduction sequence shows that our strategy $\mathcal{S}_\omega$ normalizes the constant c:

$$c \to_{\mathcal{S}_\omega} g(c) \to_{\mathcal{S}_\omega} f(c,g(c)) \to_{\mathcal{S}_\omega} f(g(c),g(c)) \to_{\mathcal{S}_\omega} a,$$

whereas the parallel-outermost strategy produces an infinite outermost-fair sequence:

$$c \to^* g(c) \to^* f(c,g(c)) \to^* f(g(c),f(c,g(c))) \to^* \cdots$$

Unfortunately, our strategy $\mathcal{S}_\omega$ does not normalize all terms of $\mathcal{R}$. For instance, a term like $f(g(c),g(g(c)))$ can only be normalized if we allow contraction of redexes that are not outermost. Nevertheless, it can be shown that the set of terms which can be normalized by $\mathcal{S}_\omega$ properly includes those for which parallel-outermost succeeds. Of course, if we drop the rewrite rule $g(x) \to f(x, g(x))$ from $\mathcal{R}$ then we obtain a confluent TRS for which our strategy $\mathcal{S}_\omega$, unlike parallel-outermost, is normalizing.

This example shows in particular that Theorem 6.8 doesn't hold for non-left-linear TRSs (without critical pairs).

References

1. J.A. Bergstra and J.W. Klop, *Conditional Rewrite Rules: Confluence and Termination*, Journal of Computer and System Sciences **32**(3), pp. 323–362, 1986.

2. N. Dershowitz and J.-P. Jouannaud, *Rewrite Systems*, in: Handbook of Theoretical Computer Science, Vol. B (ed. J. van Leeuwen), North-Holland, pp. 243–320, 1990.

3. G. Huet and J.-J. Lévy, *Computations in Orthogonal Rewriting Systems, I and II*, in: Computational Logic, Essays in Honor of Alan Robinson (eds. J.-L. Lassez and G. Plotkin), The MIT Press, pp. 396–443, 1991. Previous version: *Call by Need Computations in Non-Ambiguous Linear Term Rewriting Systems*, report 359, INRIA, 1979.

4. J.R. Kennaway, *Sequential Evaluation Strategies for Parallel-Or and Related Reduction Systems*, Annals of Pure and Applied Logic **43**, pp. 31–56, 1989.

5. J.W. Klop, *Combinatory Reduction Systems*, Ph.D. thesis, Mathematical Centre Tracts **127**, Centre for Mathematics and Computer Science, Amsterdam, 1980.

6. J.W. Klop, *Term Rewriting Systems*, in: Handbook of Logic in Computer Science, Vol. II (eds. S. Abramsky, D. Gabbay and T. Maibaum), Oxford University Press, pp. 1–116, 1992.

7. M.J. O'Donnell, *Computing in Systems Described by Equations*, Lecture Notes in Computer Science **58**, 1977.

8. M. Oyamaguchi, *NV-Sequentiality: A Decidable Condition for Call-by-Need Computations in Term Rewriting Systems*, SIAM Journal on Computation **22**(1), pp. 114-135, 1993.

9. S. Porat and N. Francez, *Fairness in Term Rewriting Systems*, Proceedings of the 1st International Conference on Rewriting Techniques and Applications, Bordeaux, Lecture Notes in Computer Science **202**, pp. 287–300, 1985.

10. R.C. Sekar and I.V. Ramakrishnan, *Programming in Equational Logic: Beyond Strong Sequentiality*, Proceedings of the 5th IEEE Symposium on Logic in Computer Science, Philadelphia, pp. 230–241, 1990.

11. Y. Toyama, *Strong Sequentiality of Left-Linear Overlapping Term Rewriting Systems*, Proceedings of the 7th IEEE Symposium on Logic in Computer Science, Santa Cruz, pp. 274–284, 1992.

On Modularity of Termination and Confluence Properties of Conditional Rewrite Systems

Bernhard Gramlich*

Fachbereich Informatik, Universität Kaiserslautern
Postfach 3049, D-67653 Kaiserslautern, Germany
gramlich@informatik.uni-kl.de

Abstract. We investigate the modularity behaviour of termination and confluence properties of conditional term rewriting systems. In particular, we show how to obtain sufficient conditions for the modularity of weak termination, weak innermost termination, (strong) innermost termination, (strong) termination, confluence and completeness of conditional rewrite systems.

1 Introduction, Motivation and Overview

Starting with the seminal work of Toyama [Toy87b] the investigation of preservation properties of term rewriting systems (TRSs for short) under various forms of combinations has become a very interesting and active area of research. From a practical point of view this field has a great potential in applications of rewriting techniques since it provides the theoretical basis for a systematic construction of large systems of rewrite rules with some desired properties from smaller ones with corresponding properties. Vice versa, it is also crucial for analyzing properties of large systems by decomposing them into smaller units where corresponding properties are often easier to verify.

In [Toy87b] it was shown that confluence is indeed preserved under disjoint unions of (unconditional) TRSs whereas termination is not (cf. also [Toy87a]). This phenomenon was the starting point of a couple of investigations about how to obtain sufficient criteria for the preservation of termination, completeness (i.e. termination plus confluence) and of other interesting properties of TRSs under disjoint combinations (cf. e.g. [Rus87], [Mid89], [TKB89], [Mid90], [KO90], [Gra92a], [Gra92b], [Ohl93b]). Non-disjoint unions of TRSs with common constructors have been considered e.g. in [MT91], [KO92], [Gra92a], [Gra92b], [Ohl93b], [Ohl93a]. More general hierarchical combinations of TRSs have recently been dealt with in [Kri93], [Der93], [Kri94], [Gra93b], [FJ93]. Some preservation results for (disjoint and non-disjoint, but non-hierarchical) combinations of conditional TRSs (CTRSs for short) finally have been obtained in [Mid90] (cf. also [Mid93b]), [Mid93a], [Gra93c], [Ohl93b].

As shown in [TKB89] (by a very involved proof), completeness is preserved under disjoint union of left-linear (unconditional) TRSs. Instead of left-linearity

* This research was supported by the 'Deutsche Forschungsgemeinschaft, SFB 314 (D4-Projekt)'.

one may also require a stronger confluence property. More precisely, termination (and hence also completeness) is preserved under disjoint unions of non-overlapping TRSs as well as of locally confluent overlay systems ([Gra92b], [Gra93b]). The crucial point is that for such TRSs (strong) innermost termination implies already (strong) termination. Recently we have been able to show that this latter property does indeed also hold for CTRSs ([Gra93a]). In the present paper we shall exploit this property and show how to obtain corresponding preservation results for disjoint unions of CTRSs. However, this generalization of [Gra92b] to the conditional case turned out to be pretty more complicated than expected, due to reasons which will be explained later on.

Before going into details let us give a summary of our main results (for join CTRSs admitting extra variables in the conditions):

- We give counterexamples showing that weak termination, weak innermost termination and (strong) innermost termination are not preserved under signature extensions in general (cf. Example 4 which contradicts Theorem 5.2 in [Mid93b]) whereas (strong) termination is indeed preserved under signature extensions (cf. Lemma 17).
- We give abstract sufficient conditions for the preservation of weak termination, weak innermost termination and (strong) innermost termination under signature extensions and more generally, for their modularity (cf. Theorem 19, Lemmas 20-26). In particular we show that these restricted termination properties are modular for confluent CTRSs and for CTRSs without extra variables (cf. Theorem 27).
- We show that (strong) termination and completeness are modular properties for non-overlapping CTRSs as well as for conditional overlay systems with joinable critical pairs (cf. Theorems 28, 29).

The rest of the paper is structured as follows. In the next section we shall introduce some necessary terminology. Then, in section 3, we shall summarize results of [Gra92b], [Gra93b], [Gra93b] on restricted and general termination and confluence properties of (C)TRSs. In the main section 4, we shall develop a couple of new preservation results for termination and confluence properties of CTRSs. Finally we summarize known and new results and discuss some open problems and related work.

2 Preliminaries

We assume familiarity with the basic theory for term rewriting (cf. e.g. [DJ90], [Klo92]). For brevity we shall make use of the following abbreviations which apply to TRSs (and, if sensible, also to terms): SN (strongly) terminating (strongly normalizing), WN weakly terminating (weakly normalizing), WIN weakly innermost terminating (weakly innermost normalizing), SIN (strongly) innermost terminating (strongly innermost normalizing), JCP (all) critical pairs are joinable, CR confluent (or equivalently, having the Church-Rosser property), WCR locally confluent, COMP complete, i.e. terminating and confluent, NE non-erasing (or variable-preserving), NO non-overlapping, OS overlay system, NF set of normal forms. Innermost reduction steps $s \to t$ are denoted by $s \underset{i}{\to} t$. In order to indicate the position p of the contracted redex in $s \to t$, the applied rule $l \to r$ and the matching substitution σ we shall also use the notation $s \to_{p,\sigma,l\to r} t$. If $p = \lambda$ (the root position) then we speak of a ***root reduction step***. The identity substitution is denoted by id.

2.1 Basic Notions and Notations for Disjoint Unions

We adopt usual basic notions and notations for disjoint unions of rewrite systems as described e.g. in [Toy87b], [Mid90], [Mid93b], but repeat some conventions here for the sake of readability. When considering a disjoint union $\mathcal{R}^{\mathcal{F}} = \mathcal{R}_1^{\mathcal{F}_1} \oplus \mathcal{R}_2^{\mathcal{F}_2}$ we say that $\mathcal{R}_1^{\mathcal{F}_1}$ ($\mathcal{R}_2^{\mathcal{F}_2}$) is the black (white) system. Symbols from $\mathcal{F}_1$ ($\mathcal{F}_2$) are black (white). Variables have no colour. A black (white) term does not contain white (black) symbols. A term is top black (top white) if its top symbol is black (white). The *special subterms* (or *aliens*), *principal subterms* and the *rank* of terms in $\mathcal{T}(\mathcal{F}, \mathcal{V})$ are defined as usual. If in a reduction step $s \to_{\mathcal{R}^{\mathcal{F}}} t$ the contracted redex is inside some principal alien of s, we speak of an *inner* step and write $s \overset{i}{\to}_{\mathcal{R}^{\mathcal{F}}} t$. Otherwise it is an *outer* step, which is denoted by $s \overset{o}{\to}_{\mathcal{R}^{\mathcal{F}}} t$. If s is a term with $rank(s) > 1$ then it has the form $s = C[\![s_1, \ldots, s_n]\!]$ where the s_i, $1 \leq i \leq n$ are the principal aliens of s and $C[, \ldots,]$ is a *context*, i.e. a term with 'holes' (represented by some fresh constant $\Box$). By $C[]_p$ we mean a context with one occurrence of $\Box$ at position p. Similarly, $C[]_\Pi$ denotes a context with $\Box$ at all positions from Π (which are required to be mutually disjoint). For terms $s_1, \ldots, s_n, t_1, \ldots, t_n$ we write $\langle s_1, \ldots, s_n \rangle \propto \langle t_1, \ldots, t_n \rangle$ if $t_i = t_j$ whenever $s_i = s_j$, for all $1 \leq i, j \leq n$. This notion extends in straightforward way to substitutions. Following [Mid90], [Mid93b] we introduce some special notations in order to enable a compact treatment of 'degenerate' cases of '$t = C[\![t_1, \ldots, t_n]\!]$'. We write $C\langle, \ldots, \rangle$ for a term containing zero or more occurrences of $\Box$ and $C\{, \ldots, \}$ denotes a term different from $\Box$ itself, containing zero or more occurrences of $\Box$. If $t_1, \ldots, t_n$ are the (possibly zero) principal subterms of some term t (from left to right), then we write $t = C\{\!\{t_1, \ldots, t_n\}\!\}$ provided $t = C\{t_1, \ldots, t_n\}$. We write $t = C\langle\!\langle t_1, \ldots, t_n\rangle\!\rangle$ if $t = C\langle t_1, \ldots, t_n\rangle$ and either $C\langle, \ldots, \rangle \neq \Box$ and $t_1, \ldots, t_n$ are the principal subterms of t or $C\langle, \ldots, \rangle = \Box$ and $t \in \{t_1, \ldots, t_n\}$.

Lemma 1. *(cf. [Mid93b], Prop. 2.23) Let $\mathcal{R}_1^{\mathcal{F}_1}$, $\mathcal{R}_2^{\mathcal{F}_2}$ be disjoint CTRSs. Then every substitution σ can be decomposed into $\sigma_2 \circ \sigma_1$ such that σ_1 is black (white), σ_2 is top white (top black), and $\sigma_2 \propto \epsilon$.*

2.2 Conditional Term Rewriting Systems

Moreover, we need some basic terminology about conditional term rewriting systems (CTRSs) (cf. e.g. [DJ90], [Klo92], [Mid93b]).

Definition 2. A *CTRS* is a pair $(\mathcal{R}, \mathcal{F})$ consisting of a signature $\mathcal{F}$ and a set of *conditional rewrite rules* of the form $s_1 = t_1 \wedge \ldots \wedge s_n = t_n \implies l \to r$ with $s_1, \ldots, s_n, t_1, \ldots, t_n, l, r \in \mathcal{T}(\mathcal{F}, \mathcal{V})$. Moreover, we require $l \notin \mathcal{V}$ and $V(r) \subseteq V(l)$ as for unconditional TRSs, i.e. no variable left hand sides and no extra variables on the right hand side. Extra variables in conditions are allowed if not stated otherwise. Instead of $(\mathcal{R}, \mathcal{F})$ we also write $\mathcal{R}^{\mathcal{F}}$ or simply $\mathcal{R}$ when $\mathcal{F}$ is clear from the context or irrelevant.

Depending on the interpretation of the equality sign in the conditions of rewrite rules, different reduction relations may be associated with a given CTRS as usual (yielding a *join*, *normal* or *semi-equational* CTRS). For the sake of readability we shall use in the following some compact notations for conditional rules and conjunctions of conditions. When writing $P \Longrightarrow l \rightarrow r$ for some conditional rewrite rule then P stands for the conjunction of all conditions. Similarly, if P is $s_1 = t_1 \wedge \ldots \wedge s_n = t_n$, then $P \downarrow$ means $s_1 \downarrow t_1 \wedge \ldots\ldots \wedge s_n \downarrow t_n$, and $\sigma(P)$ is to denote $\sigma(s_1) = \sigma(t_1) \wedge \ldots \wedge \sigma(s_n) = \sigma(t_n)$.

Definition 3. Let $\mathcal{R}$ be a join CTRS, and let $P_1 \Longrightarrow l_1 \rightarrow r_1$ and $P_2 \Longrightarrow l_2 \rightarrow r_2$ be two rewrite rules of $\mathcal{R}$ which have no variables in common. Suppose $l_1 = C[t]_p$ with $t \notin \mathcal{V}$ for some (possibly empty) context $C[]_p$ such that t and l_2 are unifiable with most general unifier σ, i.e. $\sigma(t) = \sigma(l_1/p) = \sigma(l_2)$. Then $\sigma(P_1) \wedge \sigma(P_2) \Longrightarrow \sigma(C[r_2]) = \sigma(r_1)$ is said to be a *(conditional) critical pair* of $\mathcal{R}$. If the two rules are renamed versions of the same rule of $\mathcal{R}$, we do not consider the case $C[] = \Box$, i.e. we do not overlap a rule with itself at root position. A (conditional) critical pair $P \Longrightarrow s = t$ is said to be *joinable* if $\sigma(s) \downarrow_{\mathcal{R}} \sigma(t)$ for every substitution σ with $\sigma(P) \downarrow$. A substitution σ which satisfies the conditions, i.e. for which $\sigma(P) \downarrow$ holds, is said to be *feasible*. Otherwise σ is *unfeasible*. Analogously, a (conditional) critical pair is said to be *feasible (unfeasible)* if there exists some (no) feasible substitution for it.

Note that testing joinability of conditional critical pairs is in general much more difficult than in the unconditional case since one has to consider all substitutions which satisfy the correspondingly instantiated conditions. Moreover, the critical pair lemma does not hold for CTRSs in general as shown e.g. by the following example.

Example 1. ([BK86]) Consider the join CTRS

$$\mathcal{R} = \begin{cases} x \downarrow f(x) \Longrightarrow f(x) \rightarrow a \\ \qquad\qquad\qquad\quad b \rightarrow f(b)\,. \end{cases}$$

Here we get $f(b) \rightarrow a$ due to $b \downarrow f(b)$ and hence $f(f(b)) \rightarrow f(a)$. We also have $f(f(b)) \rightarrow a$ because of $f(b) \downarrow f(f(b))$. But a and $f(a)$ do not have a common reduct which is easily shown. Thus $\mathcal{R}$ is not locally confluent despite the lack of critical pairs.

Definition 4. Let $\mathcal{R}$ be a CTRS and let $\mathcal{R}_u$ be its unconditional version, i.e. $\mathcal{R}_u := \{l \rightarrow r \mid P \Longrightarrow l \rightarrow r \in \mathcal{R}\}$. Then $\mathcal{R}$ is said to be *non-overlapping (NO)/ orthogonal / a (conditional) overlay system (OS)* if $\mathcal{R}_u$ is non-overlapping / orthogonal / an (unconditional) overlay system.

According to this definition Example 1 above shows that orthogonal CTRSs need not be confluent. But note that the CTRS $\mathcal{R}$ defined in Example 1 is not (strongly) innermost terminating.

The careful reader may have observed that the definition of being non-overlapping above is somehow rather restrictive. Namely, the case that there exist conditional critical pairs all of which are infeasible (and hence should not be 'properly critical') is not covered. Analogously, for a CTRS to be an overlay system one might allow critical pairs which are not overlays but require that all of them are infeasible, hence not 'properly critical'). These slightly generalized *semantical* versions of the properties of being non-overlapping and being an overlay system are treated in detail in [Gra93a]. For the sake of readability and due to lack of space we shall dispense here with an analogous treatment concerning preservation properties.[2] The other basic notions for unconditional TRSs introduced above generalize in a straightforward manner to CTRSs.

In the following we shall tacitly assume that all CTRSs considered are join CTRSs (which is the most important case in practice), except for cases where another kind of CTRSs is explicitly mentioned.

3 Restricted Termination and Confluence Properties of Conditional Term Rewriting Systems

Here we shall summarize some known and recently obtained new results on restricted termination and confluence properties of unconditional and conditional TRSs.

Theorem 5. *(cf. e.g. [Ros73], [O'D77], [Klo92]) Let $\mathcal{R}$ be an orthogonal, i.e. non-overlapping and left-linear (unconditional) TRS. Then $\mathcal{R}$ is confluent, and the following properties hold:*

(1a) $\forall t : [\, WIN(t) \implies SIN(t) \,]$.
(1b) $WIN(\mathcal{R}) \implies SIN(\mathcal{R})$.
(2a) $\forall t : [\, SIN(t) \implies SN(t) \,]$.
(2b) $SIN(\mathcal{R}) \implies SN(\mathcal{R})$.
(3) $\forall s,t : [\, s \underset{i}{\to} t \wedge SN(t) \implies SN(s) \,]$.
(4a) $NE(\mathcal{R}) \implies [\forall t : [\, WN(t) \implies SN(t) \,]]$.
(4b) $NE(\mathcal{R}) \implies [\, WN(\mathcal{R}) \implies SN(\mathcal{R}) \,]$.

For CTRSs the following technical result, which is a stronger local version of a result from [DOS88b], is crucial in order to obtain analogous relations between restricted and general termination and confluence properties of CTRSs.

Theorem 6. *([Gra93a]) Let $\mathcal{R}$ be a CTRS with $OS(\mathcal{R})$ and $JCP(\mathcal{R})$ and let s be a term with $SN(s)$. Furthermore let $C[]_\Pi$ be a context, and t, u, v be terms. Then we have:* $u = C[s]_\Pi \to^* v \wedge s \to^* t \implies C[t]_\Pi \downarrow v$.

Straightforward consequences of Theorem 6 are the following.

[2] In fact, concerning preservation properties there are indeed crucial differences between the usual syntactical and the slightly more general semantical versions of NO and OS. For instance, NO and OS are obviously modular which is not the case for the semantical version of OS.

Lemma 7. *([Gra93a]) Let $\mathcal{R}$ be a CTRS with OS($\mathcal{R}$) and JCP($\mathcal{R}$), and let s, t be terms with $s \rightarrow_{p,\sigma,P \Longrightarrow l \rightarrow r} t$. Furthermore let σ' be given with $\sigma \rightarrow^* \sigma'$, i.e. $\sigma(x) \rightarrow^* \sigma'(x)$ for all $x \in dom(\sigma)$, such that $SN(\sigma(x))$ holds for all $x \in dom(\sigma)$. Then we have: $s = C[\sigma(l)]_p \rightarrow^* C[\sigma'(l)]_p \rightarrow_{p,\sigma',P \Longrightarrow l \rightarrow r} C[\sigma'(r)]_p$ (due to $\sigma'(P) \downarrow$) and $t = C[\sigma(r)]_p \rightarrow^* C[\sigma'(r)]_p$ for some context $C[]_p$.*

Corollary 8. *([Gra93a]) Let $\mathcal{R}$ be a CTRS with OS($\mathcal{R}$) and JCP($\mathcal{R}$), and let s be a term with SN(s). Then we have CR(s) and hence COMP(s), too.*

The termination assumption concerning s in this result is crucial as demonstrated by the following example.

Example 2. (Example 1 continued) Here $\mathcal{R} = \{x \downarrow f(x) \Longrightarrow f(x) \rightarrow a,\ b \rightarrow f(b)\}$ is clearly an overlay system with joinable critical pairs (it is even non-overlapping). Moreover we have $f(f(b)) \rightarrow a$ and $f(f(b)) \rightarrow f(a)$ but not $a \downarrow f(a)$. Obviouly, SN($f(f(b))$) does not hold due to the presence of the rule $b \rightarrow f(b)$ in $\mathcal{R}$ (note that we even do not have SIN($f(f(b))$)).

Under the stronger assumption of global termination we get from Corollary 8 the following known critical pair criterion for confluence of conditional overlay systems.

Theorem 9. *([DOS88b]) A terminating CTRS which is an overlay system such that all its conditional critical pairs are joinable is confluent, hence complete.*

Concerning termination properties of CTRSs we have obtained the following results which generalize Theorem 5 to the conditional case and moreover, do not require left-linearity.

Theorem 10. *([Gra93a]) Let $\mathcal{R}$ be a non-overlapping CTRS. Then the following properties hold:*

(1a) $\forall t : [\, WIN(t) \Longrightarrow SIN(t)\,]$.
(1b) $WIN(\mathcal{R}) \Longrightarrow SIN(\mathcal{R})$.
(2a) $\forall t : [\, SIN(t) \Longrightarrow SN(t)\,]$.
(2b) $SIN(\mathcal{R}) \Longrightarrow SN(\mathcal{R})$.
(3) $\forall s,t : [\, s \xrightarrow{i} t \wedge SN(t) \Longrightarrow SN(s)\,]$.
(4a) $NE(\mathcal{R}) \Longrightarrow [\forall t : [\, WN(t) \Longrightarrow SN(t)]]$.
(4b) $NE(\mathcal{R}) \Longrightarrow [\, WN(\mathcal{R}) \Longrightarrow SN(\mathcal{R})]$.

Moreover, it is possible to generalize Theorem 10(2) by allowing root overlaps but guaranteeing joinability of critical pairs.

Theorem 11. *([Gra93a]) For any CTRS $\mathcal{R}$ we have:*

(a) $OS(\mathcal{R}) \wedge JCP(\mathcal{R}) \wedge SIN(\mathcal{R}) \Longrightarrow SN(\mathcal{R}) \wedge CR(\mathcal{R})$, *and*
(b) $OS(\mathcal{R}) \wedge JCP(\mathcal{R}) \Longrightarrow [\forall s : [SIN(s) \Longrightarrow SN(s) \wedge CR(s)]]$,

i.e. any (strongly) innermost terminating overlay system with joinable critical pairs is terminating and confluent, hence complete (part (a)) which also holds in the stronger local version (b).

4 Modularity Results for Disjoint Unions of CTRSs

Modular properties of (C)TRSs, i.e. properties which are preserved under disjoint unions, have attracted an increasing attention within the last few years.

Toyama [Toy87b] has shown that confluence is modular (for TRSs). The termination property, however, is in general not modular for TRSs (cf. [Toy87b], [Toy87a]).

When investigating the modularity behaviour of CTRSs the situation is much more complicated than for (unconditional) TRSs. For instance, as exhibited in [Mid90], the fundamental property of TRSs

$$s \to_{\mathcal{R}_1 \oplus \mathcal{R}_2} t \quad \Longrightarrow \quad s \to_{\mathcal{R}_1} t \vee s \to_{\mathcal{R}_2} t$$

does not hold any more. This is due to the fact that when a rule of one of the systems is applied rules of the other system may be needed in order to satisfy the conditions. Nevertheless, confluence has turned out to be a modular property of (join) CTRSs, too, as shown by Middeldorp.

Theorem 12. *([Mid90], [Mid93b]) Confluence is a modular property of CTRSs.*

For some sufficient conditions for modularity of termination of CTRSs we refer to [Mid90] (cf. also [Mid93b]), [Mid93a], [Gra93c]). Here we shall concentrate on CTRSs satisfying some structural restrictions. In [Gra92b], [Gra93b] we have proved that any (strongly) innermost terminating, locally confluent (unconditional) overlay system is terminating, and hence confluent and complete. Moreover – by exploiting the fact that (strong) innermost termination is modular (for TRSs) in contrast to the non-modularity of (strong) termination – we have shown there how to derive from this result new modularity results and simplified proofs of known ones. Here we would also like to follow the same line of reasoning – exploiting Theorems 10 and 11 – in order to obtain derived modularity results for CTRSs. But again the situation is much more complicated for CTRSs than for TRSs since neither weak termination, nor weak innermost termination nor strong innermost termination are modular in general for CTRSs. This can be seen e.g. from the next example.

Example 3. (cf. [Mid93b] for similar examples)

$$\mathcal{R}_1 = \{\ x \downarrow b \wedge x \downarrow c \implies a \to a\ \} \text{ over } \mathcal{F}_1 = \{a, b, c\},$$
$$\mathcal{R}_2 = \{G(x,y) \to x, G(x,y) \to y\} \text{ over } \mathcal{F}_2 = \{G, A\}.$$

Here, we have $a \to_{\mathcal{R}_1 \oplus \mathcal{R}_2} a$ by applying the $\mathcal{R}_1$-rule (x is substituted by $G(b,c)$), but neither $a \to_{\mathcal{R}_1} a$ nor $a \to_{\mathcal{R}_2} a$. Hence, a is an $\mathcal{R}_i$-normal form (for $i = 1, 2$) but not a normal form w.r.t. $\mathcal{R}_1 \oplus \mathcal{R}_2$. Obviously, both $\mathcal{R}_1$ and $\mathcal{R}_2$ are strongly (hence also weakly and innermost) terminating but their disjoint union is not. For instance, $a \to_{\mathcal{R}_1 \oplus \mathcal{R}_2} a \to_{\mathcal{R}_1 \oplus \mathcal{R}_2} a \to_{\mathcal{R}_1 \oplus \mathcal{R}_2} \dots$ is an infinite innermost derivation, and a does not have a normal from w.r.t. $(\mathcal{R}_1 \oplus \mathcal{R}_2)$.

4.1 Preservation Behaviour under Signature Extensions

From the observation in Example 3 above one might be tempted to conjecture (as it is done in [Mid93b]) that the preservation of normal forms, defined by (with $\mathcal{F} := \mathcal{F}_1 \uplus \mathcal{F}_2$, $\mathcal{R}^{\mathcal{F}} = \mathcal{R}_1^{\mathcal{F}_1} \oplus \mathcal{R}_2^{\mathcal{F}_2}$)

$$\mathrm{NFP}(\mathcal{R}_1, \mathcal{R}_2): \quad \mathrm{NF}(\mathcal{R}^{\mathcal{F}}) = \mathrm{NF}(\mathcal{R}_1^{\mathcal{F}}) \cap \mathrm{NF}(\mathcal{R}_2^{\mathcal{F}}),$$

should be a sufficient condition for the modularity of weak termination. But this is also not true in general.[3] The situation is even worse, since – surprisingly – it may happen that a weakly terminating CTRS may become not weakly terminating under the disjoint union with another 'empty' CTRS, i.e. simply by extending the signature without adding new rules. The same phenomenon may happen with weak and strong innermost termination as illustrated next.

Example 4. Consider the CTRSs $\mathcal{R}_1^{\mathcal{F}_1}$, $\mathcal{R}_2^{\mathcal{F}_2}$ given by

$$\mathcal{R}_1 = \begin{cases} x \downarrow z \wedge z \downarrow y \implies & f(g(x,y)) \to f(g(x,y)) \\ & g(x,x) \to x \\ & g(x,a) \to c \\ & g(x,b) \to c \\ & g(x,f(y)) \to c \\ & g(x,g(y,z)) \to c \\ & g(a,x) \to c \\ & g(b,x) \to c \\ & g(f(y),x) \to c \\ & g(g(y,z),x) \to c \\ & c \to a \\ & c \to b \end{cases}$$

over $\mathcal{F}_1 := \{f, g, a, b, c\}$ and $\mathcal{R}_2 := \emptyset$ over $\mathcal{F}_2 := \{G\}$ (with G unary). It is straightforward to verify that $\mathcal{R}_1^{\mathcal{F}_1}$ is weakly terminating, weakly innermost terminating and even strongly innermost terminating. The crucial point is that any arbitrary infinite $\mathcal{R}_1^{\mathcal{F}_1}$- derivation must contain rewrite steps using the first rule. But whenever this rule is applicable, the contracted redex cannot be innermost, since some proper subterm must then be reducible by the remaining rules which constitute a (strongly) terminating CTRS. Nevertheless, in the extended system $\mathcal{R}^{\mathcal{F}} = \mathcal{R}_1^{\mathcal{F}_1 \uplus \{G\}}$ we get the cyclic (hence infinite) innermost $\mathcal{R}^{\mathcal{F}}$-derivation:

$$f(g(G(a), G(b))) \xrightarrow{i}_{\mathcal{R}^{\mathcal{F}}} f(g(G(a), G(b))) \xrightarrow{i}_{\mathcal{R}^{\mathcal{F}}} f(g(G(a), G(b))) \xrightarrow{i}_{\mathcal{R}^{\mathcal{F}}} \cdots$$

by applying the first rule (instantiating the extra variable z by $G(c)$). Note moreover that there is no other way of reducing $f(g(G(a), G(b)))$ (all its proper subterms are in normal form w.r.t. $\mathcal{R}^{\mathcal{F}}$, and the second rule is clearly not applicable). Hence, $\mathcal{R}^{\mathcal{F}} = \mathcal{R}_1^{\mathcal{F}_1 \uplus \{G\}}$ is neither strongly innermost terminating nor weakly innermost terminating nor weakly terminating.

[3] contradicting Theorem 5.2 in [Mid93b] (cf. also Theorem 4.3.20 in [Mid90]) the proof of which implicitly relies on the incorrect assumption $\mathrm{WN}(\mathcal{R}_1^{\mathcal{F}_1}) \iff \mathrm{WN}(\mathcal{R}_1^{\mathcal{F}_1 \uplus \mathcal{F}_2})$.

By a thorough analysis of abstraction and innermost reduction properties which allow to project reduction sequences on mixed terms to certain reduction sequences on pure terms we shall show below how the monotonicity of WN, WIN and SIN under signature extensions can be guaranteed. More generally, we also develop sufficient criteria for the modularity of these properties. This analysis heavily relies on some very useful terminology and technical results from [Mid93b].

Definition 13. (cf. Def. 3.2 in [Mid93b]) Let $\mathcal{R}_1^{\mathcal{F}_1}, \mathcal{R}_2^{\mathcal{F}_2}$ be disjoint CTRSs with $\mathcal{R} = \mathcal{R}_1 \oplus \mathcal{R}_2$. Then the rewrite relation $\rightarrow_1$ is defined as follows: $s \rightarrow_1 t$ if there exists a rule $s_1 \downarrow t_1 \wedge \ldots \wedge s_n \downarrow t_n \implies l \rightarrow r$ in $\mathcal{R}_1$, a context $C[]$ and a substitution σ such that $s = C[\sigma(l)]$, $t = C[\sigma(r)]$ and $\sigma(s_i) \downarrow_1^o \sigma(t_i)$ for $i = 1, \ldots, n$, where $\sigma(s_i) \downarrow_1^o \sigma(t_i)$ means that s_i and t_i are joinable using only $\xrightarrow{o}_1$-reduction steps. The relation $\rightarrow_2$ is defined analogously. The union of $\rightarrow_1$ and $\rightarrow_2$ is denoted by $\rightarrow_{1,2}$.

Lemma 14. *(cf. [Mid93b], Prop. 3.5) ('injective abstraction' is possible for $\xrightarrow{o}_1$-steps)*
Let $\mathcal{R}_1$, $\mathcal{R}_2$ be disjoint CTRSs, s, t be black terms and σ be a top white substitution with $\sigma(s) \xrightarrow{o}_1 \sigma(t)$. Then, for any substitution τ with $\sigma \propto \tau$, we have $\tau(s) \xrightarrow{o}_1 \tau(t)$.

Note that this result implies in particular that a step $\sigma(s) \xrightarrow{o}_1 \sigma(t)$ on mixed terms can be injectively abstracted into a 'pure' step $\tau(s) \rightarrow_{\mathcal{R}_1} \tau(t)$ by injectively replacing the maximal top white aliens of $\sigma(s)$ and $\sigma(t)$ by fresh variables. One may wonder whether such an injective abstraction is also possible for an arbitrary outer step $\sigma(s) \xrightarrow{o}_{\mathcal{R}_1} \sigma(t)$, where for verifying the conditions of applied $\mathcal{R}_1$-rules also inner $\mathcal{R}_1$-steps are allowed. This is not the case as shown next.

Example 5. Consider the CTRSs $\mathcal{R}_1^{\mathcal{F}_1}, \mathcal{R}_2^{\mathcal{F}_2}$ given by

$$\mathcal{R}_1 = \begin{cases} x \downarrow y \implies & f(x,y) \rightarrow x \\ & a \rightarrow b \end{cases}$$

over $\mathcal{F}_1 := \{f, a, b\}$ and $\mathcal{R}_2 := \emptyset$ over $\mathcal{F}_2 := \{G\}$ (with G unary). Here we have $f(G(a), G(b)) \xrightarrow{o}_{\mathcal{R}_1} G(a)$ (due to $G(a) \downarrow_{\mathcal{R}_1} G(b)$), but not $f(G(a), G(b)) \xrightarrow{o}_1 G(a)$ since for satisfying $G(a) \downarrow_{\mathcal{R}_1} G(b)$ we need an inner $\mathcal{R}_1$-step. Note that after injective abstraction of $s = f(G(a), G(b))$ and $t = G(a)$ into $f(x,y)$ and x, respectively, the reduction $f(x,y) \rightarrow_{\mathcal{R}_1} x$ is not possible any more.

The above example somehow suggests that by forbidding the possibility of inner reduction steps injective abstraction of reduction steps might still be possible. But even if all maximal top white aliens are irreducible, this is not possible in general.

Example 6. Consider the CTRSs $\mathcal{R}_1^{\mathcal{F}_1}, \mathcal{R}_2^{\mathcal{F}_2}$ given by

$$\mathcal{R}_1 = \begin{cases} x \downarrow z \wedge z \downarrow y \implies & f(x,y) \rightarrow x \\ & c \rightarrow a \\ & c \rightarrow b \end{cases}$$

with $\mathcal{F}_1 := \{f, a, b, c\}$, $\mathcal{R}_2 := \emptyset$, $\mathcal{F}_2 := \{G\}$ (with G unary). Here all proper subterms of $f(G(a), G(b))$ are ($\mathcal{R}^{\mathcal{F}}$-) irreducible and $f(G(a), G(b)) \overset{o}{\rightarrow}_{\mathcal{R}_1} G(a)$ but not $f(G(a), G(b)) \overset{o}{\rightarrow}_1 G(a)$ since for satisfying $G(a) \downarrow_{\mathcal{R}_1} z \wedge z \downarrow_{\mathcal{R}_1} G(b)$ we have to instantiate the extra variable z in the condition of the first rule by a mixed term of the form $G(u)$, e.g. $G(c)$, and to use inner $\mathcal{R}_1$-steps for establishing $G(a) \downarrow_{\mathcal{R}_1} G(u)$, $G(u) \downarrow_{\mathcal{R}_1} G(b)$. Note again that after injective abstraction of $s = f(G(a), G(b))$ and $t = G(a)$ into $f(x, y)$ and x, respectively, the reduction $f(x, y) \rightarrow_{\mathcal{R}_1} x$ is not possible any more.

Whereas in the above examples an injective abstraction of certain reduction steps on mixed terms to a corresponding reduction step on pure terms is not possible, a non-injective 'identifying' one, which replaces all maximal top white aliens by the *same* fresh variable, is indeed possible. This is shown next.

Lemma 15. *('identifying abstraction' is always possible)*
Let $\mathcal{R}_1^{\mathcal{F}_1}$, $\mathcal{R}_2^{\mathcal{F}_2}$ be disjoint CTRSs, s and t be black terms, σ be a top white substitution, and $\tilde{\sigma}$ be defined by $\tilde{\sigma}(x) := z$ for all $x \in dom(\sigma)$ where z is a 'fresh' variable, i.e. not occurring in s. Then we have:

(a) $\sigma(s) \overset{o}{\rightarrow}_{\mathcal{R}_1} \sigma(t) \quad \Longrightarrow \quad \tilde{\sigma}(s) \overset{o}{\rightarrow}_{\mathcal{R}_1} \tilde{\sigma}(t)$, *and*
(b) $\sigma(s) \overset{i}{\rightarrow}_{\mathcal{R}_1} \sigma(t) \quad \Longrightarrow \quad \tilde{\sigma}(s) = \tilde{\sigma}(t)$.

Proof. (b) is trivially satisfied by definition of $\overset{i}{\rightarrow}$ and of $\tilde{\sigma}$. (a) can be proved by induction on n, the depth of rewriting (using the same proof structure as in [Mid93b] for Prop. 3.5, see Lemma 14 above). ∎

Corollary 16. *Let $\mathcal{R}^{\mathcal{F}}$ be a CTRS, $\mathcal{F}'$ be a signature with $\mathcal{F} \subseteq \mathcal{F}'$, and $s \in \mathcal{T}(\mathcal{F}, \mathcal{V})$. Then we have: $s \rightarrow_{\mathcal{R}^{\mathcal{F}'}} t \Longrightarrow s \rightarrow_{\mathcal{R}^{\mathcal{F}}} t$.*

Using Lemma 15 we are now able to show that at least termination (strong normalization) is preserved under signature extensions.

Lemma 17. *Let $\mathcal{R}^{\mathcal{F}}$ be a CTRS and $\mathcal{F}'$ be a signature with $\mathcal{F} \subseteq \mathcal{F}'$. Then the following holds: $SN(\mathcal{R}^{\mathcal{F}}) \iff SN(\mathcal{R}^{\mathcal{F}'})$.*

Proof. It clearly suffices to show: $\text{SN}(\mathcal{R}^{\mathcal{F}}) \Longrightarrow \text{SN}(\mathcal{R}^{\mathcal{F}'})$. Hence, assuming $\text{SN}(\mathcal{R}^{\mathcal{F}})$, we prove $\text{SN}(s)$ for all $s \in \mathcal{T}(\mathcal{F}', \mathcal{V})$ by induction on $n = rank(s)$.[4] For $rank(s) = 1$ we get $\text{SN}(s)$ by assumption. Let $rank(s) > 1$. If the root symbol of s is a new one, i.e. from $(\mathcal{F}' \setminus \mathcal{F})$, then $\text{SN}(s)$ follows by induction hypothesis, since rewrite steps in the top layer of s are impossible. If $root(s) \in \mathcal{F}$ then – again by induction hypothesis and the fact that $(\mathcal{F}' \setminus \mathcal{F})$-layers cannot collapse – any infinite $\mathcal{R}^{\mathcal{F}'}$-derivation starting with s would have to contain infinitely many outer $\mathcal{R}^{\mathcal{F}'}$-steps. But then identifying abstraction using Lemma 15 would yield an infinite $\mathcal{R}^{\mathcal{F}}$-derivation contradicting the assumption $\text{SN}(\mathcal{R}^{\mathcal{F}})$. ∎

[4] Note that we may consider here $\mathcal{R}^{\mathcal{F}'}$ as disjoint union $\mathcal{R}_1^{\mathcal{F}_1} \oplus \mathcal{R}_2^{\mathcal{F}_2}$ with $\mathcal{R}_1^{\mathcal{F}_1} = \mathcal{R}^{\mathcal{F}}$, $\mathcal{R}_2 = \emptyset$ and $\mathcal{F}_2 = \mathcal{F}' \setminus \mathcal{F}$.

In order to present sufficient criteria for the preservation of restricted termination properties under signature extensions and – more generally – under disjoint unions, we will introduce now some more notations, in particular for certain innermost reductions steps.

Definition 18. Let $\mathcal{R}_1^{\mathcal{F}_1}, \mathcal{R}_2^{\mathcal{F}_2}$ be disjoint CTRSs and $\mathcal{R}^{\mathcal{F}} = \mathcal{R}_1^{\mathcal{F}_1} \oplus \mathcal{R}_2^{\mathcal{F}_2} = (\mathcal{R}_1 \uplus \mathcal{R}_2)^{\mathcal{F}_1 \uplus \mathcal{F}_2}$ be their disjoint union. If (for $s \in \mathcal{T}(\mathcal{F}, \mathcal{V})$) $s \to_{\mathcal{R}^{\mathcal{F}}} t$ by applying some $\mathcal{R}_1$-rule (where for satisfying the conditions also $\mathcal{R}_2$-rules are allowed) we denote this by $s \to_{\mathcal{R}_1^{\mathcal{F}}/\mathcal{R}^{\mathcal{F}}} t$ or simply $s \to_{\mathcal{R}_1/\mathcal{R}} t$. Furthermore, for $j = 1, 2$ we define the innermost reduction properties $\mathrm{IRP}_1(\mathcal{R}_j, \mathcal{R})$, $\mathrm{IRP}_2(\mathcal{R}_j, \mathcal{R})$ and $\mathrm{IRP}_3(\mathcal{R}_j, \mathcal{R})$

$$\text{by}^5 \begin{cases} \mathrm{IRP}_1(\mathcal{R}_j, \mathcal{R}) : \forall s \in \mathcal{T}(\mathcal{F}, \mathcal{V}) : \quad s \xrightarrow{i}_{\mathcal{R}_j} t \implies s \xrightarrow{i}_j t, \\ \mathrm{IRP}_2(\mathcal{R}_j, \mathcal{R}) : \forall s \in \mathcal{T}(\mathcal{F}, \mathcal{V}) : s \xrightarrow{i}_{\mathcal{R}_j/\mathcal{R}} t \implies \exists t' \in \mathcal{T}(\mathcal{F}, \mathcal{V}) : s \xrightarrow{i}_{\mathcal{R}_j} t' \\ \mathrm{IRP}_3(\mathcal{R}_j, \mathcal{R}) : \forall s \in \mathcal{T}(\mathcal{F}, \mathcal{V}) : s \xrightarrow{i}_{\mathcal{R}_j/\mathcal{R}} t \implies s \xrightarrow{i}_{\mathcal{R}_j} t. \end{cases}$$

Note that IRP_1 enables injective abstraction (via Lemma 14) which will be useful for establishing preservation results under signature extensions. Combined with IRP_2 or the stronger property IRP_3 it will turn out to capture the essence for obtaining modularity results later on.

Using the first innermost reduction property IRP_1 defined above we obtain a sufficient criterion for the preservation of WN, WIN and SIN under signature extensions as follows.

Theorem 19. *Let $\mathcal{R}_1^{\mathcal{F}_1}, \mathcal{R}_2^{\mathcal{F}_2}$ be disjoint CTRSs with $\mathcal{R}_2 = \emptyset$ (and $\mathcal{R}^{\mathcal{F}} := \mathcal{R}_1^{\mathcal{F}_1} \oplus \mathcal{R}_2^{\mathcal{F}_2} = \mathcal{R}_1^{\mathcal{F}_1 \uplus \mathcal{F}_2}$) such that $\mathrm{IRP}_1(\mathcal{R}_1^{\mathcal{F}_1}, \mathcal{R}_1^{\mathcal{F}})$ holds. Then we have the following equivalences:*

(a) $WN(\mathcal{R}_1^{\mathcal{F}_1}) \iff WN(\mathcal{R}_1^{\mathcal{F}_1 \cup \mathcal{F}_2})$.
(b) $WIN(\mathcal{R}_1^{\mathcal{F}_1}) \iff WIN(\mathcal{R}_1^{\mathcal{F}_1 \cup \mathcal{F}_2})$.
(c) $SIN(\mathcal{R}_1^{\mathcal{F}_1}) \iff SIN(\mathcal{R}_1^{\mathcal{F}_1 \cup \mathcal{F}_2})$.

Proof. Let $\mathcal{R}_1^{\mathcal{F}_1}, \mathcal{R}_2^{\mathcal{F}_2}, \mathcal{R}^{\mathcal{F}}$ be given as above satisfying $\mathrm{IRP}_1(\mathcal{R}_1^{\mathcal{F}_1}, \mathcal{R}_1^{\mathcal{F}})$. The '$\Longleftarrow$'-directions of (a), (b) and (c) are easy by Corollary 16.

(a) For proving $\mathrm{WN}(\mathcal{R}_1^{\mathcal{F}_1}) \implies \mathrm{WN}(\mathcal{R}_1^{\mathcal{F}})$ we assume $\mathrm{WN}(\mathcal{R}_1^{\mathcal{F}_1})$ and show that every term $s \in \mathcal{T}(\mathcal{F}, \mathcal{V})$ has a normal form w.r.t. $\mathcal{R}^{\mathcal{F}} = \mathcal{R}_1^{\mathcal{F}}$ by induction on $rank(s)$. If $rank(s) = 1$, this is easy by the assumption $\mathrm{WN}(\mathcal{R}_1^{\mathcal{F}_1})$, Corollary 16 and the fact that $\mathcal{R}_2 = \emptyset$. If $rank(s) > 1$ then s has the form $s = C[\![s_1, \ldots, s_m]\!]$. If the top layer $C[, \ldots,]$ is white then by induction hypothesis and $\mathcal{R}_2 = \emptyset$ we get $\mathrm{WN}(s, \mathcal{R}_1^{\mathcal{F}})$. Otherwise, in the interesting case where $C[, \ldots,]$ is black, we know by induction hypothesis that every s_i $(1 \le i \le m)$ has a normal form w.r.t. $\mathcal{R}_1^{\mathcal{F}}$, let's say t_i. Hence, we get

$$s = C[\![s_1, \ldots, s_m]\!] \to^*_{\mathcal{R}_1^{\mathcal{F}}} C[t_1, \ldots, t_m] = C' \{\!\{ u_1, \ldots, u_n \}\!\}$$

[5] The notation used here for innermost reduction is slightly ambiguous (for the sake of readability). When writing $s \xrightarrow{i}_{\mathcal{R}_j/\mathcal{R}} t$, $s \xrightarrow{i}_{\mathcal{R}_j} t$ or $s \xrightarrow{i}_j t$, we always mean that the reduced subterm is an innermost redex of s w.r.t. $\to_{\mathcal{R}}$ which is also an innermost redex of s w.r.t. $\xrightarrow{i}_{\mathcal{R}_j/\mathcal{R}}$, $\xrightarrow{i}_{\mathcal{R}_j}$ or $\to_j$, respectively, since $\xrightarrow{i}_{\mathcal{R}_j/\mathcal{R}}$, $\xrightarrow{i}_{\mathcal{R}_j}$ and $\to_j$ are subsets of $\to_{\mathcal{R}}$.

for some black context $C'\{,\ldots,\}$ and top white normal forms u_j w.r.t. $\mathcal{R}_1^{\mathcal{F}}$. Choosing fresh variables $x_1,\ldots,x_n$ injectively, i.e. $\langle u_1,\ldots,u_n\rangle \propto \langle x_1,\ldots,x_n\rangle$, we have $rank(C'\{x_1,\ldots,x_n\}) = 1$, hence by induction hypothesis $C'\{x_1,\ldots,x_n\}$ can be reduced in $\mathcal{R}_1^{\mathcal{F}_1}$ to a normal form $C''\langle x_{i_1},\ldots,x_{i_p}\rangle$. Thus we get

$$s \rightarrow^*_{\mathcal{R}_1^{\mathcal{F}}} C'\{\!\{u_1,\ldots,u_n\}\!\} \rightarrow^*_{\mathcal{R}_1^{\mathcal{F}}} C''\langle\!\langle u_{i_1},\ldots,u_{i_p}\rangle\!\rangle$$

with $u_{i_1},\ldots,u_{i_p} \in \mathrm{NF}(\mathcal{R}_1^{\mathcal{F}})$. Now, denoting u_{i_j} by v_j, it suffices to show $C''\langle\!\langle v_1,\ldots,v_p\rangle\!\rangle \in \mathrm{NF}(\mathcal{R}_1^{\mathcal{F}})$. If this were not the case then there would exist an (outer) innermost $\mathcal{R}_1^{\mathcal{F}}$-reduction step of the form

$$C''\langle\!\langle v_1,\ldots,v_p\rangle\!\rangle \overset{o}{\underset{i}{\rightarrow}}_{\mathcal{R}_1^{\mathcal{F}}} C'''\langle\!\langle v_{k_1},\ldots,v_{k_q}\rangle\!\rangle$$

with $1 \le k_l \le p$, $1 \le l \le q$. But then, due to the assumption $\mathrm{IRP}_1(\mathcal{R}_1^{\mathcal{F}_1},\mathcal{R}_1^{\mathcal{F}})$, we could apply Lemma 14 which would yield (denoting x_{i_j} by y_j, $1 \le j \le p$)

$$C''\langle y_1,\ldots,y_p\rangle \rightarrow_{\mathcal{R}_1^{\mathcal{F}_1}} C'''\langle y_{k_1},\ldots,y_{k_q}\rangle\,.$$

But this is a contradiction to $C''\langle y_1,\ldots,y_p\rangle \in \mathrm{NF}(\mathcal{R}_1^{\mathcal{F}_1})$. Hence we are done.

(b) For proving $\mathrm{WIN}(\mathcal{R}_1^{\mathcal{F}_1}) \Longrightarrow \mathrm{WIN}(\mathcal{R}_1^{\mathcal{F}})$ the same proof structure as for (a) can be used, but the argumentation is slightly different.

(c) For proving $\mathrm{SIN}(\mathcal{R}_1^{\mathcal{F}_1}) \Longrightarrow \mathrm{SIN}(\mathcal{R}_1^{\mathcal{F}})$ we assume $\mathrm{SIN}(\mathcal{R}_1^{\mathcal{F}_1})$ and show by contradiction that for every term $s \in \mathcal{T}(\mathcal{F},\mathcal{V})$ we have $\mathrm{SIN}(s,\mathcal{R}_1^{\mathcal{F}})$. Consider a counterexample which is minimal w.r.t. the subterm relation, i.e. a term s which has an infinite innermost $\mathcal{R}_1^{\mathcal{F}}$-derivation

$$(D) \quad s =: s_0 \underset{i}{\rightarrow}_{\mathcal{R}_1^{\mathcal{F}}} s_1 \underset{i}{\rightarrow}_{\mathcal{R}_1^{\mathcal{F}}} s_2 \underset{i}{\rightarrow}_{\mathcal{R}_1^{\mathcal{F}}} \cdots$$

such that all proper subterms of s are strongly innermost terminating (w.r.t. $\mathcal{R}_1^{\mathcal{F}}$). Then, necessarily s is a top black term with $rank(s) > 1$. By the minimality assumption we know that there is some (first) innermost $\mathcal{R}_1^{\mathcal{F}}$-step

$$s_k = C_k[\![t_1,\ldots,t_n]\!] \underset{i}{\rightarrow}_{\mathcal{R}_1^{\mathcal{F}}} C'\langle\!\langle t_{i_1},\ldots,t_{i_p}\rangle\!\rangle = s_{k+1}$$

in (D) which is a root reduction step. This implies in particular that all maximal top white aliens of s_k (as well as of all $s_{k'}$, $k' > k$) are $\mathcal{R}_1^{\mathcal{F}}$-irreducible. Hence all steps in

$$s_k \underset{i}{\rightarrow}_{\mathcal{R}_1^{\mathcal{F}}} s_{k+1} \underset{i}{\rightarrow}_{\mathcal{R}_1^{\mathcal{F}}} s_{k+2} \underset{i}{\rightarrow}_{\mathcal{R}_1^{\mathcal{F}}} \cdots$$

are outer steps. Due to the assumption $\mathrm{IRP}_1(\mathcal{R}_1^{\mathcal{F}_1},\mathcal{R}_1^{\mathcal{F}}))$ we may apply now Lemma 14 which yields an infinite innermost $\mathcal{R}_1^{\mathcal{F}_1}$ derivation

$$\widehat{s_k} \underset{i}{\rightarrow}_{\mathcal{R}_1^{\mathcal{F}_1}} \widehat{s_{k+1}} \underset{i}{\rightarrow}_{\mathcal{R}_1^{\mathcal{F}_1}} \widehat{s_{k+2}} \underset{i}{\rightarrow}_{\mathcal{R}_1^{\mathcal{F}_1}} \cdots$$

by injectively abstracting the maximal top white aliens by fresh variables. But this is a contradiction to $\mathrm{SIN}(\mathcal{R}_1^{\mathcal{F}_1})$. ■

4.2 Preservation Results for WN, WIN and SIN

Using the second innermost reduction property from Definition 18, we get the following preservation result for weak and weak innermost termination.

Lemma 20. *Let $\mathcal{R}_1^{\mathcal{F}_1}$, $\mathcal{R}_2^{\mathcal{F}_2}$ be disjoint CTRSs and $\mathcal{R}^{\mathcal{F}} = (\mathcal{R}_1^{\mathcal{F}_1} \oplus \mathcal{R}_2^{\mathcal{F}_2})$. Then we have:*

(a) $IRP_2(\mathcal{R}_1, \mathcal{R}) \wedge IRP_2(\mathcal{R}_2, \mathcal{R}) \Longrightarrow [\, WN(\mathcal{R}_1^{\mathcal{F}}) \wedge WN(\mathcal{R}_2^{\mathcal{F}}) \Longleftrightarrow WN(\mathcal{R}^{\mathcal{F}})].$
(b) $IRP_2(\mathcal{R}_1, \mathcal{R}) \wedge IRP_2(\mathcal{R}_2, \mathcal{R}) \Longrightarrow [\, WIN(\mathcal{R}_1^{\mathcal{F}}) \wedge WIN(\mathcal{R}_2^{\mathcal{F}}) \Longleftrightarrow WIN(\mathcal{R}^{\mathcal{F}})].$

Proof. Let $\mathcal{R}_1^{\mathcal{F}_1}$, $\mathcal{R}_2^{\mathcal{F}_2}$, $\mathcal{R}^{\mathcal{F}}$ be given as above satisfying $\mathrm{IRP}_2(\mathcal{R}_1^{\mathcal{F}_1}, \mathcal{R}^{\mathcal{F}})$. The '$\Longleftarrow$'-directions of the equivalences in (a) and (b)) are easy by Corollary 16.

(a) For proving $\mathrm{WN}(\mathcal{R}_1^{\mathcal{F}}) \wedge \mathrm{WN}(\mathcal{R}_2^{\mathcal{F}}) \Longrightarrow \mathrm{WN}(\mathcal{R}^{\mathcal{F}})$ we assume $\mathrm{WN}(\mathcal{R}_1^{\mathcal{F}})$, $\mathrm{WN}(\mathcal{R}_2^{\mathcal{F}})$ and show that every term $s \in \mathcal{T}(\mathcal{F}, \mathcal{V})$ has a normal form w.r.t. $\mathcal{R}^{\mathcal{F}}$ by induction on $rank(s)$. If $rank(s) = 1$, this is easy by the assumptions $\mathrm{WN}(\mathcal{R}_j^{\mathcal{F}})$, $\mathrm{IRP}_2(\mathcal{R}_j, \mathcal{R})$ (for $j = 1, 2$). If $rank(s) > 1$ then s has the form $s = C[\![s_1, \ldots, s_m]\!]$ with s top black w.l.o.g., and we know by induction hypothesis that every s_i $(1 \le i \le m)$ has a normal form w.r.t. $\mathcal{R}^{\mathcal{F}}$, let's say t_i. Hence, we get

$$s = C[\![s_1, \ldots, s_m]\!] \rightarrow^*_{\mathcal{R}^{\mathcal{F}}} C[t_1, \ldots, t_m] = C' \{\!\{ u_1, \ldots, u_n \}\!\}$$

for some black context $C'\{, \ldots, \}$ and top white normal forms u_j w.r.t. $\mathcal{R}^{\mathcal{F}}$. By assumption, we can reduce $C' \{\!\{ u_1, \ldots, u_n \}\!\}$ to some normal form w.r.t. $\mathcal{R}_1^{\mathcal{F}}$, i.e.

$$s \rightarrow^*_{\mathcal{R}^{\mathcal{F}}} C' \{\!\{ u_1, \ldots, u_n \}\!\} \rightarrow^*_{\mathcal{R}_1^{\mathcal{F}}} C'' \langle\!\langle u_{i_1}, \ldots, u_{i_p} \rangle\!\rangle$$

with $C'' \langle\!\langle u_{i_1}, \ldots, u_{i_p} \rangle\!\rangle$ irreducible w.r.t. $\rightarrow_{\mathcal{R}_2/\mathcal{R}}$. Now it suffices to show $C'' \langle\!\langle u_{i_1}, \ldots, u_{i_p} \rangle\!\rangle \in \mathrm{NF}(\mathcal{R}^{\mathcal{F}})$. If this were not the case then $C'' \langle\!\langle u_{i_1}, \ldots, u_{i_p} \rangle\!\rangle$ would be innermost $\rightarrow_{\mathcal{R}_1^{\mathcal{F}}/\mathcal{R}^{\mathcal{F}}}$-reducible, hence by the assumption $\mathrm{IRP}_2(\mathcal{R}_1^{\mathcal{F}_1}, \mathcal{R}^{\mathcal{F}})$ it would also be (innermost) $\rightarrow_{\mathcal{R}_1^{\mathcal{F}}}$-reducible, contradicting $C'' \langle\!\langle u_{i_1}, \ldots, u_{i_p} \rangle\!\rangle \in \mathrm{NF}(\mathcal{R}_1^{\mathcal{F}})$. Hence we are done.

(b) For proving $\mathrm{WIN}(\mathcal{R}_1^{\mathcal{F}_1}) \Longrightarrow \mathrm{WIN}(\mathcal{R}_1^{\mathcal{F}})$ the same proof structure as for (a) can be used, but the argumentation is slightly different. ∎

An equivalent characterization of the precondition in Lemma 20 is given by the normal form property defined above. More precisely, we obtain the following result (the proof of which is omitted due to lack of space).

Lemma 21. *Let $\mathcal{R}_1^{\mathcal{F}_1}$, $\mathcal{R}_2^{\mathcal{F}_2}$ be disjoint CTRSs and $\mathcal{R}^{\mathcal{F}} = (\mathcal{R}_1^{\mathcal{F}_1} \oplus \mathcal{R}_2^{\mathcal{F}_2})$. Then we have:* $NF(\mathcal{R}^{\mathcal{F}}) = NF(\mathcal{R}_1^{\mathcal{F}}) \cap NF(\mathcal{R}_2^{\mathcal{F}}) \Longleftrightarrow IRP_2(\mathcal{R}_1, \mathcal{R}) \wedge IRP_2(\mathcal{R}_2, \mathcal{R})$.

Now, considering Lemma 20 above, the property $\mathrm{IRP}_2(\mathcal{R}_1, \mathcal{R}) \wedge \mathrm{IRP}_2(\mathcal{R}_2, \mathcal{R})$ does not yet suffice for the equivalence $\mathrm{SIN}(\mathcal{R}_1^{\mathcal{F}}) \wedge \mathrm{SIN}(\mathcal{R}_2^{\mathcal{F}}) \Longleftrightarrow \mathrm{SIN}(\mathcal{R}^{\mathcal{F}})$. To see this, consider the following slightly modified version of Example 3.

Example 7. Consider the following disjoint CTRSs.

$\mathcal{R}_1 = \{x \downarrow b \wedge x \downarrow c \Longrightarrow a \rightarrow a,\ a \rightarrow d\}$ over $\mathcal{F}_1 = \{a, b, c, d\}$,

$\mathcal{R}_2 = \{G(x,y) \to x, G(x,y) \to y\}$ over $\mathcal{F}_2 = \{G, A\}$.

Here, both $\mathcal{R}_1^{\mathcal{F}_1 \uplus \mathcal{F}_2}$ and $\mathcal{R}_2^{\mathcal{F}_1 \uplus \mathcal{F}_2}$ are (strongly) innermost terminating – and even (strongly) terminating (it is easily shown that the first $\mathcal{R}_1$-rule is never applicable) – but their disjoint union $\mathcal{R}^{\mathcal{F}} = (\mathcal{R}_1 \uplus \mathcal{R}_2)^{\mathcal{F}_1 \uplus \mathcal{F}_2}$ is not (strongly) innermost terminating due to $a \xrightarrow[i]{}_{\mathcal{R}_1 \oplus \mathcal{R}_2} a \xrightarrow[i]{}_{\mathcal{R}_1 \oplus \mathcal{R}_2} a \xrightarrow[i]{}_{\mathcal{R}_1 \oplus \mathcal{R}_2} \cdots$. Nevertheless $\mathcal{R}_1$ and $\mathcal{R}_2$ satisfy the normal form property NFP$(\mathcal{R}_1, \mathcal{R}_2)$: NF$(\mathcal{R}^{\mathcal{F}})$ = NF$(\mathcal{R}_1^{\mathcal{F}}) \cap$ NF$(\mathcal{R}_2^{\mathcal{F}})$ or equivalently IRP$_2(\mathcal{R}_1, \mathcal{R}) \wedge$ IRP$_2(\mathcal{R}_2, \mathcal{R})$ (since a is now both $\mathcal{R}_1^{\mathcal{F}}$- and $\mathcal{R}^{\mathcal{F}}$-reducible due the presence of the rule $a \to d$ in $\mathcal{R}_1$).

Requiring instead of IRP$_2(\mathcal{R}_1, \mathcal{R}) \wedge$ IRP$_2(\mathcal{R}_2, \mathcal{R})$ the stronger property IRP$_3(\mathcal{R}_1, \mathcal{R}) \wedge$ IRP$_3(\mathcal{R}_2, \mathcal{R})$ accounts for this fact.

Lemma 22. *Let $\mathcal{R}_1^{\mathcal{F}_1}$, $\mathcal{R}_2^{\mathcal{F}_2}$ be disjoint CTRSs and $\mathcal{R}^{\mathcal{F}} = (\mathcal{R}_1^{\mathcal{F}_1} \oplus \mathcal{R}_2^{\mathcal{F}_2})$. Then we have: IRP$_3(\mathcal{R}_1, \mathcal{R}) \wedge$ IRP$_3(\mathcal{R}_2, \mathcal{R}) \Longrightarrow$ [SIN$(\mathcal{R}_1^{\mathcal{F}}) \wedge$ SIN$(\mathcal{R}_2^{\mathcal{F}}) \Longleftrightarrow$ SIN$(\mathcal{R}^{\mathcal{F}})$].*

Proof. Let $\mathcal{R}_1^{\mathcal{F}_1}$, $\mathcal{R}_2^{\mathcal{F}_2}$ and $\mathcal{R}^{\mathcal{F}}$ be given as above satisfying IRP$_3(\mathcal{R}_1, \mathcal{R}) \wedge$ IRP$_3(\mathcal{R}_2, \mathcal{R})$. Now, the "$\Longleftarrow$"-direction is straightforward using Corollary 16. Vice versa, for proving SIN$(\mathcal{R}_1^{\mathcal{F}}) \wedge$ SIN$(\mathcal{R}_2^{\mathcal{F}}) \Longrightarrow$ SIN$(\mathcal{R}^{\mathcal{F}})$ we proceed by contradiction assuming SIN$(\mathcal{R}_1^{\mathcal{F}})$ and SIN$(\mathcal{R}_2^{\mathcal{F}})$. Consider a minimal counterexample, i.e. an infinite innermost $\mathcal{R}^{\mathcal{F}}$-derivation $s_0 \xrightarrow[i]{}_{\mathcal{R}^{\mathcal{F}}} s_1 \xrightarrow[i]{}_{\mathcal{R}^{\mathcal{F}}} s_2 \xrightarrow[i]{}_{\mathcal{R}^{\mathcal{F}}} \cdots$ such that no proper subterm of s_0 admits infinite innermost $\mathcal{R}^{\mathcal{F}}$-derivations. By the minimality assumption some step $s_k \xrightarrow[i]{}_{\mathcal{R}^{\mathcal{F}}} s_{k+1}$ in the above derivation must be a root reduction step, let's say using a black rule. But then we know that all subsequent steps must also be $\to_{\mathcal{R}_1/\mathcal{R}}$-steps. Thus, by the assumption IRP$_3(\mathcal{R}_1, \mathcal{R})$ we can conclude that $s_k \xrightarrow[i]{}_{\mathcal{R}_1^{\mathcal{F}}} s_{k+1} \xrightarrow[i]{}_{\mathcal{R}_1^{\mathcal{F}}} s_{k+2} \xrightarrow[i]{}_{\mathcal{R}_1^{\mathcal{F}}} \cdots$ is an infinite innermost $\mathcal{R}_1^{\mathcal{F}}$-derivation contradicting SIN$(\mathcal{R}_1^{\mathcal{F}})$. ∎

Next we shall provide sufficient conditions for the innermost reduction properties IRP$_1$, IRP$_2$ and IRP$_3$. Having again a look at Examples 4 and 6 we see that in both cases the system $\mathcal{R}_1$ is non-confluent and has a rule with extra variables which seems to be essential. And indeed, forbidding extra variables or requiring confluence turns out to be crucial as will be shown next.

Lemma 23. *Let $\mathcal{R}_1^{\mathcal{F}_1}$, $\mathcal{R}_2^{\mathcal{F}_2}$ be disjoint CTRSs without extra variables, with $\mathcal{R}^{\mathcal{F}} = (\mathcal{R}_1^{\mathcal{F}_1} \oplus \mathcal{R}_2^{\mathcal{F}_2})$. Then the innermost reduction properties IRP$_k(\mathcal{R}_j, \mathcal{R})$ hold for $j = 1, 2$ and $k = 1, 2, 3$.*

Proof. It suffices to show the following for $j = 1, 2$:

$$\forall s \in \mathcal{T}(\mathcal{F}, \mathcal{V}) : s \xrightarrow[i]{}_{\mathcal{R}_j/\mathcal{R}} t \Longrightarrow s \xrightarrow[i]{}_{\mathcal{R}_j} t \Longrightarrow s \xrightarrow[i]{}_{j} t$$

This is straightforward by induction on the depth of rewriting, and exploiting the absence of extra variables (since the step $s \xrightarrow[i]{}_{\mathcal{R}_j/\mathcal{R}} t$ is innermost and due to the absence of extra variables we know that for verifying the conditions of the applied $\mathcal{R}_j$-rule only outer $\to_j$-steps are possible). ∎

For the case of confluent CTRSs we need two more technical lemmas from [Mid93b].

Lemma 24. *(cf. Propositions 3.6 and 3.8 in [Mid93b]) Let $\mathcal{R}_1$, $\mathcal{R}_2$ be two disjoint confluent CTRSs and $\mathcal{R} = \mathcal{R}_1 \oplus \mathcal{R}_2$. Then $\rightarrow_{1,2}$ is confluent and $\downarrow_{1,2}$ coincides with $\overset{*}{\leftrightarrow}_{\mathcal{R}}$.*

Lemma 25. *(cf. Prop. 3.13 in [Mid93b]) Let $\mathcal{R}_1$, $\mathcal{R}_2$ be two disjoint, confluent CTRSs, $\mathcal{R} = \mathcal{R}_1 \oplus \mathcal{R}_2$ and $s_1, \ldots, s_n, t_1, \ldots, t_n$ be black terms. Then, for every substitution σ with $\sigma(s_i) \downarrow_{1,2} \sigma(t_i)$ for $i = 1, \ldots, n$ there exists a substitution τ such that $\sigma \rightarrow^*_{1,2} \tau$ and $\tau(s_i) \downarrow^o_1 \tau(t_i)$ for $i = 1, \ldots, n$.*

Lemma 26. *Let $\mathcal{R}_1^{\mathcal{F}_1}$, $\mathcal{R}_2^{\mathcal{F}_2}$ be disjoint confluent CTRSs, with $\mathcal{R}^{\mathcal{F}} = (\mathcal{R}_1^{\mathcal{F}_1} \oplus \mathcal{R}_2^{\mathcal{F}_2})$. Then the innermost reduction properties $IRP_k(\mathcal{R}_j, \mathcal{R})$ hold for $j = 1, 2$ and $k = 1, 2, 3$.*

Proof. It suffices to show the following for $j = 1, 2$:

$$\forall s \in \mathcal{T}(\mathcal{F}, \mathcal{V}) : s \underset{i}{\rightarrow}_{\mathcal{R}_j/\mathcal{R}} t \implies s \underset{i}{\rightarrow}_{\mathcal{R}_j} t \implies s \underset{i}{\rightarrow}_j t$$

Now consider a step $s \underset{i}{\rightarrow}_{\mathcal{R}_j/\mathcal{R}} t$ using some $\mathcal{R}_j$-rule $P \implies l \rightarrow r$ with matching substitution σ (which may also instantiate the extra variables in the conditions P). Hence, we have $\sigma(u) \downarrow_{\mathcal{R}} \sigma(v)$ for all conditions $u \downarrow v$ in P. By Lemma 24 and Lemma 25 we obtain the existence of some substitution τ with $\sigma \rightarrow^*_{1,2} \tau$ and $\tau(u) \downarrow^o_1 \tau(v)$ for all $u \downarrow v$ in P. Since the step $s \underset{i}{\rightarrow}_{\mathcal{R}_j/\mathcal{R}} t$ is innermost we know that σ is irreducible for all $x \in dom(\sigma) \cap \mathcal{V}(l)$, hence σ and τ coincide on $\mathcal{V}(l)$. Thus we get $\sigma(l) = \tau(l)$, $\sigma(r) = \tau(r)$ which implies $s \underset{i}{\rightarrow}_j t$ as desired. ■

4.3 Modularity Results

By combining Theorem 19 and the Lemmas 20, 22, 23 and 26 we now obtain the following modularity results (which obviously also cover the case of signature extensions).

Theorem 27. *Weak termination, weak innermost termination and (strong) innermost termination are modular properties for confluent CTRSs and for CTRSs without extra variables (in the conditions).*

Let us come back now to the question under which conditions termination and completeness are modular for CTRSs. Combining different results now enables us to prove the following.

Theorem 28. *Termination and completeness are modular for the class of non-overlapping CTRSs.*

Proof. Let $\mathcal{R}_1$, $\mathcal{R}_2$ be two disjoint non-overlapping and terminating CTRSs. Applying Theorem 9 yields confluence of $\mathcal{R}_i$ for $i = 1, 2$. By assumption we know in particular that both systems are (strongly) innermost terminating. Hence, by Theorem 27 we get that $\mathcal{R}_1 \oplus \mathcal{R}_2$ is (strongly) innermost terminating, too. The property of being non-overlapping is obviously modular for CTRSs. Hence $\mathcal{R}_1 \oplus \mathcal{R}_2$ is (strongly) innermost terminating and non-overlapping. Finally, applying Theorem 10 yields (strong) termination of $\mathcal{R}_1 \oplus \mathcal{R}_2$ which – again by Theorem

9 – implies confluence of $\mathcal{R}_1 \oplus \mathcal{R}_2$. Hence, $\mathcal{R}_1 \oplus \mathcal{R}_2$ is a confluent, (strongly) terminating and non-overlapping CTRS. Vice versa, assume that $\mathcal{R}_1 \oplus \mathcal{R}_2$ is non-overlapping and terminating, hence complete. Then we know that both $\mathcal{R}_1$ and $\mathcal{R}_2$ are non-overlapping and terminating, hence complete. ∎

Similarly, we can show that termination and completeness are modular for the class of conditional overlay systems with joinable critical pairs.

Theorem 29. *Termination and completeness are modular for the class of conditional overlay systems with joinable critical pairs.*

Proof. Let $\mathcal{R}_1, \mathcal{R}_2$ be two disjoint terminating, conditional overlay systems with joinable critical pairs. Applying Theorem 9 yields confluence of $\mathcal{R}_i$ for $i = 1, 2$. By assumption we know in particular that both systems are (strongly) innermost terminating. Hence, by Theorem 27 we get that $\mathcal{R}_1 \oplus \mathcal{R}_2$ is (strongly) innermost terminating, too. The property of being a conditional overlay system is obviously modular for CTRSs. Hence $\mathcal{R}_1 \oplus \mathcal{R}_2$ is a (strongly) innermost terminating, conditional overlay system. Now, in order to be able to apply Theorem 11 for inferring (strong) termination of $\mathcal{R}_1 \oplus \mathcal{R}_2$ we need to establish joinability of all (conditional) critical pairs of $\mathcal{R}_1 \oplus \mathcal{R}_2$. Since both $\mathcal{R}_1$ and $\mathcal{R}_2$ are confluent we know by Theorem 12 that $\mathcal{R}_1 \oplus \mathcal{R}_2$ is confluent, too. Hence, in particular, all critical pairs of $\mathcal{R}_1 \oplus \mathcal{R}_2$ must be joinable. Applying Theorem 11 now yields that $\mathcal{R}_1 \oplus \mathcal{R}_2$ is a (strongly) terminating and confluent conditional overlay system (with joinable critical pairs, of course). Vice versa, assume that $\mathcal{R}_1 \oplus \mathcal{R}_2$ is a conditional overlay system with joinable critical pairs which is terminating, hence confluent and complete. Then we know that both $\mathcal{R}_1$ and $\mathcal{R}_2$ are terminating conditional overlay systems. By Theorem 12 confluence of $\mathcal{R}_1 \oplus \mathcal{R}_2$ implies confluence of both $\mathcal{R}_1$ and $\mathcal{R}_2$ (hence in particular also joinability of critical pairs). ∎

Note that – compared to the unconditional case – the proofs of Theorem 28 and Theorem 29 are more complicated. This is due to the fact that both local confluence and joinability of all critical pairs are not modular for CTRSs in general ([Mid93b]) as well as (strong) innermost termination (cf. Example 4 above).

5 Discussion, Related Work and Open Problems

Our results above and the counterexamples falsifying a couple of quite obvious and tempting conjectures demonstrate once more the inherent complexity and intricacy of CTRSs. Allowing extra variables in the conditions gives rise to some additional complications and phenomena. We have also seen that some termination and confluence properties of CTRSs depend on each other in a very subtle manner (cf. e.g. Theorems 27, 28, 29 and their proofs). Compared to unconditional TRSs the compositional behaviour of CTRSs under disjoint unions and even under signature extensions has turned out to be much more complicated (cf. e.g. Example 4). In particular, the properties of having (only) joinable critical pairs (JCP), being locally confluent (WCR) and being weakly, weakly innermost and (strongly) innermost terminating (WN, WIN and SIN, respectively) are in general not preserved under disjoint unions, in contrast to the unconditional case.

In the presentation we have focussed on join CTRSs which – from an operational point of view – is the most interesting type. It needs some further investigations (but should not be too difficult) to find out which of our results do also hold for semi-equational CTRSs. Note for instance, that the counterexample 4 does not work anymore for the semi-equational case.

Due to the aforementioned bad compositional behaviour of CTRSs concerning joinability of (all) critical pairs, local confluence and (strong) innermost termination, it is not straightforward to generalize our modularity results, in particular Theorems 28 and 29 to less restrictive non-disjoint combination mechanisms. Up to now – and as far as we know – the only comparable positive results in this direction have been obtained in [Mid93a] for 'combinations of conditional constructor systems', using a quite different proof technique. There, the disjointness requirement is weakened but extra variables are not allowed[6] and only a proper subclass of (conditional) overlay systems, namely (conditional) constructor systems, is considered. It remains to be seen to what extent our analysis here – combined with ideas of [Mid93b] – can be generalized to such non-disjoint combinations of CTRSs.

References

[BK86] J. A. Bergstra and J. W. Klop. Conditional rewrite rules: Confluence and termination. *Journal of Computer and System Sciences*, 32:323–362, 1986.

[Der93] N. Dershowitz. Hierarchical termination, Department of Computer Science, Hebrew University, Jerusalem, Israel. November 1993.

[DJ90] N. Dershowitz and J.-P. Jouannaud. Rewrite systems. In J. van Leeuwen, ed., *Formal models and semantics, Handbook of Theoretical Computer Science*, vol. B, chapter 6, pp. 243–320. Elsevier - The MIT Press, 1990.

[DOS88a] N. Dershowitz, M. Okada, and G. Sivakumar. Canonical conditional rewrite systems. In E. Lusk and R. Overbeek, eds., *Proc. 9th CADE, LNCS 310*, pp. 538–549. Springer, 1988.

[DOS88b] N. Dershowitz, M. Okada, and G. Sivakumar. Confluence of conditional rewrite systems. In S. Kaplan and J.-P. Jouannaud, eds., *Proc. 1st CTRS, LNCS 308*, pp. 31–44. Springer, 1988.

[FJ93] M. Fernandez and J.-P. Jouannaud. Modularity properties of term rewriting systems revisited. Rapport de Recherche 875, LRI, Orsay, France, 1993.

[Gra92a] B. Gramlich. Generalized sufficient conditions for modular termination of rewriting. In H. Kirchner and G. Levi, eds., *Proc. 3rd ALP, LNCS 632*, pp. 53–68. Springer, 1992. Ext. version in *AAECC* 5:131–158, 1994.

[Gra92b] B. Gramlich. Relating innermost, weak, uniform and modular termination of term rewriting systems. In A. Voronkov, editor, *3rd LPAR, St. Petersburg, LNAI 624*, pp. 285–296. Springer, 1992.

[6] In fact, in [Mid93a] it is conjectured that the main results, namely preservation of weak normalization, semi-completeness and completeness under combinations of conditional constructor systems, do also hold when allowing extra variables (in the conditions of the rules).

[Gra93a] B. Gramlich. New abstract criteria for termination and confluence of conditional rewrite systems. SEKI-Report SR-93-17, FB Informatik, Universität Kaiserslautern, 1993, ext. abstract to appear in Proc. *4th CTRS*, 1994.

[Gra93b] B. Gramlich. Relating innermost, weak, uniform and modular termination of term rewriting systems. SEKI-Report SR-93-09, FB Informatik, Universität Kaiserslautern, 1993.

[Gra93c] B. Gramlich. Sufficient conditions for modular termination of conditional term rewriting systems. In M. Rusinowitch and J.L. Remy, eds., *Proc. 3rd CTRS, Pont-à-Mousson, 1992, LNCS 656*, pages 128–142. Springer, 1993.

[Kap84] S. Kaplan. Conditional rewrite rules. *TCS*, 33:175–193, 1984.

[Klo92] J.W. Klop. Term rewriting systems. In S. Abramsky, D. Gabbay, and T. Maibaum, editors, *Handbook of Logic in Computer Science*, vol. 2, chapter 1, pp. 2–117. Clarendon Press, Oxford, 1992.

[KO90] M. Kurihara and A. Ohuchi. Modularity of simple termination of term rewriting systems. *Journal of IPS, Japan*, 34:632–642, 1990.

[KO92] M. Kurihara and A. Ohuchi. Modularity of simple termination of term rewriting systems with shared constructors. *TCS*, 103:273–282, 1992.

[Kri93] M.R.K. Krishna Rao. Completeness of hierarchical combinations of term rewriting systems. In R.K. Shyamasundar, editor, *Proc. 13th FSTTCS, LNCS 761*, pp. 125–138. Springer, 1993.

[Kri94] M.R.K. Krishna Rao. Simple termination of hierarchical combinations of term rewriting systems. In *Proc. TACS, LNCS 789*, pp. 203–223, 1994.

[Mid89] A. Middeldorp. A sufficient condition for the termination of the direct sum of term rewriting systems. In *Proc. 4th LICS*, pp. 396–401, 1989.

[Mid90] A. Middeldorp. *Modular Properties of Term Rewriting Systems*. PhD thesis, Free University, Amsterdam, 1990.

[Mid93a] A. Middeldorp. Completeness of combinations of conditional constructor systems. In M. Rusinowitch and J.L. Remy, editors, *Proc. 3rd CTRS, July 1992, Pont-à-Mousson, LNCS 656*, pp. 82–96. Springer, 1993.

[Mid93b] A. Middeldorp. Modular properties of conditional term rewriting systems. *Information and Computation*, 104(1):110–158, May 1993.

[MT91] A. Middeldorp and Y. Toyama. Completeness of combinations of constructor systems. In R.V. Book, editor, *Proc. 4th RTA, LNCS 488*, pp. 174–187. Springer, 1991.

[O'D77] M.J. O'Donnell. *Computing in Systems Described by Equations, LNCS 58*. Springer, 1977.

[Ohl93a] E. Ohlebusch. On the modularity of confluence of constructor-sharing term rewriting systems. Technical Report 13, Universität Bielefeld, 1993.

[Ohl93b] E. Ohlebusch. On the modularity of termination of term rewriting systems. Technical Report 11, Universität Bielefeld, March 1993.

[Ros73] B.K. Rosen. Tree-manipulating systems and Church-Rosser theorems. *Journal of the ACM*, 20:160–187, 1973.

[Rus87] M. Rusinowitch. On termination of the direct sum of term rewriting systems. *Information Processing Letters*, 26:65–70, 1987.

[TKB89] Y. Toyama, J.W. Klop, and H.P. Barendregt. Termination for the direct sum of left-linear term rewriting systems. In N. Dershowitz, editor, *Proc. 3rd RTA, LNCS 355*, pp. 477–491. Springer, 1989.

[Toy87a] Y. Toyama. Counterexamples to termination for the direct sum of term rewriting systems. *Information Processing Letters*, 25:141–143, 1987.

[Toy87b] Y. Toyama. On the Church-Rosser property for the direct sum of term rewriting systems. *Journal of the ACM*, 34(1):128–143, 1987.

Syntactical analysis of total termination

M. C. F. Ferreira* and H. Zantema

Utrecht University, Department of Computer Science
P.O. box 80.089, 3508 TB Utrecht, The Netherlands
e-mail: {maria, hansz}@cs.ruu.nl, fax: +30-513791

Abstract. Termination is an important issue in the theory of term rewriting. In general termination is undecidable. There are nevertheless several methods successful in special cases. In [5] we introduced the notion of *total termination*: basically terms are interpreted compositionally in a total well-founded order, in such a way that rewriting chains map to descending chains. Total termination is thus a semantic notion. It turns out that most of the usual techniques for proving termination fall within the scope of total termination. This paper consists of two parts. In the first part we introduce a generalization of *recursive path order* presenting a new proof of its well-foundedness without using Kruskal's theorem. We also show that the notion of total termination covers this generalization. In the second part we present some syntactical characterizations of total termination that can be used to prove that many term rewriting systems are not totally terminating and hence outside the scope of the usual techniques. One of these characterizations can be considered as a sound and complete description of totality of orderings on terms.

1 Introduction

Most of the usual techniques for proving termination of term rewriting systems (TRS's) make use of total term orders. In [5] this notion of *total termination* was investigated in detail, with the emphasis on the underlying ordinal theory. Here we provide a syntactical analysis of total termination. A typical property of total orders is that if f is a strictly monotone function and $f(a) > f(b)$, then $a > b$. The main topic of this paper is to characterize totality of an order by properties like this. These characterizations are useful to prove that a TRS is *not* totally terminating. For example, the TRS

$$f(g(x)) \to f(f(x))$$
$$g(f(x)) \to g(g(x))$$

is terminating. Assume it is also totally terminating. Then according to the above observation it would still be terminating if the outer f from the first rule and the outer g from the second rule were stripped, yielding

* Supported by NWO, the Dutch Organization for Scientific Research, under grant 612-316-041.

$$g(x) \to f(x)$$
$$f(x) \to g(x)$$

which is clearly non-terminating. Hence the system is not totally terminating.

One way to define total termination is the following: a TRS is totally terminating if and only if there is a total well-founded order $>$ on ground terms closed under ground contexts such that $l\sigma > r\sigma$ for each rewrite rule $l \to r$ and each ground substitution σ. In practical applications it is very natural to require this totality: for example in Knuth-Bendix completion such a well-founded term ordering is required, and a highly desirable property is that all new critical pairs can be ordered by the ordering. Totality on non-ground terms can not be achieved since commutativity conflicts with well-foundedness; totality on ground terms is the strongest feasible requirement. The totality property is essential for unfailing completion strategies. In the case of ground AC-equational theories finitely presented, the existence of a reduction ordering AC-compatible and total on $\mathcal{T}(\mathcal{F})/=_{AC}$ ensures that such theories always admit a canonical rewrite system. For more information on AC-compatible total orders see for example [13, 15]. Additionally most of the usual techniques for proving termination of TRS's like *polynomial interpretations* [11, 1], *elementary interpretations* [12], *Knuth-Bendix order* (KBO), prove in fact total termination.

In section 2 we give some basic definitions and properties over term rewriting in general and total termination in particular. The rest of the paper can be divided into two independent parts: section 3 on precedence based orders, and sections 4 and 5 on syntactical characterization of total termination.

In section 3 we present a slightly generalized version of the *recursive path order* (RPO). For this order we give a new proof of well-foundedness which is independent of Kruskal's theorem. We also show that the class of TRS's whose termination can be proved by RPO falls within the class of totally terminating TRS's. The same holds for other precedence based orders like the Knuth-Bendix ordering.

In section 4 we describe a characterization of total termination that is effective in the sense that it provides a powerful technique to prove that TRS's are not totally terminating. However, it is not a complete characterization: we construct a system that is not totally terminating, but can not be dealt with this technique. Such a system is rather tricky, and it is unlikely that it will appear in any application. In section 5 we describe a complete characterization of total termination: a system is totally terminating if and only if its rewrite relation is contained in a strict partial order having some syntactical properties. These properties cover the characterization of section 4. However, this new characterization is not effective any more.

2 Basic definitions and properties

Below we give some basic notions over TRS's. For more information the reader is referred to [3].

Let $\mathcal{F}$ be a *signature*, i. e. $\mathcal{F}$ is a (non-empty) set of function symbols each with a fixed arity ≥ 0, denoted by $arity()$. Let $\mathcal{X}$ denote a set of variables, such that $\mathcal{F} \cap \mathcal{X} = \emptyset$. The set of terms over $\mathcal{F}$ and $\mathcal{X}$ is denoted by $\mathcal{T}(\mathcal{F}, \mathcal{X})$ and the set of ground terms over $\mathcal{F}$ by $\mathcal{T}(\mathcal{F})$.

A *term rewriting system* (TRS) is a tuple $(\mathcal{F}, \mathcal{X}, R)$, where R is a subset of $\mathcal{T}(\mathcal{F}, \mathcal{X}) \times \mathcal{T}(\mathcal{F}, \mathcal{X})$. The elements of R are called the rules of the TRS and are usually denoted by $l \to r$. They obey the restriction that l must be a non-variable and every variable in r must also occur in l. In the following, unless otherwise specified, we identify the TRS with R, being $\mathcal{F}$ the set of function symbols occurring in R.

Given a function symbol f with arity $n \geq 0$, its *embedding rules* are n rules of the form $f(x_1, \ldots, x_n) \to x_i$, with $1 \leq i \leq n$, where $x_1, \ldots, x_n$ are pairwise different variables. We denote by $\mathcal{E}mb_{\mathcal{F}}$ all embedding rules for all function symbols occurring in R.

A TRS R induces a *rewrite relation* over $\mathcal{T}(\mathcal{F}, \mathcal{X})$, denoted by $\to_R$, as follows: $s \to_R t$ iff $s = C[l\sigma]$ and $t = C[r\sigma]$, for some context C, substitution σ and rule $l \to r \in R$. The transitive closure of $\to_R$ is denoted by $\to_R^+$ and its reflexive-transitive closure by $\to_R^*$. A TRS is called *terminating* (strongly normalizing or noetherian) if there exists no infinite sequence of the form $t_0 \to_R t_1 \to_R \ldots$.

We define a *well-founded monotone $\mathcal{F}$-algebra* $(A, >)$ to be an $\mathcal{F}$-algebra A for which the underlying set is provided with a well-founded order $>$ and each algebra operation is monotone[2] in all of its coordinates, more precisely: for each operation symbol $f \in \mathcal{F}$ and all $a_1, \ldots, a_n, b_1, \ldots, b_n \in A$ for which $a_i > b_i$ for some i, and $a_j = b_j$ for all $j \neq i$, we have $f_A(a_1, \ldots, a_n) > f_A(b_1, \ldots, b_n)$.

Given a well-founded monotone $\mathcal{F}$-algebra $(A, >)$, let $A^{\mathcal{X}} = \{\sigma : \mathcal{X} \to A\}$; the interpretation function $[\,]_A : \mathcal{T}(\mathcal{F}, \mathcal{X}) \times A^{\mathcal{X}} \to A$ is defined inductively by

$$[x, \sigma]_A = \sigma(x),$$
$$[f(t_1, \ldots, t_n), \sigma]_A = f_A([t_1, \sigma]_A, \ldots, [t_n, \sigma]_A)$$

for $x \in \mathcal{X}, \sigma \in A^{\mathcal{X}}, f \in \mathcal{F}, t_1, \ldots, t_n \in \mathcal{T}(\mathcal{F}, \mathcal{X})$. The algebra $(A, >)$ induces an order $>_A$ over $\mathcal{T}(\mathcal{F}, \mathcal{X})$ as follows: $s >_A t \iff \forall \sigma \in A^{\mathcal{X}} : [s, \sigma] > [t, \sigma]$. Intuitively $t >_A t'$ means that for each interpretation of the variables in A the interpreted value of t is greater than that of t'. The order $>_A$ is closed under substitutions and contexts.

A well-founded monotone $\mathcal{F}$-algebra $(A, >)$ and a TRS R are said to be *compatible* if $l >_A r$, for all rules $l \to r$ in R. From [17] we recall:

Theorem 1. *A TRS is terminating if and only if admits a compatible non-empty well-founded monotone algebra.*

Definition 2. A TRS is called *totally terminating* if it admits a compatible non-empty well-founded monotone algebra in which the corresponding well-founded order is total.

---

[2] By monotone we mean *strictly increasing*.

Theorem 3. *R is totally terminating if and only if $R \cup \mathcal{E}mb_{\mathcal{F}}$ is totally terminating.*

A useful characterization of total termination without referring to monotone algebras is the following.

Theorem 4. *Let $\mathcal{F}'$ be $\mathcal{F}$ extended with a new constant if $\mathcal{F}$ does not contain any. Then R is totally terminating if and only if there is a strict partial order $>$ on $\mathcal{T}(\mathcal{F}')$, such that*

- *$>$ is total and well-founded;*
- *$>$ is closed under ground contexts, i. e. if $C[\,]$ is a ground context with exactly one hole, and t and s are ground terms with $s > t$ then $C[s] > C[t]$;*
- *$l\sigma > r\sigma$ for every rule $l \to r$ in R and every ground substitution σ.*

Proof. First, consider the if part. Since $>$ is total and well-founded on $\mathcal{T}(\mathcal{F}')$, we can make $(\mathcal{T}(\mathcal{F}'), >)$ a well-founded total monotone algebra over $\mathcal{F}$ by interpreting each function symbol in $\mathcal{F}$ by itself. From the properties of $>$ follows that R is compatible with this interpretation, yielding the total termination of R.

For the only-if part, first note that total termination of $(\mathcal{F}, \mathcal{X}, R)$ implies total termination of $(\mathcal{F}', \mathcal{X}, R)$ (see lemma 15), so we consider total monotone algebras over $\mathcal{F}'$.

The essential step in this part is the existence of any total order on the set of ground terms, well-founded and closed under contexts. To construct such an order, consider the set of function symbols $\mathcal{F}'$. By Zermelo's Theorem (see [10]) there is a total, well-founded order on $\mathcal{F}'$. Let $\succ$ be such an order, called a precedence. Consider the order $>_{lpo}$ associated with this precedence and taking lexicographic sequences from left to right. In section 3 we prove that this order has all the required properties.

Since R is totally terminating, we know that R is compatible with a (non-empty) monotone $\mathcal{F}'$-algebra $(A, >)$, with $>$ total and well-founded. Again let $[t]$ be the interpretation in A of a ground term t.

In $\mathcal{T}(\mathcal{F}')$ we define the order $\sqsupset$ by

$$s \sqsupset t \iff ([s] > [t]) \text{ or } ([s] = [t] \text{ and } s >_{lpo} t)$$

Irreflexivity and transitivity of $\sqsupset$ follows from irreflexivity and transitivity of both $>$ and $>_{lpo}$. Given any two ground terms s, t then either $[s] > [t]$ or $[t] > [s]$ or $[t] = [s]$, since $>$ is total. In the first two cases we conclude $s \sqsupset t$ or $t \sqsupset s$ respectively. In the last case, since $>_{lpo}$ is total we know that either $s >_{lpo} t$ or $t >_{lpo} s$ or $s = t$, hence the order $\sqsupset$ is total. Well-foundedness of $\sqsupset$ follows directly from well-foundedness of both $>$ and $>_{lpo}$. The same holds for closedness under ground contexts.

If $\sigma : \mathcal{X} \to \mathcal{T}(\mathcal{F}')$ is any ground substitution and $l \to r$ is a rule in R, then $[l\sigma] > [r\sigma]$, since $(A, >)$ is compatible with R, and therefore $l\sigma \sqsupset r\sigma$, concluding the proof. □

3 Precedence based orderings

In [8], Hofbauer proved that for a finite TRS proved terminating by recursive path order with only multiset status, a proof of total termination can be given in the natural numbers with primitively recursive operations. In this section we show that orders like RPO or KBO, even in their most general form, actually prove total termination, i. e. if a TRS R is proven terminating by RPO (or KBO), then R is totally terminating. The reverse is not true; the system

$$f(g(x)) \rightarrow g(f(f(x)))$$

is totally terminating (see [5]), but it cannot be proven terminating by RPO or KBO.

We introduce some needed definitions; mainly conventions and notations of [2, 16] will be followed.

Given a poset $(S, >)$ we consider two useful extensions of $>$, namely *lexicographic extension* (denoted by $>_{lex}$) defined as usual over sequences of elements of S, and *multiset extension* (denoted by $>_{mul}$) and defined over $M(S)$, the finite multisets over S (see [4, 16]).

Quasi-orders over a set S are transitive and reflexive relations over S. They will be denoted in general by $\succeq$. Any quasi-order defines an equivalence relation, namely $\succeq \cap \preceq$, and a partial order, namely $\succeq \setminus \preceq$ (or vice-versa). We usually denote the equivalence relation by $\sim$. Conversely, given a partial order $\succ$ and an equivalence $\sim$, their union does not always define a quasi-order (the transitive closure of their union does). However if $\succ$ and $\sim$ satisfy

$$(\sim \cap \succ = \emptyset) \text{ and } (\sim \circ \succ \circ \sim) \subseteq \succ \tag{1}$$

where $\circ$ represents composition, then $\succ \cup \sim$ is a quasi-order, of which $\succ$ is the strict part and $\sim$ the equivalence part.

From now on if we characterize a quasi-order via $\succ \cup \sim$, we assume that the conditions of (1) are satisfied. Also we take as partial order defined by a quasi-order $\succeq$ the relation $\succ \; = \; \succeq \setminus \preceq$.

Given a quasi-order $\succeq$ over S, the quotient $S/\sim$ consists of the equivalence classes of $\sim$; such classes are denoted by $\langle \, \rangle$. We can extend $\succ$ to $S/\sim$ in a natural way, namely $\langle s \rangle \sqsupset \langle t \rangle$ iff $s \succ t$. Since $\succ$ and $\sim$ satisfy condition (1), the relation $\sqsupset$ does not depend on the class representative and thus is well-defined. Furthermore $\sqsupset$ is a partial order over $S/\sim$. When this extension is well-defined we abusively write $\succ$ instead of $\sqsupset$.

Given two quasi-orders $\succeq$ and $\succeq'$ over the same set, we say that $\succeq'$ extends $\succeq$ iff $\succ \; \subseteq \; \succ'$ and $\sim \; \subseteq \; \sim'$.

For any quasi-order $\succeq$, $\succeq_{lex}$ and $\succeq_{mul}$ denote its lexicographic and multiset extensions, respectively. These quasi-orders are defined as in the partial order case, with equality being replaced by the more general equivalence $\sim$.

Lexicographic and multiset extensions preserve well-foundedness, more precisely:

Lemma 5. *$\succeq$ is well-founded over a set A iff $\succeq_{mul}$ is well-founded over $M(A)$.*

Lemma 6. *$\succeq$ is well-founded over a set A iff $\succeq_{lex}$ is well-founded over A^n, the set of sequences over A of size at most n, for a fixed $n \geq 1$.*

To each function $f \in \mathcal{F}$ we associate a status $\tau(f)$. Status indicates how the arguments of the function symbol are to be taken. We consider two possible cases:

- $\tau(f) = mul$; indicates that, for the purpose of ordering, the arguments of f are to be taken as a multiset.
- $\tau(f) = lex_\pi$, where π is a permutation of the set $\{1, \ldots, arity(f)\}$; indicates that, for the purpose of ordering, the arguments are to be taken as a lexicographic sequence whose order is given by π.

Given the set of function symbols $\mathcal{F}$, let $\trianglerighteq$ denote a quasi-order over $\mathcal{F}$ usually called a *quasi-precedence*. We reserve the term *precedence* to partial orders over $\mathcal{F}$.

From now on we assume that a quasi-precedence over $\mathcal{F}$ is given as well as a status function τ, under the following restriction: lexicographic and multiset status cannot be mixed, i. e.

$$\text{if } f \sim g \text{ and } \tau(f) = mul \text{ then } \tau(g) = mul \tag{2}$$

Write $>_{rpo}^{=}$ for recursive path order with status as it appears in [16]. This definition is not suitable to our purposes. We need to define a total well-founded monotone algebra $(A, >)$ and a good candidate is $(\mathcal{T}(\mathcal{F}), >_{rpo}^{=})$. If we define the congruence $\simeq$ over $\mathcal{T}(\mathcal{F}, \mathcal{X})$ as follows: $s \simeq t$ iff $s = t$ or $s = f(s_1, \ldots, s_m)$, $t = g(t_1, \ldots, t_n)$, $f \sim g$, $m = n$ and either

- $\tau(f) = \tau(g) = mul$ and there is a permutation π of $\{1, \ldots m\}$ such that $s_i \simeq t_{\pi(i)}$, for any $1 \leq i \leq m$;
- $\tau(f) = lex_{\pi_f}$ and $\tau(g) = lex_{\pi_g}$ and $s_{\pi_f(i)} \simeq t_{\pi_g(i)}$ for all $1 \leq i \leq m$.

Then if for ground terms s, t, $s \simeq t$ and $s \neq t$, both $s \not>_{rpo}^{=} t$ and $t \not>_{rpo}^{=} s$. So $(\mathcal{T}(\mathcal{F}), >_{rpo}^{=})$ is not total and it seems reasonable to take $A = \mathcal{T}(\mathcal{F})/\simeq$. But unfortunately the natural extension of $>_{rpo}^{=}$ to the congruence classes of $\mathcal{T}(\mathcal{F}, \mathcal{X})/\simeq$ is not well-defined even for total precedences (condition (1) does not hold). This can be repaired by extending the definition of $>_{rpo}^{=}$ to $>_{rpo}$, namely replace equality by $\simeq$.

Definition 7. **(RPO with status)** Given two terms s, t we say that $s \sim_{rpo} t$ if $s \simeq t$, and $s >_{rpo} t$ iff $s = f(s_1, \ldots, s_m)$ and either

1. $t = g(t_1, \ldots, t_n)$ and
   (a) $f \triangleright g$ and $s >_{rpo} t_i$, for all $1 \leq i \leq n$, or
   (b) $f \sim g$ and $(s_1, \ldots, s_m) >_{rpo,\tau} (t_1, \ldots, t_n)$ and $s >_{rpo} t_i$, for all $1 \leq i \leq n$; or
2. $\exists 1 \leq i \leq m:\ s_i >_{rpo} t$ or $s_i \sim_{rpo} t$.

It can be seen by straightforward induction proofs that $>_{rpo}$ and $\sim_{rpo}$ have the following properties:

- $>_{rpo}$ is a strict partial order and $\sim_{rpo}$ is an equivalence, both defined over $\mathcal{T}(\mathcal{F},\mathcal{X})$. Furthermore $>_{rpo}$ and $\sim_{rpo}$ satisfy condition (1).
- $>_{rpo}$ and $\sim_{rpo}$ are closed under contexts and substitutions and $>_{rpo}$ has the subterm property, i. e. $C[t] >_{rpo} t$, for any term t and non-trivial context $C[\,]$.
- $\succeq_{rpo}$ is monotone with respect to quasi-precedences, i. e. if $\trianglerighteq, \trianglerighteq'$ are quasi-precedences over $\mathcal{F}$ such that $\trianglerighteq'$ extends $\trianglerighteq$, then $>_{rpo}$ associated with $\trianglerighteq'$ extends $>_{rpo}$ associated with $\trianglerighteq$. Consequently $>_{rpo}$ extends $>^{=}_{rpo}$, for any fixed quasi-precedence and status.
- If $\trianglerighteq$ is total over $\mathcal{F}$ then $>_{rpo}$ is total over $\mathcal{T}(\mathcal{F})/\sim_{rpo}$.
- If all function symbols have *lex* status then $>_{rpo}$ coincides with Kamin and Lévy's ([9]) *lexicographic path order* (that we denote by $>_{lpo}$). If $\triangleright$ is total and $\sim$ is syntactical equality then, as a consequence of the previous remark, we have that $>_{lpo}$ is total over $\mathcal{T}(\mathcal{F})$.

In order for $>_{rpo}$ to be useful for proving termination of term rewriting systems, the order has to be well-founded. Unfortunately, well-foundedness of $\trianglerighteq$ alone is not sufficient to guarantee well-foundedness of $>_{rpo}$ as the following example shows. Let $\mathcal{F}$ consist of two constants $a \triangleright b$ and function symbols f_i, $i \geq 1$, such that f_i has arity i, $\tau(f_i) = lex_{Id}$ and $f_i \sim f_j$, for any i,j. Then we have the following infinite descending chain

$$f_1(a) >_{rpo} f_2(b,a) >_{rpo} f_3(b,b,a) >_{rpo} f_4(b,b,b,a) >_{rpo} \cdots$$

The problem stems from the fact that lexicographic sequences of unbounded size are not well-founded.[3] Kamin and Lévy ([9]) proved that $>_{lpo}$ is well-founded provided that equivalent function symbols have the same arity. In the following we prove that this restriction can be weakened. It is enough to require that for every equivalence class of function symbols with lexicographic status, there is a natural number bounding the arities of the function symbols in the class. That is

$$\forall f \in \mathcal{F}:\ \tau(f) = lex_\pi \Rightarrow (\exists n \geq 0:\ \forall g \in \langle f \rangle:\ arity(g) \leq n) \tag{3}$$

Before proving well-foundedness of $>_{rpo}$, we need some additional definitions and results from [7].

Definition 8. A quasi-order $\succeq$ over a set S is a *well quasi-order*, abbreviated to *wqo*, iff every quasi-order extending it (including $\succeq$ itself) is well-founded.

There are several equivalent characterizations of *wqo*'s. We also use the following (see [7]): "Every infinite sequence $(s_i)_{i\geq 0}$ of elements of S contains some infinite subsequence $(s_{\phi(i)})_{i\geq 0}$ such that $s_{\phi(i+1)} \succeq s_{\phi(i)}$, for all $i \geq 0$".

[3] Note that even if $\trianglerighteq$ would be total or $\mathcal{F}$ finite, with a function symbol f allowing different arities, the same problem would arise.

A traditional way of proving well-foundedness of $>_{rpo}$ is via Kruskal's theorem. Given our extended definition of $>_{rpo}$, we cannot apply Kruskal's theorem in a straightforward way. This is so because $>_{rpo}$ no longer contains the embedding relation. Let us elaborate some more here. Given a quasi-order $\trianglerighteq$ over $\mathcal{F}$, the *embedding relation* $>_{emb}$ over $\mathcal{T}(\mathcal{F}, \mathcal{X})$ is defined as follows ([7]). Either:

- $f(t_1, \ldots, t_n) \geq_{emb} g$ iff $f \trianglerighteq g$; or
- $f(\ldots, t, \ldots) \geq_{emb} t$; or
- $f(s_1, \ldots, s_m) \geq g(t_1, \ldots, t_n)$ iff $f \trianglerighteq g$, $n \leq m$ and there are integers $j_1, \ldots, j_n$ such that $1 \leq j_1 < \ldots < j_n \leq m$ and $s_{j_i} \geq_{emb} t_i$, for all $1 \leq i \leq n$.

Kruskal's theorem states that if $\trianglerighteq$ is a *wqo* on $\mathcal{F}$ then $\geq_{emb}$ is also a *wqo* on $\mathcal{T}(\mathcal{F}, \mathcal{X})$. Consequently any relation containing the embedding relation is well-founded. Previous versions of $>_{rpo}$ fall within this category. For definition 7 this does no longer hold: in the example above we have $f_2(b, a) >_{emb} f_1(a)$, however $f_2(b, a) \not>_{rpo} f_1(a)$.

A way of dealing with orders for which Kruskal's theorem is not applicable is given in [6]. Well-foundedness of $>_{rpo}$ can be derived from results presented there. Nevertheless here we present a proof of well-foundedness of $>_{rpo}$ inspired by the proof of Kruskal's theorem itself as presented in [7, 14] and closely following [6]. We should emphasize that the proof given does not rely on Kruskal's theorem and is therefore simpler if you consider the degree of difficulty involved in Kruskal's theorem itself.

Theorem 9. *Let $\trianglerighteq$ be a quasi-precedence over $\mathcal{F}$ and τ a status function such that conditions (2) and (3) are satisfied. Then $>_{rpo}$ is well-founded over $\mathcal{T}(\mathcal{F}, \mathcal{X})$ iff $\trianglerighteq$ is well-founded over $\mathcal{F}$.*

Proof. For the if part, let $\trianglerighteq$ be a well-founded quasi-precedence over $\mathcal{F}$ and τ a status function such that conditions (2) and (3) are satisfied. We first extend $\trianglerighteq$ to a total well-founded quasi-order $\trianglerighteq'$ such that $\sim' = \sim$. This is done in the "usual" way: using Zorn's Lemma we extend the well-founded partial order $\triangleright$[4] over $\mathcal{F}/\sim$ to a total well-founded partial order $>'$ over $\mathcal{F}/\sim$. Then $\triangleright'$ and $\sim$ are compatible and $\trianglerighteq'$ (with $\sim' = \sim$), is total and well-founded over $\mathcal{F}$, where as expected $\triangleright'$ is defined as $\forall f, g \in \mathcal{F} : f \triangleright' g \iff \langle f \rangle >' \langle g \rangle$. The reason why we require that $\sim' = \sim$ is to avoid problems with the status of equivalent symbols, i. e. to guarantee that conditions (2) and (3) still hold for the extended quasi-precedence.

Since $\trianglerighteq'$ is total and well-founded, every extension of it is well-founded, hence $\trianglerighteq'$ is a *wqo* over $\mathcal{F}$. Suppose now that $>_{rpo}$ taken over this total well-founded quasi-precedence, is not well-founded. Take then an infinite descending chain

$$t_0 >_{rpo} t_1 >_{rpo} t_2 >_{rpo} \cdots$$

minimal in the following sense:

---

[4] Itself a natural extension of $\triangleright$ to $\mathcal{F}/\sim$ that we abusively denote equally.

- $|t_0| \leq |s_0|$, for all infinite chains $s_0 >_{rpo} s_1 >_{rpo} \cdots$
- $|t_{i+1}| \leq |s_{i+1}|$, for all infinite chains $s_0 >_{rpo} s_1 >_{rpo} \cdots$, such that $t_j = s_j$ for $0 \leq j < i+1$.

where $|t|$ represents the number of function symbols occurring in t.

We remark that no proper subterm of a term t_i, $i \geq 0$, in the above chain, can initiate an infinite descending chain; for, suppose u_j^i is such a subterm, then the chain

$$t_0 >_{rpo} \cdots >_{rpo} t_{i-1} >_{rpo} u_j^i >_{rpo} u_1 >_{rpo} \cdots$$

will be an infinite descending chain contradicting the minimality of $(t_i)_{i \geq 0}$ (since $|u_j^i| < |t_i|$).

Let $root(t)$ be the head function symbol of the term t. We see that there is no infinite subsequence $(t_{\phi(i)})_{i \geq 0}$ of $(t_i)_{i \geq 0}$ such that $root(t_{\phi(i)}) \sim root(t_{\phi(j)})$, for all $i, j \geq 0$. Suppose it is not so and let $(t_{\phi(i)})_{i \geq 0}$ be such a subsequence. Due to condition (2), all root symbols in this sequence have the same status (either *mul* or *lex*). By definition of $>_{rpo}$, and since $t_{\phi(i)} >_{rpo} t_{\phi(i+1)}$, for all $i \geq 0$, we must have

$$args(t_{\phi(0)}) >_{rpos,\tau} args(t_{\phi(1)}) >_{rpos,\tau} \cdots$$

where $args(t)$ are the proper subterms of t. From lemma 5 or 6, we conclude that $>_{rpo}$ is not well-founded over $\bigcup_{i \geq 0} Args(t_{\phi(i)})$ (where $Args(t)$ is the set of proper subterms of t), contradicting the minimality of $(t_i)_{i \geq 0}$.

Consider the sequence $(root(t_i))_{i \geq 0}$. This sequence is infinite and since $\trianglerighteq'$ is a *wqo* over $\mathcal{F}$, an infinite subsequence $(root(t_{\phi(i)}))_{i \geq 0}$ of $(root(t_i))_{i \geq 0}$ exists such that $root(t_{\phi(i+1)}) \trianglerighteq' root(t_{\phi(i)})$, for all $i \geq 0$. But since every $\sim$-equivalence class appears only finitely many times in the sequence $(root(t_i))_{i \geq 0}$, we can say without loss of generality that the subsequence $(root(t_{\phi(i)}))_{i \geq 0}$ fulfils $root(t_{\phi(i+1)}) \triangleright' root(t_{\phi(i)})$, for all $i \geq 0$[5]. But $t_{\phi(i)} >_{rpo} t_{\phi(i+1)}$ (for all $i \geq 0$), then, by definition of $>_{rpo}$, both $t_{\phi(i)}$ and $t_{\phi(i+1)}$ are not constants and we must have $u_{\phi(i)} >_{rpo} t_{\phi(i+1)}$ or $u_{\phi(i)} \sim_{rpo} t_{\phi(i+1)}$, for some $u_{\phi(i)} \in Args(t_{\phi(i)})$. In both cases a contradiction with the minimality of $(t_i)_{i \geq 0}$ arises.

Well-foundedness of $>_{rpo}$ over the original quasi-precedence $\trianglerighteq$ follows from the fact that $>_{rpo}$ is monotone with respect to precedences (since $\trianglerighteq'$ is an extension of $\trianglerighteq$).

For the only-if part, suppose that $>_{rpo}$ is well-founded over $\mathcal{T}(\mathcal{F}, \mathcal{X})$ and that $\trianglerighteq$ is not well-founded on $\mathcal{F}$. Let $f_0 \triangleright f_1 \triangleright \cdots$ be an infinite descending sequence in $\mathcal{F}$. This sequence does not contain an infinite subsequence consisting only of constants, since if $(f_{\phi(i)})_{i \geq 0}$ would be such a sequence, we would have $f_{\phi(0)} >_{rpo} f_{\phi(1)} >_{rpo} \cdots$, contradicting the well-foundedness of $>_{rpo}$. Let then $(f_{\phi(i)})_{i \geq 0}$ be an infinite subsequence of $(f_i)_{i \geq 0}$ such that $arity(f_{\phi(i)}) \geq 1$, for all $i \geq 0$. Let x be any variable. By definition of $>_{rpo}$, we conclude that

$$f_{\phi(0)}(x, \ldots, x) >_{rpo} f_{\phi(1)}(x, \ldots, x) >_{rpo} \cdots$$

contradicting the well-foundedness of $>_{rpo}$. □

[5] Strictly speaking there is a subsequence of $(root(t_{\phi(i)}))_{i \geq 0}$ with this property.

Another approach to prove well-foundedness of our version of $>_{rpo}$ is the following. Every function symbol with status *lex* has its arity augmented to the maximal arity associated with its equivalence class. The new arguments are filled with a dummy constant. By this construction all function symbols in the same equivalence class are forced to have the same arity, hence the old version of $>_{rpo}$ is applicable, provided we change the status function consistently. Well-foundedness of our version of $>_{rpo}$ then follows from well-foundedness of previous $>_{rpo}$ versions. However the classical proof of this well-foundedness makes use of Kruskal's theorem.

The following TRS's

$$\begin{array}{ll} f(1,x) & \to g(0,x,x) \\ g(x,1,y) & \to f(x,0) \end{array}$$

and

$$\begin{array}{ll} a & \to g(c) \\ g(a) & \to b \\ f(g(x),b) & \to f(a,x) \end{array}$$

are totally terminating. Just take quasi-precedences $\trianglerighteq$ and status function τ satisfying $1 \triangleright 0$, $f \sim g$, $\tau(f) = \tau(g) = lex_{Id}$, for the first TRS, and $a \triangleright g$, $a \triangleright c$, $a \sim b$ and $\tau(f) = mul$, for the second TRS. Earlier versions or $>_{rpo}$ fail to prove termination of these TRS's: for the first TRS we cannot choose $f \triangleright g$ nor $g \triangleright f$ nor uncomparability of f and g, and if $f \sim g$, the status of these symbols cannot be the multiset status.

Theorem 10. *Given a TRS R, suppose $\trianglerighteq$ is a well-founded quasi-precedence over $\mathcal{F}$ and τ is a status function such that conditions (2) and (3) are satisfied. If $l >_{rpo} r$ for every rule $l \to r \in R$ then R is totally terminating.*

Proof. We give a sketch of the proof. In order to establish total termination of R we need to define a total well-founded monotone algebra. For that we choose $\mathcal{T}(\mathcal{F})/\sim_{rpo}$, where $\sim_{rpo}$ is the congruence associated with $>_{rpo}$. If $\mathcal{F}$ does not contain any constant, we introduce one to force $\mathcal{T}(\mathcal{F})$ to be non-empty. With respect to the quasi-precedence $\trianglerighteq$, the relative order of this new element is irrelevant and does not influence the behaviour of $>_{rpo}$. We extend $\trianglerighteq$ to a total well-founded quasi-precedence $\trianglerighteq^t$ such that the equivalence part remains the same (done using Zorn's lemma as described in the proof of theorem 9) and consider $>_{rpo}$ over this extended quasi-precedence. By theorem 9, we know that $>_{rpo}$ is well-founded, and as remarked before $>_{rpo}$ extended to $\mathcal{T}(\mathcal{F})/\sim_{rpo}$ is total and well-founded. In $\mathcal{A} = (\mathcal{T}(\mathcal{F})/\sim_{rpo}, >_{rpo})$ we interpret the function symbols of $\mathcal{F}$ by $f_{\mathcal{A}}(\langle s_1\rangle, \ldots, \langle s_{arity(f)}\rangle) = \langle f(s_1, \ldots, s_{arity(f)})\rangle$. Since $\sim_{rpo}$ is a congruence $f_{\mathcal{A}}$ is well-defined. The interpretation function $[\,] : \mathcal{T}(\mathcal{F}, \mathcal{X}) \times \mathcal{A}^{\mathcal{X}} \to \mathcal{A}$ is given as usual.

Since $\mathcal{A}$ is total and well-founded, the only condition we need to check to establish total termination is compatibility with the rules of R. It can be seen, by induction on t, that

$$\forall t \in \mathcal{F}\, \forall \tau \in \mathcal{A}^{\mathcal{X}} : \ [t, \tau] = \langle t\sigma \rangle$$

where σ is any ground substitution satisfying $\sigma(x) \in \tau(x)$, for all $x \in \mathcal{X}$. Note that the class $\langle t\sigma \rangle$ does not depend on the choice of σ. Let $l \to r$ be a rule in R and let $\tau : \mathcal{X} \to \mathcal{A}$ be an assignment. Let σ be a ground substitution satisfying $\sigma(x) \in \tau(x)$ for all $x \in \mathcal{X}$. Since $>_{rpo}$ is monotone with respect to quasi-precedences and by hypothesis $l >_{rpo} r$, with $>_{rpo}$ taken over $\trianglerighteq$, we also have $l >_{rpo} r$, where now the $>_{rpo}$ is based on the total quasi-precedence $\trianglerighteq^t$. Consequently $\langle l, \sigma \rangle >_{rpo} \langle r, \sigma \rangle$, thus $[l, \tau] >_{rpo} [r, \tau]$, and we conclude that R is totally terminating , with $\mathcal{T}(\mathcal{F})/\sim_{rpo}$ as total well-founded monotone algebra. □

The Knuth-Bendix order uses the concept of *weight function.*
Let $\phi : \mathcal{F} \cup \mathcal{X} \to \mathbb{N}$ be a function such that

$$\phi(f) \text{ is } \begin{cases} = \phi_0 > 0 \text{ if } f \in \mathcal{X} \\ \geq \phi_0 \qquad \text{if arity}(f) = 0 \\ > 0 \qquad \text{if arity}(f) = 1 \end{cases}$$

We extended ϕ to terms as follows: $\phi(f(s_1, \ldots, s_m)) = \phi(f) + \sum_{i=1}^{m} \phi(s_i)$.

Let $\#_x(t)$ denote the number of occurrences of variable x in term t. The Knuth-Bendix order with status is defined as follows ([16]).

Definition 11. (KBO with status) We say that $s >_{kbo} t$ iff $\forall x \in \mathcal{X} : \#_x(s) \geq \#_x(t)$ and

1. $\phi(s) > \phi(t)$ or
2. $\phi(s) = \phi(t)$, $s = f(s_1, \ldots, s_m)$, $t = g(t_1, \ldots, t_n)$ and
   (a) $f \triangleright g$ or
   (b) $f \sim g$ and $s_1, \ldots, s_m >_{kbos,\tau} t_1, \ldots, t_n$

Knuth-Bendix order has properties similar to $>_{rpo}$ (see [16]), namely it is a partial order closed under substitutions and contexts and monotone with respect to quasi-precedences.

The order $>_{kbo}$ can be used to define a congruence $\sim_{kbo}$ over $\mathcal{T}(\mathcal{F}, \mathcal{X})$ as follows: $s \sim_{kbo} t$ iff $s = t$ or $s = f(s_1, \ldots, s_m)$, $t = g(t_1, \ldots, t_n)$, $f \sim g$, $m = n$, $\phi(s) = \phi(t)$ and either

- $\tau(f) = mult$ and $s_i \sim_{kbo} t_{\pi(i)}$, for any $1 \leq i \leq m$, where π is a permutation of $\{1, \ldots m\}$;
- $\tau(f) = lex_{\pi_f}$, $\tau(g) = lex_{\pi_g}$ and $s_{\pi_f(i)} \sim_{kbo} t_{\pi_g(i)}$ for all $1 \leq i \leq m$.

It can be seen that $\sim_{kbo}$ is indeed a congruence i. e. a reflexive, symmetric and transitive relation, closed under contexts. Further $\sim_{kbo}$ is also closed under substitutions and it is not difficult to see that $>_{kbo}$ and $\sim_{kbo}$ are compatible, so we can extend $>_{kbo}$ to $\mathcal{T}(\mathcal{F}, \mathcal{X})/\sim_{kbo}$ in the usual way. As with $>_{rpo}$, given a total quasi-precedence over $\mathcal{F}$, $>_{kbo}$ is total over $\mathcal{T}(\mathcal{F})/\sim_{kbo}$. As for well-foundedness we have

Theorem 12. *Let $\trianglerighteq$ be a well-founded quasi-precedence over $\mathcal{F}$ and τ a status function such that condition (2) is satisfied. Then $>_{kbo}$ is well-founded over $\mathcal{T}(\mathcal{F},\mathcal{X})$.*

This theorem can be proven in a way similar to theorem 9. Notice that condition (3) is not necessary since the use of the weight function ensures that the lexicographic extension is well-founded.

Theorem 13. *Given a TRS R, suppose $\trianglerighteq$ is a well-founded quasi-precedence over $\mathcal{F}$ and τ is a status function such that condition (2) is satisfied. Let ϕ be a weight function. If $l >_{kbo} r$ for every rule $l \to r \in R$ then R is totally terminating.*

Proof. **(Sketch)** We proceed in a manner similar as for $>_{rpo}$. Namely we extend the well-founded quasi-precedence $\trianglerighteq$ to a total one whose underlying equivalence is the same, and take $>_{kbo}$ over this total well-founded quasi-precedence. As total well-founded monotone algebra we choose $\mathcal{T}(\mathcal{F})/\sim_{kbo}$[6] and interpret the function symbols of $\mathcal{F}$ in the same way. It is not difficult to see that all requirements of total termination are met. □

4 Proving non-total termination

From theorem 3 we know that a TRS R is totally terminating if and only if $R \cup \mathcal{E}mb_{\mathcal{F}}$ is totally terminating. So if $R \cup \mathcal{E}mb_{\mathcal{F}}$ is non-terminating then R is not totally terminating. A next step is context removal: if $C[t] \to_R^+ C[u]$ then R is totally terminating if and only if $R \cup \{t \to u\}$ is totally terminating. Further if $C_0[t] \to_R^+ C_1[u]$ and $C_1[t] \to_R^+ C_0[u]$ then adding $t \to u$ to R still does not affect total termination. We combine these ideas in the following definition.

Definition 14. Given a TRS R we define the relation $\gg \subseteq \mathcal{T}(\mathcal{F}) \times \mathcal{T}(\mathcal{F})$ as follows: $s \gg t$ if

- $s \to_R^+ t$ or $s \to_{\mathcal{E}mb_{\mathcal{F}}}^+ t$
- $s = C[a]$ and $t = C[b]$ and $a \gg b$
- for some $n > 0$, there are contexts $C_0[\,], \ldots, C_n[\,]$ such that $C_0[\,] = C_n[\,]$ and $C_i[s] \gg C_{i+1}[t]$, for each $0 \le i < n$,
- $\exists u \in \mathcal{T}(\mathcal{F}) :\ s \gg u$ and $u \gg t$

This relation can be used to characterize non-total terminating TRS's as we see below. First we need some auxiliary results.

Lemma 15. *$(\mathcal{F}, \mathcal{X}, R)$ is totally terminating if and only if $(\mathcal{F} \cup \{\bot\}, \mathcal{X}, R)$ is totally terminating, where $\bot$ is a constant not occurring in R.*

[6] If $\mathcal{F}$ is empty, we add a dummy constant to it and assign weight ϕ_0 to that constant.

Proof. For the if part, since $(\mathcal{F} \cup \{\bot\}, \mathcal{X}, R)$ is totally terminating there is a total monotone algebra compatible with $(\mathcal{F} \cup \{\bot\}, \mathcal{X}, R)$. The same algebra is obviously compatible with R.

For the only-if part, we take a total monotone algebra compatible with R and define the interpretation of $\bot$ to be an arbitrary element of the algebra. The interpretations of the other symbols do not change. It follows that this algebra is compatible with $(\mathcal{F} \cup \{\bot\}, \mathcal{X}, R)$, proving its total termination. □

Lemma 16. *Suppose R is totally terminating and let $(A, >)$ be a total well-founded monotone algebra compatible with R. If $s, t \in \mathcal{T}(\mathcal{F}, \mathcal{X})$ and $[s, \sigma] \geq [t, \sigma]$, for some $\sigma \in A^{\mathcal{X}}$, then $[C[s], \sigma] \geq [C[t], \sigma]$, for any context $C[\,]$.*

Proof. We proceed by induction. The assertion holds for the trivial context □ by hypothesis. Suppose it also holds for a context $C'[\,]$. Then

$$\begin{array}{ll} [f(\ldots, C'[s], \ldots), \sigma] & = \text{(by definition of } [\,]) \\ f_A(\ldots, [C'[s], \sigma], \ldots) & \geq \text{(by IH and monotonicity of } f_A) \\ f_A(\ldots, [C'[t], \sigma], \ldots) & \geq \text{(by definition of } [\,]) \\ [f(\ldots, C'[t], \ldots), \sigma] & \end{array}$$

□

Lemma 17. *Let $(A, >)$ be any total well-founded monotone algebra compatible with R. Then $C[s] >_A C[t] \Rightarrow s >_A t$, for any terms s, t and context $C[\,]$, where $>_A$ is the order over terms induced by $(A, >)$. Furthermore if $(A, >)$ is also compatible with $\mathcal{E}mb_{\mathcal{F}}$, then $C[s] >_A s$, for any non-trivial context $C[\,]$ and term s.*

Proof. Let then $C[s] >_A C[t]$. We have to see $\forall \sigma \in A^{\mathcal{X}} : [s, \sigma] > [t, \sigma]$. Suppose $\exists \tau \in A^{\mathcal{X}} : [s, \tau] \not> [t, \tau]$. Due to the totality of $>$, this means that $[s, \tau] \leq [t, \tau]$. By lemma 16 we have $[C[s], \tau] \leq [C[t], \tau]$, contradicting $C[s] >_A C[t]$. So $s >_A t$.

Suppose now that A is compatible with $\mathcal{E}mb_{\mathcal{F}}$. Let $C[s] = f(t_1, \ldots, s, \ldots, t_n)$, with s occurring in position i, $1 \leq i \leq n$.

Since the rule $f(\ldots, x_i, \ldots) \to x_i$ is part of $\mathcal{E}mb_{\mathcal{F}}$, compatibility ensures that $f(\ldots, x_i, \ldots) >_A x_i$. We define a substitution $\tau : \mathcal{X} \to \mathcal{T}(\mathcal{F}, \mathcal{X})$ by

$$\tau(x) = \begin{cases} t_j \text{ if } x = x_j, \text{ for some } j \neq i \\ s \text{ if } x = x_j \\ x \text{ otherwise} \end{cases}$$

Since $>_A$ is closed under substitutions, we have $C[s] = f(x_1, \ldots, x_n)\tau >_A \tau(x_i) = s$.

Suppose $C'[s] >_A s$ for some context $C'[\,]$. Since $>_A$ is closed under contexts, we get $f(t_1, \ldots, C'[s], \ldots, t_n) >_A f(t_1, \ldots, s, \ldots, t_n)$. But $f(t_1, \ldots, s, \ldots, t_n) >_A s$, so transitivity of $>_A$ yields the result. □

Theorem 18. *If R is totally terminating then $\gg$ is well-founded.*

Proof. Due to lemma 15 we can assume without loss of generality that $\mathcal{F}$ contains at least one constant, so $\mathcal{T}(\mathcal{F})$ is not empty. Since R is totally terminating, from theorem 3 we know that $R \cup \mathcal{E}mb_\mathcal{F}$ is also totally terminating. By theorem 4 we know there is a total well-founded order $>$ over $\mathcal{T}(\mathcal{F})$ such that:

- $l\sigma > r\sigma$, for any rule $l \to r \in R \cup \mathcal{E}mb_\mathcal{F}$ and any ground substitution σ.
- $>$ is closed under ground contexts.

We will see, by induction on the definition of $\gg$, that $s \gg t \Rightarrow s > t$. Well-foundedness of $>$ will then yield the result. Suppose that $s \gg t$, for some terms s, t.

- If $s \to_R^+ t$ or $s \to_{\mathcal{E}mb_\mathcal{F}}^+ t$, since $>$ is compatible with $R \cup \mathcal{E}mb_\mathcal{F}$ we have $\to_{R\cup\mathcal{E}mb_\mathcal{F}}^+ \subseteq >$ and therefore $s > t$.
- If $s = C[a]$, $t = C[b]$ with $a \gg b$ and $a > b$ (by induction hypothesis) then $s > t$, since $>$ is closed under ground contexts.
- If $s \gg t$ because for some $n > 0$, there are contexts $C_0[\,], \ldots, C_n[\,]$ such that $C_0[\,] = C_n[\,]$ and for each $0 \leq i < n$, $C_i[s] \gg C_{i+1}[t]$, then by induction hypothesis we have $C_0[s] > C_1[t], C_1[s] > C_2[t]$, etc. . Since $>$ is total either $s > t$ or $t \geq s$. Suppose that $t \geq s$. Using the induction hypothesis, the fact that $>$ is closed under ground contexts and its transitivity, we get

$$C_0[s] > C_1[t] \geq C_1[s] > C_2[t] > \ldots > C_n[t] \geq C_n[s] = C_0[s]$$

  contradicting well-foundedness of $>$; therefore $s > t$.
- Finally if $\exists u \in \mathcal{T}(\mathcal{F}) :\; s \gg u$ and $u \gg t$, then also by induction hypothesis $s > u$ and $u > t$ and transitivity of $>$ gives the result.

□

The previous result can be used to show that a TRS is not totally terminating and in particular that it cannot be proven terminating by any $>_{rpo}$ (or $>_{kbo}$). For example let R be:

$$\begin{array}{ll} p(f(f(x))) \to q(f(g(x))) & \quad p(g(g(x))) \to q(g(f(x))) \\ q(f(f(x))) \to p(f(g(x))) & \quad q(g(g(x))) \to p(g(f(x))) \end{array}$$

This system (actually $R \cup \mathcal{E}mb_\mathcal{F}$) is terminating (in each step the number of redexes decreases) but not totally terminating. Let c be a constant, then from the leftmost rules we get $p(f(f(c))) \gg q(f(g(c)))$ and $q(f(f(c))) \gg p(f(g(c)))$ and consequently $f(c) \gg g(c)$ (with $C_0 = p(f(\square)) = C_2$ and $C_1 = q(f(\square))$). Similarly using the rightmost rules we get $g(c) \gg f(c)$; therefore $\gg$ is not well-founded and so R cannot be totally terminating.

One can wonder whether the reverse of theorem 18 holds. This is not the case. For example one can prove that the system[7]

[7] Due to U. Waldmann.

$$f(0,a) \to f(1,b) \qquad h(1,a) \to h(0,b)$$
$$g(0,b) \to g(1,a) \qquad k(1,b) \to k(0,a)$$

is not totally terminating while $>$ is well-founded. To see this note that $>$ coincides with $\to_{R \cup \mathcal{E}mb_{\mathcal{F}}}$ and $R \cup \mathcal{E}mb_{\mathcal{F}}$ is terminating since in each R-rewriting step the number of redexes decreases and R is length-preserving (for every rule the length of the lhs equals the length of the rhs). It is easy to see that the interpretations of a and b (or 0 and 1) have to be incomparable and so the system is not totally terminating.

It is not clear whether the reverse of theorem 18 holds for string rewriting systems.

5 A complete characterization

The results presented so far apply to TRS's over finite or infinite signatures. In this section we assume that $\mathcal{F}$ is finite.

As we saw the characterization of section 4 is not complete. One can wonder whether completeness can be obtained by adding purely syntactical rules to definition 14. We did not succeed, but closely related we arrived at the following result. As in theorem 4 we assume that $\mathcal{T}(\mathcal{F})$ is non-empty (again lemma 15 justifies that assumption).

Theorem 19. *A TRS R is totally terminating if and only if there exists a strict partial order $\gg$ on $\mathcal{T}(\mathcal{F})$ satisfying*

1. $\to^{+}_{R \cup \mathcal{E}mb_{\mathcal{F}}} \subseteq \gg$.
2. *$\gg$ is closed under ground contexts.*
3. *if for some $n \geq 1$, there exists some contexts $D_0[\,], \ldots, D_n[\,]$ and terms $s_0, \ldots, s_{n-1}, t_0, \ldots, t_n \in \mathcal{T}(\mathcal{F})$ such that $D_0[\,] = D_n[\,]$, $t_0 = t_n$ and for each $0 \leq i < n$, $D_i[s_i] \gg D_{i+1}[t_{i+1}]$, then $s_i \gg t_i$, for some $i \in \{0, \ldots, n-1\}$.*

Proof. For the only if part since R is totally terminating so is $R \cup \mathcal{E}mb_{\mathcal{F}}$ (theorem 3). By theorem 4, there is a total well-founded order $>$ over $\mathcal{T}(\mathcal{F})$, closed under ground contexts and verifying $l\sigma > r\sigma$, for any ground substitution σ and rule $l \to r \in R \cup \mathcal{E}mb_{\mathcal{F}}$. Consequently $>$ satisfies conditions (1) and (2). We check that $>$ also satisfies (3). Suppose that for some $n \geq 1$ there are contexts $C_0[\,], \ldots, C_n[\,]$ and terms $s_0, \ldots, s_{n-1}, t_0, \ldots, t_n \in \mathcal{T}(\mathcal{F})$ such that $C_0[\,] = C_n[\,]$, $t_0 = t_n$ and for each $0 \leq i < n$, $C_i[s_i] > C_{i+1}[t_{i+1}]$. We have to see that there is an index $i \in \{0, \ldots, n-1\}$, such that $s_i > t_i$. Suppose no such index exists, then $\forall j \in \{0, \ldots n-1\}$ we have $t_j \geq s_j$, since $>$ is total. From the hypothesis and the fact that $>$ is closed under ground contexts, we get

$$C_0[s_0] > C_1[t_1] \geq C_1[s_1] > C_2[t_2] \geq \ldots > C_n[t_n] = C_0[t_0] \geq C_0[s_0]$$

which is a contradiction. Since $>$ fulfils all the conditions of the theorem, the result holds.

For the if part, suppose there is an order $>$ fulfilling conditions $(1)-(3)$. Let Z_R denote the set of all partial orders over $\mathcal{T}(\mathcal{F})$ satisfying those conditions, and which is non empty by hypothesis. We order Z_R by $\subset$, the strict set inclusion and will see that in this poset every chain has an upper bound. Then by Zorn's lemma, Z_R has a maximal element.

Let then $\theta_0 \subset \theta_1 \subset \ldots \subset \theta_n \subset \ldots$, be a chain in Z_R and let $\Theta = \bigsqcup_{i \in \mathbb{N}} \theta_i$. We shall prove that $\Theta \in Z_R$. Irreflexivity and transitivity of Θ are not difficult to check. It is also easy to check that Θ fulfils conditions (1) and (2).

For condition (3), suppose that for some $n \geq 1$, contexts $C_0[\,], \ldots, C_n[\,]$ and terms $s_0, \ldots, s_{n-1}, t_0, \ldots, t_n \in \mathcal{T}(\mathcal{F})$ exist such that $C_0[\,] = C_n[\,]$, $t_0 = t_n$ and for each $0 \leq i < n$, $C_i[s_i] \; \Theta \; C_{i+1}[t_{i+1}]$. We have to see that $s_i \Theta t_i$, for some index $i \in \{0, \ldots, n-1\}$. For each pair $(C_i[s_i], C_{i+1}[t_{i+1}]) \in \Theta$ there is an index $k_i \in \mathbb{N}$ such that $(C_i[s_i], C_{i+1}[t_{i+1}]) \in \theta_{k_i}$. Take $k = max\{k_0, \ldots, k_{n-1}\}$, then $(C_i[s_i], C_{i+1}[t_{i+1}]) \in \theta_k$, for all $0 \leq i < n$. Since θ_k satisfies condition (3), we conclude that $\exists i \in \{0, \ldots, n-1\}$ such that $s_i \theta_k t_i$ and therefore $s_i \Theta t_i$.

We have seen that every chain in Z_R is majorated in Z_R. Since Z_R is not empty, we can apply Zorn's lemma to conclude that Z_R has a maximal element that we denote by Θ_m. The last main step of our proof is to show that Θ_m is a total order over $\mathcal{T}(\mathcal{F})$. We proceed by contradiction. Suppose there are two ground terms $p \neq q$ such that $(p, q), (q, p) \notin \Theta_m$. Consider the relation

$$\Upsilon = (\Theta_m \cup \{(C[p], C[q]) : C[\,] \text{ is any ground context }\})^+$$

By definition Υ is transitive. For irreflexivity, suppose that there is a ground term a such that $a \Upsilon a$. Then one of the following three cases must hold:

1. $a \Theta_m a$
2. $C[p] = a = C[q]$
3. for some $n \geq 0$ there are contexts $C_0[\,], \ldots, C_n[\,]$ such that $a \Theta_m C_0[p]$, $C_i[q] \Theta_m C_{i+1}[p]$, for $0 \leq i < n$, and $C_n[q] \Theta_m a$

In the first two cases we immediately get a contradiction since Θ_m is irreflexive and $p \neq q$. The last case is an instance of condition (3) with $D_0 = \Box$, $s_0 = a = t_0 = t_{n+1}$, $s_i = q$ and $t_i = p$, for all $1 \leq i \leq n$. Since Θ_m satisfies the aforementioned condition, we have that either $a \Theta_m a$ or $q \Theta_m p$, contradicting either irreflexivity of Θ_m or the choice of p and q.

We check that Υ is closed under ground contexts. Suppose that $s \Upsilon t$ for some ground terms s, t, and let $C[\,]$ be any ground context. As for irreflexivity we have to distinguish three cases, namely

1. $s \Theta_m t$
2. $s = D[p]$ and $t = D[q]$, for some ground context $D[\,]$
3. for some $n \geq 0$ there are contexts $C_0[\,], \ldots, C_n[\,]$ such that $s \Theta_m C_0[p]$, $C_i[q] \Theta_m C_{i+1}[p]$, for $0 \leq i < n$, and $C_n[q] \Theta_m t$

In the first case we can conclude that $C[s] \Theta_m C[t]$. In the second case we have $C[s] = C[D[p]]$ and $C[t] = C[D[q]]$. In both cases we conclude that $C[s] \Upsilon C[t]$. For the last case, since Θ_m is closed under ground contexts, we derive

$C[s]\ \Theta_m\ C[C_0[p]]$, $C[C_i[q]]\ \Theta_m\ C[C_{i+1}[p]]$, for $0 \leq i < n$, and $C[C_n[q]]\ \Theta_m\ C[t]$

Again we have an instance of condition (3), with $D_0 = \Box$, $s_0 = C[s]$, $t_0 = C[t] = t_{n+1}$, and $s_i = q$ and $t_i = p$, for all $1 \leq i \leq n$. Since Θ_m satisfies the condition, either $C[s]\Theta_m C[t]$ or $q\Theta_m p$. In the first case we get the desired result and in the second we have a contradiction.

We finally check that Υ satisfies condition (3). Suppose then that for some $n \geq 1$ there are contexts $F_0[\,], \ldots, F_n[\,]$ and terms $u_0, \ldots, u_{n-1}, v_0, \ldots, v_n$ such that $F_0 = F_n$, $t_0 = t_n$ and $F_i[u_i]\Upsilon F_{i+1}[v_{i+1}]$, for $0 \leq i < n$. We want to conclude that $u_i \Upsilon v_i$, for some $0 \leq i < n$. Fix any $0 \leq i < n$. Then since $F_i[u_i]\ \Upsilon\ F_{i+1}[v_{i+1}]$, there is $k_i \geq 0$ and there are ground contexts $C_1[\,], \ldots, C_{k_i}[\,]$ such that

- $F_i[u_i]\ \Theta_m\ C_1[p]$
- $C_j[q]\ \Theta_m\ C_{j+1}[p]$, for $1 \leq j < k_i$
- $C_{k_i}[q]\ \Theta_m\ F_{i+1}[v_{i+1}]$

Again we have an instance of condition (3) with

- $n = k_i + 1$
- $D_0 = D_n = \Box$
- $s_0 = F_i[u_i]$, $t_0 = t_n = F_{i+1}[v_{i+1}]$, and $s_j = q$ and $t_j = p$, for $1 \leq j \leq k_i$

So we conclude that $F_i[u_i]\Theta_m F_{i+1}[v_{i+1}]$ or $q\Theta_m p$. Since the last case gives a contradiction, the first must hold. Given the arbitrariety of i and since Θ_m satisfies condition (3), we conclude that $\exists 0 \leq j < n :\ u_j \Theta_m v_j$, implying $u_j \Upsilon v_j$, as we wanted.

We have seen that $\Upsilon \in Z_R$ and since Υ is strictly bigger that Θ_m, this contradicts the maximality of Θ_m. Therefore Θ_m is total on $\mathcal{T}(\mathcal{F})$. Since Θ_m contains the embedding relation ($\rightarrow_{R \cup \mathcal{E}mb_{\mathcal{F}}} \subseteq \Theta_m$) and $\mathcal{F}$ is finite, by Kruskal's theorem Θ_m is well-founded so we can apply theorem 4 to conclude that R is totally terminating. □

Although this result yields completeness, it is not easy to apply for proving that a particular TRS is not totally terminating, in contrast to the result of section 4.

The type of orders described in theorem 19 are not necessarily total, but combining this result with theorem 4, we see that existence of a total well-founded order compatible with a TRS R is equivalent to the existence of a compatible order of the type described in theorem 19, so we can say that this results provides another characterization of totality.

6 Conclusions

In this paper the notion of total termination is treated syntactically in two ways. On the one hand we analyzed how total termination covers precedence based orderings like recursive path order. Surprisingly this led to a slight generalization of versions of recursive path order as they appeared in the literature and to a new proof of well-foundedness. Only after this generalization could we prove total termination.

On the other hand we tried to find a syntactical characterization of total termination of the following shape: if a TRS is totally terminating then some syntactically defined order is well-founded. This led to a method of proving non-total termination: if the constructed order admits an infinite descending chain then the TRS is not totally terminating. The converse is not true: we constructed a TRS for which the constructed order is well-founded while the TRS is not totally terminating. Finally we found an "if and only if"-characterization of total termination covering the order construction. However, this characterization is not of practical use to determine whether a given TRS is totally terminating or not.

Acknowledgements. We would like to thank the referees for their useful remarks.

References

1. BEN-CHERIFA, A., AND LESCANNE, P. Termination of rewriting systems by polynomial interpretations and its implementation. *Science of Computing Programming 9*, 2 (1987), 137–159.
2. DERSHOWITZ, N. Termination of rewriting. *Journal of Symbolic Computation 3*, 1 and 2 (1987), 69–116.
3. DERSHOWITZ, N., AND JOUANNAUD, J.-P. Rewrite systems. In *Handbook of Theoretical Computer Science*, J. van Leeuwen, Ed., vol. B. Elsevier, 1990, ch. 6, pp. 243–320.
4. DERSHOWITZ, N., AND MANNA, Z. Proving termination with multiset orderings. *Communications ACM 22*, 8 (1979), 465–476.
5. FERREIRA, M. C. F., AND ZANTEMA, H. Total termination of term rewriting. In *Proceedings of the 5th Conference on Rewriting Techniques and Applications* (1993), C. Kirchner, Ed., vol. 690 of *Lecture Notes in Computer Science*, Springer, pp. 213–227. Full version submitted for publication.
6. FERREIRA, M. C. F., AND ZANTEMA, H. Well-foundedness of term orderings. To appear at CTRS 94 (Workshop on Conditional and Typed Term Rewriting Systems).
7. GALLIER, J. H. What's so special about Kruskal's theorem and the ordinal Γ_0? A survey of some results in proof theory. *Annals of Pure and Applied Logic 53* (1991), 199–260.
8. HOFBAUER, D. Termination proofs by multiset path orderings imply primitive recursive derivation lengths. *Theoretical Computer Science 105*, 1 (1992), 129–140.

9. Kamin, S., and Lévy, J. J. Two generalizations of the recursive path ordering. University of Illinois, 1980.
10. Kuratowski, K., and Mostowski, A. *Set Theory.* North-Holland Publishing Company, 1968.
11. Lankford, D. S. On proving term rewriting systems are noetherian. Tech. Rep. MTP–3, Louisiana Technical University, Ruston, 1979.
12. Lescanne, P. Termination of rewrite systems by elementary interpretations. In *Algebraic and Logic Programming* (1992), H. Kirchner and G. Levi, Eds., vol. 632 of *Lecture Notes in Computer Science*, Springer, pp. 21 – 36.
13. Narendran, P., and Rusinowitch, M. Any ground associative-commutative theory has a finite canonical system. In *Proceedings of the 4th Conference on Rewriting Techniques and Applications* (1991), R. V. Book, Ed., vol. 488 of *Lecture Notes in Computer Science*, Springer, pp. 423–434.
14. Nash-Williams, C. S. J. A. On well-quasi ordering finite trees. *Proc. Cambridge Phil. Soc. 59* (1963), 833–835.
15. Rubio, A., and Nieuwenhuis, R. A precedence-based total AC-compatible ordering. In *Proceedings of the 5th Conference on Rewriting Techniques and Applications* (1993), C. Kirchner, Ed., vol. 690 of *Lecture Notes in Computer Science*, Springer, pp. 374–388.
16. Steinbach, J. Extensions and comparison of simplification orderings. In *Proceedings of the 3rd Conference on Rewriting Techniques an Applications* (1989), N. Dershowitz, Ed., vol. 355 of *Lecture Notes in Computer Science*, Springer, pp. 434–448.
17. Zantema, H. Termination of term rewriting by interpretation. In *Conditional Term Rewriting Systems, Proceedings Third International Workshop CTRS-92* (1993), M. Rusinowitch and J. Rémy, Eds., vol. 656 of *Lecture Notes in Computer Science*, Springer, pp. 155–167. Full version to appear in Journal of Symbolic Computation.

Logic Programs as Term Rewriting Systems

Massimo Marchiori

Department of Pure and Applied Mathematics
University of Padova
Via Belzoni 7, 35131 Padova, Italy
max@hilbert.math.unipd.it

Abstract

This paper studies the relationship between logic programs and term rewriting systems (TRSs). A compositional transform is defined which given a logic program computes a TRS. For a relevant class of logic programs, called Simply Well Moded (SWM), there is a one-to-one correspondence between computed answer substitutions of the logic program and normal forms of the corresponding TRS. Moreover the transform preserves termination, i.e., a logic program terminates iff the corresponding TRS terminates. This transform is refined in such a way that the above results hold for a relevant class of unification free programs containing SWM, the class of Flatly Well Moded (FWM) programs.

Note: This work was done during an author's stay at CWI, Amsterdam.

1 Introduction

The study of transforms from logic programs into term rewriting systems (TRSs for short) is an important topic. Theoretically, it is interesting to analyze which classes of logic programs can be regarded as TRSs in disguise. Practically, using an appropriate transform allows to infer properties of a logic program from properties of the corresponding TRS. For instance, this method has been successfully applied in a number of works, to study termination of logic programs ([SKRK90, KRKS92, GW92, AM93]), using transforms that preserve non-termination.

Transforms that compute TRSs which not only preserve non-termination, but are equivalent to the corresponding logic programs, have been investigated only very recently ([Mar93, AM93]). Equivalence means that the logic program terminates iff the corresponding TRS terminates, and that computed answer substitutions of the logic program and normal forms of the TRS are in one-to-one correspondence.

The aim of this paper is to provide a *compositional* transform which maps a logic program into an equivalent TRS. Compositionality is fundamental because, for instance, a compositional transform allows to transform a logic program into a TRS in a modular way, i.e., clause by clause. The classes of logic programs we consider are contained in the so-called well moded programs ([DM85]). Moreover the transform can deal with a broader class of programs, where types instead of modes are considered.

The contribution of this paper can be summarized as follows.

First, a compositional transform Tswm is introduced which allows to translate into a class of equivalent TRSs both the class of Simply Well Moded programs of [AE93] and a wider class of programs which are *not well moded*, namely the Simply and Well Typed programs (SWT) of [AE93].

It is also shown how with little modifications Tswm can be extended to the whole class of Well Moded programs, losing equivalence, but still providing a relevant correspondence, in the sense that if the TRS terminates then the corresponding logic program terminates as well.

Finally, it is introduced a second transform called Tfwm that extends Tswm by translating the class of *flatly well moded* programs (FWM), introduced in [Mar94], into equivalent TRSs. The FWM class has been proven to be locally *maximal* among the unification free ones. Moreover, it is the locally greatest class of unification free programs containing SWM. Informally, a class of logic programs is locally maximal (resp. greatest) among the unification free programs if it is maximal (resp. greatest) among those classes of unification free programs that can be characterized by means of clause by clause syntactical criterions (see [Mar94] for a formal definition). Recall that a logic program is *unification free* if unification in the resolution process can be performed by means of iterated applications of the simpler pattern matching ([MK85]). These results can be roughly summarized in the following slogan:

Logic Programs – Unification $\subseteq$ Term Rewriting Systems

1.1 Relations with Previous Work

The idea to transform logic programs into TRSs started with [SKRK90], and has been further refined in [KRKS92, GW92, AM93]. The main stimulus in this field was the study of termination of logic programs: a transform is defined with the property that if a logic program does not terminate, then the corresponding TRS does not terminate as well. Thus, a *sufficient* criterion for proving the termination of a logic program consists of checking whether the transformed TRS terminates.

This approach is attractive because TRSs enjoy powerful techniques to prove termination, as path orderings for instance (see [Der87, DJ90]), whereas for logic programs the situation is far more complicated.

In this paper the above transformational methodology is taken a step further, in the sense that we introduce transforms that fully translate a logic program: this way a *sufficient* but also *necessary* criterion for termination can be given.

A transform treating this kind of correspondence was introduced in [AM93]. However, this transform is not compositional. Also, the transform Tfwm here presented is able to transform classes of logic programs that are completely *out of scope* from the previous transforms, a drawback observed also by the same authors of [GW92, AM93].

The paper is organized as follows: Section 2 gives the necessary preliminaries; Section 3 introduces the concept of transform and a formal setting for its analysis. In Section 4 we specify the languages used both for the logic programs and the corresponding TRSs, and the basic rewrite rules used in the transforms. In Section 5 the transform Tswm is defined, and its completeness is proven w.r.t. the class SWM. Section 6 introduces some techniques to simplify the output of a transform, and illustrates its application to prove the termination of a logic program by means of an example. Section 7 introduces the transform Tfwm, that is proven complete for the class FWM. The relevance of this transform is illustrated by means of a significant example. Finally, Section 8 concludes with some important remarks. Proofs are here omitted or only sketched: they can be found in the full version of this paper.

2 Preliminaries

We assume familiarity with the basic notions regarding logic programs ([Llo87, Apt90]) and term rewriting systems ([Klo92]).

In this paper we will deal only with so-called *LD-derivations* (briefly *derivations*), that is SLD-derivations in which the leftmost selection rule is used.

With TERM(F) we will denote the set of terms built up from some function set F. Sequences of terms will be written in vectorial notation (e.g. $\bar{t}$), and with $t^{(i)}$ we will denote the i-th term in $\bar{t}$.

Given a family S of objects (terms, atoms, etc.), Var(S) is the set of all the variables contained in it; moreover, S is said *linear* iff no variable occurs more than once in it; objects $O_1, \ldots, O_n$ will be said *disjoint* iff $1 \leq i < j \leq n \Rightarrow \mathrm{Var}(O_i) \cap \mathrm{Var}(O_j) = \emptyset$. $s\mathcal{U}t$ will mean that the terms s and t are disjoint and unifiable. With $t[A_1/t_1, \ldots, A_n/t_n]$ we will mean the term obtained by t replacing every occurrence in t of the symbol A_i with t_i ($1 \leq i \leq n$). For the sake of simplicity, we will sometimes omit brackets from the argument of unary functions (e.g. $f(g(X))$ may be written fgX), and if $\bar{t} = t_1, \ldots, t_n$ the sequence $f(t_1), \ldots, f(t_n)$ will be indicated with $f\bar{t}$. Also, given two sequences $\bar{s} = s_1, \ldots, s_n$ and $\bar{t} = t_1, \ldots, t_m$, we will denote by $\bar{s}, \bar{t}$ the sequence $s_1, \ldots, s_n, t_1, \ldots, t_m$.

2.1 Programs

We call (logic) program a finite set of Horn clauses and goals. If the program has no goals, it is called a *proper program*.

Let P be a program, P_2 the set of all the goals in P, and $P_1 = P \setminus P_2$. We call *derivation of P* a derivation of $P_1 \cup \{G\}$, when G is in P_2. Analogously, we call *computed answer substitution of P* a computed answer substitution of $P_1 \cup \{G\}$, where G is in P_2. The set of all the computed answer substitutions of P is denoted by $cas(P)$.

This formalism is well suited when formulating program properties, since it allows not to treat separately the clauses and the goal. Moreover, it is a natural choice when using *regular* properties (see below), that essentially do not distinguish between goals and clauses.

Since we are going to transform logic programs in term rewriting systems, the same convention will be adopted for TRSs as well (reading 'goal' as 'term', 'clause' as 'rewrite rule' and 'derivation' as 'reduction'): hence an extended TRS is a finite set of rules and a possibly infinite set of terms. The analogous of the set $cas(P)$ for a TRS T is the set $NF(T)$ of its normal forms.

The class of these 'extended' logic programs (resp. TRSs) will be denoted by LPext (resp. TRSext).

2.2 Regularity

Definition 2.1 A property $\mathcal{P}$ is said *regular* if

$$\leftarrow B_1, \ldots, B_n \in \mathcal{P} \Leftrightarrow \mathtt{START} \leftarrow B_1, \ldots, B_n \in \mathcal{P}$$

where START is a new nullary predicate symbol. □

Using regularity will prove useful to elegantly shorten the description of the properties we will use in this paper, like well modedness for example, and also the definition of the transforms, since from now on *we identify a goal with the corresponding clause having the special symbol* START *in the head, and analogously for TRSs, we identify a term with the corresponding rule having the special symbol START in the left hand side* (cf. Subsection 4.1 for the language setting).

Although this will not concern us, it is worthwhile to notice that regularity is far from being merely a 'syntactic sugaring' tool, but has an importance for its own (see [Mar94]).

2.3 Modes and Well Modedness

Definition 2.2 A *mode* for a n-ary predicate p is a map from $\{1, \ldots, n\}$ to $\{\text{in}, \text{out}\}$. A *moding* is a map associating to every predicate p a mode for it. □

An argument position of a moded predicate is therefore said input (output) if it is mapped by the mode into in (out). For every predicate p, the number of its arguments (i.e. the arity), input positions and output positions will be denoted respectively by $\#\mathtt{p}$, $\#_{\mathtt{in}}\mathtt{p}$ and $\#_{\mathtt{out}}\mathtt{p}$. Moreover, we adopt the convention to write $\mathtt{p}(\bar{s}, \bar{t})$ to denote a moded atom p having its input positions filled in by the sequence of terms $\bar{s}$, and its output positions filled in by $\bar{t}$.

Now let us recall the following well-known property:

Definition 2.3 A program is *data driven* if every time an atom is selected in a goal during a derivation, its input arguments are ground. □

We now state the basic notion of well moding:

Definition 2.4 A program satisfies the (regular) *well modedness (WM)* property if for every its clause $C = \mathtt{p}_0(\bar{t}_0, \bar{s}_{n+1}) \leftarrow \mathtt{p}_1(\bar{s}_1, \bar{t}_1), \ldots, \mathtt{p}_n(\bar{s}_n, \bar{t}_n)$ it holds:

$$\forall i \in [1, n+1]: \ \mathrm{Var}(\bar{s}_i) \subseteq \bigcup_{j=0}^{i-1} \mathrm{Var}(\bar{t}_j)$$ □

Well Moded programs enjoy the following relevant property:

Theorem 2.5 ([DM85]) *Well Moded programs are data driven.*

2.4 Simply Well Modedness

First we introduce the following class of programs:

Definition 2.6 A program satisfies the (regular) ***Simply Modedness (SM)*** property if for every its clause $C = p_0(\mathbf{s}_0, \mathbf{t}_0) \leftarrow p_1(\mathbf{s}_1, \mathbf{t}_1), \ldots, p_n(\mathbf{s}_n, \mathbf{t}_n)$ it holds:
- The sequence $\mathbf{t}_1, \ldots, \mathbf{t}_n$ is linear, composed only by variables and disjoint with $\mathbf{s}_0$
- $\forall i \in [1, n] : \mathrm{Var}(\mathbf{s}_i) \cap \bigcup_{j=i}^{n} \mathrm{Var}(\mathbf{t}_j) = \emptyset$ □

We will call ***simply well moded (SWM)*** a program which is both SM and WM: this is the main class proved in [AE93] to be unification free. Interestingly, this class is quite large (see for instance the list of programs presented in the paper just cited).

3 Transforms

We introduce here a formal setting for the analysis of fundamental properties of transforms. In this paper, S will always denote a class of logic programs, $GOALS$ and $SUBST$ the sets of all the goals and substitutions, respectively. Moreover, $\wp$ is the usual powerset operator.

Definition 3.1 A *transform* is a map τ : LPext $\rightarrow$ TRSext □

Definition 3.2 A transform τ is *semi-complete (resp. sound) for* S if:
1) If $P \in S$, then P has an infinite derivation $\Longrightarrow$ (resp. $\Longleftarrow$) $\tau(P)$ has an infinite reduction.
2) There is a computable map γ_τ : $GOALS \times \mathrm{TRSext} \rightarrow \wp(SUBST)$ such that for every goal $G \in S$ and every proper program $P \in S$ it holds $\gamma(G, NF(\tau(G \cup P))) \supseteq$ (resp. $\subseteq$) $cas(G \cup P)$. □

Notice that transforms in [SKRK90, KRKS92, GW92] are trivially semi-complete in the sense that their γ map is just $\gamma(G, NF(\tau(G \cup P))) = SUBST$.

Definition 3.3 A transform τ is said *complete for* S if:
1) If $P \in S$, then P has an infinite derivation if and only if $\tau(P)$ has an infinite reduction.
2) There is a computable map α_τ : $GOALS \times \mathrm{TRSext} \rightarrow \wp(SUBST)$ (called an *answer map* of τ) such that for every goal $G \in S$ and every proper program $P \in S$ it holds $\alpha_\tau(G, NF(\tau(G \cup P))) = cas(G \cup P)$. □

3.1 Compositionality

A transform, as defined in Def. 3.1, can be arbitrarily complex as far as the computational aspect is concerned. A very important concept in developing a satisfactory transform is the following:

Definition 3.4 A transform τ is *compositional* if for every two programs P, P'

$$\tau(P \cup P') = \tau(P) \cup \tau(P')$$ □

Thus, a compositional transform of a program is equal to the union of the transforms of its clauses.

The advantages of a compositional definition are well-known: to compute the transform of a program the transforms of its clauses can be executed in parallel. Moreover, to understand the relationship between logic programs and TRSs it suffices to consider a logic program with one clause. Finally, in case a new set of clauses D is added to P obtaining a new program P', to calculate the transformed $\tau(P')$ we don't have to redo the whole computation again, but only to transform D, since $\tau(P') = \tau(P \cup D) = \tau(P) \cup \tau(D)$. This may be of great advantage, especially when the program P is big enough. The general case in which P is modified into P', possibly also *deleting* some of its clauses, will be treated later in Section 8.

4 Setting the Stage

4.1 Languages

A *moded language* is a pair (L, m) where L is a language and m is a moding for L. Every logic program is written in a moded language $\mathcal{L}_{LP} = (\{\mathtt{p}_0, \mathtt{p}_1, \ldots; \mathtt{f}_0, \mathtt{f}_1, \ldots\}, m)$ where the $\mathtt{p}_i$ are the relation symbols and the $\mathtt{f}_i$ are the function symbols (we consider constants like functions of null arity).

For every natural n, we assume that in $\mathcal{L}_{LP}$ there is an n-ary function $\otimes_n$: such functions are used as 'cartesian product' operators.

The functional language $\mathcal{L}_{TRS}$ for the TRS that will be associated with the considered programs is described as follows:

- a function p_i for every $\mathtt{p}_i \in \mathcal{L}_{LP}$, with $\#p_i = \#_{\mathrm{in}}\mathtt{p}_i$
- a function f_i for every $\mathtt{f}_i \in \mathcal{L}_{LP}$, with $\#f_i = \#\mathtt{f}_i$
- functions $(f_i)^{-1}_1, \ldots, (f_i)^{-1}_{\#\mathtt{f}_i}$ for every $\mathtt{f}_i \in \mathcal{L}_{LP}$, with $\#(f_i)^{-1}_j = 1$ (called 'inverse functions')
- an unary function $\mathcal{N}$
- unary functions $\underset{n}{\mathcal{T}}$ (for every $n \in \mathbb{N}$) called 'transition functions'.

$\mathcal{N}$ is a marker associated to terms t (of $\mathcal{L}_{TRS}$): $\mathcal{N}t$ indicates that the term t is in normal form in the considered TRS (hence the name $\mathcal{N}$). Intuitively this means that t has already been computed.

Inverse functions are used to select an argument from a term which is marked (thus already computed): for instance the function $(f_i)^{-1}_j$ applied to the term $\mathcal{N}f_i(t_1, \ldots, t_n)$ yields the term $\mathcal{N}t_j$.

Transition functions are used to rewrite a term which is marked: for example to rewrite a term $\mathcal{N}X$ into the term $f(\pi_1\mathcal{N}X, \mathcal{N}X)$ the function $\underset{\rho(f(\pi_1\bullet,\bullet))}{\mathcal{T}}$ is used, where $\bullet$ is a placeholder (that will be replaced with $\mathcal{N}X$) and $\rho(f(\pi_1\bullet, \bullet))$ is an appropriate natural number encoding of $f(\pi_1\bullet, \bullet)$.

Since the $\otimes_n$ are used to represent cartesian products, the notation π^n_i is used to indicate the inverse function $(\otimes_n)^{-1}_i$; usually instead of π^n_i and $\otimes_n(t_1, \ldots, t_n)$ we will simply write π_i, and $\langle t_1, \ldots, t_n\rangle$, respectively.

The subset $\{f_i \mid \#f_i > 0\}$ of $\mathcal{L}_{TRS}$, that is the corresponding of the proper functions in $\mathcal{L}_{LP}$, will be denoted by FUNC_{TRS}, whereas the set of all terms built on $\mathcal{L}_{TRS}$, i.e. $\mathcal{T}(\mathcal{L}_{TRS})$, will be denoted by TERM_{TRS}.

4.2 Propagation

The following definition specifies the only rules that rewrite terms of the form $f(t_1, \ldots, t_n)$, with $f \in \text{FUNC}_{TRS}$.

Definition 4.1 The *propagation rules* are:

$$\begin{array}{ll} f(\mathcal{N}X_1, \ldots, \mathcal{N}X_n) \to \mathcal{N}f(X_1, \ldots, X_n) & (f \in \text{FUNC}_{TRS}) \\ (f)_i^{-1}\mathcal{N}f(X_1, \ldots, X_n) \to \mathcal{N}X_i & (f \in \text{FUNC}_{TRS}, 1 \leq i \leq n = \#f) \end{array} \qquad \Box$$

The first schema of rules expresses the fact the $\mathcal{N}$ operator 'propagates' thru terms in FUNC_{TRS}.

The second schema is more interesting: it shows that to apply an inverse function we have to wait for the argument to be computed (marked by $\mathcal{N}$). Naïve rules of the form $f_i^{-1}f(X_1, \ldots, X_n) \to X_i$ won't work: intuitively, suppose a term t reduces to two normal forms (i.e. it gives two 'results'), say $\langle t_1, t_2 \rangle$ and $\langle s_1, s_2 \rangle$, and suppose that the first projection π_1 as well as the second projection π_2 are used. Then by applying the naïve rules $\pi_1\langle X, Y \rangle \to X$ and $\pi_2\langle X, Y \rangle \to Y$ one can obtain the following two reductions $\pi_1 t \twoheadrightarrow \pi_1\langle t_1, t_2 \rangle \to t_1$ and $\pi_2 t \twoheadrightarrow \pi_2\langle s_1, s_2 \rangle \to s_2$, thus violating the fundamental property of the projections, i.e. $\langle \pi_1 t, \pi_2 t \rangle = t$. The rules of Definition 4.1 allow to avoid such 'splitting' phenomena; we will see later (Subsection 6.3) how to relax these rules whenever these bad cases do not happen.

4.3 Transition

Transition rules will be used in the transform to encode a clause of a program by means of a rewrite rule. In $\mathcal{T}_n$, the index n encodes the transition that has to be performed, using the following (injective and computable) encoding function ρ:

$$\rho : \text{TERM}(\mathcal{L}_{TRS} \cup \{\bullet\}) \to \mathbb{N}$$

The new symbol $\bullet$ is introduced to represent the argument of the transition function, as will become clear from the following definition:

Definition 4.2 The *transition rules* are defined as follows:

$$\mathcal{T}_{\rho(t)} \mathcal{N}X \to t[\bullet/\mathcal{N}X] \quad (t \in \text{TERM}(\mathcal{L}_{TRS} \cup \{\bullet\})) \qquad \Box$$

For simplicity, we write $\mathcal{T}_t$ instead of $\mathcal{T}_{\rho(t)}$; so for example $\mathcal{T}_{f(\pi_1\bullet,\bullet)}$ will have as corresponding transition rule $\mathcal{T}_{f(\pi_1\bullet,\bullet)} \mathcal{N}X \to f(\pi_1\mathcal{N}X, \mathcal{N}X)$.

5 The Transform Tswm

We introduce here the *T*ransform for *s*imply *w*ell *m*oded programs, called Tswm.

Roughly, a clause $C : A \leftarrow B_1, \ldots, B_n$ is transformed into a rewrite rule r, where the left hand side (lhs) of r is a TRS term obtained transforming the head of C, while the right hand side (rhs) of r is constructed incrementally in a sequence of $n+1$ steps, where in the i-th step ($1 \leq i \leq n$) the (partial) rhs so far constructed is modified using the atom B_i, and in the $n+1$-th step the atom A is used. To this end two variables rhs and V are used, where rhs contains the part of the right end side of r so far computed, and V is a sequence of terms in TERM_{TRS} used to store the output arguments of the atoms in the clause.

First, we need the following definition to 'extract' arguments from a term:

Definition 5.1 Given a term $t \in \text{TERM}_{TRS}$ and a variable $X \in \text{Var}(t)$, a *suitable expression of* X *from* t (notation $\text{SE}_X(t)$) is defined as $SE_X(t)(\bullet)$, where:

i) $SE_X(X)(u) = u$

ii) $SE_X(f(t_1, \ldots, t_n))(u) = SE_X(t_i)(f_i^{-1}(u))$ if $X \in \text{Var}(t_i)$, $i \in [1, n]$

Generalizing, in case $t, s \in \text{TERM}_{TRS}$ and $\text{Var}(t) \supseteq \{X_1, \ldots, X_n\} = \text{Var}(s)$ the suitable expression of s from t is defined as $\text{SE}_s(t) = \tilde{s}[X_1/\text{SE}_{X_1}(t), \ldots, X_n/\text{SE}_{X_n}(t)]$, where $\tilde{s}$ is obtained from s replacing every constant c by $\mathcal{N}c$. □

Note that a suitable expression is in general not unique because in point ii) there may be more than one t_i containing X. However this is not a problem, since we don't care about different occurrences of the same variable: to obtain uniqueness, one can simply change the definition taking the minimum i.

Example 5.2 If $t = f(X, g\langle Y\rangle)$ then $\text{SE}_X(t) = f_1^{-1}\bullet$, $\text{SE}_Y(t) = \pi_1 g^{-1} f_2^{-1}\bullet$, and $\text{SE}_{\langle X, f(a,Y)\rangle}(t) = \langle X, f(\mathcal{N}a, Y)\rangle[X/\text{SE}_X(t), Y/\text{SE}_Y(t)] =$
$\langle X, f(\mathcal{N}a, Y)\rangle[Z/f_1^{-1}\bullet, Y/\pi_1 g^{-1} f_2^{-1}\bullet] = \langle f_1^{-1}\bullet, f(\mathcal{N}a, \pi_1 g^{-1} f_2^{-1}\bullet)\rangle$. □

Definition 5.3 (Transform Tswm)
Let the clause be $C = \mathtt{p}(\bar{\mathtt{t}}_0, \bar{\mathtt{s}}_{n+1}) \leftarrow \mathtt{p}_1(\bar{\mathtt{s}}_1, \bar{\mathtt{t}}_1), \ldots, \mathtt{p}_n(\bar{\mathtt{s}}_n, \bar{\mathtt{t}}_n)$.
The lhs of the rewrite rule is $lhs := p(\mathcal{N}\bar{t}_0)$.
The rhs is built iteratively: the atoms in the body are transformed in left to right order from $\mathtt{p}_1$ to $\mathtt{p}_n$, using a sequence V of terms. The following sequence of actions is used:

- $rhs := \mathcal{N}\langle X_1, \ldots, X_k\rangle$ and $V := X_1, \ldots, X_k$ (where $\{X_1, \ldots, X_k\} = \text{Var}(\bar{t}_0)$).
- For $i := 1$ to n do $\left\{ rhs := \underset{\text{SE}_{\langle V, p_i(s_i)\rangle}(V)}{\mathcal{T}}(rhs) \;\; ; \;\; V := V, \langle \bar{t}_i \rangle \right\}$
- If C is not a goal (viz. $\mathtt{p} \neq \mathtt{START}$) then let $rhs := \underset{\text{SE}_{\langle s_{n+1}\rangle}(V)}{\mathcal{T}}(rhs)$

The produced rewrite rule is then $lhs \rightarrow rhs$.
This rule has occurrences of functions (inverse or not) and of $\mathcal{T}$ operators: for each of them, include the corresponding propagation and transition rules. □

Assumption: Since propagation and transition rules can be inferred from the rule $lhs \rightarrow rhs$, henceforth we will omit them when writing the TRS obtained from the transform of a program.

Example 5.4 Take the classical append program, with moding ap(out,out,in):

```
ap([],X,X) ←
ap([A|X],Y,[A|Z]) ← ap(X,Y,Z)
```

Then its transform is:

$$apNX \rightarrow \underset{\langle \mathcal{N}[\,],\pi_1\bullet\rangle}{\mathcal{T}} \langle \mathcal{N}X\rangle$$
$$ap\mathcal{N}[A|Z] \rightarrow \underset{\langle[\pi_1\bullet|\pi_1\pi_3\bullet],\pi_2\pi_3\bullet\rangle}{\mathcal{T}} \; \underset{\langle\pi_1\bullet,\pi_2\bullet,ap\pi_2\bullet\rangle}{\mathcal{T}} \mathcal{N}\langle A,Z\rangle$$

□

5.1 Built-in

As seen, the transform Tswm translates each clause C into a (finite) TRS consisting of one rule ($lhs \rightarrow rhs$) together with the corresponding propagation and transition rules. We call $lhs \rightarrow rhs$ the *main rule* produced by the transform, denoted by $\mathsf{Tswm}_{\mathcal{M}}(C)$, while the remaining rules are called *built-in rules* (notation $\mathsf{Tswm}_{\mathcal{B}}(C)$): hence $\mathsf{Tswm}(C) = \mathsf{Tswm}_{\mathcal{M}}(C) \cup \mathsf{Tswm}_{\mathcal{B}}(C)$.

The intuition is that these built-in rules are just toolbox accessories for the main rule.

Thus, let us say the *built-in* $\mathcal{B}$ is the TRS composed by both the propagation and transition rules (note this is an infinite TRS, so not in TRSext).

Later on, we will improve the transform adding rules to the built-in: *so we assume that, when translating a clause C, its transform is given by the main rule(s) plus the rules from $\mathcal{B}$ that have some symbol in common with the symbols in the main rule(s).* This assumption will stay valid also for the subsequent transform Tfwm of Section 7.

It is evident we could replace $\mathsf{Tswm}_{\mathcal{B}}(C)$ with $\mathcal{B}$ itself without affecting the properties of the TRS produced by Tswm. Thus we can study $\mathcal{B}$ as a whole instead of its finite subTRSs that are generated by Tswm.

A first relevant property $\mathcal{B}$ should enjoy is *completeness*. This is not the case, because $\mathcal{B}$ is terminating but not confluent (consider the term $f^{-1}\mathcal{N}f\mathcal{N}X$: in $\mathcal{B}$ it reduces to two different normal forms $\mathcal{N}\mathcal{N}X$ and $f^{-1}\mathcal{N}\mathcal{N}fX$). To recover completeness, one can add the following rule:

$$\mathcal{N}\mathcal{N}X \rightarrow \mathcal{N}X \qquad (\textit{idempotence rule})$$

that is plausible, expressing the fact that marking twice a term (by means of $\mathcal{N}$) is the same than marking it once. Nevertheless, $\mathcal{B}$ is complete *relatively* to the terms produced by Tswm itself.

Summing up, we have the following:

Lemma 5.5 *$\mathcal{B} \cup \{\mathcal{N}\mathcal{N}X \rightarrow \mathcal{N}X\}$ is complete, whereas $\mathcal{B}$ is complete only relatively to the terms produced by the transform itself.*

To have a theoretically cleaner treatment, we *include* the idempotence rule in the built-in, being aware it does not play a role operationally. So we can reformulate the above lemma saying that $\mathcal{B}$ is complete.

Another important property the built-in enjoys is the following (roughly speaking, two TRSs *commute* if it does not matter in which order we apply rules from a TRS or from the other, see [Klo92] for a formal definition):

Lemma 5.6 *For every program P, the built-in commutes with* $\mathsf{Tswm}_{\mathcal{M}}(P)$.

5.2 Completeness of Tswm

The transform Tswm satisfies the following fundamental property:

Theorem 5.7 Tswm *is a complete (compositional) transform for SWM.*

The proof of the above theorem is not easy and quite long. The idea is that we define an *embedded sequence* from the sequence of goals $G_0, G_1,, \ldots$ of an LD-derivation $G_0, C_0, G_1, C_1, \ldots$ in the following way ($\downarrow_T$ means normalization w.r.t. the TRS T):

$$\mathcal{E}(G_0) = \mathsf{Tswm}_{\mathcal{M}}(G_0)\downarrow_{\mathcal{B}}$$
$$\mathcal{E}(G_i + 1) = (\mathcal{E}(G_i)\downarrow_{\mathsf{Tswm}_{\mathcal{M}}(C_i)})\downarrow_{\mathcal{B}}$$

Notice that Lemma 5.5 guarantees that the normalization process w.r.t. $\mathcal{B}$ is well-defined, i.e. it terminates and yields an unique result. Moreover, Lemma 5.6 ensures that normalization w.r.t. $\mathcal{B}$ does not prevent the applicability of the main rules. To show that $\downarrow_{\mathsf{Tswm}_{\mathcal{M}}(C_i)}$ is well-defined the following two lemmata are used (in fact, this normalization process reduces to just a one-step reduction):

Lemma 5.8 *A goal $G \in$ SWM and a clause $C \in$ SWM have a resolvent iff the rule* $\mathsf{Tswm}_{\mathcal{M}}(C)$ *can be applied to the term* $\mathsf{Tswm}_{\mathcal{M}}(G)\downarrow_{\mathcal{B}}$.

Lemma 5.9 *For every goal G and clause C, the rule* $\mathsf{Tswm}_{\mathcal{M}}(C)$ *can be applied to the term* $\mathsf{Tswm}_{\mathcal{M}}(G)\downarrow_{\mathcal{B}}$ *at most in one position (that is, there are no ambiguities).*

Then, a map is defined that associates to every member $\mathcal{E}(G_i)$ of the embedded sequence the partial answer substitution of G_i. This map, when $G_i = \square$, gives precisely the answer map α_{Tswm} of Definition 3.3, which is now defined:

If the goal is $G = \leftarrow \mathtt{p}_1(\bar{\mathtt{s}}_1, \bar{\mathtt{t}}_1), \ldots, \mathtt{p}_n(\bar{\mathtt{s}}_n, \bar{\mathtt{t}}_n)$ and $W = \mathrm{Var}(\bar{\mathtt{t}}_1, \ldots, \bar{\mathtt{t}}_n)$, then the answer map α_{Tswm} is

$$\alpha_{\mathsf{Tswm}}(G, NF(\mathsf{Tswm}(G \cup P))) := \{\theta|_W : \langle\langle \bar{t}_1\rangle, \ldots, \langle \bar{t}_n\rangle\rangle\theta = t, \mathcal{N} t \in NF(\mathsf{Tswm}(G \cup P))\}$$

where $\theta|_W$ is the restriction of θ to the variables in W.

6 Simplifying the Transform

In this section we show how, by using simple techniques, the output produced by the transform can be greatly simplified, providing a more readable (and easier to analyze) TRS.

6.1 Normalization

One great simplification comes from normalizing the rhs of the main rewrite rule obtained by the transform w.r.t. its built-in. This in general proves quite useful because in Subsection 6.3 we will increase the power of the built-in adding simplifying rules, that enter in action just thanks to this technique (that is, we will normalize w.r.t. the extended built-in).

Example 6.1 As a first example of what is possible using this technique, consider the program append seen previously in Example 5.4. If the obtained main rules are normalized w.r.t. the built-in, we obtain finally:

$$ap\mathcal{N}X \rightarrow \mathcal{N}\langle [\,], X\rangle$$
$$ap\mathcal{N}[A|Z] \rightarrow \underset{([\pi_1\bullet|\pi_1\pi_2\bullet],\pi_2\pi_2\bullet)}{\mathcal{T}} \langle \mathcal{N}A, ap\mathcal{N}Z\rangle \qquad \square$$

6.2 Smart Referencing

The transition functions used in the construction of the transform maintain a growing sequence (V) of all the output arguments in the body of the clause: however, all this information is not needed in case no further references are made to a variable occurring either in some output argument or in the input arguments of the head of the clause. To prevent such a waste, we can refine the transform letting V be the set of variables really needed in the sequel (*smart referencing*): more formally, the difference with the old transform is that we drop from V the variables no more present neither in the input arguments of the remaining atoms to be processed, nor in the output arguments of the head atom.

An example will clarify the situation.

Example 6.2 Consider the clause

$$p(X,Y,Z) \leftarrow q(X,W), r(Y,Z)$$

with moding p(in,in,out), q(in,out), r(in,out).
Its transform via Tswm gives

$$p(\mathcal{N}X,\mathcal{N}Y) \rightarrow \underset{(\pi_1\pi_3\bullet)}{\mathcal{T}} \quad \underset{(\pi_1\bullet,\pi_2\bullet,(\pi_1\pi_3\bullet),r\pi_2\pi_1\bullet)}{\mathcal{T}} \quad \underset{(\pi_1\bullet,\pi_2\bullet,q\pi_1\bullet)}{\mathcal{T}} \quad \mathcal{N}(X,Y)$$

$$\underset{(3)}{\vdots} \qquad \underset{(2)}{\vdots} \qquad \underset{(1)}{\vdots}$$

$$\boxed{(V)=(X,Y,(W),(Z))} \quad \boxed{(V)=(X,Y,(W))} \quad \boxed{(V)=(X,Y)}$$

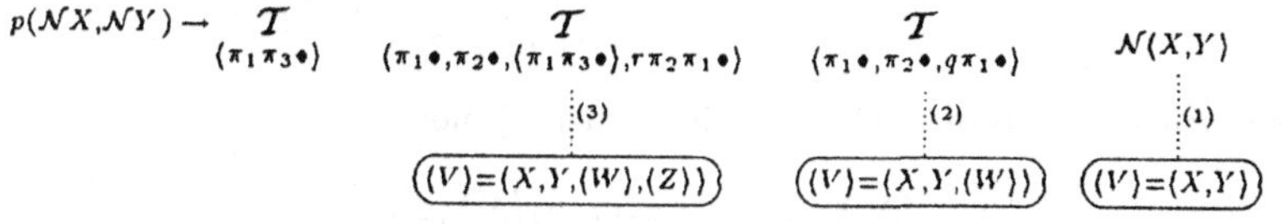

But note how in (2) X is not needed, and in (3) Y and W are not needed as well: so the revised transform gives

$$p(\mathcal{N}X,\mathcal{N}Y) \rightarrow \underset{(\pi_1\pi_1\bullet)}{\mathcal{T}} \quad \underset{(r\pi_2\pi_1\bullet)}{\mathcal{T}} \quad \underset{(\pi_2,q\pi_1\bullet)}{\mathcal{T}} \quad \mathcal{N}(X,Y) \qquad \square$$

$$\boxed{(V)=((Z))} \quad \boxed{(V)=(Y,(W))} \quad \boxed{(V)=(X,Y)}$$

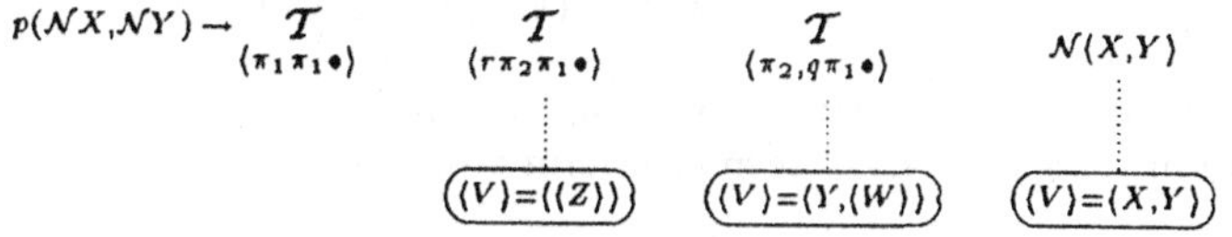

6.3 Relaxing the Built-in

Both the propagation and transition rules aim at constraining the calculus, forcing their argument(s), via the $\mathcal{N}$ operator, to be completely calculated before being further utilized.

As said, it is the possibility of 'splitting' that forces to behave this way (review Subsection 4.2): anyway, when this is not the case we can get rid of this imposed extra structure.

One such case is when unary functions are concerned: thus we add the following rules to the propagation rules that relax their behaviour (recovering the symmetry between a function and its inverse that was missing in the original propagation rules):

$$\begin{array}{ll} f^{-1}\mathcal{N}X \rightarrow \mathcal{N}f^{-1}X & (f \in \text{FUNC}_{\mathcal{TRS}}, \#f = 1) \\ f^{-1}fX \rightarrow X & \quad '' \\ ff^{-1}X \rightarrow X & \quad '' \end{array}$$

Regarding the transition rules, instead, the following rules are added:

$$\underset{\rho(t)}{\mathcal{T}} X \rightarrow t[\bullet/X] \qquad \left(\begin{array}{c} t \in \text{TERM}(\mathcal{L}_{\mathcal{TRS}} \dot{\cup} \{\bullet\}) \text{ with} \\ \text{only one occurrence of } \bullet \end{array} \right)$$

This case is in all similar to the previous one since transition functions are 'masquerade' functions with argument $\bullet$, and hence their arity should be calculated in terms of occurrences of $\bullet$.

Adding all these rules to the built-in is useful because, as said earlier in Subsection 6.1, when we normalize w.r.t. the built-in much of the extra structure imposed disappears, simplifying a lot the obtained rules. Note also that for this extended built-in Lemmata 5.5 and 5.6 still hold.

Example 6.3 Consider the previous Example 6.2:

```
p(X,Y,Z) ← q(X,W),r(Y,Z)
```

was transformed, using smart referencing, into

$$p(\mathcal{N}X, \mathcal{N}Y) \rightarrow \underset{\langle\pi_1\pi_1\bullet\rangle}{\mathcal{T}} \underset{\langle r\pi_2\pi_1\bullet\rangle}{\mathcal{T}} \underset{\langle\pi_2, q\pi_1\bullet\rangle}{\mathcal{T}} \mathcal{N}\langle X, Y\rangle$$

This rewrite rule, normalized w.r.t. the built-in, is now

$$p(\mathcal{N}X, \mathcal{N}Y) \rightarrow \pi_1 r \pi_2 \pi_1 \langle \mathcal{N}Y, q\mathcal{N}X\rangle$$ □

Example 6.4 Take the clause

```
p(X,Y) ← q(X,V),r(V,W,Z),s(Z,Y)
```

moded p(in,out), q(in,out), r(in,out,out) and s(in,out).
Its transform using the naïve Tswm transform gives

$$p\mathcal{N}X \rightarrow \underset{\langle\pi_1\pi_4\bullet\rangle}{\mathcal{T}} \underset{\langle\pi_1\bullet,\pi_2\bullet,\pi_3\bullet,s\pi_2\pi_3\bullet\rangle}{\mathcal{T}} \underset{\langle\pi_1\bullet,\pi_2\bullet,r\pi_2\bullet\rangle}{\mathcal{T}} \underset{\langle\pi_1\bullet,q\pi_1\bullet\rangle}{\mathcal{T}} \mathcal{N}\langle X\rangle$$

whereas using (smart referencing and) the built-in extended with the aforementioned unary functions rules we get

$$p\mathcal{N}X \rightarrow s\pi_2 rq\mathcal{N}X$$ □

6.4 Termination of Logic Programs: an Example

***Semi-complete* transforms can be used to provide a *sufficient* criterion for proving termination of logic programs: a logic program P terminates if its transformed TRS $\tau(P)$ terminates. Clearly, a *complete* transform provides a *sufficient* and also *necessary* criterion, hence strengthening the analysis power.**

Now, consider the following program taken from [KRKS92] (and further cited in [GW92, AM93]), computing the transitive closure of a relation p:

```
p(a,b) ←          tc(X,Y) ← p(X,Y)
p(b,c) ←          tc(X,Y) ← p(X,Z),tc(Z,Y)
```

with moding p(in,out) and tc(in,out).

The transform developed in [KRKS92] transforms this terminating logic program into a *non-terminating* TRS, whereas the transform Tswm, since the above program is SWM, obtains a TRS

$$p\mathcal{N}a \rightarrow \mathcal{N}\langle b\rangle \qquad tc\mathcal{N}X \rightarrow p\mathcal{N}X$$
$$p\mathcal{N}b \rightarrow \mathcal{N}\langle c\rangle \qquad tc\mathcal{N}X \rightarrow tc\, p\mathcal{N}X$$

that can be proven terminating using standard techniques of term rewriting.

Another application of this technique to prove termination of logic programs is given in Subsection 7.1, using transform Tfwm.

7 The Transform Tfwm

Transform Tswm is complete for SWM. In this section we modify Tswm to get a more powerful, yet more complicated, transform which is complete for the broader class of *Flatly Well Moded* programs (FWM), after [Mar94].

The idea underlying this subclass of well moded programs is that, roughly, every time an atom is selected to resolve the head of a clause, its output arguments are all filled in with *flattening expression*: a flattening expression (briefly *FE*) is either a *variable* or a *ground term* or a so-called *steady term*, where a term t is said to be *steady* if t is linear and $t = f_{(1)}\cdots f_{(k)}(X_{(1)},\ldots,X_{(n)})$ with $k>0$ and $\#f_{(1)} = \ldots = \#f_{(k-1)} = 1 \leq \#f_{(k)}$. For example, $f(g(h(X,Y)))$ is steady, whereas $f(X,X)$, $f(g(X),Y)$ and $f(g(X),h(Y))$ are not.

FWM has the remarkable property of being not only locally maximal among the unification free classes of programs, but even the locally greatest one containing SWM (see the Introduction and see [Mar94] for details).

To define Tfwm, we need the following concepts:

Definition 7.1 The *degree* of a flattening expression is the map

$$\begin{array}{lll} ||t|| & = 0 & \text{if } t \text{ is ground} \\ ||t|| & = 1 & \text{if } t \text{ is a variable} \\ ||t|| & = k+1 & \text{if } t = f_1\cdots f_k(X_1,\ldots,X_n) \end{array}$$

□

Definition 7.2 The *truncation of a term t at level k* ($Trunc_k(t)$) is:
$Trunc_0(t) = t$
$Trunc_k(t) = s$ for s an FE, $||s|| = k$, $s\,\mathcal{U}t$ □

The transform Tfwm acts like the previous Tswm, except that it keeps track of the structure of the terms occurring in the output positions of the selected atom in the goal. When the head of the clause is considered, a number of terms are produced, and each of them is used as lhs of a corresponding rewrite rule. These terms are computed by considering the degrees of all the *FE*s which unify with the output arguments of the head. Each of these degrees combined with the head yields the lhs of a rewrite rule. To this end for an atom $p(t, s)$ a triple $\langle t, s, d\rangle$ is used, where t is the input argument, s is the output argument and d is the degree of s. Notice that in Tswm only the input argument t is used to define the lhs of the correspondent rule. The rhs's of these rules are computed in a similar way as in the case of Tswm, only that this time, when processing the atoms in the body, also the structure of the current output, and its degree, is taken into account (the starting one is calculated by means of the clause head).

For example, consider the clause `p(X,f(a,Y))` ← `q(X,Y)` moded p(in, out), q(in, out); `p(X,f(a,Y))` yields three rules: the first has lhs $p\mathcal{N}\langle X, f(a,Y), 0\rangle$ (corresponding to the case that a 0-degree term, i.e. a ground one, is present in the output argument of the atom the clause head unifies with), and rhs $q\mathcal{N}\langle X, Y, 0\rangle$ (if $f(a,Y)$ unifies with a ground term then Y is set to a ground term, hence a 0-degree FE as well); the second has lhs $p\mathcal{N}\langle X, Y, 1\rangle$ (corresponding to the 1-degree case, i.e. a variable), and rhs $q\mathcal{N}\langle X, Y, 1\rangle$ (if $f(a,Y)$ unifies with a variable then Y remains a variable, hence again a 1-degree GE); the third has lhs $p\mathcal{N}\langle X, f(Z,Y), 2\rangle$ (corresponding to the 2-degree case, i.e. a steady term), and rhs $q\mathcal{N}\langle X, Y, 1\rangle$ (if $f(a,Y)$ unifies with a 2-degree FE, the latter has the form $f(W_1, W_2)$, and so Y remains a variable, viz. a 1-degree FE).

The construction process of the main rule(s) is similar to the one in Tswm, hence for space reasons we simply state the *lhs* and the start *rhs*.

Definition 7.3 (**Transform** Tfwm) For simplicity, we assume that relation symbols have only one output argument, the general case being in all similar. Moreover, we apply at once smart referencing (Subsection 6.2).
So, consider a clause $\mathtt{p}(\bar{\mathtt{t}}_0, \mathtt{s}_{n+1}) \leftarrow \mathtt{p}_1(\bar{\mathtt{s}}_1, \mathtt{t}_1), \ldots, \mathtt{p}_n(\bar{\mathtt{s}}_n, \mathtt{t}_n)$; we distinguish the following cases:

1. $\mathrm{Var}(s_{n+1}) \subseteq \mathrm{Var}(\bar{t}_0)$
This means, for the data driveness property of WM programs, that s_{n+1} is instantiated to a ground term; the transformed rule is then:

$$p\mathcal{N}\langle \bar{t}_0, Y, Z\rangle \xrightarrow[\text{likewise Tswm}]{\text{Transition functions}} T(s_{n+1}, Y, Z, \mathcal{N}\langle \bar{t}_0\rangle)$$

where $T(X, Y, Z, W)$ is a 'Test' operator that checks whether unification between the head and the selected atom in the goal can occur, and in affirmative case yields W. This can be done because we have the information (i.e. Z) about the *degree* of the flattening expression present in the output argument of the goal atom (i.e. Y). T is defined by the following rules:

i) $T(f(X), f(Y), sss(Z), W) \rightarrow T(X, Y, ss(Z), W)$	$(f \in \mathrm{FUNC}_{TRS})$	(deg.≥ 3)
ii) $T(f(X_1, \ldots, X_n), f(Y_1, \ldots, Y_n), ss(0), W) \rightarrow W$	$(f \in \mathrm{FUNC}_{TRS})$	(deg.$= 2$)
iii) $T(X, Y, s(0), W) \rightarrow W$		(deg.$= 1$)
iv) $T(X, X, 0, W) \rightarrow W$		(deg.$= 0$)

(all these T-rules are included in the built-in rules in i) and ii)), albeit in infinite number, are manageable by the transform since they are needed only when the corresponding functions of FUNC$_{TRS}$ are present, and so are treated analogously to the propagation and transition rules).

Note that the output eventually obtained after the T-test has been passed is just $\mathcal{N}\langle \bar{t}_0 \rangle$ and not the full description $\mathcal{N}\langle \bar{t}_0, s_{n+1}, 0\rangle$ because this extra information is utterly superfluous (variables in s_{n+1} are already contained in $\bar{t}_0$).

2. $\mathrm{Var}(s_{n+1}) \not\subseteq \mathrm{Var}(\bar{t}_0)$

Two cases are possible: whether the degree of a flattening expression unifying with s_{n+1} is *bounded* or *unbounded*:

A) $k = \max\{||t|| : t \text{ is an } FE, t\mathcal{U}s_{n+1}\} < \infty$ (bounded degree)
Then the transform produces $k+1$ rewrite rules:

$$p\mathcal{N}\langle \bar{t}_0, \mathit{Trunc}_i(s_{n+1}), \underbrace{s\cdots s}_{i}(0)\rangle \xrightarrow[\text{likewise Tswm}]{\text{Transition functions}} \mathcal{N}\langle \bar{t}_0 \rangle \quad (0 \le i \le k)$$

(where $\mathit{Trunc}_i(s_{n+1})$ is required to be disjoint with $\bar{t}_0$). Again, note that just $\mathcal{N}\langle \bar{t}_0 \rangle$ is used and not a full description of the output because, for properties of the FWM class, no references to variables in s_{n+1} are possible in this case.

B) $\max\{||t|| : t \text{ is an } FE, t\mathcal{U}\, s_{n+1}\} = \infty$ (unbounded degree)
This case can only happen when s_{n+1} is a steady term or a variable, so let $k = ||s_{n+1}||$.
The transform produces $k+2$ rewrite rules.

The first $k+1$ are, analogously to the previous case A,

$$p\mathcal{N}\langle \bar{t}_0, \mathit{Trunc}_i(s_{n+1}), \underbrace{s\cdots s}_{i}(0)\rangle \xrightarrow[\text{likewise Tswm}]{\text{Transition functions}} \mathcal{N}\langle \bar{t}_0, s'_{n+1}, \underbrace{s\cdots s}_{k}(0)\rangle$$

(with $0 \le i \le k$, $\bar{t}_0$ and $\mathit{Trunc}_i(s_{n+1})$ disjoint), where s'_{n+1} is a ground instance of s_{n+1}: this is done only to ensure the above rules satisfy the condition of a rewrite rule to have all of the variables in the right hand side contained in the left hand side. For instance, if $s_{n+1} = f(g(X,Y))$ and $\mathit{Trunc}_2(s_{n+1}) = f(X)$, to put s_{n+1} in the rhs we would need to introduce another variable (Y) in the lhs.

Acting this way is safe for we are only interested in $\mathit{Trunc}_k(s_{n+1})$ and not in s_{n+1} itself, and so we can pass to s'_{n+1} since $\mathit{Trunc}_k(s_{n+1}) = \mathit{Trunc}_k(s'_{n+1})$ (up to a renaming).

The $k+2$-th rule corresponds to the infinite cases in which the degree of the output part in the goal atom is greater than k: the key fact is just that we can parametrize in a single rewrite rule an otherwise infinite sequence of cases. The rule is

$$p\mathcal{N}\langle \bar{t}_0, s_{n+1}, \underbrace{s\cdots s}_{k+1}(Z)\rangle \xrightarrow[\text{likewise Tswm}]{\text{Transition functions}} \mathcal{N}\langle \bar{t}_0, s_{n+1}, \underbrace{s\cdots s}_{k+1}(Z)\rangle$$

□

The main result is

Theorem 7.4 *The map* Tfwm *is a complete (compositional) transform for FWM.*

The proof uses the same techniques employed in proving the analogous Theorem 5.7 for Tswm.

7.1 An example

Consider the following logic program after [GW92, AM93]:

```
p(X,g(X)) ←
p(X,f(Y)) ← p(X,g(Y))
```

with moding p(in, out). This program, albeit very simple, is completely *out of scope* from all the other transforms presented in the literature ([SKRK90, KRKS92, AM93]) and even the one in [GW92] transforming logic programs into the more powerful conditional TRSs. The problem, as already noticed in [GW92], is that all these transforms consider only the input arguments (which in this example are fixed), and not the output ones. Instead, since the above program belongs to FWM, its transform via Tfwm gives

$$
\begin{aligned}
&p\mathcal{N}\langle X,Y,Z\rangle \to \underset{\langle g\pi_1\bullet\rangle}{\mathcal{T}} T(g(X),Y,Z,\mathcal{N}\langle X\rangle)\\
&p\mathcal{N}\langle X,f(Y),0\rangle \to \underset{\langle fg^{-1}\pi_1\bullet\rangle}{\mathcal{T}}\ \underset{p(\pi_1\bullet,gf^{-1}\pi_2\bullet,\pi_3\bullet)}{\mathcal{T}} \mathcal{N}\langle X,f(Y),0\rangle\\
&p\mathcal{N}\langle X,Y,s(0)\rangle \to \underset{\langle fg^{-1}\pi_1\bullet\rangle}{\mathcal{T}}\ \underset{p(\pi_1\bullet,g\pi_2\bullet,\pi_3\bullet)}{\mathcal{T}} \mathcal{N}\langle X,g(c),ss(0)\rangle\\
&p\mathcal{N}\langle X,f(Y),ss(0)\rangle \to \underset{\langle fg^{-1}\pi_1\bullet\rangle}{\mathcal{T}}\ \underset{p(\pi_1\bullet,g\pi_2\bullet,\pi_3\bullet)}{\mathcal{T}} \mathcal{N}\langle X,g(c),ss(0)\rangle\\
&p\mathcal{N}\langle X,f(Y),sss(Z)\rangle \to \underset{\langle fg^{-1}\pi_1\bullet\rangle}{\mathcal{T}}\ \underset{p(\pi_1\bullet,gf^{-1}\pi_2\bullet,\pi_3\bullet)}{\mathcal{T}} \mathcal{N}\langle X,f(Y),sss(Z)\rangle
\end{aligned}
$$

that is a *terminating* TRS, whose termination can be proved for every goal belonging to FWM (these include, e.g., `← p(a ground term,X)`, and all the goals of the form `← p(a ground term,a flattening expression)`).

The transform Tfwm enhanced with the 'normalizing' technique of Subsection 6.1 gives finally:

1. $p\mathcal{N}\langle X,Y,Z\rangle \to \langle g\pi_1 T(g(X),Y,Z,\mathcal{N}\langle X\rangle)\rangle$
2. $p\mathcal{N}\langle X,f(Y),0\rangle \to \langle fg^{-1}\pi_1 p\mathcal{N}\langle X,g(Y),0\rangle\rangle$
3. $p\mathcal{N}\langle X,Y,s(0)\rangle \to \langle fg^{-1}\pi_1 p\mathcal{N}\langle X,g(c),ss(0)\rangle\rangle$
4. $p\mathcal{N}\langle X,f(Y),ss(0)\rangle \to \langle fg^{-1}\pi_1 p\mathcal{N}\langle X,g(c),ss(0)\rangle\rangle$
5. $p\mathcal{N}\langle X,f(Y),sss(Z)\rangle \to \langle fg^{-1}\pi_1 p\mathcal{N}\langle X,g(Y),sss(Z)\rangle\rangle$

Now we illustrate some reductions in the TRS, to clarify how the mimicking of the logic program is performed:

$$\leftarrow \mathrm{p(a,X)} \longmapsto \langle p\mathcal{N}(a,X,s(0))\rangle \xrightarrow{\quad 1 \quad} \langle\langle g\pi_1 T(g(a),X,s(0),\mathcal{N}(a))\rangle\rangle$$

$$\downarrow 3 \qquad\qquad\qquad\qquad\qquad\qquad \downarrow \mathcal{B}$$

$$\langle\langle fg^{-1}\pi_1 p\mathcal{N}(a,g(c),ss(0))\rangle\rangle \qquad\qquad \langle\langle g\pi_1\mathcal{N}(a)\rangle\rangle$$

$$\downarrow \mathcal{B} \qquad\qquad\qquad\qquad\qquad\qquad \downarrow \mathcal{B}$$

$$\langle\langle fg^{-1}\pi_1\langle g\pi_1 T(g(a),g(c),ss(0),\mathcal{N}(a))\rangle\rangle\rangle \qquad \boxed{\mathcal{N}(\langle g(a)\rangle)}$$

$$\downarrow \mathcal{B}$$

$$\boxed{\mathcal{N}(\langle f(a)\rangle)}$$

$$\leftarrow \mathrm{p(a,f(X))} \longmapsto \langle p\mathcal{N}(a,f(X),ss(0))\rangle \xrightarrow{\quad 4 \quad} \langle\langle fg^{-1}\pi_1 p\mathcal{N}(a,g(c),ss(0))\rangle\rangle$$

$$\downarrow 1 \qquad\qquad\qquad\qquad\qquad\qquad \downarrow 1$$

$$\langle\langle g\pi_1 T(g(a),f(X),ss(0),\mathcal{N}(a))\rangle\rangle \qquad \langle\langle fg^{-1}\pi_1\langle g\pi_1 T(g(a),g(c),ss(0),\mathcal{N}(a))\rangle\rangle\rangle$$

$$\downarrow \mathcal{B}$$

$$\langle\langle fg^{-1}\pi_1\langle g\pi_1\mathcal{N}(a)\rangle\rangle\rangle$$

$$\downarrow \mathcal{B}$$

$$\boxed{\mathcal{N}(\langle f(a)\rangle)}$$

$$\leftarrow \mathrm{p(a,f(a))} \longmapsto \langle p\mathcal{N}(a,f(a),0)\rangle \xrightarrow{\quad 2 \quad} \langle\langle fg^{-1}\pi_1 p\mathcal{N}(a,g(a),0)\rangle\rangle$$

$$\downarrow 1 \qquad\qquad\qquad\qquad\qquad\qquad \downarrow 1$$

$$\langle\langle g\pi_1 T(g(a),f(a),0,\mathcal{N}(a))\rangle\rangle \qquad \langle\langle fg^{-1}\pi_1\langle g\pi_1 T(g(a),g(a),0,\mathcal{N}(a))\rangle\rangle\rangle$$

$$\downarrow \mathcal{B}$$

$$\langle\langle fg^{-1}\pi_1\langle g\pi_1\mathcal{N}(a)\rangle\rangle\rangle$$

$$\downarrow \mathcal{B}$$

$$\boxed{\mathcal{N}(\langle f(a)\rangle)}$$

$$\leftarrow \mathrm{p(a,fh(X,Y))} \longmapsto \langle p\mathcal{N}(a,fh(X,Y),sss(0))\rangle \xrightarrow{\quad 5 \quad} \langle\langle fg^{-1}\pi_1 p\mathcal{N}(a,gh(X,Y),sss(0))\rangle\rangle$$

$$\downarrow 1$$

$$\langle\langle fg^{-1}\pi_1\langle g\pi_1 T(g(a),gh(X,Y),sss(0),\mathcal{N}(a))\rangle\rangle\rangle$$

$$\downarrow \mathcal{B}$$

$$\langle\langle fg^{-1}\pi_1\langle g\pi_1 T(a,h(X,Y),ss(0),\mathcal{N}(a))\rangle\rangle\rangle$$

$$\leftarrow \mathrm{p(a,fh(a,g(a)))} \longmapsto \langle p\mathcal{N}(a,fh(a,g(a)),0)\rangle \xrightarrow{\quad 1 \quad} \langle\langle g\pi_1 T(g(a),fh(a,g(a)),0,\mathcal{N}(a))\rangle\rangle$$

$$\downarrow 2$$

$$\langle\langle fg^{-1}\pi_1 p\mathcal{N}(a,gh(a,g(a)),0)\rangle\rangle$$

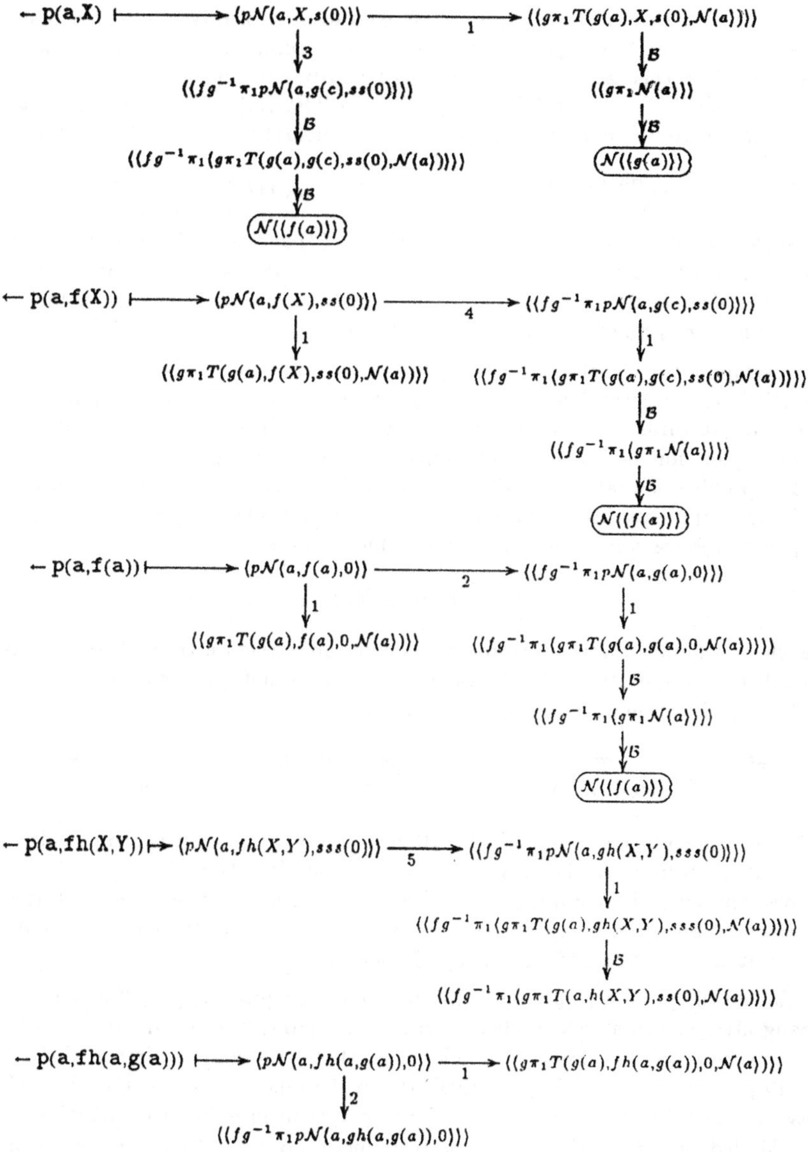

8 Remarks

– We mentioned in Subsection 3.1, among the advantages of a compositional transform, that in case of modifications of a program P adding new rules to obtain a new program P', only the transform of the difference program has to be calculated.

The general case, in which from P we pass to an arbitrary P', is readily much more worthwhile in case of practical applications. It turns out that, for the transform here developed, this case can be coped satisfactorily as before.

For two TRSs T_1 and T_2, define $T_1 \setminus_{\mathcal{M}} T_2$ as the TRS $\{r | (r \in T_1 \setminus T_2) \vee (r \in T_1 \cap \mathcal{B})\}$, that is we cut from T_1 only its main rules. Then it holds (τ stands for Tswm or Tfwm)

$$\tau(P') = \tau(P \setminus (P \setminus P') \cup (P' \setminus P)) = \tau(P) \setminus_{\mathcal{M}} \tau(P \setminus P') \cup \tau(P' \setminus P)$$

and since $\tau(P)$ was already calculated, only $\tau(P \setminus P')$ and $\tau(P' \setminus P)$ remain; hence we can generalize the case treated in Subsection 3.1 saying that when from P we pass to P', to calculate the transform of P' once given the one of P only the transforms of the *difference programs* need to be calculated.

- In developing the transforms of this paper we paid attention to completeness only. Nevertheless, semi-completeness is important in deriving sufficient criterions for termination. It turns out that we can easily extend our transforms to make them semi-complete for the broader class of Well Moded programs.

  The problem is that the result of Lemma 5.8 does not hold any more, since only the input arguments discriminate the application of a rule to a term. To cope with this, we introduce *conditional operators* defined via the rules

$$\mathcal{C}_t(t) \rightarrow t \quad (t \in \text{TERM}_{TRS})$$

  that check whether a given argument has a certain structure (provided by t): if it has not, the computation stays blocked (that is $\mathcal{N}$ cannot 'propagate').

  The modification of the transform Tswm is simply to put

$$rhs := \mathcal{T}_{\text{SE}_{(V, c_{\mathcal{N}(\bar{t}_i)} p_i(\bar{s}_i))}(V)}(rhs) \quad \text{in place of} \quad rhs := \mathcal{T}_{\text{SE}_{(V, p_i(\bar{s}_i))}(V)}(rhs)$$

  viz. every time $p_i(\bar{s}_i)$ is computed it is checked whether the result is compatible with the term structure of $\bar{t}_i$. The same technique is used for Tfwm.

  We gain only semi-completeness and not completeness because the check is performed only after the computation of $p_i(\bar{s}_i)$ is finished, and therefore new infinite computations could be added, destroying soundness.

- So far, all the proposals of transformation from logic programs to TRSs have been staying always within well moded programs. However, Transform Tswm has been built in such a way to support a broader class, that is the class of *Simply Well Typed* (SWT) programs introduced in [AE93]: this is the generalization of the SWM class to types, much like the class of Well Typed programs introduced in [BLR92] is for Well Moded programs; thanks to the introduction of types, it allows *non-ground inputs*, thus giving much more flexibility than the SWM class. Using almost the same proof used for the SWM case, it can be shown that Tswm is *complete* for SWT as well.

Acknowledgments

I wish to heartly thank Krzysztof R. Apt: without him this paper would have never been written; thanks also to Jan Willem Klop for his continuous support. Thanks also to Franca Tressoldi and to Orfeo and Elena Marchiori.

References

[AE93] K.R. Apt and S. Etalle. On the unification free Prolog programs. In S. Sokolowski, editor, *MFCS'93*, LNCS, pp. 1–19. Springer, 1993.

[AM93] G. Aguzzi and U. Modigliani. Proving termination of logic programs by transforming them into equivalent term rewriting systems. *FST&TCS'93*, LNCS. Springer, 1993.

[Apt90] K.R. Apt. Logic programming. In J. van Leeuwen, editor, *Handbook of Theoretical Computer Science*, volume B, chapter 10, pp. 495–574. Elsevier - MIT Press, 1990.

[BLR92] F. Bronsard, T.K. Lakshman, and U.S Reddy. A framework of directionality for proving termination of logic programs. In K.R. Apt, editor, *JICSLP'92*, pp. 321–335. MIT Press, 1992.

[Der87] N. Dershowitz. Termination of rewriting. *JSC*, 3:69–116, 1987.

[DJ90] N. Dershowitz and J. Jouannaud. Rewrite systems. In J. van Leeuwen, editor, *Handbook of Theoretical Computer Science*, volume B, chapter 6, pp. 243–320. Elsevier - MIT Press, 1990.

[DM85] P. Dembinski and J. Małuszyński. AND-parallelism with intelligent backtracking for annotated logic programs. *ILPS'85*, pp. 29–38, 1985.

[GW92] H. Ganzinger and U. Waldmann. Termination proofs of well-moded logic programs via conditional rewrite systems. In M. Rusinowitch and J.L Rémy, editors, *CTRS'92*, pp. 216–222, July 1992.

[Klo92] J.W. Klop. Term rewriting systems. In S. Abramsky, Dov M. Gabbay, and T.S.E. Maibaum, editors, *Handbook of Logic in Computer Science*, volume 2, chapter 1, pp. 1–116. Clarendon Press, Oxford, 1992.

[KRKS92] M.R.K. Krishna Rao, D. Kapur, and R.K. Shyamasundar. A transformational methodology for proving termination of logic programs. In *CSL'92*, volume 626 of *LNCS*, pp. 213–226, Berlin, 1992. Springer.

[Llo87] J.W. Lloyd. *Foundations of Logic Programming*. Springer, 2nd ed., 1987.

[Mar93] M. Marchiori. Logic programming, matching and term rewriting systems. Master's thesis, Dep. of Pure and Applied Mathematics, University of Padova, Italy, July 1993. In Italian.

[Mar94] M. Marchiori. Localizations of unification freedom through matching directions. Submitted, March 1994.

[MK85] J. Maluszyński and H.J. Komorowski. Unification-free execution of logic programs. *IEEE Symposium on Logic Programming*, pp. 78–86, 1985.

[SKRK90] R.K. Shyamasundar, M.R.K. Krishna Rao, and D. Kapur. Termination of logic programs. Computer science group, Tata Institute of Fundamental Research, Bombay, India, 1990. Revised version: Rewriting concepts in the study of termination of logic programs, *ALPUK*, 1992.

Higher-Order Minimal Function Graphs

Neil D Jones and Mads Rosendahl

Datalogisk Institut, University of Copenhagen
Universitetsparken 1, DK-2100 Copenhagen Ø
Denmark
{neil, rose}@diku.dk

Abstract. We present a minimal function graph semantics for a higher-order functional language with applicative evaluation order. The semantics captures the intermediate calls performed during the evaluation of a program. This information may be used in abstract interpretation as a basis for proving the soundness of program analyses. An example of this is the "closure analysis" of partial evaluation.

Program flow analysis is concerned with obtaining an approximate but safe description of a program's run-time behaviour without actually having to run it on its (usually infinite) input data set.

Consider a functional program. The meaning of a simple function definition

$$f(x_1, \ldots, x_k) = e$$

is typically given by a semantic function M of type

$$\mathsf{M}[\![f(x_1, \ldots, x_k) = e]\!] : V^k \to V_\perp$$

where V is a set of values. Denotational semantics traditionally proceeds by defining $\mathsf{M}[\![p]\!]$ by recursion on syntax. Semantics-based program approximation can be done naturally by approximating a function on precise values by another function defined on abstract values (eg. $\perp, \top$). This approach is taken in [2] for strictness analysis and may be used for other *compositional* analyses where program parts can be analysed independently of the contexts in which they occur.

In contrast, a *top-down* analysis has as goal to describe the effects of applying the program to a given set of input values and so is context-dependent. This type of analysis cannot easily be related to a usual denotational semantics without some extra instrumentation. A well-known alternative is to describe functions by their graphs. It is natural to think of function f as a set of input-output pairs $IO_f = \{(a, f(a)), (b, f(b)), \ldots\}$, so a set of needed function values corresponds to a perhaps proper subset of IO_f. This leads to an approach described in [4]. In the minimal function graph approach to semantics the idea is to describe functions by the sets of argument-result pairs sufficient to identify the function as used. From a given argument tuple the minimal function graph description should give the smallest set of argument-result pairs that is needed to compute the result. As a semantic function it may have the type

$$\mathsf{M}[\![f(x_1, \ldots, x_k) = e]\!] : V^k \to \mathcal{P}(V^k \times V_\perp)$$

and the informal definition may be

$$\mathbf{M}[\![f(x_1,\ldots,x_k)=e]\!]\vec{v}=\{\langle\vec{u},r\rangle \mid f(\vec{u}) \text{ is needed to compute } f(\vec{v}) \wedge f(\vec{u})=r\}$$

By this approach one analyses a program by approximating its MFG semantics, as outlined in [4] and developed in several places since.

The stating point of this paper is: how can one approximate the behaviour of higher-order programs using the minimal function graph approach of only describing reachable values?

Our approach is again semantically based, but on a more operational level than for example [2]. Three steps are involved.

A Define a closure-based semantics for higher-order programs (in a now traditional way).

B Define a minimal function graph variant of this, which collects only reachable function arguments and results.

C Verify safety of program analyses by reference to this higher-order MFG semantics.

In this paper we present A and B in some detail and sketch an application as in C.

1 Language

Consider a small language based on recursion equation systems. The language allows higher-order functions and the evaluation order is eager. A program is a number of function definitions:

$$\begin{array}{lcl} f_1 \;\; x_1\cdots x_k & = & e_1 \\ \vdots & & \vdots \\ f_n \;\; x_1\cdots x_k & = & e_n \end{array}$$

An expression is built from parameters and function names by application and basic operations.

x_i	Parameters
f_i	Function names
$a_i(e_1,\ldots,e_k)$	Basic operations
$e_1(e_2)$	Application
if e_1 **then** e_2 **else** e_3	Conditional

For notational simplicity we assume that all functions have the same number of arguments, mainly to avoid subscripted subscripts. A function with fewer than k parameters can be padded to one of k parameters by adding dummy parameters to the left of the parameter list and adding dummy arguments to every use of the function symbol. An actual implementation of an analysis based on this framework should not make this assumption, nor should it assume that the functions are named $f_1,\ldots,f_n$, parameters $x_1,\ldots,x_k$, and basic operations $a_1,a_2,\ldots$.

The language is in a sense weakly typed since each function has a fixed arity, *i.e.* number of arguments. Result of functions can, on the other hand, be functions partially applied to various numbers of arguments.

Example As an example of how to use the curried style in the language, consider the following program.

$$\begin{array}{lll} f & = & taut\ g\ 2 \\ g\ x\ y & = & x \wedge \neg y \\ taut\ h\ n & = & h, \quad \text{if } n = 0 \\ & = & taut\ (h\ true)\ (n-1) \wedge taut\ (h\ false)\ (n-1), \quad \textbf{otherwise} \end{array}$$

The function *taut* is a function in two arguments. If h is an n-argument function then a call *taut h n* returns *true* if h is a tautology, otherwise it returns *false*.

2 Closure semantics

We have not specified which basic operations and datatypes the language should contain. The details are not important as long as the underlying datatype contains the truth values. We will therefore assume that the language has an underlying datatype represented with the set *Base* and that the basic operations $a_1, a_2, \ldots$ have standard meanings as functions $\underline{a}_i : Base^k \rightarrow Base_\perp$. This is actually a restriction on the language as we do not allow basic operations on higher order objects. This means that we cannot have, say, `map` or `mapcar` as basic operations (but it will be easy to define those as user defined functions).

2.1 Closures

The semantics presented below is based on "closures" so a partially applied function will be represented as a closure or tuple $[i, v_1, \ldots, v_j]$ of the function identification i for the function name f_i and the so far computed arguments $(v_1, \ldots, v_j)$. Only when all arguments are provided, *i.e.* when $j = k$ will the expression e_i defining the ith function be evaluated. The arguments in the closure may belong to the base type but, as the language is higher-order, they may also be closures themselves. The set of values that may appear in computations may then be defined recursively as either base type values or closures of values:

$$V \quad = Base \cup (\{1, \ldots, n\} \times V^*)$$

We here use the numbers $1, \ldots, n$ instead of the function names so as to remove the syntactic information from the semantic domains. As an example $[i, \epsilon]$, with ϵ as the empty sequence, denotes the ith function before being applied to any arguments. We will use square brackets to construct and denote closures in expressions like $[i, e_1, \ldots, e_l]$. Closures do not contain any information about the results from calling the (partially applied) functions. This means that there is no natural ordering between closures or base values and we may use $V_\perp$ as a flat domain. In the semantics we will use a function *isbase* to test whether a value in V is of base type or is a closure.

2.2 Fixpoint semantics with closures

Semantic domains

$$V = Base \cup (\{1,\dots,n\} \times V^*) \qquad v,d \in V,\ \ \rho \in V^k$$
$$\Phi = V^k \to V_\perp \qquad \phi \in \Phi^n$$

Semantic functions.

$$\mathbf{E}_c[\![e]\!] : \Phi^n \to V^k \to V_\perp \qquad \text{Expression meanings}$$
$$\mathbf{U}_c[\![p]\!] : \Phi^n \qquad \text{Program meanings}$$

with definitions:

$$\mathbf{E}_c[\![x_i]\!]\phi\rho = \quad \rho_i$$

$$\mathbf{E}_c[\![f_i]\!]\phi\rho = \quad [i,\epsilon]$$

$$\begin{aligned}\mathbf{E}_c[\![a_j(e_1,\dots,e_k)]\!]\phi\rho = &\\ &\textbf{let } v_i = \mathbf{E}_c[\![e_i]\!]\phi\rho \textbf{ for } i=1,\dots,k \textbf{ in}\\ &\textbf{if some } v_i = \perp \textbf{ then } \perp \textbf{ else } \underline{a}_j(v_1,\dots,v_k)\end{aligned}$$

$$\begin{aligned}\mathbf{E}_c[\![e_1(e_2)]\!]\phi\rho = &\ \textbf{let } d_1 = \mathbf{E}_c[\![e_1]\!]\phi\rho \textbf{ and } d_2 = \mathbf{E}_c[\![e_2]\!]\phi\rho \textbf{ in}\\ &\textbf{if } d_1 = \perp \textbf{ or } d_2 = \perp \textbf{ or } isbase(d_1) \textbf{ then } \perp \textbf{ else}\\ &\textbf{let } [i, v_1,\dots,v_\ell] = d_1 \textbf{ in if } \ell+1 < k \textbf{ then } [i,v_1,\dots,v_\ell,d_2]\\ &\textbf{else } \phi_i(v_1,\dots,v_\ell,d_2)\end{aligned}$$

$$\begin{aligned}\mathbf{E}_c[\![\textbf{if } e_1 \textbf{ then } e_2 \textbf{ else } e_3]\!]\phi\rho = &\\ &\textbf{if } \mathbf{E}_c[\![e_1]\!]\phi\rho = true \textbf{ then } \mathbf{E}_c[\![e_2]\!]\phi\rho\\ &\textbf{if } \mathbf{E}_c[\![e_1]\!]\phi\rho = false \textbf{ then } \mathbf{E}_c[\![e_3]\!]\phi\rho \textbf{ else } \perp\end{aligned}$$

$$\mathbf{U}_c[\![f_1\ x_1\cdots x_k = e_1\ \ \dots\ \ f_n\ x_1\cdots x_k = e_n]\!] = \textbf{fix } \lambda\phi.\langle \mathbf{E}_c[\![e_1]\!]\phi,\dots,\mathbf{E}_c[\![e_n]\!]\phi\rangle$$

3 Minimal function graph

We will now present the minimal function graph semantics for the language. The function environment is somewhat special in this semantics as the functions are not represented by functions but by sets of argument-result pairs. These will be the smallest sets sufficient to include all calls resulting from applying the program to an *initial call description*. This is on the form $\langle c_1,\dots,c_k\rangle$ where each c_i is the set of arguments with which f_i is called externally.

3.1 Function environment

As indicated earlier, in the minimal function graph approach a function is represented as a set of argument-result pairs. We will use the power-set

$$\Psi = \mathcal{P}(V^k \times V_\perp)$$

with the ordering

$$\psi_1 \sqsubseteq \psi_2 \Leftrightarrow \forall \langle \vec{v}, r\rangle \in \psi_1 . \langle \vec{v}, r\rangle \in \psi_2 \vee (r = \perp \wedge \langle \vec{v}, s\rangle \in \psi_2 \text{ for some } s \in V$$

to represent the meaning of functions. The domain Ψ^n will be used for function environments. The set Ψ may be used as a domain with set inclusion as partial ordering. In the minimal function graph approach the function environment plays a dual role. It keeps the results of function calls and, as well, holds the list of "needed" calls. The "argument needs" is the set of argument tuples on which a function must be evaluated to complete the computation. They may be described in a power-set

$$C = \mathcal{P}(V^k)$$

The needs for the tuple of program functions are C^n, a domain partially ordered by component-wise set inclusion. The domain C may be seen as an abstraction of the domain of function denotations Ψ using the following two functions.

$$\begin{array}{ll} getcalls : \Psi \rightarrow C & getcalls(\psi) = \{\vec{v} \mid \langle \vec{v}, r\rangle \in \psi_1\} \\ savecalls : C \rightarrow \Psi & savecalls(c) = \{\langle \vec{v}, \bot\rangle \mid \vec{v} \in c_1\} \end{array}$$

clearly $getcalls \circ savecalls$ is the identity on C and $\forall \psi \in \Psi.\ savecalls(getcalls(\psi)) \sqsubseteq \psi$. The functions $getcall$ and $setcall$ are extended to Ψ^n and C^n component-wise.

3.2 Fixpoint semantics with minimal function graphs

We are now ready to introduce the minimal function graph semantics by defining two semantic functions $\mathbf{E}_m$ and $\mathbf{U}_m$. The function $\mathbf{E}_m$ has two uses: to evaluate; and to collect function arguments needed to do the evaluation.

Semantic domains

V	$= Base \cup (\{1, \ldots, n\} \times V^*)$	Closures
D	$= V_\bot \times C^n$	A result and a "needed calls" tuple
C	$= \mathcal{P}(V^k)$	Sets of arguments
Ψ	$= \mathcal{P}(V^k \times V_\bot)$	Function graphs

Semantic functions

$$\mathbf{E}_m[\![e]\!] : \Psi^n \rightarrow V^k \rightarrow D$$
$$\mathbf{U}_m[\![p]\!] : C^n \rightarrow \Psi^n$$

The function $\mathbf{U}_m$ maps program input needs to an n-tuple of minimal function graphs, one for each f_i.

$$
\begin{aligned}
&\mathbf{E}_m[\![x_i]\!]\psi\rho = \quad \langle \rho_i, \emptyset^n \rangle \\
&\mathbf{E}_m[\![f_i]\!]\psi\rho = \quad \langle [i,\epsilon], \emptyset^n \rangle \\
&\mathbf{E}_m[\![a_j(e_1,\ldots,e_k)]\!]\psi\rho = \\
&\qquad \textbf{let } \langle d_i, \vec{c_i} \rangle = \mathbf{E}_m[\![e_i]\!]\psi\rho \textbf{ for } i = 1,\ldots,k \textbf{ in} \\
&\qquad \textbf{if some } d_i = \bot \textbf{ then } \langle \bot, \vec{c}_1 \sqcup \cdots \sqcup \vec{c}_k \rangle \\
&\qquad \textbf{else } \langle \underline{a}_j(d_1,\ldots,d_k), \vec{c}_1 \sqcup \cdots \sqcup \vec{c}_k \rangle \\
&\mathbf{E}_m[\![e_1(e_2)]\!]\psi\rho = \textbf{let } \langle d_1, \vec{c}_1 \rangle = \mathbf{E}_m[\![e_1]\!]\psi\rho \textbf{ and} \\
&\qquad\qquad \langle d_2, \vec{c}_2 \rangle = \mathbf{E}_m[\![e_2]\!]\psi\rho \textbf{ in} \\
&\qquad \textbf{if } d_1 = \bot \textbf{ or } d_2 = \bot \textbf{ or } \mathit{isbase}(d_1) \textbf{ then } \langle \bot, \vec{c}_1 \sqcup \vec{c}_2 \rangle \\
&\qquad \textbf{else let } [i, v_1, \ldots, v_\ell] = d_1 \textbf{ in} \\
&\qquad \textbf{if } \ell + 1 < k \textbf{ then } \langle [i, v_1, \ldots, v_\ell, d_2], \vec{c}_1 \sqcup \vec{c}_2 \rangle \\
&\qquad \textbf{else } \langle \mathit{lookup}_i(\langle v_1, \ldots, v_\ell, d_2 \rangle, \psi), \\
&\qquad\qquad \vec{c}_1 \sqcup \vec{c}_2 \sqcup \mathit{only}_i(\langle v_1, \ldots, v_\ell, d_2 \rangle) \rangle \\
&\mathbf{E}_m[\![\textbf{if } e_1 \textbf{ then } e_2 \textbf{ else } e_3]\!]\psi\rho = \\
&\qquad \textbf{let } \langle d_1, \vec{c}_1 \rangle = \mathbf{E}_m[\![e_1]\!]\psi\rho \\
&\qquad\qquad \langle d_2, \vec{c}_2 \rangle = \mathbf{E}_m[\![e_2]\!]\psi\rho \\
&\qquad\qquad \langle d_3, \vec{c}_3 \rangle = \mathbf{E}_m[\![e_3]\!]\psi\rho \textbf{ in} \\
&\qquad \textbf{if } d_1 = \mathit{true} \textbf{ then } \langle d_2, \vec{c}_1 \sqcup \vec{c}_2 \rangle \\
&\qquad \textbf{else if } d_1 = \mathit{false} \textbf{ then } \langle d_3, \vec{c}_1 \sqcup \vec{c}_3 \rangle \textbf{ else } \langle \bot, \vec{c}_1 \rangle
\end{aligned}
$$

$$
\begin{aligned}
&\mathbf{U}_m[\![f_1\ x_1 \cdots x_k = e_1 \quad \ldots \quad f_n\ x_1 \cdots x_k = e_n]\!]\vec{c} = \\
&\quad \mathbf{fix}\lambda\psi.\ \mathit{savecalls}(\vec{c}) \sqcup \\
&\qquad \langle \mathit{map}_1(\mathbf{E}_m[\![e_1]\!]\psi, \mathit{getcalls}(\psi)_1), \ldots, \\
&\qquad\ \ \mathit{map}_1(\mathbf{E}_m[\![e_n]\!]\psi, \mathit{getcalls}(\psi)_n) \rangle \sqcup \\
&\qquad \mathit{savecalls}(\mathit{map}_2(\mathbf{E}_m[\![e_1]\!]\psi, \mathit{getcalls}(\psi)_1)) \sqcup \cdots \sqcup \\
&\qquad \mathit{savecalls}(\mathit{map}_2(\mathbf{E}_m[\![e_n]\!]\psi, \mathit{getcalls}(\psi)_n))
\end{aligned}
$$

with $\mathit{lookup} : V^k \times \Psi \to V_\bot$ and $\mathit{only}_i : V^k \to C^n$

$$
\begin{aligned}
&\mathit{lookup}_i(\vec{v}, \psi) = \bigsqcup\{ r \mid \langle \vec{v}, r \rangle \in \psi_i \} \\
&\mathit{only}_i(\vec{v}) = \langle \underbrace{\emptyset, \ldots, \emptyset}_{i-1}, \{\vec{v}\}, \emptyset, \ldots, \emptyset \rangle \\
&\mathit{map}_1(f, s) = \{ \langle \vec{v}, r \rangle \mid \vec{v} \in s \wedge f(\vec{v}) = \langle r, \_ \rangle \} \\
&\mathit{map}_2(f, s) = \bigsqcup\{ c \mid \vec{v} \in s \wedge f(\vec{v}) = \langle \_, c \rangle \}
\end{aligned}
$$

In words the fixpoint computation says that the function environment should contain: all the original calls, results from functions with the arguments in the environment, and all new calls found when calling the functions with the arguments in the environment.

3.3 Safety

The two semantics may be proven equivalent in the sense that everything that may be computed by either semantics may also be computed by the other. This may be expressed as

$$\forall p, \vec{v}, j.(\mathbf{U}_c[\![p]\!])_j(\vec{v}) = lookup_j(\vec{v}, \mathbf{U}_m[\![p]\!]only_j(\vec{v}))$$

This may be done as for the first-order case in [5] where also the stronger condition that the minimal function graph semantics only contains the needed computations is proved. The proofs are included in an extended version of this paper.

4 Closure analysis

As an example of how one may use this semantics in program analysis we will here sketch a closure analysis for the language. A closure analysis will for each use of a functional expression compute a superset (usually small) of the user defined functions that the expression may yield as value. The result of a closure analysis provides control-flow information which may greatly simplify later data-flow analyses of such higher-order languages. A closure analysis for a strict language was first constructed by Peter Sestoft [6]. He later extended the work to a lazy language in his PhD thesis. Closure analysis is central to the working of the Similix partial evaluator [1], and was independently rediscovered by Shivers [7].

4.1 Abstract closures

An abstract closure is a pair of a function identification in $\{1, \ldots, n\}$ and a number of provided arguments $\{0, \ldots, k-1\}$. An abstract value is either a set of abstract closures or the symbol $\underline{atom}$ denoting that the value is of base type. The domain of abstract values will be denoted $\tilde{V}$.

$$\tilde{V} = \mathcal{P}(\{\underline{atom}\} \cup (\{1, \ldots, n\} \times \{0, \ldots, k-1\}))$$

An abstract closure will then no longer contain information about values of arguments to partially applied functions. This information may, however, be retrieved from a function environment so an abstract closure $[i, j]$ denotes the set of all closures built from the ith function with j arguments whose descriptions may in turn be found in the function environment. More formally we define the domain of abstract function environments to be

$$\tilde{\Psi} = (\tilde{V}^k \times \tilde{V})$$

4.2 Relating abstract and concrete closures

The concretisation function is of functionality

$$\gamma : \tilde{\Psi} \times \tilde{V} \rightarrow \mathcal{P}(V)$$

and may be defined as the least function satisfying:

$$\gamma(\psi', S) = \bigcup_{[i,j] \in S} \{[i, v_1, \ldots, v_j] \mid v_1 \in \gamma(\psi', \psi'_i \downarrow 1), \ldots, v_j \in \gamma(\psi', \psi'_i \downarrow j)\}$$

for $\psi' \in \tilde{\Psi}^n$.

As the concretisation function depends on two arguments there will be two abstraction functions: a function generating abstract function environments and a function returning abstract closures.

$$\begin{aligned}
&\alpha_1([i, v_1, \ldots, v_j]) = \\
&\quad \langle \underbrace{\langle\langle\emptyset, \ldots, \emptyset\rangle, \emptyset\rangle, \ldots,}_{i-1} \langle\langle\alpha_2(v_1), \ldots, \alpha_2(v_j), \emptyset, \ldots\rangle, \emptyset\rangle, \langle\langle\emptyset, \ldots, \emptyset\rangle, \emptyset\rangle, \ldots\rangle \\
&\quad \sqcup \alpha_1(v_1) \sqcup \cdots \sqcup \alpha_1(v_j) \\
&\alpha_2([i, v_1, \ldots, v_j]) = \{[i, j]\}
\end{aligned}$$

The abstraction and concretisation functions may be extended to base values by the definitions $\gamma(\psi', \underline{atom}) = Base$ for any ψ' and $\alpha_2(c) = \underline{atom}$ for $c \in Base$. The functions α_1 and α_2 may further be extended to $\mathcal{P}(V)$ as the $\sqcup$ and $\cup$-closure, respectively so that we have the functionalities

$$\begin{aligned}
\gamma \ &: \tilde{\Psi} \times \tilde{V} \to \mathcal{P}(V) \\
\alpha_1 &: \mathcal{P}(V) \to \tilde{\Psi} \\
\alpha_2 &: \mathcal{P}(V) \to \tilde{V}
\end{aligned}$$

which constitutes a Galois connection between $\tilde{\Psi} \times \tilde{V}$ and $\mathcal{P}(V)$.

$$\begin{array}{ll}
\alpha_1(\gamma(\psi', v')) \sqsubseteq \psi' & \psi' \in \tilde{\Psi}, \quad v' \in \tilde{V} \\
\alpha_2(\gamma(\psi', v')) \subseteq v' & \psi' \in \tilde{\Psi}, \quad v' \in \tilde{V} \\
v \subseteq \gamma(\alpha_1(v), \alpha_2(v)) & v \in \mathcal{P}(V)
\end{array}$$

4.3 Closure analysis

The closure analysis should map a program into an abstract function environment which safely approximates the minimal function graph interpretation.

$$\begin{aligned}
\tilde{\mathsf{E}}[\![e]\!] &: \tilde{\Psi}^n \to \tilde{V}^k \to \tilde{V} \times (\tilde{V}^k)^n \\
\tilde{\mathsf{U}}[\![p]\!] &: (\tilde{V}^k)^n \to (\tilde{V}^k \times \tilde{V})^n
\end{aligned}$$

$$\begin{array}{ll}
\tilde{\mathsf{E}}[\![x_i]\!]\psi\rho = & \langle \rho_i, \emptyset^n \rangle \\
\tilde{\mathsf{E}}[\![f_i]\!]\psi\rho = & \langle \{[i, 0]\}, \emptyset^n \rangle \\
\tilde{\mathsf{E}}[\![a_j(e_1, \ldots, e_k)]\!]\psi\rho = & \mathbf{let}\ \langle d_i, c_i \rangle = \tilde{\mathsf{E}}[\![e_i]\!]\psi\rho\ \mathbf{for}\ i = 1, \ldots, k\ \mathbf{in} \\
& \mathbf{if}\ \underline{atom} \notin d_i\ \mathbf{for\ some}\ i\ \mathbf{then}\ \langle \emptyset, c_1 \sqcup \cdots \sqcup c_k \rangle \\
& \mathbf{else}\ (\{\underline{atom}\}, c_1 \sqcup \cdots \sqcup c_k) \\
\tilde{\mathsf{E}}[\![e_1(e_2)]\!]\psi\rho = & \mathbf{let}\ \langle d_1, c_1 \rangle = \tilde{\mathsf{E}}[\![e_1]\!]\psi\rho\ \mathbf{and} \\
& \qquad \langle d_2, c_2 \rangle = \tilde{\mathsf{E}}[\![e_2]\!]\psi\rho\ \mathbf{in} \\
& (\bigcup_{[i,j] \in d_1} \{\mathbf{if}\ j = k - 1\ \mathbf{then}\ lookup'_i(\psi)\ \mathbf{else}\ [i, j+1]\}, \\
& \bigsqcup_{[i,j] \in d_1} only_i(\underbrace{\bot, \ldots, \bot,}_{j} d2, \bot, \ldots))
\end{array}$$

$$\begin{array}{ll}
\multicolumn{2}{l}{\tilde{\mathsf{E}}[\![\mathbf{if}\ e_1\ \mathbf{then}\ e_2\ \mathbf{else}\ e_3]\!]\psi\rho =} \\
& \mathbf{let}\ \langle d_1, c_1 \rangle = \tilde{\mathsf{E}}[\![e_1]\!]\psi\rho \\
& \qquad \langle d_2, c_2 \rangle = \tilde{\mathsf{E}}[\![e_2]\!]\psi\rho \\
& \qquad \langle d_3, c_3 \rangle = \tilde{\mathsf{E}}[\![e_3]\!]\psi\rho\ \mathbf{in} \\
& \mathbf{if}\ \underline{atom} \in d_1\ \mathbf{then}\ \langle d_2 \cup d_3, c_1 \sqcup c_2 \sqcup c_3 \rangle \\
& \mathbf{else}\ (\emptyset, c_1)
\end{array}$$

$$\tilde{\mathbf{U}}[\![f_1\ x_1\cdots x_k = e_1 \quad \ldots \quad f_n\ x_1\cdots x_k = e_n]\!]\tilde{c} =$$
$$\mathbf{fix}\lambda\psi.\,savecalls'(\tilde{c}) \sqcup$$
$$\langle map'_1(\mathbf{E}_m[\![e_1]\!]\psi, getcalls'(\psi)\downarrow 1), \ldots,$$
$$map'_1(\mathbf{E}_m[\![e_n]\!]\psi, getcalls'(\psi)\downarrow n\rangle \sqcup$$
$$savecalls'(map'_2(\mathbf{E}_m[\![e_1]\!]\psi, getcalls'(\psi)\downarrow 1)) \sqcup \cdots \sqcup$$
$$savecalls'(map'_2(\mathbf{E}_m[\![e_n]\!]\psi, getcalls'(\psi)\downarrow n))$$

with

$$lookup'_i(\psi) = \mathbf{let}\ \langle\langle v_1, \ldots, v_k\rangle, v_r\rangle = \psi \downarrow i\ \mathbf{in}\ v_r$$
$$only'_i(\vec{v}) = \langle \underbrace{\emptyset^k, \ldots, \emptyset^k}_{i-1}, \vec{v}, \emptyset^k, \ldots\rangle$$
$$map'_1(f, \vec{v}) = \langle \vec{v}, f(\vec{v}) \downarrow 1\rangle$$
$$map'_2(f, \vec{v}) = f(\vec{v}) \downarrow 2$$
$$savecalls'(\langle \vec{v}_1, \ldots, \vec{v}_n\rangle) = \langle\langle \vec{v}_1, \emptyset\rangle, \ldots, \langle \vec{v}_n, \emptyset\rangle\rangle$$
$$getcalls'(\langle\langle \vec{v}_1, r_1\rangle, \ldots, \langle \vec{v}_n, r_n\rangle\rangle) = \langle \vec{v}_1, \ldots, \vec{v}_n\rangle$$

4.4 Example

Consider the factorial function written in continuation passing style:

$$f\ n\ k \quad = \mathbf{if}\ n = 0\ \mathbf{then}\ k\ 1\ \mathbf{else}\ f\ (n-1)\ (m\ n\ k)$$
$$m\ n\ k\ x = k(n * x)$$
$$id\ x \quad = x$$
$$fac\ x \quad = f\ x\ id$$

The initial call description states that only the factorial function fac can be called externally and that its argument will be a base value. We will in this example use function names for function identification in closures. The initial call will then be: $only'_{fac}(\langle \underline{atom}\rangle)$ The closure analysis computes the following function environment:

$$f: \quad \langle\{\underline{atom}\}, \{[id, 0], [m, 2]\}, \{\underline{atom}\}\rangle$$
$$m: \quad \langle\{\underline{atom}\}, \{[id, 0], [m, 2]\}, \{\underline{atom}\}, \{\underline{atom}\}\rangle$$
$$id: \quad \langle\{\underline{atom}\}, \{\underline{atom}\}\rangle$$
$$fac: \langle\{\underline{atom}\}, \{\underline{atom}\}\rangle$$

The second argument to the functions f and m will either be id with no further arguments or k with two arguments.

4.5 Example

Consider the tautology function from the introduction

$$f \qquad = taut\ g\ 2$$
$$g\ x\ y \quad = x \wedge \neg y$$
$$taut\ h\ n \ = h, \quad \mathbf{if}\ n = 0$$
$$= taut\ (h\ true)\ (n-1) \wedge taut\ (h\ false)\ (n-1), \quad \mathbf{otherwise}$$

The initial call description states that only the function f may be called externally. With this the closure analysis computes the following function environment:

$$\begin{array}{ll} f: & \langle\{\underline{atom}\}\rangle \\ g: & \langle\{\underline{atom}\},\{\underline{atom}\},\{\underline{atom}\}\rangle \\ taut: & \langle\{[g,0],[g,1],\underline{atom}\},\{\underline{atom}\},\{\underline{atom}\}\rangle \end{array}$$

4.6 Safety

The safety condition states that the closure analysis from a call description will compute a superset of the set of closures that an expression may yield as value. More formally we extend the abstraction function to call descriptions α_c and function environments α_ψ :

$$\alpha_c : C^n \to (\tilde{V}^k)^n \qquad \text{or } (\mathcal{P}(V^k))^n \to (\tilde{V}^k)^n$$
$$\alpha_c(\langle c_1,\ldots,c_n\rangle) = \langle\langle \alpha_2(\{\rho_1 \mid \rho \in c_1\}),\ldots,\alpha_2(\{\rho_k \mid \rho \in c_1\}),\ldots\rangle$$

$$\alpha_\psi : \Psi^n \to \tilde{\Psi} \qquad \text{or } (\mathcal{P}(V^k \times V_\perp))^n \to (\tilde{V}^k \times \tilde{V})^n$$
$$\begin{aligned} &\alpha_\psi(\langle\psi_1,\ldots,\psi_n\rangle) = \\ &\quad \langle\langle\langle \alpha_2(\{\rho_1 \mid \langle\rho,r\rangle \in \psi_1\}),\ldots,\alpha_2(\{\rho_k \mid \langle\rho,r\rangle \in \psi_1\}), \\ &\qquad\qquad \alpha_2(\{\rho_k \mid \langle\rho,r\rangle \in \psi_1 \wedge r \neq \perp\}),\ldots\rangle \\ &\quad \sqcup \bigsqcup_{\langle\langle v_1,\ldots,v_k\rangle,v_r\rangle \in \psi_i} (\alpha_1(v_1) \sqcup \cdots \sqcup \alpha_1(v_k) \sqcup \alpha_1(v_r)) \end{aligned}$$

Global safety The global safety condition states that the semantic function $\tilde{\mathbf{U}}$ from a safe description of initial calls will compute a safe description of argument and result closures for the functions.

$$\forall c' \in (\tilde{V}^k)^n, \vec{c} \in C^n.\ \alpha_c(\vec{c}) \sqsubseteq c' \Rightarrow \alpha_\psi(\mathbf{U}_m[\![p]\!]\vec{c}) \sqsubseteq \tilde{\mathbf{U}}[\![p]\!]c'$$

Local safety Given function and parameter environments

$$\begin{array}{ll} \rho \in V^k & \rho' \in \tilde{V}^k \\ \psi \in \Psi^n & \psi' \in \tilde{\Psi}^n \end{array}$$

where

$$\begin{array}{ll} \alpha_2(\rho_i) \sqsubseteq \rho'_i & i \in \{1,\ldots,k\} \\ \multicolumn{2}{l}{\alpha_\psi(\psi) \sqcup \alpha_1(\rho_1) \sqcup \cdots \sqcup \alpha_1(\rho_k) \sqsubseteq \psi'} \end{array}$$

the safety condition for the semantic function $\tilde{\mathbf{E}}$ is

$$\alpha_2(\{\mathbf{E}_m[\![e]\!]\psi\rho \downarrow 1\} \setminus \{\perp\}) \subseteq \tilde{\mathbf{E}}[\![e]\!]\psi'\rho' \downarrow 1$$
$$\alpha_c(\mathbf{E}_m[\![e]\!]\psi\rho \downarrow 2) \sqsubseteq \tilde{\mathbf{E}}[\![e]\!]\psi'\rho' \downarrow 2$$

for any expression e.

The safety proof is based on structural induction over expressions and fixpoint induction. The proof may be found in the extended version of this paper.

5 Conclusion

The paper describes a minimal function graph semantics for a higher order strict functional language. The semantics is related to a closure semantics for the language. The minimal function graph semantics may be used as a basis for program analysis. This is illustrated by the construction of a closure analysis for the language.

Acknowledgement. The work was supported in part by the Danish Research Council under the DART project.

References

1. A Bondorf. *Similix user manual.* Tech. Report. Univ. of Copenhagen, Denmark, 1993.
2. G L Burn, C L Hankin, and S Abramsky. Strictness analysis for higher-order functions. *Sci. Comp. Prog.*, 7:249–278, 1986.
3. P Cousot and R Cousot. *Static determination of dynamic properties of recursive procedures.* In Formal Description of Programming Concepts (E J Neuhold, ed.). North-Holland, 1978.
4. N D Jones and A Mycroft. *Data Flow Analysis of Applicative Programs using Minimal Function Graphs.* In 13th POPL, St. Petersburg, Florida, pp. 296–306, Jan., 1986.
5. A Mycroft and M Rosendahl. *Minimal Function Graphs are not instrumented.* In WSA'92, Bordeaux, France, pp. 60–67. Bigre. Irisa Rennes, France, Sept., 1992.
6. P Sestoft. *Replacing Function Parameters by Global Variables.* M.Sc. Thesis 88-7-2. DIKU, Univ. of Copenhagen, Denmark, Oct., 1988.
7. O Shivers. *Control flow analysis in Scheme.* In SIGPLAN '88 Conference on PLDI, Atlanta, Georgia, pp. 164–174. Volume 23(7) of ACM SIGPLAN Not., July, 1988.

Reasoning about Layered, Wildcard and Product Patterns

Delia Kesner

CNRS and LRI
Bât 490, Université de Paris-Sud
91405 Orsay Cedex
France
e-mail:Delia.Kesner@lri.fr

Abstract

We study the extensional version of the simply typed λ-calculus with product types and fixpoints enriched with *layered*, *wildcard* and *product patterns*. Extensionality is expressed by the surjective pairing axiom and a generalization of the η-conversion to patterns. We obtain a *confluent* reduction system by turning the extensional axioms as *expansion* rules, and then adding some restrictions to these expansions in order to avoid reduction loops. Confluence is proved by composition of modular properties of the extensional and non-extensional subsystems of the reduction calculus.

1 Introduction

Pattern-matching function definitions is one of the most popular features of functional languages, allowing to specify the behavior of functions by cases, according to the form of their arguments. Left-hand sides of function definitions are usually expressed using *Layered, Wildcard* and *Product Patterns* (LWPP), as for example the following Caml Light [ea93] program where the function `cons_new_pair` takes any pair (m_1, m_2) of type `'a * 'b` and yields the pair $(m_1, (m_1, m_2))$:

```
# let cons_new_pair = function (y,_) as z -> (y,z) ;;

cons_new_pair : 'a * 'b -> 'a * ('a * 'b) = <fun>
```

The previous declaration can be written in the calculus we are studying in this paper, called the LWPP calculus, that is just the simply typed lambda calculus with product types and fixpoints, enriched with layered, wildcard and product patterns. These pattern constructors allow to make abstractions of functions not only with respect to variables, but also with respect to patterns, specifying in this way the form of the arguments of a function. Other formalisms for λ-calculi with nested patterns can be found in [vO90, Jon87, How92, BTKP93]. In particular, the LWPP calculus can also be viewed as a sub-calculus of the Typed Pattern Calculus (TPC) that was recently proposed in [BTKP93]. More precisely, the LWPP calculus can be encoded in the TPC following standard techniques: this last one is designed in the spirit of the Curry-Howard isomorphism as a computational interpretation of the Gentzen sequent proofs system for intuitionistic propositional logic, and so the application and projection constructors of the LWPP calculus are encoded in the TPC following the usual translation of natural deduction proofs into sequent proofs. See [Kes93] for details.

There is anyway something else that one likes to do with programs modeled by λ-calculi besides using λ-terms as programs to be computed: one would like to *reason* about programs, to *prove* that they enjoy certain properties and to *identify* expressions having the same meaning. For example, there are *at least* three ways to write the previous function `cons_new_pair` in the LWPP calculus:

Example 1.1

(1) $\lambda\langle x,y\rangle : A\times B.\langle x,\langle x,y\rangle\rangle$ (2) $\lambda x : A\times B.\langle \pi_1(x), x\rangle$ (3) $\lambda x@\langle y,\ \_\rangle : A\times B.\langle y,x\rangle$

Here is where conversion rules and extensional equalities come into play. In the case of the λ-calculus, there is deep correspondence between its axiomatic and operational semantics and the reduction rules may be derived by orienting each equational axiom. The choice to turn the equalities into rules has to be computationally reasonable and the reduction system has to be confluent. In this way the reduction rules play at the same time the rôle of a natural model of execution and a decision method for equational provability.

By far, the best known extensional equalities in the theory of typed λ-calculus are the (η) and (sp) axioms. They are essential to prove properties about pairs and functions.

The traditional (η) axiom for arrow types, is written in the λ-calculus formalism as follows:

$$(\eta) \qquad \lambda x : A.Mx = M \qquad \text{provided } x \text{ is not free in } M$$

Now, the existence of patterns in the scope of lambda abstractions suggests a natural extension of the (η)-axiom in order to express equalities between pattern abstractions [CCMS86]. The new axiom is called $(\widehat{\eta})$-axiom:

$$(\widehat{\eta}) \qquad \lambda P : A.MP = M \text{ provided } \begin{cases} P \text{ contains only variables and pairs} \\ \text{the variables of } P \text{ are not free in } M \end{cases}$$

On the other hand, there is also an extensional rule for pairs, called *surjective pairing*, which is the analog for product types of the usual (η)-axiom for arrow types, and can be specified by the equality:

$$(sp) \qquad \langle \pi_1(M), \pi_2(M) \rangle = M$$

where π_1 and π_2 are the first and second projection functions.

Note that the $\widehat{\eta}$-equality implies the categorical uniqueness of the product type as we can show $\langle fst\ z, snd\ z \rangle = z$, for $fst \equiv \lambda\langle x, y\rangle.x$ and $snd \equiv \lambda\langle x, y\rangle.y$. We refer the reader to [CCMS86] for details.

When one wants to turn these equalities into rules, there are two different choices. When turning them from left to right as *contractions*, they just state that a term $\langle \pi_1(M), \pi_2(M) \rangle$ is more complex than M and a term $\lambda x.Mx$ is more complex than M. Otherwise, the equalities can be turned as *expansions*, and they state that a term M of arrow type must really be a function, built by λ-abstraction, and a term M of product type has to be really a pair, built via the pair constructor.

The (η) and the (sp) axioms have traditionally been turned into contractions carrying the same name. Such an interpretation is well behaved in the simply typed λ-calculus as it preserves confluence [Pot81].

But surprisingly, recursion together with the (sp)-axiom oriented as contraction causes confluence to fail [Nes89]. Moreover, the contractive interpretation of the $(\widehat{\eta})$-axiom for patterns breaks confluence, as the following example shows:

Example 1.2

$$\lambda\langle x, y\rangle : A \times B.\langle x, y\rangle \xleftarrow{\beta} \lambda\langle x, y\rangle : A \times B.(\lambda z : A \times B.z)\langle x, y\rangle \xrightarrow{\widehat{\eta}} \lambda z : A \times B.z$$

Both terms $\lambda\langle x, y\rangle : A \times B.\langle x, y\rangle$ and $\lambda z : A \times B.z$ are in normal form and they are different, so the previous diagram cannot be closed.

This inconvenient can be fortunately overcome in the LWPP calculus by turning the extensional equalities into *expansion* rules. The idea was suggested by Prawitz [Pra71] in the field of proof theory, and further studied by Huet [Hue76] in the field of higher order unification, and by Mints [Min79] who was motivated by problems in category theory. But expansions seem however to have passed unnoticed for a long time, until these last two years, where many extensional λ-calculi (without patterns) have been investigated [Jay92, JG92, Cub92, Dou93, Aka93, DCK93a].

Mainly inspired by [Aka93, DCK93a], we use *expansion* rules to provide a *confluent* reduction system for the extensional typed pattern calculus with layered, wildcard and product patterns equipped with fixpoints and product types. In particular, our system allows to rewrite *any* function $\lambda P : A.M$ into another function $\lambda P' : A.M'$ such that the pattern P' contains only variables and pairs. This corresponds to the fact that wildcard and layered patterns are *redundant* but gives at the same time another interpretation: we can discard at compile time such redundant patterns (using our reduction system) as a form of optimization of programs that will be then evaluated by simpler computation rules.

Our reduction system may be regarded as an ideal (non-deterministic) implementation that allows to study arbitrary evaluation orders. We give however in the appendix A two evaluators, lazy and eager, and we refer the reader to [BTKP93] for more details about particular implementations of the Typed Pattern Calculus. We show that our reduction system is adequate for the axiomatic theory, *i.e*, that we do not loose equalities by the reduction relation. In particular, we can prove the three functions of example 1.1 to be equal since they have all the same normal form.

We show the confluence of the full system by a divide and conquer lemma that requires different properties: the confluence of the system without expansions (relation noted $\stackrel{B}{\Longrightarrow}$), the confluence and strong normalization of the system having only expansions (noted $\stackrel{E}{\Longrightarrow}$) and the property of *preservation of E-normal forms*: every time that a term M reduces to a term N in the system without expansions, then there is a non-empty $\stackrel{B}{\Longrightarrow}$-reduction sequence from the E-normal form of M to the E-normal form of N. This technique clarifies the relation between the reduction $\stackrel{B}{\Longrightarrow}$ and E-normalization and have also an independent interest since the explicit description of E-normal forms helps to understand the behavior of expansions in a pattern framework.

We introduce now the typing rules (section 2.1), the equalities (section 2.2) and the reduction system (section 2.3). We study the main properties of the reduction relations in section 3: confluence of $\stackrel{B}{\Longrightarrow}$ (section 3.1), strong normalization and confluence of $\stackrel{E}{\Longrightarrow}$ (section 3.2) and preservation of E-normal forms (section 3.3). We conclude with ideas for further work. Since we cannot go into all the details of the proofs by lack of space, we include as appendices the proofs that are mainly related to the expansionary interpretation of extensional rules in a pattern framework, and we refer the interested reader to [Kes93] for full details.

2 The Calculus

2.1 Terms and Types

It is now time to introduce the calculus LWPP. The set of *types* of our calculus is the least set containing a denumerable set of base types (as for example natural numbers and booleans), and closed w.r.t. formation of function and product types, *i.e*, if A and B are types, then also $A \rightarrow B$ and $A \times B$ are types.

In order to introduce the syntax of patterns and terms, we first fix a denumerable set of variables $\{x, y, z, \ldots\}$. The well-typed terms are given by the set of *typing judgements* in figure 1 which have the form $\Gamma \triangleright M : A$ where Γ, called a *pattern type assignment*, is a set of elements of the form $P : A$. Intuitively, the judgement $P_1 : A_1 \ldots P_n : A_n \triangleright M : A$ means that if patterns $P_1 \ldots P_n$ have types $A_1 \ldots A_n$ (respectively), then M is a well-typed term of type A.

Variables are typed by the following *axiom*:

$$x_1 : A_1, \ \ldots, \ x_n : A_n \triangleright x_i : A_i \quad (1 \leq i \leq n)$$

where the x_j's are pairwise distinct.

And terms are typed by the following *rules*:

Left rules :

$(\times left)$	If Γ, $P_1 : A_1$, $P_2 : A_2 \triangleright M : B$,	then Γ, $\langle P_1, P_2\rangle : A_1 \times A_2 \triangleright M : B$
$(layered)$	If Γ, $P_1 : A$, $P_2 : A \triangleright M : B$,	then Γ, $P_1 @ P_2 : A \triangleright M : B$
$(wildcard)$	If $\Gamma \triangleright M : B$,	then Γ, $\_ : A \triangleright M : B$

Right rules :

$(\times right)$	If $\Gamma \rhd M_1 : A_1 \quad \Gamma \rhd M_2 : A_2$,	then $\Gamma \rhd \langle M_1, M_2\rangle : A_1 \times A_2$
(app)	If $\Gamma \rhd M : A \to B \quad \Gamma \rhd N : A$,	then $\Gamma \rhd (MN) : B$
(abs)	If $\Gamma,\ P : A \rhd M : B$,	then $\Gamma \rhd \lambda P : A.M : A \to B$
$(proj_1)$	If $\Gamma \rhd M : A \times B$,	then $\Gamma \rhd \pi_1(M) : A$
$(proj_2)$	If $\Gamma \rhd M : A \times B$,	then $\Gamma \rhd \pi_2(M) : B$
$(recursion)$	If $\Gamma,\ x : A \rhd M : A$,	then $\Gamma \rhd \mu x : A.M : A$

Figure 1: Typing Rules for the LWPP Calculus

We use the left rules $(\times left)$, $(layered)$ and $(wildcard)$ to introduce patterns that correspond to devices long used in programming languages, and the right rules to introduce the terms of typed lambda calculus. The (abs) rule allows to abstract a function with respect to a pattern. The layered pattern $\_@\_$ introduced by the $(layered)$ rule is used to name in a unique way two different patterns of the same type and it corresponds to the construction *as* of ML, but here $P_1@P_2$ might contain any pattern P_1 and not just a variable. The pattern $\_$ introduced by the $(wildcard)$ rule is the usual wildcard pattern in ML and it denotes any possible argument, while the pattern $\langle P_1, P_2\rangle$ introduced by the $(\times left)$ rule is the usual product pattern (also called pair pattern).

We say that M is a well-typed term if there exists a pattern type assignment Γ and a type A such that $\Gamma \rhd M : A$ is either an axiom or follows from axioms by the application of the typing rules. We use the notion of *context* for terms with "holes", assuming that holes do not appear in the patterns of λ-abstractions. We write $C[\,]$ for a context and we use $C[M]$ to denote the context $C[\,]$ where all the holes are replaced by M. We may omit types of patterns in $\lambda-$abstractions when they are clear from the context writing $\lambda P.M$ instead of $\lambda P : A.M$.

Free and bound occurrences of variables are defined as usual with the understanding that a term of the form $\lambda P : A.M$ defines bindings whose scope is M for all the variables occurring in P. A pattern is said to be *linear* if variables can occur at most once in it (note that all the patterns that can be constructed using the rules in figure 1 are linear). We denote by $Var(P)$ the set of variables that occurs in the pattern P, by $FV(M)$ the set of free variables that occurs in the term M, by $BV(M)$ the set of bound variables in the term M, and by $\mathcal{P}(M)$ the set of *positions* of the term M. We write $[N_1, \ldots, N_n/x_1, \ldots, x_n]$ (often abbreviated $[\overline{N}/\overline{x}]$) for the typed substitution mapping each variable $x_i : A_i$ to a term $N_i : A_i$ and $M[\overline{N}/\overline{x}]$ for the term M where each variable x_i free in M is replaced by N_i. In what follows, for every substitution θ, we assume $Dom(\theta) \cap \bigcup_{x \in Dom(\theta)} FV(\theta(x)) = \emptyset$.

As opposed to the simply typed λ-calculus, here a judgement may have several derivations. However, this is not so problematic as the left rules $(layered)$, $(wildcard)$ and $(\times left)$ commute with all the other rules - they have the so-called *commutation property* - and therefore, for every *non-variable* term M there exists *exactly one* rule such that every judgement $\Gamma \rhd M : E$ has a derivation ending with the application of that rule. Indeed, for any judgement of a pair $\langle M, N\rangle$ there is a derivation ending with the $(\times left)$ rule, for any judgement of an abstraction $\lambda P : A.M$ there is a derivation ending with the (abs) rule, in the case of an application (MN) the associated rule is (app), for the recursion term $\mu x : A.M$ the associated rule is $(recursion)$, and finally the $(proj_i)$ rule corresponds to the terms of the form $\pi_i(M)$.

We only use patterns built from variables and the pair constructor in order to define the extensional equalities. For that, we introduce the notion of *specification* and *full specification* of a pattern P by a type A, writing $P :\cdot A$ and $P :: A$ respectively. The notion of specification avoids the association of non product types to pair patterns, and the notion of full specification, besides that, forbid the association of product types to variables, *i.e*, a full specified pattern has a product type if and only if it is a pair pattern. A similar notion is defined for terms.

Definition 2.1 (Specification of Patterns) For every variable x and every type A we have $x :\cdot A$ and, whenever $P_1 :\cdot A_1$ and $P_2 :\cdot A_2$, then $\langle P_1, P_2\rangle :\cdot A_1 \times A_2$.

Definition 2.2 (Full Specification of Patterns) For every variable x and every non product type A we have $x :: A$ and, whenever $P_1 :: A_1$ and $P_2 :: A_2$, then $\langle P_1, P_2\rangle :: A_1 \times A_2$.

Definition 2.3 (Full Specification of Terms) A term M is *fully specified* if M is fully specified by its type, and M is *fully specified* by a type A if and only if M is of type A and they correspond to one of the following cases:

- If $M \neq \langle M_1, M_2 \rangle$ and $A \neq A_1 \times A_2$, then $M :: A$
- If $M_1 :: A_1$ and $M_2 :: A_2$, then $\langle M_1, M_2 \rangle :: A_1 \times A_2$.

Example 2.4 Let A and B be two base type, z and $\langle x, y \rangle$ be two patterns, and $\pi_1(w)$ and $\langle \pi_1(w), z \rangle$ two terms. Then $z :\cdot A \times B$ and $\langle x, y \rangle :\cdot A \times B$ but $z \not:\cdot A \times B$ and $\langle x, y \rangle \not:\cdot A$. In the case of terms, suppose that w is of type $A \times B$ and z is of type B. Then $\pi_1(w) :: A$ and $\langle \pi_1(w), z \rangle :: A \times B$, but $w \not:: A \times B$ and $\langle w, z \rangle \not:: A$.

It is clear that a fully specified pattern is also a specified pattern and whenever a term M is fully specified by a type A and σ is a well-typed substitution, then $N[\sigma]$ is also fully specified by A.

2.2 Equalities

First of all we define a function $Match(M, P)$ on every term M and every pattern P that allows to generalize the usual β rule to the case of patterns. This function explains clearly the operational semantics of layered, wildcard and product patterns by the notion of matching substitution, which is defined as follows:

$$\begin{array}{lll}
Match(N, _) & = \emptyset & \\
Match(N, x) & = [N/x] & \\
Match(N, P_1 @ P_2) & = Match(N, P_1) \cup Match(N, P_2) & \\
Match(\langle N_1, N_2 \rangle, \langle P_1, P_2 \rangle) & = Match(N_1, P_1) \cup Match(N_2, P_2) & \\
Match(M, P) & = \mathbf{fail} & \text{Otherwise}
\end{array}$$

Note that $Match(\_, \_)$ is well-defined in terms of the operation $\cup$ because all patterns are linear according to the typing rules in figure 1. Using this definition we can show the existence of matching substitutions between fully specified terms and specified patterns, and also, that the substitution lemma holds for our calculus.

Lemma 2.5 *If P is a pattern such that $P :\cdot A$ and N is a term such that $N :: A$, then there is a substitution σ such that $Match(N, P) = \sigma$ and $\sigma(P) = N$.*

Lemma 2.6 (Substitution Lemma)
If $\Gamma, P : C \rhd M : A$, $\Gamma \rhd N : C$ and $Match(N, P) = \theta$, then $\Gamma \rhd M[\theta] : A$.

We are now able to define the equalities between terms of our calculus. The α-conversion is the most natural one, it allows to rename bound variables. If ψ is a renaming substitution, the α-equality for λ-abstractions corresponds to the equation:

$$(\alpha) \qquad \lambda P : A.M =_\alpha \lambda P[\psi] : A.M[\psi], \text{ where } \left\{ \begin{array}{l} Var(P[\psi]) \cap (FV(M) - Var(P)) = \emptyset \\ Var(P[\psi]) \cap BV(M) = \emptyset \end{array} \right.$$

For example, $\lambda\langle x, y \rangle.x =_\alpha \lambda\langle z, w \rangle.z$ and $\lambda x @ y.\langle x, y \rangle =_\alpha \lambda y @ x.\langle y, x \rangle$.
Besides α conversion, our calculus is equipped with the following equalities between terms:

$$\begin{array}{llll}
(\beta) & (\lambda P : A.M)N & =_\beta & M[\theta], \text{ If } Match(N, P) = \theta \\
(@) & (\lambda P_1 @ P_2 : A.M)N & =_@ & (\lambda\langle P_1, P_2 \rangle : A \times A.M)\langle N, N \rangle \\
(\pi_i) & \pi_i\langle M_1, M_2 \rangle & =_{\pi_i} & M_i, \text{ for } i = 1, 2 \\
(rec) & \mu x : C.M & =_{rec} & M[\mu x : C.M/x]
\end{array}$$

Axiom $(@)$ tells us that both terms $(\lambda P_1 @ P_2 : A.M)N$ and $(\lambda\langle P_1, P_2 \rangle : A \times A.M)\langle N, N \rangle$ have the same behavior (since $Match(N, P_1 @ P_2)$ and $Match(\langle N, N \rangle, \langle P_1, P_2 \rangle)$ yield the same substitution), and therefore, we can translate the first into the second one. However, the term $(\lambda P_1@P_2 : A.M)$ is completely different from $(\lambda\langle P_1, P_2\rangle : A \times A.M)$: the first one is an abstraction on just one argument that is denoted in two different ways, whereas the second one is an abstraction on two different arguments.

We define the conversion $=_{LWPP}$ as the least congruence containing $=_\alpha$, $=_\beta$, $=_@$, $=_{\pi_1}$, $=_{\pi_2}$ and $=_{rec}$.

Definition 2.7 (The LWPP calculus) The *LWPP calculus* is equipped with the typing rules in figure 1 and the conversion $=_{LWPP}$.

The following conversion axioms are the extensional rules of the LWPP calculus, where the axiom $\widehat{\eta}$ is the natural extension of the η-equality in the simply typed λ-calculus.

$$(\widehat{\eta}) \quad M =_{\widehat{\eta}} \lambda P : A.(MP) \quad \text{If} \begin{cases} Var(P) \cap FV(M) = \emptyset \\ M \text{ is of type } A \rightarrow B \\ P :\cdot A \end{cases}$$

$$(sp) \quad M =_{sp} \langle \pi_1(M), \pi_2(M)\rangle \quad \text{If } M \text{ is of type } A \times B$$

Definition 2.8 (The extensional calculus LWPP) The *extensional calculus LWPP* contains the typing rules in figure 1 and the conversion $\doteq$ defined as the $=_{LWPP}$ equality enriched with $=_{\widehat{\eta}}$ and $=_{sp}$.

2.3 The reduction system

While equations correspond to the axiomatic semantics of the calculus, reduction rules give the operational semantics as a form of symbolic computation, *i.e,* it models program execution. For that, a reduction system has to verify some general properties, as for example *confluence* and *uniqueness of normal forms.* It is well-known that the first property guarantees the second one, so we are left to insure confluence by means of an appropriate reduction system.

Traditionally, a reduction system is obtained from the equational one by simply orienting the equations in a convenient way. But this is not the case for our calculus, where a reduction system with good properties needs to be defined in a more delicate way.

In order to obtain a reduction system for the LWPP calculus we first turn the *non extensional rules* from left to right in the following way:

Definition 2.9 (The reduction relation $\overset{\beta,@,\pi_1,\pi_2,rec}{\longrightarrow}$)

$$\begin{array}{lrcl} (\beta) & (\lambda P : A.M)N & \longrightarrow & M[\theta], \text{ If } Match(N, P) = \theta \\ (@) & (\lambda P_1@P_2 : A.M)N & \longrightarrow & (\lambda\langle P_1, P_2\rangle : A \times A.M)\langle N, N\rangle \\ (\pi_i) & \pi_i(\langle M_1, M_2\rangle) & \longrightarrow & M_i \ (i = 1, 2) \\ (rec) & \mu x : C.M & \longrightarrow & M[\mu x : C.M/y] \end{array}$$

When turning the *extensional equalities* into reduction rules, the contractive choice breaks confluence (example 1.2) while the expansive choice breaks strong normalization (example 2.10).

Example 2.10

$$\langle M, N\rangle \rightsquigarrow \langle \pi_1(\langle M, N\rangle), \pi_2(\langle M, N\rangle)\rangle \rightsquigarrow \langle M, \pi_2(\langle M, N\rangle)\rangle \rightsquigarrow \langle M, N\rangle$$

Even if recursion gives a natural mechanism to produce non terminating sequences, we prefer to keep expansions as strongly normalizing rules to provide a characterization of $(\widehat{\eta}, sp)$-normal forms that are usually very useful when working with η-long normal forms in higher order unification. For that, strong normalization for extensional rules is recovered when some restrictions are imposed to them. In order to define an appropriate reduction system for our calculus let us analyze in detail all the loops generated by the arbitrary application of extensional rules turned as expansions.

There are two different situations in which such loops may arise, we call them *structural loops* and *contextual loops* respectively. Structural loops are caused by the application of an expansion rule to a term having a *structure* that is sufficiently specified, while contextual loops are caused by the application of an expansion rule to a subterm that appears in a particular *context*. Let us see all that in detail.

Structural Loops

The structural loop caused by *sp* expansions appears in the example 2.10 and can be avoided by forbidding expansions on terms that are yet pairs as follows:

Definition 2.11 (The reduction relation $\xrightarrow{sp}$)

$$(sp)\ M \xrightarrow{sp} \langle \pi_1(M), \pi_2(M)\rangle,\ \text{If} \begin{cases} M \text{ is of type } A \times B \\ M \text{ is not a pair} \end{cases}$$

Let see now the loops caused by the application of the $\widehat{\eta}$ expansion, and in particular let us start by a case that is also problematic in the typed λ-calculus:

$$\lambda x : A.M \leadsto \lambda x' : A.(\lambda x : A.M)x' \leadsto \lambda x' : A.M[x'/x] =_\alpha \lambda x : A.M$$

We can reproduce this situation in the presence of more complicated patterns, where the loop starts in a term having a pair as abstraction.

$$\lambda\langle x, y\rangle : A \times B.M \leadsto \lambda\langle x', y'\rangle : A \times B.(\lambda\langle x, y\rangle : A \times B.M)\langle x', y'\rangle \leadsto$$
$$\lambda\langle x', y'\rangle : A \times B.M[x'/x][y'/y] =_\alpha \lambda\langle x, y\rangle : A \times B.M$$

In general, each time M is a λ-abstraction $\lambda Q : A.N$, and it reduces via the $\widehat{\eta}$-rule to a term $\lambda P : A.(\lambda Q : A.N)P$, where the pattern P is "as specific as" Q (*i.e*, α-equivalent to Q), we can always perform a β step to close the loop. As a consequence, whenever an $\widehat{\eta}$ expansion is applied to a λ-abstraction $\lambda Q : A.N$, it has to introduce a pattern P strictly "less specific" or "more specific" than Q. This suggests that it is necessary to chose a canonical form of applying an $\widehat{\eta}$ expansion to λ-abstractions : either we always introduce less specific patterns, or we always use more specific ones.

But the interpretation of extensional equalities as expansions have the intention to capture as much information as possible: if a term is of product type, then it is a pair, and if a term is of functional type, then it is a λ-abstraction. It is then reasonable, according to our interpretation, to chose the largest patterns, and it is now that the notions of *specification* and *full specification* come into play. The general form of the $\widehat{\eta}$-rule is:

Definition 2.12 (The reduction relation $\xrightarrow{\widehat{\eta}}$)

$$(\widehat{\eta})\ M \xrightarrow{\widehat{\eta}} \lambda P : A.(MP),\ \text{If} \begin{cases} Var(P) \cap FV(M) = \emptyset \\ P :: A \\ M \text{ is of type type } A \to B \\ M = \lambda Q : A.N \text{ implies } Q \not\lhd A \end{cases}$$

We can immediately verify that all the loops that we have previously shown are now ruled out.

Contextual Loops

Now, let us analyze the contextual loops, that are produced by the application of expansions to subterms that are placed in particular positions of a term. For example, in the case of the *sp*-rule, a loop arises when applying the *sp* expansion to a term M that is the argument of a projection:

$$\pi_1(M) \leadsto \pi_1(\langle \pi_1(M), \pi_2(M)\rangle) \leadsto \pi_1(M)$$

In order to avoid this kind of loops, the *sp* expansions will not be allowed on terms that are projected.

We can also produce some contextual loops by applying an $\widehat{\eta}$ expansion to a term M that is applied to another term N of base type: indeed, $MN \rightsquigarrow (\lambda x.Mx)N \rightsquigarrow MN$.

In the presence of patterns the situation is more complex as the application of the $\widehat{\eta}$ expansion does not always cause a loop. Suppose for example that A and B are base types and let N be a term of type $A \times B$ but different from a pair. Then, $MN \rightsquigarrow (\lambda\langle z, w\rangle : A \times B.M\langle z, w\rangle)N$. However, if we take N to be a pair $\langle N_1, N_2\rangle$ we obtain:

$$M\langle N_1, N_2\rangle \rightsquigarrow (\lambda\langle z, w\rangle : A \times B.M\langle z, w\rangle)\langle N_1, N_2\rangle \rightsquigarrow M\langle N_1, N_2\rangle$$

In general, this situation corresponds to the case of a term M applied to another term L that is fully specified by its type (in the example $\langle N_1, N_2\rangle$ is fully specified by the type $A \times B$), and thus the term $\lambda P.MP$ coming from the application of the $(\widehat{\eta})$-rule to the term M, produces by lemma 2.5 a matching substitution θ such that $\theta(P) = L$. The loops starting at ML are of the form:

$$ML \rightsquigarrow (\lambda P.MP)L \rightsquigarrow ML$$

To break this kind of loops, we will also forbid an $\widehat{\eta}$ expansion on a subterm that is applied to a fully specified term.

In summary, the one-step reduction relation $\Longrightarrow$ cannot be defined as the least congruence on terms containing the relation $\longrightarrow$ above, as is done traditionally. We proceed as follows:

Definition 2.13 (Relation $\Longrightarrow$) The one-step reduction relation between terms, denoted $\Longrightarrow$, is defined to be the closure of the reduction rules $\beta, @, \pi_1, \pi_2, rec, \widehat{\eta}, sp$ for all the contexts *except* application and projection, *i.e*:

- If $M \Longrightarrow M'$, then $MN \Longrightarrow M'N$ except in the case where $M \xrightarrow{\eta} M'$ and N is fully specified.
- If $M \Longrightarrow M'$, then $\pi_i(M) \Longrightarrow \pi_i(M')$ for $i = 1, 2$ except in the case where $M \xrightarrow{sp} M'$

Notation 2.1 The transitive and the reflexive transitive closure of $\Longrightarrow$ are noted $\Longrightarrow^+$ and $\Longrightarrow^*$ respectively.

We will use some standard notions from the theory of rewriting system, such as redex, normal form, confluence, weak confluence, strong normalization, etc, without explicitly redefining them here.

Using lemma 2.6 and the commutation property, it is easy to show that the one-step reduction relation preserves types.

Theorem 2.14 (Subject Reduction) *If* $\Gamma \triangleright M : A$ *and* $M \Longrightarrow M'$, *then* $\Gamma \triangleright M' : A$

The following theorem states the redundancy of layered and wildcard patterns by means of our reduction system. Indeed, every pattern abstraction $\lambda P : A.M$ can be rewritten to a function $\lambda P' : A.M'$ such that P' contains only variables and pairs, and so we can show the following:

Theorem 2.15 (Redundancy of Layered and Wildcard Patterns) *Any term M can be reduced to a term M' which contains no layered and no wildcard patterns.*

Proof. See Appendix B.

□

Coming back to example 1.1, we can check the three terms to verify the property stated in theorem 2.15. Indeed, the property is trivial for $\lambda\langle x, y\rangle : A \times B.\langle x, \langle x, y\rangle\rangle$ and $\lambda x : A \times B.\langle \pi_1(x), x\rangle$ because they have no layered and no wildcard patterns, while for $\lambda x@\langle y, \_\rangle : A \times B.\langle y, x\rangle$ we have to perform the following reduction sequence:

$$\begin{array}{ll}
\lambda x@\langle y, _\rangle : A \times B.\langle y, x\rangle & \stackrel{\widehat{\eta}}{\Longrightarrow} \\
\lambda\langle w, z\rangle : A \times B.(\lambda x@\langle y, _\rangle : A \times B.\langle y, x\rangle)\langle w, z\rangle & \stackrel{@}{\Longrightarrow} \\
\lambda\langle w, z\rangle : A \times B.(\lambda\langle x, \langle y, _\rangle\rangle : (A \times B) \times (A \times B).\langle y, x\rangle)\langle\langle w, z\rangle, \langle w, z\rangle\rangle & \stackrel{\beta}{\Longrightarrow} \\
\lambda\langle w, z\rangle : A \times B.\langle w, \langle w, z\rangle\rangle &
\end{array}$$

The adequacy of expansions for extensional equalities comes from the following theorem, which states that the limitations imposed on the reduction system do not make us loose any valid equality as they are introduced exactly to avoid reduction loops.

Theorem 2.16 **($\Longrightarrow$ generates $\doteq$)** *$M \doteq N$ if and only if $M \stackrel{*}{\Longleftrightarrow} N$.*

Proof. See Appendix B.

□

Coming back again to example 1.1, the three terms can be proved to be equal using the reduction relation $\Longrightarrow$ as follows:

$$\begin{array}{llll}
\lambda x : A \times B.\langle \pi_1(x), x\rangle & \stackrel{\widehat{\eta}}{\Longrightarrow} & \lambda\langle w, z\rangle : A \times B.(\lambda x : A \times B.\langle \pi_1(x), x\rangle)\langle w, z\rangle & \stackrel{\beta}{\Longrightarrow} \\
\lambda\langle w, z\rangle : A \times B.\langle \pi_1(\langle w, z\rangle), \langle w, z\rangle\rangle & \stackrel{\pi_1}{\Longrightarrow} & \lambda\langle w, z\rangle : A \times B.\langle w, \langle w, z\rangle\rangle &
\end{array}$$

and as previously shown:

$$\lambda x@\langle y, \_\rangle : A \times B.\langle y, x\rangle \Longrightarrow^* \lambda\langle w, z\rangle : A \times B.\langle w, \langle w, z\rangle\rangle$$

3 Confluence of the extensional LWPP calculus

We have now to show that the relation $\Longrightarrow$ is confluent. Standard techniques for showing confluence of the typed λ-calculus will not work directly, because of the extensional expansions. To overcome this annoyance, we use a divide-and-conquer technique as in [Aka93]: we separate the reduction $\Longrightarrow$ in two reduction relations: $\stackrel{B}{\Longrightarrow}$ denotes the relation $\Longrightarrow$ generated only by $\stackrel{\beta,\pi_1,\pi_2,@,rec}{\longrightarrow}$ and $\stackrel{E}{\Longrightarrow}$ denotes the relation $\Longrightarrow$ generated only by $\stackrel{\widehat{\eta},sp}{\longrightarrow}$. The confluence property of $\Longrightarrow$ comes from the following proposition:

Proposition 3.1 *If*

1. *$\stackrel{B}{\Longrightarrow}$ is confluent*
2. *$\stackrel{E}{\Longrightarrow}$ is confluent and strongly normalizing*
3. *$\forall M, N \;\; M \stackrel{B}{\Longrightarrow} N$ implies $M^E \stackrel{B}{\Longrightarrow}{}^+ N^E$, where M^E and N^E are respectively the E-normal forms of M and N*

then the relation $\stackrel{E}{\Longrightarrow} \cup \stackrel{B}{\Longrightarrow}$ is confluent.

Proof. See for example [Har87].

□

Next sections discuss the techniques to prove the three properties required by the previous lemma: confluence of the relation $\stackrel{B}{\Longrightarrow}$, confluence and strong normalization of the relation $\stackrel{E}{\Longrightarrow}$, and the third property called *preservation of E-normal forms.*

3.1 Confluence of $\stackrel{B}{\Longrightarrow}$

The confluence property of $\stackrel{B}{\Longrightarrow}$ is shown by the Tait-Martin Löf's technique. The first step is to define a reduction relation $\blacktriangleright$ in order to capture *parallel* reduction, then to check that $\blacktriangleright$ enjoys the diamond property (which immediately implies confluence) and finally, to relate the reflexive-transitive closures of the relations $\blacktriangleright$ and $\stackrel{B}{\Longrightarrow}$. We start by defining the relation $\blacktriangleright$:

- $M \blacktriangleright M$
- If $M \blacktriangleright M'$, then $\pi_1(\langle M,N\rangle) \blacktriangleright M'$, $\pi_2(\langle N,M\rangle) \blacktriangleright M'$, $\mu x : A.M \blacktriangleright M'[\mu x : A.M'/x]$ and $C[M] \blacktriangleright C[M']$, where $C[\,]$ is a context $\lambda P.[\,]$, $\mu x : A.[\,]$ or $\pi_i([\,])$.
- If $M \blacktriangleright M'$ and $N \blacktriangleright N'$, then $\langle M,N\rangle \blacktriangleright \langle M',N'\rangle$, $MN \blacktriangleright M'N'$ and $(\lambda P : A.N)M \blacktriangleright N'[Match(M',P)]$ if $Match(M,P)$ is defined
- If $M \blacktriangleright M'$, $M \blacktriangleright M''$ and $N \blacktriangleright N'$, then $(\lambda P_1 @ P_2 : A.N)M \blacktriangleright (\lambda\langle P_1,P_2\rangle : A{\times}A.N')\langle M',M''\rangle$

The following lemma states that parallel reduction is stable by substitution and it plays an important rôle in the confluence proof.

Lemma 3.2 *If $M \blacktriangleright M'$, $N \blacktriangleright N'$ and $Match(N,P)$ is defined, then $M[Match(N,P)] \blacktriangleright M'[Match(N',P)]$*

Theorem 3.3 *The reduction relation $\stackrel{B}{\Longrightarrow}$ is confluent.*

Proof. By Tait-Martin Löf's technique: we first show the following three properties:

- The relation $\blacktriangleright$ satisfies the the diamond property (use lemma 3.2).
- A relation satisfying the diamond property is confluent.
- The reflexive transitive closures of $\blacktriangleright$ and $\stackrel{B}{\Longrightarrow}$ are the same relation.

We can now derive the confluence property of the relation $\stackrel{B}{\Longrightarrow}$ in terms of the confluence property of the relation $\blacktriangleright$.

□

3.2 Strong Normalization and Confluence of $\stackrel{E}{\Longrightarrow}$

We show in this section that the reduction relation $\stackrel{E}{\Longrightarrow}$ is strongly normalizing and confluent. For the strong normalization property, we adapt the proof of [Min79] for the typed λ-calculus. We assign to every term T a natural number $E(T)$ and we prove that $T \stackrel{E}{\Longrightarrow} T'$ implies $E(T) > E(T')$, which shows that $E(T)$ is an upper bound for the length of any $\stackrel{E}{\Longrightarrow}$-reduction sequence. We note $|A|$ the number of operations and base types in the type A.
For every $u \in \mathcal{P}(T)$:

$$D_T(u) = \begin{cases} 2^{\Sigma_{1 \le i \le n}|A_i|} & \text{If } T/u \text{ is an } E\text{-redex} \\ 1 & \text{Otherwise} \end{cases}$$

where $A_1 \ldots A_n$ are the types of E-redexes in T that contain T/u (even T/u and T)

For each $u \in \mathcal{P}(T)$ such that $u \neq \epsilon$:

$$C_T(u) = \begin{cases} 2^{\Sigma_{1 \le i \le n}|A_i|} & \text{If } T/u \text{ is an } E\text{-redex} \\ 1 & \text{Otherwise} \end{cases}$$

where $A_1 \ldots A_n$ are the types of E-redexes in T that are different from T and contain T/u.

To each term T we associate the natural number $E(T)$:

$$E(T) = \Sigma_{u \in \mathcal{RP}(T)} D_T(u), \text{ where } \mathcal{RP}(T) \text{ is the set of } E\text{-redexes positions in } T.$$

Theorem 3.4 *The relation $\stackrel{E}{\Longrightarrow}$ is strongly normalizing.*

Proof. We show that $E(M) > E(M')$ if $M \stackrel{E}{\Longrightarrow} M'$ by case-analysis and then induction on the structure of terms. See [Kes93] for details.

□

Theorem 3.5 *The relation $\stackrel{E}{\Longrightarrow}$ is confluent.*

Proof. Is a consequence of theorem 3.4 and Newman's lemma because the relation $\stackrel{E}{\Longrightarrow}$ is easily checked to be weakly confluent.

□

3.3 Characterization and Preservation of E-normal forms

An important property of a one-step expansion $M \stackrel{\widehat{\eta}}{\longrightarrow} M'$ or $M \stackrel{sp}{\longrightarrow} M'$ is that the term M appears as a subterm of the term M', *i.e,* M' is obtained by inserting M in a special *expansor context*[1], which represents the scheme of the expansion rules $\stackrel{\widehat{\eta}}{\longrightarrow}$ and $\stackrel{sp}{\longrightarrow}$. Let us see that on a simple example:

Example 3.6 Let z be a variable of type $A_1 \times A_2$, where the A_i's are base types. Applying a *sp*-expansion to z, we obtain its E-normal form $\langle \pi_1(z), \pi_2(z)\rangle$, that can be obtained by inserting the variable z in the holes of the context $\langle \pi_1([\,]), \pi_2([\,])\rangle$.

In the general case, there are many positions of a term M where an expansion can be performed, so the characterization of its E-normal form have to take into account the *structure* of M. In the previous example 3.6, to define the E-normal form of the term $\langle z, z\rangle$, each occurrence of the variable z has to be inserted in the holes of an expansor context but the pair itself does not. This is due to the fact that each occurrence of z in $\langle z, z\rangle$ is reducible by $\stackrel{sp}{\Longrightarrow}$ but the pair $\langle z, z\rangle$ is not reducible at the root position.

On the other hand, expansor contexts must be carefully defined to correctly represent not only the expansion step arising from a redex already present in M, but also all the expansion sequences that such step can create: if in the previous example A_1 is taken to be an arrow type and A_2 a product type, then the term $\pi_1(z)$ can be further $\widehat{\eta}$-expanded and the term $\pi_2(z)$ can be expanded by the *sp*-expansion. However, the expansor context $\langle \pi_1([\,]), \pi_2([\,])\rangle$ cannot simulate these further possible reductions. This can only be done by storing in the expansor contexts all the information on possible future expansions, that is fully contained in the *type* of the term we are marking.

Definition 3.7 (Expansor Contexts) We associate to every type C an *expansor context* $\Delta_C[\,]$, defined by induction on the size of C as follows:

$$\Delta_{A\to B}[\,] \;=\; \lambda P : A.\Delta_B[[\,]\widehat{P}], \text{ where } P :: A \text{ and } \widehat{P} = \begin{cases} \langle \widehat{P_1}, \widehat{P_2}\rangle & \text{If } P = \langle P_1, P_2\rangle \\ \Delta_A[P] & \text{Otherwise} \end{cases}$$

$$\Delta_{A\times B}[\,] \;=\; \langle \Delta_A[\pi_1[\,]], \Delta_B[\pi_2[\,]]\rangle$$

$\Delta_A[\,]$ is the empty context in any other case

We write $\Delta_A?[M]$ to denote either $\Delta_A[M]$ or M.

Definition 3.8 (Translation) For every term M of type A, its *translation* M° is defined as follows:

$$M^\circ = \begin{cases} M^{\circ\circ} & \text{If } \begin{cases} M = \langle P_1, P_2\rangle \text{ or} \\ M = \lambda P : B.N \text{ and } P :: B \end{cases} \\ \Delta_A[M^{\circ\circ}] & \text{otherwise} \end{cases}$$

and $M^{\circ\circ}$ is defined by induction on the structure of M as:

$$\begin{array}{lll} x^{\circ\circ} = x & \pi_i(M)^{\circ\circ} = \pi_i(M^{\circ\circ}) & (\lambda P : B.M)^{\circ\circ} = \lambda P : B.M^\circ \\ \langle M, N\rangle^{\circ\circ} = \langle M^\circ, N^\circ\rangle & (MN)^{\circ\circ} = (M^{\circ\circ}N^\circ) & \mu y : A.M^{\circ\circ} = \mu y : A.M^\circ \end{array}$$

Example 3.9 Let z_1 be of type $(A \times A') \to B$ and z_2 be of type $C \times D$, where A, A', B, C and D are base types. We have $\langle z_1, z_2\rangle^\circ = \langle z_1, z_2\rangle^{\circ\circ} = \langle z_1^\circ, z_2^\circ\rangle = \langle \Delta_{(A\times A')\to B}[z_1], \Delta_{C\times D}[z_2]\rangle$, where

[1] To differentiate with the expansor *terms* defined in [DCK93a]

$$\Delta_{(A\times A')\to B}[z_1] = \lambda\langle x,y\rangle : A\times A'.z_1\langle x,y\rangle \quad \text{and} \quad \Delta_{C\times D}[z_2] = \langle \pi_1(z_2), \pi_2(z_2)\rangle$$

It is quite easy to proof that the translation preserves types and characterizes E-normal forms, so we can now complete the proof of confluence of $\Longrightarrow$ by showing that for every one-step reduction $\stackrel{B}{\Longrightarrow}$ from M to N, there is a non-empty $\stackrel{B}{\Longrightarrow}$-reduction sequence from the E-normal form of M to the E-normal form of N.

Theorem 3.10 (Preservation of E-normal forms) *If $\Gamma \rhd M : A$ and $M \stackrel{B}{\Longrightarrow} N$, then $M^\circ \stackrel{B}{\Longrightarrow}{}^+ N^\circ$.*

Proof. By induction on the structure of M using the fact that $\Delta_A?[M^\circ[\overline{N^\circ}/\overline{x}]] \stackrel{\beta,\pi_i}{\Longrightarrow}{}^* (M[\overline{N}/\overline{x}])^\circ$. □

Theorem 3.11 (Confluence of $\Longrightarrow$) *The relation $\Longrightarrow$ is confluent.*

Proof. Using proposition 3.1 and theorems 3.3, 3.4, 3.5 and 3.10. □

The confluence property guarantees uniqueness of normal forms, so that results are independent of the evaluation strategy. This is a minimal requirement for our calculus to model program execution and is essential for parallel implementations of functional languages.

4 Conclusion and Future Work

We have provided a confluent reduction system for the extensional typed λ-calculus with wildcard, layered and product patterns equipped with fixpoints and product types.

We have shown that even if wildcard and layered patterns allow more friendly specifications of function definitions (as example 1.1 shows), they are redundant and can be eliminated. That is, for *any* function $\lambda P : A.M$, there is another function $\lambda P' : A.M'$ equal to $\lambda P : A.M$ modulo our equational theory such that the pattern P' only contain variables and product patterns.

This is not very surprising because it corresponds to the fact that contraction and weakening rules are redundant in intuitionist logic [Gal93] and gives at the same time another possible reading: to remove at compile time wildcard and layered patterns from λ-abstractions using our reduction system, could lead to optimizations of programs which will be then interpreted by simpler computation rules. In fact, the (@) rule does not make more sense and the pattern matching function *Match*(_, _) become simpler.

The reduction system for the LWPP calculus without recursion can also be used as a decision method for equational provability as a consequence of theorem 2.16 and theorem 3.11. This is clearly illustrated by the example at the end of section 2.3.

This work clarifies the relation between extensionality and layered, wildcard and product patterns, but it rests as future work the development of an axiomatic theory for the Typed Pattern Calculus, especially in the presence of patterns of sum type. It is also important to remark that this approach can be applied to many other calculi with expansionary rules: for example, the weak extensionality for the sum type as in [DCK93b] or combinations of algebraic rewriting systems with extensional lambda calculi [DCK94]. We also believe that polymorphic calculi like Girard's Systems F can be handled within an expansionary interpretation of extensional rules.

Acknowledgements

I would like to thank Roberto Di Cosmo for the valuable comments made on an earlier version of this paper and for his careful proofreading. I am also very grateful to Val Breazu-Tannen for stimulating and helpful discussions about various topics related to this work.

References

[Aka93] Yohji Akama. On mints' reductions for ccc-calculus. In *Typed Lambda Calculus and Applications*, number 664 in LNCS. Springer Verlag, 1993.

[BTKP93] Val Breazu-Tannen, Delia Kesner, and Laurence Puel. A typed pattern calculus. In *Proceedings of the Symposium on Logic in Computer Science (LICS)*, Montreal, Canada, June 1993.

[CCMS86] Guy Cousineau, Pierre-Louis Curien, Michel Mauny, and Ascánder Suárez. Combinateurs catégoriques et implémentation des langages fonctionnels. Technical Report LIENS-86-3, Laboratoire d'Informatique du Département de Mathématiques et d'Informatique de l'École Normale Supérieur, 1986.

[Cub92] Djordje Cubric. On free ccc. Distributed on the `types` mailing list, 1992.

[DCK93a] Roberto Di Cosmo and Delia Kesner. A confluent reduction for the extensional typed λ-calculus with pairs, sums, recursion and terminal object. In Andrzej Lingas, editor, *Intern. Conf. on Automata, Languages and Programming (ICALP)*, number 700 in LNCS. Springer-Verlag, 1993.

[DCK93b] Roberto Di Cosmo and Delia Kesner. Simulating expansions without expansions. *Mathematical Structures in Computer Science*, 1993. To appear. Available also as INRIA Technical Report 1911.

[DCK94] Roberto Di Cosmo and Delia Kesner. Combining first order algebraic rewriting systems, recursion and extensional typed lambda calculi. In *Intern. Conf. on Automata, Languages and Programming (ICALP)*, LNCS. Springer-Verlag, 1994. To appear.

[Dou93] Daniel Dougherty. Some lambda calculi with categorical sums and products. In *Proc. of the Fifth International Conference on Rewriting Techniques and Applications (RTA)*, 1993.

[ea93] Xavier Leroy et al. The Caml Light system, release 0.6. Software and documentation distributed by anonymous FTP on `ftp.inria.fr`, 1993.

[Gal93] Jean Gallier. Constructive logics part i : A tutorial on proof systems and typed λ-calculi. *Theoretical Computer Science*, 110:249–339, 1993.

[Har87] Thérèse Hardin. *Résultats de confluence pour les règles fortes de la logique combinatoire catégorique et liens avec les lambda-calculs*. Thèse de doctorat, Université de Paris VII, 1987.

[How92] Brian Howard. *Fixed Points and Extensionality in Typed Functional Programming Languages*. PhD thesis, Stanford University, August 1992.

[Hue76] Gérad Huet. *Résolution d'équations dans les langages d'ordre* $1, 2, \ldots, \omega$. Thèse de doctorat d'état, Université Paris VII, 1976.

[Jay92] Colin Barry Jay. Long $\beta\eta$ normal forms and confluence (and its revised version). Technical Report ECS-LFCS-91-183, LFCS, University of Edimburgh, 1992.

[JG92] Colin Barry Jay and Neil Ghani. The virtues of eta-expansion. Technical Report ECS-LFCS-92-243, LFCS, University of Edimburgh, 1992.

[Jon87] Simon Peyton Jones. *The implementation of functional programming languages*. Prentice-Hall, 1987.

[Kes93] Delia Kesner. *La définition de fonctions par cas à l'aide de motifs dans des langages applicatifs*. Thèse de doctorat, Université de Paris XI, Orsay, december 1993.

[Min79] Grigori Mints. Teorija categorii i teoria dokazatelstv.I. *Aktualnye problemy logiki i metodologii nauky*, pages 252–278, 1979.

[Nes89] Dan Nesmith. An application of Klop's counterexample to a higher-order rewrite system. Seki-Report SR-94-06, Department of Computer Science, University of the Saarland, 1989.

[Pot81] Garrel Pottinger. The Church Rosser Theorem for the Typed lambda-calculus with Surjective Pairing. *Notre Dame Journal of Formal Logic*, 22(3):264–268, 1981.

[Pra71] Dag Prawitz. Ideas and results in proof theory. *Proceedings of the 2nd Scandinavian Logic Symposium*, pages 235–307, 1971.

[vO90] Vincent van Oostrom. Lambda calculus with patterns. Technical Report IR 228, Vrije Universiteit, Amsterdam, November 1990.

Appendix A: Evaluators in Natural Semantics Style

$$\frac{L \Downarrow_l \langle M,N\rangle \qquad M \Downarrow_l K}{\pi_1(L) \Downarrow_l K} \qquad \frac{L \Downarrow_l \langle M,N\rangle \qquad N \Downarrow_l K}{\pi_2(L) \Downarrow_l K}$$

$$\frac{}{\langle M,N\rangle \Downarrow_l \langle M,N\rangle} \qquad \frac{}{\lambda P:A.M \Downarrow_l \lambda P:A.M}$$

$$\frac{M[\mu x:A.M/x] \Downarrow_l K}{\mu x:A.M \Downarrow_l K}$$

$$\frac{M \Downarrow_l \lambda P:A.L \qquad \mathit{match}\ N\ \mathit{on}\ P \Downarrow_l \sigma \qquad L[\sigma] \Downarrow_l K}{MN \Downarrow_l K}$$

$$\frac{}{\mathit{match}\ L\ \mathit{on}\ x \Downarrow_l [L/x]} \qquad \frac{}{\mathit{match}\ L\ \mathit{on}\ \_ \Downarrow_l \emptyset}$$

$$\frac{L \Downarrow_l \langle M,N\rangle \quad \mathit{match}\ M\ \mathit{on}\ P \Downarrow_l \sigma \quad \mathit{match}\ N\ \mathit{on}\ Q \Downarrow_l \theta \quad \mathit{Dom}(\sigma)\cap \mathit{Dom}(\theta)=\emptyset}{\mathit{match}\ L\ \mathit{on}\ \langle P,Q\rangle \Downarrow_l \sigma\cup\theta}$$

$$\frac{\mathit{match}\ L\ \mathit{on}\ P \Downarrow_l \sigma \quad \mathit{match}\ L\ \mathit{on}\ Q \Downarrow_l \theta \quad \mathit{Dom}(\sigma)\cap \mathit{Dom}(\theta)=\emptyset}{\mathit{match}\ L\ \mathit{on}\ P@Q \Downarrow_l \sigma\cup\theta}$$

Table 1: A Lazy Evaluator for the LWPP Calculus in Natural Semantics Style

$$\frac{L \Downarrow_e \langle M,N\rangle}{\pi_1(L) \Downarrow_e M} \qquad \frac{L \Downarrow_e \langle M,N\rangle}{\pi_2(L) \Downarrow_e N} \qquad \frac{M \Downarrow_e K \quad N \Downarrow_e L}{\langle M,N\rangle \Downarrow_e \langle K,L\rangle}$$

$$\frac{M[\mu x:A.M/x] \Downarrow_e K}{\mu x:A.M \Downarrow_e K} \qquad \frac{}{\lambda P:A.M \Downarrow_e \lambda P:A.M}$$

$$\frac{M \Downarrow_e \lambda P:A.J \qquad N \Downarrow_e K \qquad \mathit{Match}(K,P)=\sigma \qquad J[\sigma] \Downarrow_e L}{MN \Downarrow_e L}$$

$$\begin{array}{lll}
\mathit{Match}(N,_) & = \emptyset & \\
\mathit{Match}(N,x) & = [N/x] & \\
\mathit{Match}(N,P_1@P_2) & = \mathit{Match}(N,P_1)\cup \mathit{Match}(N,P_2) & \\
\mathit{Match}(\langle N_1,N_2\rangle,\langle P_1,P_2\rangle) & = \mathit{Match}(N_1,P_1)\cup \mathit{Match}(N_2,P_2) & \\
\mathit{Match}(M,P) & = \mathbf{fail} & \text{Otherwise}
\end{array}$$

Table 2: A Strict Evaluator for the LWPP Calculus in Natural Semantics Style

Appendix B

Lemma 4.1 *If* $\Gamma \triangleright M : A$, *then there is a term* N *such that* $M \Longrightarrow^* N$ *and* $N :: A$.

Proof. By definition of the structure of the type A.

□

Theorem 2.15 (Redundancy of Layered and Wildcard Patterns) Any term M can be reduced to a term M' having no layered nor wildcard patterns.

Proof. Let $\overset{-}{\Longrightarrow}$ be the reduction $\Longrightarrow$ without recursion. We show that the $\overset{-}{\Longrightarrow}$-normal form of any term M contains no layered and no wildcard patterns. We proceed by induction on the structure of the term M.

- If $M = x$, the property is trivial.
- If $M = \langle M_1, M_2 \rangle$ or $M = \mu x : A.N$, the property holds by induction hypothesis.
- If $M = \lambda P : A.N$, then P is fully specified and so it has no layered and no wildcard patterns. As N is also in $\overset{-}{\Longrightarrow}$-normal form, the property holds by induction hypothesis.
- If $M = \pi_i(N)$, then N is only reducible at the root position, and thus all its proper subterms are in $\overset{-}{\Longrightarrow}$-normal form and do not contain layered nor wildcard patterns by induction hypothesis. Since N is of product type, it is not a λ-abstraction which concludes the proof.
- If $M = NL$, then the property holds for L by i.h. because it is a $\overset{-}{\Longrightarrow}$-normal form. By definition N is only reducible at the root position, and thus all its proper subterms are in $\overset{-}{\Longrightarrow}$-normal form and do not contain layered nor wildcard patterns by induction hypothesis. If N is not a λ-abstraction we are done, so suppose $N = \lambda P : A.N'$. Since L in in normal form it is fully specified by lemma 4.1 and so $Match(N, P)$ is defined and M is reducible. This leads to a contradiction so we can conclude that $N \neq \lambda P : A.N'$.

□

Lemma 4.2 *The relation* $\overset{*}{\Longleftrightarrow}$ *is closed by context.*

Proof. In order to show that $\overset{*}{\Longleftrightarrow}$ is stable by context closure, it is sufficient to show the property for the relation $\Longleftrightarrow$. According to the definition 2.13 there are just two cases where this is not immediately evident but we show how to use $\Longleftrightarrow$, or more precisely $\Longleftarrow$, to obtain the result:

- If $M \overset{\eta}{\Longrightarrow} (\lambda P : A.MP)$, then the relation is immediately closed for all contexts *except* in the case where the terms are applied to a term L that is fully specified. By lemma 2.5 there is a substitution σ such that $Match(L, P) = \sigma$ and since $Var(P) \cap FV(M) = \emptyset$ holds by definition, then $M[\sigma] = M$ and:

$$(\lambda P : A.MP)L \overset{\beta}{\Longrightarrow} (MP)[\sigma] = (M[\sigma]P[\sigma]) = ML$$

- If $M \overset{sp}{\Longrightarrow} \langle \pi_1(M), \pi_2(M) \rangle$, then the relation is immediately closed for all the contexts *except* in the case where the terms are projected. We can use in this case the rules π_i as follows:

$$\pi_i(M) \overset{\pi_i}{\Longleftarrow} \pi_i(\langle \pi_1(M), \pi_2(M) \rangle)$$

□

Theorem 2.16 ($\Longrightarrow$ generates $\doteq$) $M \doteq N$ if and only if $M \overset{*}{\Longleftrightarrow} N$.

Proof. If $M \overset{*}{\Longleftrightarrow} N$, then $M \Longleftrightarrow M_1 \Longleftrightarrow \ldots \Longleftrightarrow M_n \Longleftrightarrow N$, which implies $M \doteq M_1 \doteq \ldots \doteq M_n \doteq N$ because $\Longleftrightarrow$ is trivially included in $\doteq$. As $\doteq$ is an equivalence relation, then $M \doteq N$ holds by transitivity.

To prove that $M \doteq N$ implies $M \overset{*}{\Longleftrightarrow} N$, we proceed by induction on the depth of the derivation $M \doteq N$. If the depth of the derivation $M \doteq N$ is 0, then N is exactly M and $M \overset{*}{\Longleftrightarrow} M$ is trivial. Otherwise, we consider the following cases:

- If $M \doteq N$ comes from $N \doteq M$ by symmetry or comes from $M \doteq L$ and $L \doteq N$ by transitivity, then the results immediately follows by the induction hypothesis.
- If $M \doteq N$ comes from an equality $M' \doteq N'$ by a context closure, then by i.h. $M' \overset{*}{\Longleftrightarrow} N'$ and by lemma 4.2 we have $M \overset{*}{\Longleftrightarrow} N$.

- If $M \doteq N$ comes from an axiom, we have to show how to obtain $M \stackrel{*}{\Longleftrightarrow} N$ explicitly. We list only the problematic cases:
  - $\lambda P : A.M =_\eta \lambda Q : A.(\lambda P : A.M)Q$. The cases to consider are:
    - $P :: A$.
      - $Q :: A$. Then P and Q are necessarily α-equivalent, and if ψ is the renaming substitution between P and Q, then:

$$\lambda P : A.M =_\alpha \lambda Q : A.M[\psi] \stackrel{\beta}{\Longleftarrow} \lambda Q : A.(\lambda P : A.M)Q$$

      - Q is not fully specified by A (but $Q :\cdot A$). By lemma 2.5 $Match(P, Q) = \sigma$, so:

$$\begin{array}{lcl} \lambda Q : A.(\lambda P : A.M)Q & \stackrel{\eta}{\Longrightarrow} & \lambda P : A.(\lambda Q : A.(\lambda P : A.M)Q)P \quad \stackrel{\beta}{\Longrightarrow} \\ \lambda P : A.(\lambda P : A.M)Q[\sigma] & = & \lambda P : A.(\lambda P : A.M)P \quad \stackrel{\beta}{\Longrightarrow} \quad \lambda P : A.M \end{array}$$

    - P is not fully specified by A.
      - $Q :: A$. Then

$$\lambda P : A.M \stackrel{\eta}{\Longrightarrow} \lambda Q : A.(\lambda P : A.M)Q$$

      - Q is not fully specified by A. Let us take $R :: A$ and let σ be the substitution such that $Match(R, Q) = \sigma$ (it exists by lemma 2.5). We then have :

$$\begin{array}{ccc} \lambda Q : A.(\lambda P : A.M)Q & & \\ \Downarrow_\eta & & \\ \lambda R : A.(\lambda Q : A.(\lambda P : A.M)Q)R & & \lambda P : A.M \\ \Downarrow_\beta & & \Downarrow_\eta \\ \lambda R : A.(\lambda P : A.M)Q[\sigma] & = & \lambda R : A.(\lambda P : A.M)R \end{array}$$

  - $\langle M, N\rangle =_{sp} \langle \pi_1(\langle M, N\rangle), \pi_2(\langle M, N\rangle)\rangle$. We cannot apply an expansion to a term that is a pair, but we can use the reductions π_i as follows:

$$\langle M, N\rangle \stackrel{\pi_2}{\Longleftarrow} \langle M, \pi_2(\langle M, N\rangle)\rangle \stackrel{\pi_1}{\Longleftarrow} \langle \pi_1(\langle M, N\rangle), \pi_2(\langle M, N\rangle)\rangle$$

□

Preserving universal termination through unfold/fold

Annalisa Bossi (*), Nicoletta Cocco (**)

(*)Dipartimento di Matematica Pura ed Applicata, Università di Padova,
Via Belzoni 7, 35131 Padova, Italy.
(**)Dipartimento di Informatica, Università di Venezia-Ca' Foscari
Via Torino, 155, Mestre-Venezia, Italy

Abstract. We study how to preserve universal termination besides computed answer substitutions while transforming definite programs. We consider the unfold operation both alone and combined with the introduction of a new definition and fold operations. We prove that unfold always preserves universal termination. Moreover we define a restricted version of the Tamaki-Sato's transformation sequence and show that it preserves universal termination as well.

Keywords and Phrases: program transformations, universal termination.

1 Introduction

Logic program transformations which preserve relevant properties of the original program have been extensively studied. The basic operations, namely defining a new predicate, unfolding and folding, have been considered either in isolation [15, 6, 4], or combined in a fixed sequence of transformation steps [24, 12, 21, 23, 11, 19], and wrt various semantics representing the different properties to be preserved through the transformation. Thus the least Herbrand model semantics [24], the computed answer substitution semantics [12, 4] and the finite failure set [22], have been considered for characterizing definite programs. While for normal programs, Kunen's semantics [20], Fitting's semantics [7], the Well Founded semantics [21, 23], the Stable Model semantics [21, 2], stratification and the Perfect Model semantics [15, 22, 2], Clark's two-valued completion semantics [11], just to quote some, have been taken into account.

In this paper we consider *definite programs* and we study *how to preserve universal termination* besides computer answer substitutions. A universal terminating query [25, 9] is a query with no infinite LD-derivation, hence it has a finite LD-tree (*SLD*-tree with *leftmost* selection rule) with some computed answer substitutions or it is finitely failing. Universal termination is a very important property to be preserved in practice, in fact it guarantees termination also with a Prolog interpreter, but it is not a declarative property and as a consequence it is rather complicate to deal with. We study here both the unfold operation alone and a transformation schema similar (even if more restrictive) to the one introduced by Tamaki and Sato in [24]. Some new restrictions are clearly needed since in Tamaki and Sato's original schema the ordering among body's atoms is not taken into account.

We already know [12, 4] that unfold preserves the computed answer substitutions semantics. On the other hand unfold does not preserve infinite derivations as the following simple examples show.

Example 1. Let us consider P_1:

```
p ← q, r.
t ← r, q.
q ← q.
```

In P_1, the query p has only an infinite *LD*-derivation and the query t finitely fails. If we now unfold r in the first clause we obtain:

```
t ← r, q.
q ← q.
```

In the transformed program the query p finitely fails.

This example shows that ***unfolding can eliminate infinite derivations and it can introduce failing ones.*** On the other hand in this paper we prove that ***unfold cannot introduce further infinite LD-derivations.*** This property is not sufficient to unfold freely when we consider the unfold/fold transformation sequence, unless we impose further conditions.

Let us consider again the initial program P_1, by unfolding q in the second clause, we obtain exactly the same program. If we now apply *recursive folding* to the second clause, we get:

```
p ← q, r.
t ← t.
q ← q.
```

In this program, the query t has only an infinite *LD*-derivation. Note that the previous fold would be allowed in Tamaki and Sato [24] schema since the folding clause derives from a previous unfolding operation. On the contrary, it would not be allowed in Seki's modified folding [22].

Hence in order to preserve universal termination while applying the unfold/fold transformation sequence, and in particular while folding, we have to impose some restrictive conditions also on the initial unfolding. In this paper we introduce the notion of ***decreasing unfolding of a definition*** and show that if the the first operation in the sequence is a decreasing unfolding of a definition, then the subsequent folding operations cannot introduce infinite derivations. We give also simple sufficient conditions for being decreasing unfoldings. These conditions derive directly from the proof that unfolding cannot introduce infinite derivations.

Proietti and Pettorossi in [18] also studied transformation sequences for Prolog programs. They adopted a denotational semantics similar to the one introduced by

[16, 3] and consider program equivalence wrt sequences of c.a.s. and existential termination [25], which is a finer, but more complicated, property to study than universal termination. Unfolding does not preserve such a semantics in general. In [18] some very restrictive conditions are given for the transformation operations wrt such a semantics.

The next section introduces the basic notions about substitutions and derivations and the terminology adopted. In Section 3 the semantics representing both c.a.s. and universal termination is defined with the associated equivalence and the two complementary notions of *complete transformation* and *non-increasing transformation*. The conjunction of these two properties ensures the preservation of our semantics for all queries which are universal terminating in the original program. In section 4 the unfolding operation is studied wrt universal termination and we prove that it is always non-increasing, thus preserving universal termination. The introduction of a new definition and the folding operation are then considered, they are combined with unfolding into an unfold/fold transformation sequence. We prove that if the first unfolding of the new definition is strictly decreasing, then the transformation is non-increasing and hence it preserves universal termination. Section 5 concludes with a short discussion on possible extensions. The proof that unfold is non-increasing is given in the Appendix.

2 Preliminaries

We review here the notation and terminology used in the paper. Given a substitution η, we denote by $Dom(\eta)$ its domain, by $Ran(\eta)$ the set of variables that appear in the terms of the range of η and $Var(\eta) = Dom(\eta) \cup Ran(\eta)$. Recall that, [10, 1], a substitution η is called *idempotent* when $\eta\eta = \eta$ holds, that a substitution η is idempotent if and only if $Dom(\eta) \cap Ran(\eta) = \emptyset$. *A renaming* is a substitution which is a permutation of its domain.

Given a substitution η and a set of variables X, we denote by $\eta_{|X}$ the substitution obtained from η by restricting its domain to X.

Given an expression (term, atom, query,...) E, we denote the set of variables occurring in it by $Var(E)$. Given a set V of variables and an expression E, we say that E *is disjoint from* V, if $var(E) \cap V = \emptyset$. We often write $\eta_{|E}$ to denote $\eta_{|Var(E)}$. Given two expressions E_1 and E_2, we say that E_1 *is less instantiated than* (or equivalently *more general than*) E_2, if there exists a substitution θ such that $E_2 = E_1\theta$, then E_2 *is an instance of* E_1. This defines an order relation and we also write $E_1 \leq E_2$. We write $E \sim E'$ to denote that E and E' are *variant expressions*, that is $E_1 \leq E_2$ and $E_2 \leq E_1$ or equivalently there exists a renaming ρ such that $E = E'\rho$. Analogously, we write $\eta \leq \eta'$ to denote that there exists a substitution θ such that $\eta = \eta'\theta$ and $\eta \sim \eta'$ to denote that there exists a renaming τ such that $\eta = \eta'\tau$. Let E_1, E_2 and E_3 be expressions such that $E_1 \sim E_2$ and $E_2 \sim E_3$, then $E_1 \sim E_3$, that is the variant relation is transitive.

Given a set E of equations, we use the notation $mgu(E)$ to denote any idempotent mgu of the set E; recall that idempotent mgu's are *relevant* [1], namely $Var(mgu(E)) \subseteq Var(E)$. We make use of the following lemma.

Lemma 1 [17]. *Let E_1, E_2 be two sets of equations. Suppose that θ_1 is an mgu of E_1 and θ_2 is an mgu of $E_2\theta_1$. Then $\theta_1\theta_2$ is an mgu of $E_1 \cup E_2$. Moreover, if $E_1 \cup E_2$ is unifiable, then θ_1 exists and for any such θ_1 an appropriate θ_2 exists as well.* □

We consider definite logic programs executed by means of the *LD-resolution*, which consists of the usual *SLD*-resolution combined with the leftmost selection rule. Throughout the paper we use queries instead of goals. A *query* is a sequence of atoms. We denote sequences by bold characters. Then a goal is a construct $\leftarrow \mathbf{Q}$, where $\mathbf{Q}$ is a query. □ stands for the *empty query*. An *LD*-derivation ending with □ is a *successful LD-derivation.* We consider only *well-formed derivations*, namely all the mgu's employed are idempotent and every input clause (variant of the clause applied at each step) is standardized apart wrt both the initial query and all the input clauses used in the previous steps.

We use the notation $l : \mathbf{Q} \longmapsto^{\sigma}_{P} \mathbf{R}$ for "there exists a (partial) *LD*-derivation, l, of the query $\mathbf{Q}$ in P ending in the query $\mathbf{R}$ and σ is the composition of the *mgu's* applied during the derivation". Similarly $l : \mathbf{Q} \mid\!\leadsto^{\sigma}_{P} \mathbf{R}$ stands for "there exists a (partial) *SLD*-derivation, l', of the query $\mathbf{Q}$ in P ending in the query $\mathbf{R}$ and σ is the composition of the mgu's applied in the derivation". $\mathbf{Q} \longmapsto^{\sigma}_{P} \Box$ denotes a successful *LD*-derivation of $\mathbf{Q}$ in P with *computed answer substitution (c.a.s.)* $\sigma_{|\mathbf{Q}}$. The *length* of an (*S*)*LD*-derivation l is denoted by $\mid l \mid$.

The rest of the notation is more or less standard and essentially follows [14, 1].

3 Query Equivalence

We now define an operational semantics which is appropriate for our purposes. In this semantics both the outcomes of successful computations and the existence of a non-terminating computation are recorded. Thus this semantics is analogous with the total correctness semantics of imperative programs.

Definition 2. Given a program P and a query $\mathbf{Q}$ we define

$$\begin{aligned}\mathcal{M}[\![P]\!](\mathbf{Q}) = \quad & \{\sigma \mid \text{there is a successful } LD\text{-derivation of } \mathbf{Q} \text{ in } P \text{ with c.a.s. } \sigma\} \\ \cup\ & \{\bot \mid \text{there is an infinite } LD\text{-derivation of } \mathbf{Q} \text{ in } P\}.\end{aligned}$$

□

Note that in this semantics all variants of c.a.s., appropriately restricted on $Var(\mathbf{Q})$, are included. Note also that the termination we are representing with this semantics is exactly *universal termination* [25].

Definition 3. *A query* $\mathbf{Q}$ *is universally terminating in* P iff all *LD*-derivations for $\mathbf{Q}$ in P are finite, that is $\bot \notin \mathcal{M}[\![P]\!](\mathbf{Q})$. □

Next, we define a notion of equivalence that compares the computational behaviour of a query wrt two programs. This is the equivalence to be insured by the program transformations.

Definition 4. Let P_1, P_2 be programs and $\mathbf{Q}$ a query. We say that $\mathbf{Q}$ is *equivalent in P_1 and P_2*, and write

$$\mathbf{Q} \text{ in } P_1 \simeq \mathbf{Q} \text{ in } P_2,$$

iff $\mathcal{M}[\![P_1]\!](\mathbf{Q}) = \mathcal{M}[\![P_2]\!](\mathbf{Q})$. □

To identify program transformations which preserve the computational behaviour, we consider the two inclusions of Definition 4 separately and introduce two corresponding requirements on transformations.

Definition 5. Let P' be obtained by transforming a program P. We say that *the transformation of P into P' is complete*, iff for any query $\mathbf{Q}$:

– *if* $\mathbf{Q} \overset{\theta}{\longmapsto}_P \square$, then there exists $\mathbf{Q} \overset{\theta'}{\longmapsto}_{P'} \square$ and $\mathbf{Q}\theta = \mathbf{Q}\theta'$. □

Complete transformations do not lose c.a.s, but they could lose or add infinite derivations.

Lemma 6. *Let P be a program and let P' be obtained from P by means of a complete transformation. Then for every query $\mathbf{Q}$, universally terminating in P, $\mathcal{M}[\![P]\!](\mathbf{Q}) \subseteq \mathcal{M}[\![P']\!](\mathbf{Q})$.*

Proof. Let $\mathbf{Q}$ be a query universally terminating in P. Since the transformation is complete, any c.a.s. for $\mathbf{Q}$ in P is a c.a.s. for $\mathbf{Q}$ in P' too. Moreover $\{\perp\} \notin \mathcal{M}[\![P]\!](\mathbf{Q})$. □

In order to obtain the other inclusion we need a further concept.

Definition 7. Let P' be obtained by transforming a program P. We say that *the transformation of P into P' is non-increasing* iff for any query $\mathbf{Q}$

– for any partial LD-derivation of $\mathbf{Q}$ in P': $l' : \mathbf{Q} \overset{\delta'}{\longmapsto}_{P'} \mathbf{R}'$, there exists a partial LD-derivation of $\mathbf{Q}$ in P, $l : \mathbf{Q} \overset{\delta}{\longmapsto}_P \mathbf{R}$, of length greater or equal to the one in P', $| l | \geq | l' |$; furthermore, (*correctness*) if $\mathbf{R}' = \square$ (i.e. we are considering a successful LD-derivation of $\mathbf{Q}$ in P') then $\mathbf{R} = \square$ and $\mathbf{Q}\delta \sim \mathbf{Q}\delta'$. □

A non-increasing transformation preserves universal termination and cannot add c.a.s. This is also a rather weak property when considered alone. In fact a transformation which produces an empty program is non-increasing.

Lemma 8. *Let P be a program and let P' be obtained from P by means of a non-increasing transformation. Then for every query $\mathbf{Q}$, universally terminating in P, $\mathcal{M}[\![P']\!](\mathbf{Q}) \subseteq \mathcal{M}[\![P]\!](\mathbf{Q})$.*

Proof. Let $\mathbf{Q}$ be a query. The LD-tree for $\mathbf{Q}$ in P is finitely branching. Since $\mathbf{Q}$ is universally terminating in P, by König's lemma this tree is finite and consequently for some $n \geq 0$, all its branches are of length less or equal to n. Since the transformation is non-increasing all LD-derivations of $\mathbf{Q}$ in P' are of length less or equal to n as well. Then $\{\perp\} \notin \mathcal{M}[\![P']\!](\mathbf{Q})$. Thus to obtain the inclusion we have to prove that all c.a.s for $\mathbf{Q}$ in P' are c.a.s for $\mathbf{Q}$ in P too. This follows from the correctness of the transformation. In fact, let θ' be a c.a.s for $\mathbf{Q}$ in P', then $\theta' = \delta' |_{\mathbf{Q}}$ where δ' is the composition of mgu's in a successful derivation of $\mathbf{Q}$ in P'. By correctness, there exists δ such that $\theta = \delta |_{\mathbf{Q}}$ is a c.a.s. for $\mathbf{Q}$ in P and $\mathbf{Q}\delta' \sim \mathbf{Q}\delta$. Then $\mathbf{Q}\theta' \sim \mathbf{Q}\theta$ and, since $\theta' = \theta' |_{\mathbf{Q}}$, θ' is also a c.a.s. for $\mathbf{Q}$ in P. □

Theorem 9. *Let P' be obtained from P through a transformation which is complete and non-increasing. Then for all queries $\mathbf{Q}$, universally terminating in P,*

$$\mathbf{Q} \text{ in } P \simeq \mathbf{Q} \text{ in } P'.$$

Proof. Immediate by Lemmas 8 and 6. □

Another important aspect of non-increasing transformations is connected to the intuition that transformations must not increase program complexity (and possibly make programs more efficient). In fact non-increasing transformations satisfy this property if we take the depth of LD-trees as complexity measure.

4 How to preserve universal termination through transformations

All program transformation strategies are based on very basic transformation operations which are applicable to single clauses of the program. They are *defining a new predicate, unfolding an atom in the body of a clause, folding a predicate.* In this section we see that unfolding, when considered alone, does not require any restrictive condition in order to preserve universal termination and c.a.s. But when the three basic operations are combined together in an unfold/fold transformation sequence, a restrictive condition becomes necessary on unfolding, in order to preserve universal termination. The restriction is not too difficult to satisfy since it is sufficient that the first unfolding step of the new definition strictly decreases the length of LD-derivations. By analyzing the proof of these results, we can give a rather simple characterization of when an unfolding actually satisfies this property.

4.1 Unfolding

Unfolding an atom in the body of a clause consists in substituting the clause with all possible expansions of the selected atom. Unfold in logic programs was originally considered in Komorowski [13] and formally studied by Sato and Tamaki [24] and others. We recall the definition.

Definition 10. Let $c = H \leftarrow \mathbf{A}, B, \mathbf{C}$ be a clause of P. Suppose that $d_1, \ldots, d_n$ are all the clauses of P whose head unifies with B and for $i \in [1, n]$, $d'_i = H_i \leftarrow \mathbf{B_i}$ is a variant of d_i with no common variables with c. Let, for $i \in [1, n]$, $\theta_i = mgu(B, H_i)$ and $c_i = (H \leftarrow \mathbf{A}, \mathbf{B_i}, \mathbf{C})\theta_i$. Then we define

$$unfold(P, B, c) = (P - \{c\}) \cup \{c_1, \ldots, c_n\},$$

and say that $unfold(P, B, c)$ is the result of *unfolding B in c in P*, briefly it is *an unfolding of P.* □

Unfolding is a complete transformation for all queries. The result follows from the independence from the selection rule and the fact that unfolding preserves the computed answer substitution semantics [12, 4].

Theorem 11. *Let P be a program and P' an unfolding of P. Then the transformation of P into P' is complete.* □

This theorem states nothing about universal termination. Moreover we cannot hope to be able to prove that our equivalence is preserved for any query, namely the statement: let P' be an unfolding of P, then for any query $\mathbf{Q}$, $\mathbf{Q}$ in $P \simeq \mathbf{Q}$ in P', does not hold, as the example in Section 1 shows. However, we can prove that the equivalence is preserved for any query universally terminating in P. The next theorem allows us to prove this statement.

Theorem 12. *Let P be a program and P_1 an unfolding of P. The transformation of P into P_1 is non-increasing.*

Proof. See the Appendix.

Corollary 13. *Let P be a program, P_1 an unfolding of P. For all queries $\mathbf{Q}$, universally terminating in P,*

$$\mathbf{Q} \text{ in } P \simeq \mathbf{Q} \text{ in } P_1.$$

Proof. By Theorems 11, 12 and 9. □

This corollary tells us that no restrictive condition is necessary in order to preserve universal termination and c.a.s. when using unfolding alone.

The proof of Theorem 12 (see Appendix) is rather long, since it follows LD-derivations, but it also supplies some more information. In fact we can see that, except for the case in which the partial LD-derivation stops in P_1 before reaching the unfolded part, **Case 1** in the proof, we can prove that a strict decreasing relation holds between the length of derivations in the transformed program and the associated ones in P. This stronger relation becomes useful when composing unfolding with folding.

Definition 14. Let P be a program and P' be obtained from P by unfolding an atom A in a clause c in P and let $\mathbf{G}$ be a class of queries. *Unfolding A in c in P is decreasing wrt* $\mathbf{G}$, iff for any query $\mathbf{Q} \in \mathbf{G}$, for any partial LD-derivation, which uses an unfolding of c as input clause, $l' : \mathbf{Q} \overset{\theta'}{\longmapsto}_{P'} \mathbf{R}'$, there exists an LD-derivation $l : \mathbf{Q} \overset{\theta}{\longmapsto}_{P} \mathbf{R}$ such that $| l' | < | l |$. □

Corollary 15. *Let $c = N \leftarrow B, \mathbf{C}$ be the only clause in P defining the predicate symbol of N. Moreover, let P_1 be obtained from P by unfolding B in c in P. Then, for any substitution α, unfolding B in c in P is decreasing wrt $\mathbf{G} = \{N\alpha\}$.*

Proof. Let, for $i \in [1, n]$, $c_i = (N \leftarrow \mathbf{B}_i, \mathbf{C})\theta_i$ be the clauses in P_1 resulting from the unfolding. Since c is the only clause in P defining the predicate symbol of N, the c_i's are the only clauses defining the predicate symbol of N. Then no derivation of a query in $\mathbf{G}$ falls in **Case 1** of the proof of Theorem 12. □

This sufficient condition for being a decreasing unfolding seems to be rather intuitive. In fact unfolding the first atom in a clause, corresponds exactly to one evaluation step in an LD-derivation. It seems very reasonable that any non-trivial LD-derivation in P_1 for the queries in $\{N\alpha\}$, namely the queries using exactly one of the unfolded clauses as the first derivation step, is one step shorter than the corresponding one in the original, not unfolded, program.

4.2 Introduction of New Definitions

It is a common technique in program transformation to group the predicates one wants to manipulate under a new name. It corresponds to extend the program with a new definition clause which abstracts such predicates.

Definition 16. Let P be a program, $N = new(\mathbf{t})$ be an atom where new is a new predicate symbol not occurring in P, $\mathbf{B}$ a sequence of atoms defined in P such that $Var(N) \subseteq Var(\mathbf{B})$ and $def = N \leftarrow \mathbf{B}$ a new clause. Then the program $P' = P \cup \{def\}$ is an extension of P and def is *a new definition in* P'. □

Example 2. Let us consider the program P_2:

```
1: prefix(L, N) ← app(L1, [s(0)| Xs], L), all0(L1), length(L1, N).
2: all0([]).
3: all0([0| Xs]) ← all0(Xs).
4: length([], 0).
5: length([X| Xs],s(N)) ← length(Xs, N).
6: app([], Xs, Xs).
7: app([X| Xs], Y, [X| Zs]) ← app(Xs, Y, Zs).
```

where $prefix(L, N)$ relates a list L with the length N of the longest prefix of 0 elements which is followed by an $s(0)$ element.
Then we can extend P_2 with a new definition:

```
def: length0(L1, N) ← all0(L1), length(L1, N).
```

thus obtaining the program $P_2' = P_2 \cup \{def\}$.

The following theorem trivially holds.

Theorem 17. *Let P' be obtained as an extension of P with a new definition $N \leftarrow \mathbf{B}$. Then for any substitution θ such that $Dom(\theta) \subseteq Var(N)$,*

$$\mathcal{M}[\![P]\!](\mathbf{B}\theta)_{|N\theta} = \mathcal{M}[\![P']\!](N\theta)$$

and for any query Q *in* P

$$\mathrm{Q} \text{ in } P \simeq \mathrm{Q} \text{ in } P'.$$

□

After a new definition is introduced, the next natural transformation step consists of unfolding the body of the new clause. We allow such unfolding only if it is *decreasing* in the sense of definition 14. This prevents a loss of equivalence when further transformations are applied and in particular with folding. This is necessary for our semantics which also represents non-terminating computations.

4.3 Folding

Folding a predicate in the body of a clause replaces a conjunction of atoms with an equivalent atom, which are in general instances respectively of the body and the head of a definition clause. Fold is generally performed as a final transformation step in order to pack back unfolded predicates in a definition and to introduce recursion, then it is called *recursive folding*. Then the right side of the definition is substituted by the corresponding left side also in clauses not related with the definition itself, thus trying to bypass some or all the body predicates which recursive folding has already eliminated from the definition. In this case it is called *propagation folding*. We give a definition of fold which is completely general and valid both for recursive and propagation folding. It does not specify any restrictive condition apart from the obvious ones preventing from incorrect instantiations of variables. Note that in our definition the order of atoms is relevant.

Definition 18. Let P be a program, $def = N \leftarrow \mathbf{B}$ a new definition in P and $Y = Var(\mathbf{B}) \backslash Var(N)$. Let P_1 be obtained by transforming P and $c = H \leftarrow \mathbf{A}, \mathbf{B}\tau, \mathbf{C}$ a clause in P_1. If

1. τ restricted to $(Dom(\tau) - Var(N))$ is a renaming;
2. $Var(Y\tau) \cap Var(H, \mathbf{A}, \mathbf{C}, N\tau) = \emptyset$;

then we define

$$fold(P_1, c, \mathbf{B}\tau, def) = (P_1 \setminus \{c\}) \cup \{c'\}$$

where $c' = H \leftarrow \mathbf{A}, N\tau, \mathbf{C}$ and we say that $fold(P_1, c, \mathbf{B}\tau, def)$ is the result of *folding c with def in* P_1. □

Note that if the conditions for folding hold, then we also have:
$Var(H, \mathbf{A}, \mathbf{C}) \cap Var(\mathbf{B}\tau) = Var(H, \mathbf{A}, \mathbf{C}) \cap Var(N\tau)$.

4.4 Unfold/fold transformation sequence

By combining new definition, unfold and fold operations, we get a transformation schema which is similar to the one defined by Tamaki and Sato in [24] but more restrictive. The first restriction consists in the fact that our schema requires the operations to be performed in a fixed order: in particular it requires an initial unfolding step to be applied to a definition clause and does not allow a *propagation folding* to take place before a *recursive folding*. In practice this restriction does not bother so much, as it corresponds to the natural procedure followed in the process of transforming a program. The second restriction is that the order of the atoms in the bodies of the clauses is taken into account, since we are considering LD-derivations and universal termination. This could be a serious limitation, since it requires that the atoms to be folded are all next to each other exactly in the same sequence as in the body of the definition clause. This introduces the need for a *switch* operation, namely switching two atoms in the body of a clause, in order to extend the possibilities of folding. The last restriction is that we require the first unfolding of the definition to be decreasing wrt the defined predicate. This is necessary in order to preserve universal termination. In fact on one hand it forbids recursive folding to

introduce infinite loops, on the other hand it maintains the non-increasing property for propagation folding.
In this paper we consider only unfold and fold operations, while in [24] also other operations are considered. The most interesting is *goal replacement*, namely replacing a conjunction of atoms in a body of a clause by another conjunction. This operation includes and generalizes both folding and switching. We have identified conditions under which other transformation operations could be performed in order to preserve universal termination and we are now studying how to restrict replacement (and switching) in order to satisfy such conditions.
We split the overall transformation sequence into two parts, an initial part which may include recursive folding steps and a final part where propagation folding is performed.

Definition 19. Let P be a program, and

(i) P_0 be an extension of P with a new definition, $def = N \leftarrow \mathbf{B}$:

$$P_0 = P \cup \{def\};$$

(ii) P_1 be obtained from P_0 by a decreasing unfolding of def wrt $\{N\theta\}$:

$$P_1 = P \cup Q_1;$$

(iii) P_2, be obtained from P_1 by a non-increasing and complete transformation applied to clauses which are not in P:

$$P_2 = P \cup Q_2;$$

(iv) P_3, be obtained from P_2 by recursive folding with def in Q_2:

$$P_3 = P \cup Q_3;$$

(v) P_4, be obtained from P_3 by propagation folding with def to clauses in P:

$$P_4 = P_{fold} \cup Q_3.$$

then P_4 *is obtained from* P *and* def *by a safe transformation sequence.* □

Lemma 20. *Let* P' *be obtained from* P *and* def *by a safe transformation sequence. Then*

1. *the transformation of* P *and* def *into* P' *is complete;*
2. *the transformation of* P *and* def *into* P' *is non-increasing.*

Proof. See [5] □

Theorem 21. *Let* P' *be obtained from* P *and* def *by a safe transformation sequence. Then for all queries* $\mathbf{Q}$*, universally terminating in* $P_0 = P \cup \{def\}$,

$$\mathbf{Q} \text{ in } P_0 \simeq \mathbf{Q} \text{ in } P'.$$

□

Example 3. Let us consider the program P_2' of the previous example. If we unfold *all*0 in *def*, we obtain:

```
def1: length0([], N)  ←  length([], N).
def2: length0([0| Xs], N)  ←  all0(Xs), length([0 | Xs], N).
```

This is a decreasing unfolding because we have unfolded the first atom in the body of *def* and by corollary 15 this is a sufficient condition for being decreasing.
By unfolding also the predicate *length* in the definition of *length*0, we get:

```
def1': length0([], 0).
def2': length0([0| Xs], s(N))  ←  all0(Xs), length(Xs, N).
```

We can then apply folding of *def*2′ with *def* (recursive fold), thus obtaining:

```
def1': length0([], 0).
def3 : length0([0| Xs], s(N))  ←  length0(Xs, N).
```

Now *length*0 is defined only in terms of itself.
We can also fold *length*0 in the clause defining *prefix* (propagation fold) and by restricting the program to the deductive closure of *prefix*:

```
1'   : prefix(L, N)  ←  app(L1, [s(0)| Xs], L), length0(L1, N).
6    : app([], Xs, Xs).
7    : app([X| Xs], Y, [X| Zs])  ←  app(Xs, Y, Zs).
def1': length0([], 0).
def3 : length0([0| Xs], s(N))  ←  length0(Xs, N).
```

We have then applied a safe transformation sequence.

5 Conclusion

In this paper we study how to preserve c.a.s. and universal termination while transforming definite programs. We have examined the unfold operation both alone and combined with the new definition and fold operations in a transformation sequence. In order to capture c.a.s. and universal termination, we define an appropriate operational semantics and split the equivalence condition to be satisfied into two complementary conditions: the completeness condition, already studied by [12, 4], and the condition of being non-increasing. The validity of this second condition ensures us that the transformation cannot introduce infinite derivations. We prove that unfold alone is always non-increasing and then it cannot add infinite derivations. Moreover we show that, by introducing some restrictions on the Tamaki-Sato's original definition, the whole transformation sequence is non-increasing and then it preserves also universal termination.

The proof of the non-increasing property of unfold is rather intricate, due to the fact that we are dealing with a non-declarative semantics. On the other hand such a detailed proof enables us to find a very simple sufficient condition to ensure that the first unfold step in a transformation sequence is decreasing, thus making possible to fold later.

Our transformation sequence lets unspecified some transformation steps (from P_1 to P_2) only requiring that they are non-increasing and complete. In most transformations we make use not only of unfold and fold but also of other transformation operations. A very useful one is surely *switching two atoms in the body of a clause* in order to be able to apply folding. This operation does not make sense with a declarative semantics which ignores the order of atoms, but it becomes relevant when considering termination properties and a fixed selection rule. Switching atoms is a special case of a more general operation called *replacement* [24, 15, 8]. We are now studying how to restrict replacement operation in order to preserve universal termination and to be able to deal with more practical transformation strategies.

Acknowledgements

We are much indebted to Krzysztof R. Apt for many stimulating and clarifying discussions on this and related topics and for the encouragement to continue this work.
This work has been partially supported by "Progetto Finalizzato Sistemi Informatici e Calcolo Parallelo" of CNR under grant n. 89.00026.69

References

1. K. R. Apt. Introduction to Logic Programming. In J. van Leeuwen, editor, *Handbook of Theoretical Computer Science*, volume B: Formal Models and Semantics. Elsevier, Amsterdam and The MIT Press, Cambridge, 1990.
2. C. Aravidan and P. M. Dung. On the correctness of Unfold/Fold transformation of normal and extended logic programs. Technical report, Division of Computer Science, Asian Institute of Technology, Bangkok, Thailand, April 1993.
3. M. Baudinet. *Logic Programming Semantics: Techniques and Applications*. PhD thesis, Stanford University, Stanford, California, 1989.
4. A. Bossi and N. Cocco. Basic Transformation Operations which preserve Computed Answer Substitutions of Logic Programs. *Journal of Logic Programming*, 16:47–87, 1993.
5. A. Bossi and N. Cocco. Preserving universal termination through unfold/fold. Technical Report 16, Dip. Matematica Pura e Applicata, Università di Padova, Italy, June 1994.
6. A. Bossi, N. Cocco, and S. Etalle. On Safe Folding. In M. Bruynooghe and M. Wirsing, editors, *Programming Language Implementation and Logic Programming - Proceedings PLILP'92*, volume 631 of *Lecture Notes in Computer Science*, pages 172–186. Springer-Verlag, Berlin, 1992.
7. A. Bossi, N. Cocco, and S. Etalle. Transforming normal program by replacement. In *Third Workshop on Metaprogramming in Logic, META92: Uppsala, Sweden*, June 1992.
8. A. Bossi, N. Cocco, and S. Etalle. Simultaneous replacement in normal programs. Technical Report CS-R9357, Centre for Mathematics and Computer Science, Amsterdam, The Netherlands, August 1993.
9. A. Bossi, N. Cocco, and M. Fabris. Proving termination of logic programs by exploiting term properties. In S. Abramsky and T.S.E. Maibaum, editors, *TAPSOFT '91, Brighton, United Kingdom, April 1991, (Lecture Notes in Computer Science 494)*, pages 153–180. Springer-Verlag, 1991.

10. E. Eder. Properties of substitutions and unifications. *Journal of Symbolic Computation*, 1(1):31–48, 1985.
11. P.A. Gardner and J.C. Shepherdson. Unfold/fold transformations of logic programs. In J-L Lassez and editor G. Plotkin, editors, *Computational Logic: Essays in Honor of Alan Robinson*. 1991.
12. T. Kawamura and T. Kanamori. Preservation of Stronger Equivalence in Unfold/Fold Logic Programming Transformation. In *Proc. Int'l Conf. on Fifth Generation Computer Systems*, pages 413–422. Institute for New Generation Computer Technology, Tokyo, 1988.
13. H. Komorowski. Partial evaluation as a means for inferencing data structures in an applicative language: A theory and implementation in the case of Prolog. In Ninth ACM Symposium on Principles of Programming Languages, Albuquerque, New Mexico, pages 255–267. ACM, 1982.
14. J. W. Lloyd. *Foundations of Logic Programming*. Springer-Verlag, Berlin, 1987. Second edition.
15. M.J. Maher. Correctness of a logic program transformation system. IBM Research Report RC13496, T.J. Watson Research Center, 1987.
16. Mycroft A. N.Jones. Stepwise development of operational and denotational semantics for Prolog. In *International Symposium on Logic Programming, Atlantic City, NJ, (U.S.A.)*, pages 289–298, 1984.
17. C. Palamidessi. Algebraic properties of idempotent substitutions. In M. S. Paterson, editor, *Proc. of the 17th International Colloquium on Automata, Languages and Programming*, volume 443 of *Lecture Notes in Computer Science*, pages 386–399. Springer-Verlag, Berlin, 1990.
18. M. Proietti and A. Pettorossi. Semantics preserving transformation rules for Prolog. In *PEPM 91, New Haven, CT (U.S.A.) (SIGPLAN NOTICES, Vol.26 (9))*, pages 274–284, 1991.
19. M. Proietti and A. Pettorossi. Unfolding, definition, folding, in this order for avoiding unnesessary variables in logic programs. In Maluszynski and M. Wirsing, editors, *PLILP 91, Passau, Germany (Lecture Notes in Computer Science, Vol.528)*, pages 347–358. Springer-Verlag, 1991.
20. T. Sato. An equivalence preserving first order unfold/fold transformation system. In *Second Int. Conference on Algebraic and Logic Programming, Nancy, France, October 1990, (Lecture Notes in Computer Science, Vol. 463)*, pages 175–188. Springer-Verlag, 1990.
21. H. Seki. A comparative study of the Well-Founded and Stable model semantics: Transformation's viewpoint. In D. Pedreschi W. Marek, A. Nerode and V.S. Subrahmanian, editors, *Workshop on Logic Programming and Non-Monotonic Logic, Austin, Texas, October 1990*, pages 115–123, 1990.
22. H. Seki. Unfold/fold transformation of stratified programs. *Journal of Theoretical Computer Science*, 86:107–139, 1991.
23. H. Seki. Unfold/fold transformation of general logic programs for the Well-Founded semantics. *Journal of Logic Programming*, 16:5–23, 1993.
24. H. Tamaki and T. Sato. Unfold/Fold Transformations of Logic Programs. In Sten-Åke Tärnlund, editor, *Proc. Second Int'l Conf. on Logic Programming*, pages 127–139, 1984.
25. T. Vasak and J. Potter. Characterization of Terminating Logic Programs. In *Proc. Third IEEE Int'l Symp. on Logic Programming*, pages 140–147. IEEE Comp. Soc. Press, 1986.

6 Appendix

In our proofs we construct $(S)LD$-derivations which must satisfy the standardization apart condition. This condition is necessary for proving properties of c.a.s.. The following simple lemmas give us the necessary framework in order to construct well-formed LD-derivations by composing and transforming existing ones. The proof of lemma 28 is given in [5].

Definition 22. Two $(S)LD$-derivations are called *similar* iff (i) their first queries are equal and, (ii) for every resolution step, atoms in the same position are selected and the *input clauses* employed are variant of each other.
Two $(S)LD$-derivations are called *corresponding* iff only condition (ii) holds, namely for every resolution step, atoms in the same position are selected and the input clauses employed are variant of each other. □

Clearly, when LD-derivations are considered, the first requirement in (ii) on atoms selection is redundant.
The following theorem is a generalization of the Lifting Lemma, specialized to LD-derivations.

Lemma 23. *Let* $\mathbf{Q} = \mathbf{Q}'\alpha$ *and* $l : \mathbf{Q} \overset{\sigma}{\longmapsto}_P \mathbf{R}$ *be a partial LD-derivation for* $\mathbf{Q}$ *in* P. *Then there exists a partial LD-derivation for* $\mathbf{Q}'$ *in* P, $l' : \mathbf{Q}' \overset{\sigma'}{\longmapsto}_P \mathbf{R}'$, *such that*

- l *and* l' *are corresponding derivations;*
- $(\mathbf{Q}'\sigma', \mathbf{R}') \leq (\mathbf{Q}\sigma, \mathbf{R})$. □

Corollary 24. *In the hypothesis of lemma 23, if* α *is a renaming then* $(\mathbf{Q}'\sigma', \mathbf{R}') \sim (\mathbf{Q}\sigma, \mathbf{R})$. □

Definition 25. Let l, l' be two LD-derivations. l' is *compatible* wrt l iff all the input clauses in l' are standardized apart wrt l. □

Lemma 26. *Let* $l_1 : \mathbf{A} \overset{\alpha}{\longmapsto}_P \mathbf{B}$ *and* $l_2 : \mathbf{B} \overset{\beta}{\longmapsto}_P \mathbf{R}$ *be two LD-derivations. Then, there exists an LD-derivation* $l_2' : \mathbf{B} \overset{\beta'}{\longmapsto}_P \mathbf{R}'$ *similar to* l_2 *and compatible wrt* l_1. □

Lemma 27. *Let* $l_1 : \mathbf{A} \overset{\alpha}{\longmapsto}_P \mathbf{B}$ *and* $l_2 : \mathbf{B} \overset{\beta}{\longmapsto}_P \mathbf{R}$ *be two LD-derivations such that* l_2 *is compatible wrt* l_1. *Then, there exists the LD-derivation* $l : \mathbf{A} \overset{\alpha\beta}{\longmapsto}_P \mathbf{R}$ *which applies the same input clauses of* l_1 *and* l_2 *ordinately.* □

Lemma 28. *Let* $l_1 : \mathbf{B} \overset{\alpha}{\longmapsto}_P \mathbf{E}\alpha$ *and* $l_2 : \mathbf{A}\alpha \overset{\beta}{\longmapsto}_P \Box$ *be two LD-derivations such that* l_1 *is standardized apart wrt* $\mathbf{A}$ *and* l_2 *is compatible wrt* l_1. *Then, there exists the LD-derivation* $l : \mathbf{A}, \mathbf{B} \overset{\alpha\beta}{\longmapsto}_P \mathbf{E}\alpha\beta$ *which has an initial part corresponding to* l_2 *and the rest of the derivation corresponding to* l_1. □

Now let us consider the proof which ensures us that unfold preserves universal termination.

Theorem 29. *Let P be a program and P_1 an unfolding of P. The transformation of P into P_1 is non-increasing.*

Proof. Let $P_1 = unfold(P, B, c)$, where $c = H \leftarrow \mathbf{A}, B, \mathbf{C}$. We have to prove that for any query $\mathbf{Q}$ and for any partial LD-derivation $l : \mathbf{Q} \stackrel{\delta}{\longmapsto}_{P_1} \mathbf{R}$ in P_1 there exists a partial LD-derivation $l* : \mathbf{Q} \stackrel{\delta*}{\longmapsto}_P \mathbf{R}*$ in P with $| l* | \geq | l |$. Moreover, if $\mathbf{R} = \Box$ then $\mathbf{R}* = \Box$ and $\mathbf{Q}\delta \sim \mathbf{Q}\delta*$.
Let c be $H \leftarrow \mathbf{A}, B, \mathbf{C}$ and suppose $d_1, \ldots, d_n$ are the clauses of P available for c via B where, for $i \in [1, n]$, $d'_i = H_i \leftarrow \mathbf{B}_i$, is a variant of d_i with no common variables with c, $\theta_i = mgu(H_i, B)$ and c_i is the corresponding resolvent of c and d_i via B.
The proof is by induction on k, the number of times a clause c_i is applied in l.
$k = 0$. In P we have exactly the same LD-derivation.
$k > 0$. l can be decomposed into three parts: *init*, the initial part preceding the first application of a clause c_i, res_{c_i}, the resolution step applying c_i, and *last*, the last part of l.

Let us first assume that all the clauses $d'_1, \ldots, d'_n, c, c_1, \ldots, c_n$ are standardized apart wrt *init* and that the resolution step res_{c_i} is formed by using c_i as input clause. In the following, this assumption, together with the assumption that the clause c is disjoint from the clauses $d'_i s$, is referred to as *the assumption on init*. Subsequently we will consider the case when the assumption does not hold. Then:

$$
\begin{aligned}
&init : \mathbf{Q} \stackrel{\alpha}{\longmapsto}_{P_1} F, \mathbf{D}, \\
&res_{c_i} : F, \mathbf{D} \stackrel{\theta}{\longmapsto}_{P_1} (\mathbf{A}', \mathbf{B}'_i, \mathbf{C}', \mathbf{D})\theta, \\
&\qquad \text{where } \theta = mgu(H', F), \text{ and } c_i : \quad H' \leftarrow \mathbf{A}', \mathbf{B}'_i, \mathbf{C}' = (H \leftarrow \mathbf{A}, \mathbf{B}_i, \mathbf{C})\theta_i, \\
&last : (\mathbf{A}', \mathbf{B}'_i, \mathbf{C}', \mathbf{D})\theta \stackrel{\gamma}{\longmapsto}_{P_1} \mathbf{R}.
\end{aligned}
$$

In P there exist the LD-derivations: $init : \mathbf{Q} \stackrel{\alpha}{\longmapsto}_P F, \mathbf{D}$, since the clauses in *init* are in $P \cap P_1$.
Moreover, $\theta = mgu(H', F) = mgu(H\theta_i, F)$ and, by the assumption on *init*, $Var(F, \mathbf{D})$, $Var(c)$ and $Var(\theta_i)$ are disjoint sets. Then, there exists $\theta' = mgu(H, F)$, such that $(F, \mathbf{D})\theta' \leq (F, \mathbf{D})\theta$ and $(\mathbf{A}, B, \mathbf{C})\theta' \leq (\mathbf{A}, B, \mathbf{C})\theta_i\theta = (\mathbf{A}', B\theta_i, \mathbf{C}')\theta$.

Hence we can extend *init* by using c as input clause; we obtain:

$$first' : \mathbf{Q} \stackrel{\alpha}{\longmapsto}_P F, \mathbf{D} \stackrel{\theta'}{\longmapsto}_P (\mathbf{A}, B, \mathbf{C}, \mathbf{D})\theta'$$

where $| first' | = | init | + | res_{c_i} |$. Note that this extension is well formed by the assumption on *init*.

We have now to construct in P an LD-derivation $last' : (\mathbf{A}, B, \mathbf{C}, \mathbf{D})\theta' \stackrel{\gamma'}{\longmapsto}_P \mathbf{R}*$ compatible wrt $first'$, with $| last' | \geq | last |$ and such that if $\mathbf{R} = \Box$ then $\mathbf{R}* = \Box$ and $\mathbf{Q}\alpha\theta\gamma \sim \mathbf{Q}\alpha\theta'\gamma'$.

We distinguish three cases depending on the construction of *last*.

Case 1. In P_1 the LD-derivation *last* stops inside $\mathbf{A}'\theta$, i.e. $\mathbf{R} = \mathbf{E}, (\mathbf{B}'_i, \mathbf{C}', \mathbf{D})\theta\gamma \neq \Box$, and there exists the derivation

$$last_A : \mathbf{A}'\theta \overset{\gamma}{\longmapsto}_{P_1} \mathbf{E}$$

corresponding to *last*, and then with the same length.

By applying the inductive hypothesis to $last_A$, we find an LD-derivation $last_A* : \mathbf{A}'\theta \overset{\gamma*}{\longmapsto}_P \mathbf{E}*$, with $| last_A* | \geq | last_A |$.

Since $\mathbf{A}'\theta \geq \mathbf{A}\theta'$, by lemma 23, there exists also an LD-derivation $last'_A : \mathbf{A}\theta' \overset{\gamma_1}{\longmapsto}_P \mathbf{E}_1$, corresponding to $last_A*$ and then with the same length.

Then there exists

$$last' : (\mathbf{A}, B, \mathbf{C}, \mathbf{D})\theta' \overset{\gamma'}{\longmapsto}_P \mathbf{E}', (B, \mathbf{C}, \mathbf{D})\theta'\gamma',$$

corresponding to $last'_A$ and then with the same length.

By lemma 26 there exists a derivation similar to *last'* and compatible with *first'*, hence we may directly assume that *last'* is compatible with *first'*.

Then, since $| last' | = | last'_A | = | last_A* | \geq | last_A | = | last |$, we prove the claim in this first case.

Case 2. In P_1 the LD-derivation *last* goes further wrt $\mathbf{A}'\theta$, but it does not reach the success. Namely, there exist:

$$last_1 : \mathbf{A}'\theta \overset{\gamma_1}{\longmapsto}_{P_1} \Box \qquad \text{and} \qquad last_2 : (\mathbf{B}'_i, \mathbf{C}', \mathbf{D})\theta\gamma_1 \overset{\gamma_2}{\longmapsto}_{P_1} \mathbf{R}$$

with $\mathbf{R} \neq \Box$, $\gamma_1\gamma_2 = \gamma$ and $| last | = | last_1 | + | last_2 |$.

Let us recall that $\theta = mgu(H', F) = mgu(H\theta_i, F), \theta' = mgu(H, F), \theta_i = mgu(H_i, B)$ and that $Var(H_i)$, $Var(H, B)$ and $Var(F)$ are disjoint sets. Then $F\theta_i = F$ and, by lemma 1, $\theta_i\theta$ is an mgu of the set of equations $\{H_i = B\} \cup \{H = F\}$. Moreover, by the same lemma, there exists $\tau = mgu(H_i\theta', B\theta')$ such that $\theta_i\theta = \theta'\tau$. But $H_i\theta' = H_i$, then $\tau = mgu(H_i, B\theta')$.

Hence in P we can apply the input clause d'_i to $(B, \mathbf{C}, \mathbf{D})\theta'$ and obtain the LD-derivation:

$$res_{d_i} : (B, \mathbf{C}, \mathbf{D})\theta' \overset{\tau}{\longmapsto}_P (\mathbf{B}_i, \mathbf{C}\theta', \mathbf{D}\theta')\tau.$$

By the assumption on *init*, res_{d_i} is standardized apart wrt $\mathbf{A}\theta'$ and compatible wrt *first'*.

Note that

$$\mathbf{A}'\theta = \mathbf{A}\theta_i\theta = \mathbf{A}\theta'\tau \tag{1}$$

and there exists $last_1$ in P_1, then by inductive hypothesis, there also exists

$$last'_1 : \mathbf{A}\theta'\tau \overset{\gamma'_1}{\longmapsto}_P \Box, \quad \text{with} \quad | last'_1 | \geq | last_1 | \quad \text{and such that}$$

$$\mathbf{A}'\theta\gamma_1 \sim \mathbf{A}\theta'\tau\gamma'_1. \tag{2}$$

By the assumption on *init* and lemma 26, we may also assume that $last'_1$ is compatible wrt $first'$ and res_{d_i}. Then, by lemma 28, in P there is also:

$$newlast_1 : (\mathbf{A}, B, \mathbf{C}, \mathbf{D})\theta' \overset{\tau\gamma'_1}{\longmapsto}_P (\mathbf{B}_i, \mathbf{C}\theta', \mathbf{D}\theta')\tau\gamma'_1$$

compatible wrt $first'$ and such that $| newlast_1 |>| last'_1 |\geq| last_1 |$.

Now observe that

$$\begin{aligned}(\mathbf{B}_i, \mathbf{C}\theta', \mathbf{D}\theta')\tau &= (\mathbf{B}_i, \mathbf{C}, \mathbf{D})\theta'\tau && \text{since } Var(d'_i) \cap Var(\theta') = \emptyset \\ &= (\mathbf{B}_i, \mathbf{C}, \mathbf{D})\theta_i\theta && \text{since } \theta_i\theta = \theta'\tau \\ &= (\mathbf{B'}_i, \mathbf{C'}, \mathbf{D}\theta_i)\theta && \text{since } (\mathbf{B}_i, \mathbf{C})\theta_i = (\mathbf{B'}_i, \mathbf{C'}) \\ &= (\mathbf{B'}_i, \mathbf{C'}, \mathbf{D})\theta && \text{by the assumption on } init.\end{aligned}$$

Then

$$(\mathbf{B}_i, \mathbf{C}\theta', \mathbf{D}\theta')\tau = (\mathbf{B'}_i, \mathbf{C'}, \mathbf{D})\theta. \tag{3}$$

Let $V = Var(\mathbf{A}'\theta)$. Since l is a well-formed derivation, $Var((\mathbf{B'}_i, \mathbf{C'}, \mathbf{D})\theta) \cap Dom(\gamma_1) \subseteq V$, hence $(\mathbf{B'}_i, \mathbf{C'}, \mathbf{D})\theta\gamma_1 = (\mathbf{B'}_i, \mathbf{C'}, \mathbf{D})\theta(\gamma_1 |_V)$.

By (1) and (2), we obtain $\gamma_1 |_V \sim \gamma'_1 |_V$.
Then $(\mathbf{B'}_i, \mathbf{C'}, \mathbf{D})\theta(\gamma_1 |_V) \sim (\mathbf{B'}_i, \mathbf{C'}, \mathbf{D})\theta(\gamma'_1 |_V)$.

From the assumptions on $last'_1$ and res_{d_i}, and (3) we get that $Var((\mathbf{B'}_i, \mathbf{C'}, \mathbf{D})\theta) \cap Dom(\gamma'_1) \subseteq V$, hence $(\mathbf{B'}_i, \mathbf{C'}, \mathbf{D})\theta(\gamma'_1 |_V) = (\mathbf{B'}_i, \mathbf{C'}, \mathbf{D})\theta\gamma'_1$. Then

$$(\mathbf{B'}_i, \mathbf{C'}, \mathbf{D})\theta\gamma_1 \sim (\mathbf{B'}_i, \mathbf{C'}, \mathbf{D})\theta\gamma'_1. \tag{4}$$

Let us consider now the LD-derivation $last_2$. By inductive hypothesis there exists

$$last_2* : (\mathbf{B'}_i, \mathbf{C'}, \mathbf{D})\theta\gamma_1 \overset{\gamma_2*}{\longmapsto}_P \mathbf{R'} \quad \text{with} \quad | last_2* |\geq| last_2 |.$$

By (4), and corollary 24, there exists also: $last'_2 : (\mathbf{B'}_i, \mathbf{C'}, \mathbf{D})\theta\gamma'_1 \overset{\gamma'_2}{\longmapsto}_P \mathbf{R}*$ corresponding to $last_2*$. By lemma 26, we may also assume that $last'_2$ is compatible wrt $newlast_1$ and $first'$. Then, by lemma 27, we obtain:

$$last' : (\mathbf{A}, B, \mathbf{C}, \mathbf{D})\theta' \overset{\tau\gamma'_1\gamma'_2}{\longmapsto}_P \mathbf{R}*.$$

compatible with $first'$ and such that $| last' |>| last |$.

Let

$$l* :\ \mathbf{Q} \overset{\alpha}{\longmapsto}_P F, \mathbf{D} \overset{\theta'}{\longmapsto}_P (\mathbf{A}, B, \mathbf{C}, \mathbf{D})\theta' \overset{\tau\gamma'_1\gamma'_2}{\longmapsto}_P \mathbf{R}*$$

and observe that $| l* |=| first' | + | last' |>| l |$.

Thus we prove the claim also in this second case.

Case 3. In P_1 the LD-derivation *last* is successful, namely $\mathbf{R} = \Box$. In this case we may first construct a successful SLD-derivation and then the claim follows by the switching lemma.

The first step of this *SLD*-derivation is performed by using the input clause d'_i, thus:

$$last_1 : (\mathbf{A}, B, \mathbf{C}, \mathbf{D})\theta' \mid\!\stackrel{\tau}{\leadsto}_P (\mathbf{A}\theta', \mathbf{B_i}', \mathbf{C}\theta', \mathbf{D}\theta')\tau = (\mathbf{A}', \mathbf{B}'_i, \mathbf{C}', \mathbf{D})\theta$$

where the last equation holds because of (1) and (3). By the assumption on *init*, $last_1$ is compatible with *first'*.

By inductive hypothesis applied to *last*, there exists:

$$last_2 : (\mathbf{A}', \mathbf{B}'_i, \mathbf{C}', \mathbf{D})\theta \stackrel{\gamma'}{\longmapsto}_P \Box$$

with $| last_2 | \geq | last |$ and $(\mathbf{A}', \mathbf{B}'_i, \mathbf{C}', \mathbf{D})\theta\gamma \sim (\mathbf{A}', \mathbf{B}'_i, \mathbf{C}', \mathbf{D})\theta\gamma'$.

By lemma 26, we may also assume that $last_2$ is compatible with $last_1$ and *first'*. Then we have the *SLD*-derivation

$$l* : \mathbf{Q} \stackrel{\alpha}{\longmapsto}_P F, \mathbf{D} \stackrel{\theta'}{\longmapsto}_P (\mathbf{A}, B, \mathbf{C}, \mathbf{D})\theta' \mid\!\stackrel{\tau}{\leadsto}_P (\mathbf{A}', \mathbf{B}'_i, \mathbf{C}', \mathbf{D})\theta \stackrel{\gamma'}{\longmapsto}_P \Box$$

where $| l* | = | first' | + | last_1 | + | last_2 | > | l |$.

Since l is well-formed, $Var(\mathbf{Q}\alpha\theta) \cap Dom(\gamma) \subseteq Var((\mathbf{A}', \mathbf{B}'_i, \mathbf{C}', \mathbf{D})\theta)$.

$l*$ is well-formed too: $Var(\mathbf{Q}\alpha\theta'\tau) \cap Dom(\gamma') \subseteq Var((\mathbf{A}', \mathbf{B}'_i, \mathbf{C}', \mathbf{D})\theta)$.

Hence, from $(\mathbf{A}', \mathbf{B}'_i, \mathbf{C}', \mathbf{D})\theta\gamma \sim (\mathbf{A}', \mathbf{B}'_i, \mathbf{C}', \mathbf{D})\theta\gamma'$, we obtain $\mathbf{Q}\alpha\theta\gamma \sim \mathbf{Q}\alpha\theta'\tau\gamma'$.

By the switching lemma we prove the claim in this third case.

Let us consider now the case when the assumption on *init* does not hold. Let V be the set of variables in $d'_1, \ldots, d'_n, c, c_1, \ldots, c_n$. Then there exists $\mathbf{Q}' = \mathbf{Q}\rho$, such that $Var(\mathbf{Q}') \cap V = \emptyset$, and a partial *LD*-derivation $l' : \mathbf{Q}' \stackrel{\delta'}{\longmapsto}_{P_1} \mathbf{R}'$ whose first part corresponds to *init* and is standardized apart wrt V. Then, by corollary 24, (i) $(\mathbf{Q}\delta, \mathbf{R}) \sim (\mathbf{Q}'\delta', \mathbf{R}')$.

We could then prove our theorem for l', namely that there exists a partial derivation $l'^* : \mathbf{Q}' \stackrel{\delta'^*}{\longmapsto}_P \mathbf{R}'^*$, with $| l'^* | \geq | l' |$, and if $\mathbf{R}' = \Box$, then $\mathbf{R}'^* = \Box$ and (ii) $\mathbf{Q}'\delta' \sim \mathbf{Q}'\delta'^*$.

By lemma 23 and its corollary 24, since $\mathbf{Q}' = \mathbf{Q}\rho$, there exists also a partial *LD*-derivation $l* : \mathbf{Q} \stackrel{\delta*}{\longmapsto}_P \mathbf{R}*$, corresponding to $l'*$, such that (iii) $(\mathbf{Q}'\delta'^*, \mathbf{R}'*) \sim (\mathbf{Q}\delta*, \mathbf{R}*)$.

Hence, by (i), (ii) and (iii), $\mathbf{Q}\rho \sim \mathbf{Q}\rho*$, which completes the proof. $\Box$

A Logic for Variable Aliasing in Logic Programs

Elena Marchiori

CWI, P.O. Box 94079, 1090 GB Amsterdam, The Netherlands, e-mail:elena@cwi.nl

Abstract. This paper introduces a logic for a class of properties - in particular variable aliasing - used in static analysis of logic programs. The logic is shown to be sound, complete and decidable. Moreover, it is illustrated how this logic can be applied to automatize some parts of the reasoning when proving the partial correctness of a logic program.

1 Introduction

A number of properties of substitutions have been identified as crucial when analyzing the run-time behaviour of logic programs. They involve groundness and aliasing: for a substitution α, a variable x is said to be ground if $x\alpha$ does not contain variables; x and y are said to share, or to be aliasing if $x\alpha$ and $y\alpha$ have at least a variable in common. These properties are relevant in static analysis of logic programs. For instance, detection of groundness of certain variables of the program at run-time allows to improve efficiency, by using matching instead of unification. Also, if the arguments of two atoms at run-time do not share any variable, then they may be executed in parallel.

Various assertional methods to prove the correctness and termination of a logic program incorporate these properties in the assertion language ([DM88], [CM91]; see [AM94] for an overview and comparison of various assertional methods). These properties play an even more fundamental role in abstract interpretation of logic programs, where they are used to compute approximations of the set of all possible substitutions which can occur at each step of the execution of the program. The abstract interpretation approach, developed in [CC77] for data-flow analysis of imperative programs, has been successfully applied to logic programs (see [AH87] for a brief introduction to the major stages in the development of the field; see [CC92] for a survey on its applications to logic programs). Since both the problems of groundness and of sharing among program variables at run-time is undecidable, it remains a hard problem to find an abstract interpretation framework for the study of aliasing that is efficient and that provides an accurate analysis.

We introduce a logic where the relation symbols *var*, *ground* and *share* are used to express the basic properties we intend to study and the logical operators $\wedge$ and $\neg$ are used to express composite properties. Then the semantics of the resulting assertions consists of a set of substitutions, where $\wedge$ and $\neg$ are interpreted as set-theoretic intersection and complementation; the atoms $var(t)$ and $ground(t)$ are interpreted as the set of substitutions which map the term t to a variable and a ground term, respectively; finally the semantics of $share(t_1, \ldots, t_n)$

is the set of substitutions which map the terms $t_1, \ldots, t_n$ to terms sharing some variable. A system of inference rules (used as rewrite rules) is introduced which allows the definition of a terminating procedure which decides truth (hence satisfiability) of assertions in the logic. As an example, we illustrate how this procedure can be applied to mechanize some parts of the reasoning when proving the partial correctness of a logic program.

In [CM92] unification in logic programming is characterized by means of a predicate transformer, where also the assertions of our logic are considered. Moreover, a number of rules occurring in the present paper (viz. the singleton rules of Table 1) are there implicitly used to simplify the form of an assertion. However, the problem of finding a complete axiomatization of these properties is not investigated.

A formalization of groundness by means of a propositional logic has been given in [MS89]. The propositional logic is used as an abstract domain, to analyze variable groundness in logic programs. That logic has further been studied in [CFW91]. However, to the best of our knowledge our contribution is the first rigorous study of those properties of substitutions expressed by *groundness*, *var* and *aliasing* together with their relationship.

2 A Logic for Properties of Substitutions

Syntax

We shall consider terms containing variables. Formally, consider a countable set Var of *variables*. Let Fun be a set of *functors with rank*, containing a set $Const$ of *constants* consisting of the functors with rank zero. The class $Term$ of *terms* is the smallest set T containing $Const \cup Var$ and with the property that if $t_1, \ldots, t_n$ are in T and $f \in Fun$ has rank n then $f(t_1, \ldots, t_n)$ is in T. Then a substitution σ is a map from Var to $Term$ such that its domain $dom(\sigma) = \{x \in Var \mid x\sigma \neq x\}$ is finite. The definition of substitution is extended in the standard way to terms in $Term$, where for a substitution σ and a term t the term $t\sigma$ is obtained by simultaneously replacing every variable x of t by the term $x\sigma$. Moreover for a set S of terms and for a substitution σ we denote by $S\sigma$ the set $\{t\sigma \mid t \in S\}$. The set of substitutions is denoted by $Subst$.

For a syntactic expression o, $Var(o)$ denotes the set of variables occurring in o. Variables are denoted by v, x, y, z. Functors are indicated by f, g and constants by a, b, c. Terms are denoted by the letters r, s, t. The capital letter S is used to denote a finite set of terms, while $|S|$ indicates the cardinality of S.

Properties are expressed by means of formulas called assertions.

Definition 1. (Assertions) The set $\mathcal{A}$ of *assertions* is the smallest set A of formulas containing the atoms $var(t)$, $ground(t)$ for all terms t in $Term$, and $share(S)$ for all sets S of terms in $Term$, and with the property that if ϕ is in A then $\neg\phi$ is in A, and if ϕ and ψ are in A then $\phi \wedge \psi$ is in A.

The notation $\phi \vee \psi$ is used as a shorthand for $\neg(\neg\phi \wedge \neg\psi)$. Atoms and their negation form the class of *literals*, where a literal is denoted by L.

Semantics

An assertion ϕ is interpreted as a set $[\![\phi]\!]$ of substitutions. Logical connectives are interpreted set-theoretically in such a way that set intersection and union correspond to $\wedge$ and $\vee$, respectively, while complementation (w.r.t. *Subst*) corresponds to $\neg$. Atoms are interpreted as follows: $var(t)$ is the set of substitutions which map t to a variable, $ground(t)$ is the set of substitutions which map t to a term containing no variables, and $share(\{t_1, \ldots, t_n\})$ is the set of substitutions which map $t_1, \ldots, t_n$ to terms containing at least one common variable.

Definition 2. (Semantics)

$$[\![var(t)]\!] = \{\sigma \in Subst \mid t\sigma \in Var\};$$

$$[\![ground(t)]\!] = \{\sigma \in Subst \mid Var(t\sigma) = \emptyset\};$$

$$[\![share(\{s_1, \ldots, s_n\})]\!] = \{\sigma \in Subst \mid \bigcap_{i=1}^{n} Var(s_i\sigma) \neq \emptyset\};$$

$$[\![\phi \wedge \psi]\!] = [\![\phi]\!] \cap [\![\psi]\!];$$

$$[\![\neg\phi]\!] = Subst - [\![\phi]\!].$$

□

If $[\![\phi]\!] = Subst$ then ϕ is said to be true; if there exists σ s.t. $\sigma \in [\![\phi]\!]$ then ϕ is said to be satisfiable. Two assertions ϕ and ψ are said to be equivalent if $[\![\phi]\!] = [\![\psi]\!]$. Notice that $share(\{t\})$ is equivalent to $\neg ground(t)$. Therefore we will assume in the following that only atoms of the form $share(S)$, with $|S| \geq 2$ occur in an assertion. Moreover it is convenient to introduce the propositional constants *true* and *false* where $[\![true]\!] = Subst$ and $[\![false]\!] = \emptyset$.

Assertions satisfy the classical replacement theorem.

Theorem 3. *Let ψ be a sub-assertion of an assertion ϕ. Suppose that ψ is equivalent to ψ'. Let ϕ' be the assertion obtained replacing zero or more occurrences of ψ in ϕ by the assertion ψ'. Then ϕ is equivalent to ϕ'.*

Proof. Easy, by induction on the number of connectives occurring in ϕ. □

3 Axiomatization

In this section, a system of axioms and inference rules is introduced, where all the rules are of a particular simple form $\frac{\phi}{\psi}$, where ϕ and ψ are assertions in $\mathcal{A}$. The meaning of a rule is that ϕ and ψ are equivalent. Equivalence is required because rules will be used as rewrite rules: ψ will be replaced by ϕ. We shall apply then rules also to formulas that occur as subformulas of a larger formula. This will still preserve equivalence because of Theorem 3. For instance, the application of the rule $\frac{\phi}{\psi}$ to the formula $\psi \vee \neg\phi$ produces the formula $\phi \vee \neg\phi$.

The system is used to define, in the following section, a terminating procedure which reduces an assertion ϕ to *true* if and only if ϕ is true.
The following collection of *general rules* will be used to simplify the form of assertions.

$$\textbf{G1}\ \mathit{true} \quad \textbf{G2}\ \neg\mathit{false} \quad \textbf{G3}\ \phi \vee \neg\phi \quad \textbf{G4}\ \phi \vee \mathit{true}$$

$$\textbf{G5}\ \frac{\phi \vee \psi}{\psi \vee \phi} \quad \textbf{G6}\ \frac{\phi}{\phi \vee \mathit{false}} \quad \textbf{G7}\ \frac{\phi}{\phi \wedge \mathit{true}} \quad \textbf{G8}\ \frac{\phi}{\phi \vee \phi}$$

We consider two other collections of rules, given in Tables 1 and 2: the *singleton rules* which describe the semantics of an atom by investigating the structure of its arguments and the *combination rules* which describe the semantics of disjunctions of literals.

Notice that, in the singleton rules, k is greater or equal than 0. Moreover if $k = 0$ then $\bigvee_{i\in[1,k]} \phi_i$ and $\bigwedge_{i\in[1,k]} \phi_i$ should be read as *false* and *true*, respectively. Moreover, in the combination rules S, S_1 and S_2 denote sets of variables.

$$\textbf{S1}\quad \frac{\mathit{false}}{\mathit{var}(f(s_1,\ldots,s_k))}$$

$$\textbf{S2}\quad \frac{\bigwedge_{i\in[1,k]} \mathit{ground}(s_i)}{\mathit{ground}(f(s_1,\ldots,s_k))}$$

$$\textbf{S3}\quad \frac{\bigvee_{i\in[1,k]} \mathit{share}(S \cup \{s_i\})}{\mathit{share}(S \cup \{f(s_1,\ldots,s_k)\})}$$

Table 1. Singleton Rules

Theorem 4. *General rules, singleton rules and combination rules are equivalences.*

Proof. For the general rules the result follows direct from Definition 2. For a rule $\frac{\phi}{\psi}$ we have to show that a substitution is in $[\![\phi]\!]$ if and only if it is in $[\![\psi]\!]$;

C1	$\neg ground(x) \vee \neg var(x)$
C2	$\dfrac{\neg var(x)}{ground(x) \vee \neg var(x)}$
C3	$\dfrac{\neg ground(x)}{\neg ground(x) \vee var(x)}$
C4	$\dfrac{\neg ground(x)}{\neg ground(x) \vee share(S \cup \{x\})}$
C5	$\neg ground(x) \vee \neg share(S \cup \{x\})$
C6	$\dfrac{\neg share(S \cup \{x\})}{ground(x) \vee \neg share(S \cup \{x\})}$
C7	$\dfrac{\neg var(x) \vee \neg share(S_1 \cup S_2 \cup \{x\})}{\neg var(x) \vee \neg share(S_1 \cup \{x\}) \vee \neg share(S_2 \cup \{x\})}$
C8	$share(S_1) \vee \neg share(S_1 \cup S_2)$

Table 2. Combination Rules

for an axiom ϕ we have to show that every substitution is in $[\![\phi]\!]$. Let α be an arbitrary substitution. Notice that

$$Var(f(s_1, \ldots, s_k)\alpha) = \bigcup_{i=1}^{k} Var(s_i\alpha). \tag{1}$$

S1: $f(s_1, \ldots, s_k)\alpha$ is not in Var.
S2: From (1) it follows that $Var(f(s_1, \ldots, s_k)\alpha) = \emptyset$ if and only if $Var(s_i\alpha) = \emptyset$ for $i \in [1, k]$.
S3: From (1) it follows that $\bigcap_{s \in S} Var(s\alpha) \cap Var(f(s_1, \ldots, s_k)\alpha) \neq \emptyset$ if and only if $\bigcap_{s \in S} Var(s\alpha) \cap Var(s_i) \neq \emptyset$ for some $i \in [1, k]$.
C2: $\alpha \in [\![ground(x)]\!]$ implies $Var(x\alpha) = \emptyset$ which implies $\alpha \in [\![\neg var(x)]\!]$.
C6: $\alpha \in [\![ground(x)]\!]$ implies $Var(x\alpha) = \emptyset$ which implies $\alpha \in [\![\neg share(S \cup \{x\})]\!]$.
C7: If $x\alpha \notin Var$ then the result follows immediate; if $x\alpha \in Var$ then $Var(x\alpha) \cap \bigcap_{y \in S_1} Var(y\alpha) \cap \bigcap_{z \in S_2} Var(z\alpha) = \emptyset$ if and only if $x\alpha \notin \bigcap_{y \in S_1} Var(y\alpha)$ or $x\alpha \notin \bigcap_{z \in S_2} Var(z\alpha)$.
C8: If $\bigcap_{y \in S_1} Var(y\alpha) \neq \emptyset$ then $\alpha \in [\![share(S_1)]\!]$; if $\bigcap_{y \in S_1} Var(y\alpha) = \emptyset$ then $\bigcap_{y \in S_1 \cup S_2} Var(y\alpha) = \emptyset$ which implies $\alpha \in [\![\neg share(S_1 \cup S_2)]\!]$.

Moreover it is easy to check that rules **C1** and **C3** can be derived from rule **C2** by straightforward set operations. Analogously, rules **C4** and **C5** can be derived from rule **C6**. These rules are useful in the following section.

□

4 Soundness, Completeness and Decidability of the Logic

The system of rules introduced in the previous section allows to define a terminating procedure which applied to an assertion ϕ yields *true* if and only if ϕ is true. For technical reasons, it is convenient to have only one axiom, namely (G1): thus every other axiom ϕ is translated into the rule $\frac{true}{\phi}$. First, the singleton rules are used to reduce ϕ to a form called flat form; next the conjunctive normal form $\phi_1 \wedge \ldots \wedge \phi_n$ is computed; finally every conjunct ϕ_i is reduced to a normal form by means of the combination rules and the general rules and the outcome *true* is given if and only if the resulting conjuncts are equal to *true*.

4.1 Flat Form and Normal Form

Definition 5. (Flat Form) An assertion is in *flat form* if it does not contain any functors.

For example the assertion $share(\{f(x), y\}) \wedge var(x)$ is not in flat form (because the term $f(x)$ contains a functor) while the assertion $\neg var(x) \vee (ground(x) \wedge share(\{y, z\}))$ is in flat form.
The (proof of the) following lemma provides an algorithm to transform an assertion in flat form.

The following function *size* is used to prove that the algorithm terminates: *size* maps a term s to the natural number n, and is defined as follows:

$$size(s) = \begin{cases} 1 & \text{if } s \in Var \\ 1 + \sum_{i=1}^{n} size(s_i) & \text{if } s = f(s_1, \ldots, s_n),\ n \geq 0, \end{cases}$$

where $\sum_{i=1}^{0} size(s_i)$ is assumed to be equal to 0.

Lemma 6. *ϕ is equivalent to an assertion in flat form.*

Proof. The flat form of ϕ is obtained by applying repeatedly the singleton rules to every atom occurring in ϕ. The process terminates because the quantity

$$m(\phi) = \begin{cases} 0 & \text{if } \phi \in \{false, true\} \\ \sum_{s \in S} size(s) & \text{otherwise,} \end{cases}$$

where S is the union of the arguments of the literals which occur in ϕ (thus counting multiple occurrences of terms only once; here an argument which is a term, say t, is identified with the singleton set $\{t\}$) decreases when a rule is applied to ϕ. It follows from Theorem 4 and Theorem 3 that the resulting assertion is equivalent to ϕ. □

Notice that from the proof of the previous lemma it follows that the flat form of an assertion computed using the singleton rules is unique modulo the order in which the literals occur in the assertion.

We introduce now the class of assertions in *normal form*.

Definition 7. (Normal Form) An assertion ϕ is in *normal form* if ϕ is in flat form and $\phi = \bigvee_{i=1}^{n} L_i$, $n \geq 1$ such that either ϕ is a propositional constant or ϕ does not contain any propositional constant, $L_i \neq L_j$ for $i \neq j$ and the following conditions hold:

(a) if $L_i = \neg ground(x)$ for some $i \in [1, n]$ then $x \notin Var(L_j)$ for every $j \neq i$;
(b) if $L_i = ground(x)$ for some $i \in [1, n]$ then every other literal containing x is either equal to $var(x)$ or it is of the form $share(S \cup \{x\})$;
(c) if $L_i = \neg var(x)$ for some $i \in [1, n]$ then every other literal containing x is of the form $*share(S \cup \{x\})$ and at most one of them is of the form $\neg share(S \cup \{x\})$ ($*$ denotes $\neg$ or a blank);
(d) if $L_i = share(S)$ for some $i \in [1, n]$ then for every other literal of the form $\neg\, share(S')$ we have that $S \not\subseteq S'$.

For example the assertion $\neg ground(x) \vee var(x)$ is not in normal form (because condition (a) of the definition is not satisfied), the assertion $share(\{x, y\}) \vee \neg share(\{x, y, z\})$ is not in normal form (because condition (d) of the definition is not satisfied) while the assertion $\neg ground(x) \vee ground(y) \vee var(y) \vee share(\{y, z\})$ is in normal form.

The (proof of the) following lemma provides an algorithm to transform into normal form any assertion in flat form consisting of a disjunction of literals.

Lemma 8. *Let $\phi = \bigvee_{i \in [1,n]} L_i$. Suppose that ϕ is in flat form. Then ϕ is equivalent to an assertion in normal form.*

Proof. The normal form of ϕ is obtained as follows. For every variable x contained in ϕ the disjunction of literals of ϕ containing x is considered and the combination rules are applied, using the general rules when applicable and using rule $(G5)$ only a finite number of times. Notice that all the rules preserve the flat form. The result will be either a propositional constant, by application of rules (G2), (G3), (G4), (G5), (G6), (C1), (C5) and (C8); otherwise the result will not contain any propositional constant, by application of rules (G5) and (G6): moreover it will satisfy (a) by application of rules (C1), (C3), (C4), (C5) and (G3), (G5) and (G8); it will satisfy (b) by application of rules (C2), (C6) and (G3), (G5) and (G8); it will satisfy (c) by application of rules (C1), (C2), (C7) and (G3),(G5) and (G8); finally it will satisfy (d) by application of the rules (G5) and (C8).

The process terminates because by assumption rule (G5) is applied only finitely many times, and the application of every other rule decreases the number of connectives of the assertion. Finally, Theorem 4 and Theorem 3 imply that the resulting assertion is equivalent to ϕ. □

Notice that from the proof of the previous lemma it follows that the normal form of an assertion consisting of a disjunction of literals, computed using the general rules and the combination rules, is unique modulo the order in which the literals occur in the assertion.

The following example illustrates the application of the axiomatization.

Example 1. Consider the assertion ϕ:

$$var(f(w)) \vee ground(x) \vee \neg share(\{x,y\}) \vee \neg share(\{y,z\}) \vee \neg share(\{z,w\}) \vee share(\{x, g(a,y), z\}).$$

1. Application of rule (S1) to $var(f(w))$ yields
$false \vee ground(x) \vee \neg share(\{x,y\}) \vee \neg share(\{y,z\}) \vee \neg share(\{z,w\}) \vee share(\{x, g(a,y), z\})$;
2. application of rule (S3) to $share(\{x, g(a,y), z\})$ yields
$false \vee ground(x) \vee \neg share(\{x,y\}) \vee \neg share(\{y,z\}) \vee \neg share(\{z,w\}) \vee share(\{x,a,z\}) \vee share(\{x,y,z\})$;
3. application of rule (S3) to $share(\{x,a,z\})$ yields
$false \vee ground(x) \vee \neg share(\{x,y\}) \vee \neg share(\{y,z\}) \vee \neg share(\{z,w\}) \vee false \vee share(\{x,y,z\})$,
which is in flat form.
4. Application of rule (G5) yields
$ground(x) \vee \neg share(\{x,y\}) \vee \neg share(\{y,z\}) \vee \neg share(\{z,w\}) \vee false \vee share(\{x,y,z\}) \vee false$;
5. application of rule (G6) yields
$ground(x) \vee \neg share(\{x,y\}) \vee \neg share(\{y,z\}) \vee \neg share(\{z,w\}) \vee false \vee share(\{x,y,z\})$;
6. application of rule (G5) yields
$share(\{x,y,z\}) \vee ground(x) \vee \neg share(\{x,y\}) \vee \neg share(\{y,z\}) \vee \neg share(\{z,w\}) \vee false$;
7. application of rule (G6) yields
$share(\{x,y,z\}) \vee ground(x) \vee \neg share(\{x,y\}) \vee \neg share(\{y,z\}) \vee \neg share(\{z,w\})$;
8. application of rule (C6) to $ground(x) \vee \neg share(\{x,y\})$ yields
$$share(\{x,y,z\}) \vee \neg share(\{x,y\}) \vee \neg share(\{y,z\}) \vee \neg share(\{z,w\}),$$
which is in normal form.

4.2 Decidability Procedure

The previous results are used to define the following decidability procedure.

Definition 9. (Truth Procedure) The *truth procedure* TP reduces an assertion ϕ as follows. First the flat form ϕ_1 of ϕ is computed by means of Lemma 6. Next ϕ_1 is transformed (using standard methods) into a conjunctive normal form $\phi_2 = \psi_1 \wedge \ldots \wedge \psi_n$, where every ψ_i is a disjunction of literals. Finally every ψ_i is reduced to normal form by means of Lemma 8 and rule (G7) is applied to the resulting conjunction as many times as possible. □

Thus ϕ is reduced by TP to a conjunction of assertions in normal form. We prove now that TP is correct and terminating. Let $TP(\phi)$ denote the outcome of TP applied to ϕ.

Theorem 10. *TP is a terminating procedure and $TP(\phi)$ is equal to true if and only if ϕ is equivalent to true.*

To prove the above statement it is necessary to assume that *Fun* contains a functor of rank 0 (i.e., a constant) and one of rank 2. If it is not the case, then we add such functors to the language. Moreover some preliminary results are necessary. First, an algorithm called *Prod* is defined: given as input an assertion ψ in normal form which is neither equal to *true* nor to *false*, *Prod* produces a substitution σ such that $\sigma \notin [\![\psi]\!]$. This σ is computed in a number of steps. After each step, the intermediate result (still called σ) is applied to the resulting formula, called $A(\psi)$. Thus, two variables are used: a variable σ which contains the part of the substitution actually computed and a variable $A(\psi)$, which contains the assertion obtained from ψ applying σ. Moreover in the algorithm we need to know which of the variables of $A(\psi)$ stem from the application of the computed σ. For instance, suppose $\psi = share(\{x, y\})$ and $\sigma = \{x/f(z)\}$: then $A(\psi) = share(\{f(z), y\})$ and z is a variable which stems from the application of σ. Then to recognize these variables we assume that they are chosen from the set $IVar = Var \setminus Var(\phi)$. Variables of $IVar$ are denoted by capital letters $U, V, \ldots$. In the remainder of this section, the variables of $IVar$ occurring in a syntactic object o are called *image variables*, denoted by $Ivar(o)$, while the other variables occurring in o are called simply *variables*, denoted by $Var(o)$. Finally some other variables are used in the algorithm: for every literal L in ψ of the form $\neg share(S)$ for some S, a variable im_L is introduced which either is equal to a image variable or is undefined. The role of these variables will be explained afterwards. Initially im_L is undefined, and once im_L is set to a particular image variable, it will never change. For a image variable U the notation $U = im_L$ means that im_L is defined and that U is equal to (the value of) im_L.

The algorithm *Prod* is now defined as follows. Let g be a functor of rank 2 and let a be a constant. Let $g_1(t)$ denote the term $g(t, t)$ and for $n \geq 2$ let $g_n(t_1, \ldots, t_n)$ denote the term $g(t_1, g(t_2, \ldots, g(t_{n-1}, t_n) \ldots))$.

Initially $A(\psi)$ is set to ψ and σ is set to ϵ, the empty substitution. The algorithm consists of the following sequence of three steps.

1 For every variable x occurring in ψ, perform the following sequence of actions:
- **1.1** If the antecedent of (a) holds then set σ to $\sigma \cup \{x/a\}$;
- **1.2** If the antecedent of (b) holds then set σ to $\sigma \cup \{x/g_1(U)\}$, where U is a fresh image variable (i.e. an image variable not yet used);
- **1.3** If the antecedent of (c) holds then set σ to $\sigma \cup \{x/U\}$, where:
  - **1.3.1** if a literal L of the form $\neg share(S \cup \{x\})$ occurs in ψ then either $U = im_L$ or, if im_L is undefined, U is chosen to be a fresh image variable and im_L is set to U;
  - **1.3.2** otherwise (i.e., if no literal of the form $\neg share(S \cup \{x\})$ occurs in ψ) U is a fresh image variable;

1.4 set $A(\psi)$ to $A(\psi)\sigma$.

2 For every variable x occurring in $A(\psi)$, perform the following sequence of actions:

2.1 If $L_1\sigma, \ldots, L_m\sigma$ are all the disjuncts of $A(\psi)$ of the form $\neg share(S \cup \{x\})$, with $m \geq 1$, then set σ to $\sigma \cup \{x/g_m(V_1, \ldots, V_m)\}$, where $V_1, \ldots, V_m$ are distinct image variables such that: either $V_i = im_{L_i}$ or, if im_{L_i} is undefined, V_i is chosen to be a fresh image variable and im_{L_i} is set to V_i.

2.2 Set $A(\psi)$ to $A(\psi)\sigma$.

3 For every variable x occurring in $A(\psi)$ set σ to $\sigma \cup \{x/a\}$. Set $A(\psi)$ to $A(\psi)\sigma$. □

Some explanation of the steps of the algorithm is needed: as already said, the aim of *Prod*, when applied to an assertion ψ in normal form which is not a propositional constant, is to produce a substitution σ which is not in the semantics $[\![\psi]\!]$ of ψ. Such substitution is built incrementally, by binding each variable of ψ to a suitable term. The first three subcases of step 1 are mutually exclusive, and correspond to the first three cases in the definition of normal form. Thus after step 1 is executed, literals of the form $\neg ground(x)\sigma$, $ground(x)\sigma$, and $\neg var(x)\sigma$ become false. Moreover the variables which are not yet bound by σ occur either in literals of the form $\neg share(S)$, or of the form $share(S)$ or of the form $var(x)$. Step 2 of *Prod* takes care of all the literals of the form $\neg share(S)$: the variables of S are mapped by the substitution to terms having exactly one image variable in common. Finally step 3 of *Prod* takes care of all the literals of the form $var(x)\sigma$ or $share(S)\sigma$ which contain some variable.

To avoid that in step 2 the variables of some literal of the form $share(S')$ become bound to terms having some common image variable, it is sufficient (as will be proven in Lemma 14) that the image variables which are shared by the terms of distinct literals of the form $\neg share(S)$, be distinct. This is obtained by means of the variables im_L, which fix once for all the image variable which will be shared eventually by all the terms of L.

We illustrate now the application of *Prod* with an example.

Example 2. Let ψ be the formula obtained in Example 1:

$$share(\{x, y, z\}) \vee \neg share(\{x, y\}) \vee \neg share(\{y, z\}) \vee \neg share(\{z, w\}).$$

Since ψ is in normal form, we can apply *Prod*. Let L_1 denote $\neg share(\{x, y\})$, let L_2 denote $\neg share(\{y, z\})$ and let L_3 denote $\neg share(\{z, w\})$. The values of the variables of *Prod* corresponding to one possible execution are given below, where only the initial and the final value of $A(\psi)$ are shown:

1. Initialization:
   $A(\psi) = \psi$, $\sigma = \epsilon$, im_{L_i} undefined for $i \in [1, 3]$;
2. Step 2, suppose *Prod* has chosen the variable y:
   $\sigma = \{y/g(V_1, V_2)\}$, $im_{L_1} = V_1$, $im_{L_2} = V_2$, im_{L_3} undefined;

3. Step 2, suppose *Prod* has chosen the variable x:
   $\sigma = \{y/g(V_1, V_2), x/g(V_1, V_1)\}$, $im_{L_1} = V_1$, $im_{L_2} = V_2$, im_{L_3} undefined;
4. Step 2, suppose *Prod* has chosen the variable z:
   $\sigma = \{y/g(V_1, V_2), x/g(V_1, V_1), z/g(V_2, V_3)\}$,
   $im_{L_1} = V_1$, $im_{L_2} = V_2$, $im_{L_3} = V_3$;
5. Step 2, suppose *Prod* has chosen the variable w:
   $\sigma = \{y/g(V_1, V_2), x/g(V_1, V_1), z/g(V_2, V_3), w/g(V_3, V_3)\}$,
   $im_{L_1} = V_1$, $im_{L_2} = V_2$, $im_{L_3} = V_3$;
6. stop (all the variables of ψ have been considered):
   $A(\psi) = \neg share(\{g(V_1, V_1), g(V_1, V_2)\}) \vee \neg share(\{g(V_1, V_2), g(V_2, V_3)\}) \vee$
   $share(\{g(V_1, V_1), g(V_1, V_2), g(V_2, V_3)\}) \vee \neg share(\{g(V_2, V_3), g(V_3, V_3)\})$.

Notice that *Prod* terminates because the number of variables occurring in a formula ψ is finite. Moreover σ is well-defined because the first three cases of step 1 are mutually exclusive and variables of type im_L are distinct, as Lemma 11 will show. To show that *Prod* is correct (i.e., that if *Prod* is applied to ψ then the produced substitution σ is not in $[\![\psi]\!]$), we need some preliminary results. The following lemma states a crucial property of the variables of type im_L.

Lemma 11. *Let im_L and $im_{L'}$ be two distinct variables of Prod. If im_L and $im_{L'}$ are defined then they are equal to two distinct image variables.*

Proof. Notice that im_L is initially undefined and it becomes defined only when it is bound by *Prod* to a fresh image variable. □

In the following lemma a property is proven to be invariant under the execution of *Prod*. Notice that σ is considered as a variable of the algorithm and that at every step of the algorithm, $A(\psi)$ is equal to $\psi\sigma$, for a suitable *value* of σ. Therefore in the following a literal of $A(\psi)$ is sometimes denoted by $L\sigma$, where L is the corresponding literal of ψ and σ is the actual value of the computed substitution.

Lemma 12. *If $x \in dom(\sigma)$ and x occurs in m disjuncts of ψ of the form $\neg share(S)$, for some $m \geq 1$, then*

$$x\sigma = \begin{cases} im_{L_1} & \text{if } m = 1 \text{ and the antecedent of (c) holds,} \\ g_m(im_{L_1}, \ldots, im_{L_m}) & \text{if } m \geq 1 \text{ and the antecedent of (c) does not hold,} \end{cases}$$

where L_1, ..., L_m are all the disjuncts of ψ of the form $\neg share(S)$ such that $x \in S$.

Proof. Initially *Prod* satisfies trivially the property because $\sigma = \epsilon$. Step 1 preserves the property: for every variable x considered in that step, if the first or second subcase was applied then x does not occur in disjuncts of the form $\neg share(S)$; if the third subcase was applied then if im_L was undefined then x is bound to one fresh image variable and im_L is set to that image variable; otherwise (i.e., im_L defined) x is bound to im_L. Step 2 preserves the property because, for every variable x considered in that step, x is bound to a term t such that: if $m \geq 1$ then t is $g_m(V_1, \ldots, V_m)$, where for $i \in [1, m]$ if im_{L_i} was defined then V_i is equal to im_{L_i}, otherwise V_i is a fresh image variable and im_{L_i} is set to V_i. Finally step 3 preserves the property because the variables considered do not occur in disjuncts of the form $\neg share(S)$. □

Lemma 13. *If $S \subseteq dom(\sigma)$ is such that*

1. *$S \not\subseteq S'$, for every disjunct of ψ of the form $\neg share(S')$;*
2. *for every x in S there exists a disjunct of ψ of the form $\neg share(S')$ such that $x \in S'$.*

Then $\bigcap_{x \in S} Ivar(x\sigma) = \emptyset$.

Proof. From the hypothesis it follows that S contains at least two elements, i.e., $S = \{x_1, \ldots, x_n\}$, $n \geq 2$. Then by Lemma 12 we have that for $i \in [1, n]$

$$x_i\sigma = \begin{cases} im_{L_1^{x_i}} & \text{if } m_i = 1 \text{ and the antecedent of (c) holds,} \\ g_{m_i}(im_{L_1^{x_i}}, \ldots, im_{L_{m_i}^{x_i}}) & \text{if } m_i \geq 1 \text{ and the antecedent of (c) does not hold,} \end{cases}$$

where $L_1^{x_i}, \ldots, L_{m_i}^{x_i}$ are all the disjuncts of ψ of the form $\neg share(S')$ such that $x_i \in S'$. By 2 we have that $m_i \geq 1$ for $i \in [1, n]$. Suppose by absurd that $\bigcap_{x \in S} Ivar(x\sigma)$ is not empty. Then there exist $j_1, \ldots, j_n$ such that for $i \in [1, n]$: $1 \leq j_i \leq m_i$ and $im_{L_{j_1}^{x_1}} = im_{L_{j_2}^{x_2}} = \ldots = im_{L_{j_n}^{x_n}}$. Then by Lemma 11 it follows that $L_{j_1}, L_{j_2}, \ldots, L_{j_n}$ are all the same literal, say L and $x_1, \ldots, x_n$ are all contained in L. This contradicts 1. □

Lemma 14. *Let $share(S)$ be a disjunct of ψ. Suppose that $Var(A(\psi)) = \emptyset$. Then $\bigcap_{x \in S} Ivar(x\sigma) = \emptyset$.*

Proof. From $Var(A(\psi)) = \emptyset$ it follows that $S \subseteq dom(\sigma)$. If for some $x \in S$, $x\sigma$ is obtained from step 1.2 or from step 3 of *Prod* then it is a term containing only one fresh variable or it is a constant. Then the result follows immediate (recall that $|S| \geq 2$, by assumption). Otherwise every x in S occurs in a disjunct of ψ of the form $\neg share(S')$. Moreover since ψ is in normal form then $S \not\subseteq S'$ for every disjunct of ψ of the form $\neg share(S')$. Then 1 and 2 of Lemma 13 are satisfied. Thus $\bigcap_{x \in S} Ivar(x\sigma) = \emptyset$. □

Lemma 15. *If L, with relation symbol var or ground, is a disjunct of $A(\psi)$ such that $Var(L) = \emptyset$ then L is equivalent to false.*

Proof. Initially $A(\psi)$ satisfies the property because ψ is in flat form, hence the argument of an unary atom is a variable. The application of step 1 transforms all literals of the form $\neg ground(x)$ (first subcase) or $ground(x)$ (second subcase) or $\neg var(x)$ (third subcase) into an assertion equivalent to *false*. Finally step 2 and step 3 transform all atoms of the form $var(x)$ into an assertion equivalent to *false*. □

Theorem 16. *Let ψ be an assertion in normal form. Suppose that ψ is not a propositional constant. Then the algorithm Prod applied to ψ produces a substitution σ which does not belong to $[\![\psi]\!]$.*

Proof. *Prod* terminates when all the variables of ψ have been considered, hence $Var(A(\psi))$ becomes empty. Then the result follows by Lemma 12, Lemma 14 and Lemma 15. □

Proof of Theorem 10

By Lemma 6, Lemma 8 and the fact that (G7) can be applied only a finite number of times, it follows that TP terminates. Suppose that $TP(\phi) = true$. Then ϕ true follows from Lemma 6, Lemma 8 and Theorem 4.

We prove the converse by contraposition. Suppose that $TP(\phi)$ is not equal to *true*. Then $TP(\phi)$ is a conjunction of assertions in normal form, none of them equal to *true*, since rule (G7) has been applied. If one conjunct of $TP(\phi)$ is equal to the propositional constant *false* then ϕ is equivalent to *false*. Otherwise consider a conjunct ψ of $TP(\phi)$. Let σ be the substitution produced by applying the algorithm *Prod* to ψ. Then by Theorem 16 it follows that σ does not belong to $[\![\psi]\!]$. Hence ϕ is not true. □

5 Application

We illustrate how the truth procedure TP can be applied to mechanize some parts of the reasoning when proving the partial correctness of a logic program. Partial correctness will here be described in terms of properties of substitutions that are the intermediate results of the computations of a logic program, starting with a certain class of goals, by associating an assertion to each program point before or after an atom in the body of a clause. The class of goals considered is described by means of a goal and an assertion, called precondition, which specifies the possible values of the variables of the goal. Then every clause $h \leftarrow b_1 \ldots b_n$ of the program is annotated with assertions $h \leftarrow I_0\ b_1\ I_1 \ldots b_n\ I_n$, one assertion for every program point. An assertion associated with a program point is said to be a global invariant for the class of goals considered, if it holds every time a computation (of a goal of the considered class) reaches the correspondent program point. If the I_i's are shown to be global invariants for the class of goals considered, then the annotated program is said to be *partially correct* (with respect to the class of goals considered and with respect to these assertions). For instance, consider the following (fragment of the) annotated Prolog program `contained`:

$c1$: `contained(empty,y)` $\leftarrow I_0^{c1}$.
$c2$: `contained(node(x`$_l$`,x,x`$_r$`),y)` $\leftarrow$
  I_0^{c2} `member(x,y)` I_1^{c2} `contained(x`$_l$`,y)` I_2^{c2} `contained(x`$_r$`,y)` I_3^{c2}.

This program defines the binary relation *contained*, such that `contained(t,l)` holds if t is a binary tree whose nodes are contained in the list l. The program is used in [JL89] to illustrate the relevance of having information about aliasing of program variables at compile time. In particular, it is argued that the recursive calls in $c2$ may be executed in parallel if every time one of them is called, y is ground and x_l and x_r do not share. As an example, we show that `contained` satisfies this condition when the following class of goals is considered: $g = \leftarrow$ `contained(x,y)` with precondition $I_0^g = var(x) \wedge ground(y)$. In this example, the program computes all the trees whose nodes are contained in the list described by the ground term y. To this end, we prove that `contained` is partially correct with respect to this class of goals and with respect to the following assertions associated with the corresponding program points.

$$I_0^{c1} = true,$$
$$I_0^{c2} = var(x_l, x_r) \wedge \neg share(\{x_l, x_r\}) \wedge ground(y),$$
$$I_1^{c2} = I_0^{c2},$$
$$I_2^{c2} = var(x_r) \wedge \neg share(\{x_l, x_r\}) \wedge ground(y),$$
$$I_3^{c2} = \neg share(\{x_l, x_r\}) \wedge ground(y),$$

where, for a relation symbol p which is equal to *ground* or *var*, $p(x_1, \ldots, x_n)$ is used as shorthand for $p(x_1) \wedge \ldots \wedge p(x_n)$.

To prove the partial correctness of `contained`, we apply an inductive method informally illustrated as follows: let a be either (the atom of) g or an atom of the body of some clause of `contained`. Let I_1 and I_2 be the two assertions associated with the program points before and after a, respectively (in case a is the atom of g, assume that $I_1^g = true$ is the assertion associated with the point after g). Let I_1^t denote an assertion obtained from I_1 as follows: for all the variables $x_1, \ldots, x_k$ which could share with some variable occurring in a, replace $x_1, \ldots, x_k$ with the fresh variables $z_1, \ldots, z_k$, and set the sequence $(x_1, \ldots, x_k)$ to be equal to an instance of $(z_1, \ldots, z_k)$. Consider a variant $ci' : h' \leftarrow I_0^{ci'}\, b_1\, I_1^{ci'} \ldots b_n\, I_n^{ci'}$ of a (annotated) clause ci of the program, $i \in [1, 2]$, such that ci' has no variables in common with $I_1^t\, a\, I_2$.

1. For an arbitrary substitution α in the semantics of I_1 consider the following conditions: a) $ci'\alpha$ is a variant of ci' having no variable in common with $(I_1\, a\, I_2)\alpha$; b) $a\alpha$ and $h'\alpha$ are unifiable. If a) and b) are satisfied then show that $\alpha\beta$ is in the semantics of $I_0^{ci'}$, where β is a fixed most general unifier of $a\alpha$ and h'.
2. For an arbitrary substitution δ in the semantics of the rightmost assertion $I_n^{ci'}$ of ci', consider the following conditions: a) δ is in the semantics of I_1^t; b) for every variable x occurring in I_1^t but not in $\{x_1, \ldots, x_k\}$, $x\delta$ and $ci'\delta$ have no variables in common; c) $h'\delta$ and $a\delta$ are equal. If a), b) and c) are satisfied then show that δ is in the semantics of I_2.

Step 1 corresponds to showing that when an atom calls a clause then the leftmost assertion of the clause is satisfied. Step 2 corresponds to showing that when the execution of a clause is terminated, then the assertion after the atom that has called the clause is satisfied. The variables $z_1, \ldots, z_k$ of I_1^t represent the values of $x_1, \ldots, x_k$ before ci' is called. The call of ci' can affect the values of $x_1, \ldots, x_k$, which become instances of $z_1, \ldots, z_k$. Notice that this is the only information about $x_1, \ldots, x_k$ given by I_1^t. Moreover, I_1^t together with condition b) of step 2 are used to retrieve information about those variables occurring in I_1 which do not share with any variable occurring in a. Finally, the equality in condition c) of step 2 is used to retrieve information about the variables occurring in a. Notice that the Prolog selection rule, which selects atoms in the body of a clause from left to right, is assumed.

To describe step 1 syntactically, i.e., without referring to substitutions and most general unifiers, one can view the unification of a and h' as a function $sp_{a,h'}$ which maps a set of substitutions (the α's) into a set of substitutions (the γ's obtained by composing α with β). This has been done in [CM92], where a set of substitutions is expressed by means of an assertion and the unification of two atoms is described by means of a predicate transformer.

To describe step 2 syntactically, we define I_1^t as follows:

$$I_1^t \stackrel{\text{def}}{=} inst((x_1, \ldots, x_k), (z_1, \ldots, z_k)) \wedge I_1{}^{x_1,\ldots,x_k}_{z_1,\ldots,z_k},$$

where $(x_1, \ldots, x_k)$ denotes the sequence of elements of the set $Var(I_1 a I_2) \setminus Y$, with

$$Y = \{y \mid I_1 \Rightarrow \neg share(y, x), \text{ for all } x \text{ occurring in } a\},$$

and $(z_1, \ldots, z_k)$ is a variant of $(x_1, \ldots, x_k)$ consisting of fresh variables. Moreover, $\phi^{x_1,\ldots,x_k}_{z_1,\ldots,z_k}$ denotes the assertion obtained from ϕ by replacing every occurrence of x_i with z_i, for $i \in [1, k]$.
The semantics of the new assertions $r = s$ and $inst(r, s)$ is defined as follows:

$$[\![r = s]\!] = \{\alpha \mid r\alpha = s\alpha\},$$

$$[\![inst(r, s)]\!] = \{\alpha \mid r\alpha = s\alpha\beta \text{ for some } \beta\}.$$

Using the function $sp_{a,h'}$ and the above definition of I_1^t, one can formalize steps 1 and 2 by means of the following implications, which are based on the assertional method of Colussi and Marchiori [CM91] (see also [AM94]).

$$sp_{a,h'}(I_1 \wedge var(ci') \wedge \neg share(ci', I_1 a I_2 \cup ci')) \Rightarrow I_0^{ci'}; \qquad \textbf{CALL}$$

$$(I_n^{ci'} \wedge I_1^t \wedge \neg share(Y \cup \{z_1, \ldots, z_k\}, ci') \wedge a = h') \Rightarrow I_2, \qquad \textbf{EXIT}$$

where Y, $z_1, \ldots, z_k$ and I_1^t are defined as above.
The assertion $var(ci') \wedge \neg share(ci', I_1 a I_2 \cup ci')$ used in $CALL$ expresses the fact that when ci' is called, it is renamed apart. Notice that we have used here $share(o_1, o_2)$ as shorthand for

$$\bigvee_{x \in Var(o_1), y \in (Var(o_2) \setminus \{x\})} share(\{x, y\}),$$

for some syntactic objects o_1, o_2. Moreover, the notation $var(o_1)$ is used as shorthand for $\bigwedge_{x \in Var(o_1)} var(x)$.

So the proof that `contained` is partially correct reduces to the verification of a number of implications. The truth procedure TP can be used to mechanize some of these tests. For instance, consider I_1^{c2} **contained(x$_l$,y)** I_2^{c2} and the variant $c2'$ of $c2$ obtained replacing x with x', for every variable x occurring in the atoms or in the assertions of $c2$. The following two implications are obtained:

(a) $x_l = node(x'_l, x', x'_r) \wedge y = y' \wedge var(x', x'_l, x'_r, x_r) \wedge ground(y) \wedge$
$\neg share(\{x'_l, x'_r\}) \wedge \neg share(x_r, \{x'_l, x'_r, x'\}) \Rightarrow$
$var(x'_l, x'_r) \wedge \neg share(\{x'_l, x'_r\}) \wedge ground(y')$;

(b) $\neg share(\{x'_r, x'_l\}) \wedge ground(y') \wedge inst(x_l, z) \wedge var(z, x_r) \wedge \neg share(\{z, x_r\}) \wedge$
$ground(y) \wedge \neg share(\{x_r, y, z\}, \{x'_l, x'_r, x', y'\}) \wedge$
$x_l = node(x'_l, x', x'_r) \wedge y = y' \Rightarrow$
$var(x_r) \wedge \neg share(\{x_l, x_r\}) \wedge ground(y)$.

These implications contain the relation symbols $=$ and *inst* which are not in the assertion language $\mathcal{A}$ of our logic (see Definition 1). Then (a) and (b) can be transformed in assertions of $\mathcal{A}$ as follows:

(i) replace every assertion of the form $inst(s, t)$ by the following conjunction:

$$(ground(t) \Rightarrow ground(s)) \wedge (var(s) \Rightarrow var(t));$$

(ii) replace every equality $s = t$ by the following conjunction:

$$(ground(s) \Leftrightarrow ground(t)) \wedge (var(s) \Leftrightarrow var(t)) \wedge (\neg ground(s) \Rightarrow share(s, t)).$$

Notice that the transformations (i) and (ii) are sound, in the sense that the information about groundness and sharing given by the transformed assertion holds also for the original one. To show this formally, let $\mathcal{A}'$ be the smallest set A of formulas containing $\mathcal{A}$, containing the atoms $s = t$ and $inst(s, t)$ for all terms s, t in $Term$, and with the property that if ϕ and ψ are in A then both $\psi \wedge \phi$ and $\psi \vee \phi$ are in A. Then the following result holds.

Lemma 17. *Let ϕ be an assertion in $\mathcal{A}'$. Let $ap(\phi)$ be the assertion of $\mathcal{A}$ obtained applying the transformations specified by (i) and (ii). For every assertion ψ of $\mathcal{A}$ if $ap(\phi) \Rightarrow \psi$ is true then $\phi \Rightarrow \psi$ is true.*

Proof. $\phi \Rightarrow ap(\phi)$ is true in $\mathcal{A}'$. □

Now, apply the transformation to the assertions (a) and (b) and apply the truth procedure TP to the resulting assertions (after having eliminated all the "$\Rightarrow$" symbols using the equivalence $\phi \Rightarrow \psi = \neg\phi \vee \psi$). The outcome is *true*, as expected. Then from Lemma 17, implications (a) and (b) are true.

6 Conclusion

In this paper a logic has been introduced, which allows to model some relevant properties used in static analysis of logic programs, namely *var*, *ground* and *share*. Soundness, completeness and decidability of this logic have been proven. It has been illustrated how the truth procedure TP introduced to prove the decidability of the logic can be applied to mechanize some parts of the reasoning when proving the partial correctness of a logic program.

Another possible area of application of the results of this paper we intend to investigate is abstract interpretation. Our logic could be used as abstract domain in an abstract interpretation framework for the study of aliasing in logic programs. This framework could be defined as follows: the logic is used as abstract domain and the axiomatization of the unification as predicate transformer *sp*, given in [CM92], is used to model unification. Since the assertion obtained by applying *sp* is not in general in the assertion language of the logic, one would have to provide a suitable approximation of the result. Alternatively, the logic can be used as abstract domain to approximate a suitable semantics for logic programs, as the one given in [CMM94]: since this semantics is based on a predicate transformer, an abstract interpretation framework can be defined, based on the theory given in [CC79]. We have the impression that the two approaches sketched above would provide information about aliasing and groundness with a high degree of accuracy; however they would be rather expensive, thus penalizing the efficiency of the resulting analysis.

Acknowledgments I would like to thank Jan Rutten and one anonymous referee of an earlier draft: with their helpful suggestions and detailed comments, both the content and the exposition of this paper have improved. Thanks also to Livio Colussi for useful discussions and to the referees of this conference. Krzysztof Apt suggested, already some years ago, the topic of this paper. This research was partly supported by Esprit BRA 6810 (Compulog 2).

References

[AH87] S. Abramsky and C. Hankin. An Introduction to Abstract Interpretation. *In Abstract Interpretation of declarative languages*, pp. 9–31, eds. S. Abramsky and C. Hankin, Ellis Horwood, 1987.

[AM94] K.R. Apt and E. Marchiori. Reasoning about Prolog programs: from Modes through Types to Assertions. *Formal Aspects of Computing*, 1994. In print.

[CM91] L. Colussi and E. Marchiori. Proving Correctness of Logic Programs Using Axiomatic Semantics. *Proceedings of the Eight International Conference on Logic Programming*, pp. 629–644, 1991.

[CM92] L. Colussi and E. Marchiori. Unification as Predicate Transformer. Preliminary version in *Proceedings JICSLP' 92*, 67–85, 1992. Revised version submitted.

[CMM94] L. Colussi, E. Marchiori and M. Marchiori. Combining Logic and Control to Characterize Global Invariants for Prolog Programs. *CWI Report*, The Netherlands, 1994.

[CC77] P. Cousot and R. Cousot. Abstract Interpretation : a Unified Lattice Model for Static Analysis of Programs by Construction or Approximation of Fixpoints. *Proceedings of the 4th ACM Symposium on Principles of Programming Languages*, pp. 238–251, 1977.

[CC79] P. Cousot and R. Cousot. Systematic Design of Program Analysis Frameworks. *Proceedings of the 6th ACM Symposium on Principles of Programming Languages*, pp. 269–282, 1979.

[CC92] P. Cousot and R. Cousot. Abstract Interpretation and Application to Logic Programs. *Report LIX/RR/92/08*, 1992. To appear in the special issue on Abstract Interpretation of the Journal of Logic Programming.

[CFW91] A. Cortesi, G. Filé and W. Winsborough. *Prop* Revisited: Propositional Formula as Abstract Domain. *Proceedings of the Sixth Annual IEEE Symposium on Logic in Computer Science*, pp. 322–327, 1991.

[DM88] W. Drabent and J. Małuszyński. Inductive Assertion Method for Logic Programs. *Theoretical Computer Science 59:1*, pp. 133–155, 1988.

[JL89] D. Jacobs and A. Langen. Accurate and Efficient Approximation of Variable Aliasing in Logic Programs. *Proceedings of the North American Conference on Logic Programming*, pp. 155–165, 1989.

[MS89] K. Marriott and H. Søndergaard. Notes for a Tutorial on Abstract Interpretation of Logic Programs. *North American Conference on Logic Programming*, 1989.

Springer-Verlag and the Environment

We at Springer-Verlag firmly believe that an international science publisher has a special obligation to the environment, and our corporate policies consistently reflect this conviction.

We also expect our business partners – paper mills, printers, packaging manufacturers, etc. – to commit themselves to using environmentally friendly materials and production processes.

The paper in this book is made from low- or no-chlorine pulp and is acid free, in conformance with international standards for paper permanency.

Lecture Notes in Computer Science

For information about Vols. 1–774
please contact your bookseller or Springer-Verlag

Vol. 775: P. Enjalbert, E. W. Mayr, K. W. Wagner (Eds.), STACS 94. Proceedings, 1994. XIV, 782 pages. 1994.

Vol. 776: H. J. Schneider, H. Ehrig (Eds.), Graph Transformations in Computer Science. Proceedings, 1993. VIII, 395 pages. 1994.

Vol. 777: K. von Luck, H. Marburger (Eds.), Management and Processing of Complex Data Structures. Proceedings, 1994. VII, 220 pages. 1994.

Vol. 778: M. Bonuccelli, P. Crescenzi, R. Petreschi (Eds.), Algorithms and Complexity. Proceedings, 1994. VIII, 222 pages. 1994.

Vol. 779: M. Jarke, J. Bubenko, K. Jeffery (Eds.), Advances in Database Technology — EDBT '94. Proceedings, 1994. XII, 406 pages. 1994.

Vol. 780: J. J. Joyce, C.-J. H. Seger (Eds.), Higher Order Logic Theorem Proving and Its Applications. Proceedings, 1993. X, 518 pages. 1994.

Vol. 781: G. Cohen, S. Litsyn, A. Lobstein, G. Zémor (Eds.), Algebraic Coding. Proceedings, 1993. XII, 326 pages. 1994.

Vol. 782: J. Gutknecht (Ed.), Programming Languages and System Architectures. Proceedings, 1994. X, 344 pages. 1994.

Vol. 783: C. G. Günther (Ed.), Mobile Communications. Proceedings, 1994. XVI, 564 pages. 1994.

Vol. 784: F. Bergadano, L. De Raedt (Eds.), Machine Learning: ECML-94. Proceedings, 1994. XI, 439 pages. 1994. (Subseries LNAI).

Vol. 785: H. Ehrig, F. Orejas (Eds.), Recent Trends in Data Type Specification. Proceedings, 1992. VIII, 350 pages. 1994.

Vol. 786: P. A. Fritzson (Ed.), Compiler Construction. Proceedings, 1994. XI, 451 pages. 1994.

Vol. 787: S. Tison (Ed.), Trees in Algebra and Programming – CAAP '94. Proceedings, 1994. X, 351 pages. 1994.

Vol. 788: D. Sannella (Ed.), Programming Languages and Systems – ESOP '94. Proceedings, 1994. VIII, 516 pages. 1994.

Vol. 789: M. Hagiya, J. C. Mitchell (Eds.), Theoretical Aspects of Computer Software. Proceedings, 1994. XI, 887 pages. 1994.

Vol. 790: J. van Leeuwen (Ed.), Graph-Theoretic Concepts in Computer Science. Proceedings, 1993. IX, 431 pages. 1994.

Vol. 791: R. Guerraoui, O. Nierstrasz, M. Riveill (Eds.), Object-Based Distributed Programming. Proceedings, 1993. VII, 262 pages. 1994.

Vol. 792: N. D. Jones, M. Hagiya, M. Sato (Eds.), Logic, Language and Computation. XII, 269 pages. 1994.

Vol. 793: T. A. Gulliver, N. P. Secord (Eds.), Information Theory and Applications. Proceedings, 1993. XI, 394 pages. 1994.

Vol. 794: G. Haring, G. Kotsis (Eds.), Computer Performance Evaluation. Proceedings, 1994. X, 464 pages. 1994.

Vol. 795: W. A. Hunt, Jr., FM8501: A Verified Microprocessor. XIII, 333 pages. 1994.

Vol. 796: W. Gentzsch, U. Harms (Eds.), High-Performance Computing and Networking. Proceedings, 1994, Vol. I. XXI, 453 pages. 1994.

Vol. 797: W. Gentzsch, U. Harms (Eds.), High-Performance Computing and Networking. Proceedings, 1994, Vol. II. XXII, 519 pages. 1994.

Vol. 798: R. Dyckhoff (Ed.), Extensions of Logic Programming. Proceedings, 1993. VIII, 362 pages. 1994.

Vol. 799: M. P. Singh, Multiagent Systems. XXIII, 168 pages. 1994. (Subseries LNAI).

Vol. 800: J.-O. Eklundh (Ed.), Computer Vision – ECCV '94. Proceedings 1994, Vol. I. XVIII, 603 pages. 1994.

Vol. 801: J.-O. Eklundh (Ed.), Computer Vision – ECCV '94. Proceedings 1994, Vol. II. XV, 485 pages. 1994.

Vol. 802: S. Brookes, M. Main, A. Melton, M. Mislove, D. Schmidt (Eds.), Mathematical Foundations of Programming Semantics. Proceedings, 1993. IX, 647 pages. 1994.

Vol. 803: J. W. de Bakker, W.-P. de Roever, G. Rozenberg (Eds.), A Decade of Concurrency. Proceedings, 1993. VII, 683 pages. 1994.

Vol. 804: D. Hernández, Qualitative Representation of Spatial Knowledge. IX, 202 pages. 1994. (Subseries LNAI).

Vol. 805: M. Cosnard, A. Ferreira, J. Peters (Eds.), Parallel and Distributed Computing. Proceedings, 1994. X, 280 pages. 1994.

Vol. 806: H. Barendregt, T. Nipkow (Eds.), Types for Proofs and Programs. VIII, 383 pages. 1994.

Vol. 807: M. Crochemore, D. Gusfield (Eds.), Combinatorial Pattern Matching. Proceedings, 1994. VIII, 326 pages. 1994.

Vol. 808: M. Masuch, L. Pólos (Eds.), Knowledge Representation and Reasoning Under Uncertainty. VII, 237 pages. 1994. (Subseries LNAI).

Vol. 809: R. Anderson (Ed.), Fast Software Encryption. Proceedings, 1993. IX, 223 pages. 1994.

Vol. 810: G. Lakemeyer, B. Nebel (Eds.), Foundations of Knowledge Representation and Reasoning. VIII, 355 pages. 1994. (Subseries LNAI).

Vol. 811: G. Wijers, S. Brinkkemper, T. Wasserman (Eds.), Advanced Information Systems Engineering. Proceedings, 1994. XI, 420 pages. 1994.

Vol. 812: J. Karhumäki, H. Maurer, G. Rozenberg (Eds.), Results and Trends in Theoretical Computer Science. Proceedings, 1994. X, 445 pages. 1994.

Vol. 813: A. Nerode, Yu. N. Matiyasevich (Eds.), Logical Foundations of Computer Science. Proceedings, 1994. IX, 392 pages. 1994.

Vol. 814: A. Bundy (Ed.), Automated Deduction—CADE-12. Proceedings, 1994. XVI, 848 pages. 1994. (Subseries LNAI).

Vol. 815: R. Valette (Ed.), Application and Theory of Petri Nets 1994. Proceedings. IX, 587 pages. 1994.

Vol. 816: J. Heering, K. Meinke, B. Möller, T. Nipkow (Eds.), Higher-Order Algebra, Logic, and Term Rewriting. Proceedings, 1993. VII, 344 pages. 1994.

Vol. 817: C. Halatsis, D. Maritsas, G. Philokyprou, S. Theodoridis (Eds.), PARLE '94. Parallel Architectures and Languages Europe. Proceedings, 1994. XV, 837 pages. 1994.

Vol. 818: D. L. Dill (Ed.), Computer Aided Verification. Proceedings, 1994. IX, 480 pages. 1994.

Vol. 819: W. Litwin, T. Risch (Eds.), Applications of Databases. Proceedings, 1994. XII, 471 pages. 1994.

Vol. 820: S. Abiteboul, E. Shamir (Eds.), Automata, Languages and Programming. Proceedings, 1994. XIII, 644 pages. 1994.

Vol. 821: M. Tokoro, R. Pareschi (Eds.), Object-Oriented Programming. Proceedings, 1994. XI, 535 pages. 1994.

Vol. 822: F. Pfenning (Ed.), Logic Programming and Automated Reasoning. Proceedings, 1994. X, 345 pages. 1994. (Subseries LNAI).

Vol. 823: R. A. Elmasri, V. Kouramajian, B. Thalheim (Eds.), Entity-Relationship Approach — ER '93. Proceedings, 1993. X, 531 pages. 1994.

Vol. 824: E. M. Schmidt, S. Skyum (Eds.), Algorithm Theory – SWAT '94. Proceedings. IX, 383 pages. 1994.

Vol. 825: J. L. Mundy, A. Zisserman, D. Forsyth (Eds.), Applications of Invariance in Computer Vision. Proceedings, 1993. IX, 510 pages. 1994.

Vol. 826: D. S. Bowers (Ed.), Directions in Databases. Proceedings, 1994. X, 234 pages. 1994.

Vol. 827: D. M. Gabbay, H. J. Ohlbach (Eds.), Temporal Logic. Proceedings, 1994. XI, 546 pages. 1994. (Subseries LNAI).

Vol. 828: L. C. Paulson, Isabelle. XVII, 321 pages. 1994.

Vol. 829: A. Chmora, S. B. Wicker (Eds.), Error Control, Cryptology, and Speech Compression. Proceedings, 1993. VIII, 121 pages. 1994.

Vol. 830: C. Castelfranchi, E. Werner (Eds.), Artificial Social Systems. Proceedings, 1992. XVIII, 337 pages. 1994. (Subseries LNAI).

Vol. 831: V. Bouchitté, M. Morvan (Eds.), Orders, Algorithms, and Applications. Proceedings, 1994. IX, 204 pages. 1994.

Vol. 832: E. Börger, Y. Gurevich, K. Meinke (Eds.), Computer Science Logic. Proceedings, 1993. VIII, 336 pages. 1994.

Vol. 833: D. Driankov, P. W. Eklund, A. Ralescu (Eds.), Fuzzy Logic and Fuzzy Control. Proceedings, 1991. XII, 157 pages. 1994. (Subseries LNAI).

Vol. 834: D.-Z. Du, X.-S. Zhang (Eds.), Algorithms and Computation. Proceedings, 1994. XIII, 687 pages. 1994.

Vol. 835: W. M. Tepfenhart, J. P. Dick, J. F. Sowa (Eds.), Conceptual Structures: Current Practices. Proceedings, 1994. VIII, 331 pages. 1994. (Subseries LNAI).

Vol. 836: B. Jonsson, J. Parrow (Eds.), CONCUR '94: Concurrency Theory. Proceedings, 1994. IX, 529 pages. 1994.

Vol. 837: S. Wess, K.-D. Althoff, M. M. Richter (Eds.), Topics in Case-Based Reasoning. Proceedings, 1993. IX, 471 pages. 1994. (Subseries LNAI).

Vol. 838: C. MacNish, D. Pearce, L. Moniz Pereira (Eds.), Logics in Artificial Intelligence. Proceedings, 1994. IX, 413 pages. 1994. (Subseries LNAI).

Vol. 839: Y. G. Desmedt (Ed.), Advances in Cryptology - CRYPTO '94. Proceedings, 1994. XII, 439 pages. 1994.

Vol. 840: G. Reinelt, The Traveling Salesman. VIII, 223 pages. 1994.

Vol. 841: I. Prívara, B. Rovan, P. Ružička (Eds.), Mathematical Foundations of Computer Science 1994. Proceedings, 1994. X, 628 pages. 1994.

Vol. 842: T. Kloks, Treewidth. IX, 209 pages. 1994.

Vol. 843: A. Szepietowski, Turing Machines with Sublogarithmic Space. VIII, 115 pages. 1994.

Vol. 844: M. Hermenegildo, J. Penjam (Eds.), Programming Language Implementation and Logic Programming. Proceedings, 1994. XII, 469 pages. 1994.

Vol. 845: J.-P. Jouannaud (Ed.), Constraints in Computational Logics. Proceedings, 1994. VIII, 367 pages. 1994.

Vol. 846: D. Shepherd, G. Blair, G. Coulson, N. Davies, F. Garcia (Eds.), Network and Operating System Support for Digital Audio and Video. Proceedings, 1993. VIII, 269 pages. 1994.

Vol. 847: A. L. Ralescu (Ed.) Fuzzy Logic in Artificial Intelligence. Proceedings, 1993. VII, 128 pages. 1994. (Subseries LNAI).

Vol. 848: A. R. Krommer, C. W. Ueberhuber, Numerical Integration on Advanced Computer Systems. XIII, 341 pages. 1994.

Vol. 849: R. W. Hartenstein, M. Z. Servít (Eds.), Field-Programmable Logic. Proceedings, 1994. XI, 434 pages. 1994.

Vol. 850: G. Levi, M. Rodríguez-Artalejo (Eds.), Algebraic and Logic Programming. Proceedings, 1994. VIII, 304 pages. 1994.

Vol. 851: H.-J. Kugler, A. Mullery, N. Niebert (Eds.), Towards a Pan-European Telecommunication Service Infrastructure. Proceedings, 1994. XIII, 582 pages. 1994.

Vol. 853: K. Bolding, L. Snyder (Eds.), Parallel Computer Routing and Communication. Proceedings, 1994. IX, 317 pages. 1994.

Vol. 854: B. Buchberger, J. Volkert (Eds.), Parallel Processing: CONPAR 94 – VAPP VI. Proceedings, 1994. XVI, 893 pages. 1994.

Vol. 855: J. van Leeuwen (Ed.), Algorithms – ESA '94. Proceedings, 1994. X, 510 pages.1994.

Vol. 856: D. Karagiannis (Ed.), Database and Expert Systems Applications. Proceedings, 1994. XVII, 807 pages. 1994.